Fodor's

ESSENTIAL
ITALY

2nd Edition

Excerpted from *Fodor's Italy*
Fodor's Travel Publications   New York, Toronto, London, Sydney, Auckland
www.fodors.com

W9-AGC-301

Be a Fodor's Correspondent

Your opinion matters. It matters to us. It matters to your fellow Fodor's travelers, too. And we'd like to hear it. In fact, we need to hear it.

When you share your experiences and opinions, you become an active member of the Fodor's community. That means we'll not only use your feedback to make our books better, but we'll publish your names and comments whenever possible. Throughout our guides, look for "Word of Mouth," excerpts of your unvarnished feedback.

Here's how you can help improve Fodor's for all of us.

Tell us when we're right. We rely on local writers to give you an insider's perspective. But our writers and staff editors—who are the best in the business—depend on you. Your positive feedback is a vote to renew our recommendations for the next edition.

Tell us when we're wrong. We're proud that we update most of our guides every year. But we're not perfect. Things change. Hotels cut services. Museums change hours. Charming cafés lose charm. If our writer didn't quite capture the essence of a place, tell us how you'd do it differently. If any of our descriptions are inaccurate or inadequate, we'll incorporate your changes in the next edition and will correct factual errors at fodors.com immediately.

Tell us what to include. You probably have had fantastic travel experiences that aren't yet in Fodor's. Why not share them with a community of like-minded travelers? Maybe you chanced upon a beach or bistro or B&B that you don't want to keep to yourself. Tell us why we should include it. And share your discoveries and experiences with everyone directly at fodors.com. Your input may lead us to add a new listing or highlight a place we cover with a "Highly Recommended" star or with our highest rating, "Fodor's Choice."

Give us your opinion instantly at our feedback center at www.fodors.com/feedback. You may also e-mail editors@fodors.com with the subject line "Essential Italy Editor." Or send your nominations, comments, and complaints by mail to Essential Italy Editor, Fodor's, 1745 Broadway, New York, NY 10019.

You and travelers like you are the heart of the Fodor's community. Make our community richer by sharing your experiences. Be a Fodor's correspondent.

Buon Viaggio! (Or simply: Happy traveling!)

Tim Jarrell, Publisher

FODOR'S ESSENTIAL ITALY

Editor: Matthew Lombardi

Editorial Contributors: Linda Cabasin, Joanna Cantor, Erica Duecy, Robert Fisher, Cate Wells, Mark Sullivan

Writers: Lynda Albertson, Nicole Arriaga, Martin Wilmot Bennett, Peter Blackman, Ruth Edenbaum, Shannon Essa, Erica Firpo, Madeleine Johnson, Dana Klitzberg, Jen Laskey, Bruce Leimsidor, Nan McElroy, Eric J. Lyman, Megan McCaffrey-Guerrara, Ann Reavis, Patricia Rucidlo, Pamela Santini, Jonathan Willcocks, Megan K. Williams

Editorial Production: Astrid deRidder

Maps & Illustrations: Mark Stroud, Henry Colomb, Moon Streak Cartography, *cartographers*; Bob Blake, Rebecca Baer, and William Wu *map editors*

Design: Fabrizio La Rocca, *creative director*; Guido Caroti, Siobhan O'Hare, *art directors*; Tina Malaney, Chie Ushio, Ann McBride, *designers*; Melanie Marin, *senior picture editor*; Moon Sun Kim, *cover designer*

Cover Photo: Gondolier hat, Venice: Peter Adams/Alamy. Colosseum, Rome: Nic Cleave Photography/Alamy. Glass of red wine: Alain Proust/Alamy. Spaghetti: Campania Tourism. Shoe: Bobo/Alamy. Coffee: Jochem Wijnands/Alamy.

Production/Manufacturing: Angela L. McLean

ISBN 978-1-4000-0728-8

ISSN 1934-5550

SPECIAL SALES

This book is available at special discounts for bulk purchases for sales promotions or premiums. Special editions, including personalized covers, excerpts of existing books, and corporate imprints, can be created in large quantities for special needs. For more information, write to Special Markets/Premium Sales, 1745 Broadway, MD 6-2, New York, New York 10019, or e-mail specialmarkets@randomhouse.com.

AN IMPORTANT TIP & AN INVITATION

Although all prices, opening times, and other details in this book are based on information supplied to us at press time, changes occur all the time in the travel world, and Fodor's cannot accept responsibility for facts that become outdated or for inadvertent errors or omissions. So **always confirm information when it matters**, especially if you're making a detour to visit a specific place. Your experiences—positive and negative—matter to us. If we have missed or misstated something, **please write to us**. We follow up on all suggestions. Contact the Essential Italy editor at editors@fodors.com or c/o Fodor's at 1745 Broadway, New York, NY 10019.

PRINTED IN SINGAPORE

10 9 8 7 6 5 4

CONTENTS

CONTENTS

ABOUT
THIS BOOK

Our Ratings

Sometimes you find terrific travel experiences and sometimes they just find you. But usually the burden is on you to select the right combination of experiences. That's where our ratings come in.

As travelers we've all discovered a place so wonderful that its worthiness is obvious. And sometimes that place is so experiential that superlatives don't do it justice: you just have to be there to know. These sights, properties, and experiences get our highest rating, **Fodor's Choice,** indicated by orange stars throughout this book.

Black stars highlight sights and properties we deem **Highly Recommended,** places that our writers, editors, and readers praise again and again for consistency and excellence.

By default, there's another category: any place we include in this book is by definition worth your time, unless we say otherwise. And we will.

Disagree with any of our choices? Care to nominate a place or suggest that we rate one more highly? Visit our feedback center at www.fodors.com/feedback.

Budget Well

Hotel and restaurant price categories from ¢ to $$$$ are defined in the opening pages of each chapter. For attractions, we always give standard adult admission fees; reductions are usually available for children, students, and senior citizens. Want to pay with plastic? **AE, DC, MC, V** following restaurant and hotel listings indicate if American Express, Diners Club, MasterCard, and Visa are accepted.

Restaurants

Unless we state otherwise, restaurants are open for lunch and dinner daily. We mention dress only when there's a specific requirement and reservations only when they're essential or not accepted—it's always best to book ahead.

Hotels

Hotels have private bath, phone, TV, and air-conditioning. We indicate whether they operate on the European Plan (aka EP, meaning without meals), Breakfast Plan (BP, with a full breakfast), Modified American Plan (MAP, with breakfast and dinner) or American Plan (AP, including all meals). We always list facilities but not whether you'll be charged an extra fee to

use them, so when pricing accommodations, find out what's included.

Many Listings	
★	Fodor's Choice
★	Highly recommended
⊠	Physical address
⊹	Directions
⊡	Mailing address
☎	Telephone
🖷	Fax
⊕	On the Web
✎	E-mail
☞	Admission fee
☉	Open/closed times
Ⓜ	Metro stations
▭	Credit cards
Hotels & Restaurants	
🏨	Hotel
⇖	Number of rooms
⅋	Facilities
⏹	Meal plans
✕	Restaurant
⏎	Reservations
⎙	Smoking
⅋⅋	BYOB
✕🏨	Hotel with restaurant that warrants a visit
Outdoors	
🏌	Golf
⚠	Camping
Other	
☾	Family-friendly
⇨	See also
⊠	Branch address
☞	Take note

Experience Italy

1

WHAT'S WHERE

Numbers correspond to the book's chapter numbers.

2 Rome. Italy's capital is one of the great cities of Europe. It's a large, busy metropolis that lives in the here and now, yet there's no other place on earth where you'll encounter such powerful evocations of a long and spectacular past, from the Colosseum to the dome of St. Peter's.

3 Between Rome & Florence. Umbria, north of Rome, is a region of beautiful rolling hills topped by attractive old towns. **Orvieto** sits atop a tufa plateau that gives a warm glow to its magnificent Duomo when seen from a distance. **Spoleto** is a quiet, elegant hill town, but each summer it brims with activity during the Festival dei Due Mondi. **Perugia** is Umbria's largest city, but it's far from overwhelming, and it has a well-preserved medieval core. In **Assisi,** birthplace of Saint Francis, the grand basilica draws millions of pilgrims annually. In **Tuscany, Siena,** once Florence's main rival, remains one of Italy's most appealing medieval towns. To its west, **San Gimignano** is famous for its 15th-century towers, and farther west still is **Volterra,** a town dating back to the Etruscans. The hills spreading south from Florence to Siena make up **Chianti,** a region of sublime wine and fabulous views.

4 Florence. In the 15th century, Florence was at the center of the artistic revolution that would come to be known as the Renaissance. Today, the Renaissance remains the main reason people visit here—the abundance of art treasures is mind-boggling.

5 Between Florence & Venice. Many of Italy's signature foods come from the region of **Emilia–Romagna**—including Parmigiano-Reggiano cheese, prosciutto di Parma, and balsamic vinegar—and the pasta is considered Italy's finest. But there's more than food to draw you here. **Bologna** is a significant cultural center, and the mosaics of **Ravenna** are glittering Byzantine treasures. Farther north in the **Veneto** region, the plains stretching west of Venice hold three of northern Italy's most appealing midsize cities: **Padua, Vicenza,** and **Verona.**

6 Venice. One of the world's most novel cities, Venice has canals where the streets should be and an atmosphere of faded splendor that practically defines the word decadent.

MT. BLANC

VALLE D'AOSTA

Aosta

ALPI

Lake Como

Lugano

Lake Maggiore

Como

Turin

Po

Milan

Pavia

PIEDMONT

Asti

ALPI

LIGURIA

FRANCE

San Remo

RIVIERA

Genoa

MONACO

Ligurian Sea

CORSICA

Olbia

Sassari

SARDINIA

SARDINIA

Cagliari

ALGERIA

ITALY PLANNER

Getting Here

The major gateways to Italy are Rome's Aeroporto Leonardo da Vinci (FCO), better known as Fiumicino, and Milan's Aeroporto Malpensa (MIL). There are some direct flights to Venice and Pisa, but to fly into most other Italian cities you need to make connections at Fiumicino and Malpensa or another European airport. You can also take the FS airport train to Rome's Termini station or a bus to Milan's central train station (Centrale) and catch a train to any other location in Italy. It will take about one hour to get from either Fiumicino or Malpensa to the appropriate train station.

Italy's major airports are not known for being new, fun, or efficient. Airports in Italy have been ramping up security measures, which include random baggage inspection and bomb-detection dogs. All of the airports have restaurants and snack bars, and there is Internet access. Each airport has at least one nearby hotel. In the case of Florence and Pisa, the city centers are only a 15-minute taxi ride away—so if you encounter a long delay, spend it in town.

For further information about getting where you want to go, see "Getting Here" at the beginning of each part section of this book.

What to Pack

In summer, stick with light clothing, as things can get steamy in June, July, and August, but throw in a sweater in case of cool evenings, especially if you're headed for the mountains and/or islands. Sunglasses, a hat, and sunblock are essential. Brief summer afternoon thunderstorms are common in inland cities, so an umbrella will come in handy. In winter, bring a coat, gloves, hats, scarves, and boots. In winter, weather is generally milder than in the northern and central United States, but central heating may not be up to your standards, and interiors can be cold and damp; take wools or flannel rather than sheer fabrics. Bring sturdy shoes for winter and comfortable walking shoes in any season.

As a rule, Italians dress exceptionally well. They do not usually wear shorts. Men aren't required to wear ties or jackets anywhere, except in some of the grander hotel dining rooms and top-level restaurants, but are expected to look reasonably sharp—and they do. Formal wear is the exception rather than the rule at the opera nowadays, though people in expensive seats usually do get dressed up.

A certain modesty of dress (no bare shoulders or knees) is expected in churches, and strictly enforced in many.

For sightseeing, **pack a pair of binoculars**; they will help you get a good look at painted ceilings and domes. If you stay in budget hotels, **take your own soap.** Many such hotels do not provide it or give guests only one tiny bar per room. Washcloths, also, are rarely provided even in three- and four-star hotels.

Restaurants: The Basics

A meal in Italy has traditionally consisted of five courses, and every menu you encounter will still be organized along this five-course plan:

First up is the antipasto (appetizer), often consisting of cured meats or marinated vegetables. Next to appear is the primo, usually pasta or soup, and after that the secondo, a meat or fish course with, perhaps, a contorno (vegetable dish) on the side. A simple dolce (dessert) rounds out the meal.

This, you've probably noticed, is a lot of food. Italians have noticed as well—a full, five-course meal is an indulgence usually reserved for special occasions. Instead, restaurant meals are a mix-and-match affair: you might order a primo and a secondo, or an antipasto and a primo, or a secondo and a contorno.

The crucial rule of restaurant dining is that you should order at least two courses. It's a common mistake for tourists to order only a secondo, thinking they're getting a "main course" complete with side dishes. What they wind up with is one lonely piece of meat.

Hotels: The Basics

Hotels in Italy are usually well maintained (especially if they've earned our recommendation in this book), but in some respects they won't match what you find at comparably priced U.S. lodgings. Keep the following points in mind as you set your expectations, and you're likely to have a good experience:

■ First and foremost, rooms are usually smaller, particularly in cities. If you're truly cramped, ask for another room, but don't expect things to be spacious.

■ A "double bed" is commonly two singles pushed together.

■ In the bathroom, tubs are not a given—request one if it's essential. In budget places, showers sometimes use a drain in the middle of the bathroom floor. And washcloths are a rarity.

■ Most hotels have satellite TV, but there are fewer channels than in the United States, and only one or two will be in English.

■ Don't expect wall-to-wall carpeting. Particularly outside the cities, tile floors are the norm.

Speaking the Language

In most cities and many towns, you won't have a hard time finding locals who speak at least rudimentary English. Odds are if the person you want to talk with doesn't know English, there will be someone within earshot who can help translate. The farther south you travel, the fewer English speakers you'll encounter, but if nothing else someone at your hotel will know a few words. No matter where in Italy you're going, if you learn some common phrases in Italian, your effort will be appreciated.

Italy from Behind the Wheel

Americans tend to be well schooled in defensive-driving techniques. Many Italians are not. When you hit the road, don't be surprised to encounter tailgating and high-risk passing. Your best response is to take the same safety-first approach you use at home. On the upside, Italy's roads are very well maintained. Note that wearing a seat belt and having your lights on at all times are required by law. Bear in mind that a vehicle in Italian cities is almost always a liability, but outside of the cities it's often crucial. An effective strategy is to start and end your Italian itinerary in major cities, car-free, and to pick up wheels for countryside touring in between.

ITALY TODAY

Soccer

Soccer stands without rival as the national sport of Italy, but recent years have seen some changes to the beautiful game. On the positive side, Italy won its fourth World Cup in 2006, giving the country more world titles than any other this side of Brazil. But since then, soccer lovers have digested a series of unwelcome developments involving alleged match fixing, backroom deals for television contracts, drug scandals among players, and a rising level of violence between rival fans.

Italian professional soccer leagues are trying to put those issues behind them and focus on on-the-field play, where the Italian leagues rank with England and Spain as the best in Europe. One emerging positive trend is geographic parity. After several years of the top Serie A league being dominated by northern teams, along with a small handful from the central part of the country, success recently has been spread more evenly around the country, much to the joy of soccer-mad fans from the south.

The Beloved Lira

Italy was among a dozen European Union countries that switched to the euro currency at the start of 2002. For many Italians, the change was not a welcome one.

In day-to-day conversations, the euro is blamed for higher prices and for the handing over of more control of the Italian economy to bureaucrats in Brussels, the seat of the European government. The most common complaint is that many vendors simply took the old prices in lire and erased three zeros, meaning something that used to cost 1,000 lire (around 0.52 euro) now costs one euro.

Many Italians still value purchases in their beloved lira. Years after the switch, it is still common to hear someone in the midst of a negotiation argue the price in the now-dead currency, "Eight euros? But that's 16,000 lire!"

Politics

The political landscape in Italy is less stable than in any other industrialized nation. The country has endured a new government an average of about once a year since the end of World War II, and hopes are slim that the situation will change much in the near future.

This virtual turnstile outside the prime minister's office takes a toll on Italy in any number of ways: economic growth is slow in part because businesses are continually adapting to new sets of government policies, and polls show that rank-and-file Italians are increasingly cynical about their political institutions. As a result, they're much less likely to trust in or depend upon the government than neighbors elsewhere in Europe do.

National Parks

Italy boasts 22 national parks covering a total of around 1.5 million hectares (58,000 square mi), or about 5% of the entire surface area of the country—more than twice as much as 25 years ago. And a new park is added or an existing park is expanded every few months. (In 2008, three new parks were in line to join the existing 22.)

Part of the reason for the expansion has been a growing environmental movement in Italy, which has lobbied the government to annex undeveloped land for parks, thus protecting against development. But the trend is a boon for visitors and nature lovers, who can enjoy huge expanses of unspoiled territory.

Old Italy

Italy has the oldest populace in Europe (worldwide, only Japan is older)—the result of its low birth rate, relatively strict immigration standards, and one of the highest life expectancy rates in the world. As of 2008, the average Italian was 42.5 years old, and the number keeps rising.

The result is a remarkably stable population: the total number of Italian residents rises just 0.1% per year. But the situation is putting a strain on the country's pension system and on families, since elderly family members are likely to live with their children or grandchildren in a country where nursing homes are rare.

The trend also has an impact on other areas, including politics (where older politicians are eager to promote policies aimed at older voters) and the popular culture (where everything from fashion to television programming takes older consumers into consideration).

The Black Market

Nobody knows how big Italy's black-market economy is, though experts all agree it's massive. Estimates place it at anywhere from a fourth to a half of the official, legal economy. Put another way, if the highest estimates are correct, Italy's black-market economy is about as large as the entire economy of Mexico or India, and if the black-market figures were added to Italy's official GDP the country would leapfrog France, the U.K., and China to become the world's fourth-largest economy.

The presence of the black market isn't obvious to the casual observer, but whenever a customer is not given a printed receipt in a store or restaurant, tobacco without a tax seal is bought from a street seller, or a product or service is exchanged for another product or service, that means the transaction goes unrecorded, unreported, and untaxed.

Television

For most of the last generation, the two biggest players in the Italian television business have been Mediaset and RAI. Together, they control six of the seven television networks and about 90% of viewer hours.

Mediaset is owned by media-tycoon-turned-politician Silvio Berlusconi, Italy's richest citizen, while the Italian government controls RAI. For years, these two giants dominated the airwaves in Italy. But, now, competition is slowly developing a presence on the scene.

The most obvious newcomer is satellite broadcaster Sky Italia, owned by News Corp., the world's largest media conglomerate. And rules requiring television broadcasters to switch to digital television technologies by the end of 2009 are partially aimed at freeing up frequencies for new broadcasters itching to get a place in the Italian market. Stay tuned.

TOP ITALY ATTRACTIONS

The Vatican

(D) The home of the Catholic Church, a tiny independent state tucked within central Rome, holds some of the city's most spectacular sights, including St. Peter's Basilica, the Vatican Museums, and Michelangelo's Sistine ceiling. (⇨ Chapter 2.)

Ancient Rome

(A) The Colosseum and the Roman Forum are remarkable ruins from Rome's ancient past. Sitting above it all is the Campidoglio, with a piazza designed by Michelangelo and museums containing Rome's finest collection of ancient art. (⇨ Chapter 2.)

Galleria Borghese, Rome

Only the best could only satisfy the aesthetic taste of Cardinal Scipione Borghese, and that means famed Bernini sculptures, great paintings by Titian and Raphael, and the most spectacular 17th-century palace in Rome. (⇨ Chapter 2.)

Basilica di San Francesco, Assisi

(G) The giant basilica—made up of two churches, one built on top of the other—honors St. Francis with its remarkable fresco cycles. (⇨ Chapter 3.)

Piazza del Campo, Siena

(C) Siena is Tuscany's classic medieval hill town, and its heart is the Piazza del Campo, the beautiful, one-of-a-kind town square. (⇨ Chapter 3.)

Galleria degli Uffizi, Florence

The Uffizi—Renaissance art's hall of fame—contains masterpieces by Leonardo, Michelangelo, Raphael, Botticelli, Caravaggio, and dozens of other luminaries. (⇨ Chapter 4.)

Duomo, Florence

(B) The massive dome of Florence's Cathedral of Santa Maria del Fiore (aka the

Duomo) is one of the world's great feats of engineering. (⇨ Chapter 4.)

Ravenna's Mosaics

This small, out-of-the-way city houses perhaps the world's greatest treasure trove of early Christian art. The exquisite and surprisingly moving 5th and 6th century mosaics decorating several churches and other religious buildings still retain their startling brilliance. (⇨ Chapter 5.)

Giotto's Frescoes in the Scrovegni Chapel, Padua

(E) Dante's contemporary Giotto decorated this chapel with an eloquent and beautiful fresco cycle. Its convincing human dimension helped to change the course of western art. (⇨ Chapter 5.)

Palladio's Villas & Palazzi

(F) The 16th-century genius Andrea Palladio is one of the most influential figures in the history of architecture. You can visit his creations in his hometown of Vicenza, in and around Venice, and outside Treviso. (⇨ Chapter 5.)

Venice's Piazza San Marco

The centerpiece of Venice's main square is the Basilica di San Marco, arguably the most beautiful Byzantine church in the West. Right next door is the Venetian Gothic Palazzo Ducale, which was so beloved by the Venetians that when it burnt down in the 16th century, they had their palace rebuilt come era, dove era—exactly how and where it was. (⇨ Chapter 6.)

Venice's Grand Canal

(H) No one ever forgets a first trip down the Grand Canal. The sight of its magnificent palaces, with the light reflected from the canal's waters shimmering across their facades, is one of Italy's great experiences. (⇨ Chapter 6.)

TOP EXPERIENCES

Hanging Out in Rome's Piazzas

For Italians young and old, la piazza serves as a punto d'incontro—a meeting place—for dinner plans, drinks, people-watching, catching up with friends and, as Romans would say, exchanging due chiacchere (two words). One of the most popular piazzas is Campo de' Fiori, right in the heart of the historic center. By day, the piazza is famous for its fresh food and flower market—no rival to Piazza Navona for sheer beauty, the market is nevertheless a favorite photo-op, due to the ombrelloni (canvas umbrella) food stands. By night, the piazza turns into a popular hangout for Romans and foreigners lured by its pubs and street cafés, so much so that it has been dubbed "the American college campus of Rome." As dinner approaches at 9, the big question is: Are you "in" or "out" (inside or outside table)? No matter: the people-watching is unrivaled anywhere you sit.

Church Going

Few images are more identifiable with Italy than the country's great churches, amazing works of architecture that often took centuries to build. The name Duomo (derived from the Latin for "house," domus, and the root of the English "dome") is used to refer to the principal church of a town or city. Generally speaking, the bigger the city, the more splendid its duomo. Still, some impressive churches inhabit some unlikely places—in the Umbrian hill towns of **Assisi** and **Orvieto**, for example (⇨ Chapter 3).

In Venice, the Byzantine-influenced **Basilica di San Marco** (⇨ Chapter 6) is a testament to the city's East-meets-West character. **Milan's Duomo** (⇨ Chapter 5) is the largest, most imposing Gothic cathedral in Italy. The spectacular dome of Florence's Duomo (⇨ Chapter 4) is a work of engineering genius. The **Basilica di San Pietro** in Rome (⇨ Chapter 2) has all the grandeur you'd expect from the seat of the Catholic Church.

Hiking in the Footsteps of Saint Francis

Umbria, which bills itself as "Italy's Green Heart," is fantastic hiking country. Among the many options are two with a Franciscan twist: from the town of Cannara, 16 km (10 mi) south of Assisi, an easy half-hour walk leads to the fields of Pian d'Arca, where Saint Francis delivered his sermon to the birds. For slightly more demanding walks, you can follow the saint's path from Assisi to the Ermeo delle Carceri (Hermitage of Prisons), where Francis and his followers went to "imprison" themselves in prayer, and from here continue along the trails that crisscross Monte Subasio.

Wine-Tasting in Chianti

The gorgeous hills of the Chianti region, between Florence and Siena, produce exceptional wines, and they never taste better than when sampled on their home turf. Many Chianti vineyards are visitor-friendly, but the logistics of a visit are different from what you may have experienced in other wine regions. If you just drop in, you're likely to get a tasting, but for a tour you usually need to make an appointment several days ahead of time. The upside is, your tour may end up being a half day of full emersion—including extended conversation with the winemakers and even a meal.

Taking in the View from Florence's Piazzale Michelangelo

One of the best ways to introduce yourself to Florence is by walking up to this square on the hill south of the Arno. From here you can take in the whole city, and much of the surrounding countryside, in one spectacular vista. To extend the experience, linger at one of the outdoor cafés, and for the finest view of all, time your visit to correspond with sunset.

Discovering the Cinque Terre

Along the Italian Riviera to the west of Lucca and Pisa are five tiny, remote fishing villages known collectively as the Cinque Terre. Tourism here was once limited to backpackers, but the beauty of the landscape—with steep, vine-covered hills pushing smack-dab against an azure sea—and the charm of the villages have turned the area into one of Italy's top destinations. The number-one activity is hiking the trails that run between the villages—the views are once-in-a-lifetime gorgeous—but if hiking isn't your thing, you can still have fun lounging about in cafés, admiring the water, and perhaps sticking a toe in it.

Eating in Bologna

Italians recognize the region of Emilia as the star of its culinary culture and Bologna as its epicenter. Many dishes native to Bologna, such as the slow-cooked meat-and-tomato sauce sugo alla Bolognese, have become so famous that they are widely available in all regions of Italy and abroad. But you owe it to yourself to try them in the city where they were born and are a subject of local pride. Take note, however: in Bologna a sugo isn't served with spaghetti, but rather with an egg pasta in the form of tagliatelle, lasagne, or tortellini.

Picking Up Some Style in Milan

Italian clothing and furniture design are world famous, and the center of the Italian design industry is Milan. The best way to see what's happening in the world of fashion is to browse the designer showrooms and boutiques of the fabled quadrilatero della moda, along and around Via Montenapoleone. The central event in the world of furniture design is Milan's annual Salone Internazionale del Mobile, held at the Milan fairgrounds for a week in April. Admission is generally restricted to the trade, but the Salone is open to the general public for one day, generally on a Sunday, during the week of the show.

Going by Gondola in Venice

A ride down the Grand Canal by vaporetto (water bus) is a classic introduction to the unique character of Venice. But for a more intimate experience, there's nothing that can match a glide along one of the city's narrow side canals in a gondola—an escorted trip to nowhere in particular, watched over by Gothic palaces with delicately arched eyebrows.

Il Dolce Far Niente

"The sweetness of doing nothing" has long been an art form in Italy. This is a country in which life's pleasures are warmly celebrated, not guiltily indulged.

Of course, doing "nothing" doesn't really mean nothing. It means doing things differently: lingering over a glass of wine for the better part of an evening just to watch the sun slowly set; savoring a slow and flirtatious evening passeggiata along the main street of a little town; and making a commitment—however temporary—to thinking that there is nowhere that you have to be next, that there is no other time than the magical present.

QUINTESSENTIAL ITALY

Il Caffè (Coffee)

The Italian day begins and ends with coffee, and more cups of coffee punctuate the time in between. To live like the Italians do, drink as they drink, standing at the counter or sitting at an outdoor table of the corner bar. (In Italy, a "bar" is a coffee bar.) A primer: *caffè* means coffee, and Italian standard issue is what Americans call espresso—short, strong, and usually taken very sweet. *Cappuccino* is a foamy half-and-half of espresso and steamed milk; cocoa powder *(cacao)* on top is acceptable, cinnamon is not. If you're thinking of having a cappuccino for dessert, think again—Italians drink only caffè or caffè *macchiato* (with a spot of steamed milk) after lunchtime. Confused? Homesick? Order caffè *americano* for a reasonable facsimile of good-old filtered joe.

Il Calcio (Soccer)

Imagine the most rabid American football fans—the ones who paint their faces on game day and sleep in pajamas emblazoned with the logo of their favorite team. Throw in a dose of melodrama along the lines of a tear-jerking soap opera. Ratchet up the intensity by a factor of 10, and you'll start to get a sense of how Italians feel about their national game, soccer—known in the mother tongue as *calcio*. On Sunday afternoons throughout the long September-to-May season, stadiums are packed throughout Italy. Those who don't get to games in person tend to congregate around television sets in restaurants and bars, rooting for the home team with a passion that feels like a last vestige of the days when the country was a series of warring medieval city-states. How calcio mania affects your stay in Italy depends on how eager you are to get involved. At the very least, you may notice

If you want to get a sense of contemporary Italian culture and indulge in some of its pleasures, start by familiarizing yourself with the rituals of daily life. These are a few highlights—things you can take part in with relative ease.

an eerie Sunday-afternoon silence on the city streets, or erratic restaurant service around the same time, accompanied by cheers and groans from a neighboring room. If you want a memorable, truly Italian experience, attend a game yourself. Availability of tickets may depend on the current fortunes of the local team, but they often can be acquired with help from your hotel concierge.

Il Gelato (Ice Cream)

During warmer months, *gelato*—the Italian equivalent of ice cream—is a national obsession. It's considered a snack rather than a dessert, bought at stands and shops in piazzas and on street corners, and consumed on foot, usually at a leisurely stroll *(see La Passeggiata, below)*. Gelato is softer, less creamy, and more intensely flavored than its American counterpart. It comes in simple flavors that capture the essence of the main ingredient. (You won't find Chunky Monkey or Cookies 'n' Cream.) Standard choices include pistachio, *nocciola* (hazelnut), caffè, and numerous fresh-fruit varieties. Quality varies; the surest sign that you've hit on a good spot is a line at the counter.

La Passeggiata (Strolling)

A favorite Italian pastime is the *passeggiata* (literally, the promenade). In the late afternoon and early evening, especially on weekends, couples, families, and packs of teenagers stroll the main streets and piazzas of Italy's towns. It's a ritual of exchanged news and gossip, window-shopping, flirting, and gelato-eating that adds up to a uniquely Italian experience. To join in, simply hit the streets for a bit of wandering. You may feel more like an observer than a participant, until you realize that observing is what la passeggiata is all about.

A GREAT ITINERARY

ROME, FLORENCE, VENICE & HIGHLIGHTS IN BETWEEN

This itinerary works like an accordion: it can expand or contract, depending on the amount of time you have and where your interests lie. If your top priority is seeing Italy's most famous sights, extend your visits to the great cities of Rome, Florence, and Venice. If you're more drawn by beautiful landscapes, exceptional food and wine, and the Italians' knack for living well, then devote a good part of your trip to the other stops along the way, where the pace of life is more relaxed.

Getting there: Rome and Milan have Italy's busiest international airports, but there are also direct flights between the United States and Venice. To follow the itinerary outlined here, look into "open-jaw" tickets, with which you fly into one city (in this case Rome) and out of another (Venice). You could also finish up your trip by making the three-hour train ride from Venice to Milan, where you'll have more return-flight options (and you can see yet another side of Italy). Or you could go back to Rome (one-way plane tickets for flights within Italy are surprisingly inexpensive; the train takes about five hours), and fly home from there. For transportation details, see Essentials at the end of this book.

Getting around: Your main decision is whether to rent a car or to use Italy's efficient, reasonably priced railway system. The smartest strategy may be to do some of both. Within the cities, a car is a liability: both driving and parking are generally worse in Italian cities than anything you'll find in the United States. Outside of the cities, though, a car has its clear advantages: it gives you the freedom and flexibility to go places not served (or poorly served) by public transit. Particularly in Tuscany, there are significant limits on what you'll be able to see and do without a car.

Stop 1: Rome (2–4 Days)

Rome is a large, bustling city that lives in the here and now, yet there's no other place on earth where you'll encounter such powerful evocations of a long and spectacular past. Take a few steps from Piazza del Campidoglio, designed by Michelangelo, and you're looking down upon the ruins of ancient Rome, smack dab in the middle of the city. Exit a baroque church housing a masterpiece by Caravaggio, turn the corner, and find yourself face-to-face with the Pantheon. Such mind-bending juxtapositions are everywhere.

If you're arriving on an international flight, you'll settle into your hotel in the afternoon. Resist the temptation to nap; instead head outside and spend some time getting to know the surrounding neighborhood. In the evening, check out **Piazza Navona** and the **Trevi Fountain**—the energy of the city at night will perk you up like a shot of good espresso. For your first dinner, you can't miss with one of Rome's exceptional pizzerias.

In the morning, head to the Vatican to see **St. Peter's Basilica** and Michelangelo's glorious Sistine Chapel at the **Vatican Museums**. Have lunch back in Rome proper in the area around the Pantheon, then visit the **Pantheon** itself and spend the afternoon wandering the cobblestone streets of the neighborhood, taking time for a break at one the famous coffee shops in the area.

Begin the next day at **Campo de' Fiori**, where you'll find Rome's most colorful open-air market in full swing. Then head to the **Campidolgio**, and from there explore the ruins of ancient Rome, topped off by a visit to the **Colosseum**. In the afternoon, hop across town to **Piazza di Spagna**, a good place shop, lick gelato, and watch the sunset.

On further days here, follow the same basic strategy: devote mornings to significant sights (**Galleria Borghese** is a great choice; note that it requires a reservation) and afternoons to exploring neighborhoods (such as **Trastevere** and the **Jewish Ghetto**). In the evening, do as the Romans do: make a long, relaxed dinner the main event.

Extend your stay if: you're fascinated by Rome's mix of the ancient and the modern, and you love city life. You won't encounter such an intensely urban environment anywhere else on this trip.

Keep your visit short if: an urban environment is what you're on vacation to get away from.

Stop 2: Perugia (1–2 Days)
Perugia is about 2½ hours north of Rome by car or train, but consider a short detour along the way to **Orvieto**, a town with an impressive hilltop setting and one of Italy's great Gothic cathedrals. Both towns are in the largely rural **Umbria** region. The more relaxed pace of life makes a nice contrast to the energy of Rome.

Perugia is Umbria's largest city, but with a population of about 150,000 it's far from overwhelming, and it has a well-preserved medieval core. The pedestrian-only street through the heart of town, **Corso Vannucci**, is a classic place for a passeggiata (evening stroll), and there's a cluster of sights along the street that are worth checking out the next morning—particularly the **Collegio del Cambio**, a Renaissance guild hall frescoed by Perugia's greatest artist, Perugino.

Extend your stay if: you want to make a day trip to **Assisi,** the city of St. Francis, which is about half an hour (by car or train) east of Perugia.

Keep your visit short if: you're a thrill-seeker. Umbria is a beautiful region, but it's not as likely to quicken your pulse as much as some of the other stops on the itinerary.

Stop 3: Chianti (1–2 Days)
To the northwest of Umbria is the region of **Tuscany,** which is rightly famous for having Italy's most gorgeous landscapes.

A GREAT ITINERARY

Most beautiful of all is the Chianti district, between Florence and Siena, where vineyards and olive groves blanket rolling hills as far as the eye can see. To make the most of the experience, stay in the countryside at a converted villa or agriturismo (a farm taking overnight guests). Though Chianti is Tuscany's most idyllic location, you can hardly go wrong in the surrounding districts as well—particularly outside Siena and in the hills to its west.

Siena itself is a magnificent hill town that shouldn't be missed. With the exception of Florence, it has more to see than anywhere else in Tuscany, and its **Piazza del Campo** is one of Italy's most appealing town squares. If you leave Perugia in the morning, you can make the 1½-hour drive west to Siena and spend the afternoon there. Tuscany is also a great place for winery tours; the **Strada Chiantigiana**, the beautiful road through the heart of Chianti, takes you past visitor-friendly vineyards and enoteche (wineshops).

Extend your stay if: il dolce far niente (the sweetness of doing nothing) is a concept you find appealing. Tuscany has some spectacular sights, but the greatest pleasure here is relaxing and unwinding.

Keep your visit short if: you're dead-set against driving. The only town south of Florence that's easily accessible by train is Arezzo, which is worth a visit but won't give you the full Tuscan experience.

Stop 4: Florence (2–4 Days)
It's hard to think of a place that's more closely linked to one specific historical period than Florence. In the 15th century the city was at the center of the artistic revolution that would come to be known as the Renaissance. Five hundred years later, the Renaissance remains the main

reason people visit Florence—the abundance of art treasures is mind-boggling.

Begin your first day here at the heart of the city, the **Piazza del Duomo.** Check out Ghiberti's famous bronze doors on the **Battistero,** then climb the 463 steps to the top of Brunelleschi's splendid cathedral dome, from where you have an unbeatable view of the entire city and the hills beyond. Back on solid ground, take some time to visit the **Museo dell'Opera del Duomo,** which now holds much of the art that was once in the Duomo. Following lunch, spend the afternoon at the **Gallleria degli Uffizi** (reserve your ticket in advance), which houses one of the world's greatest art collections. When you're through there, step outside into the neighboring **Piazza della Signoria,** Florence's most impressive square. You'll find there a copy of Michelangelo's David, standing in the spot that was occupied by the original for centuries.

The following morning, visit the real David at his indoor home, the **Galleria dell'Accademia.** (Reserve your ticket here as well.) A few steps down the street are the works of another, completely different Renaissance master: the **Museo di San Marco,** a former convent, is decorated with simple, ethereal, occasionally bizarre frescoes of Fra Angelico. You can get another dose of Michangelo before lunch a few blocks away at the **Capelle Medici.** After a day and a half of walking and art-gazing, if a post-lunch nap appeals to you, don't resist. Later in the afternoon, use your revived energy to make the trip up to the **Piazzale Michelangelo,** high on a hill above Florence, from which you have a sweeping view of the city. Stick around for sunset, then head down to the Oltrarno neighborhood below and feast on a famed bistecca alla fiorentina (grilled T-bone steak with olive oil).

You'll have seen a lot by this point, but you've just scratched the surface here. "Must sees" for additional days are the **Santa Croce** and **Santa Maria Novella** cathedrals and the **Bargello** sculpture museum. And Florence isn't exclusively about art; some visitors come just for the shopping, from the food stalls of the **Mercato Centrale** to the show rooms of the exclusive boutiques along **Via Tournabuoni**.

Extend your stay if: you want to make a side trip to **Lucca, Pisa** (home of the leaning tower), or the gorgeous coastal villages of the **Cinque Terre**, all west of Florence.

Keep your visit short if: you put a premium on getting off the beaten path. After several hundred years of steady tourism, almost every path in Florence has been pretty well beaten.

Stop 5: Bologna (1–2 Days)

A one-hour trip by train north from Florence, or 1½ hours by car, brings you to Bologna, a city that doesn't have Florence's abundance of sights, but will give you more of a taste of the pleasures of day-to-day life in Italy. With a population of about 375,000, Bologna is the largest city in **Emilia–Romagna**, a region famed for its cuisine. Many of Italy's signature food products originate here, including Parmigiano-Reggiano cheese (aka Parmesan), prosciutto di Parma, and balsamic vinegar. The pasta is considered Italy's finest—a reputation the region's chefs earn every day. If you're going to splurge on one over-the-top meal, this is the place to do it.

But a visit here is about more than food: Bologna is home to Europe's oldest university, making it a cultural and intellectual center, and it has rows of street arcades winding through grandiose towers. After you've settled into your hotel, take a walk around **Piazza Maggiore** at the heart of the city. Following dinner, you can check out some of northern Italy's best nightlife—one of the by-products of the university. The next day, continue your exploration of the city center, including a visit to the basilica of **Santo Stefano** and a climb up Bologna's own leaning tower, the **Torre degli Asinelli**.

Extend your stay if: you're lured by a day trip east to see the glorious Byzantine mosaics in **Ravenna**.

Keep your visit short if: your priority is seeing Italy's most spectacular sights. Bologna's sights are impressive—they just don't rank with the treasures of Rome, Florence, and Venice.

Stop 6: Verona (1–2 Days)

North from Bologna (1½ hours by train, a little longer by car) is Verona, a charming midsize city with a distinctly northern Italian air. Standing alongside the fast-flowing River Adige, gazing at the rows of old palazzi along its banks and the rolling hills of cypress and beyond, it's easy to fall for this city of Romeo and Juliet. Spend your time here wandering the medieval piazzas; skip the touristy so-called "House of Juliet," but don't miss the stunning ancient Roman **Arena**, the **Castelvecchio** (old castle), and **San Zeno Maggiore**, possibly Italy's finest Romanesque church.

Verona is often mentioned in the same breath with **Vicenza** and **Padua**, two other cities of similar size located in the **Veneto** region, on the green plains to the west of Venice. Vicenza is best known for its pal-

A GREAT ITINERARY

aces designed by Andrea Palladio, one of history's most influential architects; Padua's star attraction is the **Cappella degli Scrovegni**, a chapel decorated with landmark Giotto frescoes. Both towns are well worth a visit as you make your way toward Venice.

Extend your stay if: you're here in the summer and have a chance to see an opera at Verona's Arena—a truly grand spectacle.

Keep your visit short if: you're impatient to see Venice.

Stop 7: Venice (2–4 Days)

Venice is one of the world's most novel cities, with canals where streets should be and an atmosphere of faded splendor that practically defines the word decadent. Once a great seafaring power, Venice now lives for tourism, prompting cynics to compare it to Disneyland. It's true that **Piazza San Marco,** the magnificent main square, is frequently packed with sightseers, and there are plenty of kitschy souvenirs for sale in the heavily trafficked area around the **Rialto Bridge.** But Venice is no Mickey Mouse affair: it has a rich history, it's packed with artistic treasures accumulated over a thousand years, and despite the crowds it remains inescapably romantic.

Allow yourself some time to get acclimated. If you have a rental car, return it to the offices on the city's western edge, then find your hotel (be sure to get directions in advance), and if all goes well, you'll have time left in the day left for sightseeing. Rather than making a beeline for Piazza San Marco, check out some of the other spectacular attractions, such as the church of **Santa Maria Gloriosa dei Frari** and the **Scuola Grande di San Rocco,** or just spend a couple of hours getting lost in the city's back canals before finding your way to a seafood dinner. Afterward, consider a nightcap around the **Campo San Luca** or **Campo Santa Margarita.**

Begin the next morning vaporetto (water bus) cruise along the **Grand Canal,** then make your visit to **Piazza San Marco,** home to the Byzantine splendor of the **Basilica di San Marco** and the imposing **Palazzo Ducale.** After lunch, perhaps at a traditional Venetian bacaro (wine bar), take the Accademia footbridge across the Grand Canal and see the **Gallerie dell'Accademia,** Venice's most important art gallery. Wander through the **Dorsoduro** neighborhood, finishing up with a romantic sunset stroll along the **Zattere** boardwalk before proceeding to dinner.

On subsequent days, make your sightseeing priorities the **Rialto fish market** (a foodie highlight), **Ca' Rezzonico** and **Ca' d'Oro** (classic Venetian palaces), and **Santa Maria dei Miracoli** and **Santi Giovanni e Paolo** (two spectacular churches).

Extend your stay if: you want to discover Venice beyond the crowds. Exploring the neighborhoods east of Piazza San Marco and the quieter outer islands will take you to another world.

Keep your visit short if: you don't have a tolerance for getting lost. Navigating the streets of Venice can feel like working through a maze.

BEATING THE EURO

Below are suggestions for ways to save money on your trip, courtesy of the Travel Talk Forums at Fodors.com.

Transportation

"I take regional trains instead of the Eurostar trains. For example, Florence to Rome on Eurostar is 32.50 euro; the regional train is 15.80 euro. That's half the price; so what if it takes 15 minutes longe . . . big deal." —JoanneH

"Instead of taking the Leonardo Express from Fiumicino to Termini in Rome, take the FR1 to whichever station is most convenient for you. The FR1 departs every 15 minutes (instead of every 30 minutes for the Express), costs only €5 (instead of €9.50 for the Express), and avoids the hullabaloo of Termini." —Therese

Food & Drink

"Buy snacks and bottled water in bulk at a neighborhood supermarket at the beginning of your stay and keep them cool in your apartment or hotel fridge. Grab a bottle each when leaving in the AM and that way avoid buying expensive water or snacks near tourist attractions, where prices are much higher. Save your euros for espresso or gelato." —cruisinred

"Bars always have two different prices: If you have your coffee at the counter it's cheaper than when a waiter serves it at a table (servizio al tavolo)." —quokka

"Visit wine fill-up shops in Italy; get table wine from the cask for 2-3 euros a liter. In Rome we would get them filled at the Testaccio market . . . I will usually ask at the local bar where I go for my coffee." —susanna

"If you aren't hungry, skip to secondo— the 'second course.' Rarely do Italians eat a primo e secondo when they go out." —glittergirl

Sights

"The small cities can be less expensive but still fabulous. We were just in Assisi—all the sites were free, a delicious dinner for two with wine was 22 euros, and our hotel was reasonable at 65 euros per night." —rosetravels

"For the art lover on a budget: Most of the art I saw in Rome is free. Where else can you see countless Caravaggios, two Michelangelos, and even more Berninis for the cost of the wear and tear on the soles of your shoes?" —amyb

"One way to save on the expense of guided tours is to register online at Sound Guides (www.sound-guides.com/) and download the various free self-guided tours to your Ipod or MP3 player." —monicapileggi

Lodging

"Go off-season—March or November have better air prices and also accommodations, particularly if you stay in apartments, which you can rent for much less off-season (and plan some meals in-house—make the noon meal your biggest of the day, then have a small dinner in the apartment)." —bobthenavigator

"Everyone talks about going in the off season and mentions November or March. But in Florence at least, July is a shoulder season. I got a hotel room for half to a third the cost of the same room during the high season." —isabel

"We try to book apartments whenever we can . . . and in Tuscany we rent farm houses. Especially if you are traveling with more than 2 persons these are usually much more reasonable." —caroltis

FAQS

Is it okay to drink cappuccino after noon? For most Italians, a frothy cappuccino is a morning thing: drinking milk later in the day is thought to be bad for the stomach. So, if you order a cappuccino in the afternoon or evening, you'll give yourself away as a tourist, and you may encounter a hint of condescension from the barista. But unless you're trying to pass as a local, there's no reason not to order whatever suits your fancy.

Are Italian drivers as crazy as I've heard? Yes—at least some of them are. Americans tend to be well schooled in defensive-driving techniques, but many Italians are not. When you hit the road, don't be surprised to encounter tailgating and high-risk passing. Your best response is to take the same safety-first approach you use at home; on the road is one place where you don't want to be mistaken for a local. On the up side, Italy's roads are very well maintained. Note that wearing a seat belt and having your lights on at all times are required by law.

Is the Cinque Terre a viable day trip from Florence? Technically it's doable, but we don't recommend it. You'll spend about five hours on the train round-trip, or something close to that if you go by car. And if it's summer and you want to hike the trails (which most people do), you're better off getting started early in the morning so you can beat the heat. The Cinque Terre is a beautiful, one-of-a-kind destination, and it deserves an overnight—but if you're set on a day trip, you're better off starting from Pisa or Lucca.

What's crime like in Italy? By and large, the cities of central and northern Italy are remarkably crime free. An exception, unfortunately, are the tourist-focused crimes of purse snatching and pickpocketing. It would be an overstatement to say these crimes are rampant, but they do happen on a regular basis, particularly around train stations and major tourist attractions. They're commonly perpetrated by groups of street kids and by well-dressed professionals cruising for easy targets. A little common sense goes a long way toward keeping yourself safe: if children approach you, don't be reluctant to shoo them away firmly; don't keep your wallet in your back pocket; carry a purse with a shoulder strap, and wear it across your chest, so it can't be separated from you with a simple tug.

On restaurant bills, does "coperto" mean tip, and if it doesn't, what does it mean? "Coperto" means cover, and it's a mandatory surcharge intended to cover the cost of tableware, linens, and the bread in the obligatory bread basket. It's an inescapable charge that comes with the territory—it's neither a tip nor a scam markup perpetrated on tourists.

So how do I tip then? Italians typically don't tip. This doesn't mean that you shouldn't, though. Always check your bill to see if service is included automatically (usually 10%). If it is, leave no more. If not, tip no more than 10%, remembering that Italian wait staff are paid a living wage.

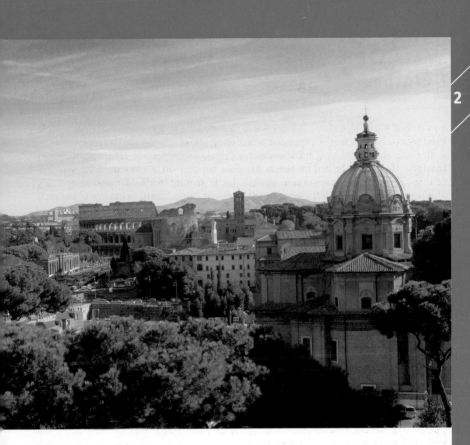

Rome

WORD OF MOUTH

"There's something very powerful to being surrounded by all that history (and I'm not a history buff). It's not a place where you walk up, snap a picture, and say, 'All right I've seen it.' It's an imposing experience (in a good way) . . . There are other beautiful scenic places in the world, but there's only one Rome."
—flatfeet

WELCOME TO ROME

TOP REASONS TO GO

★ **The Pantheon:** Of ancient Rome's remains, this is the best preserved and most impressive.

★ **St. Peter's Square and Basilica:** The primary church of the Catholic faith is truly awe-inspiring.

★ **Galleria Borghese:** With a setting as exquisite as its collection, this small, elegant museum showcases some of the finest baroque and Renaissance art in Italy.

★ **A morning walk through Campo de' Fiori:** The city comes alive in this bustling market square.

★ **Roman pizza:** Maybe it's the ovens, maybe the crust, maybe the cheese, but they just don't make it like this back home.

1 **Ancient Rome.** Backstopped by the stupendous Colosseum, the Roman Forum and Palatine Hill were once the hub of western civilization.

2 **Navona & Campo.** At the heart of Rome's historic quarter, these districts revolve around the ancient Pantheon, Campo de' Fiori, and spectacular Piazza Navona.

3 **Corso & Spagna.** Rome's "Broadway," Via del Corso, begins at Piazza Venezia and neatly divides the city center in two. A few blocks east is Piazza de Spagna, a classic area for people-watching and sophisticated shopping.

4 **Repubblica & Quirinale.** A largely 19th-century district, Repubblica lets art lovers go for baroque with a bevy of Bernini works. To the south looms the Quirinale hill, crowned by Italy's presidential palace.

5 **Villa Borghese & Piazza del Popolo.** Rome's largest park is home to the treasure-packed Galleria Borghese. Neighboring Piazza del Popolo is one of the city's main squares.

6 **The Vatican.** Hundreds of thousands of pilgrims and art-lovers come here to see St. Peter's Basilica, the Vatican Museums, and the Sistine Chapel.

GETTING ORIENTED

Rome is a sprawling city, but you'll likely spend most of your time in and around the historic center. The area is split by the River Tiber (Tevere in Italian). To its west are the Vatican and the Trastevere neighborhood. To its east is everything else you've come to see: the Colosseum, the Spanish Steps, and scores of other exceptional sights, not to mention piazzas, fountains, shops, and restaurants. This is one of the most culturally rich plots of land in the world.

7 The Ghetto & Trastevere. Once a Jewish quarter, the newly gentrified Ghetto still preserves the flavor of Old Rome. Across the Tiber, Trastevere is a neighborhood of mom-and-pop trattorias and medieval alleyways.

ROME PLANNER

Reservations Required

You should reserve tickets for the following sights. See the listings within the chapter for contact information:

Galleria Borghese requires reservations. Visitors are admitted in two-hour shifts, and prime time slots can sell out days in advance, so it pays to plan ahead. You can reserve by phone or through the gallery's Web site.

In the ancient Rome archaeological area, reservations for the Colosseum save you from standing in a ticket line that sometimes takes upward of an hour. You can reserve by phone or on the Web.

At the Vatican, you need to reserve several days in advance to see the gardens, and several weeks in advance to see the necropolis. For information about attending a papal audience, see the CloseUp box "A Morning with the Pope" several pages into this chapter.

Making the Most of Your Time

Roma, non basta una vita ("Rome, a lifetime is not enough"): this famous saying should be stamped on the passport of every first-time visitor to the Eternal City. On the other hand, it's a warning: Rome is so packed with sights that it is impossible to take them all in; it's easy to run yourself ragged trying to check off the items on your "Santa Claus" list. At the same time, the saying is a celebration of the city's abundance. There's so much here, you're bound to make discoveries you hadn't anticipated. To conquer Rome, strike a balance between visits to major sights and leisurely neighborhood strolls.

In the first category, the Vatican and the remains of ancient Rome loom the largest. Both require at least half a day; a good strategy is to devote your first morning to one and your second to the other. Leave the afternoons for exploring the neighborhoods that comprise "Baroque Rome" and the shopping district around the Spanish Steps and Via Condotti. If you have more days at your disposal, continue with the same approach. Among the sights, Galleria Borghese and the multilayered church of San Clemente are particularly worthwhile, and the neighborhoods of Trastevere and the Ghetto make for great roaming.

Since there's a lot of ground to cover in Rome, it's wise to plan your busy sightseeing schedule with possible savings in mind, and purchasing the Roma Pass (⊕ www.romapass.it) allows you to do just that. The three-day pass costs €20 and is good for unlimited use of buses, trams and the metro. It includes free admission to two of more than 40 participating museums or archaeological sites, including the Colosseum (and bumps you to the head of the long line there, to boot!), the Ara Pacis museum, the Musei Capitolini, and Galleria Borghese, plus discounted tickets to many other museums. The Roma Pass can be purchased at tourist information booths across the city, at Termini Station, or at Terminal C of the International Arrivals section of Fiumicino Airport.

How's the Weather?

Not surprisingly, spring and fall are the best times to visit, with mild temperatures and many sunny days; the famous Roman sunsets are also at their best. Summers are often sweltering. In July and August, come if you like, but learn to do as the Romans do—get up and out early, seek refuge from the afternoon heat, resume activities in early evening, and stay up late to enjoy the nighttime breeze. Come August, many shops and restaurants close as locals head out for vacation. Remember that air-conditioning is still a relatively rare phenomenon in this city. Roman winters are relatively mild, with persistent rainy spells.

Hop-On, Hop-Off

Rome has its own "hop-on, hop-off" sightseeing buses. The Trambus Open Roma 110 bus leaves with 10-minute frequencies from Piazza dei Cinquecento (at the main Termini railway station), with a two-hour loop including the Quirinale, the Colosseum, Piazza Navona, St. Peter's, the Trevi Fountain, and Via Veneto. Tickets are €16 (kids 6–12, €7). A variant is the Archeobus, which departs every 20 minutes from the Piazza dei Cinquecento and heads on out to the Via Appia Antica, including stops at the Colosseum, Baths of Caracalla, and the Catacombs. Tickets are €13 (kids 6–12, €6). The Web site for both is ⊕ www.trambu sopen.com.

Roman Hours

Virtually the entire city shuts down on Sunday, although museums, pastry shops, and most restaurants are closed Monday. However, most stores in the centro storico area, the part of town that caters to tourists, remain open. Shop hours generally run from 10 AM to 1 PM, then reopen around 4 PM until 7:30 or 8 PM. Unless advertised as having orario continuato (open all day), most businesses close from 1 to 4 PM for lunch, or riposo. On Monday, shops usually don't open until around 3 or 4 PM. Pharmacies tend to have the same hours of operation as stores unless they advertise orario notturno (night hours); two can be found at Piazza Barberini and Piazza Risorgimento (near St. Peter's Square). As for churches, most open at 8 or 9 in the morning, close from noon to 3 or 4, then reopen until 6:30 or 7. St. Peter's, however, is open 7 AM to 7 PM (6 in the fall and winter).

Information, Please

Rome's main APT (Azienda Per Turismo) Tourist Information Office is at Via Parigi 5–11 (☎ 06/488991 ⊕ www.romatur ismo.it), near the main Termini rail station. In addition, green APT information kiosks with multilingual personnel are near the most important sights and squares, as well as at Termini Station and Leonardo da Vinci Airport. These kiosks, called Tourist Information Sites (Punti Informativi Turistici, or PIT) can be found at:

PIT Castel S. Angelo, Lungotevere Vaticano; open 9:30–7 PM

PIT Cinque Lune, Piazza delle Cinque Lune (Piazza Navona); open 9:30–7 PM

PIT Fiumicino, Aeroporto Leonardo Da Vinci–Arrivi Internazionali Terminal C; open 9–7:30 PM

PIT Minghetti, Via Marco Minghetti (corner of Via del Corso); open 9:30–7 PM

PIT Nazionale, Via Nazionale (Palazzo delle Esposizioni); open 9:30–7 PM

PIT Santa Maria Maggiore, at Via dell'Olmata; open 9:30–7 PM

PIT Termini, Stazione Termini, at Via Giovanni Giolitti 34; open 8–8

PIT Trastevere, on Piazza Sidney Sonnino; open 9:30–7 PM

GETTING HERE & AROUND

Getting Here by Car

The main access routes from the north are A1 (Autostrada del Sole) from Milan and Florence and the A12-E80 highway from Genoa. All highways connect with the Grande Raccordo Anulare Ring Road (GRA), which channels traffic into the city center. For driving directions, check out ⊕ www.tuttocitta.it. Note: Parking in Rome can be a nightmare—private cars are not allowed access to the entire historic center during the day (weekdays 8–6; Saturday 2 pm–6 pm), except for residents.

Getting Here by Train

The main train stations in Rome are Termini, Tiburtina, Ostiense, and Trastevere. On long-distance routes (to Florence and Venice, for instance), you can either travel by the cheap, but slow, diretto trains, or the fast, but more expensive Intercity or the Eurostar. Trains are run by state-owned Trenitalia (☎892/2021 within Italy, 06/68475475 from abroad ⊕www.trenitalia.it); the Web site is fairly user-friendly, though it can switch from English to Italian as you navigate between pages.

Getting Here by Air

Rome's principal airport is Leonardo da Vinci Airport/Fiumicino (☎06/65951 ⊕www.adr.it) commonly known by the name of its location, Fiumicino (FCO). It's 30 km (19 mi) southwest of the city but has a direct train link with downtown Rome. Rome's other airport, with no direct train link, is Ciampino (☎06/794941 ⊕www.adr.it) or CIA, 15 km (9 mi) south of downtown and used mostly by low-cost airlines.

Two trains link downtown Rome with Fiumicino. Inquire at the APT tourist information counter in the International Arrivals hall (Terminal B) or train information counter near the tracks to determine which takes you closest to your destination in Rome. The 30-minute nonstop Airport-Termini express (called the Leonardo Express) goes directly to Track 25 at Termini Station, Rome's main train station; tickets cost €11. The FM1 train stops in Trastevere. Always stamp your tickets in the little machines near the track before you board.

As for Ciampino, COTRAL buses connect to trains that go to the city.

Getting Here by Bus

Bus lines cover all of Rome's surrounding Lazio region and are operated by the Consorzio Trasporti Lazio, or COTRAL (☎800/150008 ⊕www.cotralspa.it). These bus routes terminate either near Tiburtina Station or at outlying Metro stops, such as Rebibbia and Ponte Mammolo (Line B) and Anagnina (Line A).

COTRAL and buses run by SENA (☎800/930960 ⊕www.sena.it) are good options for taking short day trips from Rome, such as those that leave daily from Rome's Ponte Mammolo (Line B) metro station for the town of Tivoli, where Hadrian's Villa and Villa D'Este are located.

Rome Public Transit

Rome's integrated transportation system, ATAC (☎06/46952027 or 800/431784 ⊕ www.atac.roma.it), includes the Metropolitana subway, city buses, and trams. A ticket (BIT) valid for 75 minutes on any combination of buses and trams and one entrance to the metro costs €1. Day passes can be purchased for €4, and weekly passes for €16. Tickets (singly or in quantity—it's a good idea to have a few extra tickets handy) are sold at tobacconists, newsstands, some coffee bars, automatic ticket machines in metro stations, some bus stops, and ATAC and COTRAL ticket booths. Time-stamp tickets at metro turnstiles and in little yellow machines on buses and trams when boarding the first vehicle and stamp it again when boarding for the last time within 75 minutes.

Getting Around by Bus & Tram

ATAC city buses and trams are orange, gray-and-red, or blue-and-orange. You board at the rear and to exit at the middle; you must buy your ticket before boarding and stamp it in a machine when you enter.

Buses and trams run from 5:30 am to midnight, plus there's an extensive network of night (notturno) buses. ATAC has a Web site (⊕ www.atac.roma.it) that will help you determine your route. To navigate the site, look for "Muoversi a Roma" and then click on "Calcola il percorso" to get to a page that changes the site into English.

Be aware that festivi buses run only on Sunday and holidays; regular buses will either say feriali, (daily) or are unlabeled. Free Metro Routes maps are available at tourist info booths.

Getting Around by Metro

The Metropolitana (or metro) subway is the easiest and fastest way to get around Rome. The A line—known as the linea turistica (tourist line) will take you to many of Rome's main attractions, including Piazza di Spagna (Spagna stop), Piazza del Popolo (Flaminio), St. Peter's Square and the Vatican Museums (Cipro-Musei Vaticani), and the Trevi Fountain (Barberini). The B line will take you to the Colosseum (Colosseo stop) and Circus Maximus (Ostiense Station), and also lead you to the heart of Testaccio, Rome's nightlife district. The two lines intersect at Rome's main station, Termini. Street entrances are marked with red "M" signs. The metro runs from 5:30 am to 11:30 pm (Saturday: 12:30 am).

Getting Around by Taxi

Taxis in Rome do not normally cruise, but if free they will stop if you flag them down. They wait at stands and can also be called by phone (☎06/6645, 06/3570, 06/4994, 06/5551, or 06/4157). Always ask for a receipt (ricevuta) to make sure the driver charges you the correct amount. Use only licensed cabs with a plaque next to the license plate reading "Servizio Pubblico."

EATING & DRINKING WELL IN ROME

In Rome, traditional cuisine reigns supreme. Most chefs follow the mantra of freshness over fuss, simplicity of flavor and preparation over complex cooking methods.

So when Romans continue ordering the standbys, it's easy to understand why. And we're talking about very old standbys: some restaurants re-create dishes that come from ancient recipes of Apicius, probably the first celebrity chef (to Emperor Tiberius) and cookbook author of the Western world. Today, Rome's cooks excel at what has taken hundreds, or thousands, of years to perfect.

Still, if you're hunting for newer-than-now developments, things are slowly changing. Talented young chefs are exploring new culinary frontiers, with results that tingle the taste buds: potato gnocchi with sea urchin sauce, artichoke strudel, and oysters with red-onion foam are just a few recent examples. Of course, there's grumbling about the number of chefs who, in a clumsy effort to be nuovo, end up with collision rather than fusion. That noted, Rome is the capital city, and the influx of residents from other regions of the country allows for many variations on the Italian theme.

FOODIE FINDS

Via Cola di Rienzo is home to two of Rome's best specialty shops: **Castroni** (⊠Via Cola di Rienzo 200, Prati ☎06/6874651), pictured above, a gastroshop that sells high-quality cured meats, Italian cheeses, wines, pastas, and fresh truffles. Next door, **Franchi** (⊠Via Cola di Rienzo 196, Prati ☎06/68743382) is well known among expats for its imported foreign foods from the United States, Great Britain, Japan, India, and Mexico, as well as its impressive selection of candies, preserves, olive oils, and balsamic vinegars. Franchi is a great place to stop in for caffè and a cornetto (an Italian croissant).

ARTICHOKES

If there's one vegetable Rome is known for, it's the artichoke, or *carciofo*. The classic Roman preparation, *carciofo alla romana*, is a large, globe-shaped artichoke stuffed with wild mint and garlic, then braised. It's available at restaurants throughout the city in spring, when artichokes are in season. For the excellent Roman-Jewish version, *carciofo alla giudia*—a younger artichoke that is deep-fried until crisp and leathery brown in color—head to any restaurant in the Ghetto.

BUCATINI ALLA MATRICIANA

What may appear to the naked eye as spaghetti with red sauce is actually *bucatini alla matriciana*—a spicy, rich, and complex dish that owes its flavor to an important ingredient: *guanciale,* or cured pig's cheek. The simple sauce features crushed tomatoes and red pepper flakes. It is served over bucatini, a hollow, spaghetti-like pasta, and topped with grated pecorino romano cheese.

CODA ALLA VACCINARA

Rome's largest slaughterhouse in the 1800s was housed in the Testaccio neighborhood. That's where you'll find dishes like *coda alla vaccinara,* or "oxtail in the style of the slaughterhouse." This sweet-and-sour dish is made from oxtails stewed with tomatoes and wine, and seasoned with garlic, cinnamon, pancetta, and myriad other flavorings. The stew cooks for a day or two, then is finished with the sweet-and-sour element—often raisins or bittersweet chocolate. It often is served over polenta or pasta.

GELATO

For many travelers, the first taste of *gelato*—Italian ice cream—is one of the most memorable moments of their Italian trip. Almost a cross between regular American ice cream and soft serve, gelato's texture is dense but softer than hard ice cream because of the process by which it's whipped when freezing. A few common flavors are *stracciatella* (chocolate chip), *caffè* (coffee), *nocciola* (hazelnut), *fragola* (strawberry), and *cioccolato* (chocolate).

PIZZA

Roman pizza comes in two types: *pizza rustica* and *pizza al taglio* (by the slice), which have a thicker focaccia-like crust and is cut into squares. These slices are sold by weight and are available all day. The other type, *pizza tonda* (whole rounds), has a very thin crust. *Pizza tonda* is cooked in wood-burning ovens that reach extremely high temperatures. Since they're so hot, the ovens are usually fired up only in the evenings, which is why Roman pizzerias are only open for dinner.

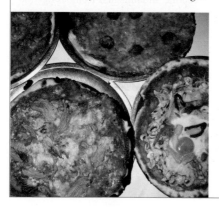

Updated by
Megan K.
Williams,
Dana
Klitzberg,
Jen Laskey,
Erica Firpo
& Lynda
Albertson

COMING OFF THE AUTOSTRADA AT Roma Nord or Roma Sud, you know by the convergence of heavily trafficked routes that you are entering a grand nexus: All roads lead to Rome. And then the interminable suburbs, the railroad crossings, the intersections—no wonder they call it the Eternal City. As you enter the city proper, features that match your expectations begin to take shape: a bridge with heroic statues along its parapets; a towering cake of frothy marble decorated with allegorical figures in extravagant poses; a piazza and an obelisk under an umbrella of pine trees. Then you spot what looks like a multistory parking lot; with a gasp, you realize it's the Colosseum.

Yours truly, have arrived. You're in the city's heart. You step down from your excursion bus onto the broad girdle of tarmac that encircles the great stone arena of the Roman emperors, and scurry out of the way of the passing Fiats—the motorists behind the wheels seem to display the panache of so many Ben-Hurs. The excitement of arriving here jolts the senses and sharpens expectations.

The timeless city to which all roads lead, Mamma Roma enthralls visitors today as she has since time immemorial. More than Florence, more than Venice, this is Italy's treasure storehouse. Here, the ancient Romans made us heirs-in-law to what we call Western Civilization; where centuries later Michelangelo painted in the Sistine Chapel; where Gian Lorenzo Bernini's baroque nymphs and naiads still dance in their marble fountains; and where, at Cinecittà Studios, Fellini filmed *La Dolce Vita* and 8½. Today, the city remains a veritable Grand Canyon of culture: Ancient Rome rubs shoulders with the medieval, the modern runs into the Renaissance, and the result is like nothing so much as an open-air museum.

Little wonder Rome's enduring popularity feeds a gluttonous tourism industry that can feel more like *National Lampoon's European Vacation* than *Roman Holiday*. As tour buses belch black smoke and the line at the Vatican Museums stretches on into eternity, even the steeliest of sightseers have been known to wonder, why am I here? The answer, with apologies to Dorothy, is: There's no place like Rome. Yesterday's Grand Tourists thronged the city for the same reason today's Expedians do. Majestic, complicated, enthralling, romantic, chaotic, monumental Rome is one of the world's great cities—past, present, and, probably, future.

But always remember: *Bisogna vivere a Roma coi costumi di Roma* ("When you are in Rome, do as Rome does"). Don't feel intimidated by the press of art and culture. Instead, contemplate the grandeur from a table at a sun-drenched caffè on Piazza Navona; let Rome's colorful life flow around you without feeling guilty because you haven't seen everything. It can't be done, anyway. There's just so much here that you will have to come back again, so be sure to throw a coin in the Trevi Fountain. It works.

EXPLORING ROME

Updated by
Megan K.
Williams

Most everyone begins by discovering the grandeur that was Rome: the Colosseum, the Forum, and the Pantheon. Then many move on to the Vatican, the closest thing to heaven on earth for some.

The historical pageant continues with the 1,001 splendors of the baroque era: glittering palaces, jewel-studded churches, and Caravaggio masterpieces. Arrive refreshed—thanks to an espresso at Antico Caffè Greco—at the foot of the Spanish Steps, where the picturesque world of the classic Grand Tour (peopled by such spirits as John Keats and Tosca) awaits you.

Thankfully, Rome provides delightful ways to catch your historic breath along the way: a walk through the cobblestone valleys of Trastevere or an hour stolen alongside a splashing Bernini fountain. Keep in mind that an uncharted ramble through the heart of the old city can be just as satisfying as the contemplation of a chapel or a trek through marbled museum corridors. No matter which aspect of Rome you end up enjoying the most, a visit to the Eternal City will live up to its name in memory.

Continued on page 50

ADMISSION

ADMISSION	
Rome Archeologia Card**	€20
Arco di Constantino	Free
Circo Massimo	Free
Foro di Traiano	€6.50
Colosseo, Colle Palatino & Foro Romano*	€12
Domus Aurea	€4.50
Musei Capitolini	€6.50
Piazza del Campidoglio	Free
Santa Maria d'Aracoeli	Free
Terme di Caracalla	€6

*Reservation fee €1.50
**This is a combination ticket for the Colosseo, Colle Palatino, and the various branches of the Museo Nazionale Romano (Palazzo Altemps, Crypta Balbi, Terme di Diocleziano, Terme di Caracalla, Villa dei Quintili, the Mausoleo di Cecilia Metella, and Palazzo Massimo alle Terme), good for seven consecutive days.

0   100 yards
0   100 meters

CAPITOLINE HILL: The original capitol hill. The seat of government in Rome since its founding now also holds the Capitoline Museums, chock-full of the treasures of antiquity.

ROMAN FORUM: Downtown Ancient Rome. People from all corners of the empire crowded into the Forum to do business, to hear the latest news, and to worship.

PALATINE HILL: Home of the empire's rich and famous. Luxurious villas lined Palatine Hill; emperors held court on its heights and vied with their predecessors for lasting renown.

CAMPIDOGLIO   FORO ROMANO   COLLE PALATINO

ANCIENT ROME
GLORIES OF
THE CAESARS

Domus Aurea

COLOSSEO

Colosseo

Pza. del Colosseo

Vibenna

Villa Celimontana

Viale del Monte Oppio

Parco Traiano

V. Terme di Tito

V. Nicola Salvi

V. d. Domus Aurea

V. Labicana

V. S. Giov. in Laterano

V. S. S. Quattro Coronati

☕ **Ai Tre Scalini**

V. Ostilia

V. Celimontana

V. Claudia

Cl. d. Scauro

KEY

☕ *Cafe / Restaurant*

COLOSSEUM: Gladiators fought for the chance to live another day on the floor of the Colosseum, iconic symbol of ancient Rome.

Time has reduced ancient Rome to fields of silent ruins, but the powerful impact of what happened here, of the genius and power that made Rome the center of the Western world, echoes across the millennia.

In this one compact area of the city, you can step back into the Rome of Cicero, Julius Caesar, and Virgil. Walk along the streets they knew, cool off in the shade of the Colosseum that loomed over the city, and see the sculptures poised above their piazzas. At the end of a day of exploring, climb one of the famous seven hills and watch the sun set over what was once the heart of the civilized world.

Today, this part of Rome, more than any other, is a perfect example of that layering of historic eras, the overlapping of ages, of religions, of a past that is very much a part of the present. Christian churches rise from the foundations of ancient pagan temples. An immense marble monument to a 19th-century king shares a square with a medieval palace built by a pope. Still, the history and memory of ancient Rome dominate the area. It's fitting that in the aftermath of centuries of such pageantry Percy Bysshe Shelley and Edward Gibbon reflected here on the meaning of *sic transit gloria mundi* (so passes away the glory of the world).

CAMPIDOGLIO

The Capitoline Museums are closed on Monday. Late evening is an option for this area. Though the Santa Maria d'Aracoeli church is closed, the museums are open until 9 PM, and the views of the city lights and the illuminated Victor Emmanuel II monument and the Foro Romano are striking.

CLIMB MICHELANGELO'S DRAMATIC RAMP TO THE SUMMIT of one of Rome's seven hills, the Campidoglio (also known as Capitoline Hill), for views across the rooftops of modern Rome in one direction and across the ruins of ancient Rome in the other. Check out the stellar Musei Capitolini, crammed with a collection of masterpieces rivaled only by the Vatican museums.

★ **Piazza del Campidoglio.** In Michelangelo's piazza at the top of the Campidoglio stands a bronze equestrian statue of Marcus Aurelius (AD 121–180). A legend foretells that some day the statue's original gold surface will return, heralding the end of the world. Pending the arrival of that day, the original 2nd century statue was moved inside the Musei Capitolini; a copy sits on the piazza. Stand with your back to it to survey central Rome.

The Campidoglio, the site of the Roman Empire's first and holiest temples, had fallen into ruin by the Middle Ages and was called *Monte Caprino* (Goat Hill). In 1536 Pope Paul III (1468–1549) decided to restore its grandeur for the triumphal entry into the city of Charles V (1500–1558), the Holy Roman Emperor. He called upon Michelangelo to create the staircase ramp, the buildings and facades on the square, the pavement decoration, and the pedestal for the bronze statue.

The two buildings that make up the **Musei Capitolini** are on the piazza, flanking the **Palazzo Senatorio**. The Campidoglio has always been the seat of Rome's government; its Latin name is the root for the word capitol. Today, Rome's city hall occupies the Palazzo Senatorio. Head to the vantage points in the belvederes on the sides of the palazzo for great views of the ruins of ancient Rome.

★ **Musei Capitolini** (Capitoline Museums). Housed in the twin Palazzi del Museo Capitolino and Palazzo dei Conservatori buildings, this is a greatest hits collection of Roman art through the ages, from the ancients to the baroque.

The **Palazzi del Museo Capitolino** contains hundreds of Roman busts of phi-

AN EMPEROR CHEAT SHEET

OCTAVIAN/AUGUSTUS (27 BC–AD 14)

After the death of Julius Caesar, Octavian gained control of Rome after a series of battles that culminated with the defeat of Antony and Cleopatra at Actium. Later known as Caesar Augustus, he was Rome's first emperor. His rule began a 200-year period of peace known as the Pax Romana.

Colle Palatino

CALIGULA (AD 37–41)

Caligula was tremendously popular when he came to power at the age of 25, but he very soon became infamous for his excessive cruelty, immorality, and erratic behavior. His contemporaries universally considered him to be insane. He was murdered by his own guard within four years.

losophers and emperors—a fascinating Who's Who of the ancient world. Forty-eight Roman emperors are represented. Unlike the Greeks, whose portraits are idealized, the Romans preferred the warts-and-all school of representation. Other notable sculptures include the poignant *Dying Gaul* and the regal *Capitoline Venus*. In the Capitolino courtyard is a gigantic, reclining sculpture of Oceanus, found in the Roman Forum and later dubbed *Marforio*. This was one of Rome's "talking statues" to which citizens from the 1500s to the 1900s affixed anonymous satirical verses and notes of political protest. Opened in 2007, the Esedra di Marco Aurelio displays the famous bronze equestrian statue of emperor Marcus Aurelius (180 AD).

Lining the courtyard of the **Palazzo dei Conservatori** are the colossal fragments of a head, leg, foot, and hand—all that remains of the famous statue of the emperor Constantine the Great, who believed that Rome's future lay with Christianity. These immense effigies were much in vogue in the later days of the Roman Empire. The renowned symbol of Rome, the *Capitoline Wolf*, a 6th-century BC Etruscan bronze, holds a place of honor in the museum; the suckling twins were added during the Renaissance to adapt the statue to the legend of Romulus and Remus. The Palazzo also contains some of baroque painting's great masterpieces, including Caravaggio's *La Buona Ventura* (1595) and *San Giovanni Battista* (1602), Peter Paul Rubens's *Romulus and Remus* (1614), and Pietro da Cortona's sumptuous portrait of Pope Urban VIII (1627). When museum fatigue sets in, enjoy the view and refreshments on a large open terrace in the Palazzo dei Conservatoria. ☎ *06/39967800 or 06/82059127* ⊕ *www.pierreci.it* ⊙ *Tues.–Sun. 9–8.*

Santa Maria d'Aracoeli. Seemingly endless, steep stairs climb from Piazza Venezia to the Santa Maria. There are 15th-century frescoes by Pinturicchio (1454–1513) in the first chapel on the right. ✉ *Via del Teatro di Marcello* ⊙ *Oct.–May, daily 7–noon and 4–6; June–Sept., daily 7–noon and 4–6:30.*

NERO (AD 54–68)

Nero is infamous as a violent persecutor of Christians. He also murdered his wife, his mother, and countless others. Although it's not certain whether he actually fiddled as Rome burned in AD 64, he was well known as a singer and a composer of music.

Domus Aurea

DOMITIAN (AD 81–96)

The first emperor to declare himself "Dominus et Deus" (Lord and God), he stripped away power from the Senate. After his death, the Senate retaliated by declaring him "Damnatio Memoriae" (his name and image were erased from all public records).

Colle Palatino

FORO ROMANO

⏱ TIMING TIPS

It takes about an hour to explore the Roman Forum. There are entrances on the Via dei Fori Imperiali and near the Colosseum. Another hour's walk will cover the Imperial Fora. You can reserve tickets online or by phone—operators speak English. If you are buying tickets in person, remember there are shorter lines here than at the Colosseum and the ticket is good for both sights.

EXPERIENCE THE ENDURING ROMANCE OF THE FORUM. Wander among its lonely columns and great, broken fragments of sculpted marble and stone— once temples, palaces, and shops crowded with people from all corners of the known world. This was the heart of ancient Rome and a symbol of the values that inspired Rome's conquest of an empire.

★ **Foro Romano** (Roman Forum). Built in a marshy valley between the Capitoline and Palatine hills, the Forum was the civic core of Republican Rome, the austere era that preceded the hedonism of the emperors. The Forum was the political, commercial, and religious center of Roman life. Hundreds of years of plunder and the tendency of later Romans to carry off what was left of the better building materials reduced it to the series of ruins you see today. Archaeological digs continue to uncover more about the sight; bear in mind that what you see are the ruins not of one period but of almost 900 years, from about 500 BC to AD 400.

The **Basilica Giulia**, which owes its name to Julius Caesar who had it built, was where the Centumviri, the hundred-or-so judges forming the civil court, met to hear cases. The open space before it was the core of the forum proper and prototype of Italy's

famous piazzas. Let your imagination dwell on Mark Antony (circa 81 BC–30 BC), who delivered the funeral address in Julius Caesar's honor from the rostrum left of the **Arco di Settimio Severo**. This arch, one of the grandest of all antiquity, was built several hundred years later in AD 203 to celebrate the victory of the emperor Severus (AD 146–211) over the Parthians, and was topped by a bronze equestrian statuary group with six horses. You can explore the reconstruction of the large brick senate hall, the **Curia**; three Corinthian columns (a favorite of 19th-century poets) are all that remains of the **Tempio di Vespasiano**. In the **Tempio di Vesta**, six highly privileged vestal virgins kept the sacred fire, a tradition that dated back to the very earliest days of Rome, when guarding the community's precious fire was essential to its well-being. The cleaned and restored **Arco di Tito**, which stands in a slightly

AN EMPEROR CHEAT SHEET

TRAJAN (AD 98–117)

Trajan, from Southern Spain, was the first Roman emperor not born in Italy. He enlarged the empire's boundaries to include modern-day Romania, Armenia, and Upper Mesopotamia.

Colonna di Traiano

HADRIAN (AD 117–138)

He expanded the empire in Asia and the Middle East. He's best known for designing and rebuilding the Pantheon, constructing a majestic villa at Tivoli, and initiating myriad other constructions across the empire, including the famed wall across Britain.

Pantheon, in Baroque Rome

elevated position on a spur of the Palatine Hill, was erected in AD 81 to celebrate the sack of Jerusalem 10 years earlier, after the great Jewish revolt. A famous relief shows the captured contents of Herod's Temple—including its huge seven-branched menorah—being carried in triumph down Rome's Via Sacra. Making sense of the ruins isn't always easy; consider renting an audio guide (€4) or buying a booklet that superimposes an image of the Forum in its heyday over a picture of it today. Guided tours in English usually begin at 10:30 AM. In summer the Forum is sometimes open for midnight (guided) tours—look for signs at the entrance or ask at your hotel. ☎ 06/39967700 ⊕ *www. pierreci.it* ⊗ *Daily, May–Oct. 8:30–7:30, Nov.–April 8:30–4:30.*

THE OTHER FORA

Fori Imperiali (Imperial Fora). These five grandly conceived squares flanked with columnades and temples were built by the emperors Caesar, Augustus, Vespasian, Nerva, and Trajan. The original Roman Forum, built up over 500 years of Republican Rome, had grown crowded, and Julius Caesar was the first to attempt

to rival it. He built the **Foro di Cesare** (Forum of Caesar), including a temple dedicated to himself and the goddess Minerva. Four later emperors followed his lead, creating their own fora. The grandest was the **Foro di Traiano** (Forum of Trajan) a veritable city unto itself built by Trajan (AD 53–117). The adjoining Mercati Traianei (Trajan's Markets), a huge multilevel brick complex of shops, walkways, and terraces, was one of the marvels of the ancient world. In the 20th century, Benito Mussolini built the Via dei Fori Imperiali directly through the Imperial Fora area. Marble and bronze maps on the wall along the avenue portray the extent of the Roman Empire and Republic, and many of the remains of the Imperial Fora lay buried beneath its surface.

Colonna di Traiano (Trajan's Column). The ashes of Trajan were buried inside the base of this column (the ashes have since been removed). Remarkable reliefs spiral up its sides, celebrating his military campaigns in Dacia (Romania). The column has stood in what was once the Forum of Trajan since AD 113. ☎ 06/69780532 ⊗ *Tues.–Sun. 9–6.*

MARCUS AURELIUS (AD 161–180)

Remembered as a humanitarian emperor, Marcus Aurelius was a Stoic philosopher and his *Meditations* are still read today. Nonetheless, he was an aggressive leader devoted to expanding the empire.

Piazza del Campidoglio

CONSTANTINE I (AD 306–337)

Constantine changed the course of history by legalizing Christianity. He legitimized the once-banned religion and paved the way for the papacy in Rome. Constantine also founded Constantinople, an Imperial capital in the East.

Arco di Constantino

COLLE PALATINO

IT ALL BEGAN HERE. ACCORDING TO LEGEND, ROMULUS, THE FOUNDER OF ROME, lived on the Colle Palatino (Palatine Hill). It was an exclusive address in ancient Rome, where emperors built palaces upon the slopes. Tour the Palatine's hidden corners and shady lanes, take a welcome break from the heat in its peaceful gardens, and enjoy a view of the Circo Massimo fit for an emperor.

★ **Colle Palatino** (Palatine Hill). A lane known as the Clivus Palatinus, paved with worn stones that were once trod by emperors and their slaves, climbs from the Forum area to a site that historians identify with Rome's earliest settlement. The legend goes that the infant twins Romulus and Remus were nursed by a she-wolf on the banks of the Tiber and adopted by a shepherd. Encouraged by the gods to build a city, the twins chose this site in 735 BC, fortifying it with a wall that archaeologist Rudolfo Lanciani identified in the late 19th century when digging on Palatine Hill.

During the Republican era the hill was an important religious center, housing the Temple of Cybele and the Temple of Victory, as well as an exclusive residential area. Cicero, Catiline, Crassus, and Agrippa all had homes here. Augustus was born on the hill, and as he rose in power, he built libraries, halls, and temples here; the **House of Livia,** reserved for his wife, is best preserved. Emperor Tiberius was the first to build a palace here; others followed. The structures most visible today date back to the late 1st century AD, when the Palatine experienced an extensive remodeling under Emperor Domitian. His architects put up two separate palaces, the **Domus Augustana** and the **Domus Livia.** During the Renaissance, the powerful Farnese family built gardens atop the ruins overlooking the Forum. Known as the **Orti Farnesiani,** they were Europe's first botanical gardens. The **Museo Palatino** charts the history of the hill. Splendid sculptures, frescoes, and mosaic intarsia from various imperial buildings are on display. ☎ 06/39967700 ⊕ www.pierreci.it 🕐 Tues.–Sun. 9–1 hr before sunset.

THE RISE AND FALL OF ANCIENT ROME

ca. 800 BC	Rise of Etruscan city-states.
510	Foundation of the Roman republic; expulsion of Etruscans from Roman territory.
343	Roman conquest of Greek colonies in Campania.
264–241	First Punic War (with Carthage): increased naval power helps Rome gain control of southern Italy and then Sicily.
218–200	Second Punic War: Hannibal's attempted conquest of Italy, using elephants, is eventually crushed.

218 BC

NEAR THE COLLE PALATINO

Circo Massimo (Circus Maximus). Ancient Rome's oldest and largest racetrack lies in the natural hollow between Palatine and Aventine hills. From the imperial box in the palace on Palatine Hill, emperors could look out over the oval course. Stretching about 650 yards from end to end, the Circus Maximus could hold more than 300,000 spectators. On certain occasions there were as many as 24 chariot races a day, and competitions could last for 15 days. The central ridge was the sight of two Egyptian obelisks (now in the Piazza del Popolo and Piazza San Giovanni in Laterano). Check out the panoramic views of the Circus Maximus from the Palatine Hill's Belvedere. You can also see the green slopes of the Aventine and Celian hills, as well as the bell tower of Santa Maria in Cosmedin.

Terme di Caracalla (Baths of Caracalla). For the Romans, public baths were much more than places to wash. The baths also had recital halls, art galleries, libraries, massage rooms, sports grounds, and gardens. Even the smallest public baths had at least some of these amenities, and in the capital of the Roman Empire, they were provided on a lavish scale. Ancient Rome's most beautiful and luxurious public baths were opened by the emperor Caracalla in AD 217 and were used until the 6th century.

Taking a bath was a long and complex process, and a social activity first and foremost. Remember, too, that for all their sophistication, the Romans didn't have soap. You began by sweating in the *sudatoria*, small rooms resembling saunas. From these you moved on to the *calidarium* for the actual business of washing, using a *strigil*, or scraper, to get the dirt off. Next was the *tepidarium*, where you gradually cooled down. Finally, you splashed around in the *frigidarium*, the only actual "bath" in the place, in essence a cold water swimming pool. There was a nominal admission fee, often waived by officials and emperors wishing to curry favor with the plebeians. The baths' functioning depended on the slaves who cared for the clients and stoked the fires that heated the water. ☏06/39967700 ⊕ *www.pierreci.it* ⊗ *Tues.–Sun. 9 AM–1 hr hour before sunset, Mon. 9–2.*

44 BC

150 BC	Roman Forum begins to take shape as the principal civic center in Italy.
146	Third Punic War: Rome razes city of Carthage and emerges as the dominant Mediterranean force.
133	Rome rules entire Mediterranean Basin except Egypt.
49	Julius Caesar conquers Gaul.
44	Julius Caesar is assassinated.
27	Rome's Imperial Age begins; Octavian (now named Augustus) becomes the first emperor and is later deified. The Augustan Age is celebrated in the works of Virgil (70 BC–AD 19), Ovid (43 BC–AD 17), Livy (59 BC–AD 17), and Horace (65–8 BC).

COLOSSEO

You can give the Colosseum a cursory look in about 30 minutes, but it deserves at least an hour. Make reservations by phone (there are English-speaking operators) or online at least a day in advance to avoid long lines. Or buy your ticket for the Colosseum at the Roman Forum, where the lines are usually shorter.

LEGEND HAS IT THAT AS LONG AS THE COLOSSEUM STANDS, ROME WILL STAND; and when Rome falls, so will the world. No visit to Rome is complete without a trip to the obstinate oval that has been the iconic symbol of the city for centuries.

★ **Colosseo.** A program of games and shows lasting 100 days celebrated the opening of the massive and majestic Colosseum in AD 80. On the opening day alone, 5,000 wild beasts perished. More than 70,000 spectators could sit within the arena's 573-yard circumference, which had marble facing, hundreds of statues for decoration, and a *velarium*—an ingenious system of sail-like awnings rigged on ropes manned by imperial sailors—to protect the audience from the sun and rain. Before the imperial box, gladiators would salute the emperor and cry, "*Ave, imperator, morituri te salutant*" ("Hail, emperor, men soon to die salute you"); it is said that when one day they heard the emperor Claudius respond, "Or maybe not," they were so offended that they called a strike.

Originally known as the Flavian Amphitheater, it took the name Colosseum after a truly colossal gilt bronze statue of Nero that stood nearby. Gladiator combat and staged animal hunts ended by the 6th century. The arena later served as a quarry from which materials were looted to build Renaissance churches and palaces. Finally, it was declared sacred by the Vatican in memory of the many Christians believed martyred here. (Scholars now maintain that Christians met their death elsewhere.) During the 19th century, romantic poets lauded the glories of the ruins when viewed by moonlight. Now its arches glow at night with mellow golden spotlights—less romantic, perhaps, but still impressive.

Expect long lines at the entrance and actors dressed as gladiators who charge a hefty fee to pose for pictures. Once inside you can walk around much of the outer ring of the structure and look down into the exposed passages under what was once the arena floor, now represented by a thin gangway and a small stage at one end. Climb the steep stairs for panoramic views in the

THE RISE AND FALL OF ANCIENT ROME

AD 116

43 AD	Rome invades Britain.
50	Rome is the largest city in the world, with a population of a million.
65	Emperor Nero begins the persecution of Christians in the Empire; Saints Peter and Paul are executed.
70–80	Vespasian builds the Colosseum.
98–117	Trajan's military successes are celebrated with his Baths (98), Forum (110), and Column (113); the Roman Empire reaches its apogee.

Colosseum and out to the Forum and Arch of Constantine. A museum space on the upper floor holds temporary archaeological exhibits. ☎ 06/7005469, 06/39967700 reservations ⊕ www.pierreci.it ⊙ Daily. 8:30–1 hr before sunset.

Arco di Costantino. The largest (69 feet high, 85 feet long, 23 feet wide) and the best preserved of Rome's triumphal arches was erected in AD 315 to celebrate the victory of the emperor Constantine (280–337) over Maxentius (died 312). It was just before this battle that Constantine, the emperor who converted Rome to Christianity, had a vision of a cross in the heavens and heard the words "In this sign, thou shalt conquer."

NEAR THE COLOSSEO

Domus Aurea. Nero's "Golden House," after further restoration has now reopened—admission is by guided tour only. The site gives a good sense of the excesses of Imperial Rome. After fire destroyed much of the city in AD 64, Nero took advantage of the resulting open space to construct a lavish palace so large that it spread over four of Rome's seven hills. It

had a facade of pure gold, seawater piped into the baths, decorations of mother-of-pearl, and vast gardens. Not much has survived of all this; a good portion of the building and grounds was buried under the public works with which subsequent emperors sought to make reparation to the Roman people for Nero's phenomenal greed. As a result, the site of the Domus Aurea itself remained unknown for many centuries. A few of Nero's original halls were discovered underground at the end of the 15th century. Raphael (1483–1520) was one of the artists who had themselves lowered into the rubble-filled rooms, which resembled grottoes. The artists copied the original painted Roman decorations, barely visible by torchlight, and scratched their names on the ceilings. Raphael later used these models—known as *grotesques* because they were found in the so-called grottoes—in his decorative motifs for the Vatican Loggia.

The palace remains impressive in scale, even if a lot of imagination is required to envision the original. ⊠ *Via della Domus Aurea* ☎ 06/39967700 ⊕ *www. ticketclic.it* 🎟 €4.50 ⊙ Tues.–Fri. 10–4.

AD 450

238 AD	The first wave of Germanic invasions penetrates Italy.
293	Diocletian reorganizes the Empire into West and East.
330	Constantine founds a new Imperial capital (Constantinople) in the East.
410	Rome is sacked by Visigoths.
476	The last Roman emperor, Romulus Augustus, is deposed. The Roman Empire falls.

NAVONA & CAMPO: BAROQUE ROME

Long called Vecchia Roma ("Old Rome"), this time-burnished district is the city's most beautiful neighborhood. Set between the Corso and the Tiber bend, it is filled with narrow streets bearing curious names, airy piazzas, and half-hidden courtyards. Some of Rome's most coveted residential addresses are nestled here. So, too, are the ancient Pantheon and the medieval square of Campo de' Fiori, but the spectacular, over-the-top baroque monuments of the 16th and 17th centuries predominate.

The hub of the district is the queen of squares, Piazza Navona—a cityscape adorned with the most eyeknocking fountain by Gian Lorenzo Bernini, father of the baroque. Streets running off the square lead to many historic must-sees, including noble churches by Borromini and Caravaggio's greatest paintings at San Luigi dei Francesi. This district has been an integral part of the city since ancient times, and its position between the Vatican and Lateran palaces, both seats of papal rule, put it in the mainstream of Rome's development from the Middle Ages onward. Craftsmen, shopkeepers, and famed artists toiled in the shadow of the huge palaces built to consolidate the power of leading figures in the papal court. Artisans and artists still live here, but their numbers are diminishing as the district becomes increasingly posh and—so critics say—"Disneyfied." But three of the liveliest piazzas in Rome, Piazza Navona, Piazza del Pantheon, and the Campo de' Fiori, are lodestars in a constellation of some of Rome's most authentic cafés, stores, and wine bars.

GETTING HERE

To bus it from Termini rail station or the Vatican, take the No. 40 Express or the No. 64 and get off at Largo Torre Argentina, a 10-minute stroll to either Campo dei Fiori or Piazza Navona or take little electric No. 116 from Via Veneto past the Spanish Steps to Campo de' Fiori.

THE MAIN ATTRACTIONS

★ ⑩ **Campo de' Fiori.** Home to Rome's oldest (since 1490) daily outdoor produce market, this bustling square was originally used for public executions, making its name—"Field of Flowers"—a bit sardonic. In fact, the central statue commemorates the philosopher Giordano Bruno, who was burned at the stake here in 1600 by the Inquisition. Today, he frowns down upon food vendors galore, who, by early afternoon, are all gone, giving way to the square's caffès and bars which attract throngs of Rome's hip, young professionals as the hours wend their way into evening.

NEED A BREAK? Some of Rome's best pizza comes out of the ovens of Il Forno di Campo de' Fiori (⊠*Campo de' Fiori* ☎*06/68806662).* Choose pizza *bianca,* topped with olive oil, or *rossa,* with tomato sauce. Move to the annex next door to have your warm pizza filled with prosciutto and figs, or other mouthwatering combinations.

Navona & Campo

Piazza Pilotta
Via delle vergini
Via dell'Archetto
Via S. Marcello
Via delle Vergini
Via Minghetti
V. d. Muratte
Piazza dei SS. Apostoli
Via IV Novembre
Via del Fori
Prefettura
Piazza Venezia
Monumento Naz. a Vittorio Emanuele II
Musei Capitolini
Via del Corso
V. dei Coll. Romani
Via di Pietra
Palazzo Doria Pamphilj
V. d. St. Ignazio
Via della Gatta
Palazzo Bonaparte
Piazza Grazioli
Via d. Plebiscito
Via d. Astalli
Piazza di Montecitorio
Piazza Pietra
Via dei Pastini
Via Seminario
Sta. Maria s.Minerva
Via del Gesù
Via del Caccio
Pantheon
Piazza di Minerva
Via della Pigna
Via del Costal
Largo di Torre Argentina
AREA SACRA
Via delle Botteghe Oscure
V. Caetani
Maddalena
Via del Coppelle
Via d. Cornacchie
Via Giustiniani
Via d. Rotonda
Via di Torre Argentina
Via Monterone
Piazza St. Eustachio
Via d. T. Valle
Corso Vittorio Emanuele II
Via del Sudario
Via M.te d'Farina
V.d. St. Agostino
V.d. Vecchia Salvatore
Palazzo Madama
Corso del Rinascimento
Teatro di Pompeo
Via S. Anna
Piazza di Monte di Pietà
NAVONA
Santa Maria della Pace
Piazza Navona
V.d. Sta. M.d. Anima
Palazzo Pamphilj
Museo di Roma
Museo Barracco
Campo de' Fiori
Via del Giubbonari
Via d. Coronari
Via d. Pace
Vic. d. Cancelleri
V.d. Cartari
Via Banchi Vecchi
C. so Vittorio Emanuele II
CAMPO
Piazza Farnese
Via Monserrato
Via dei Cappellari
Via dei Baullari
Via d. Pettinari
Via di Giulia
Lgt. dei Tebaldi
Fiume Tevere
Lungara
V. M. Giordano
Via di Panico
Via di Parione
Via del Governo Vecchio
Via d. Vetrina
Via Giulia
Pie.za Mazzini
LGt. della Farnesina
Via della Lungara

❻ Palazzo Altemps. Containing some of the finest ancient Roman statues in the world, this collection formerly formed the core of the Museo Nazionale Romano. As of 1995, it was moved to these new, suitably grander digs. The palace's sober exterior belies a magnificence that appears as soon as you walk into the majestic courtyard. Set within some gorgeously frescoed, 16th-century rooms are an array of noted antiquities. Look for two

works in the famed Ludovisi collection: the large, intricately carved Ludovisi Sarcophagus and *Galata,* a poignant work portraying a barbarian warrior who chooses death for himself and his wife rather than humiliation by the enemy. ⊠*Piazza Sant'Apollinare 46, near Piazza Navona* ☎*06/39967700* ⬚*€6.50* ☉*Tues.–Sun. 9–7:45.*

⓬ Palazzo Farnese. The most beautiful Renaissance palace in Rome, the Palazzo Farnese is noted for the grandeur of its rooms, notably the Galleria Carracci, whose ceiling is to the baroque age what the Sistine ceiling is to the Renaissance. The Farnese family rose to great power and wealth during the Renaissance, in part because of the favor Pope Alexander VI and Pope Paul III paid to the family. The uppermost frieze decorations and main window overlooking the piazza are the work of Michelangelo, who also designed part of the courtyard, as well as the graceful arch over Via Giulia at the back. The showpiece of the palace is the Galleria Carracci vault painted by Annibale Carracci between 1597 and 1604, depicting the loves of the pagan gods in a swirling style that announced the birth of the baroque style. Also eye-popping is the Salon of Hercules, with its massive replica of the ancient Farnese Hercules. Now housing the French Embassy, the historic salons can be seen on free tours (in French and Italian only) four times a week. You'll need to send a letter or e-mail to reserve tickets, one to four months in advance (depending on peak season visit or not), specifying the number in your party, when you wish to visit, and a local phone number, for confirmation a few days before the visit. ⊠*French Embassy, Servizio Culturale, Piazza Farnese 67, near Piazza Navona* ☎*06/686011* ✎*visitefarnese@france-italien.it* ⬚*Free* ☉*By appointment only.*

⓫ Palazzo Spada. An impressive stuccoed facade on Piazza Capo di Ferro, west of Piazza Farnese, fronts an equally magnificent inner courtyard. On the southeast side of the inner courtyard, the gallery designed by Borromini creates an elaborate optical illusion, appearing to be much longer than it really is. On the first floor there are paintings and sculptures that belonged to Cardinale Bernardino Spada, an art connoisseur who collected works by Italian and Flemish masters. Note that the palazzo occasionally closes in the afternoon because of staff shortages. ⊠*Piazza Capo di Ferro 13, near Campo de' Fiori, Campo* ☎*06/6832409* ⊕*www.galleriaborghese.it* ⬚*€5* ☉*Tues.–Sun. 8:30–7:30.*

4 Pantheon. One of Rome's most impressive and best-preserved ancient
Fodor'sChoice monuments, the Pantheon is particularly close to the hearts of Romans.
★   The emperor Hadrian designed it around ad 120 and had it built on
the site of an earlier temple that had been damaged by fire. Although
the sheer size of the Pantheon is impressive (until 1960 the dome was
the largest ever built), what's most striking is its tangible sense of harmony. In large part this feeling is the result of the building's symmetrical
design: the height of the dome is equal to the diameter of the circular
interior. The oculus, or opening in the dome, is meant to symbolize the
all-seeing "Eye of Heaven"; in practice, it illuminates the building and
lightens the heavy stone ceiling. The original bronze doors have survived more than 1,800 years, centuries longer than the interior's rich
gold ornamentation, which was plundered by popes and emperors. Art
lovers can pay homage to the tomb of Raphael, who is buried in an
ancient sarcophagus under the altar of Madonna del Sasso. ⊠ *Piazza
della Rotonda, Navona* 🕾 *06/68300230* 🖃 *Free* 🕗 *Mon.–Sat. 8:30–
7:30, Sun. 9–5:30.*

★ ☺ **7 Piazza Navona.** With its carefree air of the days when it was the scene
of Roman circus games, medieval jousts, and 17th-century carnivals,
the beautiful Piazza Navona today often attracts fashion photogra-
phers on shoots and Romans out for their *passeggiata* (evening stroll).
Bernini's splashing **Fontana dei Quattro Fiumi** (Fountain of the Four
Rivers), with an enormous rock squared off by statues representing the
four corners of the world, makes a fitting centerpiece. Behind the fountain is the church of **Sant'Agnese in Agone,** an outstanding example
of baroque architecture built by the Pamphilj Pope Innocent X. The
facade—a wonderfully rich mélange of bell towers, concave spaces, and
dovetailed stone and marble—is by Borromini, a contemporary and
rival of Bernini, and by Carlo Rainaldi (1611–91). One story has it that
the Bernini statue nearest the church, which represents the River Plate,
has its hand up before its eye because it can't bear the sight of the Borromini facade. Though often repeated, the story is fiction: the facade
was built after the fountain. From early December through January 6
a Christmas market fills the square with games, Nativity scenes (some
well crafted, many not), and multiple versions of the Befana, the ugly
but good witch who brings candy and toys to Italian children on Epiphany. (Her name is a corruption of the Italian word for "epiphany,"
Epifania.) ⊠ *Junction of Via della Cuccagna, Corsia Agonale, Via di
Sant'Agnese, and Via Agonale, Navona*

★ **5 San Luigi dei Francesi.** A pilgrimage spot for art lovers everywhere, San
Luigi is home to the Cerasi Chapel, adorned with three stunningly dramatic works by Caravaggio (1571–1610), the baroque master of the
heightened approach to light and dark. Set in the Chapel of St. Matthew (at the altar end of the left nave), they were commissioned for
San Luigi, the official church of Rome's French colony. The inevitable
coin machine will light up his *Calling of St. Matthew, Matthew and the
Angel,* and *Matthew's Martyrdom,* seen from left to right, and Caravaggio's mastery of light takes it from there. When painted, they caused
considerable consternation to the clergy of San Luigi, who thought the

CLOSE UP

Going Baroque

Flagrantly emotional, heavily expressive, and visually sensuous, the 17th-century artistic movement known as the baroque was born in Rome. It was the creation of three geniuses: the sculptor and architect Gianlorenzo Bernini (1598–1680), the painter and architect Pietro da Cortona (1596–1669), and the architect and sculptor Francesco Borromini (1599–1667). From the drama found in the artists' paintings to the jewel-laden, gold-on-gold detail of 17th-century Roman palaces, baroque style was intended both to shock and delight by upsetting the placid, "correct" rules of proportion and scale in the Renaissance. If a building looks theatrical—like a stage or a theater, especially with curtains being drawn back—it is usually baroque. Look for over-the-top, curvaceous marble work, trompe l'oeil, allusions to other art, and high drama to identify the style. Baroque's appeal to the emotions made it a powerful weapon in the hands of the Counter-Reformation.

artist's dramatically realistic approach was scandalously disrespectful. But these paintings did to 17th-century art what Picasso's *Demoiselles d'Avignon* did to the 20th century. ⊠ *Piazza San Luigi dei Francesi, Navona* ☎ *06/688271* ☼ *Fri.–Wed. 7–12:30 and 3:30–7.*

❸ **Santa Maria sopra Minerva.** Michelangelo's *Risen Christ* and the tomb of the gentle 15th-century artist Fra Angelico are two noted sights in the only Gothic-style church in Rome. Have some coins handy to light up the Cappella Carafa in the right transept, where exquisite 15th-century frescoes by Filippino Lippi (circa 1457–1504) are well worth the small investment. (Lippi's most famous student was Botticelli.) In front of the church, Bernini's charming elephant bearing an Egyptian obelisk has an inscription on the base stating that it takes a strong mind to sustain solid wisdom. ⊠ *Piazza della Minerva, Navona* ☎ *06/6793926* ☼ *Daily 7–noon and 4–7.*

★ ⓭ **Via Giulia.** Named after Pope Julius II and serving for more than four centuries as the "salon of Rome," this street—running between Piazza Farnese and the Tiber—is still the address of choice for Roman aristocrats and rich foreigners. Built with funds garnered by taxing prostitutes, the street is lined with elegant palaces, including the Palazzo Falconieri, old churches (one, San Eligio, reputedly designed by Raphael himself), and, in springtime, glorious hanging wisteria. The area around Via Giulia is a wonderful place to wander in to get the feeling of daily life as carried on in a centuries-old setting—an experience enhanced by the dozens of antiques shops in the neighborhood. ⊠ *One block east of the Tiber river, Navona*

ALSO WORTH SEEING

❷ **Il Gesù.** Grandmother of all baroque churches, this huge structure was designed by the architect Vignola (1507–73) to be the tangible symbol of the Jesuits, a major force in the Counter-Reformation in Europe. It remained unadorned for about 100 years, but when it finally was decorated, no expense was spared: the interior drips with lapis lazuli, precious marbles, gold, and more gold. A fantastically painted ceiling by Baciccia (1639–1709) seems to merge with the painted stucco figures at its base. St. Ignatius's apartments, reached from the side entrance of the church, are also worth a visit (afternoons only) for the trompe l'oeil frescoes and relics of the saint. ⊠ *Piazza del Gesù, near Piazza Venezia, Corso* ☎ *06/3613717* ⊙ *Daily 8:30–12:30 and 4–7:30.*

9 Sant'Andrea della Valle. Topped by the second tallest dome in Rome, this huge 17th-century church looms mightily over a busy intersection. Puccini set the first act of his opera *Tosca* here; fans have been known to hire a horse-drawn carriage at night to trace the course of the opera from Sant'Andrea up Via Giulia to Palazzo Farnese—Scarpia's headquarters—to the locale of the opera's climax, Castel Sant'Angelo. Inside, above the apse, are striking frescoes depicting scenes from St. Andrew's life by the Bolognese painter Domenichino (1581–1641). ⊠ *Corso Vittorio Emanuele II, Navona* ☎ *06/6861339* ⊙ *Daily 7:30–noon and 4:30–7:30.*

8 Sant'Ivo alla Sapienza. Borromini's eccentric 17th-century church has what must surely be Rome's most unusual dome—topped by a golden spiral said to have been inspired by a bee's stinger. ⊠ *Corso Rinascimento 40, Navona* ⊙ *Sun. 10–noon.*

CORSO & SPAGNA: PIAZZA VENEZIA TO THE SPANISH STEPS

In spirit, and in fact, this section of the city is its most grandiose. The overblown Vittoriano monument, the labyrinthine treasure-chest palaces of Rome's surviving aristocracy, even the diamond-draped denizens of Via Condotti's shops—all embody the exuberant ego of a city at the center of its own universe. Here's where you'll see ladies in furs, gobbling pastries at caffè tables, and walk through a thousand snapshots as you climb the famous Spanish Steps, admired by generations from Byron to Versace. Cultural treasures abound around here: gilded 17th-century churches, glittering palaces, and the greatest example of portraiture in Rome: Velázquez's incomparable *Innocent X* at the Galleria Doria Pamphilj. Have your camera ready—along with a coin or two—for that most beloved of Rome's landmarks, the Trevi Fountain.

GETTING HERE
One of Rome's handiest subway stations, the Spagna metro station is tucked just to the left of the Spanish Steps. Buses No. 117 (from Via Veneto area) and No. 119 (from Piazza del Popolo) hum through the neighborhood.

THE MAIN ATTRACTIONS
★ **6 Fontana di Trevi** *(Trevi Fountain).* The huge fountain designed by Nicola Salvi (1697–1751) is a whimsical rendition of mythical sea creatures amid cascades of splashing water. The fountain is the world's most spectacular wishing well: legend has it that you can ensure your return to Rome by tossing a coin into the fountain. It was featured in the 1954

film *Three Coins in the Fountain* and was the scene of Anita Ekberg's aquatic frolic in Fellini's *La Dolce Vita*. By day this is one of the most crowded sites in town; at night the spotlighted piazza feels especially festive. ⊠*Piazza di Trevi, off Via del Tritone, Corso.*

❶ Monumento a Vittorio Emanuele II. Known as the Vittoriano, this vast marble monument was erected in the late 19th century to honor Italy's first king, Vittorio Emanuele II (1820–78), and the unification of Italy. Aesthetically minded Romans have derided the oversize structure, visible from many parts of the city, calling it "the typewriter," "the wedding cake," and "the eighth hill of Rome." Whatever you think of its design, the views from the top are memorable. Here also is the **Tomb of the Unknown Soldier** with its eternal flame. A side entrance in the monument leads to the rather somber **Museo del Risorgimento**, which charts Italy's struggle for nationhood. For those not interested or able to climb the many stairs, there's now an elevator to the top (to the right as you face the monument). Before you head up, stop at the museum entrances (to the left and right of the structure) to get a pamphlet identifying the sculpture groups on the monument itself and the landmarks you will be able to see once at the top. ⊠*Entrance at Piazza Ara Coeli, near Piazza Venezia, Corso* ☎*06/6991718* ⊕*www.ambienterm.arti. beniculturali.it/vittoriano/index.html* 🖃*Monument free, museum free, elevator €7* ⊘*Tues.–Sun. 10–4.*

❾ Palazzetto Zuccaro. The real treasure at the top of the Spanish Steps is not

Fodor'sChoice ★

the somewhat dull church of Trinità dei Monti, but to the right on Via Gregoriana, the street that leads off to the right of the obelisk. Shaped to form a monster's face, this Mannerist-era house was designed in 1591 by noted painter Federico Zuccaro (1540–1609). Typical of the outré style of the period, the eyes are the house's windows; the entrance portal is through the monster's mouth (this is one of the best photo-ops in Rome—have someone photograph you standing in front of the door with your own mouth gaping wide). Via Gregoriana is a real charmer and has long been one of Rome's most elegant addresses, with residents ranging from French 19th-century painters Ingres and David to famed couturier Valentino. ⊠*Via Gregoriana 30, Spagna.*

❸ Palazzo Colonna. Inside the fabulous, private Palazzo Colonna, the 17th-century **Sala Grande**—more than 300 feet long, with bedazzling chandeliers, colored marble, and enormous paintings—is best known as the site where Audrey Hepburn met the press in *Roman Holiday.* The entrance to the picture gallery, the **Galleria Colonna,** hides behind a plain, inconspicuous door. The private palace is open to the public Saturday only; reserve ahead to get a free guided tour in English. ⊠*Via della Pilotta 17, Corso, near Piazza di Trevi* ☎*06/6784350* ⊕*www. galleriacolonna.it* 🖃*€7* ⊘*Sept.–July, Sat. 9–1.*

★ ❹ Palazzo Doria Pamphilj. This bona fide patrician palace is still home to a princely family, which rents out many of its 1,000 rooms. You can visit the remarkably well-preserved **Galleria Doria Pamphilj** (pronounced pam-*fee*-lee), a picture-and-sculpture gallery that gives you a sense of the sumptuous living quarters. Numbered paintings (the bookshop's

Corso & Spagna

museum catalog comes in handy) are packed onto every available inch of wall space. The first large salon is nearly wallpapered with paintings, and not just any paintings: on one wall, you'll find no less than three pictures by Caravaggio, including his *Magdalen* and his breathtaking early *Rest on the Flight to Egypt.* Off the gilded **Galleria degli Specchi** (Gallery of Mirrors)—reminiscent of Versailles—are the famous Velázquez portrait and the Bernini bust of the Pamphilj pope Innocent X. The audio guide by Jonathan Doria Pamphilj, the current heir, provides an intimate family history well worth listening to. ✉*Piazza del Collegio Romano 2, near Piazza Venezia, Corso* ☎*06/6797323* ⊕*www.doriapamphilj.it* 🎫€*8* ⊙*Fri.–Wed. 10–5.*

★ ❺ **Sant'Ignazio.** Rome's largest Jesuit church, this 17th-century landmark harbors some of the most magnificent illusions typical of the baroque style. Capping the 17th-century nave is a trompe l'oeil oddity: the cupola is painted as, well, a cupola—but open at the top, and full of flying angels, saints, and heavenly dignitaries who float about in what appears to be a rosy sky above. To get the full effect of the illusionistic ceiling painted by Andrea del Pozzo (1642–1709), stand on the small disk set into the floor of the nave. The church also contains some of Rome's most splendid, jewel-encrusted altars. If you're lucky, you might catch an evening concert performed here (check the posters). Step outside the church to look at it from Filippo Raguzzini's 18th-century piazza, where the buildings, as in much baroque art, are arranged resembling a stage set. ✉*Piazza Sant'Ignazio, Corso* ☎*06/6794406* ⊙*Daily 7:30–12:15 and 3–7:15.*

★ ❽ **Spanish Steps.** That icon of postcard Rome, the Spanish Steps—called the Scalinatella di Spagna in Italian—and the Piazza di Spagna from which they ascend both get their names from the Spanish Embassy to the Vatican on the piazza, opposite the American Express office—in spite of the fact that the staircase was built with French funds in 1723. In an allusion to the church of Trinità dei Monti at the top of the hill, the staircase is divided by three landings (beautifully banked with azaleas from mid-April to mid-May). For centuries, the Scalinatella ("staircase," as natives refer to the Spanish Steps) has always welcomed tourists: 18th-century dukes and duchesses on their Grand Tour, 19th-century artists and writers in search of inspiration—among them Stendhal, Honoré de Balzac, William Makepeace Thackeray, and Byron—and today's enthusiastic hordes. The **Fontana della Barcaccia** (Fountain of the Old Boat) at the base of the steps is by Pietro Bernini, father of the famous Gianlorenzo. ✉*Piazza di Spagna, at head of Via Condotti Spagna*

ALSO WORTH SEEING

❼ **Keats-Shelley Memorial House.** English Romantic poet John Keats (1795–1821), famed for "Ode to a Nightingale" and "She Walks in Beauty," once lived in what is now a (very small) museum dedicated to him and his great contemporary and friend Percy Bysshe Shelley (1792–1822). You can visit his tiny rooms, at the foot of the Spanish Steps, preserved as they were when he died here. Just across the steps is Babington's Tea Shops, a relic from the 19th-century Grand Tour era and still a

DID YOU KNOW?

Andrea Pozzo's eye-popping Sant'Ignazio 1694 ceiling fresco set the standard for *trompe l'oeil* aerial perspective and made it the rage in Europe.

favorite for Rome's grande dames. ⊠ *Piazza di Spagna 26, Spagna* 🕾 *06/6784235* ⊕ *www.keats-shelley-house.org* 🔳 *€3.50* ⊘ *Weekdays 9–1 and 3–6, Sat. 11–2 and 3–6.*

② **Palazzo Venezia.** A Roman landmark on the city's busiest square, this palace is best known for the balcony over the main portal, from which Mussolini gave public addresses to crowds in Piazza Venezia during the dark days of Fascism. Today it's home to a haphazard collection of mostly early-Renaissance weapons, ivories, and paintings in its grand salons; the palace also hosts touring art exhibits. ⊠ *Piazza San Marco 49, near Piazza Venezia, Corso* 🕾 *06/32810* ⊕ *www.ticketeria.it/palazzo venezia-eng.asp* 🔳 *€4* ⊘ *Tues.–Sun. 9–7.*

PIAZZA DELLA REPUBBLICA TO QUIRINALE

This sector of Rome stretches down from the 19th-century district built up around the Piazza della Repubblica—originally laid out to serve as a monumental foyer between the Termini rail station and the rest of the city—and on to Il Quirinale. The highest of Rome's seven hills, it is crowned by the massive Palazzo Quirinale, once home to the popes and now Italy's presidential palace. Along the way, you can see ancient Roman sculptures, Early Christian churches, and highlights from the 16th and 17th centuries, when Rome was conquered by the baroque—and by Bernini. While Bernini's work feels omnipresent in much of the city center, the Renaissance-man range of his work is particularly notable here. The artist as architect considered the church of Sant'Andrea al Quirinale one of his best; Bernini the urban designer and waterworker is responsible for the muscle-bound sea gods who wrestle so provocatively in the fountain at the center of whirling Piazza Barberini. And Bernini the master gives religious passion a joltingly corporeal treatment in what is perhaps his greatest work, the *Ecstasy of St. Theresa*, in the church of Santa Maria della Vittoria.

GETTING HERE

Bus No. 40 will get you from Termini station to the Quirinale in two stops; from the Vatican take bus No. 64. The very busy and convenient Repubblica Metro stop is on the piazza of the same name. The Metro also stops at Piazza Barberini, near the Quirinale.

THE MAIN ATTRACTIONS

① **Palazzo Massimo alle Terme.** This 19th-century palace in neobaroque style holds part of the collections of antiquities belonging to the Museo Nazionale Romano (also exhibited in the Palazzo Altemps). Here you can see extraordinary examples of the fine mosaics and masterful paintings that decorated ancient Rome's palaces and villas. Don't miss the fresco—depicting a lush garden in bloom—that came from the villa that Livia, wife of Emperor Augustus, owned outside Rome. ⊠ *Largo Villa Peretti 1, Repubblica* 🕾 *06/480201* ⊕ *www.pierreci.it* 🔳 *€8* ⊘ *Tues.–Sun. 9–7:30.*

❾ **Il Quirinale.** The highest of ancient Rome's seven hills, this is where ancient Romans, and later popes, built their residences in order to escape the deadly miasmas and malaria of the low-lying area around the Forum. Framing the hilltop vista, the fountain in the square has gigantic ancient statues of Castor and Pollux reining in their unruly steeds. The **Palazzo del Quirinale** passed from the popes to Italy's kings in the 19th century; it's now the official residence of the nation's president. Every day at 4 PM the ceremony of the changing of the guard at the portal includes a miniparade complete with band. ⊠*Piazza del Quirinale, near Piazza di Trevi* ☎*06/46991* 🎟️*€5* 🕓*Sept.–June, Sun. 8:30–noon.*

Directly opposite the main entrance of the Palazzo del Quirinale sits the **Scuderie Papale al Quirinale,** *the former papal stables.* Designed by Alessandro Specchi (1668–1729) in 1722, it was among the major achievements of baroque Rome. Now remodeled by eminent architect Gae Aulenti, they serve as a venue for touring art exhibits. ⊠*Piazza del Quirinale, Quirinale* ☎*06/39967500 or 06/696271* ⊕*www.scuderiequirinale.it* 🎟️*€10* 🕓*Mon.–Thurs. 10–7, Fri. and Sat. 10–9:30.*

❻ Palazzo Barberini. Along with architect Carlo Maderno (1556–1629), Borromini helped make the splendid 17th-century Palazzo Barberini a residence worthy of Rome's leading art patron, Pope Urban VIII, who began the palace for his family in 1625. Inside, the **Galleria Nazionale d'Arte Antica** has some fine works by Caravaggio and Raphael, including the latter's portrait of his lover, *La Fornarina.* Rome's biggest ballroom is here; its ceiling, painted by Pietro da Cortona, depicts Immortality bestowing a crown upon Divine Providence escorted by a "bomber squadron"—to quote Sir Michael Levey—of mutant bees. The museum expanded its exhibition space in late 2006, opening eight newly refurbished rooms. ⊠*Via Barberini 18, Quirinale* ☎*06/32810* ⊕*www.galleriaborghese.it* 🎟️*€6* 🕓*Tues.–Sun. 9–6:30.*

★ ❿ San Clemente. Worth the long detour, this extraordinary church-cum-archaeological site lies a good 15 blocks southeast of Piazza della Repubblica, nestled at the bottom of the Esqueline Hill and just a few blocks east of the Colosseum. This ancient reference point is apropos because San Clemente is a 12th-century church built over a 4th-century church, which in turn was constructed over a 2nd-century pagan temple to the god Mithras. The upper church holds a beautiful early-12th-century mosaic showing a cross on a gold background, surrounded by swirling green acanthus leaves teeming with little scenes of everyday life. The marble choir screens, salvaged from the 4th-century church, are decorated with Early Christian symbols: doves, vines, and fish. Off the left aisle is the **Cappella Castiglioni,** with frescoes painted around 1400 by Masolino da Panicale and note for their early use of perspective. Before you leave the upper church, take a look at the pretty cloister—evening concerts are held here in summer. From the right aisle, stairs lead down to the remains of the **4th-century church**—the vestibule is decorated with marble fragments found during the excavations and in the nave are colorful 11th-century frescoes of the life of St. Clement. Another level down is the famous **Mythraeum,** a shrine dedicated to the god Mithras, whose cult spread from Persia and gained a hold in Rome during the 2nd and 3rd centuries. Farther up the Esqueline Hill

Repubblica &
Quirinale

KEY

 Metro stops

 Tourist information

are two other churches fabled for their Early Christian mosaics, Santa Prassede (Via di Santa Prassede 9/a) and Santa Pudenziana (Via Urbana 160). ⊠ *Via San Giovanni in Laterano 108, Esquelino* ☎*06/70451018* ☞*€3* ⊙*Mon.–Sat. 9–noon and 3–6, Sun. 10–12:30 and 3–6.*

👆 **⑤ Santa Maria della Concezione.** In the crypt under the main Capuchin church, the bones of some 4,000 dead Capuchin monks are arranged in peculiar decorative designs around the skeletons of their kinsmen, a macabre reminder of the impermanence of earthly life. Signs declare WHAT YOU ARE, WE ONCE WERE; WHAT WE ARE, YOU SOMEDAY WILL BE. Although not for the easily spooked, the crypt is oddly beautiful. ⊠ *Via Veneto 27, Quirinale* ☎*06/4871185* ☞*Donation expected* ⊙*Fri.–Wed. 9–noon and 3–6.*

③ Santa Maria della Vittoria. The most famous feature here is Bernini's tri-
Fodor'sChoice umph of baroque decoration of the **Cappella Cornaro,** an exceptional
★ fusion of architecture, painting, and sculpture. *The Ecstasy of St. Theresa,* an example of Counter-Reformation art at its most alluring, is the focal point. Bernini's audacious conceit was to model the chapel after a theater: members of the Cornaro family—sculpted in white marble—watch from theater boxes as, center stage, St. Theresa, in the throes of mystical rapture, is pierced by an angel's gilded arrow. To quote one

18th-century observer, President de Brosses: "If this is divine love, I know it well." ⊠ *Via XX Settembre 17, Repubblica* ☎06/42740571 ⊙ *Mon.–Sat. 9–noon and 3–6, Sun. 3–6.*

ALSO WORTH SEEING

❹ **Fontana del Tritone** *(Triton Fountain).* The centerpiece of busy Piazza Barberini is Bernini's graceful fountain designed in 1637 for the sculptor's patron, Pope Urban VIII. The pope's Barberini family coat of arms, featuring bees, is at the base of the large shell. Close by is the **Fontana delle Api** (Fountain of the Bees), the last fountain designed by Bernini. ⊠ *Piazza Barberini, Repubblica.*

❺ **Piazza della Repubblica.** Smog-blackened porticoes, a subway station, and a McDonald's can make this grand piazza feel a bit derelict. The racy **Fontana delle Naiadi** (Fountain of the Naiads), however, is anything but. An 1870 addition to the square, the fountain depicts voluptuous bronze ladies wrestling happily with marine monsters. In ancient times, the Piazza della Repubblica served as the entrance to the immense **Terme di Diocleziano** *(Baths of Diocletian)*, an archaeological site today. Built in the 4th century AD, these were the largest and most impressive of the baths of ancient Rome, with vast halls, pools, and gardens that could accommodate 3,000 people at a time. The *aula ottagonale* (octagonal hall) now holds a sampling of the ancient sculptures unearthed here, including two beautiful bronzes. ⊠ *Via Romita 8, near Termini* ☎06/4870690 💲*Free* ⊙ *Tues.–Sat. 9–2, Sun. 9–1.*

The curving ancient Roman brick facade on one side of the Piazza della Repubblica marks the church of **Santa Maria degli Angeli,** adapted by Michelangelo from the vast central chamber of the colossal baths. Look for the sundial carved on the floor. ⊠ *Via Cernaia 9,Repubblica* ☎064880812 ⊕ *www.santamariadegliangeliroma.it* ⊙ *Mon.–Sat. 7– 6:30, Sun. 7 AM–7:30 PM.*

❼ **San Carlino alle Quattro Fontane.** In a church no larger than the base of one of the piers of St. Peter's, Borromini attained geometric architectural perfection. Characteristically, he chose a subdued white stucco for the interior decoration, so as not to distract from the form. Don't miss the cloister, which you reach through the door to the right of the altar. The exterior of the church is Borromini at his bizarre best, all curves and rippling movement. (Keep an eye out for cars whipping around the corner as you're looking.) Outside the *quattro fontane* (four fountains) frame views in four directions. ⊠ *Via del Quirinale 23, Quirinale* ☎06/4883261 ⊙ *Weekdays 10–noon and 1–3, Sat. 10–1, Sun. noon–1.*

❽ **Sant'Andrea al Quirinale.** This small but imposing baroque church was designed and decorated by Bernini, Borromini's rival, who considered it one of his finest works. ⊠ *Via del Quirinale, Piazza di Trevi* ☎06/4740807 ⊙ *Mon.–Sat. 8–noon and 3:30–7, Sun. 9–noon and 4–7.*

VILLA BORGHESE & PIAZZA DEL POPOLO

Touring Rome's artistic masterpieces while staying clear of its hustle and bustle can be, quite literally, a walk in the park. Some of the city's finest sights are tucked away in or next to green lawns and pedestrian piazzas, offering a breath of fresh air for weary sightseers, especially in the Villa Borghese park. One of Rome's largest, this park can alleviate gallery gout by offering an oasis in which to cool off under the ilex, oak, and umbrella pine trees. If you feel like a picnic, have an *alimentare* (food shop) make you some *panini* (sandwiches) before you go; food carts within the park are overpriced.

GETTING HERE

Electric bus No. 119 does a loop that connects Piazza del Popolo to Piazza Venezia. The No. 116, starting at the Villa Borghese museum, motors through the park. Piazza del Popolo has a metro stop of the same name.

THE MAIN ATTRACTIONS

★ ❹ **Ara Pacis Augustae** *(Altar of Augustan Peace).* This magnificent classical monument, with an exquisitely detailed frieze, was erected in 13 BC to celebrate Emperor Augustus's triumphant return from military conflicts in Gaul and Spain. It's housed in one of Rome's newest landmarks, a glass-and-travertine structure designed by American architect Richard Meier. The building was opened in 2006 after 10 years of delays and heated controversy concerning the altar's relocation. Overlooking the Tiber on one side and the ruins of the marble-clad Mausoleo di Augusto (Mausoleum of Augustus) on the other, the result is a luminous oasis in the center of Rome. ⊠ *Lungotevere in Augusta, near Piazza di Popolo* 🖀 *06/82059127* ⊕ *www.arapacis.it* 🖳 *€6.50* ☉ *Tues.–Sun. 9–6.*

❸ **Galleria Borghese.** It's a real toss-up which is more magnificent—the villa built for Cardinal Scipione Borghese in 1615 or the collection of 17th- and 18th-century art that lies within. The luxury-loving cardinal built Rome's most splendiferous palace as a showcase for his fabulous antiquities collection. The interiors are a monument to 18th-century Roman interior decoration at its most luxurious, dripping with

FodorśChoice ★

> **WORD OF MOUTH**
>
> "The Borghese Gallery is one of the most precious places I have ever had the good fortune to visit—twice. The Bernini Statues bring tears to my eyes. The building is gorgeous. Just a little jewel box of a museum."   –bugswife1

porphyry and alabaster and they are a fitting showcase for the statues of various deities, including one officially known as *Venus Victrix*. There has never been any doubt, however, as to the statue's real subject: Pauline Bonaparte, Napoléon's sister, who married Prince Camillo Borghese in one of the storied matches of the 19th century. Sculpted by Canova (1757–1822), the princess reclines on a chaise, bare-breasted, her hips swathed in classical drapery, the very model of haughty detachment and sly come-hither. Pauline is known to have been shocked that her husband took pleasure in showing off the work to his guests. This

Villa Borghese &
Piazza del Popolo

coyness seems curious given the reply she is supposed to have made to a lady who asked her how she could have posed for the work: "Oh, but the studio was heated." Other rooms hold important sculptures by Bernini, including *David* and the breathtaking *Apollo and Daphne*. The picture collection has splendid works by Titian, Caravaggio, and Raphael, among others. Entrance is every two hours, and reservations are required. Make sure to book online or by phone at least a few days in advance. ⊠*Piazza Scipione Borghese 5, off Via Pinciana, Villa Borghese* ☎*06/8413979 information, 06/32810 reservations* ⊕*www.galleriaborghese.it* ⊠*€10.50, including €2 reservation fee; audio guide or English tour €5* ⊙*Tues.–Sun. 9–7, with sessions on hr every 2 hrs.*

① Piazza del Popolo. Designed by neoclassical architect Giuseppe Valadier (1762–1839) in the early 1800s, this piazza is one of the largest in Rome, and it has a 3,000-year-old obelisk in the middle. A favorite spot for café-sitting and people-watching, the pedestrian-only piazza is landmarked by its two bookend baroque churches, **Santa Maria dei Miracoli** and **Santa Maria in Montesanto**. On the piazza's eastern side, stairs lead uphill to Villa Borghese's **Pincio**, a formal garden that highly fashionable in 19th-century Rome. Here you'll find the magnificent park pavilion restaurant known as the Casino Valadier (⊠Piazza Bucarest, Pincio Gardens ☎06/69922090). First designed in 1814, it has always attracted celebrities like King Farouk of Egypt, Richard Strauss, Gandhi, and Mussolini, all who came to see the lavish Empire-style salons and, of course, be seen. At the north end of the piazza is the 400-year-old **Porta del Popolo,** Rome's northern city gate, and next to it the church of Santa Maria del Popolo. The city gate was designed by Bernini to welcome the Catholic convert Queen Christina of Sweden to Rome in 1605. ⊠*At head of Corso, near Villa Borghese.*

★ ❷ **Santa Maria del Popolo.** This church next to the Porta del Popolo goes almost unnoticed, but it has one of the richest art collections of any church in Rome. Here is Raphael's High Renaissance masterpiece the **Cappella Chigi** (which has found new fame as one of the "Altars of Science" in Dan Brown's *Angels & Demons* novel and 2009 Tom Hanks film), as well as two stunning Caravaggios in the **Cappella Cerasi.** Each December an exhibit of Christmas Nativity scenes is held in the adjacent building. ⊠*Piazza del Popolo, near Villa Borghese* ☎*06/3610836* ⊙*Mon.–Sat. 7–noon and 4–7, Sun. 7:30–1:30 and 4:30–7:30.*

THE VATICAN: ROME OF THE POPES

Capital of the Catholic Church, this tiny walled city-state is a place where some people go to find a work of art—Michelangelo's frescoes, rare ancient Roman marbles, or Bernini's statues. Others go to find their soul. Whatever the reason, thanks to being the seat of world Catholicism and also address to the most overwhelming architectural achievement of the Renaissance—St. Peter's Basilica—the Vatican attracts millions of travelers every year. In addition, the Vatican Museums are famed for magnificent rooms decorated by Raphael, sculptures such as the *Apollo Belvedere* and the *Laocoön,* frescoes by Fra Angelico, paintings by Giotto and Leonardo, and the celebrated ceiling of the Sistine Chapel. The Church power that emerged as the Rome of the emperors declined gave impetus to a profusion of artistic expression and shaped the destiny of the city for a thousand years. Allow yourself an hour to see the St. Peter's Basilica, two hours for the museums, an hour for Castel Sant'Angelo, and an hour to climb to the top of the dome. Note that ushers at the entrance of St. Peter's Basilica and the Vatican Museums bar entry to people with "inappropriate" clothing—which means no bare knees or shoulders.

GETTING HERE
From Termini station, hop on the No. 40 Express or the No. 64 to deliver you to Piazza San Pietro. Metro stops Cipro or Musei Vaticani will get you within about a 10-minute walk of the entrance to the Vatican Museums.

THE MAIN ATTRACTIONS
★ ❷ **Basilica di San Pietro.** The largest church of Christendom, St. Peter's Basilica covers about 18,100 square yards, extends 212 yards in length, and carries a dome that rises 435 feet and measures 138 feet across its base. Its history is equally impressive: No less than five of Italy's greatest artists—Bramante, Raphale, Peruzzi, Antonio Sangallo the

The Vatican

2

For St. Peter's, Michelangelo originally designed a dome much higher than the one ultimately built and designed by his follower Giacomo della Porta.

Younger, and Michelangelo—died while striving to erect this "new" St. Peter's. In fact, the church's history dates back to the year AD 319, when the emperor Constantine built a basilica over the site of the tomb of St. Peter (died AD 64). This early church stood for more than 1,000 years, undergoing a number of restorations, until it was on the verge of collapse.

In 1506 Pope Julius II (1443–1513) commissioned the architect Bramante to build a new and greater basilica, but construction would take more than 170 years. In 1546 Michelangelo was persuaded to take over the job, but the magnificent cupola was finally completed by Giacomo della Porta (circa 1537–1602) and Domenico Fontana (1543–1607). The new church wasn't dedicated until 1626; by that time Renaissance had given way to baroque, and many of the plan's original elements had gone the way of their designers. At the entrance, the 15th-century bronze doors by Filarete (circa 1400–69) fill the central portal. Off the entry portico, architect and sculptor Gianlorenzo Bernini's famous *Scala Regia*, the ceremonial entry to the Vatican Palace, is one of the most magnificent staircases in the world and is graced with Bernini's dramatic statue of Constantine the Great.

Entering the sanctuary, take a moment to adjust to the enormity of the space stretching in front of you. The cherubs over the holy-water fonts have feet as long as the distance from your fingertips to your elbow. It is because the proportions are in such perfect harmony that the vastness may escape you at first. The megascale was inspired by the size of the ancient Roman ruins.

Over an altar in a side chapel near the entrance is Michelangelo's *Pietà*, a sculpture of Mary holding her son Jesus's body after crucifixion—the star attraction here other than the basilica itself. Legend has it that the artist, only 22 at the time the work was completed, overheard pass-ersby expressing skepticism that such a young man could have executed such a sophisticated and moving piece. It's said that his offense at the implication was why he crept back that night and signed the piece—in big letters, on a ribbon falling from the Virgin's left shoulder across her breast.

Inlaid in the gorgeous marble pavement of the nave's central aisles are the names of the world's great cathedrals organized by church size—the message is clear, St. Peter's has them all beat. At the crossing of the aisles four massive piers support the dome, and the mighty Bernini **baldacchino** (canopy) rises high above the papal altar, where the pope celebrates Mass. "What the barbarians didn't do, the Barberini did," 17th-century wags quipped when Barberini Pope Urban VIII had the bronze stripped from the Pantheon's portico and melted down to make the baldacchino (using what was left over for cannonballs). The bronze throne behind the main altar in the apse, the *Cathedra Petri* (Chair of St. Peter), is Bernini's work (1656), and it covers a wooden-and-ivory chair that St. Peter himself is said to have used. However, scholars contend that this throne probably dates only from the Middle Ages. See how the adoration of a million kisses has completely worn down the bronze on the right foot of the statue of St. Peter in front of the near-right pillar in the transept. Free one-hour English-language tours of the basilica depart Monday–Saturday at 10 and 3, Sunday at 2:30 (sign up at the little desk under the portico). St. Peter's is closed during ceremonies in the piazza. ⊠*Piazza di San Pietro, Vatican* ⊙ *Apr.–Sept., daily 7–7; Oct.–Mar., daily 7–6.*

The **Grotte Vaticane** *(Vatican Grottoes)* in the basilica contain the tombs of many popes, including John Paul II, and the Tomb of St. Peter. The entrance is opposite the baldacchino, near a pillar where the dome begins. The only exit leads outside the church, so don't go down until you're finished elsewhere. ☎*Free* ⊙ *Apr.–Sept., daily 7–6; Oct.–Mar., daily 7–5.*

The **roof** of St. Peter's Basilica, reached by elevator or stairs, provides a view among a landscape of domes and towers. An interior staircase (170 steps) leads to the base of the dome for a dove's-eye look at the interior of St. Peter's. Only if you are stout of heart and sound of lung should you attempt the taxing and claustrophobic climb up the remaining 330 steps to the balcony of the lantern, where the view embraces the Vatican Gardens and all of Rome. The up and down staircases are one way; once you commit to climbing, there's no turning back. ☎*06/69883462* ☎*Elevator €7, stairs €4* ⊙ *Daily 8–5 (11:30–5 on Wed. if pope has audience in Piazza San Pietro).*

🐾 **⑤** **Castel Sant'Angelo.** For hundreds of years this fortress guarded the Vatican, to which it is linked by the **Passetto,** an arcaded passageway (the secret "lair of the Illuminati," according to Dan Brown's *Angels & Demons,* the Rome-based prequel to *The Da Vinci Code*). According to legend, Castel Sant'Angelo got its name during the plague of 590, when Pope Gregory the Great (circa 540–604), passing by in a religious procession, had a vision of an angel sheathing its sword atop the stone ramparts. Though it may look like a stronghold, Castel Sant'Angelo was in fact built as a tomb for the emperor Hadrian (76–138) in AD 135. By the 6th century it had been transformed into a fortress, and it remained a refuge for the popes for almost 1,000 years. It has dungeons, battlements, cannon and cannonballs, and a collection of antique weaponry and armor. The lower levels formed the base of Hadrian's mausoleum; ancient ramps and narrow staircases climb through the castle's core to courtyards and frescoed halls, where temporary exhibits are held. Off the loggia is a café.

The upper terrace, with the massive angel statue commemorating Gregory's vision, evokes memories of Tosca, Puccini's poignant heroine in the opera of the same name, who threw herself off these ramparts with the cry, *"Scarpia, avanti a Dio!"* ("Scarpia, we meet before God!") On summer evenings a book fair with musical events and food stalls surrounds the castle. One of Rome's most beautiful pedestrian bridges, **Ponte Sant'Angelo** spans the Tiber in front of the fortress and is studded with graceful angels designed by Bernini. ✉ *Lungotevere Castello 50, near Vatican* ☎ 06/39967600 ⊕ *www.pierreci.it* 🎫 €5 ⊗ *Tues.– Sun. 9–7:30.*

④ **Musei Vaticani** *(Vatican Museums).* The building on your left as you exit
Fodor'sChoice   St. Peter's Basilica is the Vatican Palace, the papal residence since 1377,
★   with an estimated 1,400 rooms, chapels, and galleries. Other than the pope and his court, the occupant is the Musei Vaticani (Vatican Museums), containing some of art's greatest masterpieces. The Sistine Chapel is the headliner here, but in your haste to get there, don't overlook the Museo Egizio, with its fine Egyptian collection; the famed classical sculptures of the Chiaramonti and the Museo Pio Clementino; and the Stanze di Raffaello (Raphael Rooms), a suite of halls covered floor-to-ceiling in some of the master's greatest works.

On a first visit to the Vatican Museums, you may just want to see the highlights—even that will take several hours and a good, long walk. In peak tourist season, be prepared for at least an hour's wait to get into the museums and large crowds once inside. The best time to avoid lines and crowds is not first thing in the morning but during lunch hour and the Wednesday papal audiences. The collection is divided among different galleries, halls, and wings connected end to end. Pick up a leaflet at the main entrance to the museums to see the overall layout. The Sistine Chapel is at the far end of the complex, and the leaflet charts two abbreviated itineraries through other collections to reach it. An audio guide (€5.50, about 90 minutes) for the Sistine Chapel, the Stanze di Raffaello, and 350 other works and locations is worth the added expense. Phone or e-mail at least a week in advance (a month

CLOSE UP

A Morning with the Pope

The pope holds audiences in a large, modern hall (or in St. Peter's Square in summer) on Wednesday morning at 10. To attend, you must get tickets; apply in writing at least 10 days in advance to the **Papal Prefecture** (*Prefettura della Casa Pontificia*) ✆ 00120 Vatican City ☎ 06/69883273 🖶 06/69885863), indicating the date you prefer, your language, and your hotel. Or go to the prefecture, through the Porta di Bronzo, the bronze door at the end of the colonnade on the right side of the piazza; the office is open Monday–Saturday 9–1, and last-minute tickets may be available.

You can also arrange to pick up free tickets on Tuesday from 5 to 6:45 at the **Santa Susanna American Church** (✉ *Via XX Settembre 15, near Termini* ☎ 06/42014554); call first. For a fee, travel agencies make arrangements that include transportation. Arrive early, as security is tight and the best places fill up fast.

for peak season) to book a guided tour (€21.50) through the Guided Visit to Vatican Museums. The main entrance to the museums, on Viale Vaticano, is a long walk from Piazza San Pietro along a busy thoroughfare. Some city buses stop near the main entrance: Bus 49 from Piazza Cavour stops right in front; buses 81 and 492 and Tram 19 stop at Piazza Risorgimento, halfway between St. Peter's and the museums. The Ottaviano–S. Pietro and the Cipro–Musei Vaticani stops on Metro A also are in the vicinity. Entry is free the first Sunday of the month, and the museum is closed on Catholic holidays, of which there are many. Last admission is an hour before closing.

Besides the galleries mentioned here, there are many other wings along your way—full of maps, tapestries, classical sculpture, Egyptian mummies, Etruscan statues, and even Aztec treasures. From the main entrance of the Vatican Museums take the escalator up to the **Pinacoteca** (Picture Gallery) on your right. This is a self-contained section, and it's worth visiting first for works by such artists as Leonardo (1452–1520), Giotto (circa 1266–1337), Fra Angelico (1387–1455), and Filippo Lippi (circa 1406–69), and the exceptional *Transfiguration, Coronation*, and *Foligno Madonna* by Raphael (1483–1564).

The **Cortile Ottagano** (Octagonal Courtyard) of the Vatican Museums displays some of sculpture's most famous works, including the 4th century BC *Apollo Belvedere* (and Canova's 1801 *Perseus*, heavily influenced by it) and the 2nd-century *Laocoön*.

The **Stanze di Raffaello** (Raphael Rooms) are second only to the Sistine Chapel in artistic interest—and draw crowds comparable. In 1508 Pope Julius II employed Raphael, on the recommendation of Bramante, to decorate the rooms with biblical scenes. The result is a Renaissance tour de force. Of the four rooms, the second and third were decorated mainly by Raphael. The others were decorated by Giulio Romano (circa 1499–1546) and other assistants of Raphael; the first room is known as the Stanza dell'Incendio, with frescoes by Romano of the *incendio* (fire) in the Borgo neighborhood.

Continued on page 80

AGONY AND ECSTASY:
THE SISTINE CEILING

Forming lines that are probably longer than those waiting to pass through the Pearly Gates, hordes of visitors arrive at the Sistine Chapel daily to view what may be the world's most sublime example of artistry;

Michelangelo: *The Creation of Adam*, Sistine Chapel, The Vatican, circa 1511.

Michelangelo's Sistine Ceiling. To paint this 12,000-square-foot barrel vault, it took four years, 343 frescoed figures, and a titanic battle of wits between the artist and Pope Julius II. While in its typical fashion, Hollywood focused on the element of agony, not ecstasy, involved in the saga of creation, a recently completed restoration of the ceiling has revolutionized our appreciation of the masterpiece of masterpieces.

By Martin Wilmot Bennett

MICHELANGELO'S
MISSION IMPOSSIBLE

Designed to match the proportions of Solomon's Temple described in the Old Testament, the Sistine Chapel is named after Pope Sixtus VI, who commissioned it as a place of worship for himself and as the venue where new popes could be elected. Before Michelangelo, the barrel-vaulted ceiling was an expanse of azure fretted with golden stars. Then, in 1504, an ugly crack appeared. Bramante, the architect, managed do some patchwork using iron rods, but when signs of a fissure remained, the new Pope Julius II summoned Michelangelo to cover it with a fresco 135 feet long and 44 feet wide.

Taking in the entire span of the ceiling, the theme connecting the various participants in this painted universe could be said to be mankind's anguished waiting. The majestic panel depicting the Creation of Adam leads, through the stages of the Fall and the expulsion from Eden, to the tragedy of Noah found naked and mocked by his own sons; throughout all runs the underlying need for man's redemption. Witnessing all from the side and end walls, a chorus of ancient Prophets and Sibyls peer anxiously forward, awaiting the Redeemer who will come to save both the Jews and the Gentiles.

APOCALYPSE NOW

The sweetness and pathos of his Pietà, carved by Michelangelo only ten years earlier, have been left behind. The new work foretells an apocalypse, its congregation of doomed sinners facing the wrath of heaven through hanging, beheading, crucifixion, flood, and plague. Michelangelo, by nature a misanthrope, was already filled with visions of doom thanks to the fiery orations of Savonarola, whose thunderous preachments he had heard before leaving his hometown of Florence. Vasari, the 16th-century art historian, coined the word "terribilità" to describe Michelangelo's tension-ridden style, a rare case of a single word being worth a thousand pictures.

Michelangelo wound up using a *Reader's Digest* condensed version of the stories from Genesis, with the dramatis personae overseen by a punitive and terrifying God. In real life, poor Michelangelo answered to a flesh-and-blood taskmaster who was almost as vengeful: Pope Julius II. Less vicar of Christ than latter-day Caesar, he was intent on uniting Italy under the power of the Vatican, and was eager to do so by any means, including riding into pitched battle. Yet this "warrior pope" considered his most formidable adversary to be Michelangelo. Applying a form of blackmail, Julius threatened to wage war on Michelangelo's Florence, to which the artist had fled after Julius canceled a commission for a grand papal tomb unless Michelangelo agreed to return to Rome and take up the task of painting the Sistine Chapel ceiling.

MICHELANGELO, SCULPTOR

A sculptor first and foremost, however, Michelangelo considered painting an inferior genre—"for rascals and sissies" as he put it. Second, there was the sheer scope of the task, leading Michelangelo to suspect he'd been set up by a rival, Bramante, chief architect of the new St. Peter's Basilica. As Michelangelo was also a master architect, he regarded this fresco commission as a Renaissance mission-impossible. Pope Julius's powerful will prevailed—and six years later the work of the Sistine Ceiling was complete. Irving Stone's famous novel *The Agony and the Ecstasy*—and the granitic 1965 film that followed—chart this epic battle between artist and pope.

THINGS ARE LOOKING UP

To enhance your viewing of the ceiling, bring along opera glasses, binoculars, or just a mirror (to prevent your neck from becoming bent like Michelangelo's). Note that no photos are permitted. Insiders know the only time to get the chapel to yourself is during the papal blessings and public audiences held in St. Peter's Square. Failing that, get there during lunch hour. Admission and entry to the Sistine Chapel is only th__ the Musei Vaticani (Vatican Museums

SCHEMATIC OF THE SISTINE CEILING

Libyan Sibyl · Daniel · Cumean Sibyl · Isaiah · Delphic Sibyl

Jonah · NOAH STORIES · ADAM & EVE STORIES · THE CREATION · Zacheriah

1 2 3 4 5 6 7 8 9

ENTRANCE

Jeremiah · Persian Sibyl · Ezekiel · Eritrean Sibyl · Joel

Prophets · Sibyls · Ignudi

HEAVEN'S ABOVE

The ceiling's biblical symbols were ideated by three Vatican theologians, Cardinal Alidosi, Egidio da Viterbo, and Giovanni Rafanelli, along with Michelangelo. As for the

ceiling's painted "framework," this *quadratura* alludes to Roman triumphal arches because Pope Julius II was fond of mounting "triumphal entries" into his conquered cities (in imitation of Christ's procession

into Jerusalem on Palm Sunday).

THE CENTER PANELS

Prophet turned art-critic or, perhaps doubling as ourselves, the ideal viewer, Jonah the prophet (painted at the altar end) gazes up at the

Creation, or Michelangelo's version of it.

1 The first of three scenes taken from the Book of Genesis: God separates Light from Darkness.

2 God creates the sun and a craterless pre-Galilean moon while the panel's other half offers an unprecedented rear view of the Almighty creating the vegetable world.

3 In the panel showing God separating the Waters from the Heavens, the Creator tumbles towards us as in a self-made whirlwind.

4 Pausing for breath, next admire probably Western Art's most famous image—God giving life to Adam.

5 The Creation of Eve from Adam's rib leads to the sixth panel.

6 In a sort of diptych divided by the trunk of the Tree of Knowledge of Good and Evil, Michelangelo retells the Temptation and the Fall.

7 Illustrating Man's fallen nature, the last three panels narrate, in un-chronological order, the Flood. In the first Noah offers a pre-Flood sacrifice of thanks.

8 Damaged by an explosion in 1794, next comes Michelangelo's version of Flood itself.

9 Finally, above the monumental Jonah, you can just make out the small, wretched figure of Noah, lying drunk—in pose, the shrunken anti-type of the majestic Adam five panels down the wall.

THE CREATION OF ADAM

Michelangelo's Adam was partly inspired by the Creation scenes Michelangelo had studied in the sculpted doors of Jacopo della Quercia in Bologna and Lorenzo Ghiberti's Doors of Paradise in Florence. Yet in Michelangelo's version Adam's hand hangs limp, waiting God's touch to impart the spark of life. Facing his Creation, the Creator—looking a bit like the pagan god Jupiter—is for the first time ever depicted as horizontal, mirroring the Biblical "in his own likeness." Decades after its completion, a crack began to appear, amputating Adam's fingertips. Believe it or not, the most famous fingers in Western art are the handiwork, at least in part, of one Domenico Carnevale.

The frescoed **Stanza della Segnatura** (Room of the Signature), where papal bulls were signed, is one of Raphael's finest works; indeed, they are thought by many to be some of the finest paintings in the history of Western art. This was Julius's private library, and the room's use is reflected in the frescoes' themes, philosophy and enlightenment. A paradigm of High Renaissance painting, the works demonstrate the revolutionary ideals of naturalism (Raphael's figures lack the awkwardness of those painted only a few years earlier); humanism (the idea that human beings are the noblest and most admirable of God's creations); and a profound interest in the ancient world, the result of the 15th-century rediscovery of classical antiquity. The *School of Athens* glorifies some of philosophy's greats, including Plato (pointing to Heaven) and Aristotle (pointing to Earth) at the fresco's center. The pensive figure on the stairs is thought to be modeled after Michelangelo, who was painting the Sistine ceiling at the same time Raphael was working here.

In 1508, just before Raphael started work on his rooms, the redoubtable Pope Julius II commissioned Michelangelo to paint single-handedly the more-than-10,000-square-foot ceiling of the **Cappella Sistina** (Sistine Chapel). The task cost the artist four years of mental and physical anguish. It's said that for years afterward Michelangelo couldn't read anything without holding it up over his head. The result, however, was the masterpiece that you now see, its colors cool and brilliant after restoration. Bring a pair of binoculars to get a better look at this incredible work (unfortunately, you're not allowed to lie down on the floor to study the frescoes above, the viewing position of choice in decades past). Tourists in the 19th century used pocket mirrors so as not to strain their necks. For an in-depth look at Michelangelo's masterpiece, see our photo feature, "Agony & Ecstasy: The Sistine Ceiling." ⊠ *Main museum entrance, Viale Vaticano; guided visit office, Piazza San Pietro* ☎ *06/69883332* ⊕ *www.vatican.va* 🎫€ *14* ◷ *Mon.–Sat. 8:30–6, last entrance at 4; closed Sun., except for last Sun. of month, when admission is free* ⬧ *Note: ushers at entrance of St. Peter's and Vatican Museums will bar entry to people with bare knees or bare shoulders* Ⓜ *Cipro-Musei Vaticani.*

❶ Piazza San Pietro. As you enter St. Peter's Square you are officially entering Vatican territory. The piazza is one of Bernini's most spectacular masterpieces. It was completed in 1667 after 11 years' work, a relatively short time, considering the vastness of the task. The piazza can hold 400,000 people—as it did in the days following the death of Pope John Paul II.

2

The piazza is surrounded by a curving pair of quadruple colonnades, topped by a balustrade and statues of 140 saints. Look for the two disks set into the pavement on either side of the obelisk at the center of the piazza. When you stand on either disk, a trick of perspective makes the colonnades seem to consist of a single row of columns. Bernini had an even grander visual effect in mind when he designed the square: the surprise of stepping into an immense, airy space after approaching it through a neighborhood of narrow, shadowy streets. The contrast was intended to evoke the metaphor of moving from darkness to light. But in the 1930s Mussolini spoiled the effect. To celebrate the "conciliation" between the Vatican and the Italian government under the Lateran Pact of 1929, he conceived of the Via della Conciliazione, the broad avenue that now forms the main approach to St. Peter's.

Remember to look for the Swiss Guards in their colorful uniforms; they've been standing at the Vatican entrances for the past 500 years. ⊠ *At head of Via delle Conciliazione*

ALSO WORTH SEEING

❸ Giardini Vaticani *(Vatican Gardens)*. Generations of popes have strolled in these beautifully manicured gardens, originally laid out in the 16th century. A two-hour guided tour, half by bus and half on foot, takes you through a haven of shady walkways, elaborate fountains, and exotic plants. Make reservations two or three days in advance and pick up your tickets in the Guided Visit to Vatican Museums Office at the museum entrance. If you have a reservation, you can skip the line (go in through the "Exit" door); the office window is inside the atrium. ⊠ *Viale Vaticano* ☎*06/69884466 reservations* ⊕*www.vatican. va* 🔁€*10* ⊗*Tours: Mon.–Sat. 10 A.M. Office: Mon.–Sat. 8:30–7.*

THE GHETTO, TIBERINA ISLAND & TRASTEVERE

Each staunchly resisting the tides of change, these three areas are hard to beat for the authentic atmosphere of Old Rome. You begin in the old Ghetto, a warren of twisting, narrow streets, where Rome's Jewish community was once confined, then deported, and now, barely, persists. Ancient bridges, the Ponte Fabricio and Ponte Cestio, link the Ghetto to Tiberina Island, the tiny island that is one of Rome's most picturesque sights. On the opposite side of the Tiber lies Trastevere—"across the Tiber"—long cherished as Rome's Greenwich Village and now subject to rampant gentrification. In spite of this, Trastevere remains about the most tightly knit community in the city, the Trasteverini proudly proclaiming their descent from the ancient Romans. This area is Rome's enchanting, medieval heart.

GETTING HERE
From Termini station, nab the No. 40 Express or the No. 64 bus to Largo Torre Argentina, where you can get off to visit the Ghetto area. Switch to Tram 8 to get to Trastevere. The No. 41 bus ascends the Janiculum Hill.

THE MAIN ATTRACTIONS

❻ Fontana delle Tartarughe. The 16th-century Fountain of the Turtles in Piazza Mattei is one of Rome's loveliest. Designed by Giacomo della Porta (1539–1602) in 1581 and sculpted by Taddeo Landini (1550–96), the piece revolves around four bronze boys, each clutching a dolphin that jets water into marble shells. Several bronze tortoises, thought to have been added by Bernini, are held in each of the boys' hands and drink from the fountain's upper basin. The piazza is lined by a few interesting cafés and shops. It was named for the Mattei family, who built the **Palazzo Mattei** on Via Caetani, famed for its sculpture-rich, bust-adorned 17th-century courtyard—one of Rome's most photogenic. ⊠ *Piazza Mattei, Ghetto.*

★ **❼ Isola Tiberina.** Tiber Island is where a city hospital stands on a site that has been dedicated to healing ever since a temple to Aesculapius was erected here in 291 BC. Back then, the ancient Romans sheathed the entire island in travertine, sculpting it into a "boat" complete with obelisk "mast." Be sure to walk down the wide river embankment to the southern tip to see one of the most astonishing remnants of ancient Rome: the island's sculpted marble "prow" carved with a figure of Aesculapius. Every July, the city's Estate Romana hosts an open-air cinema on the island's paved shores. ⊠ *Ponte Fabricio and Ponte Cestio, near Ghetto.*

Jewish Ghetto. Rome has had a Jewish community since the 1st century BC, and from that time until the present its living conditions have varied widely according to its relations with the city's rulers. In 1555 Pope Paul II established Rome's Ghetto Ebraico in the neighborhood marked off by the Portico d'Ottavia, the Tiber, and Via Arenula. The area quickly became Rome's most densely populated. The laws were rescinded around the time of the Italian unifications in the 1870s but German troops tragically occupied Rome during World War II and in 1943 wrought havoc here. Today, there are a few Judaica shops and kosher groceries, bakeries, and restaurants (especially on Via di Portico d'Ottavia) but the neighborhood mansions are now being renovated and much coveted by the rich and stylish. **Tours of the Ghetto** (€8, about two hours) that explore Rome's Jewish history can be booked through the SIDIC historical society. ⊠ *SIDIC Office, Via Garibaldi 28, Ghetto* ☎ *06/67015555* ⊕ *www.sidic.org.*

❺ Portico d'Ottavia. Along Via del Portico d'Ottavia in the heart of the Jewish Ghetto are buildings where medieval inscriptions, ancient friezes, and half-buried classical monuments attest to the venerable history of the neighborhood. The old **Chiesa di Sant'Angelo in Pescheria** was built right into the ruins of the ancient Roman Portico d'Ottavia, which was a monumental area enclosing a temple, library, and other buildings within colonnaded porticoes. ⊠ *Via del Portico d'Ottavia, Ghetto.*

Trastevere &
the Ghetto

Fodor's Choice **Santa Maria in Trastevere.** Shimmering at night thanks to its medieval
★ facade mosaics, this is one of Rome's most magnificent and oldest
⑩ churches, first built in the 4th century and then greatly enlarged in the
12th century. Inside, the nave framed by a grand processional of two
rows of columns taken from ancient Roman temples often produced
involuntary gasps from unsuspecting visitors—this is probably as close
as we can get to the imperial splendor of an ancient Roman basilica.
A shining burst of Byzantine color and light is added by the celebrated
12th-century mosaics in the apse; also note the Cosmati work, a mosaic
style from the 12th and 13th centuries in which tiny squares and triangles were laid with larger stones to form geometric patterns, in the
church floors. Outside, the **Piazza di Santa Maria in Trastevere** is a very
popular spot for afternoon coffee and evening cocktails at its outdoor
cafés. The 13th-century mosaics on Santa Maria's facade—which
add light and color to the piazza, especially at night when they are in
spotlight—are believed to represent the Wise and Foolish Virgins. In
August, processions honoring the Virgin Mary gather at the church as
part of Trastevere's famous traditional feast, called *Festa de Noantri*
(Our Own Feast). ⊠ *Piazza di Santa Maria, Trastevere* ☎ *06/5814802*
⊗ *Daily 7:30–1 and 4–7.*

4 **Teatro di Marcello.** The Teatro, hardly recognizable as a theater today, was originally designed to hold 20,000 spectators. It was begun by Julius Caesar; today, the 16th-century apartment building that sprouted out of its remains has become one of Rome's most prestigious residential addresses. The area south of the theater makes a grand stage for chamber music concerts in summer.

✉ *Via del Teatro di Marcello, Ghetto* ☎ *06/87131590 concert information* ⊕ *www.tempietto.it* ☾ *Open during concerts only.*

Trastevere. This area consists of a maze of narrow streets that is still, despite evident gentrification, one of the city's most authentically Roman neighborhoods. Literally translated, its name means "across the Tiber," and indeed the Trasteverini—the neighborhood's natives— are a breed apart. The area is hardly undiscovered, but among its self-consciously picturesque trattorias and trendy tearooms you can also find old shops and dusty artisans' workshops in alleys festooned with laundry hung out to dry. Stroll along Via dell'Arco dei Tolomei and Via dei Salumi, shadowy streets showing the patina of the ages. One of the least affected parts of Trastevere is a block in from the Tiber: on Piazza in Piscinula, north of Via dei Salumi and south of the Ponte Cestio Fabricio, the smallest medieval church in the city, San Benedetto, stands opposite the restored medieval Casa dei Mattei. ✉ *Just east of Tiber river, accessed by Ponte Sisto, Ponte Garibaldi, Ponte Fabrizio, Ponte Palatino, and Ponte Principe Amedeo, Trastevere*

★ **11** **Villa Farnesina.** Money was no object to extravagant patron Agostino Chigi, a Sienese banker who financed many a papal project. His munificence is evident in his elegant villa, built about 1511. When Raphael could steal some precious time from his work on the Vatican Stanze and wooing Fornarina, he executed some of the frescoes, notably a luminous *Galatea*. Chigi delighted in impressing guests by having his servants cast precious dinnerware into the Tiber when it was time to clear the table. The guests didn't know of the nets he had stretched under the waterline to catch everything. His extravagant ways meant that his villa had to be eventually sold to the grand Farnese family. ✉ *Via della Lungara 230, Trastevere* ☎ *06/68027268* ⊕ *www.lincei. it/informazioni/villafarnesina/index.php* ⊡ *€5* ☾ *Mon.–Sat. and 1st Sun. of month 9–1.*

ALSO WORTH SEEING

12 **Palazzo Corsini.** This elegant palace holds the 16th- and 17th-century painting collection of the **Galleria Nazionale d'Arte Antica**; even if you're not interested in the paintings, stop in to climb the extraordinary 17th-century stone staircase, itself a drama of architectural shadows and sculptural voids. The adjacent Corsini gardens, now Rome's **Giardino Botanico**, offer delightful tranquillity, with native and exotic plants and a marvelous view at the top. ✉ *Via della Lungara 10, Traste-*

WALKING TOURS OF ROME

All About Rome, American Express, Context: Rome, Enjoy Rome, Through Eternity, and Walks of Rome offer walking tours of the city and its sites. Fascinating tours are offered: Renaissance Rome and "Angels & Demons" tours are just two of the main theme walks scheduled. Here are their contact points:

All About Rome (☎ 06/7100823 ⊕ www.allaboutromewalks.net-firms.com). **American Express** (☎ 06/67641). **Context: Rome** (✉ Via Baccina 40, near Termini ☎ 06/4820911 or 888/4671986 ⊕ www.contextrome.com). **Enjoy Rome** (✉ Via Marghera 8A, near Termini ☎ 06/4451843 ⊕ www.enjoyrome.com). **Through Eternity** (☎ 06/7009336 ⊕ www.througheternity.com). **Walks of Rome** (☎ 347/7955175).

vere ☎ 06/68802323 ⊕ *www.galleriaborghese.it* 💳 €4 ⊙ *Tues.–Sun., entrance at 9:30, 11, and 12:30.*

❶ Piazza Bocca della Verità. On the site of the Forum Boarium, ancient Rome's cattle market, this square was later used for public executions. Its name is derived from the marble **Bocca della Verità** (Mouth of Truth), a huge medieval drain cover in the form of an open-mouth face that is now set into the entry portico of the magically medieval 12th-century church of **Santa Maria in Cosmedin.** In the Middle Ages, legend had it that any person who told a lie with his hand in the mouth would have it chomped off. Today tour groups line up in this noisy, traffic-jammed piazza to give this ancient lie detector (which starred with Audrey Hepburn and Gregory Peck in *Roman Holiday*) a go. *By Tiber river, along Lungotevere dei Pierleoni,* ✉ *near Ghetto.*

❾ San Francesco a Ripa. Ask the sacristan to show you the cell where St. Francis slept when he came to seek the pope's approval for his new order. Also in this church is one of Bernini's most dramatic sculptures, the figure of the *Blessed Ludovica Albertoni,* ecstatic at the prospect of entering heaven. ✉ *Piazza San Francesco d'Assisi, Trastevere* ☎ 06/5819020 ⊙ *Daily 7–noon and 4–7:30.*

☾ ❽ Santa Cecilia in Trastevere. Mothers and children love to dally in the delightful little garden in front of this church. Duck inside for a look at the 9th-century mosaics and the languid statue of St. Cecilia under the altar. Fragments of a *Last Judgment* fresco cycle by Pietro Cavallini (circa 1250–1330), dating from the late 13th century, remain one of his most important works. Though the Byzantine-influenced fragments are obscured by the structure, what's left reveals a rich luminosity in the seated apostles' drapery and a remarkable depth in their expressions. A pretty cloister and remains of Roman houses are visible under the church. To see them, ask at the booth to the left of the main nave. ✉ *Piazza Santa Cecilia, Trastevere* ☎ 06/5899289 💳 *Church free,* *frescoes €2.50* ⊙ *Daily 9:30–12:30 and 4–6:30. Frescoes Mon.–Sat. 10:15–12:15, Sun. 11:15–noon.*

❸ Tempio della Fortuna Virilis. This rectangular temple devoted to "manly fortune" dates from the 2nd century BC and is built in the Greek style, as was the norm in the early years of Rome. For its age, its remains are remarkably well preserved, in part due to its subsequent consecration as a Christian church. ✉*Piazza Bocca della Verità, near Ghetto.*

❺❸ Tempio di Ercole Victor. All but 1 of the 20 original Corinthian columns in Rome's most evocative small ruin remain intact. It was built in the 2nd century BC. Long considered a shrine to Vesta, it is now believed the temple was devoted to Hercules by a successful olive merchant. ✉*Piazza Bocca della Verità, near Ghetto.*

THE CATACOMBS & VIA APPIA ANTICA

The Early Christian sites on the ancient Appian Way are some of the religion's oldest. Catacombs, where both ancient pagan Romans and early Christians buried their dead, and where Christians gathered to worship in secret, lie below the very road where tradition says Christ appeared to St. Peter. The Via Appia Antica, built 400 years before, is a quiet, green place to walk and ponder the ancient world. The Rome APT office provides an informative free pamphlet for this itinerary.

GETTING HERE

Take Bus 660 from the Colli Albani metro stop on Line A to the end of the line, at Via Appia Antica, or opt for the Archeobus OpenTram bus from Piazza Venezia.

THE MAIN ATTRACTIONS

❸ San Sebastiano. The 4th-century catacomb, named for the saint who was buried here, burrows underground on four levels. The only one of the catacombs to remain accessible during the Middle Ages, it's the origin of the term "catacomb," for it was in a spot where the road dips into a hollow, a place the Romans called *catacumbas* ("near the hollow"). Eventually the Christian cemetery that had existed here since the 2nd century came to be known by the same name, which was applied to all underground cemeteries discovered in Rome in later centuries. ✉*Via Appia Antica 136* ☎*06/7850350* 💶*€5* ⊙*Mid-Nov.–mid-Oct., Mon.–Sat. 9–noon and 2–5.*

❹ Tomba di Cecilia Metella. The circular mausoleum of a Roman noblewoman, who lived at the time of Julius Caesar, was transformed into a fortress in the 14th century. The tomb houses a tiny museum with sculptures from the Via Appia Antica and an interesting reconstruction of the area's geological and historical past. ✉*Via Appia Antica 161* ☎*06/78021465 or 06/39967700* 🌐*www.pierreci.it* 💶*€6* ⊙*Mon.–Sat. 9* AM*–1 hr before sunset.*

★ ☾ ❶ Via Appia Antica. This Queen of Roads, "Regina Viarium," was the most important of the extensive network of roads that traversed the Roman

The Catacombs
& Via Appia Antica

Empire, a masterful feat of engineering that made possible Roman control of a vast area by allowing for the efficient transport of armies and commercial goods. Completed in 312 BC by Appius Claudius, the road was ancient Europe's first highway, connecting Rome with Brindisi, 584 km (365 mi) away on the Adriatic coast. Part of the route exists as Via Appia (SS7), but it is a paved, modern highway. The stretch indicated here is closed to traffic; the ancient roadway passes through grassy fields and shady groves and by the villas of movie stars (Marcello Mastroianni and Gina Lollobrigida had homes here) and other VIPs. This part is still paved with the ancient *basoli* (basalt stones) over which the Romans drove their carriages—look for the wheel ruts. Pick a sunny day for your visit, wear comfortable shoes, and bring a bottle of water. You can take Bus 660 from the Colli Albani metro station (Line A) for Via Cecilia Metella at Via Appia Antica. ⊠ *Exit Via Cristoforo Colombo at Circonvallazione Ardeatina, follow signs to Appia Antica parking lot.*

ALSO WORTH SEEING

❷ **San Callisto.** A friar will guide you through the crypts and galleries of the well-preserved San Callisto catacombs. ⊠ *Via Appia Antica 110* ☎ *06/4465610* 💶 *€5* ⊙ *Mar.–Jan., Thurs.–Tues. 8:30–12:30 and 2:30–5.*

WHERE TO EAT

Updated by
Dana Klitzberg
& Jen Laskey

Rome has been known since ancient times for its great feasts and banquets, and though the days of the triclinium and the Saturnalia are long past, dining out is still the Romans' favorite pastime. The city is distinguished more by its good attitude toward eating out than by a multitude of world-class restaurants; simple, traditional cuisine reigns, although things are slowly changing as talented young chefs explore new culinary frontiers. Many of the city's restaurants cater to a clientele of regulars, and atmosphere and attitude are usually friendly and informal. The flip side is that in Rome the customer is not always right—the chef and waiters are in charge, and no one will beg forgiveness if you wanted *skim* milk in that cappuccino. Be flexible and you're sure to *mangiar bene* (eat well). Lunch is served from approximately 12:30 to 2:30 and dinner from 7:30 or 8 until about 11, though some restaurants stay open later, especially in summer, when patrons linger at sidewalk tables to enjoy the parade of people and the *ponentino* (evening breeze).

WHAT IT COSTS IN EUROS					
	¢	$	$$	$$$	$$$$
At Dinner	under €15	€15–€25	€25–€35	€35–€45	over €45

Prices are for a first course (*primo*), second course (*secondo*), and dessert (*dolce*).

PANTHEON, NAVONA, TREVI & QUIRINALE

$$$$
MODERN
ITALIAN
Fodor'sChoice
★

✕ **Il Convivio.** In a tiny, nondescript vicolo north of Piazza Navona, the three Troiani brothers—Angelo in the kitchen, and brothers Giuseppe and Massimo presiding over the dining room and wine cellar—have quietly been redefining the experience of Italian eclectic *alta cucina* for many years. Antipasti include a "roast beef" of tuna fillet lacquered with chestnut honey, rosemary, red peppercorns, and ginger served with a green apple salad, while a squid ink risotto with baby cuttlefish, sea asparagus, and basil sates the appetites of those with dreams of *fantasia*. Main courses include a fabulous version of a cold-weather pigeon dish for which Il Convivio is famous. Service is attentive without being overbearing, and the wine list is exceptional. A splurge spot. ⊠ *Vicolo dei Soldati 31, Navona* 🕾*06/6869432* ⚞*Reservations essential* 🚍*AE, DC, MC, V* ⊗*Closed Sun., 1 wk in Jan., and 2 wks in Aug. No lunch.*

$$$
MEDI-
TERRANEAN
Fodor'sChoice
★

✕ **Etablí.** On a narrow vicolo off beloved Piazza del Fico, this multidimensional locale opened last year, serving as caffè by day, and becoming a hot spot by aperitivo hour. Beautifully finished with vaulted wood beam ceilings, wrought iron touches, plush leather sofas, and chandeliers, it's all modern Italian farmhouse chic. In the restaurant section (the place is sprawling), it's minimalist Provençal hip (*etablí* is French for the regionally typical tables within). And the food is clean and Mediterranean, with touches of Asia in the raw fish appetizers. Pastas are more traditional Italian, and the secondi run the gamut from

The Piazza del Pantheon is a striking restaurant location—though you'll find better food elsewhere in the neighborhood..

land to sea. Arrive early as the place fills up by dinnertime and it's a popular postdining spot for sipping and posing. ⊠ *Vicolo delle Vacche 9/a, Navona* ☏ *06/6871499* ⊕ *www.etabli.it* ⌕ *Reservations recommended* ▤ *MC, V* ☾ *Closed Sun. in summer, Mon. in winter.*

$$ ✗ **Maccheroni.** This boisterous, convivial trattoria north of the Pan-
ITALIAN theon makes for a fun evening out. The decor is basic: white walls with wooden shelves lined with wine bottles, blocky wooden tables covered in white butcher paper—but there's an "open" kitchen (with even the dishwashers in plain view of the diners) and an airy feel that attracts a young clientele as well as visiting celebrities. The menu sticks to Roman basics such as simple pasta with fresh tomatoes and basil or rigatoni *alla gricia* (with bacon, sheep's-milk cheese, and black pepper). The specialty pasta, *trofie* (short pasta twists) with a black truffle sauce, inspires you to lick your plate. Probably the best choice on the menu is the *tagliata con rughetta*, a juicy, two-inch-thick steak sliced thinly and served on arugula. ⊠ *Piazza delle Coppelle 44, Pantheon* ☏ *06/68307895* ▤ *AE, MC, V.*

$$ ✗ **Ōbikā.** If you've ever wanted to take in a "mozzarella bar," here's
ITALIAN your chance. Mozzarella is featured here much like sushi bars showcase fresh fish—even the decor is modern Japanese minimalism–meets–ancient Roman grandeur. The cheese, in all its varieties, is the focus of the dishes: there's the familiar cow's milk, the delectable water buffalo milk varieties from the Campagnia region, and the sinfully rich *burrata* from Puglia (a fresh cow's milk mozzarella encasing a creamy center of unspun mozzarella curds and fresh cream). They're all served with

various accompanying cured meats, vegetables, sauces, and breads. An outdoor deck is a great plus for dining alfresco. ⊠ *Piazza di Firenze 26, Navona* ☎ *06/6832630* ⊟ *AE, DC, MC, V*

$
WINE BAR
Fodor'sChoice
★

✕ **Cul de Sac.** This popular wine bar near Piazza Navona is among the city's oldest enoteche and offers a book-length selection of wines from Italy, France, the Americas, and elsewhere. Food is eclectic, ranging from a huge assortment of Italian meats and cheeses (try the delicious *lonza,* cured pork loin, or *speck,* a northern Italian smoked prosciutto) to various Mediterranean dishes, including delicious baba ghanoush, a tasty Greek salad, and a spectacular wild boar pâté. Outside tables get crowded fast, so arrive early, or come late, as they serve until about 1 AM. ⊠ *Piazza Pasquino 73, 00186, Navona* ☎ *06/68801094* ⊟ *AE, MC, V* ⊘ *Closed 2 wks in Aug.*

$
PIZZA
Fodor'sChoice
★

✕ **Da Baffetto.** Down a cobblestone street not far from Piazza Navona, this is Rome's most popular pizzeria and a summer favorite for street-side dining. The plain interior is mostly given over to the ovens, but there's another room with more paper-covered tables. Outdoor tables (enclosed and heated in winter) provide much-needed additional seating. Turnover is fast and lingering is not encouraged. ⊠ *Via del Governo Vecchio 114, Navona* ☎ *06/6861617* ⊟ *No credit cards* ⊘ *Closed Aug. No lunch.*

CAMPO DE' FIORI & GHETTO

$$$
MODERN
ITALIAN

✕ **Ditirambo.** Don't let the country-kitchen ambience fool you. At this little spot off Campo de' Fiori, the constantly changing selection of offbeat takes on Italian classics is a step beyond ordinary Roman fare. The place is usually packed with diners who appreciate the adventuresome kitchen, though you may overhear complaints about the brusque service. Antipasti can be delicious and unexpected, like Gorgonzola-pear soufflé drizzled with aged balsamic vinegar, or a mille-feuille of eggplant, wild fennel, and anchovies. But people really love this place for rustic dishes like osso buco, Calabrian eggplant "meatballs," and hearty pasta with rabbit ragù. Vegetarians will adore the cheesy potato gratin with truffle shavings. ⊠ *Piazza della Cancelleria 74, Campo de' Fiori* ☎ *06/6871626* ⊟ *AE, MC, V* ⊘ *Closed Aug. No lunch Mon.*

$$$
ITALIAN
Fodor'sChoice
★

✕ **Evangelista.** This restaurant seems to be so tucked away, even the locals have difficulty stumbling upon it. Everybody, however, seems to know and love its *carciofi al mattone* (roasted artichokes pressed flat between two hot bricks); this fame is well deserved, as the artichoke comes out crispy and delicious, looking almost like a perfectly seared vegetable carpaccio. Pastas are excellent, including the home-made potato gnocchi, light and fluffy and unadorned in a vegetable ragoût with a touch of saffron. Then feast on roast pork loin with juniper berries in winter, swordfish with Marsala, mint, and pistachio in summer. The arched white ceilings and decorating details lend an air of comfortable elegance. ⊠ *Via delle Zoccolette 11/a, Campo de' Fiori* ☎ *06/6875810* ⊟ *AE, MC, V* ⊘ *Closed Sun. and Aug. No lunch.*

$$$
WINE BAR

✕ **Roscioli.** This food shop and wine bar is dark and decadent, more like a Caravaggio painting than a place of business. The shop in front beckons with top-quality comestibles: whole prosciuttos, wild Alaskan smoked salmon, more than 300 cheeses, and a dizzying array of wines. Venture further inside to be seated in a wine cavelike room where you'll be served artisanal cheeses and salamis, and the same oil, vinegar, and bread that you can purchase out front. Beyond display

case items, the menu features creative dishes like homemade pasta with duck prosciutto, or potato gnocchi with a sea urchin sauce, both original uses of fairly esoteric (but steadfastly Italian) ingredients. Tip: book ahead to reserve a table in the cozy wine cellar beneath the dining room. ⊠ *Via dei Giubbonari 21/22, Campo de' Fiori* ☎06/6875287 ▤*AE, DC, MC, V* ⊘*Closed Sun.*

$$–$$$ ✕**La Taverna Degli Amici.** This restaurant, on an idyllic ivy-draped piazza
ROMAN tucked away in the Jewish Ghetto, has what is considered one of the most delightful outdoor dining settings in Rome. Generally the menu features high-quality versions of Roman and Roman-Jewish classics. The *amatriciana* and *cacio e pepe* pastas are delicious, and the secondi courses continue the friendly feast with well-executed beef fillets with rosemary, roasted sea bream with potatoes, and a veal chop, pounded extra-thin, breaded and fried and topped with chopped cherry tomatoes and arugula. A selection from the unusual dessert list is a special treat here; try the cinnamon mousse. The wine list is edited and the markup substantial, but hey, what's a few extra euros among *amici*? ⊠*Piazza Margana 36, Ghetto* ☎06/69920637 ▤*AE, DC, MC, V* ⊘*Closed Sun. and Mon. and 2 wks in Aug.*

$$ ✕**Da Sergio.** Every neighborhood has at least one "old-school" Roman
ROMAN trattoria and, for the Campo de' Fiori area, Da Sergio is it. Once you're seated (there's usually a wait), the red-and-white-check paper tablecovering, bright lights, '50s kitsch, and the stuffed boar's head on the wall remind you that you're smack in the middle of the genuine article. Go for the delicious version of pasta *all'amatriciana*, or the generous helping of gnocchi with a tomato sauce and lots of Parmesan cheese, served, as tradition dictates, on Thursday. ⊠*Vicolo delle Grotte 27, Campo de' Fiori* ☎06/6864293 ▤*DC, MC, V* ⊘*Closed Sun. and 2 wks in Aug.*

$ ✕**Brasia.** This spacious trattoria on a back street off of the Campo de'
ITALIAN Fiori is a welcome, inexpensive addition to an area filled with tourist-riddled pizzerias and overpriced restaurants. The place itself is a huge space, but remains cozy because of brick walls and arched ceilings (the space actually harks back to the 17th century, and the name of the street it's on means "street of caves"). There's a wood-burning oven for homemade pizzas, and grilled meats are the other house specialty, here less expensive than in most spots. All typical Roman menu staples are found here as well: bruschette, mixed salumi and antipasti, and a variety of pasta standards. ⊠*Vicolo delle Grotte 17, Campo de' Fiori* ☎06/97277119.

BEST BETS FOR ROME DINING

With hundreds of restaurants to choose from, how will you decide where to eat? Fodor's writers and editors have selected their favorite restaurants by price, cuisine, and experience in the Best Bets lists below. In the first column, Fodor's Choice properties represent the "best of the best" in every price category.

FODOR'S CHOICE ★

Agata e Romeo, $$$$ p. 96

Alle Fratte di Trastevere, $$ p. 99

Il Convivio, $$$$ p. 88

Cul de Sac, $ p. 90

Da Baffetto, $ p. 90

Etablì, $$$ p. 88

Evangelista, $$$ p. 90

Il Gelato di San Crispino, p. 101

La Pergola, $$$$ p. 97

Taverna Angelica, $$$ p. 98

Tazza d'Oro, ¢ p. 101

Tram Tram, $$ p. 97

Trattoria Monti, $$ p. 97

Uno e Bino, $$$ p. 96

Best by Price

¢

Caffe Sant'Eustachio p. 101

Filetti di Baccalà p. 91

Il Gelato di San Crispino p. 101

Tazza d'Oro p. 101

$

Brasia p. 91

Cul de Sac p. 90

Da Baffetto p. 90

Dar Poeta p. 99

Remo p. 100

$$

Alle Fratte di Trastevere p. 99

Da Sergio p. 91

Ōbikā p. 89

Tram Tram p. 97

Trattoria Monti p. 97

$$$

Ditirambo p. 90

Etablì p. 88

Evangelista p. 90

Taverna Angelica p. 98

Uno e Bino p. 96

$$$$

Agata e Romeo p. 96

Il Convivio p. 88

La Pergola p. 97

Best by Cuisine

CAFFÈ

GiNa p. 96

Caffè Sant'Eustachio p. 101

Tazza d'Oro p. 101

CENTRAL ITALIAN

Dal Bolognese p. 93

Trattoria Monti p. 97

MODERN ITALIAN

Agata e Romeo p. 96

Ditirambo p. 90

Il Convivio p. 88

Il Palazzetto p. 93

La Pergola p. 97

Taverna Angelica p. 98

Uno e Bino p. 96

OLD-SCHOOL ROMAN

Ai Tre Scalini p. 100

Checchino dal 1887 p. 100

Da Sergio p. 91

OSTERIA/TRATTORIA

Alle Fratte di Trastevere p. 99

Etablì p. 88

Maccheroni p. 89

Trattoria Monti p. 97

SOUTHERN ITALIAN

Siciliainbocca p. 98

Tram Tram p. 97

WINE BAR

Cul de Sac p. 90

Del Frate p. 98

Enoteca Trastevere p. 99

L'Enoteca Antica di Via della Croce p. 96

Best by Experience

CHILD-FRIENDLY

Alle Fratte di Trastevere p. 99

'Gusto p. 93

GOOD FOR GROUPS

Alle Fratte di Trastevere p. 99

Dar Poeta p. 99

'Gusto p. 93

Maccheroni p. 89

GORGEOUS SETTING

Agata e Romeo p. 96

Il Convivio p. 88

La Pergola p. 97

OUTDOOR DINING

Alle Fratte di Trastevere p. 99

Dal Bolognese p. 93

Maccheroni p. 89

Taverna degli Amici p. 91

MOST ROMANTIC

Il Convivio p. 88

La Pergola p. 97

¢ ✕**Filetti di Baccalà.** For years, Filetti di Baccalà has been serving just
ITALIAN that—battered, deep-fried fillets of salt cod—and not much else. You'll
find no-frills starters such as *bruschette al pomodoro* (garlic-rubbed
toast topped with fresh tomatoes and olive oil), sautéed zucchini, and,
in winter months, the cod is served alongside *puntarelle*, chicory stems
topped with a delicious anchovy-garlic-lemon vinaigrette. The location,
down the street from Campo de' Fiori in a little piazza in front of the
beautiful Santa Barbara church, begs you to eat at one of the outdoor
tables, weather-permitting. Long operating hours allow those still on
U.S. time to eat as early (how gauche!) as 6 PM. ⊠*Largo dei Librari
88, Campo de' Fiori* ☎*06/6864018* ⊟*No credit cards* ⊘*Closed Sun.
and Aug. No lunch.*

VENETO, BORGHESE & SPAGNA

$$$$ ✕**Dal Bolognese.** The darling of the media, film, and fashion commu-
ITALIAN nities, this classic restaurant on Piazza del Popolo is not only an "in-
crowd" dinner destination but makes a convenient shopping-spree
lunch spot. As the name promises, the cooking adheres to the hearty
tradition of Bologna. Start with a plate of sweet *San Daniele* prosciutto
with melon, then move on to the traditional egg pastas of Emilia-
Romagna. Second plates include the famous Bolognese *bollito misto*,
a steaming tray of an assortment of boiled meats (some recognizable,
some indecipherable) served with a tangy, herby green sauce. ⊠*Piazza
del Popolo 1, Spagna* ☎*06/3611426* ⊟*AE, DC, MC, V* ⊘*Closed
Mon. and 3 wks in Aug.*

$$$–$$$$ ✕**'Gusto.** There's an urban-loft feel to this trendy two-story space, a bit
MEDI- like Pottery Barn exploded in Piazza Agusto Imperatore (the name of
TERRANEAN the restaurant is a play on this location and the Italian word for taste/
flavor). The ground floor contains a buzzing pizzeria-trattoria, while
upstairs is the more upscale restaurant, where a Mediterranean-meets-
Asia menu results in some real misses. We prefer the casual-but-hop-
ping vibe of the ground-floor wine bar in the back, where a rotating
selection of wines by the glass and bottle are served up alongside a
vast array of cheeses, salami, and bread products. And for the kitchen
enthusiast, the 'Gusto "complex" includes a store, selling everything
from cookware to cookwear. ⊠*Piazza Augusto Imperatore 9, Spagna*
☎*06/3226273* ⊟*AE, DC, MC, V.*

$$–$$$ ✕**Il Palazzetto.** This small restaurant by the Piazza di Spagna is part
MODERN of the International Wine Academy of Rome. Chef Antonio Martucci
ITALIAN creates seasonal menus using traditional Roman ingredients, which he
gives a unique "twist" to in preparation and flavor pairings. Stuffed
calamari on an eggplant puree with sautéed baby peppers is a study
in contrasting flavor and texture; homemade ricotta-filled gnocchi
with sausage and asparagus hits all the right notes. It's wise to call in
advance, both for reservations and to find out about regular prix-fixe
dinners, sometimes with guest chefs, focusing on wine-food pairings.
⊠*Vicolo del Bottino 8, Spagna* ☎*06/6990878* ⊟*AE, DC, MC, V.*

$$ ✕**Margutta Vegetariano.** Parallel to posh Via del Babuino, Via Margutta
ITALIAN has long been known as *the* street where artists have their studios in

Where to Eat in Rome

2

Rome. How fitting, then, that the rare Italian vegetarian restaurant, with changing displays of modern art, sits on the far end of this gallery-lined street closest to Piazza del Popolo. Here it takes on a chic and cosmopolitan air, where you'll find meat-free versions of classic Mediterranean dishes as well as more daring tofu concoctions. Lunch is essentially a pasta/salad bar to which you help yourself, while dinner offers à la carte and prix-fixe options. ⊠ *Via Margutta 118, Spagna* ☎ *06/32650577* ⊟ *AE, DC, MC, V.*

$ ✕ **GiNa.** "Homey minimalism" isn't a contradiction at this whitewashed
ITALIAN   caffè with a modern edge. The block seats and sleek booths, the single flowers in Mason jars, white chandeliers, and multiplicity of mirrors, make this small but multilevel space a tiny gem tucked away on the street leading from Piazza di Spagna up to Villa Borghese. With a menu ranging from various bruschette to interesting mixed salads, sandwiches, and pastas, this is the perfect spot for a light lunch, an aperitivo, or a light dinner that won't break the bank in this high-end neighborhood. Also available are fully stocked gourmet picnic baskets, complete with checked tablecloth, to pick up on the way to the Villa Borghese. ⊠ *Via San Sebastianello 7A, Spagna* ☎ *06/6780251* ⊟ *AE, MC, V* ⊙ *Closed Sun. and Aug.; open only for lunch and aperitivi (until 8 pm) in summer.*

$ ✕ **L'Enoteca Antica di Via della Croce.** This wine bar is always crowded,
WINE BAR   and for good reason. It's long on personality: colorful ceramic-tile tables are always filled with locals and foreigners, as is the half-moon-shape bar where you can order from the large selection of salumi and cheeses on offer. Peruse the chalkboard highlighting the special wines by-the-glass for that day to accompany your nibbles. There's waiter service at the tables in back and out front on the bustling Via della Croce, where people-watching is in high gear. ⊠ *Via della Croce 76/b, Spagna* ☎ *06/6790896* ⊟ *AE, DC, MC, V* ⊙ *Closed 2 wks in Aug.*

MONTI, ESQUILINO, REPUBBLICA & SAN LORENZO

$$$$ ✕ **Agata e Romeo.** For the perfect marriage of fine dining, creative cui-
MODERN   sine, and rustic Roman tradition, the husband-and-wife team of Agata
ITALIAN   Parisella and Romeo Caraccio is the top. Romeo presides over the din-
Fodor'sChoice   ing room and delights in the selection of wine-food pairings. And Chef
★   Agata was perhaps the first in the capital city to put a gourmet spin on Roman ingredients and preparations, elevating dishes of the common folk to new levels, wherein familiar staples like *coda alla vaccinara* are transformed into a rich oxtail ragoût with celery root, both as a puree and as shoestring fries. From antipasti to desserts, many dishes are the best versions of classics you can get. The prices here are steep, but for those who appreciate extremely high-quality ingredients, an incredible wine cellar, and warm service, dining here is a real treat. ⊠ *Via Carlo Alberto 45, Termini* ☎ *06/4466115* ⊟ *AE, DC, MC, V* ⊙ *Closed weekends, 2 wks in July, and 2 wks in Aug.*

$$$ ✕ **Uno e Bino.** The setting is simple: wooden tables and chairs on a stone
ITALIAN   floor with little more than a few shelves of wine bottles lining the walls
Fodor'sChoice   for decor. Giampaolo Gravina's restaurant in this artsy corner of the
★   San Lorenzo neighborhood is popular with foodies and locals alike, as

the kitchen turns out inventive cuisine inspired by the family's Umbrian and Sicilian roots. Dishes like octopus salad with asparagus and carrots, and spaghetti with swordfish, tomatoes, and capers are specialties. The parmesan soufflé is a study in lightness and silky-salty. Desserts are delicious and upscale-simple as well, making this small establishment one of the top dining deals—and pleasurable meals—in Rome. ⊠ *Via degli Equi 58, San Lorenzo* ☎ *06/4460702* ▤ *MC, V* ⊘ *Closed Mon. and Aug. No lunch.*

$$ ✕**Tram Tram.** This bustling trattoria is usually snugly packed with hun-
ITALIAN   gry Romans. The name refers to its proximity to the tram tracks, but
Fodor's Choice   could also describe its size, as it's narrow-narrow and often stuffed to
★   the rafters-rafters. In warmer weather, there's a "side car" of tables enclosed along the sidewalk. The focus of the food is the cook's hometown region of Puglia. You'll find an emphasis on seafood and vegetables—maybe prawns with saffron-kissed sautéed vegetables—as well as pastas of very particular shapes. Fish is a good bet here; try the homemade *orecchiette*, ear-shaped pasta, made here with clams and broccoli. ⊠ *Via dei Reti 44/46, San Lorenzo* ☎ *06/490416* ▤ *AE, DC, MC, V* ⊘ *Closed Mon. and 1 wk in mid-Aug.*

$$ ✕**Trattoria Monti.** Not far from Santa Maria Maggiore and one of the
ITALIAN   most dependable, moderately priced trattorias in the city, Monti favors
Fodor's Choice   the cuisine of the Marches, an area to the northeast of Rome. There
★   are surprisingly few places specializing in this humble fare considering there are more *marchegiani* in Rome than in the whole region of Le Marche. The fare served up by the Camerucci family is hearty and simple, represented by various roasted meats and game and a selection of generally vegetarian timbales and soufflés that change seasonally. The region's rabbit dishes are much loved, and here the *timballo di coniglio con patate* (rabbit casserole with potatoes) is no exception. ⊠ *Via di San Vito 13, Monti* ☎ *06/4466573* ▤ *AE, DC, MC, V* ⊘ *Closed Aug., 2 wks at Easter, and 10 days at Christmas.*

$$ ✕**Trimani Il Winebar.** This is a handy address for diners in a town where
WINE BAR   most restaurants don't open before 8 PM. Trimani operates nonstop from 11 AM to 12:30 AM and serves hot food at lunch and dinner. Decor is minimalist, and the second floor provides a subdued, candlelit space to sip wine. There's always a choice of a soup and pasta plates, as well as second courses and *torte salate* (savory tarts). Around the corner is a wineshop, one of the oldest in Rome, of the same name. Call about wine tastings and classes (in Italian). ⊠ *Via Cernaia 37/b, Repubblica* ☎ *06/4469630* ▤ *AE, DC, MC, V* ⊘ *Closed Sun. and 2 wks in Aug.*

VATICAN, BORGO & PRATI

$$$$ ✕**La Pergola.** La Pergola's rooftop location offers a commanding view
MODERN   of the city, and as you're seated in your plush chair, you know you're
ITALIAN   in for a three–Michelin star experience. First, your waiter will present
Fodor's Choice   you with menus—food, wine, and water (you read correctly). Then
★   you must choose between the German Wunder-chef Heinz Beck's *alta cucina* specialties, though most everything will prove to be the best version of the dish you've ever tasted. Lobster is oh-so-lightly poached,

and melt-in-your-mouth lamb in a veggie-accented jus is deceptively simple but earthy and perfect. Each course comes with a flourish of sauces or extra touches that makes it an event in its own right, while the cheese cart is well-explained by knowledgeable servers. And the dessert course is extravagant, including tiny petits fours and treats tucked away in small drawers that make up the serving "cabinet." The wine list is as thrilling as one might expect with the financial backing of the Hilton and their investment in one of the top wine cellars in Italy. ⊠ *Cavalieri Hilton, Via Cadlolo 101, Monte Mario, Northwest Rome* ☎ *06/3509221* ⌨ *Reservations essential. Jacket and tie* ⊟ *AE, DC, MC, V* ⊘ *Closed Sun. and Mon., and 2 wks in Dec. No lunch.*

$$$–$$$$
SOUTHERN
ITALIAN

✕ **Siciliainbocca.** The owners, both natives of the southernmost Italian island, decided to open up Siciliainbocca after years of frustration at not finding decent renditions of the food for which their home region is so renowned. As a result, the pasta *alla norma*—with eggplant, tomato sauce, and aged ricotta cheese—here is one of the best versions in Rome. Try specialties like *caponata*, a sweet-and-sour eggplant ratatouille, or *risotto ai profumi di Sicilia* with lemon, orange, mozzarella, and zucchini. Be sure to try the delicious grilled swordfish, shrimp, and squid. Even in the dead of winter, Siciliainbocca's yellow walls and brightly colored ceramic plates make you feel as if you're in sunny Sicily. ⊠ *Via E. Faà di Bruno 26, Prati* ☎ *06/37358400* ⊟ *AE, DC, MC, V* ⊘ *Closed Sun.*

$$$
MODERN
ITALIAN
Fodor's Choice
★

✕ **Taverna Angelica.** The area surrounding St. Peter's Basilica isn't known for culinary excellence, but Taverna Angelica is an exception. Its tiny size allows the chef to concentrate on each individual dish, and the menu is creative without being pretentious. Dishes such as warm octopus salad on a bed of warm mashed potatoes with a basil-parsley pesto drizzle are more about taste than presentation. The lentil soup with pigeon breast brought hunter's cuisine to a new level. And the breast of duck in balsamic vinegar was exquisitely executed. It may be difficult to find, on a section of the street that's set back and almost subterranean, but it's worth searching out. ⊠ *Piazza A. Capponi 6, Borgo* ☎ *06/6874514* ⌨ *Reservations essential* ⊟ *AE, V.*

$$
WINE BAR

✕ **Del Frate.** This impressive wine bar, adjacent to one of Rome's noted wineshops, matches sleek and modern decor with creative cuisine and three dozen wines available by the glass. The house specialty is marinated meat and fish, and you can also get cheeses, smoked meats, and composed salads. For dessert, dip into the chocolate fondue. ⊠ *Via degli Scipioni 118, Prati* ☎ *06/3236437* ⊟ *AE, MC, V* ⊘ *Closed 3 wks in Aug.*

TRASTEVERE

$$$
TUSCAN

✕ **Il Ciak.** This Tuscan staple in Trastevere is a carnivore's delight. Specializing in the Tuscan *chianina* beef as well as the many game and pork dishes of the region (wild boar sausage, anyone? Or perhaps pasta with wild hare sauce?), Il Ciak prepares reliably tasty fare. It's probably best appreciated during the autumn and winter months, when hunter's dishes get accompaniments like porcini mushrooms and truffles with

Dining al fresco in Trastevere

polenta that even vegetarians will appreciate. Be prepared to share the pleasure of your oversized fiorentina steak—prepared *al sangue* (rare), of course. ⊠ *Vicolo del Cinque, Trastevere* ☎ *06/5890774* ▭ *MC, V* ✆ *Closed Sun.*

$$ ✕ **Alle Fratte di Trastevere.** Here you can find staple Roman trattoria fare
ROMAN as well as dishes with a southern slant. This means that *spaghetti alla*
Fodor'sChoice *carbonara* (with pancetta, eggs, and cheese) shares the menu with the
★ likes of penne *alla Sorrentina* (with tomato, basil, and fresh mozarella).
For starters, the bruschette here are exemplary, as is the pressed octo-
pus carpaccio on a bed of arugula. As for secondi, you can again look
south and to the sea for a mixed seafood pasta or a grilled sea bass with
oven-roasted potatoes, or go for the meat with a fillet *al pepe verde*
(green peppercorns in a brandy cream sauce). Service is always with a
smile, as the owners and their trusted waitstaff make you feel at home.
⊠ *Via delle Fratte di Trastevere 49/50* ☎ *06/5835775* ▭ *AE, DC, MC,
V* ✆ *Closed Wed. and 2 wks in Aug.*

$ ✕ **Dar Poeta.** Romans drive across town for great pizza from this neigh-
PIZZA borhood institution on a small street in Trastevere. Maybe it's the
dough—it's made from a secret blend of flours that's reputed to be
easier to digest than the competition. They offer both thin-crust pizza
and a thick-crust (*"alta"*) Neapolitan-style pizza with any of the given
toppings. For dessert, there's a ridiculously good calzone with Nutella
chocolate-hazelnut spread and ricotta cheese, so save some room. Ser-
vice from the owners and friendly waitstaff is smile-inducing. ⊠ *Vicolo
del Bologna 45, Trastevere* ☎ *06/5880516* ▭ *AE, MC, V.*

$
WINE BAR

✕ **Enoteca Trastevere.** Most wine bars in Rome seem to share the same interior decorator and this one is no exception, with its dark-wood tables, chairs, and shelves lined with bottles of Italian wines. Rome's enoteca menu consultant is a busy person as well; the usual crostini, cheeses, cured meats, and salads are all here. But what sets this wine bar apart from others is

WORD OF MOUTH

"No matter where you go, be bold and order from the list of daily specialties—usually handwritten in Italian on a chalkboard near the front door . . . it's what looked good at the market that day."

—Thomarob

its central location with a large outdoor seating space and big, white umbrellas. Its large selection of organic wine is another selling point, as well as its rich selection of grappas, distilled liquors, and *amari* (Italian bitter herbal digestives). The reasonable prices and friendly service round out the pleasant experience. ✉ *Via della Lungaretta 86, Trastevere* ☎ *06/5885659* ⊟ *AE, MC, V* ⊘ *Closed 3 wks in Jan.*

COLOSSEO, AVENTINO & TESTACCIO

$$$$
ROMAN

✕ **Checchino dal 1887.** Literally carved out of a hill of ancient shards of amphorae, Checchino remains an example of a classic, family-run Roman restaurant, with one of the best wine cellars in the region. Though the slaughterhouses of this quarter, Testaccio, are long gone, an echo of their past existence lives on in the restaurant's soul food—mostly offal and other less-traditionally appealing cuts like *trippa* (tripe), *pajata* (intestine with the mother's milk still inside), and *coratella* (sweetbreads and heart of beef) are all still on the menu for die-hard Roman purists. For the less adventuresome, house specialties include braised milk-fed lamb with seasonal vegetables. Head here for a taste of old Rome, but note that Checchino is really beginning to show its age. ✉ *Via di Monte Testaccio 30* ☎ *06/5746318* ⊟ *AE, DC, MC, V* ⊘ *Closed Sun., Mon., Aug, and 1 wk at Christmas.*

$$$
ROMAN

✕ **Ai Tre Scalini.** A traditional restaurant by the Colosseum, Ai Tre Scalini is old-school Roman with touches of the Sicilian. Some dishes don't appear as described on the menu: eggplant "flan" arrived as parmigiana, and newborn-fish fritters were dry, baked, briny balls. But seating outside in warm weather is pleasant, and some dishes highlight the chef's playfulness, like the unusual radicchio and cheese-stuffed *zagnolotti* (small ravioli) in a lobster sauce. A wide variety of second courses, from gilthead bream topped with paper-thin potato rounds, to simple beef with rosemary, are indeed what they seem, served by waiters who have clearly been around for quite some time. ✉ *Via SS. Quattro 30, Colosseo* ☎ *06/7096309* ⊟ *AE, DC, MC, V* ⊘ *Closed Mon. and 10 days in Sept.*

$
PIZZA

✕ **Remo.** Expect a wait at this perennial favorite in Testaccio frequented by students and neighborhood locals. You won't find tablecloths or other nonessentials, just classic Roman pizza and boisterous conversation. ✉ *Piazza Santa Maria Liberatrice 44, Testaccio* ☎ *06/5746270* ⊟ *No credit cards* ⊘ *Closed Sun., Aug., and Christmas wk. No lunch.*

CAFÉS

Café-sitting is a popular leisure-time activity in Rome, practiced by all and involving nothing more strenuous than gesturing to catch the waiter's eye. Part of the pleasure is resting your tired feet; you won't be rushed, even when the cafés are most crowded, just before lunch and dinner. (Be aware, though, that you pay for your seat—prices are higher at tables than at the counter.) Nearly every corner in Rome holds a faster-paced coffee bar, where locals stop for a quick caffeine hit at the counter. You can get coffee drinks, fruit juices, pastries, sandwiches, liquor, and beer there, too.

Caffé Sant'Eustachio (⊠ *P. Sant'Eustachio 82, Pantheon* ☎ *06/68802048*), traditionally frequented by Rome's literati, has what is generally considered Rome's best cup of coffee. Just walking into the blue-and-yellow spot, the smell of freshly ground beans wafts over you, letting you know that this is *the* place. Servers purposely hidden behind a huge espresso machine vigorously mix the sugar and coffee for you to protect their "secret method" for the perfectly prepared cup. (If you want your *caffè* without sugar here, ask for it *amaro*.) Don't miss the *gran caffè*, a secret concoction unlike anything else in the city.

Fodor's Choice ★ **Tazza d'Oro** (⊠ *Via degli Orfani, Pantheon* ☎ *06/6789792*) has many admirers who contend it serves the city's best cup of coffee. The hot chocolate in winter, all thick and gooey goodness, is a treat. And in warm weather, the coffee granita is the perfect cooling alternative to a regular espresso.

With its sidewalk tables taking in Santa Maria della Pace's adorable piazza, **Caffé della Pace** (⊠ *Via della Pace 3, Navona* ☎ *06/6861216*) has long been the haunt of Rome's *beau monde*. Set on a quiet street near Piazza Navona, it also has two rooms filled with old-world personality.

GELATO

For many travelers, the first taste of *gelato*—Italian ice cream—is one of the most memorable moments of their Italian trip. Almost a cross between regular American ice cream and soft serve, gelato's texture is lighter and fluffier than hard ice cream because of the process by which it's whipped when freezing.

Along with the listings here, you can find a number of gelaterias in Via di Tor Millina, a street off the west side of Piazza Navona.

Fodor's Choice ★ **Il Gelato di San Crispino** (⊠ *Via della Panetteria 54, Piazza di Trevi* ☎ *06/6793924* ☉ *Closed Tues.*) makes perhaps the most celebrated gelato in all of Italy, without artificial colors or flavors. It's worth crossing town for—nobody else creates flavors this pure. To preserve the "integrity" of the flavor, the ice cream is only served in paper cups.

For years **Giolitti** (⊠ *Via degli Uffici del Vicario 40, Pantheon* ☎ *06/6991243*) was considered the best gelateria in Rome, and it's still worth a stop if you're near the Pantheon.

Immediately beside the Pantheon is **Cremeria Monteforte** (⊠ *Via della Rotonda 22, Pantheon* ☎*06/6867720)*, which has won several awards for its flavors. Also worth trying is its chocolate sorbetto—it's an icier version of the gelato without the dairy (instead ask for whipped cream on top).

Gelateria alla Scala (⊠ *Via della Scala 51, Trastevere* ☎*06/5813174* ⊙ *Closed Dec. and Jan.*) is a tiny place, but don't let the size fool you. It does a good business offering artisanal gelato prepared in small batches, so when one flavor runs out on any given day, its finished.

Al Settimo Gelo (⊠ *Via Vodice 21/a, Prati* ☎*06/3725567)*, in Prati, has been getting rave reviews for both classic flavors and newfangled inventions. Inventive flavors, such as cardamom and chestnut, wow locals and gelato fans from all over Rome.

WHERE TO STAY

Updated by
Jen Laskey

When planning your Roman Holiday, you may be surprised to learn that you really will have to *do* as the Romans do, meaning that unless you're coveting a luxury suite at the Eden, you'll probably find yourself in a tiny room. The air-conditioning may be weak and the customer service will likely be indifferent. Naturally, there are exceptions, but the Eternal City simply doesn't offer the cushy standards that most Americans are accustomed to, though standards in general are improving.

There are more luxury lodgings, bed-and-breakfasts, and designer "boutique" hotels in Rome than ever before, but if you prefer more modest accommodations (because really, who comes to Rome to hang out in the hotel room?), you still have plenty of options. There are many mid-range and budget hotels and *pensioni* (small, family-run lodgings) available. You may also consider staying at a monastery or convent, a hostel, or an apartment.

If you're looking for luxury, you're most likely to find it around Via Veneto and the Spanish Steps area. On the contrary, many of the city's cheapest accommodations are located near Stazione Termini. But for the most authentic Roman experience, stay in or near the *centro storico* (the historic center).

WHAT IT COSTS IN EUROS					
	¢	$	$$	$$$	$$$$
For Two People	under €75	€75–€150	€151–€225	€226–€300	over €300

Prices are for a standard double room in high season.

PANTHEON, NAVONA, TREVI & QUIRINALE

$$$ 📅 **Pantheon.** The Pantheon is a superb place to stay right next door to the grand monument of the same name. The lobby is the very epitome of a Roman hotel lobby—a warm, cozy, yet opulent setting that comes

replete with Stil Liberty stained glass, sumptuous wood paneling, a Renaissance beamed ceiling, and a massive and glorious chandelier. A print of one of Rome's obelisks on the door welcomes you to your room, where you'll find antique walnut furniture, fresh flowers, and more wood-beam ceilings. **Pros:** Proximity to the Pantheon; big, clean bathrooms; friendly staff. **Cons:** Rooms are in need of some upgrading; the lighting is low and the carpets are worn; the breakfast lacks variety. ⊠ *Via dei Pastini 131, Pantheon,* ☎ *06/6787746* 🖷 *06/6787755* ⊕ *www.hotelpantheon.com* 🛏 *13 rooms, 1 suite* ⚿ *In-room: safe, refrigerator, Wi-Fi. In-hotel: bar, room service, laundry service, public Wi-Fi, no-smoking rooms* ☰ *AE, DC, MC, V* ⍟ *CP.*

$$
Fodor'sChoice
★

Albergo Santa Chiara. With its white shutters and pretty canteloupe-hue stone, this hotel is comprised of three historic buildings set behind the Pantheon. It's been in the same family for 200 years, and the personal attention shows in meticulously decorated and maintained lounges and rooms. The lobby is *alla Romana*—an all white affair; it's elegantly accented with a Venetian chandelier, a stucco statue, a gilded baroque mirror, and a walnut concierge desk. Upstairs, the pricier rooms are most fetching, with stylish yet comfortable furniture. Each room has built-in oak headboards, a marble-top desk, and a travertine bath. Double-glaze windows make a difference in those rooms that look out over the Piazza della Minerva. There are also three apartments, for two to five people, with full kitchens. **Pros:** Great location in the historical center behind the Pantheon; most of the rooms are spacious; the staff is both polite and helpful. **Cons:** Layout is mazelike (you must take two elevators to some of the rooms); rooms don't get a lot of light; no Internet access at the hotel. ⊠ *Via Santa Chiara 21, Pantheon,* ☎ *06/6872979* 🖷 *06/6873144* ⊕ *www.albergosantachiara.com* 🛏 *96 rooms, 3 suites, 3 apartments* ⚿ *In-room: safe, kitchen (some), refrigerator. In-hotel: room service, bar, laundry service, concierge, airport shuttle (fee)* ☰ *AE, DC, MC, V* ⍟ *CP.*

$$
Hotel Trevi. Location, location, location: this delightful place is tucked away down one of Old Rome's quaintest alleys near the Trevi Fountain. The smallish rooms are bright and clean, and a few of the larger ones have antique furniture and wooden ceilings with massive beams. There's also an arborlike roof-garden restaurant where you can eat marvelous pasta as you peer out at the city below. **Pros:** Pass the Trevi Fountain each day as you come and go; comfortable rooms; roof-garden restaurant. **Cons:** Breakfast room is cramped; staff is brusque; no Internet connection in the rooms or in the public spaces. ⊠ *Vicolo del Babbuccio 20/21, Piazza di Trevi,* ☎ *06/6789563* 🖷 *06/69941407* ⊕ *www.gruppotrevi.it* 🛏 *29 rooms* ⚿ *In-room: safe, refrigerator. In-hotel: restaurant, room service, laundry service, airport shuttle (fee), parking (fee), no-smoking rooms* ☰ *AE, DC, MC, V* ⍟ *CP.*

$-$$ **Genio.** Just at the ancient entrance to Piazza Navona, this medium-size hotel offers top-floor rooms with terraces and citywide views. There's also a roof terrace for all, where you can eat your breakfast. Modeled along classic Roman lines, the lobby and public areas are cozy. Rooms are decorated in warm colors and have parquet floors and a harmonious mix of modern and antique reproduction furnishings.

Pros: You can sip wine on the rooftop and take in the view; rooms are a decent size for a Roman hotel; the bathrooms have been designed especially well. **Cons:** Genio is on a busy street so there is often traffic noise; you might hear your neighbors through the walls; both the decor and the carpet have seen better days. ⊠ *Via G. Zanardelli 28, Navona,* ☎ *06/6832191* 🖷 *06/68307246* ⊕ *www.leonardihotels.com/ Genio/index.jsp* ⮐ *60 rooms* ♿ *In-room: refrigerator. In-hotel: room service, bar, laundry services, public Internet, parking (fee)* ▤ *AE, DC, MC, V* �𐃉*CP.*

CAMPO DE' FIORI AND GHETTO

$$$$ ⛨**Hotel Ponte Sisto.** With one of the prettiest patio-courtyards in Rome, this hotel offers its own blissful definition of *Pax Romana*. Peace, indeed, will be yours sitting in this enchanting spot, shadowed by palm trees, set with tables, and adorned with pink and white flowers, all surrounded by the ochre walls of the hotel. Inside, the sleek decors, replete with cherry wood accents, recessed lighting, and luminous marble floors also give a calming effect. Guest rooms are refined—suites come with Jacuzzis and furnished balconies or terraces, bathrooms can be lavishly modern, and there's also a bar and restaurant. The location is an award-winner— just off the Ponte Sisto, the pedestrian bridge that connects the Campo de' Fiori area with Trastevere (whose trattorias and bars are thus just a quick jaunt away), and a second from Via Giulia, Rome's prettiest street. **Pros:** Some rooms with views; luxury bathrooms; beautiful courtyard garden. **Cons:** Street-side rooms can be a bit noisy; some rooms are on the small side; restaurant doesn't serve lunch or dinner. ⊠ *Via dei Pettinari 64, Campo de' Fiori,* ☎ *06/686310* 🖷 *06/68301712* ⊕ *www. hotelpontesisto.it* ⮐ *103 rooms, 4 suites* ♿ *In-room: safe, refrigerator, dial-up. In-hotel: restaurant, room service, bar, laundry service, public Internet, airport shuttle (fee), parking (fee), some pets allowed, no-smoking rooms* ▤ *AE, DC, MC, V* ⟮𐃉⟯*BP.*

$$ ⛨**Hotel Campo de' Fiori.** Frescoes, exposed brickwork, and picturesque effects throughout this little hotel could well be the work of a set designer, but a recent renovation attributes the charming ambience to interior designer Dario di Blasi. Each room is entirely unique in its colors, furniture, and refined feel. The hotel underwent a complete renovation in 2006, retaining its old-world charm, but modernizing with soundproofing, air-conditioning, flat-screen TVs, pay-per-view movies, DSL, and Wi-Fi in all the rooms. There is also a marvelous view from the roof terrace. If you desire more extensive accommodations, Hotel Campo de' Fiori offers an additional selection of 15 different apartments in the area that can accommodate two to five guests. **Pros:** Newly renovated; superb location; modern amenities that many Roman hotels haven't caught up with yet; rooftop terrace. **Cons:** Some of the rooms are very small; breakfast works on a voucher system with a nearby caffè; the staff doesn't necessarily go out of their way to help you settle in. ⊠ *Via del Biscione 6, Campo de' Fiori,* ☎ *06/68806865* 🖷 *06/6876003* ⊕ *www.hotelcampodefiori.it* ⮐ *28 rooms* ♿ *In-room:*

safe, refrigerator, high-speed Internet, Wi-Fi. In-hotel: no-smoking rooms ☰MC, V ¶⃝CP.

$$ ▦ **Teatro di Pompeo.** Where else can you breakfast under the ancient stone vaults of Pompey's Theater, historic site of Julius Caesar's assassination? At this intimate and refined little hotel in the heart of Old Rome you are part of that history. At night, you sleep under restored beamed ceilings that date from the days of Michelangelo. Rooms are simple but tasteful, with terra-cotta floors, comfortable old-fashioned beds, and attractive antique furniture. The staff is also sincere and helpful. Hotel Teatro di Pompeo is the kind of place that really makes you feel like you're living among the true Romans. Do yourself a favor, and book well in advance. **Pros:** Location is central to the Campo but not right on the market square; helpful staff; affordable with an old-school Roman feel. **Cons:** It can be noisy on both the street side and the interior courtyard; rooms are small; no Wi-Fi. *⊠Largo del Pallaro 8, Campo de' Fiori, ☎06/68300170 ⎙06/68805531 ⊕www. hotelteatrodipompeo.it ↩13 rooms ♿In-room: safe, refrigerator. In-hotel: room service, bar, laundry service, public Internet ☰AE, DC, MC, V ¶⃝CP.*

$ ▦ **Arenula.** Standing on an age-worn byway off central Via Arenula, this hotel is a superb bargain by Rome standards. With an imposingly elegant stone exterior, this hotel welcomes you with a luminous and cheerful all-white interior. Guest rooms are simple in decor but have pale-wood furnishings and gleaming bathrooms, as well as double-glaze windows and air-conditioning (in summer only; ask when you reserve). Two of the rooms accommodate four beds. Of course, you can't have everything, so that the graceful oval staircase of white marble and wrought iron in the lobby cues you that there is no elevator. Those guests with rooms on the fourth floor had better be in good shape! **Pros:** It's a real bargain; conveniently located in the Ghetto (close to Campo de' Fiori and Trastevere), and it's spotless. **Cons:** Totally no-frills accommodations; four floors and no elevator; traffic and tram noise can be heard throughout the night despite the double-glazing. *⊠Via Santa Maria dei Calderari 47, off Via Arenula, Ghetto, ☎06/6879454 ⎙06/6896188 ⊕www.hotelarenula.com ↩50 rooms ♿In-room: no a/c (some). In-hotel: no elevator ☰AE, DC, MC, V ¶⃝CP.*

VENETO, BORGHESE & SPAGNA

$$$$ ▦ **Eden.** Once the preferred haunt of Hemingway, Bergman, and Fellini,
Fodor's Choice this superlative hotel combines dashing elegance and stunning vistas of
★ Rome with the warmth of Italian hospitality. Set atop a hill near the Villa Borghese (and a bit out of the historic center for serious sightseers), this hotel was opened in the late 19th century and quickly became famous for its balcony views and Roman splendor. You'll now dive deep here into the whoosh of luxury, with antiques, sumptuous Italian fabrics, linen sheets, and marble baths competing for your attention. Banquette window seats, rich mahogany furniture, soaring ceilings, Napoléon-Trois sofas are just some of the allurements here. **Pros:** gorgeous panoramic view from roof terrace; you could be rubbing elbows

BEST BETS FOR ROME LODGING

Fodor's offers a selective listing of quality lodging experiences at every price range, from the city's best budget motel to its most sophisticated luxury hotel. Here, we've compiled our top recommendations by price and experience. The very best properties—in other words, those that provide a particularly remarkable experience in their price range—are designated in the listings with the Fodor's Choice logo.

FODOR'S CHOICE ★

Albergo Santa Chiara, $$ p. 103
The Beehive, $ p. 113
Daphne Veneto, $$ p. 110
Eden, $$$$ p. 105
Hassler, $$$$ p. 107
Hotel San Pietrino, ¢ p. 117
Relais Le Clarisse, $$ p. 118
Scalinata di Spagna, $$$ p. 107
Yes Hotel, $ p. 113

By Price

¢

Hotel San Pietrino p. 117
Italia p. 115
Arenula p. 105
The Beehive p. 113
Hotel Trastevere p. 118
Yes Hotel p. 113

$$

Albergo Santa Chiara p. 103
Alimandi p. 117
Daphne Veneto p. 110
Hotel Campo de' Fiori p. 104
Hotel Santa Maria p. 117
Relais Le Clarisse p. 118
San Carlo p. 111

$$$

Pantheon p. 102
Scalinata di Spagna p. 107

$$$$

Capo d'Africa p. 119
Eden p. 105
Hassler p. 107

Best by Experience

BEST B&BS

Daphne Veneto p. 110
Relais Le Clarisse p. 118

BEST FOR BUSINESS TRAVEL

Cavalieri Hilton p. 116
Exedra p. 111

BEST CONCIERGE

The Beehive p. 113
Daphne Veneto p. 110
Hotel Lancelot p. 119
Scalinata di Spagna p. 107

BEST DESIGN

Capo d'Africa p. 119
Exedra p. 111

BEST POOLS

Cavalieri Hilton p. 116
Exedra p. 111

BEST SPAS

Cavalieri Hilton p. 116
Exedra p. 111

CHILD-FRIENDLY

Cavalieri Hilton p. 116
Hassler p. 107
Hotel Lancelot p. 119
Hotel Ponte Sisto p. 104

GREAT VIEWS

Cavalieri Hilton p. 116
Eden p. 105
Genio p. 103
Hassler p. 107
Hotel Campo de' Fiori p. 104
San Carlo p. 111

HIDDEN OASIS

Capo d'Africa p. 119
Domus Aventina p. 118
Hotel Lancelot p. 119
Hotel San Anselmo p. 119
Hotel Santa Maria p. 117
Relais Le Clarisse p. 118

MOST ROMANTIC

Daphne Veneto p. 110
Hotel Ponte Sisto p. 104
Relais Le Clarisse p. 118

NEIGHBORHOOD FEEL

Domus Aventina p. 118
Giuliana p. 112
Hotel Santa Maria p. 117
Hotel Trastevere p. 118
Relais Le Clarisse p. 118
Teatro di Pompeo p. 105

with the stars; 24-hour room service. **Cons:** expensive (unless money is no object for you); no Wi-Fi in the rooms; some say the staff can be hit-or-miss. ☒*Via Ludovisi 49, Veneto,* ☎*06/478121* 🖷*06/4821584* 🌐*www.lemeridien.com/eden* 🛏*121 rooms, 13 suites* ♿*In-room: safe, refrigerator, DVD (some), high-speed Internet. In-hotel: restaurant, room service, 2 bars, gym, concierge, laundry service, public Internet, Wi-Fi, airport shuttle (fee), parking (fee), no-smoking rooms, some pets allowed* ▭*AE, DC, MC, V* ⊙*EP.*

$$$$ ☵**Hassler.** Here, in villas atop the Pincian Hill, Poussin, Piranesi, Ingres,
Fodor's Choice   and Berlioz once enjoyed having all of Rome at their feet. Today, movie
★   stars and millionaires do the same by staying at this hotel, which sits just to the right of the church atop the Spanish Steps. The guest rooms here are among the world's most beautiful and opulent. If you're not willing to pay V.I.P prices, you'll get more standard-issue rooms at the rear of the hotel, but many are soigné and some come with views of the Villa Medici park. Better, the hotel has several elegant bars, restaurants, and retreats. The Rooftop Restaurant is world-famous for its view if not for its food; the Hassler Bar was where Princess Diana savored one of the hotel's "Veruschkas" (pomegranate juice, vodka, and champagne); and the Palm Court Garden, which becomes the hotel bar in summer, is overflowing with flowers. **Pros:** Charming old-world feel; prime location and panoramic views at the top of the Spanish Steps; just "steps" away from some of the best shopping in the world. **Cons:** V.I.P. prices; many think the staff are too standoffish; some say the cuisine at the rooftop restaurant isn't worth the gourmet price tag. ☒*Piazza Trinità dei Monti 6, Spagna,* ☎*06/699340* 🖷*06/6789991* 🌐*www.lhw.com* 🛏*85 rooms, 13 suites* ♿*In-room: safe, refrigerator, high-speed Internet. In-hotel: restaurant, room service, bar, gym, spa, concierge, laundry service, public Wi-Fi, parking (fee), no-smoking rooms* ▭*AE, DC, MC, V* ⊙*EP.*

$$$ ☵**Scalinata di Spagna.** An old-fashioned pensione that has hosted gen-
Fodor's Choice   erations of romantics, this tiny hotel is booked solid for months ahead.
★   Its location at the very top of the Spanish Steps, inconspicuous little entrance, and quiet, sunny charm add up to the feeling of your own pied-à-terre in the city's most glamorous neighborhood. Guest rooms are chic, with high-style floral fabrics and Empire-style sofas. The rooms most in demand are those overlooking the Spanish Steps, but even if you don't land one of those few, you can repair to the hotel's exquisite roof garden, where you can have breakfast with Rome unfolding before you. Amenities, such as in-room Internet access and breakfast service until noon are a nice touch. **Pros:** Friendly and helpful concierge; fresh fruit in the rooms; free Wi-Fi throughout the Scalinata. **Cons:** It's a hike up the hill to the hotel; no porter and no elevator; service can be hit-or-miss. ☒*Piazza Trinità dei Monti 17, Spagna,* ☎*06/6793006* 🖷*06/69940598* 🌐*www.hotelscalinata.com* 🛏*16 rooms* ♿*In-room: safe, refrigerator, Wi-Fi. In-hotel: room service, no elevator, laundry service, concierge, public Internet, public Wi-Fi, parking (fee), no-smoking rooms* ▭*AE, D, MC, V* ⊙*BP*

$$-$$$ ☵**Hotel Homs.** At this midsize hotel, on a quiet street in the heart of the historic center, two rooftop terraces provide fine views of the whole

Where to Stay in Rome

2

area; the larger terrace is suitable for breakfast year-round. Although room furnishings are a bit plain overall, beautiful antiques accent strategic spots for an air that's a cut above average. Rome's most complete English-language bookshop, the Anglo-American, is directly across the street. **Pros:** Walking distance to Piazza di Spagna; recently renovated; helpful staff. **Cons:** No breakfast included in the room rate; small rooms; fee for the Wi-Fi. ✉ *Via della Vite 71–72, Spagna,* ☎*06/6792976* 🖷*06/6780482* 🛏*53 rooms, 5 suites, 1 apartment* ⚬*In-room: safe, refrigerator, high-speed Internet. In-hotel: room service, bar, laundry service, public Wi-Fi, airport shuttle (fee), parking (fee), some pets allowed, no-smoking rooms* ▭*AE, DC, MC, V* ⊙*EP.*

\$\$–\$\$\$ 🎬 **Locarno.** The sort of place that inspired a movie (Bernard Weber's 1978 *Hotel Locarno,* to be exact), this has been a longtime choice for art aficionados and people in cinema. But everyone will appreciate this hotel's fin de siècle charm, intimate feel, and central location off Piazza del Popolo. Exquisite wallpaper and fabric prints are coordinated in the rooms, and some rooms are decorated with antiques. Everything is lovingly supervised by the owners, a mother-daughter duo. The buffet breakfast is ample, there's bar service on the panoramic roof garden, and complimentary bicycles are available if you feel like braving the traffic. A newly renovated annex is done in art deco style. **Pros:** Luxurious feel (it may even seem like you're in a movie); spacious rooms (even by American standards); free bicycles for exploring Rome. **Cons:** Some of the rooms are dark; the annex doesn't compare to the main hotel; the regular staff probably won't go out of their way to help you. ✉ *Via della Penna 22, Spagna,* ☎*06/3610841* 🖷*06/3215249* ⊕*www. hotellocarno.com* 🛏*64 rooms, 2 suites* ⚬*In-room: safe, refrigerator, Wi-Fi. In-hotel: restaurant, bar, bicycles, laundry service, public Internet, public Wi-Fi, airport shuttle (fee), no-smoking rooms* ▭*AE, DC, MC, V* ⊙*BP.*

\$\$
Fodor'sChoice
★ 🎬 **Daphne Veneto.** Inspired by baroque artist Gianlorenzo Bernini's exquisite Apollo and Daphne sculpture at the Borghese Gallery, the Daphne Inn at Via Veneto is an "urban B&B" run by people who love Rome and who will do their best to make sure you love it too. This boutique hotel offers an intimate lodging experience, elegantly designed rooms, comfortable beds, a cell phone to use during your stay, fresh fruit and pastries with your coffee each morning, and a small staff of people who promise to give you the opportunity to see Rome "like an insider." They will help you map out your destinations, schedule itineraries, plan day trips, and book tours. **Pros:** You get a priceless introduction to Rome by lovers of Rome; the beds have plush mattresses and fluffy comforters. **Cons:** No TVs; Daphne only accepts Visa or MasterCard to hold bookings (though you can actually pay with an AmEx); there are only seven rooms at the Daphne Veneto (and five at Daphne Trevi), and they're usually booked ahead. ✉ *Via di San Basilio 55, Veneto,* ☎*06/87450087* 🖷*06/233240967* ⊕*www.daphne-rome. com* 🛏*7 rooms, 2 suites* ⚬*In-room: safe, refrigerator, no TV, high-speed Internet. In-hotel: bicycles, laundry service, concierge, public Internet, public Wi-Fi, airport shuttle (fee), parking (fee), no-smoking rooms* ▭*AE, MC, V* ⊙*CP.*

$$ 🏨**San Carlo.** Marble accents are everywhere at this renovated 17th-century mansion, and there's an overall effect that's refined and decidedly classical. Rooms are bright and comfortable; some have their own terraces with rooftop views. A top-floor terrace is ideal for having breakfast or taking in the sun throughout the day. The rooms also feature flat-screen TVs and free Wi-Fi. **Pros:** Rooms with terraces and views of historic Rome; rooftop garden; attentive staff. **Cons:** There are a lot of stairs and no elevator; breakfast is basic Italian fare (great coffee but otherwise just cornetti, cereal, and yogurt); the rooms can be noisy. ✉ *Via delle Carrozze 92–93, Spagna,* ☎*06/6784548* 🖨*06/69941197* ⊕*www.hotelsancarloroma.com* 🛏*50 rooms, 2 suites* 🛎*In-room: refrigerator, Wi-Fi. In-hotel: bar, no elevator, laundry service, public Wi-Fi, no-smoking rooms* ⊟*AE, DC, MC, V* ⫧*CP.*

$ 🏨**Panda.** One of the best deals in Rome, the Panda is particularly remarkable given that the neighborhood is Via della Croce, one of Piazza di Spagna's chic shopping streets. Guest rooms are outfitted in terra-cotta and wrought iron; they're smallish, but quiet, thanks to double-glaze windows, and spotlessly clean. Pay even less by sharing a bath—in low season, you may have it to yourself anyway. **Pros:** Discount if you pay cash; free Wi-Fi; located on a quiet street, but still close to the Spanish Steps. **Cons:** Some say the Wi-Fi signal is weak; not all rooms have private bathrooms; Panda doesn't have an elevator; no TVs in the rooms. ✉ *Via della Croce 35, Spagna,* ☎*06/6780179* 🖨*06/69942151* ⊕*www.hotelpanda.it* 🛏*20 rooms, 14 with bath* 🛎*In-room: no a/c (some), no TV, Wi-Fi. In-hotel: no elevator, laundry service, public Wi-Fi, airport shuttle (fee)* ⊟*MC, V* ⫧*CP.*

MONTI, ESQUILINO, REPUBBLICA & SAN LORENZO

$$$$ 🏨**Exedra.** If Rome's semi-stodgy hotel scene has an It-Girl, it's the Exedra. Hardly a travel column unfolds without a mention of it, celebs vie for face time, and it's the hostess of the moment for out-of-town high rollers and Roman big spenders alike. The Exedra is a model of neoclassical respectability, all gilt-framed mirrors and fresh flowers, but there's a glint of cutting edge in the paparazzi-inspired (and inspiring) Tazio brasserie. Rooms are luscious in an uptown way, with silky linens and handsome nouveau-colonial bedsteads, and many face the spectacular fountain in the piazza outside. Why stay here, rather than at the umpteen other expensively elegant hotels in central Rome? You can think about it while you lounge by the rooftop swimming pool. **Pros:** Spacious and attractive rooms; great spa and pool; terrace with cocktail service. **Cons:** Pricey food and beverages; hotel seems overstaffed at times; beyond the immediate vicinity; parts of the neighborhood seem unsavory. ✉*Piazza della Repubblica 47, Repubblica,* ☎*06/489381* 🖨*06/48938000* ⊕*www.boscolohotels.com* 🛏*240 rooms, 18 suites* 🛎*In-room: safe, refrigerator, high-speed Internet. In-hotel: 3 restaurants, room service, 2 bars, pool, gym, spa, laundry service, concierge, public Internet, public Wi-Fi, parking (fee), some pets allowed, no-smoking rooms* ⊟*AE, DC, MC, V* ⫧*CP.*

$$ ⊡ **D'Este.** The decor in this distinguished 19th-century hotel tries to evoke turn-of-the-20th-century comfort, with brass bedsteads and lamps as well as dark-wood period furniture. Rooms are quiet, light, and spacious; many can accommodate families. The attentive owner-manager likes to have fresh flowers in the halls and sees that everything works. He encourages inquiries about special rates, particularly during the slack summer months. The location is within hailing distance of Santa Maria Maggiore and close to Termini Station. (You can arrange to be picked up there, free of charge, by the hotel car.) **Pros:** Good value for budget travelers; the cleaning staff is especially friendly; hotel car picks you up at Santa Maria Maggiore. **Cons:** The walls are thin; breakfast is the standard Continental fare; some of the beds are squeaky. ⊠ *Via Carlo Alberto 6, Monti,* ☎ *06/4465607* 📠 *06/4465601* ⊕ *www.hotel-deste.com* ⤴ *37 rooms* ⚿ *In-room: safe, refrigerator, Wi-Fi. In-hotel: room service, bar, concierge, public Wi-Fi, airport shuttle (fee), parking (fee), no-smoking rooms* ⊟ *AE, DC, MC, V* ¶⃝*CP.*

$–$$ ⊡ **Des Artistes.** The three personable Riccioni brothers have transformed their hotel into the best in the neighborhood in its price range. It's bedecked with paintings and handsome furnishings in mahogany, and rooms are decorated in attractive fabrics. Marble baths are smallish but luxurious for this price, and they're stocked with hair dryers and towel warmers. Des Artistes hasn't forgotten its roots, though: there's also a "hostel" floor with 11 simpler rooms for travelers on a budget. Book well ahead. As for location, this is somewhat on the fringe, being several blocks (in the wrong direction) from Stazione Termini. **Pros:** Good value; decent-size rooms; relaxing roof garden. **Cons:** Breakfast area is overcrowded; no Internet access in the building; reception is on the fifth floor. ⊠ *Via Villafranca 20, San Lorenzo,* ☎ *06/4454365* 📠 *06/4462368* ⊕ *www.hoteldesartistes.com* ⤴ *40 rooms, 27 with bath* ⚿ *In-room: no a/c (some), safe, refrigerator. In-hotel: bar, concierge, parking (fee), no-smoking rooms* ⊟ *AE, DC, MC, V* ¶⃝*BP.*

$–$$ ⊡ **Giuliana.** A friendly family operates this small, cozy residence with pride. The decor is unprepossessing, with 1960s modern furniture but guest rooms are large (if sparely furnished) and the tiled baths are shiny clean. Make sure to specify bath or shower when you make your reservation; it's one or the other. If you need to check your e-mail while you're on vacation, there is wireless Internet access in the rooms and in the lobby, though it's limited to daytime hours. The hotel doesn't provide laundry service, but you can drop your clothes at the laundry service right next door (and there are several coin-operated laundries in the neighborhood if you need them). **Pros:** Spacious, clean rooms; staff is warm and welcoming; with only 11 rooms, it's an intimate experi-

2

ence. **Cons:** You may hear noise from the local market; air-conditioning is an extra €10 charge; bathroom has either a shower or a tub. ✉ *Via Agostino Depretis 70, Esquilino,* ☎ *06/4880795* 🖷 *06/4824287* ⊕ *www.hotelgiuliana.com* 🖵 *11 rooms* ⚒ *In-room: no a/c (some), safe, refrigerator. In-hotel: room service, bar, concierge, parking (fee), no-smoking rooms* 🚭 *AE, MC, V* ○I *CP.*

$ 🏨 **Adler.** This tiny pensione run by the same family for more than three decades provides a comfortable stay on a quiet street near the main station for a very good price. Ideal for families, Adler has six spacious rooms that sleep three, four, or five, as well as a single and a double. Rooms are basic, but impeccably clean. Worn but cozy chairs line the lobby, and in summer, breakfast can be taken on the leafy courtyard balcony. **Pros:** Breakfast on the terrace; free Internet point in the lobby; strong a/c. **Cons:** Some rooms are dark; showers are tiny; no safes in the rooms. ✉ *Via Modena 5, Esquilino,* ☎ *06/484466* 🖷 *06/4880940* ⊕ *www.hoteladler-roma.com* 🖵 *8 rooms* ⚒ *In-room: refrigerator. In-hotel: room service, bar, public Internet, airport shuttle (fee), parking (fee)* 🚭 *AE, DC, MC, V* ○I *CP.*

$ 🏨 **The Beehive.** Rome meets the best of Southern California at the Bee-
Fodor's Choice   hive. Started by a Los Angeles couple following their dream, the Bee-
★   hive might be the most unique budget hotel in Rome—although, it's not just a hotel; it's more of an ecologically minded little empire that also offers hostel accommodations, a vegetarian café, a yoga space and an art gallery with a garden, a reading lounge, and a few off-site apartments. It offers a respite from Rome's chaos, but is conveniently located only a few blocks from Termini. The design is contemporary and hip and the vibe is mellow. All of the rooms come with shared bathrooms. There is a lovely garden with fruit trees, herbs, and flowers. The Beehive offers free Wi-Fi, but no TVs or air-conditioning (rooms do have ceiling fans). If you would prefer your own self-catering apartment (and private bathroom) for your group or family, or if you'd just like an individual room in an apartment, the Beehive also has three apartments in the neighborhood that can be rented. **Pros:** Yoga, massage, and other therapies offered on-site; free Wi-Fi and Beehive's own guidebook. **Cons:** No TV, a/c, baggage storage, or private bathroom; breakfast is not included in the room rate. ✉ *Via Marghera 8, Repubblica,* ☎ *06/44704553* ⊕ *www.the-beehive.com* 🖵 *8 rooms, 1 dormitory, 3 apartments* ⚒ *In-room: no a/c, kitchen (some), no TV, Wi-Fi. In-hotel: no elevator, public Wi-Fi, no-smoking rooms* 🚭 *MC, V* ○I *EP.*

$ 🏨 **Yes Hotel.** A newcomer to the Rome budget hotel scene, Yes was
Fodor's Choice   opened in April of 2007 by the same folks who own Hotel Des Artistes.
★   It's centrally located near Stazione Termini, and thus close to many restaurants and transportation options. One of the nicest things about Yes is that, even though it's a budget hotel, the rooms have a flair for style with a contemporary feel. Yes also offers the kind of amenities that are usually found in more expensive hotels, like flat-screen TVs and air-conditioning. Unfortunately, there is no Internet access at the hotel, but they do have a special deal with a nearby Internet Point shop that allows guests free access for 15 minutes a day. **Pros:** It doesn't feel like a budget hotel, but it is; discount if you pay cash;

Hassler

Scalinata di Spagna

Eden

Relais Le Clarisse

Daphne Veneto

Yes Hotel

CLOSE UP

Renting an Apartment in Rome

For parties of more than two, Roman hotel rooms can be a little too cozy for comfort (and too cramped to keep more than one suitcase open at a time). If you're traveling in a group or with your family, the best solution may be a short-term apartment rental that offers more space, privacy, and bang for your buck. As a renter, you can find an apartment through an agency, a hotel, or a private owner. There is usually a minimum of a three-night stay. Prices will vary, but expect them to be higher in the historic city center, the Vaticano/Borgo, the Campo de' Fiori, and Trastevere areas.

Start your research online. Rome's official Web site, ⊕ *www.romaturismo.it*, offers a search function for a number of different housing options.

The Bed & Breakfast Association of Rome is an agency that offers an online apartment rental database in addition to its B&B search, at ⊕ www. b-b.rm.it. They inspect all properties advertised on their site.

HOTELS WITH APARTMENTS

There are a number of Roman hotels that—in addition to rooms and suites—offer a selection of local apartments to their prospective guests. Albergo Santa Chiara, 3 apart-ments (⊠ *Via Santa Chiara 21, Pan-theon,* ☎ *06/6872979* 📠 *06/6873144* ⊕ *www.albergosantachiara.com).* Campo de' Fiori, 15 apartments (⊠ *Via del Biscione 6, Campo de' Fiori,* ☎ *06/68806865* 📠 *06/6876003* ⊕ *www.hotelcampodefiori.it).* Italia, 1 apartment (⊠ *Via Venezia 18, Ter-mini,* ☎ *06/4828355* 📠 *06/4745550* ⊕ *www.hotelitaliaroma.com).* Julia, 3 apartments (⊠ *Via Rasella 29, Via Veneto,* ☎ *06/4881637* 📠 *06/4817044* ⊕ *www.hoteljulia. it).* Mecenate Palace Hotel, 2 apart-ments (⊠ *Via Carlo Alberto 3, Termini,* ☎ *06/44702024* 📠 *06/4461354* ⊕ *www.mecenatepalace.com).*

RESIDENCE HOTELS

Residence hotels also specialize in short-let vacation rentals. They usually have fully equipped kitchens and offer linens, laundry, and clean-ing services. Most are available for weekly or monthly rentals. Cost for an apartment for two ranges from about €1,300 for a week to €2,600 per month. Residence Aldrovandi (⊠ *Via Ulisse Aldrovandi 11, Parioli,* ☎ *06/3221430* 📠 *06/3222181* ⊕ *www.aldrovandiresidence.it).* Resi-dence Ripetta (⊠ *Via di Ripetta 231, Piazza di Spagna,* ☎ *06/3231144* 📠 *06/3203959* ⊕ *www.ripetta.it).*

great value. **Cons:** Rooms are small; no individual climate control or refrigerators in the rooms; no Internet in the hotel. ⊠ *Via Magenta 15, San Lorenzo,* ☎ *06/44363836* 📠 *06/44363829* ⊕ *www.yeshotelrome. com* 🛏 *29 rooms, 1 suite* 🍴 *In-room: safe. In-hotel: parking (fee), no-smoking rooms* ☰*MC, V* ⧖*CP.*

¢ 🏨 **Italia.** It looks and feels like a classic pensione: low-budget with a lot of heart. A block off the very trafficky Via Nazionale, this friendly, family-run hotel offers inexpensive rooms with big windows, desks, parquet floors, and baths with faux-marble tiles, but the rooms aren't really the point. The price is, and it's made all the more tempting by a generous buffet breakfast and thoughtful touches like an ice machine and free wireless Internet access. Ask for even lower midsummer rates.

Pros: Free Wi-Fi and Internet access in the lobby; great price; individual attention and personal care. Cons: No Internet access in the rooms; it's sometimes noisy; a/c is an extra €10. ✉ *Via Venezia 18, Monti,* ☎*06/4828355* 🖷*06/4745550* ⊕*www.hotelitaliaroma.com* ⟿*31 rooms, 1 apartment* ⚹*In-room: no a/c (some), safe. In-hotel: bar, concierge, public Internet, public Wi-Fi, airport shuttle (fee), parking (fee), no-smoking rooms* ▭*AE, MC, V* ⦿*CP.*

VATICAN, BORGO & PRATI

$$$$ **Cavalieri Hilton.** Though the Cavalieri is outside the city center, slightly northwest of the Vatican, distance has its advantages. One of them is this property's magnificent view over Rome. Occupying a vast area atop modern Rome's highest hill, the Cavalieri Hilton is an oasis of good taste that feels more like a resort than a city hotel. Central to its appeal, particularly in summer, is a terraced garden that spreads out from an Olympic-size pool and smart poolside restaurant; legions of white-clothed cushioned lounge chairs are scattered throughout the greenery, so there's always a place to sun yourself. Inside, spacious rooms, often with large balconies, are done up in striped damask, puffy armchairs, and such Hiltonesque amenities as a "pillow menu." If you can tear yourself away, the city center is just a 15-minute complimentary shuttle bus ride away. The strawberry on top: La Pergola restaurant *(⇨ see the Where to Eat section)* is renowned as one of Rome's very best. Pros: Beautiful bird's-eye view of Rome; shuttle to the city center; three-Michelin-star dining. Cons: You definitely pay for the luxury of staying here—everything is expensive; outside the city center; not all rooms have the view. ✉ *Via Cadlolo 101, Monte Mario, Northwest Rome,* ☎*06/35091* 🖷*06/35092241* ⊕*www.cavalieri-hilton.com* ⟿*357 rooms, 17 suites* ⚹*In-room: safe, refrigerator, DVD (some), high-speed Internet. In-hotel: 2 restaurants, 3 bars, tennis court, pools, gym, spa, laundry service, concierge, public Internet, airport shuttle (fee), no smoking rooms* ▭*AE, DC, MC, V* ⦿*CP.*

$$–$$$ **Farnese.** Polished walnut antiques, linen sheets, and the occasional painted ceiling—it's all in the details here. An early-20th-century mansion, the Farnese is carefully authentic, preserving a polished Belle Epoque elegance that sits well with its well-traveled clientele. Add to this a comfortable sitting room you'll actually want to use and a roof garden with a view. It's also near the Metro and within walking distance of St. Peter's. Pros: Comfy linen sheets; free Internet; quick walk to the Vatican. Cons: Small rooms; small shower stalls; small and slow elevator. ✉ *Via Alessandro Farnese 30, Prati,* ☎*06/3212553* 🖷*06/3215129* ⟿*23 rooms* ⚹*In-room: safe, refrigerator, Wi-Fi. In-hotel: room service, bar, laundry service, concierge, public Internet, public Wi-Fi, parking (no fee), no smoking rooms* ▭*AE, DC, MC, V* ⦿*BP.*

$$ **Alimandi.** On a side street a block from the Vatican Museums, this family-operated hotel offers excellent value in a neighborhood with moderately priced shops and restaurants. A spiffy lobby, spacious lounges, a tavern, terraces, and roof gardens are some of the perks,

2

as is an exercise room equipped with step machines and a treadmill. Rooms are spacious and well-furnished; many can accommodate extra beds. Needless to say the location here is quite far away from Rome's historic center. **Pros:** Nice family-owned hotel with a friendly staff, a terrace, a tavern, and a gym. **Cons:** Breakfast is a good spread but it goes quickly; rooms are small; not close to much of interest other than the Vatican. ⊠ *Via Tunisi 8, Vatican,* ☎*06/39723948* 🖷*06/39723943* ⊕*www.alimandi.it* ⤳*35 rooms* ♿*In-room: safe, refrigerator (some), Wi-Fi. In-hotel: bar, gym, public Internet, airport shuttle (fee), parking (no fee), no-smoking rooms* ☰*AE, DC, MC, V* ⦿*BP.*

$–$$ ⊞ **Sant'Anna.** In the picturesque old Borgo neighborhood in the shadow of St. Peter's, this fashionable small hotel has exceedingly stylish ample bedrooms with new wood-beam ceilings, designer fabrics, and comfy beds. The frescoes in the vaulted breakfast room and fountain in the courtyard add an individual touch. The marvelously decorated and spacious attic rooms also have tiny terraces. **Pros:** Borgo Pio is a pedestrian-only zone during the day; beds are comfy; staff is eager-to-please. **Cons:** Street-side rooms are noisy; not many amenities; no bar or restaurant in the hotel. ⊠*Borgo Pio 133, Borgo,* ☎*06/68801602* 🖷*06/68308717* ⊕*www.hotelsantanna.com* ⤳*20 rooms* ♿*In-room: safe, refrigerator. In-hotel: parking (fee)* ☰*AE, DC, MC, V* ⦿*BP.*

¢ ⊞**Hotel San Pietrino.** It may seem like a miracle, but the San Pietrino
Fodor'sChoice is a well-appointed, stylish hotel with bargain prices near the Vatican.
★ It's on the third floor of a 19th-century palazzo that's only a five-minute walk to St. Peter's Square. In addition to clean, simple rooms, San Pietrino offers air-conditioning, TVs with DVD players, and high-speed Internet to guests. There is no breakfast included and no bar in the hotel, but not to worry—with all the local caffès and bars, you won't have any trouble finding yourself a *cornetto* and cappuccino in the morning or a prosecco for aperitivo in the evening. **Pros:** Heavenly prices near the Vatican; TVs with DVD players; high-speed Internet. **Cons:** A couple of metro stops away from the center of Rome; no breakfast; no bar. ⊠*Via Giovanni Bettolo 43, Prati,* ☎*06/3700132* 🖷*06/3701809* ⊕*www.sanpietrino.it* ⤳*12* ♿*In-room: DVD (some), high-speed Internet, Wi-Fi. In-hotel: public Internet, public Wi-Fi, airport shuttle (fee)* ☰*MC, V* ⦿*EP.*

TRASTEVERE

$$ ⊞**Hotel Santa Maria.** A Trastevere treasure, this hotel has a pedigree going back four centuries. This ivy-covered, mansard-roofed, rosy-brick-red, erstwhile Renaissance-era convent has been transformed by Paolo and Valentina Vetere into a true charmer. Surrounded by towering tenements, the complex is centered around a monastic porticoed courtyard, lined with orange trees—a lovely place for breakfast. The guest rooms are sweet and simple: a mix of brick walls, "cotto" tile floors, modern oak furniture, and stylishly floral bedspreads and curtains. Best of all, the location is *buonissimo*—just a few blocks from the Tiber and its *isola*. **Pros:** A quaint and pretty oasis in a chaotic city; relaxing courtyard; stocked wine bar. **Cons:** It might be tricky to find; some of the showers drain slowly; it's not always easy finding a cab in Trastevere. ✉ *Vicolo del Piede 2, Trastevere,* ☎*06/5894626* 🖷*06/5894815* ⊕*www.htlsantamaria.com* ⌕*18 rooms, 2 suites* ♿*In-room: safe, refrigerator. In-hotel: bar, bicycles, laundry service, concierge, public Internet, airport shuttle (fee), no-smoking rooms* ▭*AE, DC, MC, V* ⫾○⫾*BP.*

$$
Fodor's Choice
★

▥ **Relais Le Clarisse.** In one of Rome's most popular neighborhoods, this charming little oasis features five simple, but classically styled accommodations (two doubles and three suites) with terra-cotta-tiled floors, wrought-iron bed frames, and oak furnishings. Each room opens up onto a bright courtyard surrounded by a Mediterranean garden of grapevines and olive and lemon trees. Rooms are equipped with the most modern technologies, including individual climate control, flat-screen TVs, and Wi-Fi. It feels more like staying in a villa than a former cloister, and with only five rooms, you have a very personal experience with the staff. **Pros:** Spacious rooms with comfy beds; high-tech showers/tubs with good water pressure; staff is multilingual, friendly, and at your service. **Cons:** This part of Trastevere can be noisy at night; the rooms here fill up quickly; they only serve American coffee. ✉ *Via Cardinale Merry del Val 20, Trastevere,* ☎*06/58334437* 🖷*06/58334437* ⊕*www.leclarisse.com* ⌕*5 rooms, 3 suites* ♿*In-room: safe, refrigerator, high-speed Internet. In-hotel: room service, laundry service, public Internet, public Wi-Fi, airport shuttle (fee), parking (fee), no-smoking rooms* ▭*AE, MC, V* ⫾○⫾*CP.*

$

▥ **Hotel Trastevere.** This tiny hotel captures the villagelike charm of the Trastevere district. The entrance hall features a mural of the famous Piazza di Santa Maria, a block away, and hand-painted art nouveau wall designs add a touch of graciousness throughout. Open medieval brickwork and a few antiques here and there complete the mood. Most rooms face Piazza San Cosimato, where there's an outdoor food market every morning except Sunday. **Pros:** Cheap with a good location; convenient to transportation; friendly staff. **Cons:** No frills; few amenities; no Internet access. ✉ *Via Luciano Manara 24–25, Trastevere,* ☎*06/5814713* 🖷*06/5881016* ⊕*www.hoteltrastevere.net* ⌕*19 rooms, 3 apartments* ♿*In-room: safe (some), refrigerator (some), kitchen (some). In-hotel: no-smoking rooms* ▭*AE, DC, MC, V* ⫾○⫾*CP.*

AVENTINO, TESTACCIO & PALATINO

$$

▥ **Domus Aventina.** Set between a municipal rose garden and Rome's famous Orange Garden, this friendly little hotel is right in the heart of the historic Aventine. It's also not far from the Temple to Mithras and the House of Aquila and Priscilla (where St. Peter touched down). The 17th-century facade has been so restored it almost looks modern—ditto for the inside, where guest rooms have standard modern decors. Half of them also have balconies, and set around an ancient cloister, they all make for islands of tranquillity. **Pros:** Quiet location; walking distance to tourist attractions; complimentary Wi-Fi in rooms and public spaces. **Cons:** No elevator in the hotel; small showers; no tubs. ✉ *Via di*

Santa Prisca 11/b, Aventino, ☎*06/5746135* 🗐*06/57300044* ⊕*www. domus-aventina.com* ⥱*26 rooms* &*In room: safe, refrigerator, Wi-Fi. In-hotel: bar, no elevator, laundry service, public Wi-Fi, airport shuttle (fee), parking (fee)* ⊟*AE, DC, MC, V* ⦿*CP.*

$$ 🖵**Hotel San Anselmo.** Birdsongs emanating from the tree-lined avenues tell you the San Anselmo is as much a retreat as a hotel. It's far from the bustle of the city center, perched on top of the Aventine Hill in a residential neighborhood. This 19th-century villa glows in archetypal Roman cantaloupe-hue stone. Inside, the lobby and adjacent "tea room" are stuffed with a quirky mix of gilded mirrors, plate-glass windows, and a riot of Italianate Rococo chairs and sofas. Others will find the best features here are the verdant garden and terrace bar. Guest rooms are period in flavor, complete with huge armoires, old-fashioned painted headboards, and Empire-style drapes and chandeliers. Two of them have been specially designed with facilities for disabled guests. **Pros:** Historic building with artful decor; great showers with jets; a garden where you can enjoy your breakfast. **Cons:** Some consider it a bit of a hike to sights; limited public transportation; the wireless is pricey. ✉*Piazza San Anselmo 2, Aventino,* ☎*06/570057* 🗐*06/5783604* ⊕*www.aventinohotels.com* ⥱*45 rooms* &*In-room: safe, refrigerator, high-speed Internet. In-hotel: room service, bar, laundry service, public Wi-Fi (fee), parking (no fee), no-smoking rooms* ⊟*AE, DC, MC, V* ⦿*BP.*

COLOSSEO AREA

$$$$ 🖵**Capo d'Africa.** Many find the modern look and feel of Capo d'Africa—not to mention its plush beds and deep bathtubs—refreshing after a long day's journey through ancient Rome. Each room is decorated in warm, muted color tones with sleek furniture, stylish accents, and contemporary art. The hotel features a nonsmoking floor, fitness center, and solarium. There is also access for disabled guests. It sits on a quiet street near the Colosseum, Palatine, and Forum, and it's not far from the metro. A delicious breakfast is served on the rooftop terrace, where you can also enjoy an *aperitivo* overlooking Rome at the end of your day. **Pros:** Luxury digs near the ancient digs; quiet, comfortable rooms; fitness center. **Cons:** Despite proximity to Colosseum, there isn't a great view of it from the hotel; far from the other Roman sites and the rest of the city scene; not a lot of restaurants in the immediate neighborhood. ✉*Via Capo d'Africa 54, Colosseo,* ☎*06/772801* 🗐*06/77280801* ⊕*www.hotelcapodafrica.com* ⥱*65 rooms* &*In-room: safe, refrigerator, DVD (some), high-speed Internet. In-hotel: gym, room service, bar, concierge, airport shuttle (fee), parking (fee), no-smoking rooms* ⊟*AE, MC, V, DC* ⦿*CP.*

$$ 🖵**Hotel Lancelot.** Originally a guesthouse that started hosting visitors in the 1950s, Hotel Lancelot has been run by the same family since 1970, and is well-known for its wonderfully attentive staff and the personal care they give to those who stay here. Located in a quiet residential area near the Colosseum, rooms at Hotel Lancelot tend to have big windows, so they're bright and airy, and some have terraces or balconies as

well. Rooms have air-conditioning, bathrooms, TVs, and Wi-Fi. In the restaurant, where hearty breakfasts and dinners are served, guests sit at Lancelot's "round tables"—a play on the knight's tale and an effort to encourage communal dining among guests from around the world. They seem to be a big hit, as Hotel Lancelot boasts that most of their guests are return visitors or new guests recommended by others who've spent vacations here. **Pros:** Their motto is "hospitality" and they have the staff to prove it; secluded and quiet; very family-friendly. **Cons:** Some of the bathrooms are on the small side; no refrigerators in the rooms; the location may be a little too quiet for some travelers. ⊠ *Via Capo d'Africa 47, Colosseo,* ☏*06/70450615* 🖶*06/70450640* ⊕*www. lancelothotel.com* 🛏*60 rooms* ⚿*In-room: safe, Wi-Fi. In-hotel: restaurant, room service, bar, laundry service, concierge, public Internet, public Wi-Fi, airport shuttle (fee), parking (fee), no-smoking rooms* ▭*AE, MC, V, DC* ⦿*CP.*

NIGHTLIFE & THE ARTS

THE ARTS

Updated by
Erica Firpo

Cultural events are publicized well in advance through the city's Web site ⊕*www.comune.roma.it.* Weekly events listings can be found in the Cronaca and Cultura sections of Italian newspapers, as well in *Metro* (the free newspaper). The most comprehensive listings are in the weekly *roma c'è* booklet, which comes out every Wednesday. It has a brief yet very detailed English-language section at the back. On the Web, check out www.inromenow.com, an events site written exclusively for the English-speaking community and updated monthly, as well as the site for *Time Out Roma* (⊕*www.timeout.com/travel/rome*). Two monthly English-language periodicals (with accompanying Web sites), *Wanted in Rome* (⊕*www.wantedinrome.com*), and *The American* (⊕*www. theamericanmag.com*), available at many newsstands, have good coverage of arts events. Events and concert listings can also be found in both English and Italian at www.musicguide.it.

VENUES

★ Rome used to be a performing arts backwater until 2002, when it opened its state-of-the-art **Auditorium-Parco della Musica** (⊠ *Via de Coubertin 15, Flaminio* ☏*06/80241, 06/6880144 information and tickets* ⊕*www.musicaperroma.it*), a 10-minute tram ride from Piazza del Popolo. Three futuristic concert halls designed by famed architect Renzo Piano have excellent acoustics and a large courtyard used for concerts and other events—everything from chamber music to jazz to big-name pop, even film screenings, art exhibits, fashion shows, and "philosophy festivals." **Teatro Argentina** (⊠ *Largo Argentina 52, near Campo de' Fiori* ☏*06/68400345* ⊕*www.teatrodiroma.net*), built in 1732 by the architect Theoldi, has been the home of the Teatro Sabile theater company since 1994. The theater is a beautiful, ornate structure, with velvet seats and chandeliers, and plays host to many plays, classical music performances, operas, and dance performances. Both the city's bal-

CLOSE UP

Entertainment Alfresco

Roman nightlife moves outdoors in summertime, and that goes not only for pubs and discos but for higher culture as well. Open-air opera in particular is a venerable Italian tradition; competing companies commandeer church courtyards, ancient villas, and soccer stadiums for performances that range from student-run mom-and-poperas to full-scale extravaganzas. The same goes for dance and for concerts covering the spectrum of pop, classical, and jazz. Look for performances at the Baths of Caracalla, site of the famous televised "Three

Tenors" concert; regardless of the production quality, it's a breathtaking setting. In general, though, you can count on performances being quite good, even if small productions often resort to school-play scenery and folding chairs to cut costs. Tickets run about €15–€50. The more-sophisticated productions may be listed in newspapers and magazines such as *roma c'è*, but your best sources for information are old-fashioned posters plastered all over the city, advertising classics such as *Tosca* and *La Traviata*.

2

let and opera companies, as well as visiting international performers, appear at the **Teatro dell'Opera** (⊠*Piazza Beniamino Gigli 8, near Termini* ☎*06/481601, 06/48160255 tickets* ⊕*www.operaroma.it*). **Teatro Olimpico** (⊠*Piazza Gentile da Fabriano 17, Flaminio* ☎*06/3265991*) hosts both concerts and dance performances. **Teatro Valle** (⊠*Via del Teatro Valle 23A, near Piazza Navona* ☎*06/68803794*) hosts dramatic performances of the same caliber as its neighbor, Teatro Argentina, but often with a more-experimental bent, particularly in fall. Dance and classical music are also presented here. The ancient **Terme di Caracalla** (⊠*Via delle Terme di Caracalla 52, Aventino* ☎*No phone* ⊕*www. operaroma.it*) has one of the most spectacular and enchanting outdoor stages in the world, often hosting performances presented by Rome's opera company ranging from *Aida* (with elephants) to avant-garde.

TICKETS

Tickets for major events can be bought online at **Ticket One** (⊕*www. ticketone.it*). Tickets for larger musical performances as well as many cultural events can usually be found at **Hello Ticket** (⊕*www.helloticket. it*), which lists all cultural events and the many *punta di vendita*, ticket sellers, in Rome. Or go in person to **Orbis** (⊠*Piazza Esquilino 37, Repubblica* ☎*06/4744776*) or to **Mondadori** (⊠*Via del Corso 472, Spagna* ☎*06/684401*), a huge and central store that sells music, DVDs, books, and concert tickets.

CONCERTS

Christmastime is an especially busy classical concert season in Rome. Many small classical concert groups perform in cultural centers and churches year-round; all performances in Catholic churches are religious music and are free. Look for posters outside the churches. Pop, jazz, and world music concerts are frequent, especially in summer, although they may not be well advertised. Many of the bigger-name acts perform outside the center, so it's worth asking about transportation *before* you buy your tickets (about €10–€40).

CLASSICAL

A year-round classical concert series, often showcasing the famed Orchestra dell'Accademia di Santa Cecilia, is organized by the **Accademia di Santa Cecilia** (*Concert hall and box office* ✉ *Via Pietro de Coubertin 34, Flaminio* ☎*06/8082058* ⊕*www.santacecilia.it*). The **Accademia Filarmonica Romana** (✉ *Via Flaminia 118, near Flaminio* ☎*06/3201752, 06/3265991 tickets*) has concerts at the Teatro Olimpico. **Il Tempietto** (☎*06/87131590* ⊕*www.tempietto.it*) organizes classical music concerts indoors in winter and in the atmospheric settings of Teatro di Marcello and Villa Torlonia in summer. The internationally respected **Oratorio del Gonfalone series** (✉ *Via del Gonfalone 32/a, Campo de' Fiori* ☎*06/6875952* ⊕*www.oratoriogonfalone.it*) focuses on baroque music. The church of **Sant'Ignazio** (✉*Piazza Sant'Ignazio, near Corso* ☎*06/6794560*) often hosts classical concerts in its spectacularly frescoed setting. The Renaissance-era **Chiostro del Bramante** (✉*Vicolo della Pace 2,near Piazza Navona* ☎*06/68809098*) has a summer concert series. The **Orto Botanico** (✉*Largo Cristina di Svezia 23/a, Trastevere* ☎*06/6868441*), off Via della Lungara in Trastevere, has a summer concert series with a beautiful, verdant backdrop.

FILM

Movie tickets range in price from €4.50 for matinees and some weeknights up to €10 for reserved seats on weekend evenings. Check listings in *roma c'è* or www.inromenow.com for reviews of all English-language films currently playing or visit www.mymovies.it for a list of current features. The **Metropolitan** (✉ *Via del Corso 7, near Piazza di Popolo* ☎*06/32600500*) has four screens, one dedicated to English-language films September–June. The five-screen **Warner Village Moderno** (✉*Piazza della Repubblica 45–46, Repubblica* ☎*06/47779202*), close to the train station, usually has one theater with an English-language film.

OPERA

The season for the **Opera Theater of Rome** (☎*06/481601, 06/48160255 tickets* ⊕*www.operaroma.it*) runs from November or December to May. Main performances are staged at the Teatro dell'Opera, on Piazza Beniamino Gigli, in cooler weather and at outdoor locations, such as Piazza del Popolo and the spectacular Terme di Caracalla (Baths of Caracalla) in summer.

For a bit of comedy with a Monty Python slant, check out the **Miracle Players** (⊕*www.miracleplayers.org*), a group of English-speaking actors who write and produce free public performances every summer in the Roman Forum, presenting a perfectly balanced mix of the historical and the hilarious.

The Spanish Steps by night.

NIGHTLIFE

Rome's nightlife is decidedly more happening for locals and insiders who know whose palms to grease and when to go where. The "flavor of the month" factor is at work here, and many places fade into oblivion after their 15 minutes of fame. Smoking has been banned in all public areas in Italy (that's right, it actually happened); Roman aversion to clean air has meant a decrease in crowds at bars and clubs. The best sources for an up-to-date list of nightspots are the *roma c'è* and *Time Out Roma* magazines. Trastevere and the area around Piazza Navona are both filled with bars, restaurants, and, after dark, people. In summer, discos and many bars close to beat the heat (although some simply relocate to the beach, where many Romans spend their summer nights). The city-sponsored Estate Romana (Rome Summer) festival takes over, lighting up hot city nights with open-air concerts, bars, and discos. Pick up the event guide at newsstands.

CAFÉS, ENOTECHE & WINE BARS

First and foremost among the bar scene is the wine bar, found (often with outdoor seating) in almost every piazza and on side streets throughout the city. These *enoteche* are mostly small in size, offering a smattering of antipasti to accompany a variety of wines. In addition, the following selections, cafés included, are among the best in the city.

Ai Tre Scalini (✉ *Via Panisperna 251, Monti* ☏*06/48907495*) is a rustic local hangout with a wooden bar in the new boho section of Rome. It serves delicious antipasti and light entrées.

★ The wood-paneled walls of **L'Angolo Divino** (✉ *Via dei Balestrari 12, Campo* ☏*06/6864413*) are racked with more than 700 of bottles of wine. A quiet enoteca in a back alley behind Campo, L'Angolo Divino allows you to sidestep the crowds while enjoying homemade pastas with a vintage bottle.

Celebrities and literati hang out at the coveted outdoor tables of **Antico Caffé della Pace** (✉ *Via della Pace 5, near Piazza Navona* ☏*06/6861216*), set on the enchanting *piazzatina* (tiny piazza) of Santa Maria della Pace. The only drawbacks: overpriced table service and distracted waiters.

L'Enoteca Antica di Via della Croce (✉ *Via della Croce 76/b, near Piazza di Spagna* ☏*06/6790896*) is Piazza di Spagna's most celebrated wine bar, occupying a prime people-watching corner just below the piazza. In addition to a vast selection of wine (also available for take away), Enoteca Antica has delectable antipasti, perfect for a snack or a light lunch. **Fluid** (✉ *Via del Governo Vecchio 46/47,near Piazza Navona* ☏*06/6832361*), with its slick design and zen waterfall, is all about the scene, especially with its looking-glass front window where pretty young things primp on ice cube–shaped chairs. For the cocktail crowd, Fluid's many variations on the traditional martini are quite laudable. **Freni e Frizioni** (✉ *Via de Politeama 4–6, Trastevere* ☏*06/58334210*) is one of Rome's latest artsy hangouts—it spills out onto its Trastevere piazza and down the stairs, filling the area around Piazza Trilussa with an attractive crowd of local mojito-sippers. **Stardust** (✉ *Via Santa Maria dell'Anima 52, near Piazza Navona* ☏*06/6868986*) has cocktails and music that keep a loyal and eclectic clientele (a mix of locals, expats, and entertainment types) happy. There's occasional live music, from jazz to opera.

★ For a dip into La Dolce Vita, the **Jardin de Hotel de Russie** (✉ *Via del Babuino 9, near Piazza del Popolo* ☏*06/328881* ⊕*www.hotelderussie. it*) is the location for every Hollywood VIP, as well as up-and-coming starlets. Mixed drinks are well above par, as are the prices.

Fodor's Choice ★ **Rosé Terrazzo at the St. George Hotel** (✉ *Via Giulia 62, near Piazza Navona* ☏*06/686611* ⊕*www.stgeorgehotel.it*) is the latest front-run-ner in Rome's ever-growing list of rooftop sweet spots. With a delicious oyster selection headlining its seafood-only menu, the Rosé Terrazzo's dizzying drink selection includes cocktails, beer, and many rosés—from pink champagnes to Italian *rosati*.

Sitting in front of a 2nd-century temple, **Salotto 42** (✉*Piazza di Pietra 42, near Piazza Navona* ☏*06/6785804*) holds court from morning until late in the evening. The cozy-sleek room (high-backed velvet chairs, zebra-print rugs, chandeliers) is a smorgasbord of the own-ers' Roman–New York–Swedish pedigree. The den, complete with art books, local sophisticates, and models moonlighting as waitresses, is the fashionista's favorite choice for late-night drinks.

★ **Tazio** (✉ *Hotel Exedra, Piazza della Repubblica 47, Repubblica* ☎ *06/489381*), named after the original Italian *paparazzo* (celebrity photographer), is an Adam Tihany–designed champagne bar. The red, black, and white lacquered interior, with crystal chandeliers, has a distinct '80s feel (think Robert Palmer, *Addicted to Love*), while the outside seating area is simple and modern. The favorite pastime here is sipping champagne while watching the people parade through the colonnade. In summer, the hotel's rooftop bar **Sensus** is the place to be, with its infinity pool and terrace view overlooking downtown.

Terrace Bar of the Hotel Raphael (✉ *Largo Febo 2, near Piazza Navona* ☎ *06/682831*) is noted for its bird's-eye view of the campaniles and palazzi of the Piazza Navona. High up in the moonlit sky, the Terrace Bar tends to be the choice place for a romantic evening.

NIGHTCLUBS & DISCOS

Most dance clubs open about 10:30 PM and charge an entrance fee of about €20, which may include the first drink (subsequent drinks cost about €10). Clubs are usually closed Monday, and all those listed here close in summer, some opening instead at the beaches of Ostia or Fregene. The liveliest areas for clubs with a younger clientele are the grittier working-class districts of Testaccio and Ostiense. Any of the clubs lining Via Galvani, leading up to Monte Testaccio, are fair game for a trendy, crowded dance-floor experience—names and ownership of clubs change frequently, but the overall scene has shown some staying power.

Behind the Vatican Museums, **Alexanderplatz** (✉ *Via Ostia 9, near Vaticano* ☎ *06/39742171*), Rome's most famous jazz and blues club, has a bar and a restaurant. Local and internationally known musicians play nightly. In trendy Testaccio, **Caffè Latino** (✉ *Via Monte Testaccio 96, Aventino* ☎ *06/57288556*) is a vibrant Roman locale that has live music (mainly Latin) almost every night, followed by recorded soul, funk, and '70s and '80s revival; it's closed Monday. **Gilda** (✉ *Via Mario de' Fiori 97, near Piazza di Spagna* ☎ *06/6784838*) used to be the place to spot famous Italian actors and politicians. Now it is host to B-actors and leftover politniks. This nightspot near the Spanish Steps has a piano bar as well as a restaurant and dance floors with live and disco music. Jackets are required. **Hulala** (✉ *Via dei Conciatori 7, Aventino* ☎ *06/57300429*) is home to Rome's fashionistas. Mod films are projected on the walls, and champagne is drunk through straws.

★ Housed in a medieval palazzo is **La Cabala** (✉ *Via dei Soldati 23, near Piazza Navona* ☎ *06/68301192*), Rome's version of a supper club. This three-level space has a piano bar, restaurant, and club, and often has very dressy crowd vying to get past the velvet rope.

★ Lounge fever is all over Rome, with **La Maison** (✉ *Vicolo dei Granari 4, near Piazza Navona* ☎ *06/6833312*) as one of the best. Bedecked in purple velvet and crystal chandeliers, the club has two distinct spaces, a VIP area and a dance floor, with a DJ dishing up the latest dance tunes. Head straight to the back room and grab a couch. **Qube** (⊠ *Via di Portonaccio 212, San Lorenzo* ☎ *06/4385445*), open only Thursday through Saturday, is Rome's biggest underground disco, where bodies mix and mingle like a rugby game. Friday night hosts the **Muccassassina** (⊕ *www.muccassassina.it*), Rome's most popular gay event. It has paid a price for its fame, and is now more straight than gay.

SHOPPING

Updated by
Lynda
Albertson

They say when in Rome to do as the Romans do—and the Romans love to shop. Stores are generally open from 9 or 9:30 to 1 and from 3:30 or 4 to 7 or 7:30. There's a tendency for shops in central districts to stay open all day, and hours are becoming more flexible throughout the city. Many places close Sunday, though this is changing, too, especially in the city center. With the exception of food stores, many stores also close Monday morning from September to mid-June and Saturday afternoon from mid-June through August. Stores selling food are usually closed Thursday afternoon.

You can stretch your euros by taking advantage of the Tax-Free for Tourists V.A.T. tax refunds, available at most large stores for purchases over €155. Or hit Rome in January and early February or in late July, when stores clean house with the justly famous biannual sales. There are so many hole-in-the-wall boutiques selling top-quality merchandise in Rome's center that even just wandering you're sure to find something that catches your eye.

SHOPPING DISTRICTS

The city's most famous shopping district, **Piazza di Spagna,** is conveniently compact, fanning out at the foot of the Spanish Steps in a galaxy of boutiques selling gorgeous wares with glamorous labels. Here you can ricochet from Gucci to Prada to Valentino to Versace with less effort than it takes to pull out your credit card. If your budget is designed for lower altitudes, you also can find great clothes and accessories at less-extravagant prices. But here, buying is not necessarily the point—window displays can be works of art, and dreaming may be satisfaction enough. Via Condotti is the neighborhood's central axis, but there are shops on every street in the area bordered by Piazza di Spagna on the east, Via del Corso on the west, between Piazza San Silvestro and Via della Croce, and extending along Via del Babuino to Piazza del Popolo. Shops along **Via Campo Marzio,** and adjoining Piazza San Lorenzo in Lucina, stock eclectic, high-quality clothes and accessories—both big names (Bottega Veneta, Louis Vuitton) and unknowns—at slightly lower prices. Running from Piazza Venezia to Piazza del Popolo lies **Via del Corso,** a main shopping avenue that has more than a mile of clothing, shoes, leather goods, and home furnishings from classic to cutting-edge. Running west from Piazza Navona, **Via del Governo Vecchio** has numerous women's boutiques and secondhand-clothing stores. **Via Cola di Rienzo,** across the Tiber from Piazza del Popolo, is block after block of boutiques, shoe stores, department stores, and mid-level chain shops, as well as street stalls and upscale food shops. **Via dei Coronari,** across the Tiber from Castel Sant'Angelo, has quirky antiques and home furnishings. Via Giulia and other surrounding streets are good bets for decorative arts. Should your gift list include religious souvenirs, look for everything from rosaries to Vatican golf balls at the shops between Piazza San Pietro and **Borgo Pio.** Liturgical vestments and statues of saints make for good window-shopping on **Via dei Cestari,** near the Pantheon. **Via Nazionale** is a good bet for affordable stores of the Benetton ilk, and for shoes, bags, and gloves. The **Termini** train station has become a good one-stop place for many shopping needs. Its 60-plus shops are open until 10 PM and include a Nike store, the Body Shop, Sephora, Mango (women's clothes), a UPIM department store, and a grocery store.

MARKETS

Outdoor markets are open Monday–Saturday from early morning to about 1 PM (a bit later on Saturday), but get there early for the best selection. Remember to keep an eye on your wallet—the money changing hands draws Rome's most skillful pickpockets. And don't go if you can't stand crowds. Downtown Rome's most colorful outdoor food market is at **Campo de' Fiori,** south of Piazza Navona. The **Trionfale market** (✉ *Via Andrea Doria, near Vatican*) is big and bustling; it's about a five-minute walk north of the entrance to the Vatican Museums. There's room for bargaining at the Sunday-morning flea market at **Porta Portese** (✉ *Via Ippolito Nievo, Trastevere*). Seemingly endless rows of merchandise include new and secondhand clothing, bootleg CDs, old furniture, car stereos of suspicious origin, and all manner of old junk and hidden treasures.

SPECIALTY STORES

DESIGNER CLOTHING

All of Italy's top fashion houses and many international designers have stores near Piazza di Spagna. Buying clothes can be a bit tricky for American women, as sizes tend to be cut for a petite Italian frame. A size 12 (European 46) is not always easy to find, but the more-expensive stores should carry it. Target less-expensive stores for accessories if this is an issue.

D&G (✉ *Piazza di Spagna 82, Spagna* ☎06/69924999), a spin-off of the top-of-the-line Dolce & Gabbana, shows trendy casual wear and accessories for men and women. The flagship store for **Fendi** (✉ *Largo Carlo Goldoni 419–421, near Piazza di Spagna* ☎06/696661) is in the former Palazzo Boncompagni, renamed "Palazzo Fendi." It overlooks the intersection of famed Via Condotti and Via del Corso, and it's the quintessential Roman fashion house, presided over by the Fendi sisters. Their signature baguette bags, furs, accessories, and sexy separates are all found here. The **Giorgio Armani** (✉ *Via Condotti 77,* *near Piazza di Spagna* ☎*06/6991460)* shop is as understated and elegant as its designs. **Gucci** (✉ *Via Condotti 8, near Piazza di Spagna* ☎*06/6790405)* often has lines out the door of its two-story shop, testament to the continuing popularity of its colorful bags, wallets, and shoes in rich leathers. Edgy clothes designs are also available. Sleek, vaguely futuristic **Prada** (✉ *Via Condotti 92, near Piazza di Spagna* ☎*06/6790897)* has two entrances: the one for the men's boutique is to the left of the women's. Rome's leading local couturier, **Valentino** (*Valentino Donna* ✉ *Via Condotti 13, near Piazza di Spagna* ☎*06/6795862 Valentino Uomo* ✉ *Via Bocca di Leone 15, near Piazza di Spagna* ☎*06/6783656)*, is recognized the world over by the "V" logo. The designer has shops for the *donna* (woman) and the *uomo* (man) not far from his headquarters in Piazza Mignanelli beside the Spanish Steps. In 2008, the grand master announced his retirement and fashionistas await the anointment of a successor to continue the hyper-glamorous brand. **Versace** (*Versace Uomo* ✉ *Via Borgognona 24–25, near Piazza di Spagna* ☎*06/6795037 Versace Donna* ✉ *Via Bocca di Leone 26–27, near Piazza di Spagna* ☎*06/6780521)* sells the rock-star styles that made the house's name.

MEN'S CLOTHING

Ermenegildo Zegna (✉ *Via Borgognona 7/e, near Piazza di Spagna* ☎*06/6789143)* has the finest in men's elegant styles and accessories. **Brioni** (✉ *Via Condotti 21, near Piazza di Spagna* ☎*06/485855* ✉ *Via Barberini 79, near Piazza di Trevi* ☎*06/484517)* has a well-deserved reputation as one of Italy's top tailors. There are ready-to-wear garments in addition to impeccable custom-made apparel. **Davide Cenci** (✉ *Via Campo Marzio 1–7, near Piazza Navona* ☎*06/6990681)* is famed for conservative clothing of exquisite craftsmanship. **Il Portone** (✉ *Via delle Carrozze 71, near Piazza di Spagna* ☎*06/6793355)* embodies a tradition in custom shirt making.

WOMEN'S CLOTHING

Arsenale (✉ *Via del Governo Vecchio 64, near Piazza Navona* ☎*06/6861380)* has a sleek layout and a low-key elegance that stands out, even in Rome. Whether you are looking for a wedding dress or a seductive bustier, you are bound to find something unconventional here. Designer and owner Patriza Pieroni creates many of the pieces on display, all cleverly cut and decidedly captivating. **Galassia** (✉ *Via Frattina 21, near Piazza di Spagna* ☎*06/6797896)* has expensive, extreme, and extravagant women's styles by Gaultier, Westwood, and Yamamoto—this is the place for feather boas and hats with ostrich plumes.

Fodor'sChoice ★ **L'Anatra all'Arancia** (✉ *Via Tiburtina 105 , San Lorenzo* ☎*06/4456293)* has the locals in this bustling working class district agog at its window displays of flowing innovative designer clothes, teeny-weeny bikinis, and zany underwear. Owner Donatella Baroni believes in fashion being fun. The men's shop is across the road at No. 130, where style-conscious hipsters can find pure linen shirts and trousers in unusual colors. The clientele includes Italian TV and stage personalities who live in the trendy area.

★ **Maga Morgana** (✉ *Via del Governo Vecchio 27, near Piazza Navona* ☎*06/6879995* ✉*Via del Governo Vecchio 98, Navona* ☎*06/ 6878085*) is a family-run business where everyone's nimble fingers contribute to producing the highly original clothes and accessories. From hippie chick to bridal chic, designer Luciana Iannace creates lavishly ornate clothes that are as inventive as they are distinguishing. **Victory** (✉*Via S. Francesco a Ripa 19, Trastevere* ☎*06/5812437*) spotlights youthful, lighthearted styles created by lesser known stylists, such as Rose D, Nina, Alessandrini, and Marithé et François Girbaud. Victory's clothing is made for flaunting. A menswear version of the store is located at Piazza San Calisto 10 in Trastevere.

EMBROIDERY & LINENS

Frette (✉*Piazza di Spagna 11, Spagna* ☎*06/6790673*) is a Roman institution for luxurious linens. **Venier Colombo** (✉ *Via Frattina 79, near Piazza di Spagna* ☎*06/6787705*) is one of Rome's most historic shops. For the coquette that favors retro classicism, and has a penchant for all things Victorian, the shop offers a breathtaking selection of lace-trimmed lingerie and linens, as well as exquisite christening robes for babies and hand-embroidered lavender bags.

JEWELRY

Fodor'sChoice **Gioielli in Movimento** (✉*Via della Stelletta 22/b, near Piazza Navona* ★ ☎*06/6867431*) draws customers like Andie McDowell, hooked on Carlo Cardena's ingenious designs. Carlo's "Twice as Nice" earrings, which can be transformed from fan-shaped clips into elegant drops, were Uno Erre's best selling earrings between 1990 and 1998 and his "Up and Down" pendant, which can be worn two different ways, is set to become another hit. **Quattrocolo** (✉ *Via della Scrofa 54, near Piazza Navona* ☎*06/68801367*) has been specializing in antique micro-mosaic jewelry and baubles from centuries past since 1938.

SHOES & LEATHER ACCESSORIES

For gloves as pretty as Holly Golightly's, shop at **Sermoneta** (✉*Piazza di Spagna 61, Spagna* ☎*06/6791960*). Any color or style one might desire, from elbow-length black leather to scallop-edged lace-cut lilac suede, is available at this glove institution. **Furla** (✉*Piazza di Spagna 22, Spagna* ☎*06/69200363*) has 14 franchises in Rome alone. Its flagship store, to the left of the Spanish Steps, has been entirely refurbished in 2005 to make it even more inviting. Be prepared to fight your way through crowds of passionate handbag lovers, all anxious to possess one of the delectable bags, wallets, or watch straps in ice-cream colors. **Salvatore Ferragamo** (✉*Via Condotti 64, near Piazza di Spagna* ☎*06/6781130* ✉ *Via Condotti 73/74, Piazza di Spagna* ☎*06/6791565*) is one of the top-10 most-wanted men's footwear brands in the world and for years has been providing Hollywood glitterati and discerning clients with unique handmade designs. The Florentine design house also specializes in handbags, small leather goods, men's and women's ready-to-wear, and scarves and ties. Men's styles are found at Via Condotti 64, women's at 73/74. **Di Cori** (✉*Piazza di Spagna 53, Spagna* ☎*06/6784439*) has gloves in every color of the spectrum. **Bruno Magli** (✉ *Via Condotti 6, near Piazza di Spagna* ☎*06/69292121*) has classy shoes with simple, elegant lines for men and women that have character without compromising comfort.

Fodor's Choice **Tod's** (⊠ *Via Fontanella di Borghese 56a/c, near Piazza di Spagna*
★   🕾*06/68210066*) has become hyperfashionable again due in large part
to owner Diego Della Valle's ownership of Florence's soccer team. The
brand is known for its sporty flats and comfortable, casual styling.
Tod's occupies the ground floor in the celebrated 16th-century Palazzo Ruspoli. **Fausto Santini** (⊠ *Via Frattina 120, near Piazza di Spagna*
🕾*06/6784114*) gives a hint of extravagance in minimally decorated,
all-white show windows displaying surprising shoes that fashion
mavens love. Santini's footwear for men and women is bright, colorful,
and trendy, sporting unusual forms, especially in heels. Coordinated
bags and wallets add to the fun.

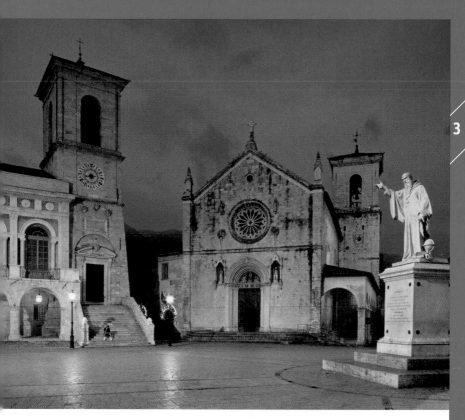

Between Rome & Florence

HIGHLIGHTS OF UMBRIA & TUSCANY

WORD OF MOUTH

"Siena is not for a daytime, 'hit the highlights' tour. It is deeper than that. I think it's Italy's most enchanting medieval city. Give it a go!"

—jtrandolph

WELCOME TO UMBRIA & TUSCANY

TOP REASONS TO GO

★ **Assisi, shrine to St. Francis:** Recharge your soul in this rose-color hill town with a visit to the gentle saint's majestic Basilica.

★ **Orvieto's Duomo:** Arresting visions of heaven and hell on the facade and brilliant frescoes within make this Gothic cathedral a dazzler.

★ **Piazza del Campo, Siena:** Sip a cappuccino, lick some gelato, and take in this spectacular piazza.

★ **Piero della Francesca's True Cross frescoes, Arezzo:** If your holy grail is great Renaissance art, seek out these 12 silently enigmatic scenes.

★ **Sunset, San Gimignano:** Grab a spot on the steps of the Collegiata church as flocks of swallows swoop in and out of the famous medieval towers.

★ **Wine tasting in Chianti:** Sample the fruits of the region's gorgeous vineyards, at either the wineries themselves or the towns' wine bars.

Assisi

Florence
Pisa
Tavarnelle   Greve
orno   San Gimignano   CHIANTI
E74
3
68
Cecina   Siena   326
Mare Tirreno   1   TUSCANY   Montalcino
223
2
Piombino
Elba   Grossieto
Pianosa
Orbetello   1
Gigilio

1 Southern Umbria. The town of **Orvieto** is famed for its cathedral, its dry white wines, and its spectacular hilltop location. Further east, **Spoleto** offers Filippo Lippi frescoes, a massive castle towering over the town, and one of the world's great summer music festivals.

2 Northern Umbria. Assisi—sanctified by St. Francis—doubles as a beautiful medieval village and a major pilgrimage site. Umbria's largest town, **Perugia**, is home to some of Perugino's great frescoes and a hilltop centro storico. It's also beloved by chocoholics: hazelnut Baci candies were born here.

3 **Central Tuscany.** The privileged hilltop site that helped **Siena** flourish in the Middle Ages keeps it one of Italy's most enchanting medieval towns today. To the west, **San Gimignano**, bristles with 15th-century stone towers. To the north, The hills of the **Chianti** district present a rolling pageant of ageless vineyards and villas.

4 **Eastern Tuscany.** The ancient stone town of **Cortona** sits high above the perfectly flat Valdichiana valley, offering great views of beautiful countryside. **Arezzo**, to the north, is best known for its sublime frescoes by Piero della Francesca.

GETTING ORIENTED

The path between Rome and Florence runs along the Apennine mountain range through the hilly regions of Tuscany and Umbria. A mix of forests, vineyards, olive groves, and poppy fields adds up the Italian countryside at its most beautiful. The hillside towns, many dating from the days of ancient Rome, wear their history on their sleeves: you'll encounter towering Gothic cathedrals, glowing Renaissance frescoes, and cobblestone streets worn smooth by a thousand years of strollers. When people close their eyes and dream of Italy, this is what they see.

Arezzo · Sansepolcro
UMBRIA
4 Cortona
E45
298
2
Perugia
Assisi
Lago Di Trasimeno
Foligno
78
448
3
Todi
Spoleto
1
Orvieto
A1
4
204
Rieti
Lago di Bolsena
Tarquinia
LAZIO
2
3
Lago di Bracciano
Terni
1
Tivoli
A24
ROME
A91
A1
Lido di Ostia
601

Duomo, Orvieto

UMBRIA & TUSCANY PLANNER

Making the Most of Your Time

The best strategy for visiting Umbria and Tuscany is to choose one town as a base for several nights and then take day trips through the surrounding region. The beauty of this plan is that it's virtually impossible to choose the wrong base: every town listed in this chapter has countless adherents who have fallen in love with it. Even places with heavy tourist traffic—Assisi, Siena, San Gimignano—seem to breathe a sigh and relax in the evening after the day-trippers have departed.

Wherever you settle, keep in mind that this isn't the place for a jam-packed itinerary. One of the great pleasures here is indulging in rustic hedonism, marked by long lunches and showstopping sunsets.

Typical Travel Times

Hours by Car/Train	
Rome–Florence	3:00/1:45
Rome–Orvieto	1:30/1:00
Rome–Assisi	2:15/2:00
Rome–Siena	2:45/3:30
Florence–Assisi	1:45/2:30
Florence–Siena	1:00/1:30
Florence–Arezzo	1:00/0:30

Getting Around

A crucial thing to know when you're traveling through the hilly terrain of Umbria and Tuscany is that the valleys primarily run north–south. That means you can move in a north–south direction, following a valley, with relative ease, but when you're going east–west, you're climbing over hills, which involves slow, winding roads.

Getting around by Car: The major highway through the regions is the north–south A1 superstrada, which runs a 277-km (172-mi) course between Rome and Florence. It passes through western Umbria, skirting the hill town of Orvieto, and eastern Tuscany, passing close to Arezzo.

For more than a fleeting glance at these two regions, you need to get off the superstrada. Fortunately, the quality of the secondary roads is good, and driving them is a pleasure in itself. In Umbria, a loop of highway (made up of road nos. 204, 3, and 75) takes you off A1 to Spoleto, Assisi, and Perugia. In Tuscany, the A14 is the major highway between Siena and Florence, whereas road no. 222, know as the Strada Chiantigiana, is the slower, more picturesque, alternative.

Getting around by Train: Like the main highway, the direct train line from Rome to Florence runs through Orvieto and Arezzo. Other towns in Umbria are accessible by regional trains, but in Tuscany, the towns of the Chianti region aren't; there's train service to Siena, but the station isn't near the center of the old city—you need to take a taxi between the two.

Getting Here

Most flights to Tuscany originating in the United States stop either in Rome, London, Paris, or Frankfurt, and then connect to Florence's small **Aeroporto A. Vespucci** (commonly called **Peretola**), or to Pisa's **Aeroporto Galileo Galilei**. The only exception at this writing is Delta's New York/JFK flight going directly into Pisa.

There are several other alternatives for getting into the region. If you want to start your trip in Umbria, it works to fly into Rome's Aeroporto Leonardo da Vinci (commonly called Fiumincino); from Rome it's an hour by train or an hour and a half by car to reach the lovely town of Orvieto.

You can also fly to Milan and pick up a connecting Alitalia flight to Pisa, Florence, or Perugia. Finally, from May through September (as of this writing), the carrier Eurofly has nonstop flights between New York and Bologna, which is an hour by train or an hour and a half by car from Florence.

Finding a Place to Stay

It's a common practice in Umbria and Tuscany to convert old villas, farms, and monasteries into first-class hotels. The natural beauty of the countryside more than compensates for being located outside of town—provided you have a car. Hotels in towns tend to be simpler than their country cousins, with a few notable exceptions.

Though it's tempting to think of this as an area where you can wander the hills and then stumble upon a charming little hotel at the end of the day, you're better off not testing your luck. Reservations are the way to go.

DINING & LODGING PRICE CATEGORIES (IN EUROS)

¢	$	$$	$$$	$$$$
Restaurants				
under €15	€15–€25	€25–€35	€35–€45	over €45
Hotels				
under €70	€70–€110	€110–€160	€160–€220	over €220

Restaurant prices are for a first course (*primo*), second course (*secondo*), and dessert (*dolce*). Hotel prices are for two people in a standard double room in high season, including tax and service.

How's the Weather?

Throughout Tuscany and Umbria, the best times to visit are spring and fall. Days are warm, nights are cool, and though there are still tourists, the crowds are smaller. In the countryside the scenery is gorgeous, with abundant greenery and flowers in spring, and burnished leaves in autumn.

July and August are the most popular times to visit. Note, though, that the heat is often oppressive and mosquitoes are prevalent. Try to start your days early and visit major sights first to beat the crowds and the midday sun.

November through March, you might wonder who invented the term "sunny Italy." The panoramas are still beautiful, even with overcast skies, frequent rain, and occasional snow. In smaller towns and in the countryside, many hotels and restaurants close for the season.

Gubbio

UMBRIA

Updated
by Jonathan
Willcocks

Umbria contains a series of character-rich hill towns, all within an hour or two drive of one another; you can choose one as your base, then explore the others, and the countryside and forest in between, on day trips. No single town here has the extravagant wealth of art and architecture of Florence, Rome, or Venice, but this can work in their favor: the towns feel knowable, not overwhelming. And there's plenty to admire: Orvieto's cathedral and Assisi's basilica are two of the most important sights in Italy, while Perugia and Spoleto are rich in art and architecture. While you're here, keep an eye out for remnants of ancient Rome, which crop up all over---expect to see Roman villas, aqueducts, theaters, walls, and temples.

ORVIETO

The natural defenses of an enormous plateau rising 1,000 feet above the flat valley proved very attractive to settlers in central Italy as far back as the Bronze Age, making Orvieto among the oldest cities in the region. The Etruscans developed the town considerably, carving a network of 1,200 wells and storage caves out of the soft tufa (volcanic stone) of the mountain on which the city was built. By 283 BC the Romans had attacked, sacked, and destroyed the city, by then known as Volsinii Veteres. Perhaps they were attracted by the golden Orvieto Classico made from grapes grown in the rich volcanic soil of the valley below—a wine the town is still famous for today.

Charlemagne (742–814) changed the name to Urbs Vetus, from which the modern name derives. The town rose steadily as an independent commune in the late Middle Ages. When the Guelphs won decisively over the Ghibellines in the 14th century, Orvieto passed under the control of the papacy and was subsequently used by the popes as a refuge from enemies or the summer heat of Rome.

In addition to wine and some of the best restaurants in the region, Orvieto has much to offer: the celebrated Duomo, with Italy's finest Gothic facade, is alone worth the trip. Inside are masterly frescoes by Luca Signorelli (circa 1450–1523)—stunningly restored—perhaps the most underrated in the entire country. A couple of good museums and some excavations round out the sights.

The festival highlight of the year is the Festa della Palombella on Pentecost Sunday (the seventh Sunday after Easter). In this unique take on a fireworks show, a tabernacle with images of the Madonna and the Apostles is set up on the steps in front of the central doorway of the Duomo. A white dove attached to a cable strung across the piazza slides down and ignites the fireworks.

A more traditional celebration is the Festa del Corpus Domini (the ninth Sunday after Easter), begun by Pope Urban IV in 1264, which may have its origin in the Miracle at Bolsena. Each year Bolsena's miraculous, bloodstained *corporale* (square linen cloth) is taken out of the chapel and led around town in a solemn procession, preceded by a rich court in sumptuous period costumes. Between Christmas and the first days of January, the Umbria Jazz Festival comes to Orvieto. Plan on big crowds, high-season rates in the hotels, and plenty of music flowing through the streets.

3

GETTING HERE

Orvieto is well connected by train to Rome, Florence, and Perugia. It's also adjacent to the A1 superstrada that runs between Florence and Rome. Parking areas in the upper town tend to be crowded. A better idea is to follow the signs for the Porta Orvetiana parking lot, then take the free funicular that carries people up the hill.

VISITOR INFORMATION

Orvieto tourism office (⊠*Piazza del Duomo 24* ☎*0763/341772* ⊕*www. orvieto.umbria2000.it*).

EXPLORING ORVIETO

If you are arriving by train, take the funicular that runs from the train station up the side of the hill and through the fortress to Piazzale Cahen. It runs every 20 minutes, daily 7:15 AM–8:30 PM, and costs €1. Although the workings have been modernized, there are a few pictures in each station of the old cog railcars, which were once run hydraulically. Keep your funicular ticket, as it will get you a discount on admission to the Museo Claudio Faina. Bus 1 makes the same trip from 8 AM to 11 PM. From Piazzale Cahen, Bus A runs to Piazza del Duomo in the town center.

A *Carta Orvieto Unica* (single ticket) is expensive but a great deal if you want to visit everything; for €18 you get admission to the four major sights in town—Cappella di San Brizio (at the Duomo), Museo Claudio Faina, Torre del Moro, and Orvieto Underground—plus a combination bus–funicular pass or five hours of free parking.

MAIN ATTRACTIONS

⑤ **Duomo.** Orvieto's Duomo is, quite simply, stunning. The church was

Fodor'sChoice built to commemorate the Miracle at Bolsena. In 1263, a young priest

★ who questioned the miracle of transubstantiation (in which the Communion bread and wine become the flesh and blood of Christ) was saying mass at nearby Lago di Bolsena. His doubts were put to rest, however, when a wafer he had just blessed suddenly started to drip blood, staining the linen covering the altar. The cloth and the host were taken to the pope, who proclaimed a miracle and a year later provided for a new religious holiday—the Feast of Corpus Domini. Thirty years later, construction began on a *duomo* to celebrate the miracle and house the stained altar cloth.

Orvieto

It is thought that Arnolfo di Cambio (circa 1245–1302), the famous builder of the Duomo in Florence, was given the initial commission for the Duomo, but the project was soon taken over by Lorenzo Maitani (circa 1275–1330), who consolidated the structure and designed the monumental facade. Maitani also made the bas-relief panels between the doorways, which graphically tell the story of the Creation (on the left) and the

> **WORD OF MOUTH**
>
> "Orvieto makes a nice day or overnight stop. Lots of great shoe shops. The nearby hilltop village of Civita makes a great side trip—you have to park your vehicle and walk across a suspension bridge to get there, but when you arrive, you'll find a quaint and cute village."   –DOCK

Last Judgment (on the right). The lower registers, now protected by Plexiglas, succeed in conveying the horrors of hell as few other works of art manage to do, an effect made all the more powerful by the worn gray marble. Above, gold mosaics are framed by finely detailed Gothic decoration.

Inside, the cathedral is rather vast and empty; the major works are in the transepts. To the left is the **Cappella del Corporale,** where the square linen cloth (corporale) is kept in a golden reliquary that's modeled on the cathedral and inlaid with enamel scenes of the miracle. The cloth is removed for public viewing on Easter and on Corpus Domini (the ninth Sunday after Easter). In the right transept is the **Cappella di San Brizio,** or Cappella Nuova. In this chapel is one of Italy's greatest fresco cycles, notable for its influence on Michelangelo's *Last Judgment,* as well as for the extraordinary beauty of the figuration. In these works, the damned fall to hell, demons breathe fire and blood, and Christians are martyred. Some scenes are heavily influenced by the imagery in Dante's (1265–1321) The *Divine Comedy.* ✉*Piazza del Duomo* ☎*0763/342477* ✇*Church free, Cappella Nuova €5* ⊙*Nov.–Feb., daily 7:30–12:45 and 2:30–5:15; Mar. and Oct., daily 7:30–12:45 and 2:30–6:15; Apr.–Sept., daily 7:30–12:45 and 2:30–7:15.*

NEED A BREAK?

Orvieto has plenty of spots to grab a quick bite—a boon in off-hours, when restaurants are closed and sightseers get peckish. Gastronomia Carraro (✉*Corso Cavour 101* ☎*0763/342870*) has an excellent selection of local sausages and cheeses. (Try the different kinds of pecorino.) It also has delicious pickled olives and tomatoes, perfect on a roll if the sightseeing has made you hungry. Alas, it's closed Sunday. For a snack or coffee on tables outside, check out Bar Sant'Andrea (✉*Piazza della Repubblica* ☎*0763/343285*). You can get simple, cheap food here, and in the summer sit on the small terrace. The service is quick and friendly, and if conversation is lacking you can always contemplate the rather odd-looking 12-sided bell tower of the church of Sant'Andrea across the piazza. Wonderful gelato in large scoops is to be had at ivy-shaded alfresco tables at L'Archetto (✉*Piazza del Duomo 14* ☎*0763/341034*). Try the delicately flavored pistachio and coconut ice cream while you admire the facade of the Duomo. It's closed mid-December through February.

④ Museo Archeologico Claudio Faina. This superb private collection, beau-
★ tifully arranged and presented, goes far beyond the usual museum offerings of a scattering of local remains. The collection is particularly rich in Greek- and Etruscan-era pottery, from large Attic amphorae (6th–4th century BC) to Attic black- and red-figure pieces to Etruscan *bucchero* (dark, reddish clay) vases. Other interesting pieces in the collection include a 6th-century sarcophagus and a substantial display of Roman-era coins. ⌧ *Piazza del Duomo 29* ☎ *0763/341511* ⊕ *www. museofaina.it* ⌧ *€4.50* ☉ *Oct.–Mar., Tues.–Sun. 11–3; Apr.–Sept., daily 9:30–6.*

⑥ Museo Emilio Greco. Another medieval building built by a pope on leave here from Rome, 13th-century Palazzo Soliano was for many years the location of the Museo dell'Opera del Duomo, a fine collection that includes works by Signorelli and other notable names like Simone Martini and Arnolfo di Cambio. But the art treasures have been locked away during an interminable restoration. Meanwhile, the ground floor has been made into the Museo Emilio Greco, a good-looking space filled with sculpture and sketches from the prolific Sicilian artist Emilio Greco (born 1913)—who also made the doors for the Duomo in the 1960s. ⌧ *Piazza del Duomo, Palazzo Soliano* ☎ *0763/344605* ⌧ *€2.50* ☉ *Weekdays 10:30–4:30.*

Orvieto Underground. More than just about any other town, Orvieto has grown from its own foundations—if one were to remove from present-day Orvieto all the building materials that were dug up from below, there would hardly be a building left standing. The Etruscans, the Romans, and those who followed dug into the tufa (the same soft volcanic rock from which catacombs were made), and over the centuries created more than 1,000 separate cisterns, caves, secret passages, storage areas, and production areas for wine and olive oil. Some of the tufa removed was used as building blocks for the city that exists today, and some was partly ground into *pozzolana*, which was made into mortar. The most thorough **Orvieto Underground tour** (⌧ *Orvieto tourism office, Piazza del Duomo 24* ☎ *0763/341772*) is run daily at 11, 12:15, 4, and 5:15. Admission for the hour-long English tour is €5.50. If you are short on time but still want a look at what it was like down there, head for the **Pozzo della Cava** (⌧ *Via della Cava 28* ☎ *0763/342373*), an Etruscan well for spring water. It's open Tuesday through Friday from 8 to 8, and costs €3.

ALSO WORTH SEEING

② Palazzo del Popolo. Built in tufa and basaltic rock, this was once the town hall. Restoration work in the late 1980s revealed the remains of an Etruscan temple underneath, and it now holds the state archives. ⌧ *Piazza del Popolo.*

① Pozzo di San Patrizio *(St. Patrick's Well).* When Pope Clement VII (1478–1534) took shelter in Orvieto during the Sack of Rome in 1527, he had to ensure a safe water supply should Orvieto come under siege. Many

UMBRIA THROUGH THE AGES

The earliest inhabitants of Umbria, the Umbri, were thought by the Romans to be the most ancient inhabitants of Italy. Little is known about them; with the coming of Etruscan culture the tribe fled into the mountains in the eastern portion of the region. The Etruscans, who founded some of the great cities of Umbria, were in turn supplanted by the Romans. Unlike Tuscany and other regions of central Italy, Umbria had few powerful medieval families to exert control over the cities in the Middle Ages—its proximity to Rome ensured that it would always be more or less under papal domination.

In the center of the country, Umbria has for much of its history been a battlefield where armies from north and south clashed. Hannibal destroyed a Roman army on the shores of Lake Trasimeno, and the bloody course of the interminable

Guelph-Ghibelline conflict of the Middle Ages was played out here. Dante considered Umbria the most violent place in Italy. Trophies of war still decorate the Palazzo dei Priori in Perugia, and the little town of Gubbio continues a warlike rivalry begun in the Middle Ages—every year it challenges the Tuscan town of Sansepolcro to a crossbow tournament. Today the bowmen shoot at targets, but neither side has forgotten that 500 years ago its ancestors shot at each other. In spite of—or perhaps because of—this bloodshed, Umbria has produced more than its share of Christian saints. The most famous is St. Francis, the decidedly pacifist saint whose life shaped the Church of his time. His great shrine at Assisi is visited by hundreds of thousands of pilgrims each year. St. Clare, his devoted follower, was Umbria-born, as were St. Benedict, St. Rita of Cascia, and the patron saint of lovers, St. Valentine.

wells and cisterns were built, and the pope commissioned one of the great architects of the day, Antonio da Sangallo the Younger (1493–1546), to build the well adjacent to the Rocca. After nearly a decade of digging, water was found at a depth of 203 feet. Two one-way spiral stairways allowed donkey-driven carts to descend and return without running into one another. Windows open onto the shaft, providing natural light in the stairwells. There are 248 steps down to the bottom, but you'll probably get the idea after just a few. The well was once compared to St. Patrick's Well in Ireland. The name stuck, and "pozzo di San Patrizio" has come to represent an inexhaustible source of wealth. ⊠ *Viale Sangallo, off Piazzale Cahen* ☎ *0763/343768* ⊠ *€4.50* ⊙ *Oct.–Mar., daily 10–5:45; Apr.–Sept., daily 9:30–7:45.*

3 **Torre del Moro.** It's hard to imagine a simpler, duller affair than this tower in the center of town. It took on a little more character in the 19th century, when the large, white-face clock was added along with the fine 14th-century bell, marked with the symbols of the 24 arts and craft guilds then operating in the city. The views, however, are worth the climb. ⊠ *Corso Cavour at Via del Duomo* ☎ *0763/344567* ⊠ *€2.80* ⊙ *May–Aug., daily 10–8; Mar., Apr., Sept., and Oct., daily 10–7; Nov.–Feb., daily 10–1 and 2:30–5.*

OFF THE BEATEN PATH
Crocefisso del Tufo. This 6th-century BC Etruscan necropolis, about 2 km (1 mi) down Viale Crispi, doesn't have the frescoes that other Etruscan tombs are famous for, and the relics that were buried within have long since been taken away (mostly to the Museo Claudio Faino). But the walk here is pleasant, and it can be interesting to see the type of site from which nearly all our knowledge of Etruscans comes. Names of the deceased are carved into the stone architraves above tomb chambers. ✛ *2 km (1 mi) from Piazzale Cahen, down Viale F. Crispi (SS71)* ☎*0763/343611* ☜*€3* ⊙*Daily 8:30–7.*

WHERE TO EAT

The streets around the Duomo are lined with all types of bars and restaurants where you can eat simple or elaborate food and try the wines by the glass.

$$–$$$
Fodor'sChoice
★
✕**Il Giglio D'Oro.** A great view of the Duomo is coupled with superb food. Eggplant is transformed into an elegant custard with black truffles in the *sformatino di melenzane con vellutata al tartuffo nero.* Pastas, like *ombrichelli al pesto umbro,* are traditional, but perhaps with a new twist like fresh coriander leaves instead of the usual basil. Lamb roasted in a crust of bread is delicately seasoned with a tomato cream sauce. The wine cellar includes some rare vintages. ✉*Piazza Duomo 8* ☎*0763/341903* ☱*AE, MC, V* ⊙*Closed Wed.*

$$–$$$
✕**Le Grotte del Funaro.** If you can't do the official hour tour of Underground Orvieto, dine here instead, inside tufa caves under central Orvieto, where the two windows have splendid views of the hilly countryside during the day. The traditional Umbrian food is average, but with good, simple grilled meats and vegetables and pizzas. Oddly, the food is outclassed by an extensive wine list with top local and Italian labels and quite a few rare vintages. ✉*Via Ripa Serancia 41* ☎*0763/343276* ☜*Reservations essential* ☱*AE, DC, MC, V* ⊙*Closed Mon. and 1 wk in July.*

$–$$$
★
✕**Trattoria La Grotta.** The owner has been in this location for more than 20 years, and locals are still fond of him. He has attracted a steady American clientele without losing his touch with homemade pasta, perhaps with a duck or wild-boar sauce. Roast lamb, veal, or pork are all good, and the desserts are homemade. Franco knows the local wines well and has a carefully selected list, including some from smaller but excellent wineries, so ask about them. ✉*Via Luca Signorelli 5* ☎*0763/341348* ☱*AE, DC, MC, V* ⊙*Closed Tues.*

WHERE TO STAY

Orvieto has a wide choice of lodging options, so if you haven't reserved a hotel in advance, take the time to wander around and choose your favorite.

$$$
★
🏠**Hotel La Badia.** One of the region's best-known country hotels occupies a 12th-century monastery. Vaulted ceilings and exposed stone walls establish the rustic elegance in the guest rooms, which have beamed

ceilings and polished terra-cotta floors covered with rugs. The rolling park around the hotel provides wonderful views of the valley. It's 4 km (2½ mi) south of Orvieto. **Pros:** Elegant atmosphere; fine views. **Cons:** Slightly overpriced; need a car to get around. ✉*Località La Badia, Orvieto Scalo* ☎*0763/301959* ⊕*www.labadiahotel.it* ↻*18 rooms, 9 suites* ⚒*In-room: refrigerator. In-hotel: restaurant, bar, tennis courts, pool, parking (no fee)* ▭*AE, MC, V* ⊗*Closed Jan. and Feb.* ℡*BP.*

$$ **▥ Hotel Palazzo Piccolomini.** This hotel is often preferred by local wine-makers and other professionals for its updated look with inviting lobby areas and a convenient location near the church of San Giovanni. From here, it's a lovely short walk past Piazza della Repubblica to the Duomo. **Pros:** Peaceful atmosphere; efficient staff; good location. **Cons:** Unattractive building; slightly overpriced. ✉*Piazza Ranieri 36* ☎*0763/341743* ⊕*www.hotelpiccolomini.it* ↻*28 rooms, 3 suites* ⚒*In-room: refrigerator, Ethernet. In-hotel: bar, laundry service, parking (fee), no-smoking rooms* ▭*AE, MC* ℡*BP.*

$ **▥ Gran Hotel Reale.** The best feature of this hotel is its location in the center of Orvieto, across a square that hosts a lively market. Facing the impressive Gothic–Romanesque Palazzo del Popolo, rooms are spacious and adequately furnished, with a traditional accent. **Pros:** Good budget option; friendly staff. **Cons:** Can be noisy; very basic rooms. ✉*Piazza del Popolo 27* ☎*0763/341247* ↻*31 rooms* ⚒*In-hotel: bar* ▭*MC, V* ⊗*Closed Jan. and Feb.* ℡*BP.*

WINE BARS

Orvieto has been known for white wine since its beginnings. There is evidence that the Etruscans grew grapes in the rich volcanic soil in the valley below and then fermented their wine in the cool caverns dug out of the tufa atop the hill. The Romans made special efforts to bring the local wine, which they blended with water and spices, back to Rome with them. Things had not changed by the early 16th century, when Signorelli was paid in part with wine for his work on the Cappella di San Brizio.

Although Orvieto Classico is the best-known wine in the region, it is no longer one of Italy's best. However, it is pleasantly drinkable and light. You will also have the chance to taste different types of Orvieto, from the well-known dry Orvieto Classico to the less-commercialized *abboccato* (semisweet) and the intensely flavored, sweeter *muffato*.

Begin your tastings at these *enoteche* (wine bars), *cantine* (wineshops), and *vinerie* (wineries).

At **Cantina Foresi** (✉*Piazza del Duomo 2* ☎*0763/341611*), a light lunch of cheese, salami, bread, and salad is hard to beat. Hundreds of bottles are stored in the cool earth of the cellar, which was built in 1290 and is worthy of a visit. The few outdoor tables are a great place for a light snack while sipping.

At **La Bottega del Buon Vino** (✉*Via della Cava 26* ☎*0763/342373*), a window in the floor looks down into the caves. It's closed Monday.

EATING & DRINKING WELL IN UMBRIA

Central Italy is mountainous, and its food is hearty and straightforward, with a stick-to-the-ribs quality that sees hardworking farmers and artisans through a long day's work and helps them make the steep climb home at night.

In restaurants here, as in much of Italy, you're rewarded for seeking out the local cuisines, and you'll often find better, and cheaper, food if you're willing to stray a few hundred yards from the main sights. Spoleto is noted for its good food and service, probably a result of high expectations from the international arts crowd. For gourmets, however, it's hard to beat Spello, which has both excellent restaurants and first-rate wineshops.

A rule of thumb for eating well throughout Umbria is to order what's in season; the trick is to stroll through local markets to see what's for sale. A number of restaurants in the region offer *degustazione* (tasting) menus, which give you a chance to try different local specialties without breaking the bank.

TASTY TRUFFLES

More truffles are found in Umbria than anywhere else in Italy. Spoleto and Norcia are prime territory for the *tartufo nero* (reddish-black interior and fine white veins), pictured below right, prized for its extravagant flavor and intense aroma. The mild summer truffle, *scorzone estivo* (black outside and beige inside), is in season from May through December. The *scorzone autunnale* (burnt brown color and visible veins inside) is found from October through December. Truffles can be shaved into omelets or over pasta, pounded into sauces, or chopped and mixed with oil.

OLIVE OIL

Nearly everywhere you look in Umbria, olive trees grace the hillsides. The soil of the Apennines allows the olives to ripen slowly, guaranteeing low acidity, a cardinal virtue of fine oil. Look for restaurants that proudly display their own oil, often a sign that they care about their food.

Umbria's finest oil is found in Trevi, where the local product is intensely green and fruity. You can sample it in the town's wine bars, which often do double duty, offering olive-oil tastings.

PORK PRODUCTS

Much of traditional Umbrian cuisine revolves around pork. It can be cooked in wood-fire stoves, sometimes basted with a rich sauce made from innards and red wine. The roasted pork known as *porchetta*, pictured at left, is grilled on a spit and flavored with fennel and herbs, leaving a crisp outer sheen. The art of pork processing has been handed down through generations in Norcia, so much so that charcuterie producers throughout Italy are often known as *norcini*. Don't miss *prosciutto di Norcia*, which is aged for two years.

LENTILS & SOUPS

The town of Castelluccio di Norcia is particularly known for its lentils and its *farro* (an ancient grain used by the

Romans, similar to wheat), and a variety of beans used in soups. Throughout Umbria, look for *imbrecciata*, a soup of beans and grain, delicately flavored with local herbs. Other ingredients that find their way into thick Umbrian soups are wild beet, sorrel, mushrooms, spelt, chickpeas, and the elusive, fragrant saffron, grown in nearby Cascia.

WINE

Sagrantino grapes are the star in Umbria's most notable red wines. For centuries they've been used in Sagrantino *passito,* a semisweet wine made by leaving the grapes to dry for a period after picking in order to intensify their sugar content. In recent decades, the *secco* (dry) Sagrantino has occupied the front stage. Both *passito* and *secco* have a deep red-ruby color, with a full body and rich flavor.

In the past few years the phenomenon of the *enoteca* (wineshop and wine bar) has taken off, making it easier to arrange wine tastings. Many also let you sample different olive oils on toasted bread, known as *bruschetta.* Some wine information centers, like La Strada del Sagrantino in Montefalco, will help set up appointments for wine tastings.

Many area wine producers create excellent variations of the standard Orvieto Classico wine. Close to town and highly recommended is **Azienda Agricola Palazzone** (⊠ *Località Rocca Ripesana* ✛ *5 km [3 mi] from Orvieto* ☎*0763/344166*), where you can sample Muffa Nobile—a warm, golden, sweet wine with a rich taste caused by the fungus that is cultivated—Grechetto, and Orvieto Classico Superior that has been aged longer than most and has a richer taste than the mass-produced Orvietos. This vintner has also won awards for his Armaleo, a rich ruby red.

Castello della Sala (✛ *20 km [12 mi] north of Orvieto, Località Sala* ☎*0763/86051*), owned by the Antinori group, produces white wines of high quality. Housed in a 14th-century castle, this is an especially interesting place to try out some of Orvieto's new-style wines—Cervaro della Sala, Grechetto, and chardonnay—all aged in oak barrels.

SHOPPING

Orvieto has a few shops selling Orvietan-style pottery, bright-white vessels with hand-painted motifs. **La Torreta** (⊠*Corso Cavour 283* ☎*0763/340248*) has a kiln right in the shop and will custom paint something for you on the spot. For copies of ancient Etruscan and Greek ceramics, try **L'Arte del Vasaio** (⊠ *Via Pedota 3* ☎*0763/342022*).

Established in 1907 to provide work for impoverished women, the tradition of lace-making, or *ars wetana*, has flourished in Orvieto. Using designs inspired by the reliefs on the facade of the Duomo, the patterns of Orvietan lace are unique and distinctive.

Specializing in *merletto* (lace) products, **Duranti** (⊠*Corso Cavour 107* ☎*No phone*) maintains the high standards set by one of the sustainers of the tradition during the last century, Eleonora Duranti. The Moretti family has long been associated with lace-making in Orvieto. Their products can be admired at **Ditta Moretti Merletti** (⊠*Via Duomo 55* ☎*0763/41714*).

Orvieto is a center for woodworking, particularly fine inlays and veneers. Corso Cavour is lined with a number of artisan woodworking shops, the best known being the **Michelangeli Family Studio** (⊠ *Via Michelangeli 3, at Corso Cavour* ☎*0763/342377*). The imaginatively designed objects range in size from a giant *armadio* (wardrobe) to a simple wooden spoon. If all those Michelangeli flourishes don't quite suit you, head over to **Patrice** (⊠ *Via Michelangeli 4* ☎*No phone*), who has a shop full of imaginative items that he has made, from crafts for children to trompe-l'oeil intarsia windows in wood.

SPOLETO

GETTING HERE
Spoleto is an hour's drive from Perugia. From the E45 highway, take the exit toward Assisi and Foligno, then merge onto the SS75 until you reach the Foligno Est exit. Merge onto the SS3, which leads to Spoleto.

There are regular trains on the Perugia-Foligno line. From the train station it's a 15-minute uphill walk to the center, so you'll probably want to take a taxi.

VISITOR INFORMATION
Spoleto tourism office (✉*Piazza della Libertà 7* ☎*0743/238921* ⊕*www. spoleto.umbria2000.it*).

EXPLORING SPOLETO

The walled city is set on a slanting hillside, with the most interesting sections clustered toward the upper portion. Parking options inside the walls include Piazza Campello (just below the Rocca) on the southeast end, Via del Trivio to the north, and Piazza San Domenico on the west end. You can also park at Piazza della Vittoria farther north, just outside the walls. There are also several well-marked lots near the train station. If you arrive by train, you can walk 1 km (½ mi) from the station to the entrance to the lower town. Regular bus connections are every 15 to 30 minutes. You can also use the "trenino," as locals call the shuttle service added in 2004, from the train station to Piazza della Libertà, near the upper part of the old town, where you'll find the tourist office.

Like most other towns with narrow, winding streets, Spoleto is best explored on foot. Bear in mind that much of the city is on a steep slope, so there are lots of stairs and steep inclines. The well-worn stones can be slippery even when dry; wear rubber-sole shoes for good traction. Several pedestrian walkways cut across Corso Mazzini, which zigzags up the hill. A €2.60 combination ticket purchased at the tourist office allows you entry to the Pinacoteca Comunale, Casa Romana, and Galleria d'Arte Moderna. It's an excellent deal, since a combination ticket purchased directly from any one of these sights is €6.

MAIN ATTRACTIONS

3 **Duomo.** The cathedral's 12th-century Romanesque facade received a
★ Renaissance face-lift with the addition of a loggia in a rosy pink stone. A stunning contrast in styles, the Duomo is one of the finest cathedrals in the region. The eight rose windows are especially dazzling in the late afternoon sun. Look under the largest rose window and you see two figures that appear to be holding up the structure; in the corners of the square surrounding the window, the four Evangelists are sculpted. Inside, the original tile floor dates from an earlier church that was destroyed by Frederick I (circa 1123–90).

Above the church's entrance is Bernini's bust of Pope Urban VIII (1568–1644), who had the rest of the church redecorated in 17th-century baroque; fortunately he didn't touch the 15th-century frescoes painted in the apse by Fra Filippo Lippi (circa 1406–69) between 1466 and 1469. These immaculately restored masterpieces—the *Annunciation, Nativity,* and *Death of Mary*—tell the story of the life of the Virgin. The *Coronation of the Virgin,* adorning the half dome, is the literal and figurative high point. Portraits of Lippi and his assistants are on the right side of the central panel. The Florentine artist priest WHOSE COLORS EXPRESSED GOD'S VOICE (the words inscribed on his tomb) died shortly after completing the work. His tomb, which you can see in the right transept (note the artist's brushes and tools), was designed by his son, Filippino Lippi (circa 1457–1504).

Another fresco cycle, including work by Pinturicchio, is in the Cappella Eroli, off the right aisle. Note the grotesques in the ornamentation, then very much in vogue with the rediscovery of ancient Roman paintings. The bounty of Umbria is displayed in vivid colors in the abundance of leaves, fruits, and vegetables that adorn the center seams of the cross vault. In the left nave, not far from the entrance, is the well-restored 12th-century crucifix by Alberto Sozio, the earliest known example of this kind of work, with a painting on parchment attached to a wood cross. To the right of the presbytery is the Cappella della Santissima Icona (Chapel of the Most Holy Icon), which contains a small Byzantine painting of a Madonna given to the town by Frederick Barbarossa as a peace offering in 1185, following his destruction of the cathedral and town three decades earlier. ⊠*Piazza Duomo* ☎*0743/44307* ☾*Mar.–Oct., daily 8:30–12:30 and 3:30–6; Nov.–Feb., daily 8:30–12:20 and 3:30–6.*

A fresco by Fra Filippo Lippi in Spoleto's Duomo.

⑤ Ponte delle Torri *(Bridge of the Towers).* Standing massive and grace-
★ ful through the deep gorge that separates Spoleto from Monteluco,
this 14th-century bridge is one of Umbria's most photographed monuments, and justifiably so. Built over the foundations of a Roman-era
aqueduct, it soars 262 feet above the forested gorge—higher than the
dome of St. Peter's in Rome. Sweeping views over the valley and a
pleasant sense of vertigo make a walk across the bridge a must, particularly on a starry night. ⊠ *Via del Ponte.*

ALSO WORTH SEEING

② Casa Romana. Spoleto became a Roman colony in the 3rd century BC,
but the best excavated remains date from the 1st century AD. Excavated
in the late 9th century, the Casa Romana was not a typical Roman residence. According to an inscription, it belonged to Vespasia Polla, the
mother of Emperor Vespasian (one of the builders of the Coliseum and
perhaps better known by the Romans for taxing them to install public
toilets, later called "Vespasians"). The rooms, arranged around a large
central atrium built over an *impluvium* (rain cistern), are decorated
with black-and-white geometric mosaics. ⊠ *Palazzo del Municipio, Via
Visiale 9* ☎ *0743/224656* ⊠ *€2.50, €6 combination ticket, includes
Pinacoteca Comunale and Galleria d'Arte Moderna* ☉ *Oct. 15–Mar.
15, daily 10–6; Mar. 16–Oct. 14, daily 10–8.*

④ La Rocca. Built in the mid-14th century for Cardinal Egidio Albornoz,
this massive fortress served as a seat for the local pontifical governors, a
tangible sign of the restoration of the Church's power in the area when

the pope was ruling from Avignon. Several popes spent time here, and one of them, Alexander VI, in 1499 sent his capable teenage daughter Lucrezia Borgia (1480–1519) to serve as governor for three months. The Gubbio-born architect Gattapone (14th century) used the ruins of a Roman acropolis as a foundation and took materials from many Roman-era sites, including the Teatro Romano.

> **WORD OF MOUTH**
>
> "In Spoleto, be sure to take the walk up through the old city and on around the big castle at the top of the hill, so you can see, and walk along, the enormous ancient Roman aqueduct."
>
> –simpsonc510

La Rocca's plan is long and rectangular, with six towers and two grand courtyards, an upper loggia, and inside some grand reception rooms. In the largest tower, Torre Maesta, you can visit an apartment with some interesting frescoes. A small shuttle bus gives you that last boost up the hill from the ticket booth to the entrance of the fortress. If you phone in advance, you may be able to secure an English-speaking guide. ⊠ *Via del Ponte* ☎*0743/223055* ⌨*€6.50* ☉*Mid-Mar.–early June and mid-Sept.–Oct., weekdays 10–noon and 3–6:45, weekends 10–7; early June–mid-Sept., daily 10–7; Nov.–mid-Mar., weekdays 10–noon and 3–5, weekends 10–5.*

❶ **Teatro Romano.** The Romans who had colonized the city in 241 BC, constructed this small theater in the first century AD; for centuries afterward it was used as a quarry for building materials. The most intact portion is the hallway that passes under the *cavea* (stands). The rest was heavily restored in the early 1950s and serves as a venue for Spoleto's Festival dei Due Mondi. The theater was the site of a gruesome episode in Spoleto's history: during the medieval struggle between Guelph (papal) and Ghibelline (imperial) forces, Spoleto took the side of the Holy Roman Emperor. Afterward, 400 Guelph supporters were massacred in the theater, their bodies burned in an enormous pyre. In the end, the Guelphs were triumphant, and Spoleto was incorporated into the states of the Church in 1354. Through a door in the west portico of the adjoining building is the **Museo Archeologico,** with assorted artifacts found in excavations primarily around Spoleto and Norcia. The collection contains Bronze Age and Iron Age artifacts from Umbrian and pre-Roman eras. Another section contains black-glaze vases from the Hellenistic period excavated from the necropolis of Saint Scolastica in Norcia. The highlight is the stone tablet inscribed on both sides with the Lex Spoletina (Spoleto Law). Dating from 315 BC, this legal document prohibited the desecration of the woods on the slopes of nearby Monteluco. ⊠ *Via Sant'Agata 18* ☎*0743/223277* ⌨*€4* ☉*Daily 8:30–7:30.*

WHERE TO EAT

$$–$$$ ✕**Apollinare.** Low wooden ceilings and flickering candlelight make this monastery from the 10th and 11th centuries Spoleto's most romantic spot. The kitchen serves sophisticated, innovative variations on local dishes. Sauces of cherry tomatoes, mint, and a touch of red pepper, or of porcini mushrooms, top the long, slender strangozzi. The *caramella*

CLOSE UP

Hiking the Umbrian Hills

Magnificent scenery makes the heart of Italy excellent walking, hiking, and mountaineering country. In Umbria, the area around Spoleto is particularly good; several pleasant, easy, and well-signed trails begin at the far end of the Ponte alle Torri bridge over Monteluco. From Cannara an easy half-hour walk leads to the fields of Pian d'Arca, the site of St. Francis's sermon to the birds. For slightly more-arduous walks, you can follow the saint's path, uphill from Assisi to the Eremo delle Carceri, and then continue along the trails that crisscross Monte Subasio. At 4,250 feet, the Subasio's treeless summit affords views of Assisi, Perugia, far-off Gubbio, and the distant mountain ranges of Abruzzo.

For even more challenging hiking, the northern reaches of the Valnerina are exceptional; the mountains around Norcia should not be missed. Throughout Umbria and the Marches, you'll find that most recognized walking and hiking trails are marked with the distinctive red-and-white blazes of the Club Alpino Italiano (CAI). Tourist offices are a good source for walking and climbing itineraries to suit all ages and levels of ability, while bookstores, *tabacchi* (tobacconists), and *edicole* (newsstands) often have maps and hiking guides that detail the best routes in their area. Depending on the length and location of your walk, it can be important that you have comfortable walking shoes or boots, appropriate attire, and plenty of water to drink.

(light puff pastry cylinders filled with local cheese and served with a creamy Parmesan sauce) is popular. In warm weather you can dine under a canopy on the piazza across from the archaeological museum. ✉ *Via Sant'Agata 14* ☎ *0743/223256* 🟰 *AE, D, MC, V* 🕙 *Closed Tues.*

\$\$–\$\$\$ ✕ **Il Pentagramma.** This stable-turned-restaurant has terra-cotta floors, stone walls, and a wood-burning oven. Its fresh local dishes change seasonally. The farro soup has a new twist here: it is pureed and served inside a bread "bowl." Pastas might include *tortelli ai carciofi e noci* (artichoke-filled pasta with a hazelnut sauce) or, in summer, homemade fettucini served with sauce made from fresh vegetables and saffron. For your main course, you might try lamb in a truffle sauce. The stuffed zucchini flowers are lighter than usual, because they are baked (not fried) and filled with ricotta. The restaurant is off the Piazza della Libertà. ✉ *Via Martani 4* ☎ *0743/223141* 🟰 *DC, MC, V* 🕙 *Closed Mon. No dinner Sun., and for about 2 wks after Christmas.*

\$\$–\$\$\$ ✕ **Il Tartufo.** As the name indicates, dishes prepared with truffles are the specialty here—don't miss the risotto al tartufo. But there are also dishes not perfumed with this expensive delicacy. Incorporating the ruins of a Roman villa, the restaurant's decor is rustic on the ground floor and more modern upstairs. In summer, tables appear outdoors and the traditional fare is spiced up to appeal to the cosmopolitan crowd attending (or performing in) the Festival dei Due Mondi. ✉ *Piazza Garibaldi 24* ☎ *0743/40236* ✍ *Reservations essential* 🟰 *AE, DC, MC, V* 🕙 *Closed Mon. and last 2 wks in July. No dinner Sun.*

$$–$$$ ✕**Ristorante Panciolle.** In the heart of Spoleto's medieval quarter, this
★   restaurant has one of the most appealing settings you could wish for:
a small garden filled with lemon trees. Dishes change throughout the
year, and may include pastas served with asparagus or mushrooms,
as well as grilled meats. More expensive dishes prepared with fresh
truffles are also available in season. ⊠ *Via Duomo 3/5* ☎ *0743/221241*
▵ *Reservations essential* ▭ *DC, MC, V* ⊘ *Closed Wed.*

$–$$ ✕**Osteria del Trivio.** At this friendly trattoria, everything is made on
the premises. The menu changes daily, depending on what's in season.
Dishes might include stuffed artichokes, pasta with local mushrooms,
or chicken with artichokes. For dessert, try the homemade biscotti,
made for dunking in sweet wine. There is a printed menu, but the
owner can explain the dishes in a number of languages. A complete
meal from appetizer to dessert with house wine is likely to cost no
more than €25. ⊠ *Via del Trivio 16* ☎ *0743/44349* ▭ *AE, DC, MC,
V* ⊘ *Closed Tues.*

WHERE TO STAY

$$–$$$ 🏨**Cavaliere Palace Hotel.** An arched passageway off one of the city's
★   busy shopping streets leads to an elegant world through a quiet courtyard. Built in the 17th century for an influential cardinal, the rooms,
particularly those on the second floor, retain their sumptuous frescoed
ceilings; care has been taken to retain a sense of old-world comfort
throughout. In warm weather enjoy breakfast on the terrace or in the
peaceful garden at the back of the hotel. **Pros:** Quiet elegance; central
position. **Cons:** Finding parking can be a problem; crowded in summer. ⊠ *Corso Garibaldi 49* ☎ *0743/220350* ⊕ *www.cavalierehotels.
com* ⇱ *29 rooms, 2 suites* ⚐ *In-room: safe, refrigerator. In-hotel: restaurant, bar* ▭ *AE, DC, MC, V* ⦿*BP.*

$$ 🏨**Hotel dei Duchi.** This well-run hotel is a favorite among performers
in the festival. It's in the center of town, near the Roman amphitheater.
The spacious rooms, some looking out onto the gardens, have simple
modern furniture. **Pros:** Central location; friendly staff. **Cons:** Unat-
tractive building; parking can be difficult in summer months. ⊠ *Viale
Matteotti 4* ☎ *0743/44541* ⊕ *www.hoteldeiduchi.com* ⇱ *47 rooms, 2
suites* ⚐ *In-hotel: restaurant, bar, parking (no fee), some pets allowed*
▭ *AE, DC, MC, V* ⦿*BP.*

$$ 🏨**Hotel San Luca.** The elegant San Luca is one of Spoleto's finest hotels,
Fodor'sChoice   thanks to its commendable attention to detail, such as the hand-painted
★   friezes that decorate the walls of the spacious guest rooms and the
generous selection of up-to-date magazines for your reading pleasure.
The service is very gracious, and the prices are surprisingly modest.
Enjoy an ample breakfast buffet, including homemade cakes, served
in a cheerful room facing the central courtyard. You can sip afternoon
tea in oversize armchairs by the fireplace, or take a walk in the hotel's
sweet-smelling rose garden. The staff will give you route maps or help
you book a guided bicycle tour. **Pros:** Very helpful staff; peaceful location. **Cons:** Outside the town center; a long walk to the main sites.
⊠ *Via Interna delle Mura 19* ☎ *0743/223399* ⊕ *www.hotelsanluca.*

com ⬇33 *rooms, 2 suites* ⬠*In-room: safe, refrigerator, Ethernet. In-hotel: restaurant, laundry service, public Internet, parking (fee)* ⊟*AE, DC, MC, V* †◎*BP.*

$–$$ 🏨**Hotel Clitunno.** A renovated 18th-century building in the center of town houses this pleasant hotel. Cozy guest rooms and intimate public rooms, some with timbered ceilings, have the sense of a traditional Umbrian home—albeit one

3

with a good restaurant. The staff is glad to light the fireplace in Room 212 in advance of winter arrivals. Upper-floor rooms look over Spoleto's rooftops. The "older style" rooms, which have wood ceilings, iron beds, and nicer textiles, are more attractive. **Pros:** Friendly staff; good restaurant. **Cons:** Difficult to find a parking space; some small rooms. ⊠*Piazza Sordini 6* 🕾*0743/223340* ⊕*www.hotelclitunno.com* ⬇*45 rooms* ⬠*In-hotel: restaurant, bar* ⊟*AE, DC, MC, V* †◎*BP.*

THE ARTS

Fodor's Choice In 1958, composer Gian Carlo Menotti chose Spoleto for the first
★ **Festival dei Due Mondi** (*Festival of Two Worlds* ⊠*Piazza Duomo 8* 🕾*0743/220320 or 800/565600* ⊕*www.spoletofestival.it*), a gathering of artists, performers, and musicians intended to bring together the "new" and "old" worlds of America and Europe. (A corresponding festival in South Carolina is no longer connected to this festival.) The annual event, held in late June to early July, is one of the most important cultural happenings in Europe, attracting big names in all branches of the arts, particularly music, opera, and theater.

ASSISI

The small town of Assisi is one of the Christian world's most important pilgrimage sites and home of the Basilica di San Francesco—built to honor Saint Francis (1182–1226) and erected in swift order after his death. The peace and serenity of the town is a welcome respite after the hustle and bustle of some of Italy's major cities.

Like most other towns in the region, Assisi began as an Umbri settlement in the 7th century BC and was conquered by the Romans 400 years later. The town was Christianized by Saint Rufino, its patron saint, in the third century, but it is the spirit of Saint Francis, a patron saint of Italy and founder of the Franciscan monastic order, that is felt throughout its narrow medieval streets. The famous 13th-century basilica was decorated by the greatest artists of the period.

GETTING HERE
Assisi lies on the Terontola–Foligno rail line, with almost hourly connections to Perugia and direct trains to Rome and Florence several

Assisi

KEY

||||| Steps

TO EREMO DELLE CARCERI →

Anfiteatro Romano

Porto Nuova

TO SAN DAMIANO →

Rocca Maggiore

San Pietro

S.444

S.147

TO TRAIN STATION

TO SANTA MARIA DEGLI ANGELI

V. Santuario d. Carceri

Pza. Matteotti

Via Dono

Via S. Gabriele

Via Galeazzo Alessi

Via Borgo Aretino

Viale Umberto I

Viale Umberto

Viale Vittorio Emanuele II

Viale Vittorio Emanuele II

Viale Vittorio

Corso Mazzini

Pza. San Rufino

Duomo Don

Perlici

Via della Rocca

Via della Porta

Via S. Maria delle Rose

Via del Colle

Via Santa Croce

Via Metastasio

Via S. Francesco

Via del Seminario

Pza. del Comune

Pza. G. di Sant'Anna

Via Rocchi

Via S. Antonio

Via S. Paolo

Via Giotto

Via Portica

Via Brizi

Via B. da Comunanza

Via A. Cristofani

Via Fontebella

Via del Fosso

Pza. San Pietro

Via Borgo S. Pietro

T. degli Ancajani

Cupa

Via Unità d'Italia

Pza. Unità d'Italia

Via Metri del Val

Via San Giacomo

Pza. San Francesco

Viale G. Marconi

0 — 200 yards
0 — 200 meters

Basilica di
San Francesco **1**

Basilica di
Santa Chiara **4**

Cattedrale di
San Rufino **3**

Santa Maria
Sopra Minerva **2**

times a day. The Stazione Centrale is 4 km (2½ mi) from town, with a bus service about every half hour. Assisi is easily reached from the A1 Motorway (Rome–Florence) and the S75b highway. The walled town is closed to traffic, so cars must be left in the parking lots at Porta San Pietro, near Porta Nuova, or beneath Piazza Matteotti. (Pay your parking fee at the *cassa* [ticket booth] before you return to your car to get a ticket to insert in the machine that will allow you to exit.) It's a short but sometimes steep walk into the center of town; frequent minibuses (buy tickets from a newsstand or tobacco shop near where you park your car) make the rounds for weary pilgrims.

VISITOR INFORMATION
Assisi tourism office (⊠ *Piazza del Commune 22* ☎ *075/812534* ⊕ *www. assisi.umbria2000.it*).

EXPLORING ASSISI

Assisi is pristinely medieval in architecture and appearance, owing in large part to relative neglect from the 16th century until 1926, when the celebration of the 700th anniversary of Saint Francis's death brought more than 2 million visitors. Since then, pilgrims have flocked here in droves, and today several million arrive each year to pay homage. But not even the constant flood of visitors to this town of just 3,000 residents can spoil the singular beauty of this significant religious center, the home of some of the Western tradition's most important works of art. The hill on which Assisi sits rises dramatically from the flat plain, and the town is dominated by a medieval castle at the very top.

Even though Assisi can become besieged with sightseers disgorged by tour buses, who clamor to visit the famous basilica, it's difficult not to be charmed by the tranquility of the town and its medieval architecture. Once you've seen the basilica, stroll through the town's narrow winding streets to see beautiful vistas of the nearby hills and valleys peeking through openings between the buildings.

MAIN ATTRACTIONS
4 **Basilica di Santa Chiara.** The lovely, wide piazza in front of this church is reason enough to visit. The red-and-white-striped facade of the church frames the piazza's panoramic view over the Umbrian plains. Santa Chiara is dedicated to Saint Clare, one of the earliest and most fervent of Saint Francis's followers and the founder of the order of the Poor Ladies—or Poor Clares—which was based on the Franciscan monastic order. The church contains Clare's body, and in the **Cappella del Crocifisso** (on the right) is the cross that spoke to Saint Francis. A heavily veiled nun of the Poor Clares order is usually stationed before the cross in adoration of the image. ⊠ *Piazza Santa Chiara* ☎ *075/812282* ⊙ *Nov.–mid-Mar., daily 6:30–noon and 2–6; mid-Mar.–Oct., daily 6:30–noon and 2–7.*

3 **Cattedrale di San Rufino.** Saint Francis and Saint Clare were among those baptized in Assisi's Cattedrale, which was the principal church in town until the 12th century. The baptismal font has since been redecorated, but it is possible to see the crypt of Saint Rufino, the bishop who brought Christianity to Assisi and was martyred on August 11, 238 (or 236 by some accounts). Admission to the crypt includes the small **Museo Capitolare,** with its detached frescoes and artifacts. ⊠*Piazza San Rufino* ☎*075/812283* ⊕*www.sistemamuseo.it* ☜*Crypt and Museo Capitolare €2.50* ☉*Cattedrale: daily 7–noon and 2–6; crypt and Museo Capitolare: mid-Mar.–mid-Oct., daily 10–1 and 3–6; mid-Oct.–mid-Mar., daily 10–1 and 2:30–5:30.*

ALSO WORTH SEEING

❷ Santa Maria Sopra Minerva. Dating from the time of the Emperor Augustus (27 BC–AD 14), this structure was originally dedicated to the Roman goddess of wisdom, in later times used as a monastery and prison before being converted into a church in the 16th century. The expectations raised by the perfect classical facade are not met by the interior, which was subjected to a thorough baroque transformation in the 17th century. ⊠*Piazza del Comune* ☎*075/812268* ☉*Weekdays 7:15 AM–7:30 PM, weekends 8–7:30.*

OFF THE BEATEN PATH

Eremo delle Carceri. About 4 km (2½ mi) east of Assisi is a monastery set in a dense wood against Monte Subasio. The "Hermitage of Prisons" was the place where Saint Francis and his followers went to "imprison" themselves in prayer. The only site in Assisi that remains essentially unchanged since Saint Francis's times, the church and monastery are the kinds of tranquil places that Saint Francis would have appreciated. The walk out from town is very pleasant, and many trails lead from here across the wooded hillside of Monte Subasio (now a protected forest), with beautiful vistas across the Umbrian countryside. True to their Franciscan heritage, the friars here are entirely dependent on alms from visitors. ⊠*Via Santuario delle Carcer* ⊹ *4 km (2½ mi) east of Assisi* ☎*075/812301* ⊕*www.eremocarceri.it* ☜*Donations accepted* ☉*Nov.–Mar., daily 6:30–6; Apr.–Oct., daily 6:30 AM–7:15 PM.*

WHERE TO EAT

Assisi is not a late-night town, so don't plan on any midnight snacks. What you can count on is the ubiquitous stringozzi pasta, as well as the local specialty *piccione all'assisana* (roasted pigeon with olives and liver). The locals eat *torta al testo* (a dense flat bread, often stuffed with vegetables or cheese) with their meals.

$$$–$$$$ ✕**San Francesco.** An excellent view of the Basilica di San Francesco is the primary reason to come here. Locals consider this the best restaurant in town, where creative Umbrian dishes are made with aromatic locally grown herbs. The seasonal menu might include gnocchi topped with a sauce of wild herbs and *oca stufata di finocchio selvaggio* (goose stuffed with wild fennel). Appetizers and desserts are especially good. ⊠*Via di San Francesco 52* ☎*075/812329* ⊟*AE, DC, MC, V* ☉*Closed Wed. and July 15–30.*

$$–$$$ ✕**Osteria Piazzetta dell'Erba.** Hip service and sophisticated presentations
★ attract locals to this trattoria. The owners carefully select wine at local

Continued on page 163

ASSISI'S BASILICA DI SAN FRANCESCO

The legacy of St. Francis, founder of the Franciscan monastic order, pervades Assisi. Each year the town hosts several million pilgrims, but the steady flow of visitors does nothing to diminish the singular beauty of one of Italy's most important religious centers. The pilgrims' ultimate destination is the massive Basilica di San Francesco, which sits halfway up Assisi's hill, supported by graceful arches.

The basilica is not one church but two. The Romanesque **Lower Church** came first; construction began in 1228, just two years after St. Francis's death, and was completed within a few years. The low ceilings and candlelit interior make an appropriately solemn setting for St. Francis's tomb, found in the crypt below the main altar. The Gothic **Upper Church**, built only half a century later, sits on top of the lower one, and is strikingly different, with soaring arches and tall stained-glass windows (the first in Italy). Inside, both churches are covered floor to ceiling with some of Europe's finest frescoes: the Lower Church is dim and full of candlelit shadows, and the Upper Church is bright and airy.

VISITING THE BASILICA

THE LOWER CHURCH

The most evocative way to experience the basilica is to begin with the dark Lower Church. As you enter, give your eyes a moment to adjust. Keep in mind that the artists at work here were conscious of the shadowy environment—they knew this was how their frescoes would be seen.

In the first chapel to the left, a superb fresco cycle by Simone Martini depicts scenes from the life of St. Martin. As you approach the main altar, the vaulting above you is decorated with the *Three Virtues of St. Francis* (poverty, chastity, and obedience) and *St. Francis's Triumph*, frescoes attributed to Giotto's followers. In the transept to your left, Pietro Lorenzetti's *Madonna and Child with St. Francis and St. John* sparkles when the sun hits it. Notice Mary's thumb; legend has it Jesus is asking which saint to bless, and Mary is pointing to Francis. Across the way in the right transept, Cimabue's *Madonna Enthroned Among Angels and St. Francis* is a famous portrait of the saint. Surrounding the portrait are painted scenes from the childhood of Christ, done by the assistants of Giotto. Nearby is a painting of the crucifixion attributed to Giotto himself.

You reach the crypt via stairs midway along the nave—on the crypt's altar, a stone coffin holds the saint's body. Steps up from the transepts lead to the cloister, where there's a gift shop, and the treasury, which contains holy objects.

THE UPPER CHURCH

The St. Francis fresco cycle is the highlight of the Upper Church. (See facing page.) Also worth special note is the 16th-century choir, with its remarkably delicate inlaid wood. When a 1997 earthquake rocked the basilica, the St. Francis cycle sustained little damage, but portions of the ceiling above the entrance and altar collapsed, reducing their frescoes (attributed to Cimabue and Giotto) to rubble. The painstaking restoration is ongoing. ⚠The dress code is strictly enforced—no bare shoulders or bare knees. Piazza di San Francesco, 075/819001, Lower Church Easter–Oct., Mon.–Sat. 6⊦ –6:45 ⊙ , Sun. 6:30⊦ –7:15 ⊙ ; Nov.–Easter, daily 6:30– 6. Upper Church Easter–Oct., Mon.–Sat. 8:30–6:45[1] Sun. 8:30–7:15; Nov.–Easter, daily 8:30–6.

FRANCIS, ITALY'S PATRON SAINT

PREGANDO ASPETTERÒ CHE TORNI

St. Francis was born in Assisi in 1181, the son of a noblewoman and a well-to-do merchant. His troubled youth included a year in prison. He planned a military career, but after a long illness Francis heard the voice of God, renounced his father's wealth, and began a life of austerity. His mystical embrace of poverty, asceticism, and the beauty of man and nature struck a responsive chord in the medieval mind; he quickly attracted a vast number of followers. Francis was the first saint to receive the stigmata (wounds in his hands, feet, and side corresponding to those of Christ on the cross). He died on October 4, 1226, in the Porziuncola, the secluded chapel in the woods where he had first preached the virtue of poverty to his disciples. St. Francis was declared patron saint of Italy in 1939, and today the Franciscans make up the largest of the Catholic orders.

THE UPPER CHURCH'S ST. FRANCIS FRESCO CYCLE

The 28 frescoes in the Upper Church depicting the life of St. Francis are the most admired works in the entire basilica. They're also the subject of one of art history's biggest controversies. For centuries they thought to be by Giotto (1267-1337), the great early Renaissance innovator, but inconsistencies in style, both within this series and in comparison to later Giotto works, have thrown their origin into question. Some scholars now say Giotto was the brains behind the cycle, but that assistants helped with the execution; others claim he couldn't have been involved at all.

Two things are certain. First, the style is revolutionary—which argues for Giotto's in-volvement. The tangible weight of the figures, the emotion they show, and the use of perspective all look familiar to modern eyes, but in the art of the time there was nothing like it. Second, these images have played a major part in shaping how the world sees St. Francis. In that respect, who painted them hardly matters.

Starting in the transept, the frescoes circle the church, showing events in the saint's life (and afterlife). Some of the best are grouped near the church's entrance—look for the nativity at Greccio, the miracle of the spring, the death of the knight at Celano, and, most famously, the sermon to the birds.

3

IN FOCUS

The St. Francis fresco cycle
1. Homage of a simple man
2. Giving cloak to a poor man
3. Dream of the palace
4. Hearing the voice of God
5. Rejection of worldly goods
6. Dream of Innocent III
7. Confirmation of the rules
8. Vision of flaming chariot
9. Vision of celestial thrones
10. Chasing devils from Arezzo
11. Before the sultan
12. Ecstasy of St. Francis
13. Nativity at Greccio
14. Miracle of the spring
15. Sermon to the birds
16. Death of knight at Celano
17. Preaching to Honorius III
18. Apparition at Arles
19. Receiving the stigmata
20. Death of St. Francis
21. Apparition before Bishop Guido and Fra Agostino
22. Verification of the stigmata
23. Mourning of St. Clare
24. Canonization
25. Apparition before Gregory IX
26. Healing of a devotee
27. Confession of a woman
28. Repentant heretic freed

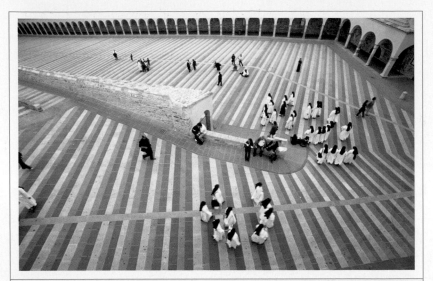

FODOR'S FIRST PERSON

Sister Marcellina,
Order of St. Bridget

Sister Marcellina of the Order of St. Bridget talks about her life in Assisi, where she and 11 other sisters live in a convent and guesthouse on the outskirts of the town:

"Before coming to Assisi, I lived in various countries. I've lived in India, and in England, and been to Holland, to Sweden, and to Finland, as well as lived in Rome. But Assisi is the place that I would never want to change for any other. I don't know, I think there is something very special about this place. I've been here 13 years now, and each year I pray that I won't be sent somewhere else. I'm very happy here.

"I like the atmosphere of Assisi, it's very friendly, and of course with St. Francis and St. Claire, but especially St. Francis, there is a simplicity to life that I like very much. Even though I'm in the Order of St. Bridget, living here I feel very much a part of Franciscan spirituality. There is also a very strong ecumenical feeling to Assisi and this is very nice. There are over 60 different religious communities, with people from all over the world. And even though they come from different religious backgrounds they still feel a part of Assisi. Living here, you don't see the people of Assisi, you see people who have come from all over the world.

"There is something you feel when you come to Assisi, something you feel in your heart that makes you want to come back. And people do return! They feel the peacefulness and tranquility. Not that there aren't other aspects, like the commercialism—but these things happen. People return for the simplicity of this place. People feel attracted to Assisi. There's always something that people feel when they come here—even the hard-hearted ones!"

Asked if she thinks Assisi is changing, Sister Marcellina answers, with laughter in her voice, "When they wanted to make all the changes in the year 2000, the Jubilee Year, our Lord said, 'I must stop everything.' They had lots of projects to build new accommodations to house the people coming for the Jubilee Year, but the Lord said, 'No!'"

vineyards, buy it in bulk, and then bottle it themselves, resulting in high quality and reasonable prices. Choose from the wide selection of appetizers, including smoked goose breast, and from four or five types of pasta, plus various salads and a good selection of torta al testo fillings. For dessert, try the homemade biscuits, which you dunk in sweet wine. Outdoor seating is available. ⊠ *Via San Gabriele dell'Addolorata 15b* ☎*075/815352* ⊟*AE, V* ⊘*Closed Mon. and a few wks in Jan. or Feb.*

$–$$$ ✕ **Buca di San Francesco.** In summer, dine in a cool green garden; in winter, under the low brick arches of the restaurant's cozy cellars. The unique settings and the first-rate fare make this central restaurant Assisi's busiest. Try homemade spaghetti *alla buca,* served with a roasted mushroom sauce. ⊠ *Via Brizi 1* ☎*075/812204* ⊟*AE, DC, MC, V* ⊘*Closed Mon. and July 20–30.*

$–$$$ ✕ **La Fortezza.** Partially enclosed by Roman walls, this family-run restaurant has excellent service and reliably good food. A particular standout is *anatra al finocchio selvatico* (duck with wild fennel). ⊠ *Vicolo della Fortezza 2b* ☎*075/812993* ⊿*Reservations essential* ⊟*AE, DC, MC, V* ⊘*Closed Thurs. and Feb.*

$–$$$
Fodor'sChoice
★ ✕ **La Pallotta.** At this homey, family-run trattoria with a crackling fireplace and stone walls, the women do the cooking and the men serve the food. Try the stringozzi *alla pallotta* (with a pesto of olives and mushrooms). Connected to the restaurant is an inn whose eight rooms have firm beds and some views across the rooftops of town. Hotel guests get a discount if they dine here. ⊠ *Vicolo della Volta Pinta* ☎*075/812649 or 075/812307* ⊟*AE, DC, MC, V* ⊘*Closed Tues. and 2 wks in Jan. or Feb.*

WHERE TO STAY

Advance reservations are essential at Assisi's hotels between Easter and October and over Christmas. Latecomers are often forced to stay in the modern town of Santa Maria degli Angeli, 8 km (5 mi) away. As a last-minute option, you can also inquire at restaurants to see if they are renting out rooms.

Until the early 1980s, pilgrim hostels outnumbered ordinary hotels in Assisi, and they present an intriguing and economical alternative to conventional lodgings. They are usually called *conventi* or *ostelli* ("convents" or "hostels") because they're run by convents, churches, or Catholic organizations. Rooms are spartan but peaceful. Check with the tourist office for a list.

$$$ ⊡ **Hotel Subasio.** The converted monastery close to the Basilica di San Francesco is well past its prime, when guests included celebrities like Marlene Dietrich and Charlie Chaplin. If you can get past the kitschy hangings on the walls, you'll notice such vestiges of glamour as Venetian chandeliers. The hotel does have splendid views, comfortable sitting rooms, and flower-decked terraces, and it's a stone's throw from all those Giotto frescoes. Some rooms are grand in size and overlook the valley, whereas others are small and rough around the edges. The

restaurant has a nice view, but the food could be better. **Pros:** Perfect location; views of the Assisi plain. **Cons:** Lobby a bit drab; some small rooms; service can be spotty. ✉ *Via Frate Elia 2* ☎*075/812206* 🖶*075/816691* ⬚*54 rooms, 8 suites* ⬚*In-room: no a/c. In-hotel: restaurant, bar, parking (fee)* ▭*AE, DC, MC, V* ⍾*BP.*

$–$$$ 🏨 **San Francesco.** You can't beat the location—the roof terrace and some of the rooms look out onto the Basilica di San Francesco, which is opposite the hotel. Rooms and facilities range from simple to dreary, but you may be reminded that looks aren't everything by the nice touches like slippers, a good-night piece of chocolate, and soundproofing. Fruit, homemade tarts, and fresh ricotta make for a first-rate breakfast. **Pros:** Excellent location; great views. **Cons:** Simple rooms; sometimes noisy in peak season. ✉ *Via San Francesco 48* ☎*075/812281* 🖶*075/816237* ⊕*www.hotelsanfrancescoassisi.it* ⬚*44 rooms* ⬚*In-room: refrigerator, Ethernet. In-hotel: restaurant, bar, public Internet, some pets allowed* ▭*AE, DC, MC, V* ⍾*BP.*

$$
Fodor'sChoice
★
🏨 **Castello di Petrata.** Built as a fortress in the 14th century, the Castello di Petrata rightfully dominates the area, with Monte Subasio, Assisi, and the distant hills and valleys of Perugia all in view. Every room is different from the last: wood beams and sections of exposed medieval stonework add character, and comfortable couches turn each room into a delightful retreat. **Pros:** Great views of Assisi hills, gardens, and walks. **Cons:** Slightly isolated; far from Assisi town center. ✉ *Via Petrata 25, Località Petrata06081* ☎*075/815451* 🖶*075/8043026* ⊕*www.castellopetrata.com* ⬚*22 rooms, 1 suite* ⬚*In-room: no a/c, ethernet. In-hotel: restaurant, bar, pool, some pets allowed* ▭*AE, DC, MC, V* ☉*Closed Jan.–Mar.* ⍾*BP.*

$ 🏨 **Hotel Umbra.** A 16th-century town house is the setting for this charming hotel near Piazza del Comune. Ask for an upper room with a view over the Assisi rooftops to the valley below. The restaurant, closed for lunch on Tuesday and Wednesday, has a charming vine-covered terrace leading to a secluded garden. **Pros:** Friendly welcome; pleasant small garden. **Cons:** Difficult parking; some small rooms. ✉ *Via degli Archi 6* ☎*075/812240* 🖶*075/813653* ⊕*www.hotelumbra.it* ⬚*6 suites, 19 rooms* ⬚*In-hotel: restaurant, bar* ▭*AE, DC, MC, V* ☉*Closed mid-Jan.–mid-Mar.* ⍾*BP.*

PERUGIA

Perugia is a majestic, handsome, wealthy city, and with its trendy boutiques, refined cafés, and grandiose architecture, it doesn't try to hide its affluence. A student population of more than 30,000 means that the city is abuzz with activity throughout the year. Umbria Jazz, one of the region's most important music festivals, attracts music lovers from around the world, and Eurochocolate, the international chocolate festival, is an irresistible draw for anyone with a sweet tooth.

GETTING HERE

The best approach to the city is by train. The area around the station doesn't attest to the rest of Perugia's elegance, but buses running from

3

Perugia

the station to Piazza d'Italia, the heart of the old town, are frequent. If you are driving to Perugia and your hotel doesn't have parking facilities, leave your car in one of the lots close to the center. Electronic signs indicate the location of lots and the number of spaces free. If you park in the Piazza Partigiani, take the escalators that pass through the fascinating subterranean excavations of the Roman foundations of the city and lead to the town center.

VISITOR INFORMATION
Umbria's regional tourism office (✉ *Piazza Matteotti 18* ☎ *075/5736458* 📠 *075/5720988* ⊕ *www.perugia.umbria2000.it*)is in Perugia. The staff is well informed about the area, and can give you a wide selection of leaflets and maps to assist you during your trip. It's open Monday to Saturday 8:30 to 1:30 and 3 to 6:30, and Sunday 8:30 to 1.

EXPLORING PERUGIA

Thanks to Perugia's hilltop position, the medieval city remains almost completely intact. It is the best-preserved hill town of its size, and few other places in Italy better illustrate the model of the self-contained city-state that so shaped the course of Italian history.

Perugia's Fontana Maggiore by night.

MAIN ATTRACTIONS

④ Collegio del Cambio *(Bankers' Guild Hall)*. These elaborate rooms, on
★ the ground floor of the **Palazzo dei Priori**, served as the meeting hall
and chapel of the guild of bankers and money changers. Most of the
frescoes were done by the most important Perugian painter of the
Renaissance, Pietro Vannucci, better known as Perugino. He included
a remarkably honest self-portrait on one of the pilasters. The iconog-
raphy includes common religious themes, such as the Nativity and the
Transfiguration seen on the end walls. On the left wall are female figures representing the virtues, beneath them the heroes and sages of
antiquity. On the right wall are figures presumed to have been painted
in part by Perugino's most famous pupil, Raphael. (His hand, experts
say, is most apparent in the figure of Fortitude.) The *cappella* (chapel)
of San Giovanni Battista has frescoes painted by Giannicola di Paolo,
another student of Perugino. ✉ *Corso Vannucci 25* ☎ *075/5728599*
💳 *€4.50, €5.50 with Collegio della Mercanzia* ☉ *Mon.–Sat. 9–12:30
and 2:30–5:30, Sun. 9–1.*

Corso Vannucci. A string of elegantly connected *palazzi* (palaces)
expresses the artistic nature of this city center, the heart of which is
concentrated along Corso Vannucci. Stately and broad, this pedestrians-only street runs from Piazza d'Italia to Piazza IV Novembre. Along
the way, the entrances to many of Perugia's side streets might tempt you
to wander off and explore. But don't stray too far as evening falls, when
Corso Vannucci fills with Perugians out for their evening *passeggiata*,
a pleasant pre-dinner stroll that may include a pause for an aperitif at
one of the many bars that line the street.

③ **Galleria Nazionale dell'Umbria.** The region's most comprehensive art gal-
Fodor'sChoice lery is housed on the fourth floor of the **Palazzo dei Priori.** Enhanced
★ by skillfully lit displays and computers that allow you to focus on the
works' details and background information, the collection includes
work by native artists—most notably Pintoricchio (1454–1513) and
Perugino (circa 1450–1523)—and others of the Umbrian and Tuscan
schools, among them Gentile da Fabriano (1370–1427), Duccio (circa
1255–1318), Fra Angelico (1387–1455), Fiorenzo di Lorenzo (1445–
1525), and Piero della Francesca (1420–92). In addition to paintings,
the gallery has frescoes, sculptures, and some superb examples of cru-
cifixes from the 13th and 14th centuries. Some rooms are dedicated to
Perugia itself, showing how the medieval city evolved. ⊠ *Corso Vannucci 19, Piazza IV Novembre* ☎ *075/5721009* ⊕ *www.gallerianazio
naleumbria.it* ⊠ *€6.50* ⊙ *Tues.–Sun. 8:30–7:30; last admission ½ hr
before closing.*

② **Palazzo dei Priori** *(Palace of Priors).* A series of elegant connected build-
★ ings, the palazzo serves as Perugia's city hall and houses three of the
city's museums. The buildings string along Corso Vannucci and wrap
around the Piazza IV Novembre, where the original entrance is located.
The steps here lead to the **Sala dei Notari** (Notaries' Hall). Other
entrances lead to the **Galleria Nazionale dell'Umbria,** the **Collegio del
Cambio,** and the **Collegio della Mercanzia.** The Sala dei Notari, which
dates back to the 13th century and was the original meeting place of
the town merchants, had become the seat of the notaries by the second half of the 15th century. Wood beams and an interesting array of
frescoes attributed to Maestro di Farneto embellish the room. Coats
of arms and crests line the back and right lateral walls; you can spot
some famous figures from *Aesop's Fables* on the left wall. The palazzo
facade is adorned with symbols of Perugia's pride and past power: the
griffin is the city symbol, and the lion denotes Perugia's allegiance to
the Guelph (or papal) cause. ⊠ *Piazza IV Novembre* ⊠ *Free* ⊙ *June–
Sept., Tues.–Sun. 9–1 and 3–7.*

Rocca Paolina. A labyrinth of little streets, alleys, and arches, this underground city was originally part of a fortress. It was built at the behest
of Pope Paul III between 1540 and 1543 to confirm papal dominion
over the city. When the papacy fell parts of it were destroyed, but much
still remains. Begin your visit by taking the escalators from Piazza Italia and Via Masi. In the summer this is the coolest place in the city.
⊙ *Daily 8–7.*

ALSO WORTH SEEING

① **Duomo.** Severe yet mystical, the Duomo, also called the Cathedral of
San Lorenzo, is most famous for being the home of the wedding ring
of the Virgin Mary, stolen by the Perugians in 1488 from the nearby
town of Chiusi. The ring, kept high up in a red-curtained vault in the
chapel immediately to the left of the entrance, is kept under lock—15
locks, to be precise—and key most of the year. It's shown to the public
on July 30 (the day it was brought to Perugia) and the second-to-last
Sunday in January (Mary's wedding anniversary). The cathedral itself
dates from the Middle Ages and has many additions from the 15th

and 16th centuries. The most visually interesting element is the altar to the Madonna of Grace; an elegant fresco on a column at the right of the entrance of the altar depicts *La Madonna delle Grazie* and is surrounded by prayer benches decorated with handwritten notes to the Holy Mother. Around the column are small amulets—symbols of gratitude from those whose prayers were answered. There are also elaborately carved choir stalls, executed by Giovanni Battista Bastone in 1520. The altarpiece (1484), an early masterpiece by Luca Signorelli (circa 1441–1523), shows the Madonna with Saint John the Baptist, Saint Onophrius, and Saint Lawrence. Sections of the church may be closed to visitors during religious services. ⊠*Piazza IV Novembre* ☏*075/5724853* ⊟*Free* ☉ *Mon.–Sat. 7–12:30 and 4–6:45, Sun. 8–12:30 and 4–6:45*

❺ **Museo Archeologico Nazionale.** The museum, next to the imposing church of San Domenico, contains an excellent collection of Etruscan artifacts from throughout the region. Perugia was a flourishing Etruscan city long before it fell under Roman domination in 310 BC. Little else remains of Perugia's mysterious ancestors, although the Arco di Augusto, in Piazza Fortebraccio, the northern entrance to the city, is of Etruscan origin. ⊠*Piazza G. Bruno 10* ☏*075/5727141* ⊕*www.archeopg.arti.benicul turali.it* ⊠*€4* ☉ *Mon. 2:30–7:30, Tues.–Sun. 8:30–7:30.*

> ### WORD OF MOUTH
>
> "Two things you must not fail to do in Perugia are to (a) join the evening walk on the Corso Vannucci beginning at about 5 pm and (b) take the escalators that go up and down and through the historic city walls. Also: Hang out as often as you dare at Sandri's, one of Italy's most marvelous cafe/pastry shops, on the Corso Vanucci."   –nessundorma

WHERE TO EAT

$$–$$$ ✕**Antica Trattoria San Lorenzo.** Brick vaults are not the only distinguishing feature of this small restaurant next to the Duomo, as both the food and the service are outstanding. Particular attention is paid to adapting traditional Umbrian cuisine to the modern palate. There is also a nice variety of seafood dishes on the menu. The *trenette alla farina di noce con pesce di mare* (flat noodles made with walnut flour topped with fresh fish) is a real treat. ⊠*Piazza Danti 19-A* ☏*075/5721956* ⊟*AE, D, MC, V* ☉ *Closed Sun.*

$–$$$ ✕**La Rosetta.** The restaurant, in the hotel of the same name, is a peaceful, elegant spot. In winter you dine inside under medieval vaults; in summer, in the cool courtyard. The food is simple but reliable and flawlessly served. ⊠*Piazza d'Italia 19* ☏*075/5720841* ⌨*Reservations essential* ⊟*AE, DC, MC, V.*

$$ ✕**La Taverna.** Medieval steps lead to a rustic two-story restaurant where wine bottles and artful clutter decorate the walls. Good choices from the regional menu include *caramelle al gorgonzola* (pasta rolls filled with red cabbage and mozzarella and topped with a Gorgonzola sauce) and grilled meat dishes, such as the *medaglioni di vitello al tartuffo*

(grilled veal with truffles). ⊠ *Via delle Streghe 8, off Corso Vannucci* ☎*075/5724128* ⊟*AE, DC, MC, V* ⊙*Closed Mon.*

$–$$ ✗**Il Falchetto.** Exceptional food at reasonable prices makes this Perugia's best bargain. Service is smart but relaxed in the two medieval dining rooms that put the chef on view. The house specialty is *falchetti* (homemade gnocchi with spinach and ricotta cheese). ⊠ *Via Bartolo 20* ☎*075/5731775* ⊟*AE, DC, MC, V* ⊙*Closed Mon. and last 2 wks in Jan.*

$ ✗**Dal Mi' Cocco.** A great favorite with Perugia's university students, this
★ place is fun, crowded, and inexpensive. You may find yourself seated at a long table with other diners, but some language help from your neighbors could come in handy—the menu is in pure Perugian dialect. The fixed-price meals change with the season, and each day of the week brings some new creation *dal cocco* (from the "coconut," or head) of the chef. ⊠*Corso Garibaldi 12* ☎*075/5732511* ⚐*Reservations essential* ⊟*No credit cards* ⊙*Closed Mon. and July 25–Aug. 15*

WHERE TO STAY

$$$ 🏨**Castello dell'Oscano.** A splendid neo-Gothic castle, a late-19th-century villa, and a converted farmhouse hidden in the tranquil hills north of Perugia offer a wide range of accommodations. Step back in time in the castle, where spacious suites and junior suites, all with high oak-beam ceilings, and some with panoramic views of the surrounding country, are decorated with 18th- and 19th-century antiques. The sweeping wooden staircase of the main lounge, and the wood-paneled reading rooms and restaurant are particularly elegant. Rooms in the villa are smaller and more modern, and the apartments of the farmhouse, in the valley below the castle, have their own kitchens. The complex is in Cenerente, 5 km (3 mi) north of Perugia. **Pros:** Quiet elegance; fine gardens; Umbrian wine list. **Cons:** Distance from Perugia; not easy to find. ⊠*Strada della Forcella 32, Cenerente* ☎*075/584371* 🖷*075/690666* ⊕*www.oscano.it* ⇥*24 rooms, 8 suites, 13 apartments* ⚙*In-room: no a/c (some), Ethernet. In-hotel: restaurant, bar, pool, gym, bicycles, no-smoking rooms* ⊟*AE, D, V* ⦿*BP*

$$ 🏨**Hotel Fortuna.** The elegant decor in the large rooms of this friendly hotel complements the frescoes, which date from the 1700s. Some rooms have balconies. The building itself, just out of sight of Corso Vannucci, dates to the 1300s. **Pros:** Central but quiet; homely atmosphere. **Cons:** Some small rooms; no restaurant. ⊠*Via Bonazzi 19* ☎*075/5722845* 🖷*075/5735040* ⊕*www.umbriahotels.com* ⇥*51 rooms* ⚙*In-hotel: restaurant, bar, parking (fee)* ⊟*AE, DC, MC, V* ⦿*BP*

$$ 🏨**Il Cantico della Natura.** Don't let the rustic appearance of the buildings fool you, this is one of the plushest agriturismi in Umbria. The rooms are furnished in varying ethnic styles, with nice little extras thrown in such as bedside kettles and an array of teas and herbal infusions. The owners also organize a series of outdoor activities. **Pros:** Views of Lake Trasimeno and the surrounding countryside. **Cons:** Not easy to find; road poor in winter. ⊠*Vocabolo Penna, Montesperello di Magione*

3

☎075/841699 ⊕*www.ilcanticodellanatura.it* ↝12 *rooms* ⟋*In-hotel: restaurant, gym, bicycles*☰*AE, DC, MC, V* �ⓞ⏐*BP*

$$ ⊡ **Locanda della Posta.** In the city's old district, this lodging is in an 18th-century palazzo. Renovations have left the lobby and other public areas rather bland, but the rooms are soothingly decorated in muted colors. Although facing busy Corso Vannucci and supposedly soundproof, they're still a bit noisy. Those on the upper floors at the back of the building are quieter and have great views. **Pros:** Some fine views; central position. **Cons:** Uninspiring lobby; some small rooms; no restaurant. ⊠*Corso Vannucci 97* ☎*075/5728925* ☐*075/5732562* ↝*38 rooms, 1 suite* ⟋*In-hotel: bar, parking (fee)* ☰*AE, DC, MC, V* ⊡ⓞ⏐*BP.*

NIGHTLIFE & THE ARTS

With its large student population, the city has plenty to offer in the way of bars and clubs. The best ones are around the city center, off Corso Vanucci. *Viva Perugia* is a good source of information about nightlife. The monthly, sold at newsstands, has a section in English.

MUSIC FESTIVALS

Summer sees two music festivals in Perugia. **Umbria Jazz** (☎*075/5732432* ⊕*www.umbriajazz.com*) is held for 10 days in July. Tickets are available starting at the end of April. The **Sagra Musicale Umbra** (☎*075/5721374* ⊕*www.perugiamusicaclassica.com*), held from mid-August to mid-September, celebrates sacred music.

SHOPPING

Take a stroll down any of Perugia's main streets, including Corso Vannucci, Via dei Priori, Via Oberdan, and Via S. Ercolano, and you'll see many well-known designer boutiques and specialty shops.

The most typical thing to buy in Perugia is some Perugina chocolate, which you can find almost anywhere. The best-known chocolates made by Perugina are the chocolate-and-hazelnut-filled nibbles called Baci (literally, "kisses"). They're wrapped in silver paper that includes a sliver of paper, like the fortune in a fortune cookie, with multilingual romantic sentiments or sayings.

TUSCANY

There's a magic about Tuscany: the right elements have all fallen into place here. The art and the culture, the food and the wine, are justly famous. The gorgeous countryside and the picture-book towns take on a certain glow in the late afternoon sun. And the people mix warmth, modesty, and pride in a way that honors their glorious past without bowing down to it.

Tuscany isn't the place for a jam-packed itinerary. One of the great pleasures here is indulging in rustic hedonism, marked by long lunches and show-stopping sunsets. Whether by car, bike, or foot, you'll want to get out into the glorious landscape, but it's smart to keep your plans modest. Set a church or a hill town or an out-of-the-way restaurant as your destination, knowing that half the pleasure is in getting there---admiring as you go the stately palazzos, the tidy geometry of row upon row of grape vines, the fields vibrant with red poppies and yellow broom.

You'll need to devise a Siena strategy. The town shouldn't be missed; it's compact enough that you can see the major sights on a day trip, and that's exactly what most people do. Spend the night, and you'll get to witness the town breath a sigh and relax upon the day-trippers' departure. The flip side is, your favorite place to stay in Tuscany is more likely to be out in the country than in town.

SIENA

With its narrow streets and steep alleys, a stunning Gothic Duomo, a bounty of early Renaissance art, and the glorious Palazzo Pubblico overlooking its magnificent Campo, Siena is often described as Italy's best-preserved medieval city. Victory over Florence in 1260 at Montaperti marked the beginning of Siena's golden age. During the following decades Siena erected its greatest buildings (including the Duomo); established a model city government presided over by the Council of Nine; and became a great art, textile, and trade center. Siena succumbed to Florentine rule in the mid-16th century, when a yearlong siege virtually eliminated the native population. Ironically, it was precisely this decline that, along with the steadfast pride of the Sienese, prevented further development, to which we owe the city's marvelous medieval condition today.

Although much looks as it did in the early 14th century, Siena is no museum. Walk through the streets and you can see that the medieval *contrade*, 17 neighborhoods into which the city has been historically divided, are a vibrant part of modern life. You may see symbols of the *contrada*—Tartuca (turtle), Oca (goose), Istrice (porcupine), Torre

TUSCANY THROUGH THE AGES

Etruscans & Romans. Tuscany was populated, at least by the 7th century BC, by the Etruscans, a mysterious lot who chose to live on hills—the better to see the approaching enemy—in such places as present-day Arezzo, Chiusi, Cortona, Fiesole, and Volterra. Some 500 years later, the Romans came, saw, and conquered; by 241 BC they had built the Aurelia, a road from Rome to Pisa that is still in use today. The crumbling of the Roman Empire and subsequent invasions by marauding Lombards, Byzantines, and Holy Roman Emperors meant centuries of turmoil. By the 12th century city-states were being formed throughout Tuscany in part, perhaps, because it was unclear exactly who was in charge.

Guelphs & Ghibellines. The two groups vying for power were the Guelphs and the Ghibellines, champions of the pope and the Holy Roman Emperor, respectively. They jostled for control of individual cities and of the region as a whole. Florence was more or less Guelph, and Siena more often than not Ghibelline. This led to bloody battles, most notably the 1260 battle of Montaperti, in which the Ghibellines roundly defeated the Guelphs.

Eventually—by the 14th century—the Guelphs became the dominant force. But this did not mean that the warring Tuscan cities settled down to a period of relative peace and tranquility. The age in which Dante wrote his *Divine Comedy* and Giotto and Piero della Francesca created their incomparable frescoes was one of internecine strife.

Florentines & Sienese. Florence was the power to be reckoned with; it coveted its main rival, Siena, which it conquered, lost, and reconquered during the 15th and 16th centuries. Finally, in 1555, following in the footsteps of Volterra, Pisa, Prato, and Arezzo, Siena fell for good. They were all united under Florence to form the grand duchy of Tuscany. The only city to escape Florence's dominion was Lucca, which remained fiercely independent until the arrival of Napoléon. Eventually, however, even Florence's influence waned, and the 17th and 18th centuries saw the decline of the entire region as various armies swept across it.

(tower)—emblazoned on banners and engraved on building walls. The Sienese still strongly identify themselves by the contrada where they were born and raised; loyalty and rivalry run deep. At no time is this more visible than during the centuries-old Palio, a twice-yearly horse race held in the Piazza del Campo, but you need not visit during the wild festival to come to know the rich culture and enchanting pleasures of Siena; those are evident at every step.

GETTING HERE

From Florence, the quickest way to Siena is via the Florence–Siena Superstrada. Otherwise, take the Via Cassia (SR2), for a scenic route. Coming from Rome, leave the A1 at Valdichiana, and follow the Siena–Bettole Superstrada. SITA provides excellent bus service between Florence and Siena. Because buses are direct and speedy, they are preferable over the train, which sometimes involves a change in Empoli.

VISITOR INFORMATION
Siena tourism office (✉ *Piazza del Campo 56* ☎ *0577/280551* ⊕ *www. comune.siena.it*).

EXPLORING SIENA

If you come by car, you're better off leaving it in one of the parking lots around the perimeter of town. Driving is difficult or impossible in most parts of the city center. Practically unchanged since medieval times, Siena is laid out in a "Y" over the slopes of several hills, dividing the city into *terzi* (thirds). Although the most interesting sites are in a fairly compact area around the Campo at the center of town in the neighborhoods of Città, Camollìa, and San Martino, be sure to leave some time to wander into the narrow streets that rise and fall steeply from the main thoroughfares, giving yourself at least two days to really explore the town. At the top on the list of things to see is the Piazza del Campo, considered by many to be the finest public square in Italy. The Palazzo Pubblico sits at the lower end of the square and is well worth a visit. The Duomo is a must-see, as is the nearby Cripta.

Tra-In (☎ *0577/204111* ⊕ *www.trainspa.it*) buses also run frequently within and around Siena, including through the centro storico. Tickets cost €0.90 and should be bought in advance at tobacconists or news-stands. Routes are marked with signposts.

The **Association of Official Tour Guides** (✉ *Piazza del Campo 56* ☎ *0577/ 288084* ⊕ *www.terredisiena.it*) offers a two-hour walking tour that takes in most of the major sights such as the Duomo, the Campo, and the exterior of Palazzo Pubblico. You can arrange for English-speaking guides.

TIMING It's a joy to walk in Siena—hills notwithstanding—as it's a rare opportunity to stroll through a medieval city rather than just a town. (There is quite a lot to explore, in contrast to tiny hill towns that can be crossed in minutes.) The walk can be done in as little as a day, with minimal stops at the sights. But stay longer and take time to tour the church building and museums, and to enjoy the streetscapes themselves. Several of the sites have reduced hours on Sunday afternoon and Monday.

THE MAIN ATTRACTIONS

③ Cripta. After it had lain unseen for possibly 700 years, a crypt was
Fodor'sChoice rediscovered under the grand *pavimento* (floor) of the Duomo dur-
★ ing routine excavation work and was opened to the public in 2003. An unknown master executed the breathtaking frescoes here sometime between 1270–80; they retain their original colors and pack an emotional punch even with sporadic damage. The *Deposition/Lamentation* gives strong evidence that the Sienese school could paint emotion just as well as the Florentine school—and did it some 20 years before Giotto. Guided tours in English take place more or less every half hour and are limited to no more than 35 persons. ✉ *Piazza del Duomo, Città* ☎ *0577/283048* 🎟️ *€6; €10 combined ticket includes the Duomo, Battistero, and Museo dell'Opera Metropolitana* ⊙ *June–Aug., daily 9:30–8; Sept.–May, daily 9:30–7.*

④ Duomo. Siena's Duomo is beyond question one of the finest Gothic
Fodor'sChoice cathedrals in Italy. The multicolor marbles and painted decoration
★ are typical of the Italian approach to Gothic architecture—lighter and much less austere than the French. The amazingly detailed facade has few rivals in the region, although it's quite similar to the Duomo in Orvieto. It was completed in two brief phases at the end of the 13th and 14th centuries. The statues and decorative work were designed by Niccolo and Giovanni Pisano, although most of what we see today are copies, the originals having been removed to the nearby Museo dell'Opera Metropolitana. The gold mosaics are 18th-century restorations. The Campanile (no entry) is among central Italy's finest, with the number of windows increasing with each level.

The Duomo's interior, with its black-and-white striping throughout and finely coffered and gilded dome, is simply striking. Step in and look back up at Duccio's (circa 1255–1319) panels of stained glass that fill the circular window. Finished in 1288, it's the oldest example of stained glass in Italy. The Duomo is most famous for its unique and magnificent inlaid-marble floors, which took almost 200 years to complete; more than 40 artists contributed to the work, made up of

56 separate compositions depicting biblical scenes, allegories, religious symbols, and civic emblems. The floors are covered for most of the year for conservation purposes, but are unveiled during September and October. The Duomo's carousel pulpit, also much appreciated, was carved by Nicola Pisano (circa 1220–84) around 1265; the *Life of Christ* is depicted on the rostrum frieze. In striking contrast to all the Gothic decoration in the nave are the magnificent Renaissance frescoes in the **Biblioteca Piccolomini,** off the left aisle. Painted by Pinturicchio (circa 1454–1513) and completed in 1509, they depict events from the life of native son Aeneas Sylvius Piccolomini (1405–64), who became Pope Pius II in 1458. The frescoes are in excellent condition and have a freshness rarely seen in work so old.

The Duomo is grand, but the medieval Sienese people had even bigger plans. They wanted to enlarge the building by using the existing church as a transept for a new church, with a new nave running toward the southeast, to make what would be the largest church in the world. But only the sidewall and part of the new facade were completed when the Black Death struck in 1348, decimating Siena's population. The city fell into decline, funds dried up, and the plans were never carried out. (The dream of building the biggest church was actually doomed to failure from the start—subsequent attempts to get the project going revealed that the foundation was insufficient to bear the weight of the proposed structure.) The beginnings of the new nave, extending from the right side of the Duomo, were left unfinished, perhaps as a testament to unfulfilled dreams, and ultimately enclosed to house the adjacent ⇨ **Museo dell'Opera Metropolitana.** The ⇨ **Cripta** was discovered during routine preservation work on the church and has been opened to the public. ✉ *Piazza del Duomo, Città* ☎ *0577/283048* 💶 *€3 Nov.–Aug.; €5 Sept. and Oct.; €10 combined ticket includes the Cripta, Battistero, and Museo dell'Opera Metropolitana* ⏰ *Mar.–Oct., Mon.–Sat. 10:30–7:30, Sun. 1:30–6:30; Nov.–Feb., Mon.–Sat. 10:30–6:30, Sun. 1:30–5:30.*

ALSO WORTH SEEING

5 Battistero. The Duomo's 14th-century Gothic Baptistery was built to prop up one side of the Duomo. There are frescoes throughout, but the highlight is a large bronze 15th-century baptismal font designed by Jacopo della Quercia (1374–1438). It's adorned with bas-reliefs by various artists, including two by Renaissance masters: the *Baptism of Christ* by Lorenzo Ghiberti (1378–1455) and the *Feast of Herod* by Donatello. ✉ *Entrance on Piazza San Giovanni* ☎ *No phone* 💶 *€3; €10 combined ticket includes the Duomo, Cripta, and Museo dell'Opera del Duomo* ⏰ *June–Aug., daily 9:30–8; Sept.–May, daily 9:30–7.*

6 Museo dell'Opera Metropolitana. Part of the unfinished nave of what was to have been a new cathedral, the museum contains the Duomo's treasury and some of the original decoration from its facade and interior. The first room on the ground floor displays weather-beaten 13th-century sculptures by Giovanni Pisano (circa 1245–1318) that were brought inside for protection and replaced by copies, as was a tondo of the *Madonna and Child* (now attributed to Donatello) that once hung on the door to the south transept. The masterpiece is unquestionably

Continued on page 180

Climbing the 400 narrow steps of the **Torre del Mangia** rewards you with unparalleled views of Siena's rooftops and the countryside beyond.

The **Palazzo Pubblico**, Siena's town hall since the 14th century.

Something about the fan-shaped, sloping design of **Il Campo** encourages people to sit and relax (except during the Palio, when they stand and scream). The communal atmosphere here is unlike that of any other Italian piazza.

PIAZZA DEL CAMPO

7 The fan-shaped **Piazza del Campo,** known simply as il Campo (The
Field), is one of the finest squares in Italy. Constructed toward the end
of the 12th century on a market area unclaimed by
any contrada, it's still the heart of town. The
bricks of the Campo are patterned in nine
different sections—representing each
member of the medieval Government
of Nine. At the top of the Campo
is a copy of the **Fonte Gaia,** decorated in the early 15th century by
Siena's greatest sculptor, Jacopo
della Quercia, with 13 sculpted
reliefs of biblical events and virtues. Those lining the rectangular
fountain are 19th-century copies;
the originals are in the Spedale di
Santa Maria della Scala. On Palio
horse race days (July 2 and August
16), the Campo and all its surrounding buildings are packed with cheering,
frenzied locals and tourists craning their
necks to take it all in.

Fodor'sChoice ★

8 The Gothic **Palazzo Pubblico,** the focal point of the Piazza del Campo,
has served as Siena's town hall since the 1300s. It now also contains
the **Museo Civico,** with walls covered in early Renaissance frescoes.
The nine governors of Siena once met in the Sala della Pace, famous
for Ambrogio Lorenzetti's frescoes called *Allegories of Good and Bad
Government,* painted in the late 1330s to demonstrate the dangers
of tyranny. The good government side depicts utopia, showing first
the virtuous ruling council surrounded by angels and then scenes of
a perfectly running city and countryside. Conversely, the bad government fresco tells a tale straight out of Dante. The evil ruler and his
advisers have horns and fondle strange animals, and the town scene
depicts the seven mortal sins in action. Interestingly, the bad government fresco is severely damaged, and the good government fresco is
in terrific condition. The **Torre del Mangia,** the palazzo's famous bell
tower, is named after one of its first bell ringers, Giovanni di Duccio
(called Mangiaguadagni, or earnings eater). The climb up to the top is
long and steep, but the view makes it worth every step. ⊠ *Piazza del
Campo 1, Città* ☎ *0577/41169* ▣ *Museo €7, Torre €6, combined
ticket €10* ⊙ *Museo Nov.–Mar. 15, daily 10–6:30; Mar. 16–Oct., daily
10–7. Torre Nov.–Mar. 15, daily 10–4; Mar. 16–Oct., daily 10–7.*

THE PALIO

The three laps around a makeshift racetrack in Piazza del Campo are over in less than two minutes, but the spirit of Siena's Palio—a horse race held every July 2 and August 16—lives all year long.

The Palio is contested between Siena's contrade, the 17 neighborhoods that have divided the city since the Middle Ages. Loyalties are fiercely felt. At any time of year you'll see on the streets contrada symbols—Tartuca (turtle), Oca (goose), Istrice (porcupine), Torre (tower)—emblazoned on banners and engraved on building walls. At Palio time, simmering rivalries come to a boil.

It's been that way since at least August 16, 1310, the date of the first recorded running of the Palio. At that time, and for centuries to follow, the race went through the streets of the city. The additional July 2 running was instituted in 1649; soon thereafter the location was moved to the Campo and the current system for selecting the race entrants established. Ten of the contrade are chosen at random to run in the July Palio. The August race is then contested between the 7 contrade left out in July, plus 3 of the 10 July participants, again chosen at random. Although the races are in theory of equal importance, Sienese will tell you that it's better to win the second and have bragging rights for the rest of the year.

The race itself has a raw and arbitrary character—it's no Kentucky Derby. There's barely room for the 10 horses on the makeshift Campo course, so falls and collisions are inevitable. Horses are chosen at random three days before the race, and jockeys (who ride bareback) are mercenaries hired from surrounding towns. Almost no tactic is considered too underhanded. Bribery, secret plots, and betrayal are commonplace—so much so that the word for "jockey," *fantino*, has come to mean "untrustworthy" in Siena. There have been incidents of drugging (the horses) and kidnapping (the jockeys); only sabotaging a horse's reins remains taboo.

Above: The tension of the starting line. Top left: The frenzy of the race. Bottom left: A solemn flag bearer follows in the footsteps of his ancestors.

17 MEDIEVAL CONTRADE

AQUILA	BRUCO	CHIOCCIOLA

Festivities kick off three days prior to the Palio, with the selection and blessing of the horses, trial runs, ceremonial banquets, betting, and late-night celebrations. Residents don their contrada's colors and march through the streets in medieval costumes. The Campo is transformed into a racetrack lined with a thick layer of sand. On race day, each horse is brought to the church of the contrada for which it will run, where it's blessed and told, "Go little horse and return a winner." The Campo fills through the afternoon, with spectators crowding into every available space until bells ring and the piazza is sealed off. Processions of flag wavers in traditional dress march to the beat of tambourines and drums and the roar of the crowds. The *palio* itself—a banner for which the race is named, dedicated to the Virgin Mary—makes an appearance, followed by the horses and their jockeys.

The race begins when one horse, chosen to ride up from behind the rest of the field, crosses the starting line. There are always false starts, adding to the frenzied mood. Once underway, the race is over in a matter of minutes. The victorious rider is carried off through the streets of the winning contrada (where in the past tradition dictated he was entitled to the local girl of his choice), while winning and losing sides use television replay to analyze the race from every possible angle. The winning contrada will celebrate into the night, at long tables piled high with food and drink. The champion horse is guest of honor.

Reserved seating in the stands is sold out months in advance of the races; contact the Siena Tourist Office (✉ Piazza del Campo 56 ☎ 0577/280551) to find out about availability, and ask your hotel if it can procure you a seat. The entire area in the center is free and unreserved, but you need to show up early in order to get a prime spot against the barriers.

CIVETTA	DRAGO
GIRAFFA	ISTRICE
LEOCORNO	LUPA
NICCHIO	OCA
ONDA	PANTERA
SELVA	TARTUCA
TORRE	VALDIMONTONE

3

IN FOCUS PIAZZA DEL CAMPO

Duccio's *Maestà*, one side with 26 panels depicting episodes from the Passion, the other side with a *Madonna and Child Enthroned*. Painted between 1308 and 1311 as the altarpiece for the Duomo (where it remained until 1505), its realistic elements, such as the lively depiction of the Christ child and the treatment of interior space, proved an enormous influence on

later painters. The second floor is divided between the treasury, with a crucifix by Giovanni Pisano and several statues and busts of biblical characters and classical philosophers, and La Sala della Madonna degli Occhi Grossi (the Room of the Madonna with the Big Eyes), named after the namesake painting it displays by the Maestro di Tressa, who painted in the early 13th century. The work originally decorated the Duomo's high altar, before being displaced by Duccio's *Maestà*. There is a fine view from the tower inside the museum. ⊠*Piazza del Duomo, Città* ☎*0577/283048* 🖃*€6; €10 combined ticket includes the Duomo, Cripta, and Battistero* ⊘*Mar.–May and Sept. and Oct., daily 9:30–7; June–Aug., daily 9:30* AM–*10* PM; *Nov.–Feb., daily 10–5.*

❾ Pinacoteca Nazionale. The superb collection of five centuries of local painting in Siena's national picture gallery can easily convince you that the Renaissance was by no means just a Florentine thing—Siena was arguably just as important a center of art and innovation as its rival to the north, especially in the mid-13th century. Accordingly, the most interesting section of the collection, chronologically arranged, has several important "firsts." Room 1 contains a painting of the *Stories of the True Cross* (1215) by the so-called Master of Tressa, the earliest identified work by a painter of the Sienese school, and is followed in Room 2 by late-13th-century artist Guido da Siena's *Stories from the Life of Christ,* one of the first paintings ever made on canvas (earlier painters used wood panels). Rooms 3 and 4 are dedicated to Duccio, a student of Cimabue (circa 1240–1302) and considered to be the last of the proto-Renaissance painters. Ambrogio Lorenzetti's landscapes in Room 8 are the first truly secular paintings in Western art. Among later works in the rooms on the floor above, keep an eye out for the preparatory sketches used by Domenico Beccafumi (1486–1551) for the 35 etched marble panels he made for the floor of the Duomo. ⊠*Via San Pietro 29, Città* ☎*0577/281161* 🖃*€4* ⊘*Tues.–Sat. 8:15–7:15; Sun. 8:15–1:15; Mon. 8:30–1:30; last entrance ½ hr before closing.*

❶ San Domenico. Although the Duomo is celebrated as a triumph of 13th-century Gothic architecture, this church, built at about the same time, turned out as an oversize, hulking brick box that never merited a finishing coat in marble, let alone a graceful facade. Named for the founder of the Dominican order, the church is now more closely associated with Saint Catherine of Siena. Just to the right of the entrance is the chapel in which she received the stigmata. On the wall is the only known contemporary portrait of the saint, made in the late 14th century by Andrea Vanni (circa 1332–1414). Farther down is the famous **Cappella di Santa Caterina,** the church's official shrine. Catherine, or bits and pieces of her, was literally spread all over the country—a foot is in Venice, most of her body is in Rome, and only her head and finger are here (kept in a reliquary on the altar). She was revered throughout the country long before she was officially named a patron saint of Italy in 1939. On either side of the chapel are well-known frescoes by Sodoma (aka Giovanni Antonio Bazzi, 1477–1549) of *St. Catherine in Ecstasy.* Don't miss the view of the Duomo and town center from the apse-side terrace. ⊠ *Costa di Sant'Antonio, Camollìa* ☎ *0577/280893* ◫ *Free* ☉ *Mid-Mar.–Oct., daily 7–1 and 2:30–6:30; Nov.–mid-Mar., daily 9–1 and 3–6.*

② Spedale di Santa Maria della Scala. For more than a thousand years, this complex across from the Duomo was home to Siena's hospital, but now it serves as a museum to display some terrific frescoes and other Sienese Renaissance treasures. Restored 15th-century frescoes in the Sala del Pellegrinaio (once the emergency room) tell the history of the hospital, which was created to give refuge to passing pilgrims and to those in need, and to distribute charity to the poor. Incorporated into the complex is the church of the Santissima Annunziata, with a celebrated *Risen Christ* by Vecchietta (also known as Lorenzo di Pietro, circa 1412–80). Down in the dark Cappella di Santa Caterina della Notte is where Saint Catherine went to pray at night. The subterranean archaeological museum contained within the *ospedale* (hospital) is worth seeing even if you're not particularly taken with Etruscan objects: the interior design is sheer brilliance—it's beautifully lighted, eerily quiet, and an oasis of cool on hot summer days. The displays—including the *bucchero* (dark, reddish clay) ceramics, Roman coins, and tomb furnishings—are clearly marked and can serve as a good introduction to the history of regional excavations. Don't miss della Quercia's original sculpted reliefs from the Fonte Gaia. Although the fountain has been faithfully copied for the Campo, there's something incomparably beautiful about the real thing. ⊠ *Piazza del Duomo, Città* ☎ *0577/224811* ◫ *€6* ☉ *Mar. 16–Jan. 9, daily 10:30–6:30; Jan. 10–Mar. 15, daily 10:30–4:30.*

WHERE TO STAY & EAT

$$$–$$$$ ✕ **Antica Trattoria Botteganova.** Along the road that leads to Chianti is
★   arguably the best restaurant in Siena. Chef Michele Sorrentino's cooking is all about clean flavors, balanced combinations, and inviting presentation. Look for inspiring dishes such as spaghetti *alla chitarra in salsa di astice piccante* (with a spicy lobster sauce), or ravioli *di ricotta con ragù d'agnello* (with sheep's-milk cheese and lamb sauce). The interior, with high vaulting, is relaxed yet elegant, and the service is first rate. ⊠ *Strada per Montevarchi 29 j 2 km (1 mi) northeast of Siena* ☎ *0577/284230* ⸙ *Reservations essential* ▭ *AE, DC, MC, V* ☉ *Closed Sun.*

EATING & DRINKING WELL IN TUSCANY

HOLD THE SALT

The influence of the ancient Etruscans—who favored the use of fresh herbs—is still felt in Tuscan cuisine three millennia later. Simple and earthy, Tuscan food celebrates the seasons with fresh vegetable dishes, wonderful bread-based soups, and meats perfumed with sage, rosemary, and thyme.

Tuscan bread is famous for what it's missing: it's made without salt. That's because it's intended to pick up seasoning from the food it accompanies; it's not to be eaten alone or dipped in a bowl of oil (which is a custom in American restaurants, but not Italian ones). Tuscans like their bread grilled and drizzled with olive oil (*crostino or fettunta*), covered with chicken-liver spread (*crostino di fegatini*), or rubbed with garlic and topped with tomatoes (*bruschetta*).

Throughout Tuscany there are excellent upscale restaurants that serve elaborate dishes, but to get a real taste of the flavors of the region, head for the family-run trattorias found in every town. The service and setting are often basic, but the food can be great.

Few places serve lighter fare at midday, so expect substantial meals at lunch and dinner, especially in out-of-the-way towns. Dining hours are fairly standard: lunch between 12:30 and 2, dinner between 7:30 and 10.

AFFETTATI MISTI

The name, roughly translated, means "mixed cold cuts," pictured left, and it's something Tuscans do exceptionally well. A platter of cured meats, served as an antipasto, is sure to include *prosciutto crudo* (ham, cut paper thin) and *salame* (dry sausage, prepared in dozens of ways—some spicy, some sweet). The most distinctly Tuscan affettati are made from *cinta senese* (a once nearly extinct pig found only in the heart of the region) and *cinghiale* (wild boar, which roam all of central Italy). You can eat these delicious slices unadorned or layered on a piece bread.

PASTA

Restaurants throughout Tuscany serve dishes similar to those in Florence, but they also have their own local specialties. Many recipes are from the *nonna* (grandmother) of the restaurant's owner, handed down through time but never written down. Look in particular for pasta creations made with *pici* (a long, thick, hand-rolled spaghetti), pictured below. *Pappardelle* (a long, flat pasta noodle), pictured upper right, is frequently paired with sauces made with game, such as *lepre* (hare) or *cinghiale*. In the northwest, a specialty of Lucca is *tordelli di carne al ragù* (meat-stuffed pasta with a meat sauce).

MEAT

Bistecca all fiorentina (a thick T-bone steak, grilled rare) is the classic meat dish of Tuscany, but there are other specialties as well. Many menus will include *tagliata di manzo* (thinly sliced, roasted beef, drizzled with olive oil), *arista di maiale* (roast pork with sage and rosemary), and *salsiccia e fagioli* (pork sausage and beans). In the southern part of the region, don't be surprised to find *piccione* (pigeon), which can be roasted, stuffed, or baked.

WINE

Grape cultivation here also dates from Etruscan times, and, particularly in Chianti, vineyards are abundant. The resulting medium-body red wine is a staple on most tables; however, you can select from a multitude of other varieties, including such reds as Brunello di Montalcino and Vino Nobile di Montepulciano and such whites as Vermentino and Vernaccia. Super Tuscans, a fanciful name given to a group of wines by American journalists, now command attention as some of the best produced in Italy; they have great depth and complexity. The dessert wine *vin santo* is made throughout the region and is often sipped with *biscotti* (twice-baked cookies), perfect for dunking.

$$$-$$$$ ✕ **Le Logge.** Bright flowers provide a dash of color at this classic Tuscan dining room, and stenciled designs on the ceilings add some whimsy. The wooden cupboards (now filled with wine bottles) lining the walls recall its past as a turn-of-the-19th-century grocery store. The menu, with four or five *primi* (first courses) and *secondi* (second courses) changes regularly, but almost always includes their classic *malfatti all'osteria* (ricotta and spinach dumplings in a cream sauce). Desserts such as *coni con mousse al cioccolato e gelato allo zafferano* (two diminutive ice-cream cones with chocolate mousse and saffron ice cream) provide an inventive ending to the meal. When not vying for one of the outdoor tables, make sure to ask for one in the main downstairs room. ⊠ *Via del Porrione 33, San Martino* ☎*0577/48013* ♣*Reservations essential* ⊟*AE, DC, MC, V* ⊙*Closed Sun. and 3 wks in Jan.*

$-$$ ✕ **Osteria del Coro.** Chef-owner Stefano Azzi promotes local produce,
Fodor'sChoice   uses age-old Sienese recipes, and backs it all up with a stellar wine
★   list. His *pici con le briciole al modo mio* (thick spaghetti with bread-crumbs), liberally dressed with fried *cinta senese* (a bacon made from a long-snouted pig), dazzles. The place was once a pizzeria, and it retains its unadorned, unpretentious air—you certainly wouldn't come because of the decor. ⊠ *Via Pantaneto 85/87Città* ☎*0577/222482* ⊟ *DC, MC, V* ⊙*Closed Mon.*

$-$$ ✕ **Trattoria Papei.** The menu hasn't changed for years, and why should
★   it? The *pici al cardinale* (handmade spaghetti with a duck and bacon sauce) is wonderful, and all the other typically Sienese dishes are equally delicious. Tucked away behind the Palazzo Pubblico in a square that serves as a parking lot for most of the day, the restaurant's location isn't great, but the food is. ⊠*Piazza del Mercato 6, Città* ☎*0577/280894* ⊟*MC, V* ⊙*Closed Mon.*

$$$ ⌷ **Hotel Santa Caterina.** Manager Lorenza Capannelli and her fine staff
★   are welcoming, hospitable, enthusiastic, and go out of their way to ensure a fine stay. Dark, straight-lined wood furniture stands next to beds with floral spreads; some have upholstered headboards. Rooms in the back look out onto the garden or the countryside in the distance. When it's warm, breakfast is served on the flower-filled garden with a view of the Siena countryside, providing a gorgeous start to the day. The well-run hotel is outside Porta Romana—a 15-minute walk south of Piazza del Campo. **Pros:** Friendly staff; a short walk to center of town; breakfast in the garden. **Cons:** On a busy intersection; outside city walls. ⊠ *Via Piccolomini 7, San Martino,* ☎*0577/221105* ⊕*www.hscsiena.it* ⇌*22 rooms* ⌂*In-room: refrigerator, dial-up. In-hotel: concierge, laundry service, public Internet, parking (fee), some pets allowed* ⊟*AE, DC, MC, V* ⦿|*BP.*

$$$ ⌷ **Palazzo Ravizza.** This romantic palazzo exudes a sense of genteel
★   shabbiness. Rooms have high ceilings, antique furnishings, and bathrooms decorated with hand-painted tiles. The location is key: from here it's just a 10-minute walk to the Duomo. Il Capriccio ($$–$$$), ably run by chef Fabio Tozzi, specializies in traditional Tuscan fare. In warm weather, enjoy your meal in the garden with a trickling fountain. "We have only positive things to say about Palazzo Ravizza ... from the amazing Tuscan view, to the proximity to Il Campo this hotel was

by far the best one we stayed at throughout our Italy vacation," says one traveler on Fodors.com. **Pros:** 10-minute walk to the center of town; pleasant garden with a view beyond the city walls; professional staff. **Cons:** Not all rooms have views; some of the rooms are a little cramped. ⊠*Pian dei Mantellini 34, Città,* ☎*0577/280462* ⊕*www. palazzoravizza.it* ⇆*38 rooms, 4 suites* ⚼*In-room: safe, refrigerator, Wi-Fi (some). In-hotel: restaurant, bar, concierge, laundry service, public Internet, public Wi-Fi, parking (no fee), some pets allowed* ⊟*AE, DC, MC, V* ⊗|*BP.*

$$ 🔲 **Antica Torre.** The cordial Landolfo family has carefully evoked a private home with their eight guest rooms inside a restored 16th-century tower. Simple but tastefully furnished rooms have ornate wrought-iron headboards, usually atop twin beds. The old stone staircase, large wooden beams, wood shutters, and original brick vaults here and there are reminders of the building's great age. Antica Torre is in a southeast corner of Siena, a 10-minute walk from Piazza del Campo. **Pros:** Near the town center; charming atmosphere. **Cons:** Narrow stairway up to the rooms; low ceilings; cramped bathrooms. ⊠*Via Fieravecchia 7, San Martino,* ☎*0577/222255* ⊕*www.anticatorresiena.it* ⇆*8 rooms* ⚼*In-hotel: no elevator* ⊟*AE, DC, MC, V* ⊗|*BP.*

AREZZO & CORTONA

The hill towns of Arezzo and Cortona carry on age-old local traditions—in June and September, for example, Arezzo's Romanesque and Gothic churches are enlivened by the Giostra del Saracino, a costumed medieval joust. Arezzo has been home to important artists since ancient times, when Etruscan potters produced their fiery-red vessels here. Fine examples of the work of Luca Signorelli are preserved in Cortona, his hometown.

AREZZO

63 km (39 mi) northeast of Siena, 81 km (50 mi) southeast of Florence.

GETTING HERE
Arezzo is easily reached by car from the A1 (Autostrada del Sole), the main highway running between Florence and Rome. Direct trains connect Arezzo with Rome (2½ hours) and Florence (1 hour). Direct bus service is available from Florence, but not from Rome.

VISITOR INFORMATION
Arezzo tourism office (⊠*Piazza della Repubblica 28* ☎*0575/377678* ⊕*www.apt.arezzo.it*).

EXPLORING
The birthplace of the poet Petrarch (1304–74) and the Renaissance artist and art historian Giorgio Vasari, Arezzo is today best known for the magnificent Piero della Francesca frescoes in the church of San Francesco. The city dates from pre-Etruscan times and thrived as an Etruscan capital from the 7th to the 4th century BC. During the Middle

Ages it was fully embroiled in the conflict between the Ghibellines (pro–Holy Roman Emperor) and the Guelphs (pro-pope), losing its independence to Florence at the end of the 14th century after many decades of doing battle.

Urban sprawl testifies to the fact that Arezzo (population 90,000) is the third-largest city in Tuscany (after Florence and Pisa). But the old town, set on a low hill, is relatively small, and almost completely closed to traffic. Look for parking along the roads that circle the lower part of town, near the train station, and walk into town from there. You can explore the most interesting sights in a few hours, adding time to linger for some window-shopping at Arezzo's many antiques shops.

> **WORD OF MOUTH**
>
> "Arezzo holds a huge antiques fair the first weekend of each month that takes over the streets in the historical center of town. You may want to check your dates, either to avoid or take advantage of it."
>
> –shellio

Fodor'sChoice The remarkable frescoes by Piero della Francesca (circa 1420–92) in ★ the **Basilica di San Francesco** were painted between 1452 and 1466. They depict scenes from the *Legend of the True Cross* on three walls of the *cappella maggiore*, or high altar choir. What Sir Kenneth Clark called "the most perfect morning light in all Renaissance painting" may be seen in the lowest section of the right wall, where the troops of the emperor Maxentius flee before the sign of the cross. A 15-year project restored the works to their original brilliance. Reservations are required to see the choir area with the frescoes. ⊠*Piazza San Francesco 6* ☎*0575/20630 church, 0575/352757 Capella Bacci reservations* ⊕*www.pierodellafrancesca.it* ✉*Church free, Capella Bacci* €*6* ☉*Church: daily 8:30–6:30. Capella Bacci: Apr.–Oct., weekdays 9–6:30, Sat. 9–5:30, Sun. 1–5:30; Nov.–Mar., weekdays 9–5:30, Sat. 9–5, Sun. 1–5.*

Some historians maintain that Arezzo's oddly shaped, sloping **Piazza Grande** was once the site of an ancient Roman forum. Now it hosts a first-Sunday-of-the-month antiques fair as well as the **Giostra del Saracino** (Joust of the Saracen), featuring medieval costumes and competition, held here in the middle of June and on the first Sunday of September. Check out the 16th-century loggia designed by native son Giorgio Vasari on the northeast side of the piazza.

The curving, tiered apse on Piazza Grande belongs to **Pieve di Santa Maria,** one of Tuscany's finest Romanesque churches, built in the 12th century. Don't miss the Portale Maggiore (great door) with its polychrome figures representing the months; restored in 2002, they are remarkably vibrant. ⊠*Corso Italia* ☎*0575/22629* ☉*May–Sept., daily 8–1 and 3–7; Oct.–Apr., daily 8–noon and 3–6.*

Arezzo's medieval **Duomo** (at the top of the hill) contains a fresco of a somber *Magdalen* by Piero della Francesca; look for it next to the large marble tomb near the organ. ⊠*Piazza del Duomo 1* ☎*0575/23991* ☉*Daily 6:30–12:30 and 3–6:30.*

WHERE TO STAY & EAT

$$–$$$ ✕**Antica Trattoria da Guido.** Owned by a southern Italian, this small trattoria serves tasty adaptations of Calabrian dishes, such as homemade pasta served with *salsa ai pomodori secchi* (a spicy sauce of sun-dried tomatoes, capers, and red peppers). The display of homemade pastries makes decisions difficult at the end of the meal. The dining room is a pleasant mix of rustic and modern, and the service is friendly. ⊠ *Via di San Francesco 1* ☎*0575/23271* ═*MC, V* ⊙*Closed Sun. and 2 wks in mid-Aug.*

$–$$ ✕**La Torre di Gnicche.** Wine lovers shouldn't miss this wine bar/eatery with more than 700 labels on the list, located just off Piazza Grande. Seasonal dishes of traditional fare, such as *acquacotta del casentino* (porcini mushroom soup) and *baccalà in umido* (salt-cod stew), are served in the simply decorated, vaulted dining room. You can accompany your meal with one, or more, of the almost 30 wines that are available by the glass. Limited outdoor seating is available in warm weather. ⊠*Piaggia San Martino 8* ☎*0575/352035* ═*AE, MC, V* ⊙*Closed Wed., Jan., and 2 wks in July.*

$$ ⊞**Cavaliere Palace Hotel.** On a quiet backstreet in the old town, the Cavaliere is moments away from the main sights. The carpeted rooms in the restored 19th-century town house are small but comfy, with contemporary furnishings. **Pros:** Location, location, location. **Cons:** Some complain of noise from nearby disco; very plain decor. ⊠ *Via Madonna del Prato 83, Arezzo,* ☎*0575/26836* 🖷*0575/21925* ⊕*www.cavaliere hotels.com* ⤷*27 rooms* ♿*In-room: refrigerator, Wi-Fi. In-hotel: public Wi-Fi, parking (fee)* ═*AE, D, MC, V* ◍*CP.*

$ ⊞**Calcione Country and Castle.** The elegant Marchesa Olivella Lotteringhi della Stufa has turned her six-centuries-old family estate (circa 1483) into a top-notch agriturismo. Think sophisticated rustic: many of the apartments have open fireplaces, and the stone houses have a private pool (the rest share the estate pool). Explore the grounds, which include olive groves, vineyards, and private lakes for fishing and windsurfing. "We hated leaving," says one user of fodors.com. To make up for the absence of room phones, mobile phones are made available to guests. From June to mid-September, a minimum one-week stay is mandatory. **Pros:** Houses can sleep up to 17; large swimming pools; quiet, beautiful, remote setting. **Cons:** Private transportation is a must: nearest village is 8 km (5 mi) away; some complain about insects in summer; no a/c. ⊠*Calcione, 26 km (15 mi) southwest of Arezzo, Lucignano* ☎*0575/837100* 🖷*0575/837153* ⊕*www.calcione. com* ⤷*2 houses, 1 cottage, 6 apartments* ♿*In-room: no a/c, no phone, kitchen, no TV (some). In-hotel: tennis court, pools, laundry facilities, some pets allowed* ═*No credit cards* ⊙*Closed Nov.–Mar.* ◍*EP.*

Fodor's Choice
★

SHOPPING

Ever since Etruscan goldsmiths set up their shops here more than 2,000 years ago, Arezzo has been famous for its jewelry. Today the town lays claim to being one of the world's capitals of jewelry design and manufacture, and you can find an impressive display of big-time baubles in the town center's shops. Arezzo is also famous, at least in Italy, for its antiques dealers.

CORTONA

29 km (18 mi) south of Arezzo, 79 km (44 mi) east of Siena, 117 km (73 mi) southeast of Florence.

GETTING HERE

Cortona is easily reached by car from the A1 (Autostrada del Sole): take the Valdichiana exit toward Perugia, then follow signs for Cortona. Regular bus service, provided by Etruria Mobilità, is available between Arezzo and Cortona (1 hour). Train service to Cortona is made inconvenient by the location of the train station, in the valley 3 km (1½ mi) steeply below the town itself. From there, you have to rely on bus or taxi service to get up to Cortona.

VISITOR INFORMATION

Cortona tourism office (✉ *Via Nazionale 42* ☎*0575/630352* ⊕*www. apt.arezzo.it*).

With olive trees and vineyards creeping up to its walls, pretty Cortona—popularized by Frances Mayes's *Under the Tuscan Sun*—commands sweeping views over Lake Trasimeno and the plain of the Valdichiana. Its two galleries and churches are rarely visited; its delightful medieval streets are a pleasure to wander for their own sake. The heart of town is formed by Piazza della Repubblica and the adjacent Piazza Signorelli; both contain pleasant shops to browse in.

The **Museo Diocesano** *(Diocesan Museum)* houses an impressive number of large and splendid paintings by native son Luca Signorelli, as well as a stunning *Annunciation* by Fra Angelico, a delightful surprise in this small town. ✉*Piazza Duomo* ☎*0575/62830* 💳*€5* ⊘*Tues.–Sun. 10–5.*

★ Legend has it that **Santa Maria del Calcinaio** was built between 1485 and 1513 after the image of the Madonna appeared on a wall of the medieval *calcinaio* (lime pit used for curing leather) that had occupied the site. The linear gray-and-white interior recalls Florence's Duomo. Sienese architect Francesco di Giorgio (1439–1502) most likely designed the sanctuary: the church is a terrific example of Renaissance architectural principles. ✉*Località Il Calcinaio 227* ✛ *3 km (2 mi) southeast of Cortona's center on Via Guelph* ☎*0575/604830* 💳*Free* ⊘*Mon.–Sat. 3:30–6, Sun. 10–12:30.*

WHERE TO STAY & EAT

$$ – $$$ ✕**Osteria del Teatro.** Photographs from theatrical productions spanning many years line the walls of this tavern off Cortona's large Piazza del Teatro. The food is simply delicious—try the *filetto al lardo di colonnata e prugne* (beef cooked with bacon and prunes); service is warm and friendly. ✉*Via Maffei 2* ☎*0575/630556* ▭*AE, DC, MC, V* ⊘*Closed Wed. and 2 wks in Nov. and in Feb.*

$$$$ ✕▦**Il Falconiere.** Choose here from rooms in an 18th-century villa,
★   suites in the *chiesetta* (chapel, or little church), or for more seclusion, Le Vigne del Falco suites at the far end of the property. Husband and wife team Riccardo and Silvia Baracchi run the show, serving an almost

exclusively American and British clientele. Their restaurant's ($$$$) inventive seasonal menu includes *pici alla carbonara con lo zafferano di Centoia e pancetta croccante* (homemade thick spaghetti with carbonara sauce), over which, if your heart desires, you can add shaved white truffles. Cooking

classes and guided wine tastings are available, and a small shop sells estate-produced olive oil and wine. **Pros:** Attractive setting, in the valley beneath Cortona; excellent service; elegant, but relaxed. **Cons:** A car is a must; some find rooms in main villa a little noisy; lacks full 24-hour service. ⊠ *Località San Martino 370* ✢ *3 km (1½ mi) north of Cortona,* ☎ *0575/612679* 🖷 *0575/612927* ⊕ *www.ilfalconiere.com* 🛏 *13 rooms, 7 suites* ♿ *In-room: safe, refrigerator, dial-up. In-hotel: restaurant, room service, bar, pools, concierge, laundry service, public Internet, parking (no fee), some pets allowed (fee)* ⊟ AE, MC, V ☉ *No lunch in restaurant Tues. Nov.–Mar. Hotel closed last 3 wks in Jan.–mid-Feb.* 🍽 BP.

HILL TOWNS WEST OF SIENA

Submit to the draw of Tuscany's enchanting fortified cities that crown the hills west of Siena, many dating to the Etruscan period. San Gimignano, known as the "medieval Manhattan" because of its forest of stout medieval towers built by rival families, is the most heavily visited. This onetime Roman outpost, with its tilted cobbled streets and ancient buildings, can make the days of Guelph-Ghibelline conflicts palpable. Rising from a series of bleak gullied hills and valleys, Volterra has always been popular for its minerals and stones, particularly alabaster, which was used by the Etruscans for many implements. Examples are now displayed in the exceptional and unwieldy Museo Etrusco Guarnacci.

VOLTERRA

48 km (30 mi) south of San Miniato, 75 km (47 mi) southwest of Florence.

GETTING HERE

By car, the best route from San Gimignano follows the SP1 south to Castel San Gimignano and then the SS68 all the way to Volterra. Coming from the west, take the SS1, a coastal road to Cecina, then follow the SS68 to Volterra. Either way, there's a long, winding climb at the end of your trip. Traveling to Volterra by bus or train is complicated; avoid it if possible, especially if you have lots of luggage. From Florence or Siena, the journey is best made by bus and involves a change in Colle di Val d'Elsa. From Rome or Pisa, it is best to take the train to Cecina and then take a bus to Volterra or a train to the Volterra-Saline station. The latter is 10 km (6 mi) from town.

VISITOR INFORMATION

Volterra tourism office (✉*Piazza dei Priori 20* ☎*0588/87257* ⊕*www. volterratur.it*).

EXPLORING

Unlike other Tuscan hill towns rising above sprawling vineyards and rolling fields of green, Volterra is surrounded by desolate terrain marred with industry and mining equipment. D.H. Lawrence described it as "somber and chilly alone on her rock" in his *Etruscan Places*. The fortress, walls, and gates still stand mightily over Le Balze, a distinctive series of gullied hills and valleys to the west that were formed by irregular erosion. The town has long been known for its alabaster, which has been mined since Etruscan times; today the Volterrans use it to make ornaments and souvenirs sold all over town. An €8 combined ticket is your only option for visiting the Museo Etrusco Guarnacci and the Pinacoteca e Museo Civico.

Volterra has some of Italy's best small museums. The extraordinarily large and unique collection of Etruscan artifacts at the **Museo Etrusco Guarnacci** is a treasure in the region. (Many of the other Etruscan finds from the area have been shipped off to state museums or the Vatican.) If only a curator had thought to cull the best of the 700 funerary urns rather than to display every last one of them. ✉*Via Don Minzoni 15* ☎*0588/86347* ⊕*www.comune.volterra.pi.it* ✇*€8, includes admission to Museo Diocesano di Arte Sacra and Pinoteca* ⊗*Mid-Mar.–early Nov., daily 9–6:45; early Nov.–mid-Mar., daily 9–1:15.*

The **Pinacoteca e Museo Civico** houses a highly acclaimed collection of religious art, including a *Madonna and Child with Saints* by Luca Signorelli (1445/50–1523) and a *Deposition* by Rosso Fiorentino (1494–1541) that is reason enough to visit Volterra. ✉*Via dei Sarti 1* ✉*Via dei Sarti 1* ☎*0588/87580* ⊕*www.comune.volterra.pi.it* ✇*€8, includes admission to Museo Etrusco Guarnacci and Museo Diocesano di Arte Sacra* ⊗*Mid-Mar.–early Nov., daily 9–7; early Nov.–mid-Mar., daily 9–1:45.*

Next to the altar in the town's unfinished **Duomo** is a magnificent 13th-century carved-wood *Deposition*. Note the fresco by Benozzo Gozzoli in the Cappella della Addolorata. Along the left wall of the nave you can see the arrival of the Magi. ✉*Piazza San Giovanni* ☎*0588/86192* ✇*Free* ⊗*Daily 7–7.*

Among Volterra's best-preserved ancient remains is the Etruscan **Porta all'Arco,** an arch dating from the 4th century BC now incorporated into the city walls.

The ruins of the 1st-century BC **Teatro Romano,** a beautifully preserved Roman theater, are worth a visit. Adjacent to the theater are the remains of the **terme** (baths). The complex is outside the town walls past Porta Fiorentina. ✉*Viale Francesco Ferrucci* ☎*0586/260837* ✇*€2* ⊗*Mar.–May and Sept.–Nov., daily 10–1 and 2–4; June–Aug., daily 10–6:45; Dec.–Feb., weekends 10–1 and 2–4.*

WHERE TO STAY & EAT

$–$$$ ✕**Il Sacco Fiorentino.** Start with the *antipasti del Sacco Fiorentino*—a
★ medley of sautéed chicken liver, porcini mushrooms, and polenta driz-
zled with balsamic vinegar. The meal just gets better when you move on
to the *tagliatelle del Sacco Fiorentino*, a riot of curried spaghetti with
chicken and roasted red peppers. The wine list is a marvel, as it's long
and very well priced. White walls, tile floors, and red tablecloths create
an understated tone that is unremarkable, but once the food starts arriv-
ing, it's easy to forgive the lack of decoration. ✉*Piazza XX Settembre
1856048* ☎*0588/88537* ▭*AF, DC, MC, V* ☾*Closed Wed.*

$ ▥**San Lino.** Within the town's medieval walls, this convent-turned-hotel
has wood-beam ceilings, graceful archways, and terra-cotta floors in
public spaces. The furnishings are contemporary wood laminate and
straight-line ironwork. Sip a beverage or write a postcard on the small
terrace filled with potted geraniums; the pool area is framed on one
side by a church with a stained-glass window of the Last Supper. The
restaurant ($–$$) serves Tuscan classics and local specialties such as
zuppa alla volterrana, a thick vegetable soup. Half board is available.
Pros: Steps away from center of town; friendly and helpful staff; convenient parking. **Cons:** A little run-down; elevators are noisy; breakfast is adequate, but nothing to write home about. ✉*Via San Lino
26,* ☎*0588/85250* 🖷*0588/80620* ⊕*www.hotelsanlino.com* ⇥*43*

rooms &*In-room: refrigerator, dial-up. In-hotel: restaurant, bar, pool, concierge, laundry service, public Internet, parking (fee), some pets allowed* ⊟*AE, DC, MC, V* ⊗*Closed Nov.–Jan.* †Ⓞ*BP.*

SAN GIMIGNANO

27 km (17 mi) east of Volterra, 57 km (35 mi) southwest of Florence.

GETTING HERE

You can reach San Gimignano by car from the Florence–Siena Superstrada. Exit at Poggibonsi Nord and follow signs for San Gimignano. Although it involves changing buses in Poggibonsi, getting to San Gimignano by bus is a relatively straightforward affair. SITA operates the service between Siena or Florence and Poggibonsi, while Tra-In takes care of the Poggibonsi to San Gimignano route. You cannot reach San Gimignano by train.

VISITOR INFORMATION

San Gimignano tourism office (⊠*Piazza Duomo 1* ☎*0577/940008* ⊕*www. sangimignano.com*).

EXPLORING

When you're on a hilltop surrounded by soaring medieval towers silhouetted against the sky, it's difficult not to fall under the spell of San Gimignano. Its tall walls and narrow streets are typical of Tuscan hill towns, but it's the medieval "skyscrapers" that set the town apart from its neighbors. Today 14 towers remain, but at the height of the Guelph–Ghibelline conflict there was a forest of more than 70, and it was possible to cross the town by rooftop rather than by road. The towers were built partly for defensive purposes—they were a safe refuge and useful for pouring boiling oil on attacking enemies—and partly for bolstering the egos of their owners, who competed with deadly seriousness to build the highest tower in town.

Today San Gimignano isn't much more than a gentrified walled city, touristy but still very much worth exploring because, despite the profusion of cheesy souvenir shops lining the main drag, there's some serious Renaissance art to be seen here. Tour groups arrive early and clog the wine-tasting rooms—San Gimignano is famous for its light white Vernaccia—and art galleries for much of the day, but most sights stay open through late afternoon, when all the tour groups have long since departed.

The town's main church is not officially a *duomo* (cathedral) because San Gimignano has no bishop. Behind the simple facade of the Romanesque **Collegiata** lies a treasure trove of fine frescoes, covering nearly every part of the interior. Bartolo di Fredi's 14th-century fresco cycle of Old Testament scenes extends along one wall. Their distinctly medieval feel, with misshapen bodies, buckets of spurting blood, and lack of perspective, contrasts with the much more reserved scenes from the *Life of Christ* (attributed to 14th-century artist Lippo Memmi), painted on the opposite wall just 14 years later. Taddeo di Bartolo's other-worldly *Last Judgment* (late 14th century), with its distorted and suffering nudes, reveals the great influence of Dante's horrifying imagery in *The Inferno* and was surely an inspiration for later painters. Proof that the town had more than one protector, Benozzo Gozzoli's arrow-riddled *St. Sebastian* was commissioned in gratitude after

the locals prayed to the saint for relief from plague. The Renaissance **Cappella di Santa Fina** is decorated with a fresco cycle by Domenico Ghirlandaio illustrating the life of Saint Fina. A small girl who suffered from a terminal disease, Fina repented for her sins—among them having accepted an orange from a boy—and in penance lived out the rest of her short life on a wooden board, tormented by rats. The scenes depict the arrival of Saint Gregory, who appeared to assure her that death was near; the flowers that miraculously grew from the wooden plank; and the miracles that accompanied her funeral, including the healing of her nurse's paralyzed hand and the restoration of a blind choirboy's vision. ⊠*Piazza Duomo* ☎*0577/940316* 💳*€3.50; €5.50 includes the Museo d'Arte Sacra* ⊙*Apr.–Oct., weekdays 9:30–7:10, Sat. 9:30–5:10, Sun. 12:30–5:10; Nov. 1–15, Dec. 1–Jan. 15, and Feb. 1–Mar., Mon.–Sat. 9:30–4:40, Sun. 12:30–5:10. Closed Nov. 16–30 and Jan. 16–31.*

★ The impressive **Museo Civico** occupies what was the "new" Palazzo del Popolo; the Torre Grossa is adjacent. Dante visited San Gimignano for only one day as a Guelph ambassador from Florence to ask the locals to join the Florentines in supporting the pope—just long enough to get the main council chamber, which now holds a 14th-century *Maestà* by Lippo Memmi, named after him. Off the stairway is a small room containing the racy frescoes by Memmo di Filippuccio (active 1288–1324) depicting the courtship, shared bath, and wedding of a young, androgynous-looking couple. That the space could have been a private room for the commune's chief magistrate may have something to do with the work's highly charged eroticism.

Upstairs, paintings by famous Renaissance artists Pinturicchio (*Madonna Enthroned*), Benozzo Gozzoli (*Madonna and Child*), and two large *tondi* (circular paintings) by Filippino Lippi (circa 1457–1504) attest to the importance and wealth of San Gimignano. Also worth seeing are Taddeo di Bartolo's *Life of San Gimignano,* with the saint holding a model of the town as it once appeared; Lorenzo di Niccolò's gruesome martyrdom scene in the *Life of St. Bartholomew* (1401); and scenes from the *Life of St. Fina* on a tabernacle that was designed to hold her head. Admission includes the steep climb to the top of the Torre Grossa, which on a clear day has spectacular views. ⊠*Piazza Duomo* ☎*0577/990312* 💳*€5* ⊙*Mar.–Oct., daily 9:30–7; Nov.–Feb., daily 10–5:30.*

There's no shortage of places to try Vernaccia di San Gimignano, the justifiably famous white wine with which San Gimignano would be singularly associated—if it weren't for all those towers. At **Enoteca Gustavo** (✉ *Via San Matteo 29* ☎*0577/940057*) you can buy a glass of Vernaccia di San Gimignano and sit down with a cheese plate or with one of the fine crostini served up in this tiny wine bar.

★ Make a beeline for Benozzo Gozzoli's superlative frescoes inside the church of **Sant'Agostino.** This Romanesque–Gothic church contains Benozzo's stunning 15th-century fresco cycle depicting scenes from the life of Saint Augustine. The saint's work was essential to the early development of church doctrine. As thoroughly discussed in his autobiographical *Confessions* (an acute dialogue with God), Augustine, like many saints, sinned considerably in his youth before finding God. But unlike the lives of other saints, where the story continues through a litany of deprivations, penitence, and often martyrdom, Augustine's life and work focused on philosophy and the reconciliation of faith and thought. Benozzo's 17 scenes on the choir wall depict Augustine as a man who traveled and taught extensively in the fourth and fifth centuries. The 15th-century altarpiece by Piero del Pollaiolo (1443–96) depicts *The Coronation of the Virgin* and the various protectors of the city. On your way out of Sant'Agostino, stop in at the **Cappella di San Bartolo,** with a sumptuously elaborate tomb by Benedetto da Maiano (1442–97). ✉*Piazza Sant'Agostino, off Via San Matteo* ☎*0577/907012* ✍*Free* ☉*Apr.–Oct., daily 7–noon and 3–7; Nov. and Dec. and Mar., daily 7–noon and 3–6; Jan. and Feb., Mon. 3–6, Tues. –Sun. 10–noon and 3–6.*

WHERE TO STAY & EAT

The **Cooperativa Hotels Promotion** (✉ *Via di San Giovanni 125* ☎*0577/ 940809* ⊕*www.hotelsiena.com*) provides commission-free booking for local hotels and farmhouses.

$–$$ ✕**La Mangiatoia.** Multicolor gingham tablecloths provide an interesting juxtaposition with rib-vaulted ceilings dating from the 13th century. The lighthearted touch might be explained by the influence of chef Susi Cuomo, who has been presiding over the kitchen for more than 20 years. The menu is seasonal—in autumn, don't miss her *sacottino di pecorino al tartufo* (little packages of pasta stuffed with pecorino and seasoned with truffles). In summer eat lighter fare on the intimate, flower-bedecked terrace in the back. ✉*Via Mainardi 5, off Via San Matteo,* ☎*0577/941528* ▬*MC, V* ☉*Closed Tues., 3 wks in Nov., and 1 wk in Jan.*

$–$$ ⌂**Pescille.** A rambling farmhouse has been transformed into a handsome hotel with understated contemporary furniture in the bedrooms and country-classic motifs such as farm implements hanging on the walls in the bar. From this charming spot you get a splendid view of San Gimignano's towers. **Pros:** Splendid views; quiet atmosphere; 10-minute walk to town. **Cons:** Furnishings a bit austere; there's an elevator for luggage but not for guests. ✉*Strada Provinciale Castel San Gimignano, Località Pescille* ⊹*4 km (2½ mi) south of San Gimignano town center,* ☎*0577/940186* ⊕*www.pescille.it* ↩*38 rooms, 12 suites*

&In-room: refrigerator, Wi-Fi. In-hotel: bar, tennis court, pool, gym, no elevator, public Internet, public Wi-Fi, parking (no fee) ⊟AE, DC, MC, V ⊗Closed Nov.–Mar. ⦿BP.

COLLE DI VAL D'ELSA

15 km (9 mi) southeast of San Gimignano, 50 km (31 mi) southwest of Florence.

GETTING HERE

You can reach Colle di Val d'Elsa by car on either the SR2 from Siena or the Florence–Siena Superstrada. Bus service to and from Siena and Florence is frequent.

VISITOR INFORMATION

Colle di Val d'Elsa (⊠ Via Campana 43 ☎0577/922791).

EXPLORING

Most people pass through on their way to and from popular tourist destinations Volterra and San Gimignano—a shame, since Colle di Val d'Elsa has a lot to offer. It's another town on the Via Francigena that benefited from trade along the pilgrimage route to Rome. Colle got an extra boost in the late 16th century when it was given a bishopric, probably related to an increase in trade when nearby San Gimignano was cut off from the well-traveled road. The town is arranged on two levels, and from the 12th century onward the flat lower portion was given over to a flourishing paper-making industry; today the area is mostly modern, and efforts have shifted toward the production of fine glass and crystal.

WHERE TO STAY & EAT

$$$$ ╳**Ristorante Arnolfo.** Food lovers should not miss Arnolfo, one of Tus-
Fodor'sChoice cany's most highly regarded restaurants. Chef Gaetano Trovato sets
★ high standards of creativity; his dishes daringly ride the line between innovation and tradition, almost always with spectacular results. The menu changes frequently and has a fixed-price option, but you are always sure to find fish and lots of fresh vegetables in the summer. You're in for a special treat if the specials include *carrè di agnello al vino rosso e sella alle olive* (rack of lamb in a red wine sauce and lamb saddle with olives). ⊠Piazza XX Settembre 52, 53034 ☎0577/920549 ⊟AE, DC, MC, V ⊗Closed Tues. and Wed., last wk in Jan.–Feb., and last wk in Aug.

$$$$ 🏨**La Suvera.** Pope Julius II once owned this luxurious estate in the
★ valley of the River Elsa. The papal villa and an adjacent building have magnificently furnished guest rooms and suites appointed with antiques. A wall-size tapestry depicting the Roman army hangs beside a red canopy bed in the Angels Room. La Suvera's first-rate facilities include drawing rooms, a library, an Italian garden, a park, and the Oliviera restaurant (serving organic estate wines). **Pros:** Luxurious accommodations; historic setting; far from the madding crowd. **Cons:** Out-of-the-way location; showing its age; some bristle at the extremely formal service. ⊠Off SS541 ✛ 15 km (9 mi) south of Colle di Val

d'Elsa, Pievescola ☎*0577/960300* ⊕*www.lasuvera.it* ⌖*36 rooms,*
12 suites ⅏*In-room: safe, refrigerator. In-hotel: restaurant, room ser-*
vice, bar, tennis court, pool, bicycles, concierge, laundry service, public
Internet, no kids under 12 ▭*AE, DC, MC, V* ⊘*Closed Nov.–Easter*
⃝*BP.*

CHIANTI

Chianti, directly south of Florence, is one of Italy's most famous
wine-producing areas; its hill towns, olive groves, and vineyards
are quintessential Tuscany. Many British and northern Europeans
have relocated here, drawn by the unhurried life, balmy climate, and
charming villages; there are so many Britons, in fact, that the area
has been nicknamed Chiantishire. Still, it remains strongly Tuscan
in character, with drop-dead views of vine-quilted hills and elegantly
elongated cypress trees.

The sinuous SS222 highway, known as the Strada Chiantigiana, runs
from Florence through the heart of Chianti. Its most scenic section connects Strada in Chianti, 16 km (10 mi) south of Florence, and Greve in
Chianti, whose triangular central piazza is surrounded by restaurants
and vintners offering *degustazioni* (wine tastings), 11 km (7 mi) farther south.

GREVE IN CHIANTI

40 km (25 mi) northeast of Colle Val d'Elsa, 27 km (17 mi) south of
Florence.

GETTING HERE
Driving from Florence or Siena, Greve is easily reached via the Strada
Chiantigiana (SR222). SITA buses travel frequently between Florence
and Greve. Tra-In and SITA buses connect Siena and Greve, but a direct
trip is virtually impossible. There is no train service to Greve.

VISITOR INFORMATION
Greve in Chianti tourism offices (✉*Via Giovanni da Verrazzano*
59 ☎*055/8546287* ✉*Via Giovanni da Verrazzano 33* ☎*055/*
8546299).

EXPLORING
If there's a capital of Chianti, it's Greve, a friendly market town with
no shortage of cafés, *enoteche* (wine bars), and craft shops lining its
main square.

The gently sloping, asymmetrical **Piazza Matteotti** is an attractive arcade
whose center holds a statue of the discoverer of New York harbor,
Giovanni da Verrazano (circa 1480–1527). Check out the lively market
held here on Saturday morning.

The church of **Santa Croce** has a triptych by Bicci di Lorenzo (1373–
1452) and an *Annunciation* painted by an anonymous Florentine mas-

ter that dates from the 14th century. ⊠*Small end of Piazza Matteotti* ☎*No phone* 🅿*Free* ⊙*Daily 9–1 and 3–7.*

About 2 km (1 mi) west of Greve in Chianti is the tiny hilltop hamlet of **Montefioralle.** This is the ancestral home of Amerigo Vespucci (1454–1512), the mapmaker, navigator, and explorer who named America. (His niece Simonetta may have been the inspiration for Sandro Botticelli's *Birth of Venus*, painted sometime in the 1480s.)

WHERE TO STAY & EAT

★ $$$$ ✕**Osteria di Passignano.** Sophisticated country dining may not get better than at this deceptively simple restaurant next to a Vallombrosan abbey. A tiny sampling (maybe *sformatino di pecorino di fosso*, a flan made with aged pecorino) whets the appetite for what's to come. The young chefs in the kitchen can do traditional as well as whimsical Tuscan—and then divine things such as the *maccheroni del Martelli al ragù bianco di agnelli e carciofi morellini* (tubular pasta with a lamb and artichoke sauce), which really isn't Tuscan at all. The wine list is unbeatable, as is the service. ⊠*Via Passignano 33, Località Badia a Passignano* ✛*15 km (9 mi) east of Greve in Chianti* ☎*055/8071278* ▭*AE, DC, MC, V* ⊙*Closed Sun., Jan. 7–Feb. 1, and 15 days in Aug.*

★ $$–$$$ ✕**Ristoro di Lamole.** Although off the beaten path (in this case, the SS222), this place is worth the effort to find—up a winding hill road lined with olive trees and vineyards. The view from the outdoor terrace is divine, as is the simple, exquisitely prepared Tuscan cuisine. Start with the bruschetta drizzled with olive oil or the sublime *verdure sott'olio* (vegetables marinated in oil) before moving on to any of the fine secondi. The kitchen has a way with *coniglio* (rabbit); don't pass it up if it's on the menu. ⊠*Off SS222, Lamole in Chianti* ☎*055/8547050* ▭*AE, DC, MC, V* ⊙*Closed Jan. 6–Feb. 28.*

★ $ ✕**Enoteca Fuoripiazza.** Detour off Greve's flower-strewn main square for food that relies heavily on local ingredients (especially those produced by nearby makers of cheese and salami). The lengthy wine list provides a bewildering array of choices to pair with *affettati misti* (a plate of cured meats) or one of their primi—the *pici* (a thick, short noodle) is deftly prepared here. All the dishes are made with great care. ⊠*Via I Maggio 2, Piazza Trenta* ☎*055/8546313* ▭*AE, DC, MC, V* ⊙*Closed Mon.*

$$$$
Fodor'sChoice
★

🏨**Villa Bordoni.** David and Catherine Gardner, Scottish expats, have transformed a ramshackle 16th-century villa into a stunning little hotel nestled in the hills above Greve. Much care has been taken in decorating the rooms, no two of which are alike. All have stenciled walls; some have four-poster beds, others small mezzanines. Bathrooms are a riot of color, with tiles from Vietri. A sitting room on the second floor, with a cozy fireplace, is the perfect place for a cup of tea or a glass of wine. The hotel's restaurant has a talented young chef who gives cooking lessons in the modern kitchen. **Pros:** Splendidly isolated; beautiful decor; wonderful hosts. **Cons:** On a long and bumpy dirt road; need a car to get around. ⊠*Via San Cresci 31/32, Località Mezzuola, 50022* ☎*055/8547453* ⊕*www.villabordoni.com* 🛏*8 rooms, 3 suites* ♿*In-room: safe, dial-up, Wi-Fi. In-hotel: restaurant, pool, bicycles,* *laundry service, public Wi-Fi, parking (no fee)* 🖹 *AE, DC, MC, V* ⊘*Closed 3 wks in Jan. and Feb.* ⦿*BP.*

$$ 🏨**Villa Vignamaggio.** Reputed to be the birthplace of the woman made famous by Leonardo da Vinci's *Mona Lisa*, the Villa Vignamaggio has origins in the 14th century. This historic estate, which includes the main building and two small cottages, is surrounded by manicured classical Italian gardens. Some rooms have exposed beams, whereas others have the genuine ancient plaster walls that faux-paint treatments attempt to replicate. The villa also produces some very fine wines; ask about tastings at the reception desk. Fodors.com users report that the villa is in a "good location for day trips in northern Tuscany." A minimum stay of two nights is required. **Pros:** Unbeatable views; informative wine tastings. **Cons:** No elevator to third floor; the staff seems less than attentive. ✉*Via Petriolo 5, Località Vicchiomaggio 50022* ☎*055/854661* ⊕*www.vignamaggio.com* 🛏*3 rooms, 4 suites, 13 apartments, 2 cottages* ⚟*In-room: kitchen (some). In-hotel: tennis court, pools, no elevator, laundry service, public Internet, some pets allowed* 🖹*AE, DC, MC, V* ⊘*Closed mid-Nov.–mid-Mar.* ⦿*BP.*

$ 🏨**Albergo del Chianti.** At a corner of the Piazza Matteotti, the Albergo del Chianti has rooms with views of the square or out over the tile rooftops toward the surrounding hills. Plain modern cabinets and wardrobes stand near wrought-iron beds. The swimming pool, sunny terrace, and grassy lawn behind the hotel are a nice surprise. **Pros:** Central location; best value in Greve. **Cons:** Rooms facing the piazza can be noisy; lobby is run-down; small bathrooms. ✉*Piazza Matteotti 86,* ☎*055/853763* ⊕*www.albergodelchianti.it* 🛏*16 rooms* ⚟*In-room: refrigerator. In-hotel: restaurant, bar, pool, public Wi-Fi* 🖹*MC, V* ⊘*Closed Jan.* ⦿*BP.*

PANZANO

⑲ *7 km (4½ mi) south of Greve, 29 km (18 mi) south of Florence.*

GETTING HERE
From Florence or Siena, Panzano is easily reached by car along the Strada Chiantigiana (SR222). SITA buses travel frequently between Florence and Panzano. From Siena, the journey by bus is extremely difficult because SITA and Tra-In do not coordinate their schedules. There is no train service to Panzano.

EXPLORING
The little town of Panzano, between Greve in Chianti and Castellina in Chianti, has inviting shops, and enoteche offering tastes of the local wine.

An ancient church even by Chianti standards, the hilltop **San Leolino** probably dates from the 10th century, but it was completely rebuilt in the Romanesque style sometime in the 13th century. It has a 14th-century cloister worth seeing. The 16th-century terra-cotta tabernacles are attributed to Giovanni della Robbia, and there's also a remarkable triptych (attributed to the Master of Panzano) that was executed sometime in the mid-14th century. Open days and hours are unpredictable; check with the tourist office in Greve in Chianti for the latest. ✛*3 km (2 mi) south of Panzano, Località San Leolino* ☎*No phone* ☞*Free.*

WHERE TO STAY & EAT

$$ ✗**Solociccia.** "Abandon all hope, ye who enter here," announces the menu, "you're in the hands of a butcher." Indeed you are, for this restaurant is the creation of Dario Cecchini, Panzano's local merchant of meat. Served at communal tables, the set meal consists of no less than six meat courses, chosen at Dario's discretion. They are accompanied by seasonal vegetables, white beans with olive oil, and focaccia bread. Though Cecchini emphasizes that steak is never on the menu, this lively, crowded place is definitely not for vegetarians. The entrance is on Via XX Luglio. ⊠*Via Chiantigiana 550022* ☎*055/852727* ✍*Reservations essential* ⊟*AE, DC, MC, V* ⊘*Closed Mon.–Wed. No dinner Sun.*

$$$$
Fodor's Choice
★
📷**Villa Le Barone.** Once the home of the Viviani della Robbia family, this 16th-century villa in a grove of ancient cypress trees retains many aspects of a private country dwelling. It feels like a "second home," according to some fodors.com users. The honor bar allows you to enjoy an *aperitivo* on the terrace while admiring the views of the pool to the rose gardens, across the hills to the town. Guest rooms have white-plaster walls, timber ceilings, and some tile floors. The restaurant uses fresh produce from the owner's farm in western Tuscany. Though the hotel staff may recommend it, the full, three-meal plan is not mandatory. **Pros:** Beautiful location; wonderful restaurant; great base for exploring the region. **Cons:** Noisy a/c; 20-minute walk to nearest town. ⊠*Via San Leolino 19,* ☎*055/852621* ⊕*www.villalebarone.it* ⟿*30 rooms* ⌂*In-room: no a/c (some), no TV. In-hotel: restaurant, bar, tennis court, pool, no elevator, concierge, laundry service, public Internet* ⊟*AE, MC, V* ⊘*Closed Nov.–Easter* ⏹*BP.*

RADDA IN CHIANTI

26 km (15 mi) south of Panzano, 52 km (32 mi) south of Florence.

GETTING HERE

Radda can be reached by car from either Siena or Florence along the SR222 (Strada Chiantigiana), and from the A1 highway. Three Tra-In buses make their way from Siena to Radda. One morning SITA bus travels from Florence to Radda. There is no train service convenient to Radda.

VISITOR INFORMATION

Radda in Chianti tourism office (⊠*Piazza Ferrucci 1* ☎*0577/738494*).

EXPLORING

Radda in Chianti sits on a hill separating two valleys, Val di Pesa and Val d'Arbia. It's one of many tiny Chianti villages that invite you to stroll their steep streets; follow the signs pointing you toward the *camminamento,* a covered medieval passageway circling part of the city inside the walls.

Continued on page 207

GRAPE ESCAPES
THE PLEASURES OF TUSCAN WINE

The vineyards stretching across the landscape of Tuscany may look like cinematic backdrops, but in fact they're working farms, and they produce some of Italy's best wines. No matter whether you're a wine novice or a connoisseur, there's great pleasure to be had from exploring this lush terrain, visiting the vineyards, and uncorking a bottle for yourself.

GETTING TO KNOW TUSCAN WINE

Most of the wine produced in Tuscany is red (though there are some notable whites as well), and most Tuscan reds are made primarily from one type of grape, sangiovese. That doesn't mean, however, that all wines here are the same. God (in this case Bacchus) is in the details: differences in climate, soil, and methods of production result in wines with several distinct personalities.

Chianti

Chianti is the most famous name in Tuscan wine, but what exactly the name means is a little tricky. It once identified wines produced in the region extending from just south of Florence to just north of Siena. In the mid-20th century, the official Chianti zone was expanded to include a large portion of central Tuscany. That area is divided into eight subregions. **Chianti Classico** is the name given to the original zone, which makes up 17,000 of the 42,000 acres of Chianti-producing vineyards.

Classico wines, which bear the *gallo nero* (black rooster) logo on their labels, are the most highly regarded Chiantis (with **Rùfina** running second), but that doesn't mean Classicos are always superior. All Chiantis are strictly regulated (they must be a minimum 75% to 80% sangiovese, with other varieties blended in to add nuance), and they share a strong, woodsy character that's well suited to Tuscan food. It's a good strategy to drink the local product—**Colli Senesi Chianti** when in Siena, for example. The most noticeable, and costly, difference comes when a Chianti is from *riserva* (reserve) stock, meaning it's been aged for at least two years.

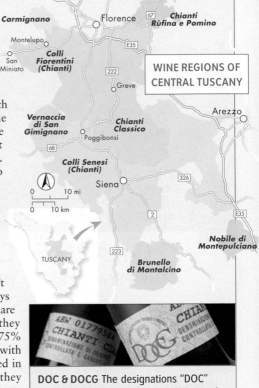

WINE REGIONS OF CENTRAL TUSCANY

DOC & DOCG The designations "DOC" and "DOCG"—Denominazione di Origine Controllata (e Garantita)—mean a wine comes from an established region and adheres to rigorous standards of production. Ironically, the esteemed Super Tuscans are labeled *vini da tavola* (table wines), the least prestigious designation, because they don't use traditional grape blends.

Brunello di Montalcino

The area surrounding the hill town of Montalcino, to the south of Siena, is drier and warmer than the Chianti regions, and it produces the most powerful of the sangiovese-based wines. Regulations stipulate that Brunello di Montalcino be made entirely from sangiovese grapes (no blending) and aged at least four years. **Rosso di Montalcino** is a younger, less complex, less expensive Brunello.

The Super Tuscans

Beginning in the 1970s, some winemakers, chafing at the regulations imposed on established Tuscan wine varieties, began blending and aging wines in innovative ways. Thus were born the so-called Super Tuscans. These pricey, French oak–aged wines are admired for their high quality, led by such star performers as **Sassicaia**, from the Maremma region, and **Tignanello**, produced at the Tenuta Marchesi Antinori near Badia a Passignano. Purists, however, lament the loss of local identity resulting from the Super Tuscans' use of nonnative grape varieties such as cabernet sauvignon and merlot.

Vino Nobile di Montepulciano

East of Montalcino is Montepulciano, the town at the heart of the third, and smallest, of Tuscany's top wine districts.

Blending regulations aren't as strict for Vino Nobile as for Chianti and Brunello, and as a result it has a wider range of characteristics. Broadly speaking, though, Vino Nobile is a cross between Chianti and Brunello—less acidic than the former and softer than the latter. It also has a less pricey sibling, **Rosso di Montepulciano**.

The Whites

Most whites from Tuscany are made from **trebbiano** grapes, which produce a wine that's light and refreshing but not particularly aromatic or flavorful—it may hit the spot on a hot afternoon, but it doesn't excite connoisseurs.

Golden-hewed **Vernaccia di San Gimignano** is a local variety with more limited production but greater personality—it's the star of Tuscan whites. Winemakers have also brought chardonnay and sauvignon grapes to the region, resulting in wines that, like some Super Tuscans, are pleasant to drink but short on local character.

TOURING & TASTING IN TUSCAN WINE COUNTRY

Strade del Vino di Toscana

Tuscany has visitor-friendly wineries, but the way you go about visiting is a bit different here from what it is in California or France. Many wineries welcome drop-ins for a tasting, but for a tour you usually need to make an appointment a few days in advance. There are several approaches you can take, depending on how much time you have and how serious you are about wine:

PLAN 1: FULL IMMERSION. Make an appointment to tour one of the top wineries (see our recommendations on the next page), and you'll get the complete experience: half a day of strolling through vineyards, talking grape varieties, and tasting wine, often accompanied by food. Groups are small; in spring and fall, it may be just you and the winemaker. The cost is usually €10 to €15 per person, but can go up to €40 if a meal is included. Remember to specify a tour in English.

PLAN 2: SEMI-ORGANIZED. If you want to spend a few hours going from vineyard to vineyard, make your first stop one of the local tourist information offices—they're great resources for maps, tasting itineraries, and personalized advice about where to visit. The offices in **Greve**, **Montalcino**, and **Montepulciano** are the best equipped. **Enoteche** (for more about them, turn the page) can also be good places to pick up tips about where to go for tastings.

PLAN 3: SPONTANEOUS. Along Tuscany's country roads you'll see signs for wineries offering **vendita diretta** (direct sales) and **degustazioni** (tastings). For a taste of the local product with some atmosphere thrown in, a spontaneous visit is a perfectly viable approach. You may wind up in a simple shop or an elaborate tasting room; either way, there's a fair chance you'll sample something good. Expect a small fee for a three-glass tasting.

THE PICK OF THE VINEYARDS

Within the Chianti Classico region, these wineries should be at the top of your to-visit list, whether you're dropping in for a taste or making a full tour. (Tours require reservations unless otherwise indicated.)

CHIANTI CLASSICO

Badia a Coltibuono

(✉ Gaiole in Chianti ☎ 0577/749498 ⊕ www.coltibuono. com). Along with an extensive prelunch tour and tasting, there are shorter afternoon tours, no reservation required, starting on the hour from 2 to 5. (See "Gaiole in Chianti" in this chapter.)

Castello di Fonterutoli

(✉ Castellina in Chianti ☎ 0577/73571 ⊕ www. fonterutoli.it). Hour-long tours include a walk through the neighboring village.

Castello di Volpaia

(✉ Radda in Chianti ☎ 0577/738066 ⊕ www. volpaia.com). The castle is part of the tiny town of Volpaia, perched above Radda.

Castello di Verrazzano

(✉ Via S. Martino in Valle 12, Greve in Chianti ☎ 055/854243 ⊕ www. verrazzano.com). Tours here take you down to the cellars, through the gardens, and into the woods in search of wild boar.

Villa Vignamaggio

(✉ Via Petriolo 5, Greve in Chianti ☎ 055/854661 ⊕ www. vignamaggio.com). Along with a wine tour, you can spend the night at this villa where Mona Lisa is believed to have been born. (See "Where to Stay" under "Greve in Chianti" in this chapter.)

Rocca delle Màcie

(✉ Località Le Màcie 45, Castellina in Chianti ☎ 0577/732236 ⊕ www.rocca dellemacie.com). A full lunch or dinner can be incorporated into your tasting here.

Castello di Brolio

(✉ Gaiole in Chianti ☎ 0577/730220 ⊕ www.ricasoli.it). One of Tuscany's most impressive castles also has a centuries-old winemaking tradition. (See "Gaiole in Chianti" in this chapter.)

REMEMBER ⚠

Always have a designated driver when you're touring and tasting. Vineyards are usually located off narrow, curving roads. Full sobriety is a must behind the wheel.

MORE TUSCAN WINE RESOURCES

Enoteche: Wine Shops

The word *enoteca* in Italian can mean "wine store," "wine bar," or both. In any event, *enoteche* (the plural, pronounced "ay-no-*tek*-ay") are excellent places to sample and buy Tuscan wines, and they're also good sources of information about local wineries. There are scores to choose from. These are a few of the best:

Enoteca Italiana, Siena (Fortezza Medicea, Viale Maccari ☎ 0577/288497 ⊕ www. enoteca-italiana.it). The only one of its kind, this *enoteca* represents all the producers of DOC and DOCG wines in Italy and stocks over 400 labels. Wine by the glass and snacks are available.

Enoteca Osticcio, Montalcino (✉ Via Matteotti 23 ☎ 0577/848271 ⊕ www. osticcio.com). There are more than one thousand labels in stock. With one of the best views in Montalcino, it is also a very pleasant place to sit and meditate over a glass of Brunello.

Enoteca del Gallo Nero, Greve in Chianti (✉ Piazzetta S. Croce 8 ☎ 055/853297). This is one of the best stocked *enoteche* in the Chianti region.

Palazzo Avignonesi, Montepulciano (Via di Gracciano nel Corso 91 ☎ 0578/757872). The streets of Montepulciano are lined with *enoteche*, but these 12th-century cellars of the Avignonesi winery merit special mention.

Wine on the Web

Tuscan wine country is well represented on the Internet. A good place for an overview is ⊕ www.terreditoscana.regione.-toscana.it. (Click on "Le Strade del Vino"; the page that opens next will give you the option of choosing an English-language version.) This site shows 14 *strade del vino* (wine roads) that have been mapped out by consortiums representing major wine districts (unfortunately, Chianti Classico isn't included), along with recommended itineraries. You'll also find links to the consortium Web sites, where you can dig up more detailed information on touring. The Chianti Classico consortium's site is ⊕ www.chianticlassico.com. The Vino Nobile di Montepulciano site is ⊕ www.vinonobiledimontepulciano.it, and Brunello di Montalcino is ⊕ www. consorziobrunellodimontalcino.it. All have English versions.

★ If you only have time for one castle, visit the stunning **Castello di Brolio.** At the end of the 12th century, when Florence conquered southern Chianti, Brolio became Florence's southernmost outpost, and it was often said, "When Brolio growls, all Siena trembles." Brolio was built about AD 1000 and owned by the monks of the Badia Fiorentina; the "new" owners, the Ricasoli family, have been in possession since 1141. Bettino Ricasoli (1809–80), the so-called Iron Baron, was one of the founders of modern Italy and is said to have invented the original formula for Chianti wine. Brolio, one of Chianti's best-known labels, is still justifiably famous. Its cellars may be toured by appointment. There's a sign at the Brolio gate that translates as RING BELL AND BE PATIENT. You pull a rope and the bell above the ramparts peals, and in a short time, the caretaker arrives to let you in. The grounds are worth visiting, even though the 19th-century manor house is not open to the public. (The current baron is very much in residence.) There are two apartments here available for rent by the week. ⊠*Località Brolio* ✚ *2 km (1 mi) southeast of Gaiole* ☎*0577/730227* ⊠€5 ⊙*June–Sept., daily 9–noon and 2–6:30; Oct.–May, Sat.–Thurs. 9–noon and 2–6:30.*

East of Radda a turnoff leads to the **Badia a Coltibuono** *(Abbey of the Good Harvest),* which has been owned by Lorenza de' Medici's family for more than a century and a half (the family isn't closely related to the Renaissance-era Medici). Wine has been produced here since the abbey was founded by Vallombrosan monks in the 11th century. Today the family continues the tradition, making Chianti Classico and other wines, along with cold-pressed olive oil and various flavored vinegars and floral honeys. A small Romanesque church with campanile is surrounded by 2,000 acres of oak, fir, and chestnut woods threaded with walking paths—open to all—that pass two small lakes. Though the abbey itself, built between the 11th and 18th centuries, serves as the family's home, parts are open for tours (in English, German, or Italian). Visit the jasmine-draped main courtyard, the inner cloister with its antique well, the musty old aging cellars, and the Renaissance-style garden redolent of lavender, lemons, and roses. In the shop, **L'Osteria,** you can taste wine and honey, as well as pick up other items like homemade beeswax hand lotion in little ceramic dishes. The Badia is closed on public holidays. ⊠*Località Badia a Coltibuono* ✚ *4 km (2½ mi) north of Gaiole* ☎*0577/749498 for tours, 0577/749479 for shop* ☎*0577/749235* ⊕*www.coltibuono.com* ⊠*Abbey €3* ⊙*Tours: May–July and Sept. and Oct., weekdays 2:30, 3, 3:30, 4; shop: Mar.– mid-Jan., daily 9–1 and 2–7.*

OFF THE BEATEN PATH

Volpaia. Perched atop a hill 10 km (6 mi) north of Radda is Volpaia, a fairy-tale hamlet that was a military outpost from the 10th to the 16th century and once a shelter for religious pilgrims. Every August, for the Festa di San Lorenzo, people come to Volpaia to watch for falling stars and a traditional fireworks display put on by the family that owns the adjacent wine estate and agriturismo lodging, **Castello di Volpaia** (⊠*Piazza della Cisterna 1* ☎*0577/738066).*

WHERE TO STAY & EAT

$-$$
Fodor'sChoice
★

✕**Osteria Le Panzanelle.** Silvia Bonechi's experience in the kitchen—and a few precious recipes handed down from her grandmother—is one of the reasons for the success of this small restaurant. The other is the front-room hospitality of Nada Michelassi. These two *panzanelle* (women from Panzano) serve a short menu of tasty and authentic dishes at what the locals refer to as *prezzi giusti* (the right prices). Both the *pappa al pomodoro* (tomato soup) and the *peposo* (peppery beef stew) are exceptional. Whether you are eating inside or under large umbrellas on the terrace near a tiny stream, the experience is always congenial. "The best food we had in Tuscany," writes one user of fodors.com. Reservations are essential in July and August. ⊠*Località Lucarelli 29 ⊹ 8 km (5 mi) northwest of Radda on road to Panzano* ☎*0577/733511* ➡*MC, V* ☉*Closed Mon. and Jan. and Feb.*

$$$-$$$$
Fodor'sChoice
★

✕🖼**Relais Fattoria Vignale.** On the outside it's a rather plain manor house with an annex across the street. Inside it's a refined and comfortable country house with numerous sitting rooms that have terracotta floors and nice stonework. Guest rooms have exposed-brick walls and wood beams and are filled with simple wooden furnishings and handwoven rugs. The grounds, flanked by vineyards and olive trees, are equally inviting, with lawns, terraces, and a pool. The sophisticated Ristorante Vignale ($–$$$) serves excellent wines and local specialties like *cinghiale in umido con nepitella e vin cotto* (wild boar stew flavored with catmint and wine). **Pros:** Intimate public spaces; excellent restaurant; helpful and friendly staff. **Cons:** North-facing rooms blocked by tall cypress trees; single rooms are small; annex across a busy road. ⊠*Via Pianigiani 9,* ☎*0577/738300 hotel, 0577/738094 restaurant, 0577/738012 enoteca* ⊕*www.vignale.it* ➹*37 rooms, 5 suites* ♿*In-room: safe, refrigerator. In-hotel: restaurant, bar, pool, concierge, laundry service, public Internet* ➡*AE, DC, MC, V* ☉*Closed Nov.–Mar. 15.* �‖*BP.*

¢

🖼**La Bottega di Giovannino.** The name is actually that of the wine bar run by Giovannino Bernardoni and his daughter Monica, who also rent rooms in the house next door. This is a fantastic place for the budget-conscious traveler, as rooms are immaculate. Most have a stunning view of the surrounding hills. All have their own bath, though most of them necessitate taking a short trip outside one's room. **Pros:** Great location in the center of town; close to restaurants and shops; super value. **Cons:** Some rooms are small; some bathrooms are down the hall; basic decor. ⊠*Via Roma 6–8,* ☎*0577/738056* ⊕*www.labottegadigiovannino.it* ➹*10 rooms, 2 apartments* ♿*In-room: no a/c, no phone. In-hotel: bar, no elevator* ➡*AE, MC, V* ❑*EP.*

CASTELLINA IN CHIANTI

14 km (8 mi) west of Radda, 59 km (35 mi) south of Florence.

GETTING HERE

As with all the towns along the Strada Chiantigiana (SR222), Castellina is an easy drive from either Siena or Florence. From Siena, Castellina is well served by the local Tra-In bus company. However, only

The Tuscan countryside in early autumn

one bus a day travels here from Florence. The closest train station is at Castellina Scalo, some 15 km (9 mi) away.

VISITOR INFORMATION
Castellina in Chianti tourism office (⊠ *Piazza del Comune 1* ☎ *0577/ 741392*).

EXPLORING
Castellina in Chianti, or simply Castellina, is on a ridge above the Val di Pesa, Val d'Arbia, and Val d'Elsa, with beautiful panoramas in every direction. The imposing 15th-century tower in the central piazza hints at the history of this village, which was an outpost during the continuing wars between Florence and Siena.

WHERE TO STAY & EAT
$$$$ ╳ **Albergaccio.** The fact that the dining room can seat only 35 guests makes a meal here an intimate experience. The ever-changing menu mixes traditional and creative dishes. In late September and October *zuppa di funghi e castagne* (mushroom and chestnut soup) is a treat; grilled meats and seafood are on the list throughout the year. There's also an excellent wine list. When the weather is warm make sure you dine on the terrace. ⊠ *Via Fiorentina 25* ☎ *0577/741042* ⌖ *Reservations essential* ⊟ *No credit cards* ⊗ *Closed Sun. No lunch Wed. and Thurs.*

$–$$ ╳ **Ristorante Le Tre Porte.** The specialty of the house, a thick slab of beef called *bistecca alla fiorentina*, is usually served very rare. Paired with grilled fresh porcini mushrooms when in season (in spring and fall), it's a heady dish. The main floor of the restaurant has a small dining room serving full-course meals. In the evening, a second room is opened downstairs where you can order pizzas from the wood-burning oven. Reservations are essential in July and August. ⊠ *Via Trento e Trieste 4* ☎*0577/741163* ⊟*AE, DC, MC, V* ⊗*Closed Tues.*

$-$$$

Fodor's Choice

★

🛏**Palazzo Squarcialupi.** In the center of Castellina, this 15th-century palace is a tranquil place to stay. Rooms are spacious, with high ceilings, tile floors, and 18th-century furnishings; bathrooms are tiled in local stone. Many of the rooms have views of the valley below, some look toward the town's main pedestrian street. Common areas are elegant, with deep, plush couches that invite you to recline. There's an ample breakfast buffet throughout the year, and you can arrange for a light lunch in the warmer months. The multilingual staff goes out of its way to be helpful. Users of fodors.com praised the "lovely room, fantastic views," and "friendly staff." **Pros:** Great location; elegant public spaces. **Cons:** On a street with no car access; across from a noisy restaurant. ⊠*Via Ferruccio 22,* ☎*0577/741186* 🖶*0577/740386* ⊕*www.palazzo squarcialupi.com* ⋑*17 rooms* ⓹*In room: refrigerator. In-hotel: bar, pool, laundry service, public Wi-Fi, some pets allowed* ⊟*AE, DC, MC, V* ⊗*Closed Nov.–Mar.* ⦿*BP.*

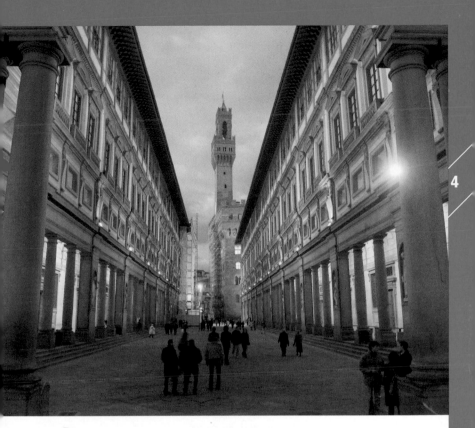

Florence

WORD OF MOUTH

"Michelangelo, Dante, Galileo. Gelato, red wine, amazing food. Some of the most wonderful art and architecture.
Firenze is a magical city (and where my fiancé and I got
engaged). It is an absolute gem."

—Kristin

WELCOME TO FLORENCE

TOP REASONS TO GO

★ **Galleria degli Uffizi:** Italian Renaissance art doesn't get much better than this vast collection bequeathed to the city by the last Medici, Anna Maria Luisa.

★ **The dome of the Duomo:** Brunelleschi's work of engineering genius is the city's undisputed centerpiece.

★ **Michelangelo's David:** One look and you'll know why this is the Western world's most famous sculpture.

★ **The view from Piazzale Michelangelo:** From this perch the city is laid out before you. The colors at sunset heighten the experience.

★ **Piazza Santa Croce:** After you've had your fill of Renaissance masterpieces, hang out here and watch the world go by.

1 The Duomo to the Ponte Vecchio. You're in the heart of Florence here. Among the numerous highlights are the city's greatest museum (the Uffizi) and its most impressive square (Piazza della Signoria).

2 San Lorenzo to the Accademia. The blocks from the church of San Lorenzo to the Accademia museum bear the imprints of the Medici and of Michelangelo, culminating in his masterful David. Just to the north, the former convent of San Marco is an oasis decorated with ethereal frescoes.

3 Santa Maria Novella to the Arno. This part of town includes the train station, 15th-century palaces, and the city's most chic shopping street, Via Tornabuoni.

4 Santa Croce. The district centers around its namesake basilica, which is filled with the tombs of Renaissance luminaries. The area is also known for its leather shops, some of which have been in operation since the 16th century.

5 The Oltrarno. Across the Arno you encounter the massive Palazzo Pitti and the narrow streets of the Santo Spirito district, which is filled with artisans' workshops and antiques stores. A climb to Piazzale Michelangelo gives you a spectacular view of the city.

Piazza del Duomo

GETTING ORIENTED

The historic center of Florence is flat and compact—you could walk from one end to the other in half an hour. In the middle of everything is the Duomo, with its huge dome towering over the city's terra-cotta rooftops. Radiating out from the Duomo are Renaissance-era neighborhoods identified by their central churches and piazzas. Though the majority of sights are north of the Arno River, the area to the south, known as the Oltrarno, has its charms as well.

San Marco

Galleria dell'Accademia

DUOMO

Piazza San Lorenzo

San Lorenzo **2**

Battistero

Duomo

Piazza del Duomo

Piazza della Repubblica

Piazza Strozzi

1

Piazza della Signoria

Piazza San Firenze

Galleria degli Uffizi

Ponte Vecchio

Piazza degli Uffizi

Piazza Santa Croce

Santa Croce

4 SANTA CROCE

5 OLTRARNO

Fiume Arno

Lungarno Acciaioli

Lungarno Torrigiani

Lungarno Generale Armando Diaz

Lungarno della Grazie

Ponte alle Grazie

0   150 M

0   500 ft

FLORENCE PLANNER

Avoiding an Art Hangover

Even for the most dedicated art enthusiast, trying to take in Florence's abundance of masterpieces can turn into a headache—there's just too much to see. Especially if you don't count yourself as an art lover, remember to pace yourself. Allow time to wander and follow your whims, and ignore any pangs of guilt if you'd rather relax in a café and watch the world go by than trudge on sore feet through another breathtaking palace or church.

Florence isn't a city that can be "done." It's a place you can return to again and again, confident there will always be more treasures to discover.

Making the Most of Your Time

With some planning, you can see Florence's most famous sights in a couple of days. Start at the city's most awe-inspiring work of architecture, the **Duomo,** climbing to the top of the dome if you have the stamina. On the same piazza, check out Ghiberti's bronze doors at the **Battistero.** (They're actually high-quality copies; the Museo dell'Opera del Duomo has the originals.) Set aside the afternoon for the **Galleria degli Uffizi,** making sure to reserve tickets in advance.

On Day 2, visit Michelangelo's David in the **Galleria dell'Accademia**—reserve tickets here, too. Linger in the **Piazza della Signoria,** Florence's central square, where a copy of David stands in the spot the original occupied for centuries, then head east a couple of blocks to **Santa Croce,** the city's most artistically rich church. Double back and walk across Florence's landmark bridge, the **Ponte Vecchio.**

Do all that, and you'll have seen some great art, but you've just scratched the surface. If you have more time, put the **Bargello,** the **Museo di San Marco,** and the **Cappelle Medicee** at the top of your list. When you're ready for an art break, stroll through the **Boboli Gardens** or explore Florence's lively shopping scene, from the food stalls of the **Mercato Centrale** to the chic boutiques of the **Via Tornabuoni.**

Piazza della Signoria

Tourist Offices

The Florence tourist office, known as the APT (☎ 055/290832 ⊕ www.comune.firenze.it), has locations next to the Palazzo Medici-Riccardi, in the main train station, and around the corner from the Basilica di Santa Croce. The offices are generally open from 9 in the morning until 7 in the evening. The multilingual staff will give you directions (but usually not free maps) and the latest on happenings in the city. It's particularly worth a stop if you're interested in finding out about performing-arts events. The APT Web site is in Italian only.

Titian's *Venus of Urbino*

Florentine Hours

Florence's sights keep tricky hours. Some are closed on Wednesday, some on Monday, some on every other Monday. Quite a few shut their doors each day (or on most days) by 2 in the afternoon. Things get even more confusing on weekends. Make it a general rule to check the hours closely for any place you're planning to visit; if it's somewhere you have your heart set on seeing, it's worthwhile to call to confirm.

Here's a selection of major sights that might not be open when you'd expect—consult the sight listings within this chapter for the full details. And be aware that, as always, hours can and do change.

■ The **Uffizi** and the **Accademia** are both closed Monday. All but a few of the galleries at Palazzo Pitti are closed Monday as well.

■ The **Duomo** closes at 3:30 on Thursday (as opposed to 5:30 on other weekdays, 4:45 on weekends). The dome of the Duomo is closed on Sunday.

■ The **Battistero** is open from noon until 7, Monday through Saturday, and on Sunday from 8:30 to 2.

■ The **Bargello** closes at 1:50 PM, and is closed entirely on alternating Sundays and Mondays.

■ The **Cappelle Medicee** are closed on alternating Sundays and Mondays.

■ **Museo di San Marco** closes at 1:50 on weekdays but stays open until 7 on weekends—except for alternating Sundays and Mondays, when it's closed entirely.

■ **Palazzo Medici-Riccardi** is closed Wednesday.

With Reservations

At most times of day you'll see a line of people snaking around the Uffizi. They're waiting to buy tickets, and you don't want to be one of them.

Instead, call ahead for a reservation (☎055/294883; reservationists speak English). You'll be given a reservation number and a time of admission—the further in advance you call, the more time slots you'll have to choose from. Go to the museum's reservation door at the appointed hour, give the clerk your number, pick up your ticket, and go inside. You'll pay €3 for this privilege, but it's money well spent.

At this writing, an on-line reservation option has also been launched at ⊕ *www.polomuseale.firenze.it; the booking process at this point is awkward, but it's likely to improve.*

Use the same reservation service to book tickets for the Galleria dell'Accademia, where lines rival those of the Uffizi. (Reservations can also be made for the Palazzo Pitti, the Bargello, and several other sights, but they aren't needed.) An alternative strategy is to check with your hotel—many will handle reservations.

GETTING HERE & AROUND

Getting Here by Car

Florence is connected to the north and south of Italy by the Autostrada del Sole (A1). It takes about 1½ hours of driving on scenic roads to get to Bologna (although heavy truck traffic over the Apennines often makes for slower going), about 3 hours to Rome, and 3 to 3½ hours to Milan. The Tyrrhenian Coast is an hour west on the A11.

Getting Here by Bus

Long-distance buses provide inexpensive if somewhat claustrophobic service between Florence and other cities in Italy and Europe. **Lazzi Eurolines** (⊠ *Via Mercadante 2, Santa Maria Novella* ☎ *055/363041* ⊕ *www. lazzi.it*) and **SITA** (⊠ *Via Santa Caterina da Siena 17/r, Santa Maria Novella* ☎ *055/214721* ⊕ *www.sita-on-line.it*) are the major lines; they have neatly divided up their routes, so there's little overlap.

Getting Here by Air

Florence's small **Aeroporto A. Vespucci** (✈ *10 km [6 mi] northwest of Florence* ☎ *055/373498* ⊕ *www.aeroporto. firenze.it*), commonly called **Peretola**, is just outside of town and receives flights from Milan, Rome, London, and Paris. To get into the city center from the airport by car, take the autostrada A11. Tickets for the local bus service into Florence are sold at the airport's second-floor bar—Bus 62 runs once an hour directly to the train station at Santa Maria Novella. The airport's bus shelter is beyond the parking lot.

Pisa's **Aeroporto Galileo Galilei** (✈ *12 km [7 mi] south of Pisa and 80 km [50 mi] west of Florence* ☎ *050/849300* ⊕ *www.pisa-airport.com*) is the closest landing point with significant international service, including (at this writing) a few direct flights from the United States each week on Delta. It's a straight shot down SS67 to Florence. A train service connects Pisa's airport station with Santa Maria Novella, roughly a 1½-hour trip. Trains start running about 7 AM from the airport, 6 AM from Florence, and continue service every hour until about 7 PM from the airport, 4 PM from Florence.

For flight information, call the airport or **Florence Air Terminal** (⊠ *Stazione Centrale di Santa Maria Novella* ☎ *055/216073*)—which, despite the misleading name, is simply an office at the Santa Maria Novella train station, around the corner from train tracks 1 and 2.

Getting Here by Train

Florence is on the principal Italian train route between most European capitals and Rome, and within Italy it is served frequently from Milan, Venice, and Rome by Intercity (IC) and nonstop Eurostar trains. **Stazione Centrale di Santa Maria Novella** (☎ *892021* ⊕ *www.trenitalia.com*) is the main station and is in the center of town. Avoid trains that stop only at the Campo di Marte or Rifredi stations, which are not convenient to the city center.

Getting Around by Bus

Neptune Fountain,
Piazza della Signoria

Florence's flat, compact city center is made for walking, but when your feet get weary, you can use the efficient bus system, which includes small electric buses making the rounds in the center. Buses also climb to Piazzale Michelangelo and San Miniato south of the Arno.

Maps and timetables for local bus service are available for a small fee at the ATAF (Azienda Trasporti Area Fiorentina) booth next to the train station, or for free at visitor information offices. Tickets must be bought in advance from tobacco shops, newsstands, automatic ticket machines near main stops, or ATAF booths. The ticket must be canceled in the small validation machine immediately upon boarding.

You have several ticket options, all valid for one or more rides on all lines. A €1.20 ticket is good for one hour from the time it is first canceled. A multiple ticket—four tickets, each valid for 70 minutes—costs €4.50. A 24-hour tourist ticket costs €5. Two-, three-, and seven-day passes are also available.

Getting Around by Taxi

Taxis usually wait at stands throughout the city (in front of the train station and in Piazza della Repubblica, for example), or you can call for one (☎ *055/4390 or 055/4798*). The meter starts at €2.30, with a €3.60 minimum and extra charges at night, on Sunday, and for radio dispatch.

Getting Around by Bike & Moped

Brave souls (cycling in Florence is difficult at best) may rent bicycles at easy-to-spot locations at Fortezza da Basso, the Stazione Centrale di Santa Maria Novella, and Piazza Pitti. Otherwise, try **Alinari** (⊠ *Via Guelfa 85/r, San Marco* ☎ *055/280500* ⊕ *www. alinarirental.com*). You'll be up against hordes of tourists and those pesky *motorini* (mopeds). (For a safer ride, try Le Cascine, a former Medici hunting ground turned into a large public park with paved pathways.) The historic center can be circumnavigated via bike paths lining the *viali*, the ring road surrounding the area. If you want to go native and rent a noisy Vespa (Italian for "wasp") or other make of motorcycle or motorino, you may do so at **Maxlrent** (⊠ *Borgo Ognissanti 155/r, Santa Maria Novella* ☎ *055/265420*) or **Massimo** (⊠ *Via Campo d'Arrigo 16/r* ☎ *055/573689*). However unfashionable, helmets must be rented at either place, and by law are mandatory.

Getting Around by Car

An automobile in Florence is a major liability. If your itinerary includes parts of Italy where you'll want a car (such as Tuscany), pick the vehicle up on your way out of town.

EATING & DRINKING WELL IN FLORENCE

Food in Florence is not about sauces, foams, or fusion. Simply prepared meats, grilled or roasted, are the stars, and pair well with seasonal vegetables like artichokes, porcini, and cannellini beans. Bistecca's big here, but there's plenty more that tastes great on the grill, too.

Traditionalists (and many Florentines are) go for their gustatory pleasures in trattorie and osterie, places where décor is unimportant, place mats are mere paper, and service is often perfunctory. Culinary innovation comes slowly in this town, though some cutting-edge restaurants have been appearing, usually with young chefs who've traveled and worked outside Italy. Some of these places lack charm (many have an international, you-could-be-anywhere feel), their menus offer exciting, updated versions of Tuscan standards

By American standards, Florentines eat late: 1:30 or 2 is typical for lunch, and 9 for dinner. Consuming a primo, secondo, and dolce is largely a thing of the past, and no one looks askance if you don't order the whole nine yards. For lunch, many Florentines simply grab a panino and a glass of wine at a bar. Those opting for a simple trattoria lunch often order a plate of pasta and dessert.

STALE AND STELLAR

Florence lacks signature pasta and rice dishes, perhaps because the town's content to have raised frugality with bread to culinary craft. Stale bread is the basis for three classic Florentine primi: pappa al pomodoro, ribollita, and panzanella. "Pappa" is made with either fresh or canned tomatoes and that stale bread. Ribollita is a vegetable soup fortified with cavolo nero (sometimes called Tuscan kale elsewhere), cannellini beans, and thickened with bread. Panzanella, a summertime dish, is reconstituted Tuscan bread combined with tomatoes, cucumber, and basil. They all are greatly enhanced with a generous application of fragrant Tuscan olive oil.

A CLASSIC ANTIPASTO: CROSTINI DI FEGATINI

This beloved dish consists of a chicken liver spread, served warm or at room temperature, on toasted, garlic-rubbed bread. It can be served smooth, like a pâté, or in a rougher spread. It's made by sautéeing chicken livers with finely diced carrot and onion, enlivened with the addition of wine, broth, or Marsala reductions, and mashed anchovies and capers.

A CLASSIC SECONDO: BISTECCA FIORENTINA

The town's culinary pride and joy is a thick slab of beef, resembling a T-bone steak, from large white oxen called Chianina. The meat's slapped on the grill and served rare, sometimes with a pinch of salt. It's always seared on both sides, and just barely cooked inside (experts say five minutes per side, and then fifteen minutes with the bone sitting perpendicularly on the grill). To ask for it more well done is to incur disdain; some restaurants simply won't serve it any other way than rare.

A CLASSIC CONTORNO: CANNELLINI BEANS

Simply boiled, they provide the perfect accompaniment to a bistecca. The small white beans are best when they go straight from the garden into the pot. They should be annointed with a gener-

ous outpouring of Tuscan olive oil; the combination is oddly felicitous, and it goes a long way toward explaining why Tuscans are referred to as *mangiafagioli* (bean eaters) by other Italians..

A CLASSIC DOLCE: BISCOTTI DI PRATO

These are sometimes the only dessert on offer, and are more or less an afterthought to the glories that have proceeded them. "Biscotti" means twice-cooked (or, in this case, twice baked) hard almond cookies which soften considerably when dipped languidly into *vin santo* ("holy wine"), a sweet dessert wine, or into a simple *caffè*.

A CLASSIC WINE: CHIANTI CLASSICO

This blend from the region just south of Florence relies mainly on the local, hardy sangiovese grape; it's aged for at least one year before hitting the market. (*Riserve*—reserves—are aged at least an additional six months.) Chianti is usually the libation of choice for Florentines, and it pairs magnificently with grilled foods and seasonal vegetables. Traditionalists opt for the younger, fruitier (and usually less expensive) versions often served in straw flasks. You can sample *Chianti classico* all over town, and buy it in local *salumerie, enoteche,* and supermarkets.

Updated
by Patricia
Rucidlo

FLORENCE, THE CITY OF THE lily, gave birth to the Renaissance and changed the way we see the world. For centuries it has captured the imagination of travelers, who have come seeking rooms with views and phenomenal art. Florence's is a subtle beauty—its staid, unprepossessing palaces built in local stone are not showy. They take on a certain magnificence when day breaks and when the sun sets; their muted colors glow in this light. A walk along the Arno offers views that don't quit and haven't much changed in 700 years; navigating Piazza Signoria, almost always packed with tourists and locals alike, requires patience. There's a reason why everyone seems to be here, however. It's the heart of the city, and home to the Uffizi—arguably the world's finest repository of Renaissance art.

Florence was "discovered" in the 1700s by upper-class northerners making the grand tour. It became a mecca for travelers, particularly the Romantics, who were inspired by the elegance of its palazzi and its artistic wealth. Today millions of modern visitors follow in their footsteps. When the sun sets over the Arno and, as Mark Twain described it, "overwhelms Florence with tides of color that make all the sharp lines dim and faint and turn the solid city to a city of dreams," it's hard not to fall under the city's spell.

THE DUOMO TO THE PONTE VECCHIO

The heart of Florence, stretching from the Piazza del Duomo south to the Arno, is as dense with artistic treasures as anyplace in the world. The churches, medieval towers, Renaissance palaces, and world-class museums and galleries contain some of the most outstanding aesthetic achievements of Western history.

Much of the *centro storico* (historic center) is closed to automobile traffic, but you still must dodge mopeds, cyclists, and masses of fellow tourists as you walk the narrow streets, especially in the area bounded by the Duomo, Piazza della Signoria, Galleria degli Uffizi, and Ponte Vecchio.

THE MAIN ATTRACTIONS

❺ Bargello. During the Renaissance, this building was headquarters for the
★ chief of police. It also was used as a prison, and the exterior served as a "most wanted" billboard: effigies of notorious criminals and Medici enemies were painted on its walls. Today it houses the **Museo Nazionale,** home to what is probably the finest collection of Renaissance sculpture in Italy. The concentration of masterworks by Michelangelo (1475–1564), Donatello (circa 1386–1466), and Benvenuto Cellini (1500–71) is remarkable; the works are distributed among an eclectic collection of arms, ceramics, and miniature bronzes, among other things. For Renaissance-art lovers, the Bargello is to sculpture what the Uffizi is to painting.

In 1401 Filippo Brunelleschi (1377–1446) and Lorenzo Ghiberti (circa 1378–1455) competed to earn the most prestigious commission of the day: the decoration of the north doors of the Baptistery in Piazza del Duomo. For the contest, each designed a bronze bas-relief panel

The Duomo to the Ponte Vecchio

V. Martelli

Piazza del Duomo

Via del Proconsolo

Piazza di S. Giovanni

Via d. Studio

Via delle Oche

Borgo degli Albizi

Via dei Calzaiuoli

Via del Corso

Via dei Tosinghi

Via dei Pandolfini

Via Ghibellina

Via degli Speziali

Via Dante Alighieri

Via della Vigna Vecchia

Via d. Burella

Piazza della Repubblica

Via dei Tavolini

Via d'Acqua

Via Calimala

V. Orsanmichele

Via dei Cimatori

Piazza S. Firenze

Via dell' Anguillara

Via dei Mazzini

Via della Condotta

Via dei Lamberti

Via d. Gondi

Borgo dei Greci

Via d. Corno

Via Porta Rossa

Via Leoni

Via Vinegia

Via d. Parlascio

C. de' Marzetti

Via Vaccherreccia

Via dei Neri

Via de' Castellani

Via delle Terme

C. N'casori

Via Por S. Maria

Piazza dei Giudici

Borgo SS. Apostoli

V. dell' Oro

Lung. Diaz

Lung. Acciaioli

Lung. Archibusieri

Arno

0   1/8 mile

0   200 meters

FLORENCE THROUGH THE AGES

Guelph vs. Ghibelline. Though Florence can lay claim to a modest importance in the ancient world, it didn't come into its own until the Middle Ages. In the early 1200s, the city, like most of the rest of Italy, was rent by civic unrest. Two factions, the Guelphs and the Ghibellines, competed for power. The Guelphs supported the papacy, and the Ghibellines supported the Holy Roman Empire. Bloody battles—most notably one at Montaperti in 1260—tore Florence and other Italian cities apart. By the end of the 13th century the Guelphs ruled securely and the Ghibellines had been vanquished. This didn't end civic strife, however: the Guelphs split into the Whites and the Blacks for reasons still debated by historians. Dante, author of The *Divine Comedy,* was banished from Florence in 1301 because he was a White.

The Guilded Age. Local merchants had organized themselves into guilds by 1250. In that year they proclaimed themselves the "*primo popolo*" (literally, "first people"), making a landmark attempt at elective, republican rule. Though the episode lasted only 10 years, it constituted a breakthrough in Western history. Such a daring stance by the merchant class was a by-product of Florence's emergence as an economic powerhouse. Florentines were papal bankers; they instituted the system of international letters of credit; and the gold florin became the international standard of currency. With this economic strength came a building boom. Palaces and basilicas were erected, enlarged, or restructured. Sculptors such as Donatello and Ghiberti decorated them; painters such as Giotto and Botticelli frescoed their walls.

Mighty Medici. Though ostensibly a republic, Florence was blessed (or cursed) with one very powerful family, the Medici, who came to prominence in the 1430s and were the de facto rulers of Florence for several hundred years. It was under patriarch Cosimo il Vecchio (1389–1464) that the Medici's position in Florence was securely established. Florence's golden age occurred during the reign of his grandson Lorenzo de' Medici (1449–92). Lorenzo was not only an astute politician but also a highly educated man and a great patron of the arts. Called "Il Magnifico" (the Magnificent), he gathered around him poets, artists, philosophers, architects, and musicians.

Lorenzo's son, Piero (1471–1503), proved inept at handling the city's affairs. He was run out of town in 1494, and Florence briefly enjoyed its status as a republic while dominated by the Dominican friar Girolamo Savonarola (1452–98). After a decade of internal unrest, the republic fell and the Medici were recalled to power, but Florence never regained its former prestige. By the 1530s most of the major artistic talent had left the city—Michelangelo, for one, had settled in Rome. The now-ineffectual Medici, eventually attaining the title of grand dukes, remained nominally in power until the line died out in 1737, after which time Florence passed from the Austrians to the French and back again until the unification of Italy (1865–70), when it briefly became the capital under King Vittorio Emanuele II.

depicting the sacrifice of Isaac; the panels are displayed together in the room devoted to the sculpture of Donatello, on the upper floor. The judges chose Ghiberti for the commission; see if you agree with their choice. ⊠ *Via del Proconsolo 4, Bargello* ☎*055/294883* ⊕*www. polomuseale.firenze.it* ☎*€4* ☉*Daily 8:15–1:50; closed 2nd and 4th Mon. of month and 1st, 3rd, and 5th Sun. of month.*

② **Battistero** *(Baptistery).* The octagonal Baptistery is one of the supreme monuments of the Italian Romanesque style and one of Florence's oldest structures. Local legend has it that it was once a Roman temple dedicated to Mars; modern excavations, however, suggest that its foundations date from the fourth to fifth and the eighth to ninth centuries AD, well after the collapse of the Roman Empire. The round Romanesque arches on the exterior probably date from the 11th century. The interior dome mosaics from the beginning of the 14th century are justly renowned, but—glittering beauties though they are—they could never outshine the building's famed bronze Renaissance doors decorated with panels crafted by Lorenzo Ghiberti. The doors—or at least copies of them—on which Ghiberti worked most of his adult life (1403–52) are on the north and east sides of the Baptistery, and the Gothic panels on the south door were designed by Andrea Pisano (circa 1290–1348) in 1330. The original Ghiberti doors were removed to protect them from the effects of pollution and acid rain and have been beautifully restored; they are now on display in the Museo dell'Opera del Duomo.

Ghiberti's north doors depict scenes from the life of Christ; his later, east doors (dating from 1425–52), facing the Duomo facade, render scenes from the Old Testament. Both merit close examination, for they are very different in style and illustrate the artistic changes that marked the beginning of the Renaissance. Look at the far right panel of the middle row on the earlier (1403–24) north doors (*Jesus Calming the Waters*). Ghiberti here captured the chaos of a storm at sea with great skill and economy, but the artistic conventions he used are basically pre-Renaissance: Jesus is the most important figure, so he is the largest; the disciples are next in size, being next in importance; the ship on which they founder looks like a mere toy.

The exquisitely rendered panels on the east doors are larger, more expansive, more sweeping—and more convincing. The middle panel on the left-hand door tells the story of Jacob and Esau, and the various episodes of the story—the selling of the birthright, Isaac ordering Esau to go hunting, the blessing of Jacob, and so forth—have been merged into a single beautifully realized street scene. Ghiberti's use of perspective suggests depth: the background architecture looks far more credible than on the north-door panels, the figures in the foreground are grouped realistically, and the naturalism and grace of the poses (look at Esau's left leg and the dog next to him) have nothing to do with the sacred message being conveyed. Although the religious content

4

remains, the figures and their place in the natural world are given new prominence and are portrayed with a realism not seen in art since the fall of the Roman Empire nearly a thousand years before.

As a footnote to Ghiberti's panels, one small detail of the east doors is worth a special look. To the lower left of the Jacob and Esau panel, Ghiberti placed a tiny self-portrait bust. From either side, the portrait is extremely appealing—Ghiberti looks like everyone's favorite uncle—but the bust is carefully placed so that you can make direct eye contact with the tiny head from a single spot. When that contact is made, the impression of intelligent life—of *modern* intelligent life—is astonishing. It's no wonder that these doors received one of the most famous compliments in the history of art from an artist known to be notoriously stingy with praise: Michelangelo declared them so beautiful that they could serve as the Gates of Paradise. ⊠ *Piazza del Duomo* ☎ *055/2302885* ⊕ *www.operaduomo.firenze.it* 🎫 *€3* ⊘ *Mon.–Sat. noon–7, Sun. 8:30–2*; 1st Sat. of month 8:30–2.

⓭ **Galleria degli Uffizi.** The venerable Uffizi Gallery occupies the top floor of the U-shaped **Palazzo degli Uffizi** fronting on the Arno, designed by Giorgio Vasari (1511–74) in 1560 to hold the *uffizi* (administrative offices) of the Medici grand duke Cosimo I (1519–74). Later, the Medici installed their art collections here, creating what was Europe's first modern museum, open to the public (at first only by request) since 1591. Hard-core museum aficionados can pick up a complete guide to the collections at bookshops and newsstands.

Fodor'sChoice
★

Among the highlights are Paolo Uccello's *Battle of San Romano,* its brutal chaos of lances one of the finest visual metaphors for warfare ever captured in paint; the *Madonna and Child with Two Angels,* by Fra Filippo Lippi (1406–69), in which the impudent eye contact established by the angel would have been unthinkable prior to the Renaissance; the *Birth of Venus* and *Primavera* by Sandro Botticelli (1445–1510), the goddess of the former seeming to float on air and the fairy-tale charm of the latter exhibiting the painter's idiosyncratic genius at its zenith; the portraits of the Renaissance duke Federico da Montefeltro and his wife, Battista Sforza, by Piero della Francesca (circa 1420–92); the *Madonna of the Goldfinch* by Raphael (1483–1520), which, though darkened by time, captures an aching tenderness between mother and child; Michelangelo's *Doni Tondo;* a *Self-Portrait as an Old Man* by Rembrandt (1606–69); the *Venus of Urbino* by Titian (circa 1488/90–1576); and the splendid *Bacchus* by Caravaggio (circa 1571/72–1610). In the last two works, the approaches to myth and sexuality are diametrically opposed, to put it mildly. Six additional exhibition rooms opened in 2004, convoluting the way you exit the museum. Many of the more than 400 works now displayed would have been better left in storage, though a couple of Caravaggios at the very end of your hike out are well worth a look.

Late in the afternoon is the least crowded time to visit. For a €3 fee, advance tickets can be reserved by phone or, once in Florence, at the Uffizi reservation booth at least one day in advance of your visit. At

GALLERIA DEGLI UFFIZI
SECOND FLOOR

Terrace

ENTRANCE

TO PALAZZO VECCHIO

Vestibolo d'entrata

1

3   4

2

5-6

7

8

9

10-14

15   16

17

18

19

20

21

22

23

24

45

44

43

42

41

35

34

31
32
33
29
28   27   26   25
30

Rembrandt
• Self-Portrait as an Old Man

Giotto & 13th Century

International Gothic

Early Renaissance
• Uccello's Battle of San Romano

Filippo Lippi
• Madonna & Child with Two Angels

Piero della Francesca
• The Portraits of the Renaissance Duke Federico da Montefeltro & his wife, Battista Sforza

Sandro Botticelli
• Birth of Venus; Primavera

Leonardo Da Vinci
• Adoration of the Magi
• Annunciation

The Tribune

Titian & Sebastiano Del Piombo
• Venus of Urbino

Michelangelo & The Florentines
• Doni Tondo

Raphael & Andrea Del Sarto
• Madonna of the Goldfinch

this writing, an on-line reservation option has also been launched at ⊕*www.polomuseale.firenze.it; the booking process at this point is awkward, but it's likely to improve.* If you book by phone, remember to keep the confirmation number and take it with you to the door at the museum marked "Reservations." Usually you're ushered in almost immediately. Come with cash, because credit cards are not accepted (though you can use a credit card when booking on-line). When there's a special exhibit on, which is often, the base ticket price goes up to €10. ⊠*Piazzale degli Uffizi 6, Piazza della Signoria* ☎*055/23885 advance tickets* ⊠*Consorzio ITA, Piazza Pitti 1,* ☎*055/294883* ⊕*www.uffizi. firenze.it; reservations: www.polomuseale.firenze.it* ⊠*€6.50, reservation fee €3* ◷*Tues.–Sun. 8:15–6:50.*

⓫ ★ **Piazza della Signoria.** This is by far the most striking square in Florence. It was here, in 1497, that the famous "bonfire of the vanities" took place, when the fanatical friar Savonarola induced his followers to hurl their worldly goods into the flames; it was also here, a year later, that he was hanged as a heretic and, ironically, burned. A bronze plaque in the piazza pavement marks the exact spot of his execution.

The statues in the square and in the 14th-century **Loggia dei Lanzi** on the south side vary in quality. Cellini's famous bronze *Perseus* holding the severed head of Medusa is certainly the most important sculpture in the loggia. Other works here include *The Rape of the Sabine* and *Hercules and the Centaur,* both late-16th-century works by Giambologna (1529–1608), and in the back, a row of sober matrons dating from Roman times.

In the square, the Neptune Fountain, created between 1550 and 1575, takes something of a booby prize. It was created by Bartolomeo Ammannati, who considered it a failure himself. The Florentines call it Il Biancone, which may be translated as "the big white man" or "the big white lump." Giambologna's equestrian statue, to the left of the fountain, pays tribute to Grand Duke Cosimo I. Occupying the steps of the Palazzo Vecchio are a copy of Donatello's proud heraldic lion of Florence, the *Marzocco* (the original is now in the Bargello); a copy of Donatello's *Judith and Holofernes* (the original is in the Palazzo Vecchio); a copy of Michelangelo's *David* (the original is in the Galleria dell'Accademia); and Baccio Bandinelli's *Hercules* (1534). The Marzocco, the Judith, and the David were symbols of Florentine civic pride—the latter two subjects had stood up to their oppressors. They provided apt metaphors for the republic-loving Florentines, who often chafed at Medici hegemony.

⓮ ★ **Ponte Vecchio** *(Old Bridge).* This charmingly simple bridge is to Florence what the Tower Bridge is to London. It was built in 1345 to replace an earlier bridge that was swept away by flood, and its shops housed first butchers, then grocers, blacksmiths, and other merchants. But in 1593 the Medici grand duke Ferdinand I (1549–1609), whose private corridor linking the Medici palace (Palazzo Pitti) with the Medici offices (the Uffizi) crossed the bridge atop the shops, decided that all this plebeian commerce under his feet was unseemly. So he threw out the butchers and blacksmiths and installed 41 goldsmiths and eight jewelers. The bridge has been devoted solely to these two trades ever since.

The **Corridoio Vasariano** (✉*Piazzale degli Uffizi 6, Piazza della Signoria* ☎*055/23885 or 055/294883*), the private Medici corridor, was built by Vasari in 1565. Though the ostensible reason for its construction was one of security, it was more likely designed so that the Medici family wouldn't have to walk amid the commoners. The corridor is notoriously fickle with its operating hours; at this writing it was temporarily closed, but it can often be visited by prior special arrangement. Call for the most up-to-date details. Take a moment to study the Ponte Santa Trinita, the next bridge downriver, from either the bridge or the corridor. It was designed by Bartolomeo Ammannati in 1567 (possibly from sketches by Michelangelo), blown up by the retreating Germans during World War II, and painstakingly reconstructed after the war. The view from the Ponte Santa Trinita is beautiful, which might explain why so many young lovers seem to hang out there.

ALSO WORTH SEEING

6 **Badia Fiorentina.** Originally endowed by Willa, Marquess of Tuscany, in 978, this ancient church is an interesting mélange of 13th-century, Renaissance, baroque, and 18th-century architectural refurbishing. Its graceful bell tower, best seen from the interior courtyard, is beautiful for its unusual construction—a hexagonal tower built on a quadrangular base. The interior of the church (open Monday afternoon only) was halfheartedly remodeled in the baroque style during the 17th century. Three tombs by Mino da Fiesole (circa 1430–84) line the walls, including the *monumento funebre di Conte Ugo* (tomb sculpture of Count Ugo), widely regarded as Mino's masterpiece. Executed in 1469–81, it shows Mino at his most lyrical: the faces seem to be lit from within—no small feat in marble. The best-known work of art here is the delicate *Vision of St. Bernard,* by Filippino Lippi (circa 1457–1504), on the left as you enter. The painting—one of Filippino's finest—is in superb condition; note the Virgin Mary's hands, perhaps the most beautifully rendered in the city. On the right side of the church, above the **cappella di San Mauro,** is a monumental organ dating from 1558. Constructed by Onofrio Zeffirini da Cortona (1510–86), it's largely intact but is missing its 16th-century keyboard. ✉*Via Dante Alighieri 1, Bargello* ☎*055/264402* 🎫*Free* ⊙*Mon. 3–6.*

3 **Campanile.** The Gothic bell tower designed by Giotto (circa 1266–1337) is a soaring structure of multicolor marble originally decorated with reliefs that are now in the Museo dell'Opera del Duomo. A climb of 414 steps rewards you with a close-up of Brunelleschi's cupola on the Duomo next door and a sweeping view of the city. ✉*Piazza del Duomo* ☎*055/2302885* ⊕*www.operaduomo.firenze.it* 🎫*€6* ⊙*Daily 8:30–7:30.*

NEED A BREAK? Calling itself a "zupperia," La Canova di GustaVino (✉*Via della Condotta 29/r, Piazza della Signoria* ☎*055/2399806*) keeps several hearty, restorative soups on hand. Solid fare includes mixed cheese plates (both French and Italian), as well as *tomino con prosciutto* (mild cow's cheese, topped

with thin slices of prosciutto) run under the broiler.

🔟 **Mercato Nuovo** *(New Market).* The open-air loggia, built in 1551, teems with souvenir stands, but the real attraction is a copy of Pietro Tacca's bronze *Porcellino* (which translates as "little pig" despite the fact the animal is, in fact, a wild boar). The Porcellino is Florence's equivalent of the Trevi Fountain: put a coin in his mouth, and if it falls through the grate below (according to one interpretation), it means you'll return to Florence someday. The statue dates from around 1612, but the original version, in Palazzo Pitti, is an ancient Greek work. ⊠*Corner of Via Por Santa Maria and Via Porta Rossa, Piazza della Repubblica* ⊙*Market: Tues.–Sat. 8–7, Mon. 1–7.*

❹ **Museo dell'Opera del Duomo** *(Cathedral Museum).* Ghiberti's original Baptistery door panels and the *cantorie* (choir loft) reliefs by Donatello and Luca della Robbia (1400–82) keep company with Donatello's *Mary Magdalene* and Michelangelo's *Pietà* (not to be confused with his more famous *Pietà* in St. Peter's in Rome). Renaissance sculpture is in part defined by its revolutionary realism, but in its palpable suffering Donatello's *Magdalene* goes beyond realism. Michelangelo's heart-wrenching *Pietà* was unfinished at his death; the female figure supporting the body of Christ on the left was added by Tiberio Calcagni (1532–65), and never has the difference between competence and genius been manifested so clearly. ⊠*Piazza del Duomo 9* ☎*055/2302885* ⊕*www.operaduomo.firenze.it* ☑*€6* ⊙*Mon.–Sat. 9–7:30, Sun. 9–1:40.*

❼ **Orsanmichele.** This multipurpose structure, which is closed indefinitely for restoration at this writing, began as an 8th-century oratory and then in 1290 was turned into an open-air loggia for selling grain. Destroyed by fire in 1304, it was rebuilt as a loggia-market. Between 1367 and 1380 the arcades were closed and two stories were added above; finally, at century's end it was turned into a church. Inside is a beautifully detailed 14th-century Gothic tabernacle by Andrea Orcagna (1308–68). The exterior niches contain sculptures dating from the early 1400s to the early 1600s by Donatello and Verrocchio (1435–88), among others, that were paid for by the guilds. Although it is a copy, Verrocchio's *Doubting Thomas* (circa 1470) is particularly deserving of attention. Here you see Christ, like the building's other figures, entirely framed within the niche, and St. Thomas standing on its bottom ledge, with his right foot outside the niche frame. This one detail, the positioning of a single foot, brings the whole composition to life. Most of the sculptures have since been replaced by copies; however, it's possible to see nearly all of them at the **Museo di Orsanmichele** (also closed at this writing for restoration). ⊠*Via dei Calzaiuoli, Piazza della Repubblica* ☎*055/284944* ☑*Free* ⊙*Closed for restoration.*

Continued on page 235

THE DUOMO
FLORENCE'S BIGGEST MASTERPIECE

For all its monumental art and architecture, Florence has one undisputed centerpiece: the Cathedral of Santa Maria del Fiore, better known as the Duomo. Its cupola dominates the skyline, presiding over the city's rooftops like a red hen over her brood. Little wonder that when Florentines feel homesick, they say they have *"nostalgia del cupolone."*

The Duomo's construction began in 1296, following the design of Arnolfo da Cambio, Florence's greatest architect of the time. By modern standards, construction was slow and haphazard—it continued through the 14th and into the 15th century, with some dozen architects having a hand in the project.

In 1366 Neri di Fioravanti created a model for the hugely ambitious cupola: it was to be the largest dome in the world, surpassing Rome's Pantheon. But when the time finally came to build the dome in 1418, no one was sure how—or even if—it could be done. Florence was faced with a 143-ft hole in the roof of its cathedral, and one of the greatest challenges in the history of architecture.

Fortunately, local genius Filippo Brunelleschi was just the man for the job. Brunelleschi won the 1418 competition to design the dome, and for the

next 18 years he oversaw its construction. The enormity of his achievement can hardly be overstated. Working on such a large scale (the dome weighs 37,000 tons and uses 4 million bricks) required him to invent hoists and cranes that were engineering marvels. A "dome within a dome" design and a novel herringbone bricklaying pattern were just two of the innovations used to establish structural integrity. Perhaps most remarkably, he executed the construction without a supporting wooden framework, which had previously been thought indispensable.

Brunelleschi designed the lantern atop the dome, but he died soon after its first stone was laid in 1446; it wouldn't be completed until 1461. Another 400 years passed before the Duomo received its façade, a 19th-century neo-Gothic creation.

DUOMO TIMELINE

1296 Work begins, following design by Arnolfo di Cambio.

1302 Arnolfo dies; work continues, with sporadic interruptions.

1331 Management of construction taken over by the Wool Merchants guild.

1334 Giotto appointed project overseer, designs campanile.

1337 Giotto dies; Andrea Pisano takes leadership role.

1348 The Black Plague; all work ceases.

1366 Vaulting on nave completed; Neri di Fioravanti makes model for dome.

1417 Drum for dome completed.

1418 Competition is held to design dome.

1420 Brunelleschi begins work on the dome.

1436 Dome completed.

1446 Construction of lantern begins; Brunelleschi dies.

1461 Michelozzo completes lantern.

1469 Gilt copper ball and cross added by Verrocchio.

1588 Original façade is torn down by Medici court.

1871 Emilio de Fabris wins competition to design new façade.

1887 Façade completed.

WHAT TO LOOK FOR INSIDE THE DUOMO

The interior of the Duomo is a fine example of Florentine Gothic with a beautiful marble floor, but the space feels strangely barren—a result of its great size and the fact that some of the best art has been moved to the nearby **Museo dell'Opera del Duomo**.

Notable among the works that remain are two towering equestrian frescoes of famous soldiers: *Niccolò da Tolentino* (1456), by Andrea del Castagno, and *Sir John Hawkwood* (1436), by Paolo Uccello. There's also fine terra-cotta work by Luca della Robbia. Ghiberti,

Brunelleschi's great rival, is responsible for much of the stained glass, as well as a reliquary urn with gorgeous reliefs. A vast fresco of the Last Judgment, painted by Vasari and Zuccari, covers the dome's interior. Brunelleschi had wanted mosaics to go there; it's a shame he didn't get his wish.

In the crypt beneath the cathedral, you can explore excavations of a Roman wall and an 11th-century cemetery; entry is near the first pier on the right. On the way down you pass Brunelleschi's modest tomb.

1. Entrance; stained glass by Ghiberti
2. Fresco of Niccolò da Tolentino by Andrea del Castagno
3. Fresco of John Hawkwood by Paolo Uccello
4. *Dante and the Divine Comedy* by Domenico di Michelino
5. Lunette: *Ascension* by Luca della Robbia
6. Above altar: two angels by Luca della Robbia. Below the altar: reliquary of St. Zenobius by Ghiberti.
7. Lunette: *Resurrection* by Luca della Robbia
8. Entrance to dome
9. Bust of Brunelleschi by Buggiano
10. Stairs to crypt
11. Campanile

500 Feet

300 Feet

MAKING THE CLIMB

Climbing the 463 steps to the top of the dome is not for the faint of heart—or for the claustrophobic—but those who do it will be awarded a smashing view of Florence ❶. Keep in mind that the way up is also the way down, which means that while you're huffing and puffing in the ascent, people very close to you in a narrow staircase are making their way down ❷.

300 Feet

75 Feet

DUOMO GOOD TO KNOW

- Even first thing in the morning during high season (May through September), a line is likely to have formed to climb the dome. Expect an hour wait.

- For an alternative to the dome, consider climbing the less trafficked campanile, which gives you a view from on high of the dome itself.

- Dress code essentials: covered shoulders, no short shorts, and hats off upon entering.

✉ Piazza del Duomo
☎ 055/2302885
⊕ www.operaduomo.firenze.it
✉ Free, crypt €3, cupola €6
🕐 Crypt: Mon.–Wed., Fri., Sun. 10–5; Thurs. 10–4:30; Sat. 10–5:45; first Sat. of month 10–3:30. Cupola: Weekdays 8:30–7, Sat. 8:30–5:40, 1st Sat. of month 8:30–4. Duomo: Mon.–Wed. and Fri. 10–5, Thurs. 10–4:30, Sat., 10–4:45, Sun 1:30–4:45, 1st Sat. of month 10–3:30.

BRUNELLESCHI vs. GHIBERTI
The Rivalry of Two Renaissance Geniuses

In Renaissance Florence, painters, sculptors, and architects competed for major commissions, with the winner earning the right to undertake a project that might occupy him (and keep him paid) for a decade or more. Stakes were high, and the resulting rivalries fierce—none more so than that between Filippo Brunelleschi and Lorenzo Ghiberti.

The two first clashed in 1401, for the commission to create the bronze doors of the Baptistery. When Ghiberti won, Brunelleschi took it hard, fleeing to Rome, where he would remain for 15 years. Their rematch came in 1418, over the design of the Duomo's cupola, with Brunelleschi triumphant. For the remainder of their lives, the two would miss no opportunity to belittle each other's work.

FILIPPO BRUNELLESCHI (1377–1446)

MASTERPIECE: The dome of Santa Maria del Fiore.

BEST FRIENDS: Donatello, whom he stayed with in Rome after losing the Baptistery doors competition; the Medici family, who rescued him from bankruptcy.

SIGNATURE TRAITS: Paranoid, secretive, bad tempered, practical joker, inept businessman.

SAVVIEST POLITICAL MOVE: Feigned sickness and left for Rome after his dome plans were publicly criticized by Ghiberti, who was second-in-command. The project proved too much for Ghiberti to manage on his own, and Brunelleschi returned triumphant.

MOST EMBARRASSING MOMENT: In 1434 he was imprisoned for two weeks for failure to pay a small guild fee. The humiliation might have been orchestrated by Ghiberti.

OTHER CAREER: Shipbuilder. He built a huge vessel, *Il Badalone*, to transport marble for the dome up the Arno. It sank on its first voyage.

INSPIRED: The dome of St. Peter's in Rome.

LORENZO GHIBERTI (1378–1455)

MASTERPIECE: *The Gates of Paradise*, the ten-paneled east doors of the Baptistery.

BEST FRIEND: Giovanni da Prato, an underling who wrote diatribes attacking the dome's design and Brunelleschi's character.

SIGNATURE TRAITS: Instigator, egoist, know-it-all, shrewd businessman.

SAVVIEST POLITICAL MOVE: During the Baptistery doors competition, he had an open studio and welcomed opinions on his work, while Brunelleschi labored behind closed doors.

OTHER CAREER: Collector of classical artifacts, historian.

INSPIRED: *The Gates of Hell* by Auguste Rodin.

The Gates of Paradise detail

9 Palazzo Davanzati. The prestigious Davanzati family owned this 14th-century palace in one of Florence's swankiest medieval neighborhoods. It reopened in May 2005 after a lengthy, 10-year restoration. The place is a delight, as you can wander through the surprisingly light-filled courtyard, and climb the steep stairs to the *piano nobile,* where the family did most of its living. The beautiful *Sala dei Pappagalli* (Parrot Room) is adorned with trompe l'oeil tapestries and gaily painted birds. Though some claim that these date from the 14th century, many art historians are much less sure. ⊠*Piazza Davanzati 13, Piazza della Repubblica* ☎*055/2388610* ⬜*Free* ⊙ *Daily 8:15–1:50. Closed 1st, 3rd, and 5th Sun. of month; closed 2nd and 4th Mon. of month.*

12 Palazzo Vecchio *(Old Palace).* Florence's forbidding, fortresslike city hall was begun in 1299, presumably designed by Arnolfo di Cambio, and its massive bulk and towering campanile dominate Piazza della Signoria. It was built as a meeting place for the heads of the seven major guilds governing the city at the time; over the centuries it has served lesser purposes, but today it is once again City Hall. The interior courtyard is a good deal less severe, having been remodeled by Michelozzo (1396–1472) in 1453; a copy of Verrocchio's bronze *puttino* cherub), topping the central fountain, softens the space.

The main attraction is on the second floor: two adjoining rooms that supply one of the most startling contrasts in Florence. The first is the vast **Sala dei Cinquecento** (Room of the Five Hundred), named for the 500-member Great Council, the people's assembly established after the death of Lorenzo the Magnificent, that met here. The sala was decorated by Giorgio Vasari, around 1563–65, with huge—almost grotesquely huge—frescoes celebrating Florentine history; depictions of battles with nearby cities predominate. Continuing the martial theme, the sala also contains Michelangelo's *Victory,* intended for the never-completed tomb of Pope Julius II (1443–1513), plus other sculptures of decidedly lesser quality.

The second room is the little **Studiolo,** to the right of the sala's entrance. It was the study of Cosimo I's son, the melancholy Francesco I (1541–87). It was designed by Vasari and decorated by Vasari and Bronzino (1503–72) and is intimate, civilized, and filled with complex, questioning, allegorical art. ⊠*Piazza della Signoria* ☎*055/2768465* ⬜*€6* ⊙ *Mon.–Wed. and Fri.–Sun. 9–7, Thurs. 9–2.*

8 Piazza della Repubblica. The square marks the site of the ancient forum that was the core of the original Roman settlement. The street plan around the piazza still reflects the carefully plotted Roman military encampment. The Mercato Vecchio (Old Market), which had been here since the Middle Ages, was demolished and the current piazza was constructed between 1885 and 1895 as a neoclassical showpiece. The piazza is lined with outdoor cafés, affording an excellent opportunity for people-watching.

SAN LORENZO TO THE ACCADEMIA

A sculptor, painter, architect, and even a poet, Florentine native son Michelangelo was a consummate genius, and some of his finest creations remain in his hometown. The Biblioteca Medicea Laurenziana is perhaps his most fanciful work of architecture. A key to understanding Michelangelo's genius can be found in the magnificent Cappelle Medicee, where both his sculptural and architectural prowess can be clearly seen. Planned frescoes were never completed, sadly, for they would have shown in one space the artistic triple threat that he certainly was. The towering yet graceful *David*, his most famous work, resides in the Galleria dell'Accademia.

After visiting San Lorenzo, resist the temptation to explore the market that surrounds the church. You can always come back later, after the churches and museums have closed; the market is open until 7 PM. Note that the Museo di San Marco closes at 1:50 on weekdays.

THE MAIN ATTRACTIONS

2 **Cappelle Medicee** *(Medici Chapels).* This magnificent complex includes
★ the **Cappella dei Principi,** the Medici chapel and mausoleum that was begun in 1605 and kept marble workers busy for several hundred years, and the **Sagrestia Nuova** (New Sacristy), designed by Michelangelo and so called to distinguish it from Brunelleschi's Sagrestia Vecchia (Old Sacristy) in San Lorenzo.

Michelangelo received the commission for the New Sacristy in 1520 from Cardinal Giulio de' Medici (1478–1534), who later became Pope Clement VII and who wanted a new burial chapel for his cousins Giuliano (1478–1534) and Lorenzo (1492–1519). The result was a tour de force of architecture and sculpture. Architecturally, Michelangelo was as original and inventive here as ever, but it is, quite properly, the powerful sculptural compositions of the sidewall tombs that dominate the room. The scheme is allegorical: on the tomb on the right are figures representing Day and Night, and on the tomb to the left are figures representing Dawn and Dusk; above them are idealized sculptures of the two men, usually interpreted to represent the active life and the contemplative life. But the allegorical meanings are secondary; what is most important is the intense presence of the sculptural figures and the force with which they hit the viewer. ⊠*Piazza di Madonna degli Aldobrandini, San Lorenzo* ☎*055/294883 reservations* 🖃*€6* ⊙*Daily 8:15–4:50. Closed 1st, 3rd, and 5th Mon. and 2nd and 4th Sun. of month.*

7 **Galleria dell'Accademia** *(Accademia Gallery).* The collection of Floren-
⟳ tine paintings, dating from the 13th to the 18th centuries, is largely
★ unremarkable, but the sculptures by Michelangelo are worth the price of admission. The unfinished *Slaves*, fighting their way out of their

San Lorenzo to the Accademia

Giardino della Gherardesca

Via Giuseppe Giusti

Via Laura

Via della Colonna

Via della Pergola

Borgo Pinti

11

0   1/8 mile

0   200 meters

10

9

Via Gino Capponi

Via C. Battisti

Piazza della SS. Annunziata

6

Via degli Alfani

Via dei Servi

Via del Castellaccio

Ospedale Santa Maria Nuova

8

Piazza San Marco

Chiostro dello Scalzo

7

Via Ricasoli

Via Cavour

🛈

Via de' Gori

Via de' Ginori

5

Via de' Pucci

Via Martelli

V. S. Gallo

Via Guelfa

Via Santa Reparata

V. della Stufa

Via Faenza

V. del Melarancio

V. del Giglio

Via dell' Ariento

Borgo la Noce

Via Taddea

Via Canto de' Nelli

Via dell' Amorino

Via Conti

Piazza Mercato Centrale

1

2

3

4

Piazza S. Lorenzo

4

marble prisons, were meant for the tomb of Michelangelo's overly demanding patron Pope Julius II (1443–1513). But the focal point is the original *David*, moved here from Piazza della Signoria in 1873. *David* was commissioned in 1501 by the Opera del Duomo (Cathe-

dral Works Committee), which gave the 26-year-old sculptor a leftover block of marble that had been ruined by another artist. Michelangelo's success with the block was so dramatic that the city showered him with honors, and the Opera del Duomo voted to build him a house and a studio in which to live and work.

Today *David* is beset not by Goliath but by tourists, and seeing the statue at all—much less really studying it—can be a trial. Save yourself a long and tiresome wait in line by reserving tickets in advance. A Plexiglas barrier surrounds it, following a 1991 attack upon the sculpture by a hammer-wielding artist who, luckily, inflicted only a few minor nicks on the toes. A 2004 restoration in honor of his 500th birthday has, at the very least, cleaned up the sculpture. The statue is not quite what it seems. It is so poised and graceful and alert—so miraculously alive—that it is often considered the definitive embodiment of the ideals of the High Renaissance in sculpture. But its true place in the history of art is a bit more complicated.

As Michelangelo well knew, the Renaissance painting and sculpture that preceded his work were deeply concerned with ideal form. Perfection of proportion was the ever-sought Holy Grail; during the Renaissance, ideal proportion was equated with ideal beauty, and ideal beauty was equated with spiritual perfection. But *David*, despite its supremely calm and dignified pose, departs from these ideals. Michelangelo didn't give the statue perfect proportions. The head is slightly too large for the body, the arms are too large for the torso, and the hands are dramatically large for the arms. The work was originally commissioned to adorn the exterior of the Duomo and was intended to be seen from a distance and on high. Michelangelo knew exactly what he was doing, calculating that the perspective of the viewer would be such that, in order for the statue to appear proportioned, the upper body, head, and arms would have to be bigger as they are farther away from the viewer's line of vision. But he also did it to express and embody, as powerfully as possible in a single figure, an entire biblical story. David's hands *are* big, but so was Goliath, and these are the hands that slew him. ⊠ *Via Ricasoli 60, San Marco* ☎ *055/294883 reservations, 055/2388609 gallery* ⬚ *€6.50, reservation fee €3* ⊙ *Tues.–Sun. 8:15–6:50.*

❽ Museo di San Marco. A former Dominican convent adjacent to the church of San Marco now houses this museum, which contains many stunning works by Fra Angelico (circa 1400–55), the Dominican friar famous for his piety as well as for his painting. When the friars' cells were restructured between 1439 and 1444, he decorated many of them with frescoes meant to spur religious contemplation. His unostentatious and

CLOSE UP

Florence's Trial by Fire

One of the most striking figures of Renaissance Florence was Girolamo Savonarola, a Dominican friar who, for a moment, captured the conscience of the city. In 1491 he became prior of the convent of San Marco, where he adopted a life of austerity and delivered sermons condemning Florence's excesses and the immorality of his fellow clergy. Following the death of Lorenzo de' Medici, Savonarola was instrumental in the formation of the republic of Florence, ruled by a representative council with Christ enthroned as monarch. In one of his most memorable acts, he urged Florentines to toss worldly possessions—from frilly dresses to Botticelli paintings—onto a "bonfire of the vanities" in Piazza della Signoria. Savonarola's antagonism toward church hierarchy led to his undoing: he was excommunicated in 1497, and the following year was hanged and burned on charges of heresy. Today, at the Museo di San Marco, you can visit Savonarola's cell and see his arresting portrait.

direct paintings exalt the simple beauties of the contemplative life. Fra Angelico's works are everywhere, from the friars' cells to the superb panel paintings on view in the museum. Don't miss the famous *Annunciation,* on the upper floor, and the works in the gallery off the cloister as you enter. Here you can see his beautiful *Last Judgment*; as usual, the tortures of the damned are far more inventive and interesting than the pleasures of the redeemed. ⊠*Piazza San Marco 1* ☎*055/2388608* ☜*€4* ⊙ *Weekdays 8:15–1:50, weekends 8:15–6:50. Closed 1st, 3rd, and 5th Sun., and 2nd and 4th Mon. of month.*

❸ San Lorenzo. Filippo Brunelleschi designed this basilica, as well as that of Santo Spirito in the Oltrarno, in the early 15th century. He never lived to see either finished. The two interiors are similar in design and effect and proclaim with ringing clarity the beginning of the Renaissance in architecture. San Lorenzo, however, has a grid of dark, inlaid marble lines on the floor, which considerably heightens the dramatic effect. The grid makes the rigorous geometry of the interior immediately visible and is an illuminating lesson on the laws of perspective. If you stand in the middle of the nave at the church entrance, on the line that stretches to the high altar, every element in the church—the grid, the nave columns, the side aisles, the coffered nave ceiling—seems to march inexorably toward a hypothetical vanishing point beyond the high altar, exactly as in a single-point-perspective painting. Brunelleschi's **Sagrestia Vecchia** (Old Sacristy) has stucco decorations by Donatello; it's at the end of the left transept. ⊠*Piazza San Lorenzo* ☎*055/2645144* ☜*€2.50* ⊙ *Mon.–Sat. 10–5; Mar.–Oct., Sun. 1:30–5. Closed Sun. Nov.–Feb.*

ALSO WORTH SEEING

❹ Biblioteca Medicea Laurenziana *(Laurentian Library).* Michelangelo the architect was every bit as original as Michelangelo the sculptor. Unlike Brunelleschi (the architect of the Spedale degli Innocenti), however, he wasn't obsessed with proportion and perfect geometry. He was interested in experimentation and invention and in the expression of a personal vision at times highly idiosyncratic.

It was never more idiosyncratic than in the Laurentian Library, begun in 1524 and finished in 1568, and its famous **vestibolo**. This strangely shaped anteroom has had scholars scratching their heads for centuries. In a space more than two stories high, why did Michelangelo limit his use of columns and pilasters to the upper two-thirds of the wall? Why didn't he rest them on strong pedestals instead of on huge, decorative curlicue scrolls, which rob them of all visual support? Why did he recess them into the wall, which makes them look weaker still? The architectural elements here do not stand firm and strong and tall, as inside San Lorenzo, next door; instead, they seem to be pressed into the wall as if into putty, giving the room a soft, rubbery look that is one of the strangest effects ever achieved by classical architecture. It's almost as if Michelangelo intentionally flouted the conventions of the High Renaissance to see what kind of bizarre, mannered effect might result. His innovations were tremendously influential and produced a period of architectural experimentation. As his contemporary Giorgio Vasari put it, "Artisans have been infinitely and perpetually indebted to him because he broke the bonds and chains of a way of working that had become habitual by common usage."

The anteroom's staircase (best viewed straight-on), which emerges from the library with the visual force of an unstoppable lava flow, has been exempted from the criticism, however. In its highly sculptural conception and execution, it is quite simply one of the most original and fluid staircases in the world. ⊠ *Piazza San Lorenzo 9, entrance to left of San Lorenzo* ☏ *055/210760* ⊕ *www.bml.firenze.sbn.it* ✉ *Special exhibitions €5,* museum *€3* ⊘ *Sun.–Fri. 9–1.*

❶ **Mercato Centrale.** Some of the food at this huge, two-story market hall is remarkably exotic. The ground floor contains meat and cheese stalls, as well as some very good bars that have *panini* (sandwiches), and the second floor teems with vegetable stands. ⊠ *Piazza del Mercato Centrale, San Lorenzo* ☏ *No phone* ⊘ *Mon.–Sat. 7–2.*

❿ **Museo Archeologico** *(Archaeological Museum).* Of the Etruscan, Egyptian, and Greco-Roman antiquities here, the Etruscan collection is particularly notable—one of the largest in Italy. The famous bronze *Chimera* was discovered (without the tail, a reconstruction) in the 16th century. ⊠ *Via della Colonna 38, Santissima Annunziata* ☏ *055/23575* ⊕ *www.comune.firenze.it/soggetti/sat/didattica/museo.html* ✉ *€4* ⊘ *Mon. 2–7, Tues. and Thurs. 8:30–7, Wed. and Fri.–Sun. 8:30–2.*

❺ **Palazzo Medici-Riccardi.** The main attraction of this palace, begun in 1444 by Michelozzo for Cosimo de' Medici, is the interior chapel, the so-called **Cappella dei Magi** on the upper floor. Painted on its walls is Benozzo Gozzoli's famous *Procession of the Magi,* finished in 1460 and celebrating both the birth of Christ and the greatness of the Medici family. Gozzoli wasn't a revolutionary painter and today is considered by some not quite first rate because of his technique, which was old-fashioned even for his day. Gozzoli's gift, however, was for entrancing the eye, not challenging the mind, and on those terms his success here is beyond question. The paintings are full of activity yet somehow frozen in time in a way that fails utterly as realism but succeeds triumphantly as soon as the demand for realism is set aside. Entering the chapel is like walking into the middle of a magnificently illustrated children's storybook, and this beauty makes it one of the most enjoyable rooms in the city. ⊠ *Via Cavour 1, San Lorenzo* ☎*055/2760340* ⌨€5 ⊙ *Thurs.–Tues. 9–7.*

⑫ **Santa Maria Maddalena dei Pazzi.** One of Florence's hidden treasures, a cool and composed *Crucifixion* by Perugino (circa 1445/50–1523), is in the chapter house of the monastery below this church. Here you can see the Virgin Mary and St. John the Evangelist with Mary Magdalene and Sts. Benedict and Bernard of Clairvaux posed against a simple but haunting landscape. The figure of Christ crucified occupies the center of this brilliantly hued fresco. Perugino's colors radiate—note the juxtaposition of the yellow-green cuff against the orange tones of the Magdalene's robe. ⊠ *Borgo Pinti 58, Santa Croce* ☎*055/2478420* ⌨*Suggested €1* ⊙ *Mon.–Sat. 9–noon, 5–5:20, and 6–7; Sun. 9–noon and 5–6:20.*

⑨ **Santissima Annunziata.** Dating from the mid-13th century, this church was restructured in 1447 by Michelozzo, who gave it an uncommon (and lovely) entrance cloister with frescoes by Andrea del Sarto (1486–1530), Pontormo (1494–1556), and Rosso Fiorentino (1494–1540). The interior is a rarity for Florence: an overwhelming example of the baroque. But it's not really a fair example, because it's merely 17th-century baroque decoration applied willy-nilly to an earlier structure—exactly the sort of violent remodeling exercise that has given the baroque a bad name. The **Cappella dell'Annunziata,** immediately inside the entrance to the left, illustrates the point. The lower half, with its stately Corinthian columns and carved frieze bearing the Medici arms, was commissioned by Piero de' Medici in 1447; the upper half, with its erupting curves and impish sculpted cherubs, was added 200 years later. Each is effective in its own way, but together they serve only to prove that dignity is rarely comfortable wearing a party hat. Fifteenth-century-fresco enthusiasts should also note the very fine Holy Trinity with St. Jerome in the second chapel on the left. Done by Andrea del Castagno (circa 1421–57), it shows a wiry and emaciated St. Jerome with Paula and Eustochium, two of his closest followers. ⊠*Piazza di Santissima Annunziata* ☎*055/266186* ⊙*Daily 7–12:30 and 4–6:30.*

⑪ **Spedale degli Innocenti.** Built by Brunelleschi in 1419 to serve as an orphanage, it takes the historical prize as the very first Renaissance building. Brunelleschi designed its portico with his usual rigor, building it out of the two shapes he considered mathematically (and therefore philosophically and aesthetically) perfect: the square and the circle. Below the level of the arches, the portico encloses a row of perfect cubes; above the level of the arches, the portico encloses a row of intersecting hemispheres. The entire geometric scheme is articulated with Corinthian columns, capitals, and arches borrowed directly from antiquity. At the time he designed the portico, Brunelleschi was also designing the interior of

San Lorenzo, using the same basic ideas. But because the portico was finished before San Lorenzo, the Spedale degli Innocenti can claim the honor of ushering in Renaissance architecture. The 10 ceramic medallions depicting swaddled infants that decorate the portico are by Andrea della Robbia (1435–1525/28), done in about 1487.

Within the Spedale degli Innocenti is a small museum, or **Pinacoteca** (🖾€4 ⊘ *Thurs.–Tues. 8:30–2*). Most of the objects are minor works by major artists, but well worth a look is Domenico Ghirlandaio's (1449–94) *Adorazione dei Magi* (*Adoration of the Magi*), executed in 1488. His use of color, and his eye for flora and fauna, shows that art from north of the Alps made a great impression on him. ⊠ *Piazza di Santissima Annunziata 12* 🕾 *055/20371* 🖾€4 ⊘ *Mon.–Sat. 8:30–7, Sun. 8:30–2.*

SANTA MARIA NOVELLA TO THE ARNO

Piazza Santa Maria Novella, near the train station, suffers a degree of squalor, especially at night. Nevertheless, the streets in and around the piazza have their share of architectural treasures, including some of Florence's most tasteful palaces. Between Santa Maria Novella and the Arno is Via Tornabuoni, Florence's finest shopping street.

THE MAIN ATTRACTIONS

❶ Santa Maria Novella. The facade of this church looks distinctly clumsy by later Renaissance standards, and with good reason: it is an architectural hybrid. The lower half was completed mostly in the 14th century; its pointed-arch niches and decorative marble patterns reflect the Gothic style of the day. About 100 years later (around 1456), architect Leon Battista Alberti was called in to complete the job. The marble decoration of his upper story clearly defers to the already existing work below, but the architectural motifs he added evince an entirely different style. The central doorway, the four ground-floor half-columns with Corinthian capitals, the triangular pediment atop the second story, the inscribed frieze immediately below the pediment—these are borrowings from antiquity, and they reflect the new Renaissance style in architecture, born some 35 years earlier at the Spedale degli Innocenti. Alberti's most important addition, however, the S-curve scrolls that surmount the decorative circles on either side of the upper story, had no precedent whatever in antiquity. The problem was to soften the abrupt transition between wide ground floor and narrow upper story. Alberti's solution turned out to be definitive. Once you start to look for them, you will find scrolls such as these (or sculptural variations of them) on churches all over Italy, and every one of them derives from Alberti's example here.

The architecture of the interior is, like that of the Duomo, a dignified but somber example of Florentine Gothic. Exploration is essential, however, because the church's store of art treasures is remarkable. Highlights include the 14th-century stained-glass rose window depicting the *Coronation of the Virgin* (above the central entrance); the

Santa Maria Novella
to the Arno

hostel

Via Taddea

Piazza
Mercato
Centrale

Via Cavour

Via Faenza

Via Panicale

Via della Stufa

Via de' Ginori

Via dei Gori

Piazza
Adoa

Via Fiume

Via dell' Ariento

Borgo
Noce

V. dei Gori

Via Nazionale

Via Vallorda

Via Canto de' Nelli

Stazione
Maria
Novella

Via S. Antonio

Via Faenza

Via Conti

Via del Melarancio

Via del Giglio

Via dell' Alloro

Via Cerretani

Piazza
dell' Unità
Italiana

Via dei Panzani

Piazza
S. Maria
Maggiore

Via Pecori

V. S. Caterina
da Siena

Via della Scala

Via dei Banchi

Via de' Rondinelli

Via de' Vecchietti

Via del
Trebbio

V. d. Belle Donne

Piazza
S. Maria
Novella

Via de' Pescioni

Via de' Corsi

Via dell'Albero

Via de' Conti

V. Benedetta

Via Strozzi

Via de' Sassetti

Via Palazzuolo

Via del Sole

Via Spada

P.za Strozzi

2

Via Maso
Finiguerra

Piazza
San Pancrazio

Via dei Fossi

Vigna Nuova

Via Tornabuoni

Borgo Ognissanti

V. del Purgatorio

Piazza
Santa
Trinità

Via Montebello

Piazza
Ognissanti

Via d. Porcellana

Via dei Federighi

Via del Moro

Via del Parione

3

Via del Parione

4

Piazza
Goldoni

Lung. Amerigo Vespucci

Lung. Corsini

Ponte
Vespucci

Ponte alla Carraia

Arno

S. Trinità

Ponte
Trinità

0   1/8 mile

0   200 meters

Lung. Guicciardini

Cappella Filippo Strozzi (to the right of the altar), containing late-15th-century frescoes and stained glass by Filippino Lippi; the *cappella maggiore* (the area around the high altar), displaying frescoes by Ghirlandaio; and the Cappella Gondi (to the left of the altar), containing Filippo Brunelleschi's famous wood crucifix, carved around 1410 and said to have so stunned the great Donatello when he first saw it that he dropped a basket of eggs.

Of special interest for its great historical importance and beauty is Masaccio's *Trinity,* on the left-hand wall, almost halfway down the nave. Painted around 1426–27 (at the same time he was working on his frescoes in Santa Maria del Carmine), it unequivocally announced the arrival of the Renaissance. The realism of the figure of Christ was revolutionary in itself, but what was probably even more startling to contemporary Florentines was the barrel vault in the background. The mathematical rules for employing perspective in painting had just been discovered (probably by Brunelleschi), and this was one of the first works of art to employ them with utterly convincing success.

In the cloisters of the **Museo di Santa Maria Novella** (✉ *Piazza Santa Maria Novella 19* ☎ *055/282187* 🎟 *€2.70* 🕐 *Mon.–Thurs. and Sat. 9– 5, Sun. 9–2*), to the left of Santa Maria Novella, is a faded fresco cycle by Paolo Uccello depicting tales from Genesis, with a dramatic vision of the Deluge. Earlier and better-preserved frescoes painted in 1348–55 by Andrea da Firenze are in the chapter house, or the **Cappellone degli Spagnoli** (Spanish Chapel), off the cloister. ☎ *055/210113* 🎟 *€2.50 for both museum and chapel* 🕐 *Mon.–Thurs. and Sat. 9–5, Sun. 9–2.*

❸ Santa Trinita. Started in the 11th century by Vallambrosian monks and originally Romanesque in style, the church underwent a Gothic remodeling during the 14th century. (Remains of the Romanesque construction are visible on the interior front wall.) Its major works are the fresco cycle and altarpiece in the Cappella Sassetti, the second to the high altar's right, painted by Ghirlandaio from around 1480 to 1485. His work here possesses such graceful decorative appeal as well as a proud depiction of his native city (most of the cityscapes show 15th-century Florence in all her glory). The wall frescoes illustrate scenes from the life of St. Francis, and the altarpiece, depicting the *Adoration of the Shepherds,* veritably glows. ✉ *Piazza Santa Trinita, Santa Maria Novella* ☎ *055/216912* 🕐 *Mon.–Sat. 8–noon and 4–6.*

ALSO WORTH SEEING

❹ Museo Salvatore Ferragamo. If there's such a thing as a temple for footwear, this is it. The shoes in this dramatically displayed collection were designed by Salvatore Ferragamo (1898–1960) beginning in the early 20th century. Born in southern Italy, the late master jump-started his career in Hollywood by creating shoes for the likes of Mary Pickford and Rudolph Valentino. He then returned to Florence and set up shop in the basement of the 13th-century Palazzo Spini Ferroni. The collection includes about 16,000 shoes, and those on exhibition are frequently rotated. ✉ *Via dei Tornabuoni 2, Santa Maria Novella* ☎ *055/3360846* 🎟 *€5* 🕐 *Mon. and Wed.–Sun. 10–6.*

CLOSE UP

Meet the Medici

The Medici were the dominant family of Renaissance Florence, wielding political power and financing some of the world's greatest art. You'll see their names at every turn around the city. These are some of the clan's more notable members:

Cosimo il Vecchio (1389–1464), incredibly wealthy banker to the popes, was the first in the family line to act as de facto ruler of Florence. He was a great patron of the arts and architecture; he was the moving force behind the family palace and the Dominican complex of San Marco.

Lorenzo il Magnifico (1449–92), grandson of Cosimo il Vecchio, presided over a Florence largely at peace with her neighbors. A collector of cameos, a writer of sonnets, and lover of ancient texts, he was the preeminent Renaissance man.

Leo X (1475–1521), also known as Giovanni de' Medici, became the first Medici pope, helping extend the family power base to include Rome and the Papal States. His reign was characterized by a host of problems, the biggest one being a former friar named Martin Luther.

Catherine de' Medici (1519–89) was married by her cousin Pope Clement VII to Henry of Valois, who later became Henry II of France. Wife of one king and mother of three, she was the first Medici to marry into European royalty. Lorenzo il Magnifico, her great-grandfather, would have been thrilled.

Cosimo I (1537–74), the first grand duke of Tuscany, should not be confused with his ancestor Cosimo il Vecchio.

4

❷ **Palazzo Strozzi.** The Strozzi family built this imposing palazzo in an attempt to outshine the nearby Palazzo Medici. Based on a model by Giuliano da Sangallo (circa 1452–1516) dating from around 1489 and executed between 1489 and 1504 under il Cronaca (1457–1508) and Benedetto da Maiaino (1442–97), it was inspired by Michelozzo's earlier Palazzo Medici-Riccardi. The palazzo's exterior is simple, severe, and massive: it's a testament to the wealth of a patrician, 15th century Florentine family. The interior courtyard, entered from the rear of the palazzo, is another matter altogether. It is here that the classical vocabulary—columns, capitals, pilasters, arches, and cornices—is given uninhibited and powerful expression. Blockbuster art shows frequently occur here. ✉ *Via Tornabuoni, Piazza della Repubblica* ☎ *055/2776461* ⊕ *www.palazzostrozzi.org* ⊕ *www.contromodafi renze.it* ✉ *Free, except during exhibitions* ☉ *Daily 10–7.*

SANTA CROCE

The Santa Croce quarter, on the southeast fringe of the historic center, was built up in the Middle Ages outside the second set of medieval city walls. The centerpiece of the neighborhood was the basilica of Santa Croce, which could hold great numbers of worshippers; the vast piazza could accommodate any overflow and also served as a fairground and, allegedly since the middle of the 16th century, as a playing field for no-holds-barred soccer games. A center of leatherworking since the Middle Ages, the neighborhood is still packed with leatherworkers and leather shops.

THE MAIN ATTRACTIONS

② Piazza Santa Croce. Originally outside the city's 12th-century walls, this piazza grew with the Franciscans, who used the large square for public preaching. During the Renaissance it was used for *giostre* (jousts), including one sponsored by Lorenzo de' Medici. "Bonfires of the vanities" occurred here, as well as soccer matches in the 16th century. Lined with many palazzi dating from the 15th century, it remains one of Florence's loveliest piazze and is a great place to people-watch.

㉝ Santa Croce. Like the Duomo, this church is Gothic, but, also like the
Fodor'sChoice Duomo, its facade dates from the 19th century. As a burial place, the
★ church probably contains more skeletons of Renaissance celebrities than any other in Italy. The tomb of Michelangelo is on the right at the front of the basilica; he is said to have chosen this spot so that the first thing he would see on Judgment Day, when the graves of the dead fly open, would be Brunelleschi's dome through Santa Croce's open doors. The tomb of Galileo Galilei (1564–1642) is on the left wall; he was not granted a Christian burial until 100 years after his death because of his controversial contention that Earth is not the center of the universe. The tomb of Niccolò Machiavelli (1469–1527), the political theoretician whose brutally pragmatic philosophy so influenced the Medici, is halfway down the nave on the right. The grave of Lorenzo Ghiberti, creator of the Baptistery doors, is halfway down the nave on the left. Composer Gioacchino Rossini (1792–1868) is buried at the end of the nave on the right. The monument to Dante Alighieri (1265–1321), the greatest Italian poet, is a memorial rather than a tomb (he is buried in Ravenna); it's on the right wall near the tomb of Michelangelo.

The collection of art within the complex is by far the most important of any church in Florence. The most famous works are probably the Giotto frescoes in the two chapels immediately to the right of the high altar. They illustrate scenes from the lives of St. John the Evangelist and St. John the Baptist (in the right-hand chapel) and scenes from the life of St. Francis (in the left-hand chapel). Time has not been kind to these frescoes; through the centuries, wall tombs were placed in the middle of them, they were whitewashed and plastered over, and in the 19th century they suffered a clumsy restoration. But the reality that Giotto introduced into painting can still be seen. He did not paint beautifully stylized religious icons, as the Byzantine style that preceded him prescribed; he instead painted drama—St. Francis surrounded by grieving friars at the very moment of his death. This was a radical shift in emphasis: before Giotto, painting's role was to symbolize the attributes of God; after him, it was to imitate life. His work is indeed primitive compared with later painting, but in the early 14th century it caused a sensation that was not equaled for another 100 years. He was, for his time, the equal of both Masaccio and Michelangelo.

Santa Croce

| 0 | | 1/8 mile |
| 0 | | 200 meters |

Via Nuova dei Caccini

Via dei Pilastri

Borgo Pinti

Via Fiesolana

Via dei Pepi

V. Luigi Carlo Farini

4

Via di Mezzo

Via Pietrapiana

Via S. Egidio

Via Martiri d. Popolo

Via M. Buonarroti

Piazza Salvemini

Piazza San Pier Maggiore

V. San Pier Maggiore

Via dell' Ulivo

Via dell' Agnolo

3

Via dei Pandolfini

Via Giuseppe Verdi

Via Ghibellina

Via delle Pinzochere

Via San Cristofano

Borgo Allegri

Via Verrazzano

Via della Vigna Vecchia

Via di S. Giuseppe

Via d.' Buretta

Via Torta

Via dell' Anguillara

2

1

i

Via d.' Acqua

Borgo dei Greci

Via de' Benci

Borgo S. Croce

V. Antonio Magliabechi

V.d.' Corno

V. d.' Parlascio

V. d.' Magalotti

V.d.' Rustici

Via Vinegia

Via dei Neri

Corso Tintori

V.d.' Vagelli

Arno

KEY
i *Tourist information*

Among the church's other highlights are Donatello's *Annunciation,* a moving expression of surprise (on the right wall two-thirds of the way down the nave); 14th-century frescoes by Taddeo Gaddi (circa 1300–66) illustrating scenes from the life of the Virgin Mary, clearly showing the influence of Giotto (in the chapel at the end of the right transept);

WORD OF MOUTH

"You can walk *anywhere* in Florence easily—it's one of my favorite cities because it's so compact. Every time I go I am surprised by how close all the major sites are."

–Travelday

and Donatello's *Crucifix,* criticized by Brunelleschi for making Christ look like a peasant (in the chapel at the end of the left transept). Outside the church proper, in the **Museo dell'Opera di Santa Croce** off the cloister, is the 13th-century *Triumphal Cross* by Cimabue (circa 1240–1302), badly damaged by the flood of 1966. A model of architectural geometry, the Cappella Pazzi, at the end of the cloister, is the work of Brunelleschi. ✉ *Piazza Santa Croce 16* ☎ *055/2466105* 💶*€5 combined admission to church and museum* ⊙ *Mon.–Sat. 9:30–5:30, Sun. 1–5.*

❻ **Sinagoga.** Jews were well settled in Florence by 1396, when the first money-lending operations became officially sanctioned. Medici patronage helped Jewish banking houses to flourish, but by 1570 Jews were required to live within the large "ghetto," near today's Piazza della Repubblica, by the decree of Cosimo I, who had cut a deal with Pope Pius V (1504–72): in exchange for ghettoizing the Jews, he would receive the title of Grand Duke of Tuscany.

Construction of the modern Moorish-style synagogue began in 1874 as a bequest of David Levi, who wished to endow a synagogue "worthy of the city." Falcini, Micheli, and Treves designed the building on a domed Greek cross plan with galleries in the transept and a roofline bearing three distinctive copper cupolas visible from all over Florence. The exterior has alternating bands of tan travertine and pink granite, reflecting an Islamic style repeated in Giovanni Panti's ornate interior. Of particular interest are the cast-iron gates by Pasquale Franci, the eternal light by Francesco Morini, and the Murano glass mosaics by Giacomo dal Medico. The gilded doors of the Moorish ark, which fronts the pulpit and is flanked by extravagant candelabra, are decorated with symbols of the ancient Temple of Jerusalem and bear bayonet marks from vandals. The synagogue was used as a garage by the Nazis, who failed to inflict much damage in spite of an attempt to blow up the place with dynamite. Only the columns on the left side were destroyed, and even then, the Women's Balcony above did not collapse. Note the Star of David in black and yellow marble inlaid in the floor. The original capitals can be seen in the garden.

Some of the oldest and most beautiful Jewish ritual artifacts in all of Europe are displayed upstairs in the small **Museo Ebraico.** Exhibits document the Florentine Jewish community and the building of the synagogue. The donated objects all belonged to local families and date from as early as the late 16th century. Take special note of the exquisite needlework and silver pieces. A small but well-stocked gift shop

Continued on page 255

WHO'S WHO IN RENAISSANCE ART

Michelangelo. Leonardo da Vinci. Raphael. This heady triumvirate of the Italian Renaissance is synonymous with artistic genius. Yet they are only three of the remarkable cast of characters whose work defines the Renaissance, that extraordinary flourishing of art and culture in Italy, especially in Florence, as the Middle Ages drew to a close. The artists were visionaries, who redefined painting, sculpture, architecture, and even what it means to be an artist.

THE PIONEER. In the mid-14th century, a few artists began to move away the flat, two-dimensional painting of the Middle Ages. **Giotto**, who painted seemingly three-dimensional figures who show emotion, had a major impact on the artists of the next century.

THE GROUNDBREAKERS. The generations of **Brunelleschi** and **Botticelli** took center stage in the 15th century. **Ghiberti**, **Masaccio**, **Donatello**, **Uccello**, **Fra Angelico**, and **Filippo Lippi** were other major players. Part of the Renaissance (or "re-birth") was a renewed interest in classical sources—the texts, monuments, and sculpture of Ancient Greece and Rome. Perspective and the illusion of three-dimensional space in painting was another discovery of this era, known as the Early Renaissance. Suddenly the art appearing on the walls looked real, or more realistic than it used to.

Roman ruins were not the only thing to inspire these artists. There was an incredible exchange of ideas going on. In Santa Maria del Carmine, Filippo Lippi was inspired by the work of Masaccio, who in turn was a friend of Brunelleschi. Young artists also learned from the masters via the apprentice system. Ghiberti's workshop (*bottega* in Italian) included, at one time or another, Donatello, Masaccio, and Uccello. Botticelli was apprenticed to Filippo Lippi.

THE BIG THREE. The mathematical rationality and precision of 15th-century art gave way to what is known as the High Renaissance. **Leonardo**, **Michelangelo**, and **Raphael** were much more concerned with portraying the body in all its glory and with achieving harmony and grandeur in their work. Oil paint, used infrequently up until this time, became more widely employed: as a result, Leonardo's colors are deeper, more sensual, more alive. For one brief period, all three were in Florence at the same time. Michelangelo and Leonardo surely knew one another, as they were simultaneously working on frescoes (never completed) inside Palazzo Vecchio.

When Michelangelo left Florence for Rome in 1508, he began the slow drain of artistic exodus from Florence, which never really recovered her previous glory.

A RENAISSANCE TIMELINE

IN THE WORLD

Black Death in Europe kills one third of the population, 1347-50.

Joan of Arc burned at the stake, 1431.

IN FLORENCE

Dante, a native of Florence, writes *The Divine Comedy*, 1302-21.

Founding of the Medici bank, 1397.

Medici family made official papal bankers.

1434, Cosimo il Vecchio becomes de facto ruler of Florence. The Medici family will dominate the city until 1494.

1300   1400

IN ART   EARLY RENAISSANCE

Masaccio and Masolino fresco Santa Maria del Carmine, 1424-28.

GIOTTO (ca. 1267-1337)

Giotto fresoes in Santa Croce, 1320-25.

BRUNELLESCHI (1377-1446)

LORENZO GHIBERTI (ca. 1381-1455)

DONATELLO (ca. 1386-1466)

PAOLO UCCELLO (1397-1475)

FRA ANGELICO (ca. 1400-1455)

MASACCIO (1401-1428)

FILIPPO LIPPI (ca. 1406-1469)

1334, 67-year-old Giotto is appointed chief architect of Santa Maria del Fiore, Florence's Duomo (below). He begins to work on the Campanile, which will be completed in 1359, after his death.

Donatello sculpts his bronze *David*, ca. 1440.

Fra Angelico frescoes friars' cells in San Marco, ca 1438-45.

Uccello's *Sir John Hawkwood*, ca. 1436.

Ghiberti wins the competition for the Baptistery doors (above) in Florence, 1401.

Brunelleschi wins the competition for the Duomo's cupola (right), 1418.

Gutenberg Bible is printed, 1455.

Columbus discovers America, 1492.

Martin Luther posts his 95 theses on the door at Wittenberg, kicking off the Protestant Reformation, 1517.

Constantinople falls to the Turks, 1453.

Machiavelli's *Prince* appears, 1513.

Copernicus proves that the earth is not the center of the universe, 1530-43.

Lorenzo "il Magnifico" (right), the Medici patron of the arts, rules in Florence, 1449-92.

Two Medici popes Leo X (1513-21) and Clement VII (1523-34) in Rome.

Catherine de'Medici becomes Queen of Fran 1547.

1450   **1500**   **1550**

HIGH RENAISSANCE   MANNERISM

4

IN FOCUS WHO'S WHO IN RENAISSANCE ART

Fra Filippo Lippi's *Madonna and Child*, ca. 1452.

1508, Raphael begins work on the chambers in the Vatican, Rome.

Giorgio Vasari publishes his first edition of *Lives of the Artists*, 1550.

1504, Michelangelo's *David* is put on display in Piazza della Signoria, where it remains until 1873.

Botticelli paints the *Birth of Venus*, ca. 1482.

Michelangelo begins to fresco the Sistine Chapel ceiling, 1508.

BOTTICELLI (ca. 1444-1510)

LEONARDO DA VINCI (1452-1519)

RAPHAEL (1483-1520)

MICHELANGELO (1475-1564)

Leonardo paints *The Last Supper* in Milan, 1495-98.

Giotto's *Nativity*   Donatello's *St. John the Baptist*   Ghiberti's *Gates of Paradise*

GIOTTO (CA. 1267-1337)
Painter/architect from a small town north of Florence.
He unequivocally set Italian painting on the course that led to the triumphs of the Renaissance masters. Unlike the rather flat, two-dimensional forms found in then prevailing Byzantine art, Giotto's figures have a fresh, life-like quality. The people in his paintings have bulk, and they show emotion, which you can see on their faces and in their gestures. This was something new in the late Middle Ages. Without Giotto, there wouldn't have been a Raphael.
In Florence: Santa Croce; Uffizi; Campanile; Santa Maria Novella Elsewhere in Italy: Scrovegni Chapel, Padua; Vatican Museums, Rome

FILIPPO BRUNELLESCHI (1377-1446)
Architect/engineer from Florence.
If Brunelleschi had beaten Ghiberti in the Baptistery doors competition in Florence, the city's Duomo most likely would not have the striking appearance and authority that it has today. After his loss, he sulked off to Rome, where he studied the ancient Roman structures first-hand. Brunelleschi figured out how to vault the Duomo's dome, a structure unprecedented in its colossal size and great height. His Ospedale degli Innocenti employs classical elements in the creation of a stunning, new architectural statement; it is the first truly Renaissance structure.
In Florence: Duomo; Ospedale degli Innocenti; San Lorenzo; Santo Spirito; Baptistery Doors Competition Entry, Bargello; Santa Croce

LORENZO GHIBERTI (CA. 1381-1455)
Sculptor from Florence.
Ghiberti won a competition—besting his chief rival, Brunelleschi—to cast the gilded bronze North Doors of the Baptistery in Florence. These doors, and the East Doors that he subsequently executed, took up the next 50 years of his life. He created intricately worked figures that are more true-to-life than any since antiquity, and he was one of the first Renaissance sculptors to work in bronze. Ghiberti taught the next generation of artists; Donatello, Uccello, and Masaccio all passed through his studio.
In Florence: Door Copies, Baptistery; Original Doors, Museo dell'Opera del Duomo; Baptistry Door Competition Entry, Bargello; Orsanmichele

DONATELLO (CA. 1386-1466)
Sculptor from Florence.
Donatello was an innovator who, like his good friend Brunelleschi, spent most of his long life in Florence. Consumed with the science of optics, he used light and shadow to create the effects of nearness and distance. He made an essentially flat slab look like a three-dimensional scene. His bronze *David* is probably the first free-standing male nude since antiquity. Not only technically brilliant, his work is also emotionally resonant; few sculptors are as expressive.
In Florence: *David*, Bargello; *St. Mark*, Orsanmichele; Palazzo Vecchio; Museo dell'Opera del Duomo; San Lorenzo; Santa Croce Elsewhere in Italy: Padua; Prato; Venice

Fra Angelico's *The Deposition*   Masaccio's *Trinity*   Filippo Lippi's *Madonna and Child*

PAOLO UCCELLO (1397-1475)
Painter from Florence.

Renaissance chronicler Vasari once observed that had Uccello not been so obsessed with the mathematical problems posed by perspective, he would have been a very good painter. The struggle to master single-point perspective and to render motion in two dimensions is nowhere more apparent than in his battle scenes. His first major commission in Florence was the gargantuan fresco of the English mercenary Sir John Hawkwood (the Italians called him Giovanni Acuto) in Florence's Duomo.

In Florence: *Sir John Hawkwood*, Duomo; *Battle of San Romano*, Uffizi; Santa Maria Novella
Elsewhere in Italy: Urbino

FRA ANGELICO (CA. 1400-1455)
Painter from a small town north of Florence.

A Dominican friar, who eventually made his way to the convent of San Marco, Fra Angelico and his assistants painted frescoes for aid in prayer and meditation. He was known for his piety; Vasari wrote that Fra Angelico could never paint a crucifix without a tear running down his face. Perhaps no other painter so successfully translated the mysteries of faith and the sacred into painting. And yet his figures emote, his command of perspective is superb, and his use of color startles even today.

In Florence: Museo di San Marco; Uffizi
Elsewhere in Italy: Vatican Museums, Rome; Fiesole; Cortona; Perugia; Orvieto

MASACCIO (1401-1428)
Painter from San Giovanni Valdarno, southeast of Florence.

Masaccio and Masolino, a frequent collaborator, worked most famously together at Santa Maria del Carmine. Their frescoes of the life of St. Peter use light to mold figures in the painting by imitating the way light falls on figures in real life. Masaccio also pioneered the use of single-point perspective, masterfully rendered in his *Trinity*. His friend Brunelleschi probably introduced him to the technique, yet another step forward in rendering things the way the eye sees them. Masaccio died young and under mysterious circumstances.

In Florence: Santa Maria del Carmine; *Trinity*, Santa Maria Novella

FILIPPO LIPPI (CA. 1406-1469)
Painter from Prato.

At a young age, Filippo Lippi entered the friary of Santa Maria del Carmine, where he was highly influenced by Masaccio and Masolino's frescoes. His religious vows appear to have made less of an impact; his affair with a young nun produced a son, Filippino (Little Philip, who later apprenticed with Botticelli), and a daughter. His religious paintings often have a playful, humorous note; some of his angels are downright impish and look directly out at the viewer. Lippi links the earlier painters of the 15th century with those who follow; Botticelli apprenticed with him.

In Florence: Uffizi; Palazzo Medici Riccardi; San Lorenzo; Palazzo Pitti
Elsewhere in Italy: Prato

Botticelli's *Primavera*

Leonardo's *Portrait of a Young Woman*

Raphael's *Madonna on the Meadow*

BOTTICELLI (CA. 1444-1510)
Painter from Florence.
Botticelli's work is characterized by stunning, elongated blondes, cherubic angels (something he undoubtedly learned from his time with Filippo Lippi), and tender Christs. Though he did many religious paintings, he also painted monumental, nonreligious panels—his *Birth of Venus* and *Primavera* being the two most famous of these. A brief sojourn took him to Rome, where he and a number of other artists frescoed the Sistine Chapel walls.

In Florence: *Birth of Venus*, *Primavera*, Uffizi; Palazzo Pitti
Elsewhere in Italy: Vatican Museums, Rome

LEONARDO DA VINCI (1452-1519)
Painter/sculptor/engineer from Anchiano, a small town outside Vinci.
Leonardo never lingered long in any place; his restless nature and his international reputation led to commissions throughout Italy, and took him to Milan, Vigevano, Pavia, Rome, and, ultimately, France. Though he is most famous for his mysterious *Mona Lisa* (at the Louvre in Paris), he painted other penetrating, psychological portraits in addition to his scientific experiments: his design for a flying machine (never built) predates Kitty Hawk by nearly 500 years. The greatest collection of Leonardo's work in Italy can be seen on one wall in the Uffizi.

In Florence: *Adoration of the Magi*, Uffizi
Elsewhere in Italy: *Last Supper*, Santa Maria delle Grazie, Milan

RAPHAEL (1483-1520)
Painter/architect from Urbino.
Raphael spent only four highly productive years of his short life in Florence, where he turned out made-to-order panel paintings of the Madonna and Child for a hungry public; he also executed a number of portraits of Florentine aristocrats. Perhaps no other artist had such a fine command of line and color, and could render it, seemingly effortlessly, in paint. His painting acquired new authority after he came up against Michelangelo toiling away on the Sistine ceiling. Raphael worked nearly next door in the Vatican, where his figures take on an epic, Michelangelesque scale.

In Florence: Uffizi; Palazzo Pitti
Elsewhere in Italy: Vatican Museums, Rome

MICHELANGELO (1475-1564)
Painter/sculptor/architect from Caprese.
Although Florentine and proud of it (he famously signed his St. Peter's *Pietà* to avoid confusion about where he was from), he spent most of his 90 years outside his native city. He painted and sculpted the male body on an epic scale and glorified it while doing so. Though he complained throughout the proceedings that he was really a sculptor, Michelangelo's Sistine Chapel ceiling is arguably the greatest fresco cycle ever painted (and the massive figures owe no small debt to Giotto).

In Florence: *David*, Galleria dell'Accademia; Uffizi; Casa Buonarroti; Bargello
Elsewhere in Italy: St. Peter's Basilica, Vatican Museums, and Piazza del Campidoglio in Rome

is downstairs. ⊠ *Via Farini 4, Santa Croce* ☎*055/2346654* ⌨*Synagogue and museum €5* ⊘*Apr., May, Sept., and Oct., Sun.–Thurs. 10–5, Fri. 10–2; June–Aug., Sun.–Thurs. 10–6, Fri. 10–2; Nov.–Mar., Sun.–Thurs. 10–3, Fri. 10–2. English guided tours: 10:10, 11, noon, 1, 2 (no tour at 2 on Fri.).*

NEED A BREAK? The only kosher–vegetarian restaurant in Tuscany is Ruth's (⊠ *Via Farini 2/ a, Santa Croce* ☎*055/2480888*), adjacent to Florence's synagogue. On the menu: inexpensive vegetarian and Mediterranean dishes and a large selection of kosher wines. It's closed for Friday dinner and Saturday lunch.

ALSO WORTH SEEING

③ Casa Buonarroti. If you are really enjoying walking in the footsteps of the great genius, you may want to complete the picture by visiting the Buonarroti family home, even though Michelangelo never actually lived there. It was given to his nephew, and it was the nephew's son, also called Michelangelo, who turned it into a gallery dedicated to his great-uncle. The artist's descendents filled it with art treasures, some by Michelangelo himself—a marble bas-relief; the *Madonna of the Steps,* carved when Michelangelo was only a teenager; and his wooden model for the facade of San Lorenzo—and some by other artists that pay homage to him. ⊠ *Via Ghibellina 70, Santa Croce* ☎*055/241752* ⊕*www. casabuonarroti.it* ⌨*€6.50* ⊘*Fri.–Wed. 9:30–2.*

THE OLTRARNO

A walk through the Oltrarno (literally "the other side of the Arno") takes in two very different aspects of Florence: the splendor of the Medici, manifest in the riches of the mammoth Palazzo Pitti and the gracious Giardino di Boboli; and the charm of the Oltrarno, a slightly gentrified but still fiercely proud working-class neighborhood with artisans' and antiques shops.

Farther east across the Arno, a series of ramps and stairs climbs to Piazzale Michelangelo, where the city lies before you in all its glory (skip this trip if it's a hazy day). More stairs (behind La Loggia restaurant) lead to the church of San Miniato al Monte. You can avoid the long walk by taking Bus 12 or 13 at the west end of Ponte alle Grazie and getting off at Piazzale Michelangelo; you still have to climb the monumental stairs to and from San Miniato, but you can then take the bus from Piazzale Michelangelo back to the center of town. If you decide to take a bus, remember to buy your ticket before you board.

THE MAIN ATTRACTIONS

⑤ Giardino di Boboli *(Boboli Gardens).* The main entrance to these landscaped gardens is from the right wing of ⇨ **Palazzo Pitti.** The gardens began to take shape in 1549, when the Pitti family sold the palazzo to Eleanor of Toledo, wife of the Medici grand duke Cosimo I. The initial landscaping plans were laid out by Niccolò Tribolo (1500–50). After his death, work was continued by Vasari, Ammannati, Giambologna, Bernardo Buontalenti (circa 1536–1608), and Giulio (1571–1635)

The Oltrarno

1/4 mile

400 meters

and Alfonso Parigi (1606–56), among others. Italian landscaping is less formal than French but still full of sweeping drama. A copy of the famous *Morgante*, Cosimo I's favorite dwarf astride a particularly unhappy tortoise, is near the exit. Sculpted by Valerio Cioli (circa 1529–99), the work seems to

illustrate the perils of culinary overindulgence. A visit here can be disappointing because the gardens are somewhat underplanted and undercared for, but it's still a great walk with some fabulous views. ⊠*Enter through Palazzo Pitti* ☎*055/294883* ⊕*www.polomuseale.firenze.it* ☞*€6, combined ticket with Galleria del Costume and Giardino Bardini* ☉*Jan., Feb., Nov., and Dec., daily 8:15–4:30; Mar., daily 8:15–5:30; Apr., May, Sept., and Oct., daily 8:15–6:30; June–Aug., daily 8:15–7:30. Closed 1st and last Mon. of month.*

❻ Piazzale Michelangelo. From this lookout you have a marvelous view of Florence and the hills around it, rivaling the vista from the Forte di Belvedere. It has a copy of Michelangelo's *David* and outdoor cafés packed with tourists during the day and with Florentines in the evening. In May, the **Giardino dell'Iris** (Iris Garden) off the piazza is abloom with more than 2,500 varieties of the flower. The **Giardino delle Rose** (Rose Garden) on the terraces below the piazza is also in full bloom in May and June.

❹ Palazzo Pitti. This enormous palace is one of Florence's largest architectural set pieces. The original palazzo, built for the Pitti family around 1460, comprised only the main entrance and the three windows on either side. In 1549 the property was sold to the Medici, and Bartolomeo Ammannati was called in to make substantial additions. Although he apparently operated on the principle that more is better, he succeeded only in producing proof that more is just that: more.

Today the palace houses several museums: The **Museo degli Argenti** displays a vast collection of Medici household treasures. The **Galleria del Costume** showcases fashions from the past 300 years. The **Galleria d'Arte Moderna** holds a collection of 19th- and 20th-century paintings, mostly Tuscan. Most famous of the Pitti galleries is the **Galleria Palatina,** which contains a broad collection of paintings from the 15th to 17th centuries. The rooms of the Galleria Palatina remain much as the Medici left them. Their floor-to-ceiling paintings are considered by some to be Italy's most egregious exercise in conspicuous consumption, aesthetic overkill, and trumpery. Still, the collection possesses high points, including a number of portraits by Titian and an unparalleled collection of paintings by Raphael, notably the double portraits of Angelo Doni and his wife, the sullen Maddalena Strozzi. The price of admission to the Galleria Palatina also allows you to explore the former **Appartamenti Reali** containing furnishings from a remodeling done in the 19th century. ⊠*Piazza Pitti* ☎*055/210323* ☞*Galleria Palatina and Galleria d'Arte Moderna, combined ticket €8.50; Gal-*

leria del Costume, Giardino Bardini, Giardino di Boboli, Museo degli Argenti, and Museo Porcelleane, combined ticket €6 ⊘ Tues.–Sun. 8:15–6:50.

❼ San Miniato al Monte. This church, like the Baptistery, is a fine example of Romanesque architecture and is one of the oldest churches in Florence, dating from the 11th century. A 12th-century mosaic topped by a gilt bronze eagle, emblem of San Miniato's sponsors, the Calimala (cloth merchants' guild) crowns the lovely green and white marble facade. Inside are a 13th-century inlaid-marble floor and apse mosaic. Artist Spinello Aretino (1350–1410) covered the walls of the **Sagrestia** with frescoes depicting scenes from the life of St. Benedict. The nearby **Cappella del Cardinale del Portogallo** (Chapel of the Portuguese Cardinal) is one of the richest 15th-century Renaissance works in Florence. It contains the tomb of a young Portuguese cardinal, Prince James of Lusitania, who died in Florence in 1459. Its glorious ceiling is by Luca della Robbia, and the sculpted tomb by Antonio Rossellino (1427–79). ✉ *Viale Galileo Galilei, Piazzale Michelangelo, Lungarno Sud* ☎ *055/2342731* ⊘ *Apr.–Oct., daily 8–7; Nov.–Mar., Mon.–Sat. 8–1 and 2:30–6, Sun. 3–5.*

❶ Santa Maria del Carmine. The **Cappella Brancacci,** at the end of the right transept of this church, houses a masterpiece of Renaissance painting: a fresco cycle that changed the course of Western art. Fire almost destroyed the church in the 18th century; miraculously, the Brancacci Chapel survived almost intact. The cycle is the work of three artists: Masaccio and Masolino (1383–circa 1447), who began it around 1424, and Filippino Lippi, who finished it some 50 years later after a long interruption during which the sponsoring Brancacci family was exiled. It was Masaccio's work that opened a new frontier for painting, as he was among the first artists to employ single-point perspective; tragically, he died in 1428 at the age of 27, so he didn't live to experience the revolution his innovations caused.

Masaccio collaborated with Masolino on several of the frescoes, but he alone painted the *Tribute Money,* on the upper-left wall; *St. Peter Baptizing,* on the upper altar wall; the *Distribution of Goods,* on the lower altar wall; and the *Expulsion of Adam and Eve,* on the chapel's upper-left entrance pier. If you look closely at the last painting and compare it with some of the chapel's other works, you should see a pronounced difference. The figures of Adam and Eve possess a startling presence primarily thanks to the dramatic way in which their bodies seem to reflect light. Masaccio here shaded his figures consistently, so as to suggest a single, strong source of light within the world of the painting but outside its frame. In so doing, he succeeded in imitating with paint the real-world effect of light on mass, and he thereby imparted to his figures a sculptural reality unprecedented in his day.

These matters have to do with technique, but with the *Expulsion of Adam and Eve* his skill went beyond mere technical innovation. In the faces of Adam and Eve, you see more than finely modeled figures; you see terrible shame and suffering depicted with a humanity rarely achieved in art. Reservations to see the chapel are mandatory, but can be booked on the same day. Your time inside is limited to 15 minutes—a frustration that's only partly mitigated by the 40-minute DVD about the history of the chapel you can watch either before or after your visit. ⊠*Piazza del Carmine, Santo Spirito* ☎*055/2768224 reservations* ⊠*€4* ⊙*Mon. and Wed.–Sat. 10–5, Sun. 1–5.*

ALSO WORTH SEEING

❸ **Santa Felicita.** This late-baroque church (its facade was remodeled between 1736 and 1739) contains the Mannerist Jacopo Pontormo's *Deposition*, the centerpiece of the Cappella Capponi (executed 1525–28) and a masterpiece of 16th-century Florentine art. The remote figures, which transcend the realm of Renaissance classical form, are portrayed in tangled shapes and intense pastel colors (well preserved because of the low lights in the church), in a space and depth that defy reality. Note, too, the exquisitely frescoed *Annunciation*, also by Pontormo, at a right angle to the *Deposition*. The granite column in the piazza was erected in 1381 and marks a Christian cemetery. ⊠*Piazza Santa Felicita, Via Guicciardini, Palazzo Pitti* ⊙*Mon.–Sat. 9–noon and 3–6, Sun. 9–1.*

❷ **Santo Spirito.** The plain, unfinished facade gives nothing away, but the interior, although it appears chilly compared with later churches, is one of the most important examples of Renaissance architecture in Italy. Unfortunately, it's closed to the public except durring mass (Mon.–Sat. 9, Sun. 9, 10:30, and 6). You're welcome to attend the service, but if you go, be prepared to sit through the whole thing.

The interior is one of a pair designed in Florence by Filippo Brunelleschi in the early 15th century (the other is San Lorenzo). It was here that Brunelleschi supplied definitive solutions to the two major problems of interior Renaissance church design: how to build a cross-shaped interior using classical architectural elements borrowed from antiquity and how to reflect in that interior the order and regularity that Renaissance scientists (among them Brunelleschi himself) were at the time discovering in the natural world around them.

Brunelleschi's solution to the first problem was brilliantly simple: turn a Greek temple inside out. While ancient Greek temples were walled buildings surrounded by classical colonnades, Brunelleschi's churches were classical arcades surrounded by walled buildings. This brilliant architectural idea overthrew the previous era's religious taboo against pagan architecture once and for all, triumphantly claiming that architecture for Christian use.

Brunelleschi's solution to the second problem—making the entire interior orderly and regular—was mathematically precise: he designed the ground plan of the church so that all its parts were proportionally related. The transepts and nave have exactly the same width; the side aisles are precisely half as wide as the nave; the little chapels off the side aisles are exactly half as deep as the side aisles; the chancel and transepts are exactly one-eighth the depth of the nave; and so on, with dizzying exactitude. For Brunelleschi, such a design technique was a

matter of passionate conviction. Like most theoreticians of his day, he believed that mathematical regularity and aesthetic beauty were flip sides of the same coin, that one was not possible without the other. In the **Santo Spirito refectory** (⊠*Piazza Santo Spirito 29* ☎*055/287043*), adjacent to the church, you can see Andrea Orcagna's painting of the

WORD OF MOUTH

"A good idea for Oltrarno: get lost between Borgo San Jacopo and Santo Spirito for wonderful antiques and restoration workshops. Extremely charming."

–lcquinn2

Crucifixion. ⊠*Piazza Santo Spirito* ☎*055/210030* ⊠*Church free, refectory €2.20* ⊗ *Church: open only during mass. Refectory: Apr.–Sept., Tues.–Sat. 9–2; Oct.–Mar., Tues.–Sat. 9–1:30.*

4

NEED A BREAK?

Cabiria (⊠*Piazza Santo Spirito 4/r* ☎*055/215732*), across the piazza from the church of Santo Spirito, draws funky locals and visitors in search of a cappuccino, a quenching ade, or an expertly mixed drink. When it's warm, sit outside on the terrace.

WHERE TO EAT

Florence's popularity with tourists means that, unfortunately, there's a higher percentage of mediocre restaurants here than you'll find in most Italian towns. Some restaurant owners cut corners and let standards slip, knowing that a customer today is unlikely to return tomorrow, regardless of the quality of the meal. So, if you're looking to eat well, it pays to do some research, starting with the recommendations here—we promise there's not a tourist trap in the bunch.

Dining hours start at around 1 for lunch and 8 for dinner. Many of Florence's restaurants are small, so reservations are a must. You can sample such specialties as creamy *fegatini* (a chicken-liver spread) and *ribollita* (minestrone thickened with bread and beans and swirled with extra-virgin olive oil) in a bustling, convivial trattoria, where you share long wooden tables set with paper place mats, or in an upscale *ristorante* with linen tablecloths and napkins.

Those with a sense of culinary adventure should not miss the tripe sandwich, served from stands throughout town. This Florentine favorite comes with a fragrant *salsa verde* (green sauce) or a piquant red hot sauce—or both. Follow the Florentines' lead and take a break at an *enoteca* (wine bar) during the day and discover some excellent Chiantis and Super Tuscans from small producers who rarely export.

WHAT IT COSTS IN EUROS					
	¢	$	$$	$$$	$$$$
At Dinner	under €15	€15–€25	€25–€35	€35–€45	over €45

Prices are for a first course *(primo)*, second course *(secondo)*, and dessert *(dolce)*.

THE DUOMO TO THE PONTE VECCHIO

$–$$ ✕ **Frescobaldi Wine Bar.** This swanky establishment serves both lunch and dinner. The food is typically Tuscan with some flights of fancy, including *acciughe marinate* (marinated anchovies) and *affettati misti* (a selection of sliced, cured meats). There's a separate wine bar within the restaurant called Frescobaldino. ⊠ *Via de' Magazzini 2–4/r, Piazza della Signoria* ☎ *055/284724* ⊟ *MC, V* ⊘ *Closed Sun. No lunch Mon.*

SAN LORENZO & BEYOND

$$$–$$$$ ✕ **Taverna del Bronzino.** Want to have a sophisticated meal in a 16th-
Fodor's Choice century Renaissance artist's studio? The former studio of Santi di Tito,
★ a student of Bronzino's, has a simple, formal decor, with white table-cloths and place settings. The classic, dramatically presented Tuscan food is superb, and the solid, afforable wine list rounds out the menu. The service is outstanding. Reservations are advised, especially for eating at the wine cellar's only table. ⊠ *Via delle Ruote 25/r, San Marco* ☎ *055/495220* ⊟ *AE, DC, MC, V* ⊘ *Closed Sun. and 3 wks in Aug.*

$ ✕ **Mario.** Florentines flock to this narrow family-run trattoria near San
★ Lorenzo to feast on Tuscan favorites served at simple tables under a wooden ceiling dating from 1536. A distinct cafeteria feel and genuine Florentine hospitality prevail: you'll be seated wherever there's room, which often means with strangers. Yes, there's a bit of extra oil in most dishes, which imparts calories as well as taste, but aren't you on vacation in Italy? Worth the splurge is *riso al ragù* (rice with ground beef and tomatoes). ⊠ *Via Rosina 2/r, corner of Piazza del Mercato Centrale, San Lorenzo* ☎ *055/218550* ⌖ *Reservations not accepted* ⊟ *No credit cards* ⊘ *Closed Sun. and Aug. No dinner.*

¢ ✕ **da Nerbone.** The place has been around since 1872, and it's easy to see why: this tiny stall in the middle of the covered Mercato Centrale has been serving up Florentine food to Florentines who like their tripe. Tasty primi and secondi are available every day, but cognoscenti come for the *panino con il lampredotto* (a type of tripe sandwich). Less adventurous sorts might want to sample the panino con il bollito (a boiled beef sandwich). Ask that the bread be "bagnato" (dipped, briefly, in the tripe cooking liquid), and have both the *salsa verde* (green sauce) and *salsa piccante* (a spicy, cayenne-laced sauce) slathered on top. ⊠ *Mercato San Lorenzo* ☎ *055/219949* ⊟ *No credit cards* ⊘ *Closed Sun. No dinner.*

SANTA MARIA NOVELLA TO THE ARNO

$$$ ✕ **Cantinetta Antinori.** After a rough morning of shopping on Via Tornabuoni, stop for lunch in this 15th-century palazzo in the company of Florentine ladies (and men) who lunch and come to see and be seen. The panache of the food matches its clientele: expect treats such as *tramezzino con pane di campagna al tartufo* (country pâté with truffles served on bread) and the *insalata di gamberoni e gamberetti con carciofi freschi* (crayfish and prawn salad with shaved raw artichokes).

BEST BETS, FLORENCE DINING

With hundreds of restaurants to choose from, how will you decide where to eat? Fodor's writers and editors have selected their favorite restaurants by price, cuisine, and experience in the Best Bets lists below. In the first column, Fodor's Choice properties represent the "best of the best."

FODOR'S CHOICE

Cibrèo p.266
Ora d'Aria p.267
Taverna del Bronzino p.262
Osteria de'Benci p.268

Best by Price

BEST ¢

All'Antico Vinaio p.269
da Nerbone p.262

BEST $

Cibrèo Trattoria p.269
La Casalinga p.270
Mario p.262
Osteria Antica Mescita San Niccolo p.271

BEST $$

Baldovino p.268
Frescobaldi Wine Bar p.262
La Mucca sul Tetto p.268
Quattro Leoni p.270

BEST $$$

Beccofino p.270
Il Latini p. 266
La Giostra p.267
Osteria de'Benci p.268

BEST $$$$

Cibrèo p.266
Ora d'Aria p.267
Simon Boccanegra p.267
Taverna del Bronzino p.262

Best Experiences

FOR KIDS

Baldovino p.268
Danny Rock p.270
Il Latini p.266

ROMANTIC

Enoteca Pinchiorri p.266
Ora d'Aria p.267

BISTECCA FIORENTINA (TUSCAN STEAK)

Il Latini p.266
La Giostra p.267
Osteria de'Benci p.268

OUTDOOR DINING

Fuori Porta p.271
Osteria de'Benci p.268
Quattro Leoni p.270

WINE BARS

Fuori Porta p.271

ALTA CUCINA (SOPHISTICATED CUISINE)

Enoteca Pinchiorri p.266
Ora d'Aria p.267
Taverna del Bronzino p.262

CASALINGA (HOME COOKING)

La Casalinga p.270
Mario p.262

LUNCH SPOTS

Antico Noe p.267
Cantinetta Antinori p.266
Benvenuto p.268
Frescobaldi Wine Bar p.262

WINE LIST

Cantinetta Antinori p.266
Enoteca Pinchiorri p.266
Taverna del Bronzino p.262

4

✉ *Piazza Antinori 3, Santa Maria Novella* ☎ *055/292234* 🚫 *AE, DC, MC, V* 🕙 *Closed weekends, 20 days in Aug., and Dec. 25–Jan. 6.*

$$$ ✕ **Il Latini**. It may be the noisiest, most crowded trattoria in Florence, but it's also one of the most fun. The genial host, Torello ("little bull") Latini, presides over his four big dining rooms, and somehow it feels as if you're dining in his home. Ample portions of *ribollita* prepare the palate for the hearty meat dishes that follow. Both Florentines and tourists alike tuck into the *agnello fritto* (fried lamb) with aplomb. Though reservations are advised, there's always a wait anyway. ✉ *Via dei Palchetti 6/r, Santa Maria Novella* ☎ *055/210916* 🚫 *AE, DC, MC, V* 🕙 *Closed Mon. and 15 days at Christmas.*

$-$$ ✕ **Osteria delle Belle Donne**. Down the street from the church of Santa Maria Novella, this gaily decorated spot, festooned with ropes of garlic and other vegetables, has an ever-changing menu and stellar service led by the irrepressible Giacinto. The kitchen has Tuscan standards, but shakes up the menu with alternatives such as *sedani con bacon, verza, e uova* (thick noodles sauced with bacon, cabbage, and egg). If you want to eat alfresco, request a table outside when booking. ✉ *Via delle Belle Donne 16/r, Santa Maria Novella* ☎ *055/2382609* 🚫 *AE, DC, MC, V.*

SANTA CROCE

$$$$ ✕ **Cibrèo**. The food at this upscale trattoria is fantastic, from the creamy

Fodor's Choice   crostini *di fegatini* (a savory chicken-liver spread) to the melt-in-your-

★   mouth desserts. Many Florentines hail this as the city's best restaurant, and Fodor's readers tend to agree—though some take issue with the prices and complain of long waits for a table (even with a reservation). If you thought you'd never try tripe—let alone like it—this is the place to lay any doubts to rest: the *trippa in insalata* (cold tripe salad) with parsley and garlic is an epiphany. The food is traditionally Tuscan, impeccably served by a staff that's multilingual—which is a good thing, because there are no written menus. Around the corner is Cibreino, Cibrèo's budget version, with a shorter menu and a no-reservations policy. ✉ *Via A. del Verrocchio 8/r, Santa Croce* ☎ *055/2341100* ⚠ *Reservations essential* 🚫 *AE, DC, MC, V* 🕙 *Closed Sun. and Mon. and July 25–Sept. 5.*

$$$$ ✕ **Enoteca Pinchiorri**. A sumptuous Renaissance palace with high, frescoed ceilings and bouquets in silver vases provides the backdrop for this restaurant, one of the most expensive in Italy. Some consider it one of the best, and others consider it a non-Italian rip-off, as the kitchen is presided over by a Frenchwoman with sophisticated, yet internationalist, leanings. Prices are high and portions are small; the vast holdings of the wine cellar, as well as stellar service, dull the pain, however, when the bill is presented. Interesting pasta combinations such as the *ignudi*—ricotta-and-spinach dumplings with a lobster-and-coxcomb fricassee—are always on the menu. ✉ *Via Ghibellina 87, Santa Croce* ☎ *055/242777* ⚠ *Reservations essential* 🚫 *AE, MC, V* 🕙 *Closed Sun., Mon., and Aug. No lunch Tues. or Wed.*

$$$$ ✕ **Ora d'Aria.** The name means "Hour of Air" and refers to the time of
Fodor'sChoice   day when prisoners were let outside for fresh air—alluding to the fact
★   that this gem is across the street from what was once the old prison.
In the kitchen, gifted young chef Marco Stabile turns out exquisite
Tuscan classics as well as more-fanciful dishes, which are as beautiful
as they are delicious; intrepid diners will be vastly rewarded for ordering the tortellini *farciti con piccione* (stuffed with pigeon) if it's on the
day's menu. Two tasting menus give Stabile even greater opportunity
to shine, and the carefully culled wine list has something to please
every palate. Do not miss his tiramisu espresso—something halfway
between a dessert and a coffee. ✉*Via Ghibellina 3/c, near Santa Croce*
☎*055/2001699* 🍴*AE, DC, MC, V* ⊘*Closed Sun. No lunch.*

$$$$ ✕**Simon Boccanegra.** Florentine food cognoscenti flock to this place
named for a condottiere (mercenary) hero in a Verdi opera. Under high
ceilings, candles on every table cast a rosy glow; the fine wine list and
superb service make a meal here a true pleasure. The chef has a deft
hand with fish dishes, as well as an inventiveness when it comes to
reinterpreting such classics as risotto with chicken liver—he adds leek
and saffron to give it a lift. Remember to save room for dessert. A less-
expensive, less-formal wine bar serving a basic Tuscan menu is also
on the premises. ✉*Via Ghibellina 124/r, Santa Croce* ☎*055/2001098*
🍴*Reservations essential* 🍴*AE, DC, MC, V* ⊘*Closed Sun. No lunch.*

$$$ ✕**La Giostra.** This clubby spot, whose name means "carousel" in Ital-
★   ian, is owned and run by Prince Dimitri Kunz d'Asburgo Lorena, and
his way with mushrooms is as remarkable as his charm. The unusually
good pastas may require explanation from Soldano, one of the prince's
good-looking twin sons. In perfect English he'll describe a favorite dish,
taglierini con tartufo bianco, a decadently rich pasta with white truf-
fles. Leave room for dessert: this might be the only show in town with a
sublime tiramisu *and* a wonderfully gooey Sacher torte. ✉*Borgo Pinti*
12/r, Santa Croce ☎*055/241341* 🍴*AE, DC, MC, V.*

$$–$$$ ✕**Antico Noe.** If Florence had diners (it doesn't), this would be the best
diner in town. The short menu at the one-room eatery relies heav-
ily on seasonal ingredients picked up daily at the market. The menu
comes alive particularly during truffle and artichoke season (don't miss
the grilled artichokes if they're on the menu). Locals rave about the
tagliatelle *ai porcini* (with mushrooms); the fried eggs liberally laced
with truffle might be the greatest truffle bargain in town. Ask for the
menu in Italian, as the English version is much more limited. The short
wine list has some great bargains. ✉*Volta di San Piero 6/r, Santa Croce*
☎*055/2340838* 🍴*AE, DC, MC, V* ⊘*Closed Sun. and 2 wks in Aug.*

$$–$$$ ✕**Osteria de'Benci.** A few minutes from Santa Croce, this charming oste-
Fodor'sChoice   ria serves some of the most eclectic food in Florence. Try the spaghetti
★   *degli eretici* (in tomato sauce with fresh herbs). The grilled meats are jus-
tifiably famous; the *carbonata* is a succulent piece of grilled beef served
rare. When it's warm, you can dine outside with a view of the 13th-cen-
tury tower belonging to the prestigious Alberti family. Right next door
is Osteria de'Benci Caffè (¢–$), serving selections from the menu from 8
AM to midnight. ✉*Via de'Benci 11–13/r, Santa Croce* ☎*055/2344923*
🍴*AE, DC, MC, V* ⊘*Closed Sun. and 2 wks in Aug.*

4

$$ ✗ **Baldovino.** David and Catherine Gardner, expat Scots, have created this lively, brightly colored restaurant down the street from the church of Santa Croce. From its humble beginnings as a pizzeria, it has evolved into something more. It's a happy thing that pizza is still on the menu, but now it shares billing with sophisticated primi and secondi. The menu changes monthly and has such treats as *filetto di manzo alla Bernaise* (filet mignon with light béarnaise sauce). Baldovino also serves pasta dishes and grilled meat until the wee hours. ⊠ *Via San Giuseppe 22/r, Santa Croce* ☏ *055/241773* ⊟ *MC, V.*

$$ ✗ **La Mucca sul Tetto.** The strangely named "Cow on the Roof" has an equally odd, but pleasing, interior: anthracite-sponged walls adorned with Moorish-style stencil work are bounded by 15th-century vaulting. The menu, which changes every few weeks, features Tuscan seasonal classics, as well as some unusual, tasty variations. Start with their light-as-a-feather *coccoli* (fried, coin-size discs of dough) served with *stracchino* (a soft, mild cheese) and prosciutto on the side. Meat lovers should not miss the fried lamb chops, whose batter is laden with pistachios. The bilingual staff is happy to guide you through the well-culled wine list, which caters to all budgets and all tastes. ⊠ *Via Ghibellina 134/r, near Santa Croce* ☏ *055/2344810* ⊟ *AE, DC, MC, V* ⊘ *Closed Sun. No lunch.*

$–$$ ✗ **Koime.** If you're looking for a break from the ubiquitous ribollita, stop in at this eatery, which may be the only Japanese restaurant in the world to be housed in a 15th-century Renaissance palazzo. High, vaulted arches frame the Kaiten sushi conveyor belt. It's Japanese food, cafeteria style: selections, priced according to the color of the plate, make their way around a bar, where diners pick whatever they find appealing. Those seeking a more substantial meal head to the second floor, where Japanese barbecue is prepared at your table. The minimalist basement provides a subtle but dramatic backdrop for a well-prepared cocktail. ⊠ *Via dei Benci 41/r, Santa Croce* ☏ *055/2008009* ⊟ *AE, DC, MC, V*

$ ✗ **Benvenuto.** At this Florentine institution, beloved for decades by locals and Anglophone Renaissance scholars alike, the service is ebullient, the menu long (with often unwittingly humorous English typographical errors), and the food simple, Tuscan, and tasty. The list of primi and secondi is extensive, and there are daily specials as well. Don't miss the *scaloppine all Benvenuto* (veal cutlets with porcini). ⊠ *Via della Mosca 16/r, at Via de' Neri, Santa Croce* ☏ *055/214833* ⊟ *AE, DC, MC, V* ⊘ *Closed Sun.*

$ ✗ **Cibrèo Trattoria.** This intimate little trattoria, known to locals as Cibreino, shares its kitchen with the famed Florentine culinary institution that also share's its name. They share the same menu, too, though Cibreino's is much shorter. Start with *il gelatina di pomodoro* (tomato gelatin) liberally laced with basil, garlic, and a pinch of hot pepper, and then sample the justifiably renowned *passato in zucca gialla* (pureed yellow-pepper soup) before moving on to any of the succulent second courses. Save room for dessert, as the pastry chef has a dangerous hand with chocolate tarts. To avoid sometimes agonizingly long waits, come early (7 PM) or late (after 9:30). ⊠ *Via dei Macci 118, Santa Croce*

What Tripe!

While in Florence, those with a sense of culinary adventure should seek out a tripe sandwich, which is just about as revered by local gourmands as the bistecca alla fiorentina. In this case, however, the treasure comes on the cheap—sandwiches are sold from small stands found in the city center, topped with a fragrant green sauce or a piquant red hot sauce, or both. *Bagnato* means that the hard, crusty roll is first dipped in the tripe's cooking liquid; it's advisable to say "*sì*" when asked if that's how you like it. Sandwiches are usually taken with a glass of red wine poured from the tripe seller's *fiasco* (flask). If you find the tripe to your liking, you might also enjoy *lampredotto*, another, some say better, cut of stomach. For an exalted,

high-end tripe treat, try Fabio Picchi's cold tripe salad, served gratis as an *amuse-bouche* at the restaurant Cibrèo. It could make a convert of even the staunchest "I'd never try *that*" kind of eater.

Tripe carts are lunchtime favorites of Florentine working men—it's uncommon, but not unheard of, to see a woman at a tripe stand. Aficionados will argue which sandwich purveyor is best; here are three that frequently get mentioned: **La Trippaia** (⊠ *Via dell'Ariento, Santa Maria Novella* ☎ *No phone* ⊙ *Closed Sun.*). **Il Trippaio** (⊠ *Via de' Macci at Borgo La Croce, Santa Croce* ☎ *No phone* ⊙ *Closed Sun.*). **Nerbone** (⊠ *Inside the Mercato Centrale, Santa Maria Novella* ☎ *No phone* ⊙ *Closed Sun.*).

☎ *055/2341100* ⊜ *Reservations not accepted* ⊟ *No credit cards* ⊙ *Closed Sun. and Mon. and July 25–Sept. 5.*

$ ✕**Pallottino.** With its tile floor, photograph-filled walls, and wooden tables, Pallottino is the quintessential Tuscan trattoria, with hearty, heartwarming classics such as *pappa al pomodoro* (bread and tomato soup) and *peposa alla toscana* (beef stew laced with black pepper). The menu changes frequently to reflect what's seasonal; the staff is friendly, as are the diners who often share a table and, eventually, conversation. They also do pizza here, as well as great lunch specials. ⊠ *Via Isola delle Stinche 1/r, Santa Croce* ☎ *055/289573* ⊟ *AE, DC, MC, V* ⊙ *Closed Mon. and 2–3 wks in Aug.*

¢ ✕**All'Antico Vinaio.** Florentines like to grab a quick bite to eat at this narrow little sandwich shop near the Uffizi. A handful of stools offer a place to perch while chowing down on one of their very fine sandwiches; most folks, however, simply grab a sandwich, pour themselves a glass of inexpensive wine in a paper cup (more serious wines can be poured into glasses) and mingle on the pedestrians-only street in front. If *porchetta* (a very rich, deliciously fatty roasted pork) is on offer, don't miss it. They also offer first-rate primi, which change daily. ⊠ *Via de' Neri 65, Santa Croce* ☎ *No phone* ⊟ *No credit cards* ⊙ *Closed Sun.*

¢ ✕**Danny Rock.** There's a bit of everything at this restaurant, which is always hopping with Italians eager to eat well-made cheeseburgers and fries or one of the many tasty crepes (served both sweet and savory). You can also find a basic plate of spaghetti as well as a respectable pizza here. Interior decor isn't high on the list: you dine at a green metal table with matching chairs. The young-at-heart feel might explain why the main dining room has a big screen showing *Looney Tunes.* ⊠ *Via Pandolfini 13/r, Santa Croce* ☎055/2340307 ☐*AE, DC, MC, V.*

¢ ✗**da Rocco.** At one of Florence's biggest markets you can grab lunch to go, or you could cram yourself into one of the booths and pour from the straw-cloaked flask (wine here is *da consumo,* which means they charge you for how much you drink). Food is abundant, Tuscan, and fast; locals pack in. The menu changes daily, and the prices are great. ⊠*In Mercato Sant'Ambrogio, Piazza Ghiberti, Santa Croce* ☎No *phone* ⌂*Reservations not accepted* ☐No *credit cards* ⊗*Closed Sun. No dinner.*

THE OLTRARNO

$$$ ✗**Beccofino.** Forget that the noise level here often reaches the pitch of the Tower of Babel, and ignore the generic urban decor. Come here for the food: chef Robbie Pepin, who's worked with such heavy hitters as Gordon Ramsey and Alain Ducasse, has breathed life into this very cool place. His cooking, while wholly Italian, has a crisp simplicity reminiscent of Japanese food. He can do just about everything, but shines with fish and shellfish. He takes the Florentine classic gnudi and tops it with prawns, calamari, and fresh tomatoes; it creates a beautiful blend in your mouth. The menu changes frequently, the wine list is divine, and service is exceptional. ⊠ *Piazza Scarlatti 1/r, Lungarno South* ☎ 055/2790076 ⌂ *Reservations essential* ☐ *MC, V* ⊗No *lunch.*

$$ ✗**Quattro Leoni.** The eclectic staff at this trattoria in a small piazza is an appropriate match for the diverse menu. In winter you can eat in one of two rooms with high ceilings, and in summer you can sit outside and admire the scenery. Traditional Tuscan favorites, such as *taglierini con porcini* (long, thin, flat pasta with porcini mushrooms), are on the menu, but so, too, are less typical dishes such as the earthy cabbage salad with avocado, pine nuts, and drops of *olio di tartufo* (truffle oil). Reservations are a good idea. ⊠ *Piazza della Passera, Via dei Vellutini 1/r, Palazzo Pitti* ☎055/218562 ☐*AE, DC, MC, V* ⊗No *lunch Wed.*

$ ✗**La Casalinga.** *Casalinga* means "housewife," and this place has the nostalgic charm of a 1950s kitchen with Tuscan comfort food to match. If you eat *ribollita* anywhere in Florence, eat it here—it couldn't be more authentic. Mediocre paintings clutter the semipaneled walls, tables are set close together, and the place is usually jammed. The menu is long, portions are plentiful, and service is prompt and friendly. Save room for dessert: the lemon sorbet perfectly caps off the meal. ⊠*Via Michelozzi 9/r, Santo Spirito* ☎055/218624 ☐*AE, DC, MC, V* ⊗*Closed Sun., 1 wk at Christmas, and 3 wks in Aug.*

$ ✗**Osteria Antica Mescita San Niccolò.** It's always crowded, always good, and always cheap. The osteria is next to the church of San Niccolò, and if you sit in the lower part you'll find yourself in what was once a chapel dating from the 11th century. The subtle but dramatic background is a nice complement to the food, which is simple Tuscan at its best. The *pollo con limone* is tasty pieces of chicken in a lemon-scented broth. In winter try the *spezzatino di cinghiale con aromi* (wild boar stew with herbs). Reservations are advised. ⊠*Via San Niccolò 60/r, San Niccolò* ☎055/2342836 ☐*AE, MC, V* ⊗*Closed Sun. and Aug.*

¢ ✕ **Fuori Porta.** One of the oldest and best wine bars in Florence, this place serves cured meats and cheeses, as well as daily specials such as the sublime spaghetti *al curry. Crostini* and *crostoni*—grilled breads topped with a mélange of cheeses and meats—are the house specialty; the *verdure sott'olio* (vegetables with oil) are divine. All this can be enjoyed at rustic wooden tables, and outdoors when weather allows. One shortcoming is the staff; the members of which are sometimes disinclined to explain the absolutely wonderful wine list. ✉ *Via Monte alle Croci 10/r, San Niccolò* ☎ *055/2342483* ▭ *AE, MC, V.*

BEYOND THE CITY CENTER

$$$ ✕ **Zibibbo.** Benedetta Vitali, formerly of Florence's famed Cibrèo, has a restaurant of her very own. It's a welcome addition to the sometimes claustrophobic Florentine dining scene—particularly as you have to drive a few minutes out of town to get here. Off a quiet piazza, it has two intimate rooms with rustic, maroon-painted wood floors and a sloped ceiling. The *tagliatelle al sugo d'anatra* (wide pasta ribbons with duck sauce) are aromatic and flavorful, and *crocchette di fave con salsa di yogurt* (fava bean croquettes with a lively yogurt sauce) are innovative and tasty. ✉ *Via di Terzollina 3/r, northwest of city center* ☎ *055/433383* ▭ *AE, DC, MC, V* ⊘ *Closed Sun.*

WHERE TO STAY

No stranger to visitors, Florence is equipped with hotels for all budgets; for instance, you can find both budget and luxury hotels in the *centro storico* (historic center) and along the Arno. Florence has so many famous landmarks that it's not hard to find lodging with a panoramic vista. The equivalent of the genteel *pensioni* of yesteryear still exist, though they are now officially classified as hotels. Generally small and intimate, they often have a quaint appeal that usually doesn't preclude modern plumbing.

Florence's importance not only as a tourist city but as a convention center and the site of the Pitti fashion collections guarantees a variety of accommodations. The high demand also means that, except in winter, reservations are a must. If you find yourself in Florence with no reservations, go to **Consorzio ITA** (✉ *Stazione Centrale, Santa Maria Novella* ☎ *055/282893*). You must go there in person to make a booking.

WHAT IT COSTS IN EUROS					
	¢	**$**	**$$**	**$$$**	**$$$$**
FOR TWO PEOPLE	under €80	€80–€140	€140–€210	€210–€290	over €290

Prices are for a standard double room in high season, including tax and service.

THE DUOMO TO THE ARNO

$$$$ **⊡ Hotel Helvetia and Bristol.** Painstaking care has gone into making this
★ hotel one of the prettiest and most intimate in town. It has the extra
plus of being in the center of the centro storico, making it a luxurious
base from which to explore the city. From the cozy yet sophisticated
lobby with its stone columns to the guest rooms decorated with prints,
you might feel as if you're a guest in a sophisticated manor house.
The restaurant serves sumptuous fare in a romantic setting. **Pros:** Central location; superb staff. **Cons:** Rooms facing the street get some
noise. ⊠ *Via dei Pescioni 2, Piazza della Repubblica,* ☎*055/26651*
🖷*055/288353* ⊕*www.hbf.royaldemeure.com* ⌁*54 rooms, 13 suites*
⌂*In-room: safe, refrigerator, VCR, Wi-Fi. In-hotel: restaurant, room*
service, bar, concierge, laundry service, parking (fee), some pets allowed
☰*AE, DC, MC, V* ⏏*EP.*

$$$$ **⊡ Hotel Savoy.** From the outside, it looks very much like the turn-of-
the-19th-century building that it is. Inside, sleek minimalism and up-
to-the-minute amenities prevail. Sitting rooms have a funky edge, their
cream-color walls dotted with contemporary prints. Muted colors dress
the rooms, which have streamlined furniture and soaring ceilings; many
have views of the Duomo's cupola or the Piazza della Repubblica. The
deep marble tubs might be reason enough to stay here—but you'll also
appreciate the efficient and courteous staff. **Pros:** Location; trendy
clientele (if that's your thing). **Cons:** Smallish rooms; trendy clientele
(if that's not your thing). ⊠ *Piazza della Repubblica 7,* ☎*055/27351*
🖷*055/2735888* ⊕*www.roccofortehotels.com* ⌁*88 rooms, 12 suites*
⌂*In-room: safe, refrigerator, VCR, dial-up, Wi-Fi. In-hotel: restau-*
rant, room service, bar, concierge, children's programs (ages infant–
12), laundry service, parking (fee) ☰*AE, DC, MC, V* ⏏*EP.*

$$–$$$ **⊡ Hermitage.** A stone's throw from the Ponte Vecchio, this is a fine
little hotel with an enviable location. All rooms are decorated differently with lively wallpaper; some have views of Palazzo Vecchio and
others of the Arno. The rooftop terrace, where you can have breakfast
or an aperitivo, is decked with flowers. The lobby suggests a friend's
living room—its warm yellow walls are welcoming. Double glaz-
ing and air-conditioning help keep street noise at bay. **Pros:** Views;
friendly; English-speaking staff. **Cons:** Short flight of stairs to reach
elevator. ⊠ *Vicolo Marzio 1, Piazza della Signoria,* ☎*055/287216*
🖷*055/212208* ⊕*www.hermitagehotel.com* ⌁*27 rooms, 1 suite* ⌂*In-*
room: safe. In-hotel: laundry service, public Wi-Fi, parking (fee), some
pets allowed ☰*MC, V* ⏏*BP.*

$$–$$$ **⊡ In Piazza della Signoria.** Proprietors Alessandro and Sonia Pini want
Fodor's Choice you to use their house—in this case, part of a 15th-century palazzo—as
★ if it were your own. Such warm sentiments extend to the cozy feeling
created in the rooms, all of which are uniquely decorated and lovingly
furnished; some have sweeping damask curtains, others fanciful frescoes in the bathroom. **Pros:** Marvelous staff; tasty breakfast with a
view of Piazza della Signoria. **Cons:** Short flight of stairs to reach elevator. ⊠ *Via dei Magazzini 2, near Piazza della Signoria,* ☎*055/2399546*
⊕*www.inpiazzadellasignoria.com* ⌁*10 rooms, 3 apartments* ⌂*In-*

room: safe, kitchen (some), refrigerator (some), Wi-Fi. In hotel: laundry service, public Internet, parking (fee) ⊟*AE, DC, MC, V* ❡|*BP.*

$$–$$$ ⊞**Palazzo Niccolini al Duomo.** This 16th-century family palace has been lovingly restored by Ginevra and Filippo Niccolini di Camugliano—the building has been in Filippo's family for more than 100 years. The sumptuous rooms have high ceilings, spacious marble-floored bathrooms (a rarity in restored Renaissance palazzi); some are decorated with sweeping frescoes. A few rooms have views of the Duomo (just down the street); others retain their original Empire furnishings. The Blue Suite accommodates up to four, and comes with its own kitchenette. **Pros:** Steps away from the Duomo. **Cons:** Street noise sometimes a problem. ✉*Via dei Servi 2,* ☎*055/282412* 🖷*055/290979* ⊕*www. niccolinidomepalace.com* ➥*5 rooms, 5 suites* ♿*In-room: safe, refrigerator, Wi-Fi. In-hotel: public Internet, Wi-Fi, parking (fee)* ⊟*AE, DC, MC, V.*

4

$ ⊞**Albergo Firenze.** A block from the Duomo, this hotel is on one of the oldest piazzas in Florence. Though the reception area and hallways have all the charm of a college dormitory, the similarity ends upon entering the spotlessly clean rooms. A good number of triple and quadruple rooms make this a good choice for families. **Pros:** For the location, a great bargain. **Cons:** No-frills public areas. ✉*Piazza Donati 4, Duomo,* ☎*055/214203* 🖷*055/212370* ⊕*www.hotelfirenze-fi.it* ➥*58 rooms* ♿ *In-hotel: public Internet (fee), parking (fee)* ⊟*MC, V* ❡|*BP.*

SAN LORENZO & BEYOND

$$–$$$ ⊞**Il Guelfo Bianco.** The 15th-century building has all modern conveniences, but its Renaissance charm still shines. Rooms have high ceilings (some are coffered) and windows are triple-glazed. Contemporary prints and paintings on the walls contrast nicely with classic furnishings. Larger-than-usual single rooms have French-style beds and are a good choice for those traveling alone. Breakfast can be enjoyed in a small outdoor garden when weather permits. Though the hotel is in the centro storico, it still feels somewhat off the beaten path. **Pros:** Stellar multilingual staff. **Cons:** Rooms facing the street can be a little noisy. ✉*Via Cavour 29, San Marco,* ☎*055/288330* 🖷*055/295203* ⊕*www. ilguelfobianco.it* ➥*40 rooms* ♿*In-room: safe, refrigerator. In-hotel: concierge, laundry service, public Internet, parking (fee), some pets allowed* ⊟*AE, DC, MC, V* ❡|*BP.*

$$–$$$ ⊞**Loggiato dei Serviti.** Though this hotel was not designed by Brunelleschi, Florence's architectural genius, it might as well have been. The Loggiato is tucked away on one of the city's loveliest squares; a mirror image of the architect's famous Spedale degli Innocenti across the way. Occupying a 16th-century former convent, the building was once an inn for traveling priests. Vaulted ceilings, tasteful furnishings (some antique), canopy beds, and rich fabrics make this spare Renaissance building with modern comforts a find. An annex named the Dependance has five rooms of comparable quality. **Pros:** Prime location; helpful, English-speaking staff. **Cons:** Some furnishings show wear; some noise in rooms facing piazza. ✉*Piazza Santissima Annunziata 3,* ☎*055/289592* 🖷*055/289595* ⊕*www.loggiatodeiservitihotel.it* ➥*43 rooms* ♿*In-*

room: safe, refrigerator, Wi-Fi (some). In-hotel: bar, laundry service, parking (fee), some pets allowed ⊟*AE, DC, MC, V* ⦿❙*BP.*

$$ ❐**Bellettini.** You're in good hands at this small hotel on three floors run by Gina Naldini and Claudio, her husband. The top floor has two rooms with a view, and all the good-size guest rooms have Venetian or Tuscan provincial furnishings; bathrooms are bright and modern. Public rooms are simple but comfortable. A handful of triples and quadruples are available. An ample buffet breakfast includes tasty homemade cakes. **Pros:** Excellent staff. **Cons:** Two rooms have shared bath (but at significantly lower rates). ✉ *Via dei Conti 7, Santa Maria Novella,* ☎*055/213561* 📠*055/283551* ⦿*www.hotelbellettini.com* ⊟*28 rooms, 26 with private bath* ⦵*In-room: safe, refrigerator, Ethernet. In-hotel: bar, parking (fee), some pets allowed* ⊟*AE, DC, MC, V* ⦿❙*BP.*

$$ ❐**Hotel Casci.** In this refurbished 14th-century palace, the home of Giacchino Rossini in 1851–55, the friendly Lombardi family runs a hotel with spotless rooms. Guest rooms are functional, and many of them open out onto various terraces (a view doesn't necessarily follow, however). It's on a very busy thoroughfare, but triple-glazed windows allow for a sound night's sleep. Many rooms easily accommodate an extra bed or two, and there are a number of triples and quads available. **Pros:** Helpful staff; good option for families. **Cons:** Bit of a college-dorm atmosphere; small elevator. ✉ *Via Cavour 13, San Marco,* ☎*055/211686* 📠*055/2396461* ⦿*www.hotelcasci.com* ⊟*25 rooms* ⦵*In-room: safe, refrigerator, Wi-Fi. In-hotel: laundry service, public Internet, parking (fee), some pets allowed* ⊟*AE, DC, MC, V* ⦿❙*BP.*

$$ ❐**Hotel delle Arti.** If Florence had town houses, this would be one: the entrance to the public room downstairs feels as if you're in someone's living room. Pale, pastel walls, polished hardwood floors, and muted fabrics give rooms a simple, elegant look. Breakfast is taken on the top floor, and a small terrace provides city views. The highly capable staff is completely fluent in English. **Pros:** Down the street from the Duomo. **Cons:** Staff goes home at 11. ✉ *Via dei Servi 38/a, Santissima Annunziata,* ☎*055/2645307* 📠*055/290140* ⦿*www.hoteldellearti.it* ⊟*9 rooms* ⦵*In-room: refrigerator. In-hotel: laundry service, some pets allowed (fee)* ⊟*AE, DC, MC, V* ⦿❙*BP.*

$–$$ ❐ **Firenze.** Each room in the intimate *residenza* is painted a different pastel color—peach, rose, powder blue. Simple furnishings and double-glazedwindows ensure a peaceful night's sleep. You might ask for one of the rooms that has a small private terrace; if you contemplate a longer stay, one of their well-located apartments might suit. Coffee, tea, and fresh fruit, available all day in the sitting room, are on the house. **Pros:** Ample DVD library, honor bar with Antinori wines. **Cons:** Staff goes home at 8, no credit cards accepted. ✉ *Via San Gallo 72, San Marco,* ☎*055/4627296* 📠*055/4634450* ⦿*www.anticadimorafirenze. it* ⊟*6 rooms* ⦵*In-room: safe, refrigerator, dial-up, Wi-Fi* ⊟*No credit cards* ⦿❙*BP.*

$ ❐**Residenza Johanna I.** Savvy travelers and those on a budget should
★ look no farther, as this *residenza* is a tremendous value for quality and location. Though it's very much in the centro storico, the place is rather

homey. You're given a large set of keys to let yourself into the building after 7 PM, when the staff goes home. Simple rooms have high ceilings and pale pastel floral prints. Morning tea and coffee (but no breakfast) are served in your room. **Pros:** Great value. **Cons:** Staff goes home at 7; no credit cards. ⊠ *Via Bonifacio Lupi 14, San Marco,* 🕿*055/481896* 🖷*055/482721* ⊕*www.johanna.it* ⇌*11 rooms* &*In-room: no a/c, no phone, no TV. In-hotel: parking (fee)* ⊟*No credit cards* †⊙†*EP.*

SANTA MARIA NOVELLA TO THE ARNO

$$$$ ⊡ **Gallery Hotel Art.** High design resides at this art showcase near the Ponte Vecchio. The coolly understated public rooms have a revolving collection of photographs by artists like Helmut Newton adorning the walls; the reception area is subtly but dramatically lit. Rooms are sleek and uncluttered and dressed mostly in neutrals. Luxe touches, such as leather headboards and kimono robes, abound. Both the bar and restaurant attract sophisticated, fashionable locals; brunch happens on the weekends. **Pros:** Cookies in the room; comfortable beds. **Cons:** Sometimes elevator is slow. ⊠*Vicolo dell'Oro 5, Santa Maria Novella,* 🕿*055/27263* 🖷*055/268557* ⊕*www.lungarnohotels.com* ⇌*65 rooms, 9 suites* &*In-room: safe, refrigerator, dial-up, Wi-Fi. In-hotel: restaurant, room service, bar, concierge, laundry service, parking (fee)* ⊟*AE, DC, MC, V* †⊙†*BP.*

$$$$
Fodor's Choice
★
⊡ **JK Place.** Ori Kafri, the manager of this boutique hotel, refers to it as a house, and indeed it is a sumptuously appointed home away from home. A library serves as the reception room; buffet breakfast is laid out on a gleaming chestnut table in an interior atrium. Soothing earth tones prevail in the rooms, some of which have chandeliers, others canopied beds. A secluded rooftop terrace makes a perfect setting for an aperitivo, as do the ground-floor sitting rooms with large, pillow-piled couches. The place is favored by young fashionistas, their entourages, and other beautiful people. **Pros:** Intimate feel; stellar staff. **Cons:** Breakfast at a shared table. ⊠*Piazza Santa Maria Novella 7,* 🕿*055/2645181* 🖷*055/2658387* ⊕*www.jkplace.com* ⇌*14 doubles, 6 suites* &*In-room: safe, refrigerator, VCR, dial-up, Wi-Fi. In-hotel: bar, concierge, laundry service, parking (fee), some pets allowed* ⊟*AE, DC, MC, V* †⊙†*BP.*

$$$
★
⊡ **Beacci Tornabuoni.** Florentine pensioni don't get any classier than this. It has old-fashioned style and enough modern comfort to keep you happy, and it's in a 14th-century palazzo. The sitting room has a large fireplace, the terrace has a tremendous view of some major Florentine monuments, and the wallpapered rooms are inviting. On Monday, Wednesday, and Friday nights from May through October, the dining room opens, serving Tuscan specialties. **Pros:** Multilingual staff; flower-filled terrace. **Cons:** Fodor's readers advise to request rooms away from reception area, which can be noisy. ⊠ *Via Tornabuoni 3, Santa Maria Novella,* 🕿*055/212645* 🖷*055/283594* ⊕*www.tornabuonihotels.com* ⇌*28 rooms* &*In-room: refrigerator. In- hotel: restaurant, bar, laundry service, public Internet, parking (fee), some pets allowed* ⊟*AE, DC, MC, V* †⊙†*BP.*

$$ Torre Guelfa. If you want to get a taste of medieval Florence, try this hotel hidden within a former 13th-century tower. The Torre Guelfa once protected the obscenely wealthy Acciaiuoli family; now it's one of the best small hotels in the center of Florence. Each guest room is different, some with canopied beds, some with balconies. Those on a budget might consider one of the six less expensive rooms on the second floor, which are comparable to the rest of the rooms but have no TV. **Pros:** Wonderful staff; some family-friendly triple rooms. **Cons:** Stairs to elevator. *Borgo Santi Apostoli 8, Santa Maria Novella, 055/2396338 055/2398577 www.hoteltorreguelfa.com 24 rooms, 2 suites In-room: safe (some), no TV (some). In-hotel: laundry service, public Wi-Fi, parking (fee), some pets allowed AE, MC, V BP.*

$$ Villa Azalee. The 19th-century villa deftly recalls its previous incarnation as a private residence. It's been in the hands of the Brizzi family for more than 100 years, and they understandably take pride in the prettiness of the place. Quilted, floral-print slipcovers dress the furniture; throw rugs pepper the floors. Many rooms have views of the hotel's garden, and some have private terraces. The hotel is five minutes on foot from the train station and steps from the Fortezza da Basso (site of the Pitti fashion shows). **Pros:** Proximity to train station; two garden apartments are wheelchair accessible. **Cons:** Feels a bit out of the way; despite being in city center. *Viale Fratelli Rosselli 44, Santa Maria Novella, 055/214242 055/268264 www.villa-azalee.it 25 rooms In-hotel: bar, bicycles, laundry service, public Internet, parking (fee), some pets allowed AE, DC, MC, V BP.*

$-$$ Alessandra. The location, a block from the Ponte Vecchio, and the clean, ample rooms make this a good choice. The building, known as the Palazzo Roselli del Turco, was designed in 1507 by Baccio d'Agnolo, a contemporary of Michelangelo. Though little remains of the original design save for the high wood ceilings, there's still an aura of grandeur. Friendly hosts Anna and Andrea Gennarini speak fluent English. **Pros:** Several rooms have views of the Arno; the spacious suite is a bargain. **Cons:** Stairs to elevator; some rooms share bath. *Borgo Santi Apostoli 17, Santa Maria Novella, 055/283438 055/210619 www.hotelalessandra.com 26 rooms, 19 with bath; 1 suite; 1 apartment In-room: safe, refrigerator, dial-up, Wi-Fi. In-hotel: laundry service, parking (fee) AE, MC, V Closed Dec. 10–26 BP.*

¢–$ Nuova Italia. The genial English-speaking Viti family runs this hotel near the train station and within walking distance of the sights. Its rooms are clean and simply furnished. Air-conditioning and triple-glazed windows ensure restful nights. Some rooms can accommodate extra beds. **Pros:** Reasonable rates. **Cons:** No elevator. *Via Faenza 26, Santa Maria Novella, 055/268430 055/210941 www.hotelnuovaitalia.it 20 rooms In-room: Wi-Fi (some). In-hotel: no elevator, laundry service, public Wi-Fi, parking (fee), some pets allowed AE, MC, V Closed Dec. 8–Dec. 26 BP.*

THE OLTRARNO & BEYOND

$$$$ ☷**Lungarno.** Many rooms and suites here have private terraces that jut out right over the Arno, granting stunning views of the Palazzo Vecchio and the Lungarno. Four suites in a 13th-century tower preserve details like exposed stone walls and old archways and look over a little square with a medieval tower covered in jasmine. The very chic interiors approximate breezily elegant homes, with lots of crisp white fabrics with blue trim. A wall of windows and a sea of white couches make the lobby bar one of the most relaxing places in the city to stop for a drink. Inquire about the Lungarno Suites, across the river; they include kitchens, making them attractive if you're planning a longer stay. **Pros:** Upscale without being stuffy. **Cons:** Rooms without Arno views feel less special. ✉*Borgo San Jacopo 14, Lungarno Sud,* ☎*055/27261* 📠*055/268437* ⊕*www.lungarnohotels.com* ⏎*60 rooms, 13 suites* ☖*In-room: dial-up, Wi-Fi. In-hotel: restaurant, bar, concierge, laundry service, parking (fee)* ▭*AE, DC, MC, V* ⍣❙*BP.*

$$ ☷**Hotel Silla.** The entrance to this slightly off-the-beaten-path hotel is through a 15th-century courtyard lined with potted plants and sculpture-filled niches. The hotel, formerly a palazzo dating from the 15th century, is up a flight of stairs and has two floors. Rooms are simply furnished and walls are papered; some have views of Via de' Renai and the Arno, while others overlook a less-traveled road. Breakfast may be taken in a room that preserves an Empire feel (including two chandeliers from the early 19th century); when it's warm, a large, sunny terrace is the perfect place to read or to write that postcard. **Pros:** A Fodor's reader raves, "It's in the middle of everything except the crowds." **Cons:** Some readers complain of street noise and too-small rooms. ✉*Via de' Renai 5, San Niccolò,* ☎*055/2342888* 📠*055/2341437* ⊕*www.hotelsilla. it* ⏎*35 rooms* ☖*In-room: safe, refrigerator, Wi-Fi. In-hotel: bar, concierge, laundry service, parking (fee), some pets allowed* ▭*AE, DC, MC, V* ⍣❙*BP.*

SANTA CROCE

$$$$ ☷**Hotel Regency.** The noise and crowds of Florence seem far from this stylish hotel in a residential district near the Sinagoga, though you're not more than 10 minutes from the Accademia and Michelangelo's *David*. Across the street is Piazza d'Azeglio, a small public park that somehow evokes 19th-century middle Europe. Rooms dressed in richly colored fabrics and antique-style furniture remain faithful to the hotel's 19th-century origins as a private mansion. The restaurant here is equally sophisticated. **Pros:** Faces one of the few green parks in the center of Florence. **Cons:** A small flight of stairs takes you to reception. ✉*Piazza d'Azeglio 3, Santa Croce,* ☎*055/245247* 📠*055/2346735* ⊕*www.regency-hotel. com* ⏎*30 rooms, 4 suites* ☖*In-room: safe, refrigerator, Wi-Fi. In-hotel: restaurant, room service, bar, concierge, laundry service, parking (fee), some pets allowed, no-smoking rooms* ▭*AE, DC, MC, V* ⍣❙*BP.*

$$$$ ☷**Monna Lisa.** Housed in a 15th-century palazzo, with parts of the
★ building dating from the 13th century, this hotel retains some of its original wood-coffered ceilings from the 1500s, as well as its original

marble staircase. Though some rooms are small, they are tasteful, and each is done in different floral wallpaper. The public rooms retain a 19th-century aura, and the intimate bar, with its red velveteen wallpaper, is a good place to unwind. **Pros:** Annex is wheelchair accessible. **Cons:** Rooms in annex are much less charming than those in palazzo. ⊠ *Borgo Pinti 27, Santa Croce,* ☎ *055/2479751* 🖷 *055/2479755* ⊕ *www.monnalisa.it* 🖙 *45 rooms* 🖧 *In-room: safe, refrigerator. In-hotel: bar, concierge, laundry service, parking (fee), some pets allowed* ⊟ *AE, DC, MC, V* ⊠|*BP.*

$$$–$$$$ 🎬 **J&J.** On a quiet street within walking distance of the sights sits this unusual hotel, a converted 16th-century convent. The large, suite-like rooms are ideal for honeymooners, families, and small groups of friends; some are on two levels, and many are arranged around a central courtyard. Pale travertine tiles used to refit some bathrooms provide a pleasing, ultramodern contrast to more traditional furnishings. Smaller rooms are more intimate, and some open onto a little shared courtyard. The gracious owners enjoy chatting in the light and airy lounge; breakfast is served in a glassed-in Renaissance loggia or in the central courtyard. **Pros:** Large rooms. **Cons:** One flight of steep stairs to get to rooms. ⊠ *Via di Mezzo 20, Santa Croce,* ☎ *055/26312* 🖷 *055/240282* ⊕ *www.cavalierehotels.com* 🖙 *19 rooms, 7 suites* 🖧 *In-room: dial-up. In-hotel: bar, no elevator, laundry service, public Wi-Fi, parking (fee)* ⊟ *AE, DC, MC, V* ⊠|*BP.*

$$–$$$ 🎬 **Morandi alla Crocetta.** You're made to feel like privileged friends of
★   the family at this charming and distinguished residence near Piazza Santissima Annunziata. The former convent is close to the sights but very quiet, and it's furnished comfortably in the classic style of a gracious Florentine home. One room retains original 17th-century fresco fragments, and two others have small private terraces. The Morandi is not only an exceptional hotel but also a good value. It's very small, so book well in advance. **Pros:** Interesting, offbeat location; terrific staff. **Cons:** Extra charge for breakfast; two flights of stairs to reach reception and rooms. ⊠ *Via Laura 50, Santissima Annunziata,* ☎ *055/2344747* 🖷 *055/2480954* ⊕ *www.hotelmorandi.it* 🖙 *10 rooms* 🖧 *In-room: safe, refrigerator, dial-up, Wi-Fi. In-hotel: no elevator, concierge, laundry service, parking (fee), some pets allowed* ⊟ *AE, DC, MC, V* ⊠|*EP.*

¢ 🎬 **Albergo Losanna.** Most major sights are within walking distance of this tiny pensione steps away from the *viali*, the edge of the city center. Though dated and a little worn around the edges, the property is impeccably clean and the rooms have high ceilings; the mother and son who run the place are enthusiastic and cordial. Try to get a room facing away from the street; though there aren't any views, you won't hear as much street noise. **Pros:** Bargain price. **Cons:** On a noisy street. ⊠ *Via V. Alfieri 9, Santa Croce,* ☎🖷 *055/245840* ⊕ *www.albergolosanna.com* 🖙 *8 rooms, 3 with bath* 🖧 *In-room: no a/c (some), no TV. In-hotel: parking (fee)* ⊟ *AE, MC, V* ⊠|*BP.*

¢ 🎬 **Istituto Oblate dell'Assunzione.** Twelve nuns run this convent, which is minutes from the Duomo. Rooms are spotlessly clean and simple; some of them have views of the cupola, and others look out onto a carefully tended garden where you are welcome to relax. Several rooms have three and four beds, making them well suited for families. Curfew is at 11:30 PM. You can join mass every morning at 7:30. For an additional three euros, you can get a simple continental breakfast, and the nuns provide half or full pension for groups of 10 or more. None of the nuns speak English, and they don't have a Web presence, so unless you speak Italian, the best way to book is by fax. **Pros:** Bargain price. **Cons:** Curfew, no credit cards. ⊠*Borgo Pinti 15, Santa Croce,* ☎*055/2480582* 🖷*055/2346291* ↪*28 rooms, 22 with bath* ⚒*In-room: no a/c (some), no phone, no TV. In-hotel: parking (fee)* ☰*No credit cards* ❘⊙❘*EP.*

OUTSIDE THE CITY

$$$ 🏨**Torre di Bellosguardo.** *Bellosguardo* means "beautiful view"; given the view of Florence you get here, the name is fitting. The hotel, perched atop a hill minutes from the *viale,* is reached via a narrow road dotted with olive trees. Dante's friend Guido Calvacanti supposedly chose this serene spot for his country villa, but little remains from the early 14th century. The reception area, a former ballroom, has soaring ceilings with frescoes by Francavilla (1553–1615). Guest rooms, all with high ceilings, are simple and have heavy wooden furniture. **Pros:** Great for escaping heat of the city in summer. **Cons:** A car is a necessity. ⊠*Via Roti Michelozzi 2,* ☎*055/2298145* 🖷*055/229008* ⊕*www.torrebel losguardo.com* ↪*9 rooms, 7 suites* ⚒*In-room: no a/c (some), refrigerator, no TV, dial-up. In-hotel: bar, pool, concierge, laundry service, parking (no fee), some pets allowed* ☰*AE, MC, V.*

$$–$$$ 🏨**Villa Poggio San Felice.** Livia Puccinelli Sannini, the descendant of a
★ famed 19th-century Florentine hotelier, and her husband have turned her family's former country villa (documented in the 15th century) into a serene hotel outside the city limits. It retains the intimate feel of a single-family home with only five high-ceilinged rooms; some have divine views of Brunelleschi's cupola down below, and others have working fireplaces. Simple landscaped gardens are peaceful. Though a daily shuttle service runs to the center of town, a car is vital. **Pros:** Affordable villa experience; pool is a great advantage in summer. **Cons:** You need a car. ⊠*Via San Matteo in Arcetri 24,* ☎*055/220016* 🖷*055/2335388* ⊕*www.villapoggiosanfelice.com* ↪*4 rooms, 1 suite* ⚒*In-hotel: pool, no elevator, laundry service, public Internet, parking (no fee), some pets allowed* ☰*AE, MC, V* ⊙*Closed Jan. 10–Feb. 28* ❘⊙❘*BP.*

NIGHTLIFE & THE ARTS

THE ARTS

Florence has a lively classical music scene. The internationally famous, annual Maggio Musicale lights up the musical calendar in early summer. Fans of rock, pop, and hip-hop might be somewhat surprised by the lack of live acts that make it to town (for such offerings, travel to Rome or Milan is often a necessity). What it lacks in contemporary music, however, is more than made up for with its many theatrical offerings.

MUSIC

The **Accademia Bartolomeo Cristofori** (✉ *Via di Camaldoli 7/r, Santo Spirito/San Frediano* ☎*055/221646* ⊕*www.accademiacristofori.it*), also known as the Amici del Fortepiano (Friends of the Fortepiano), sponsors fortepiano concerts throughout the year. **Amici della Musica** (⊕*www.amicimusica.fi.it*) organizes concerts at the **Teatro della Pergola** (*Box office* ✉ *Via Alamanni 39, Santissima Annunziata* ☎*055/210804* ⊕*www.pergola.firenze.it*).

The **Maggio Musicale Fiorentino** (✉ *Via Alamanni 39* ☎*055/210804*), a series of internationally acclaimed concerts and recitals, is held in the **Teatro Comunale** (✉*Corso Italia 16, Lungarno North* ☎*055/211158* ⊕*www.maggiofiorentino.com*). Within Italy, you can purchase tickets from late April through July directly at the box office or by phone at ☎*800/112211*. You can also buy them online. Other events—opera, ballet, and additional concerts—occur regularly throughout the year at different venues in town.

The **Orchestra da Camera Fiorentina** (✉ *Via E. Poggi 6, Piazza della Signoria* ☎*055/783374*) performs various concerts of classical music throughout the year at Orsanmichele, the grain market–turned–church.

The concert season of the **Orchestra della Toscana** (✉ *Via Ghibellina 101, Santa Croce* ☎*055/2340710*) runs from November to June. You can hear organ music in the baroque church of **Santa Margherita in Maria de' Ricci** (✉*Via il Corso, Piazza della Signoria* ☎*055/215044*). Free concerts begin every night at 9:15, except Monday.

Visiting rock stars, trendy bands from Germany, and some American groups play at **Tenax** (✉*Via Pratese 46* ⊕*www.tenax.org*).

NIGHTLIFE

Florentines are rather proud of their nightlife options. Most bars now have some sort of happy hour, which usually lasts for many hours and often has snacks that can substitute for a light dinner. (Check, though, that the buffet is free or comes with the price of a drink.) Clubs typically don't open until very late in the evening and don't get crowded until 1 or 2 in the morning. Though the cover charges can be steep, finding free passes around town is fairly easy.

BARS

Capocaccia (✉*Lungarno Corsini 12/14r, Lungarno Sud* ☎*055/210751*) makes great Bloody Marys, and it's the place to be at cocktail time. At night young Florentines crowd the doors and spill out into the street. **Colle Bereto** (✉*Piazza Strozzi 4–6/r, Piazza della Repubblica* ☎*055/283156*) draws in young Florentines and savvy tourists who like well-made cocktails and the huge spread that accompanies them. One of the hottest spots in town is the bar at the Gallery Art Hotel, **Fusion Bar** (✉*Vicolo dell'Oro 5, Santa Maria Novella* ☎*055/27263*). For a swanky experience, lubricated with trademark Bellinis and the best martinis in Florence, head to **Harry's Bar** (✉*Lungarno Vespucci 22/r, Lungarno North* ☎*055/2396700*). The oh-so-cool vibe at **La**

Dolce Vita (⊠*Piazza del Carmine 6/r, Santo Spirito* ☏*055/284595* ⊕*www.dolcevitaflorence.com*) attracts Florentines and the occasional visiting American movie star. **Negroni** (⊠*Via de' Renai 17/r, San Niccolò* ☏*055/243647* ⊕*www.negronibar.com*) teems with well-dressed young Florentines at happy hour. **Rex** (⊠*Via Fiesolana 23–25/r, Santa Croce* ☏*055/2480331*) attracts a trendy, artsy clientele. **Zoe** (⊠*Via de' Renai13/r, San Niccolò* ☏*055/243111*) calls itself a "caffetteria," and while coffee may indeed be served, elegant youngish Florentines flock here for the fine cocktails. Here's people-watching at its very best, done while listening to the latest CDs imported from England. **Zona 15** (⊠*Via del Castellaccia 53–55/r [Piazza Brunelleschi], Duomo* ☏*055/211678*) is coolly chic with its pale interior, blond woodwork, and metallic surfaces. Lunch, dinner, cocktails, and live music draw Florentine cognoscenti and others.

NIGHTCLUBS

BeBop (⊠*Via dei Servi 76/r, Santissima Annunziata* ☏*No phone*) has loud, live music, Beatles nights, and teems with American kids enjoying their junior year abroad programs. **Central Park** (⊠*Via Fosso Macinante 2* ☏*055/353505*) is a great spot for those who want to put on their dancing shoes for some house and hip-hop music. **Jazz Club** (⊠*Via Nuova de' Caccini 3, corner of Borgo Pinti, Santa Croce* ☏*055/2479700*) puts on live music in a small basement. When last call's come and gone, go where the bartenders unwind after their shift: **Loch Ness** (⊠*Via de' Benci 19/r, Santa Croce* ☏*No phone*) keeps the drinks flowing until 5 AM.

Maracaná (⊠*Via Faenza 4, Santa Maria Novella* ☏*055/210298*) is a restaurant and pizzeria featuring Brazilian specialties; at 11 PM it transforms itself into a cabaret floor show, and then into a disco until 4 AM. Book a table if you want to eat. **Meccanò** (⊠*Le Cascine, Viale degli Olmi 1* ☏*055/331371*) is a multimedia experience in a high-tech disco with a late-night restaurant. People sip cocktails against a backdrop of exotic flowers, leopard-print chairs and chintz, and red walls and floors on the two crowded floors at **Montecarla** (⊠*Via de' Bardi 2, San Niccolò* ☏*055/2340259*). **Space Electronic** (⊠*Via Palazzuolo 37, Santa Maria Novella* ☏*055/293082*) has two floors, with karaoke downstairs and an enormous disco upstairs. **Yab** (⊠*Via Sassetti 5/r, Piazza della Repubblica* ☏*055/215160*) celebrated its 25th anniversary in 2004; it never seems to go out of style, though it increasingly becomes the haunt of Florentine high schoolers and university students intent on dancing and doing vodka shots.

SHOPPING

Window-shopping in Florence is like visiting an enormous contemporary-art gallery. Many of today's greatest Italian artists are fashion designers, and most keep shops in Florence. Discerning shoppers may find bargains in the street markets. ∎TIP➔ Do not buy any knockoff goods from any of the hawkers plying their fake Prada (or any other high-end designer) on the streets. It's illegal, and fines are astronomical if the police happen to catch you. (You pay the fine, not the vendor.) Shops are generally open 9 to 1 and 3:30 to 7:30 and are closed Sunday and Monday mornings most of the year. Summer (June to September) hours are usually 9 to 1 and 4 to 8, and some shops close Saturday afternoon instead of Monday morning. When looking for addresses, you'll see two color-coded numbering systems on each street. The red numbers are commercial addresses and are indicated, for example, as 31/r. The blue or black numbers are residential addresses. Most shops take major credit cards and ship purchases, but because of possible delays it's wise to take your purchases with you.

MARKETS

Le Cascine's open-air market is held every Tuesday morning. Food, bargain clothing, and gadgets are sold. The **Mercato Centrale** (⊠*Piazza del Mercato Centrale, San Lorenzo*) is a huge indoor food market with a staggering selection of things edible. The clothing and leather-goods stalls of the **Mercato di San Lorenzo** in the streets next to the church of San Lorenzo have bargains for shoppers on a budget. It's possible to strike gold at the **Mercato di Sant'Ambrogio** (⊠*Piazza Ghiberti, off Via dei Macci, Santa Croce*), where clothing stalls abut the fruit and vegetables. Every Thursday morning from September through June, the covered loggia in Piazza della Repubblica hosts a **Mercato dei Fiori** (*flower market* ⊠*Piazza della Repubblica*); it's awash in a lively riot of plants and flowers. If you're looking for cheery, inexpensive trinkets to take home, you might want to stop and roam through the stalls under the loggia of the **Mercato del Porcellino** (⊠*Via Por Santa Maria at Via Porta Rossa, Piazza della Repubblica*). You can find bargains at the **Piazza dei Ciompi flea market** (⊠*Sant'Ambrogio, Santa Croce*) Monday through Saturday and on the last Sunday of the month. The second Sunday of every month brings the **Spirito flea market**. On the third Sunday of the month, vendors at the Fierucola organic fest sell such delectables as honeys, jams, spice mixes, and fresh vegetables.

SHOPPING DISTRICTS

Florence's most fashionable shops are concentrated in the center of town. The fanciest designer shops are mainly on **Via Tornabuoni** and **Via della Vigna Nuova**. The city's largest concentrations of antiques shops are on **Borgo Ognissanti** and the Oltrarno's **Via Maggio**. The **Ponte Vecchio** houses reputable but very expensive jewelry shops, as it has since the 16th century. The area near **Santa Croce** is the heart of the leather merchants' district.

SPECIALTY STORES

BOOKS & PAPER

Alberto Cozzi (⊠*Via del Parione 35/r, Santa Maria Novella* ☎*055/294968*) keeps an extensive line of Florentine papers and paper products. The artisans in the shop rebind and restore books

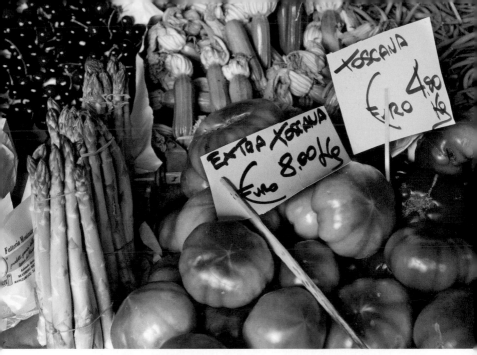

The bounty at Florence's Mercato Centrale.

☝ and works on paper. **Alice's Masks Art Studio** (✉ *Via Faenza 72/r, Santa Maria Novella* ☎*055/287370*) preserves the centuries-old technique of papier-mâché masks. On hand are masks typical of 18th-century Venice, as well as some more whimsical ones: a mask of Vincent van Gogh is painted with brushstrokes reminiscent of his own inimitable style. One of Florence's oldest paper-goods stores, **Giulio Giannini e Figlio** (✉*Piazza Pitti 37/r* ☎*055/212621*) is *the* place to buy the marbleized stock, which comes in many shapes and sizes, from flat sheets to boxes and even pencils. Photograph albums, frames, diaries, and other objects

★ dressed in handmade paper can be purchased at **Il Torchio** (✉ *Via dei Bardi 17, San Niccolò* ☎*055/2342862*). The stuff is high-quality, and

☝ the prices lower than usual. **La Tartaruga** (✉*Borgo Albizzi 60/r, Santa Croce* ☎*055/2340845*) sells brightly colored, recycled paper in lots of guises (such as calendars and stationery), as well as toys for children. **Libreria d'Arte Galleria Uffizi** (✉*Piazzale degli Uffizi 6, near Palazzo Vecchio* ☎ *055/284508*) carries monographs on famous artists, some of whose work can be found in the Uffizi; it also carries scholarly works in both Italian and English.

Long one of Florence's best art-book shops, **Libreria Salimbeni** (✉*Via Matteo Palmieri 14–16/r, Santa Croce* ☎*055/2340905*) has an outstanding selection. **Pineider** (✉*Piazza della Signoria 13/r, Piazza della Signoria* ☎*055/284655*) has shops throughout the world, but the business began in Florence and still does all its printing here. Stationery and business cards are the mainstay, but the stores also sell fine leather desk accessories as well as a less stuffy, more lighthearted line of products.

CLOTHING

The usual fashion suspects—Prada, Gucci, Versace, to name but a few—all have shops in Florence.

The sleek, classic boutique **Giorgio Armani** (⊠ *Via Tornabuoni 48/ r, Santa Maria Novella* ☎*055/219041*) is a centerpiece of the dazzling high-end shops clustered in this part of town. **Bernardo** (⊠ *Via Porta Rossa 87/r, Piazza della Repubblica* ☎*055/283333*) specializes in men's trousers, cashmere sweaters, and shirts with details like mother-of-pearl buttons. **Cabó** (⊠ *Via Porta Rossa 77–79/r, Piazza della Repubblica* ☎*055/215774*) carries that sinuous Missoni knitwear. Trendy **Diesel** (⊠ *Via dei Lamberti 13/r, Piazza della Signoria* ☎*055/2399963*) started in Vicenza; its gear is on the "must-have" list of many self-respecting Italian teens. The outlandish designs of native son **Roberto Cavalli** (⊠ *Via Tornabuoni 83/r, Santa Maria Novella* ☎*055/2396226*) appeal to Hollywood celebrities and to those who want a little bit of rock star in their wardrobe. **Emporio Armani** (⊠*Piazza Strozzi 16/r, Santa Maria Novella* ☎*055/284315*), sister store of the Giorgio Armani boutique, has slightly more affordable, funky, nightclub- and office-friendly garb. **Prada** (⊠ *Via Tornabuoni 67/r, Santa Maria Novella* ☎*055/267471*), known to mix schoolmarmish sensibility with sexy cuts and funky fabrics, appeals to an exclusive clientele. The aristocratic Marchese di Barsento, **Emilio Pucci** (⊠ *Via Tornabuoni 20–22/r, Santa Maria Novella* ☎*055/2658082*), became an international name in the late 1950s when the stretch ski clothes he designed for himself caught on with the dolce vita crowd—his pseudo-psychedelic prints and "palazzo pajamas" became all the rage. You can take home a custom-made suit or dress from **Giorgio Vannini** (⊠ *Borgo Santi Apostoli 43/r, Santa Maria Novella* ☎*055/293037*), who has a showroom for his prêt-à-porter designs. The signature couture collection of **Gianni Versace** (⊠ *Via Tornabuoni 13–15/r, Santa Maria Novella* ☎*055/2396167*) revolutionized the catwalk with rubber dresses and purple leather pants; sister Donatella continues the line of high-priced, over-the-top couture for rock stars and movie celebs. **Versus** (⊠ *Via Vigna Nuova 36–38/r, Santa Maria Novella* ☎*055/217619*) is the more playful—and more affordable—Versace line.

The intrepid shopper might want to check out some other, lesser-known shops. Young Florentines have a soft spot in their hearts for the clingy, one-of-a-kind frocks designed by Angela Baldi at her tiny shop, **Babele** (⊠*Borgo Pinti 34/r, Santa Croce* ☎*055/244729*). **Blunauta** (⊠ *Via del Proconsolo 69/r, Duomo* ☎*055/212460*) sells casual, well-made clothes for men and women. At **L'essentiel** (⊠ *Via del Corso 10/r, Piazza della Signoria* ☎*055/294713*) Lara Caldieron has spun her club-going years into fashion that also works well on the street and in the office. **Geraldine Tayar** (⊠*Sdrucciolo de' Pitti 6/r, Palazzo Pitti* ☎*055/290405*) makes clothing and accessories of her own design in eclectic fabric combinations. **Il Guardaroba/Stock House** (⊠ *Via Verdi, Santa Croce* ☎*055/2340271*) is where savvy Florentines shop for one-off designer clothes at affordable prices. If you're looking for something hot to wear to the clubs, check out **Liu-Jo** (✉ *Via Calimala 14/r, Piazza della Repubblica* ☎*055/216164*). The surreal window displays at **Luisa Via Roma** (✉ *Via Roma 19–21/r, Duomo* ☎*055/217826*) hint at the trendy yet tasteful clothing inside this fascinating, *alta moda* (high-style) boutique, which stocks the world's top designers as well as Luisa's own line. **Lo Stock di Max** (✉ *Via Pietrapiana 15/r* ☎*055/241084*) sells last year's Max Mara stuff at a fraction of the original price.

Maçel (✉ *Via Guicciardini 128/r, Palazzo Pitti* ☎*055/287355*) has collections by lesser-known Italian designers, many of whom use the same factories as the A-list. Florentine designer **Patrizia Pepe** (✉ *Piazza San Giovanni 12/r, Duomo* ☎*055/2645056*) has body-conscious clothes perfect for all ages, especially for women with a tiny streak of rebelliousness. Members of the junior set desiring to look well clad, Florentine style, should consider stopping at **Piccolo Slam** (✉ *Via dei Lamberti 13/r, Piazza della Signoria* ☎*055/214504*). **Principe** (✉ *Via del Sole 2, Santa Maria Novella* ☎*055/292764*) is a Florentine institution with casual clothes for men, women, and children at far-from-casual prices. It also has a great housewares department. For cutting-edge fashion, the fun and funky window displays at **Spazio A** (✉ *Via Porta Rossa 109–115/r, Piazza della Repubblica* ☎*055/212995*) merit a stop. The shop carries such well-known designers as Alberta Ferretti and Narciso Rodriguez, as well as lesser-known Italian, English, and French designers.

FRAGRANCES

Aromatherapy has been elevated to an art form at **Antica Officina del Farmacista Dr. Vranjes** (✉*Borgo La Croce 44/r, Santa Croce* ☎*055/241748* ✉*Via San Gallo 63/r* ☎*055/494537*). Dr. Vranjes makes scents for the body and for the house.

The essence of a Florentine holiday is captured in the sachets of the **Officina Profumo Farmaceutica di Santa Maria Novella** (✉ *Via della Scala 16, Santa Maria Novella* ☎*055/216276*), an art nouveau emporium of herbal cosmetics and soaps that are made following centuries-old recipes created by friars.

JEWELRY

Angela Caputi (✉*Borgo Santi Apostoli 44/46* ☎*055/292993*) wows Florentine cognoscenti with her highly creative, often outsized plastic jewelry. A small, but equally creative, collection of women's clothing made of fine fabrics is also on offer. **Carlo Piccini** (✉*Ponte Vecchio 31/r, Piazza della Signoria* ☎*055/292030*) has been around for several generations, selling antique jewelry as well as making pieces to order; you can also get old jewelry reset here. **Cassetti** (✉*Ponte Vecchio 54/r, Piazza della Signoria* ☎*055/2396028*) combines precious and semiprecious stones and metals in contemporary settings. **Gatto Bianco** (✉*Borgo Santi Apostoli 12/r, Santa Maria Novella* ☎*055/282989*) has breathtakingly beautiful jewelry worked in semiprecious and precious stones; the feel is completely contemporary. **Gherardi** (✉*Ponte Vecchio 5/r, Piazza della Signoria* ☎*055/211809*), Florence's king of coral, has the city's largest selection of finely crafted pieces, as well as cultured

pearls, jade, and turquoise. **Oro Due** (✉ *Via Lambertesca 12/r, Piazza della Signoria* ☎*055/292143*) sells gold jewelry the old-fashioned way: beauteous objects are priced according to the level of craftsmanship and the price of gold bullion that day. The two women who run **Oreria** (✉ *Borgo Pinti 87/a, Santa*

Croce ☎*055/244708*) create divine designs using silver and semiprecious stones. Send suitors to purchase significant gifts here. **Studio Ballerino** (✉ *Borgo Allegri 25/r, Santa Croce* ☎*055/2344658*) has one-of-a-kind pieces crafted in semiprecious stone, gold, and silver. One of Florence's oldest jewelers, **Tiffany** (✉ *Via Tornabuoni 25/r, Santa Maria Novella* ☎*055/215506*) has supplied Italian (and other) royalty with finely crafted gems for centuries. Its selection of antique-looking classics has been updated with a selection of contemporary silver.

LINENS & FABRICS

Antico Setificio Fiorentina (✉ *Via L. Bartolini 4, Santo Spirito/San Frediano* ☎*055/213861*) has been providing damasks and other fine fabrics for royalty and those who aspire to it since 1786. Visits by appointment are preferred. **Blue Home** (✉ *Borgo Santi Apostoli 58/r, Santa Maria Novella* ☎*055/2658262*) sells sumptuous fabrics, which can be rendered into sofas, rugs, and other home furnishings to create divinely inspired interiors. Antique and contemporary rugs are also on hand. **Loretta Caponi** (✉ *Piazza Antinori 4/r, Santa Maria Novella* ☎*055/213668*) is synonymous with Florentine embroidery, and the luxury lace, linens, and lingerie have earned the eponymous signora worldwide renown. Luxurious silks, beaded fabrics, lace, wool, and tweeds can be purchased at **Valli** (✉ *Via Strozzi 4/r, Piazza della Repubblica* ☎*055/282485*). It carries fabrics created by Armani, Valentino, and other high-end designers.

OUTLETS

For bargains on Italian designer clothing, you need to leave the city and hit the outlet stores. At **Barberino Designer Outlet** (✉ *Via Meucci snc,* ☎*055/842161*) you'll find Prada, Pollini, Missoni, and Bruno Magli, among others. To get here, take the A1 to the Barberino di Mugello exit, and follow signs to the mall.

One-stop bargain shopping awaits at **The Mall** (✉ *Via Europa 8* ☎*055/8657775*), where the stores sell goods by such names as Bottega Veneta, Giorgio Armani, Loro Piana, Sergio Rossi, and the decidedly non-Italian Yves St. Laurent. Cognoscenti drive 45 minutes or take the train to Montevarchi, and then taxi out of town to the **Prada Outlet** (✉ *Levanella Spacceo, Estrada Statale 69, Montevarchi* ☎*055/91911*).

SHOES & LEATHER ACCESSORIES

Florentine women with a sense of whimsical style adore the purses at **Bracciolini** (✉ *Via delle Vigna Nuova 30/r*); if you're a fan of frogs, you'll adore the frog baguette bag with matching frog wallet.

The colorful, foot-friendly shoes at **Camper** (✉ *Via Por Santa Maria 47/r, Piazza della Signoria* ☎*055/2670342*) are made in Spain, but they cost less here than they do in the United States. The ultimate fine leathers are crafted into classic shapes at **Casadei** (✉ *Via Tornabuoni 33/r, Santa Maria Novella* ☎*055/287240*), winding up as women's shoes and bags. The late Salvatore Ferragamo earned his fortune custom-making shoes for famous feet, especially Hollywood stars. The classy **Ferragamo** (✉ *Via Tornabuoni 2/r, Santa Maria Novella* ☎*055/292123*), in a 13th-century Renaissance palazzo, displays designer clothing and accessories, but elegant footwear still underlies the Ferragamo success. **Pollini** (✉ *Via Calimala 12/r, Piazza della Repubblica* ☎*055/214738*) has beautifully crafted shoes and leather accessories for those willing to pay that little bit extra.

Beltrami (✉ *Via della Vigna Nuova 70/r, Santa Maria Novella* ☎*055/ 287779*), which sells shoes and some apparel, has long been synonymous with style; classic looks are beautifully updated. **Cellerini** (✉ *Via del Sole 37/r, Santa Maria Novella* ☎*055/282533*) is an institution in a city where it seems that just about everybody wears an expensive leather jacket. **Coccinelle** (✉ *Via Por Santa Maria 49/r, Piazza della Signoria* ☎*055/2398782*) sells leather accessories in bold colors and funky designs. **Furla** (✉ *Via Calzaiuoli 47/r, Piazza della Repubblica* ☎*055/2382883*) makes beautiful leather bags and wallets in up-to-the-minute designs. **Giotti** (✉ *Piazza Ognissanti 3–4/r, Lungarno North* ☎*055/294265*) has a full line of leather goods, including clothing. Florentine perennial **Gucci** (✉ *Via Tornabuoni 73/r, Santa Maria Novella* ☎*055/264011*) puts its famous initials on just about everything it sells. Beware, however, of shop assistants with severe attitude problems. **Il Bisonte** (✉ *Via del Parione 31/r, off Via della Vigna Nuova, Santa Maria Novella* ☎*055/215722*) is known for its natural-looking leather goods, all stamped with the store's bison symbol. **Madova** (✉ *Via Guicciardini 1/r, Palazzo Pitti* ☎*055/2396526*) has high-quality leather gloves in a rainbow of colors and a choice of linings (silk, cashmere, and unlined). **Paolo Carandini** (✉ *Via de' Macci 73/r, Santa Croce* ☎*055/245397*) works exclusively in leather, producing exquisite objects such as picture frames, jewelry boxes, and desk accessories.

Shoe styles at **Romano** (✉ *Via Speziali 10/r, Piazza della Repubblica* ☎*055/216535*) span the staid to the offbeat at appealing prices. A consortium of leatherworkers plies its trade at **Scuola del Cuoio** (✉ *Piazza Santa Croce 16* ☎*055/244533* ⊕*www.leatherschool.com*), in the former dormitory of the convent of Santa Croce; high-quality, fairly priced jackets, belts, and purses are sold here.

SIDE TRIPS FROM FLORENCE

West of Florence, and easily accessible by car or train, is Pisa, the town known the world over for its great engineering mistake, the Leaning Tower. North of Pisa, and also a quick shot from Florence, is the relaxed, elegant town of Lucca, which feels like its own little world, surrounded by 16th-century ramparts that have been transformed into parklike promenades. Pisa's tower is definitely worth seeing—and there's more to see than just the tower—but ultimately Lucca has greater charms, making it a better choice if you're picking one for an overnight.

Farther west, a hop over the border from Tuscany into Liguria brings you to the Cinque Terre—five tiny, cliff-hugging coastal villages that have become one of Italy's most popular destinations. It's not impossible to visit the Cinque Terre on a day trip from Florence, but we don't recommend it; you'll spend about five hours on the train round-trip, or something close to that if you go by car. You're better off either overnighting in Lucca or Pisa and day-tripping from there, or (best of all) spending a night or two in the Cinque Terre itself.

LUCCA

Ramparts built in the 16th and 17th centuries enclose a charming town filled with churches (99 of them), terra-cotta-roof buildings, and narrow cobblestone streets, along which local ladies maneuver bikes to do their daily shopping. Here Caesar, Pompey, and Crassus agreed to rule Rome as a triumvirate in 56 BC. Lucca was later the first Tuscan town to accept Christi-

> **WORD OF MOUTH**
>
> "For history and charm the small walled city of Lucca is, I think, absolutely magical. The food in Lucca also eclipses most all of Tuscany too!"
>
> –hanabilly

anity, and it still has a mind of its own: when most of Tuscany was voting communist as a matter of course, Lucca's citizens rarely followed suit. The famous composer Giacomo Puccini (1858–1924) was born here; his work forms the nucleus of the summer Opera Theater and Music Festival of Lucca. The ramparts circling the center city are the perfect place to take a stroll, ride a bicycle, kick a ball, or just stand and look down upon Lucca.

GETTING HERE

You can reach Lucca easily by train from Florence; the historic center is a short walk from the station. If you're driving, take the A11/E76.

Side Trips from Florence

VISITOR INFORMATION
Lucca tourism office (⌂*Piazza Santa Maria 35* ☎*0583/91991* ⊕*www. lucca.turismo.toscana.it*).

EXPLORING LUCCA

The historic center of Lucca, 51 km (31 mi) west of Florence, is walled, and motorized traffic is restricted. Walking and biking are the most efficient and most enjoyable ways to get around. You can rent bicycles, and the flat center makes biking easy. A combination ticket costing €6.50 gains you admission to both the Museo Nazionale di Villa Guinigi and the Pinacoteca Nazionale di Palazzo Mansi.

THE MAIN ATTRACTIONS

❶ ★ **Duomo.** The round-arch facade of the cathedral is a fine example of the rigorously ordered Pisan Romanesque style, in this case happily enlivened by an extremely varied collection of small carved columns. Take a closer look at the decoration of the facade and that of the portico below; they make this one of the most entertaining church exteriors in Tuscany. The Gothic interior contains a moving Byzantine crucifix—called the Volto Santo, or Holy Face—brought here, according to legend, in the eighth century (though it probably dates from between the 11th and early 13th centuries). The masterpiece of the Sienese sculptor Jacopo della Quercia (circa 1371–1438) is the marble *Tomb of Ilaria del Carretto* (1407–08). ⌂*Piazza del Duomo* ☎*0583/490530* 🎫*€2* ⊙*Duomo: weekdays 7–5:30, Sat. 9:30–6:45, Sun. 11:30–11:50 and 1–5:30. Tomb: Nov.–Mar., weekdays 9:30–4:45, Sat. 9:30–6:45, Sun. 11:30–11:50 and 1–5; Apr.–Oct., weekdays 9:30–5:45, Sat. 9–6:45, Sun. 9–10 and 1–5:45.*

★ **Passeggiata delle Mura.** Any time of day when the weather is clement, you can find the citizens of Lucca cycling, jogging, strolling, or kicking a soccer ball in this green, beautiful, and very large park—neither

Lucca

0   200 yards

0   200 meters

Viale Guglielmo Marconi

Viale Catorra

Viale G. Pacini

Via Giuseppe Giusti

V. dei Bastardi

Orti

V. B. Paoli

V. delle Arti

Via Elisa

Via S. Chiara

S. Michele

Via del fosso

Via S. Nicolao

Piazza S. Francesco

Via D. St. Francesco

Fratta

V. dell'Angelo Custode

V. S. Croce

Via di Poggio

Via Giuliano Bocabranca

Piazza del Anfiteatro Romano

V. Guinigi

Piazza dei Servi

V. dell' Arcivescovado

Via di Rosa

Anastasio

Bacchettoni

Battisteri

V. S. Croce

V. del Colmetto

Via del Battistero

Piazza S. Martino

V. del Gallo

V. del Moro

V. Fillungo

Piazza dei Mercanti

Piazza del Salvatore

V. Calderia

Via Cenani

V. S. Micheletto

V. Fillungo

Via Burlamacchi

Via Beccheria

Piazza S. Giovanni

Piazza del Giglio

Via Vittorio Veneto

Via S. Giorgio

Via di Poggio

Piazza Napoleone

Via del Moro

Piazza del Palazzo Dipinto

Piazza S. Romano

Via Fontana

Via Vittorio Emanuele

V. S. Giustina

V. S. Paolino

V. Carrara

Via Garibaldi

Corso Garibaldi

Via Carrara

Viale Regina Margherita

Via Cattaneo

Piazza S. Donato

V.S. Tassi

P.L. Pelesa

V. Tommaso

Pza G. Verdi

Viale Lazzaro Papi

Viale Giosuè Carducci

V. del Fosso

inside nor outside the city but rather right on the ring of ramparts that defines Lucca. Sunlight streams through two rows of tall plane trees to dapple the *passeggiata delle mura* (walk on the walls), which is 4.2 km (2½ mi) in length. Ten bulwarks are topped with lawns, many with picnic tables, and some with play equipment for children. Be aware at all times of where the edge is—there are no railings and the drop to the ground outside the city is a precipitous 40 feet.

NEED A BREAK? Gelateria Veneta (⊠ *Via V. Veneto 74* ☏ *0583/467037*) makes outstanding gelato, sorbet, and ices (some sugar-free). They prepare their confections three times a day using the same recipes with which the Brothers Arnoldo opened the place in 1927. The pièces de résistance are frozen fruits stuffed with creamy filling: don't miss the apricot-sorbet-filled apricot. Note that they close shop in October and reopen around Easter.

 Piazza dell'Anfiteatro Romano. Here's where the ancient Roman amphitheater once stood; some of the medieval buildings built over the amphitheater retain its original oval shape and brick arches. ⊠ *Off Via Fillungo, near north side of old town.*

San Frediano. The church of San Frediano, just steps from the Anfiteatro, has a 14th-century mosaic decorating its facade and contains works by Jacopo della Quercia (circa 1371–1438) and Matteo Civitali (1436–1501), as well as the lace-clad mummy of Saint Zita (circa 1218–78), the patron saint of household servants. ⊠ *Piazza San Frediano* ☏ *No phone* ⌨ *Free* ☉ *Mon.–Sat. 8:30–noon and 3–5, Sun. 10:30–5.*

San Michele in Foro. In the middle of the centro storico is this church with a facade even more fanciful than that of the Duomo. The upper levels of the facade have nothing but air behind them (after the front of the church was built, there were no funds to raise the nave), and the winged Archangel Michael, who stands at the very top, seems precariously poised for flight. The facade, heavily restored in the 19th century, displays busts of 19th-century Italian patriots such as Garibaldi and Cavour. Check out the superb Filippino Lippi (1457/58–1504) panel painting of Saints Girolamo, Sebastian, Rocco, and Helen in the right transept. ⊠ *Piazza San Michele* ☏ *No phone* ⌨ *Free* ☉ *Daily 9–noon and 3–6.*

 Torre Guinigi. The tower of the medieval Palazzo Guinigi contains one of the city's most curious sights: a grove of ilex trees has grown at the top of the tower and their roots have pushed their way into the room below. From the top you have a magnificent view of the city and the surrounding countryside. (Only the tower is open to the public, not the palazzo.) ⊠ *Palazzo Guinigi, Via Sant'Andrea* ☏ *No phone* ⌨ *€3.50* ☉ *Mar. and Apr., daily 9:30–6; May–Sept., daily 9–midnight; Oct.–Feb., daily 9–5.*

ALSO WORTH SEEING

Museo Nazionale di Villa Guinigi. On the eastern end of the historic center, this museum has an extensive collection of local Romanesque and Renaissance art. The museum represents an overview of Lucca's artistic traditions from Etruscan times until the 17th century, housed in the former

15th-century villa of the Guinigi family. ⊠ *Villa Guinigi, Via della Quarquonia* ☎*0583/496033* 🎫*€4, combination ticket €6.50, includes Museo Nazionale di Palazzo Mansi* ⊙*Tues.–Sat. 8:30–7, Sun. 8:30–1:30.*

WHERE TO EAT

$$ ✕**Buca di Sant'Antonio.** The staying power of Buca di Sant'Antonio—
★   it's been around since 1782—is the result of superlative Tuscan food brought to the table by waitstaff that doesn't miss a beat. The menu includes the simple-but-blissful, like *tortelli lucchesi al sugo* (meat-stuffed pasta with a tomato-and-meat sauce), and more daring dishes such as roast *capretto* (kid) with herbs. A white-wall interior hung with copper pots and brass musical instruments creates a classy but comfortable dining space. ⊠ *Via della Cervia 3* ☎*0583/55881* ▤*AE, DC, MC, V* ⊙*Closed Mon., 1 wk in Jan., and 1 wk in July. No dinner Sun.*

$$ ✕**Il Giglio.** Just off Piazza Napoleone, this restaurant has quiet, late-19th-century charm and classic cuisine. It's a place for all seasons, with a big fireplace for chilly weather and an outdoor patio in summer. If mushrooms are in season, try the *tacchonni con funghi*, a homemade pasta with mushrooms and a local herb called *niepitela*. A local favorite during winter is the *coniglio con olive* (rabbit stew with olives). ⊠*Piazza del Giglio 2* ☎*0583/494508* ▤*AE, DC, MC, V* ⊙*Closed Wed. and 15 days in Nov. No dinner Tues.*

$ ✕**Trattoria da Leo.** A few short turns away from the facade of San Michele, this noisy, informal, traditional trattoria delivers *cucina alla casalinga* (home cooking) in the best sense. Try the typical minestra di farro to start or just go straight to *secondi piatti* (entrées); in addition to the usual roast meats, there's excellent chicken with olives and a good cold dish of boiled meats served with a sauce of parsley and pine nuts. Save some room for a dessert, such as the rich, sweet, fig-and-walnut torte or the lemon sorbet brilliantly dotted with bits of sage, which tastes almost like mint. ⊠ *Via Tegrimi 1, at corner of Via degli Asili* ☎*0583/492236* ▤*No credit cards* ⊙*Closed Sun. Nov.–Mar. No lunch Sun.*

WHERE TO STAY

$$$–$$$$ 🏨**Hotel Ilaria.** The former stables of the Villa Bottini have been transformed into a modern hotel within the historic center. A second-floor terrace, overlooking the villa, makes a comfortable place to relax, and there's a hot tub for the adventurous. Rooms are done in a warm wood veneer with blue and white fittings. The availability of free bicycles is a nice bonus in this bike-friendly city, and the sumptuous buffet breakfast could see you through dinner. Residenza dell'Alba, the hotel's annex across the street, was originally part of a 14th-century church; now it's a luxe accommodation with in-room hot tubs. **Pros:** A Fodor's reader sums it up as a "nice modern small hotel"; free bicycles. **Cons:** Though in city center, it's a little removed from main attractions. ⊠ *Via del Fosso 26,* ☎*0583/47615* 🖷*0583/991961* ⊕*www.hotelilaria.com* ⇨*36 rooms, 5 suites* ⚴*In-room: safe, refrigerator. In-hotel: bar, bicycles, concierge, laundry service, public Internet, parking (no fee), some pets allowed (fee)* ▤*AE, DC, MC, V* ⎟◎⎟*BP.*

Lucca's *centro storico* (including Piazza San Michele, shown here) was home to the composer Giacomo Puccini (1858–1924). His work is celebrated at Lucca's annual summer music festival.

$$$ ⌂**Palazzo Alexander.** This small, elegant boutique hotel is on a quiet side street a short walk from San Michele in Foro. The building, dating from the 12th century, has been restructured to create the ease common to Lucchesi nobility: timbered ceilings, warm yellow walls, and brocaded chairs adorn the public rooms, and the motif continues into the guest rooms, all of which have high ceilings and that same glorious damask. Top-floor suites have sweeping views of the town. One suite is on the mezzanine floor, but also has city views. **Pros:** Intimate feel; gracious staff. **Cons:** Some Fodor's readers complain of too-thin walls. ⊠ *Via S. Giustina 48,* ☎*0583/583571* 🖷*0583/583610* ⊕*www.pala-zzo-alexander.com* ↝*9 rooms, 3 suites, 1 apartment* ♿*In-room: safe, refrigerator, dial-up. In-hotel: bar, bicycles, concierge, laundry service, public Internet, parking (fee)* ⊟*AE, DC, MC, V* ⍟*BP.*

$$ ⌂**Albergo San Martino.** Down a narrow street facing a quiet, sun-sprin-kled *piazzale (small square)* stands this small hotel. The brocade bed-spreads are fresh and crisp, the proprietor friendly. Although around the corner from the Duomo, the busy Corso Garibaldi, and the great walls of Lucca, the inn, tucked away as it is, feels private—a place to retreat to when you have seen all the church facades you can stand. Two of the eight rooms are wheelchair accessible. In the cheerful apri-cot breakfast room, filled with framed prints, you can get a more-than-solid breakfast. A little terrace with wicker chairs provides a lovely place to unwind. **Pros:** Comfortable bed; great breakfast. **Cons:** Break-fast costs €20. ⊠ *Via della Dogana 9,* ☎*0583/469181* 🖷*0583/991940* ⊕*www.albergosanmartino.it* ↝*6 rooms, 2 suites* ♿*In-room: refrig-erator. In-hotel: bar, bicycles (fee), no elevator, laundry service* ⊟*AE, DC, MC, V* ⍟*EP.*

$ ⛁ **Piccolo Hotel Puccini.** Steps away from the busy square and church of San Michele, this little hotel is quiet and calm—and a great deal. Wallpaper, hardwood floors, and throw rugs are among the handsome decorations. Paolo, the genial manager, speaks fluent English and dispenses great touring advice. **Pros:** Cheery, English-speaking staff. **Cons:** Breakfast costs extra; some rooms are on the dark side. ⊠ *Via di Poggio 9,* ☎ *0583/55421* 🖷 *0583/53487* ⊕ *www.hotelpuccini.com* 📶 *14 rooms* ♿ *In-room: no a/c, safe. In-hotel: bar, laundry service, some pets allowed, no-smoking rooms* ⊟ *AE, MC, V* ⊗ *EP.*

SPORTS & THE OUTDOORS

A splendid bike ride (rental about €12.50 for the day) may be had by circling the entire historic center along the top of the bastions—affording something of a bird's-eye view. **Poli Antonio Biciclette** (⊠ *Piazza Santa Maria 42, Lucca East* ☎ *0583/493787*) is an option for bicycle rental on the east side.

SHOPPING

Lucca's justly famed olive oils are available throughout the city (and exported around the world). Look for those made by Fattoria di Fubbiano and Fattoria Fabbri—two of the best.

Antica Bottega di Prospero (⊠ *Via San Lucia 13* ☎ *No phone* ♿ sells top-quality local products, including farro, dried porcini mushrooms, olive oil, and wine.

★ Chocoholics can get their fix at **Caniparoli** (⊠ *Via S. Paolino 96, San Donato* ☎ *0583/53456*). They are so serious about their sweets here that they do not make them from June through August because of the heat. Bargain hunters won't want to miss **Benetton Stock Outlet** (⊠ *Via Mordini 17/19, Anfiteatro* ☎ *0583/464533*), with its brightly colored garments at reduced prices.

PISA

When you think Pisa, you think Leaning Tower. Its position as one of Italy's most famous landmarks is a heavy reputation to bear, and it comes accompanied by abundant crowds and kitschy souvenirs. But the building *is* interesting and novel, and even if it doesn't captivate you, Pisa has other treasures that make a visit worthwhile. Taken as a whole, the Campo dei Miracoli (Field of Miracles), where the Leaning Tower, Duomo, and Baptistery are located, is among the most dramatic architectural complexes in Italy.

Pisa may have been inhabited as early as the Bronze Age. It was certainly populated by the Etruscans and, in turn, became part of the Roman Empire. In the early Middle Ages it flourished as an economic powerhouse—along with Amalfi, Genoa, and Venice, it was one of the maritime republics. The city's economic and political power ebbed in the early 15th century as it fell under the domination of Florence, though it enjoyed a brief resurgence under Cosimo I in the mid-16th century. Pisa endured heavy Allied bombing—miraculously, the Duomo and Leaning Tower, along with some other grand Romanesque structures, were spared, though the Camposanto sustained heavy damage.

GETTING HERE
Pisa is an easy hour train ride from Florence. By car it's a straight shot on the Fi-Pi-Li autostrada. The Pisa–Lucca train runs frequently and takes about 30 minutes.

VISITOR INFORMATION
Pisa tourism office (⊠ *Piazza Vittorio Emanuele II* ☎ *050/42291*).

4

EXPLORING PISA

Pisa is 84 km (52 mi) west of Florence. Like many other Italian cities, the town is best seen on foot. The views along the Arno are particularly grand and shouldn't be missed—there's a sense of spaciousness here that the Arno in Florence lacks. You should weigh the different options for combination tickets to sights on the Piazza del Duomo when you begin your visit. Combination tickets are sold at the ticket office behind the Duomo opposite the Leaning Tower; one monument costs €5, two monuments €6, up to €8 for all the main sights, excluding the Leaning Tower.

THE MAIN ATTRACTIONS
2 **Battistero.** This lovely Gothic baptistery, which stands across from the Duomo's facade, is best known for the pulpit carved by Nicola Pisano (circa 1220–84; father of Giovanni Pisano) in 1260. Ask one of the ticket takers if he'll sing for you inside; the acoustics are remarkable. ⊠ *Piazza del Duomo* ☎ *050/3872210* ⊕ *www.opapisa.it* ☎ *€5, discounts available if bought in combination with tickets for other monuments* ☉ *Mar. 1–13, daily 9–6; Mar. 14–20, daily 9–7; Mar. 21–Sept., daily 8–8; Oct., daily 9–7; Nov.–Feb., daily 10–5.*

3 **Duomo.** Pisa's cathedral brilliantly utilizes the horizontal marble stripe motif (borrowed from Moorish architecture) that became common to Tuscan cathedrals. It is famous for the Romanesque panels on the transept door facing the tower that depict scenes from the life of Christ. The beautifully carved 14th-century pulpit is by Giovanni Pisano (son of Nicola). ⊠ *Piazza del Duomo* ☎ *050/3872210* ⊕ *www.opapisa.it* ☎ *€2, discounts available if bought in combination with tickets for other monuments* ☉ *Mar. 1–13, daily 9–6; Mar. 14–20, daily 10–7; Mar. 21–Sept., daily 10–8; Oct., daily 10–7; Nov.–Feb., daily 10–1 and 2–5.*

4 **Leaning Tower** *(Torre Pendente).* Legend holds that Galileo conducted
Fodor's Choice an experiment on the nature of gravity by dropping metal balls from
★ the top of the 187-foot-high Leaning Tower of Pisa. Historians, however, say this legend has no basis in fact—which isn't quite to say that it's false. Work on this tower, built as a campanile (bell tower) for the Duomo, started in 1173: the lopsided settling began when construction

reached the third story. The tower's architects attempted to compensate through such methods as making the remaining floors slightly taller on the leaning side, but the extra weight only made the problem worse. The settling continued, and by the late 20th century it had accelerated to such a point that many feared the tower would simply topple over, despite all efforts to prop it up. The structure has since been firmly anchored to the earth. The final phase to restore the tower to its original tilt of 300 years ago was launched in early 2000 and finished two years later. The last phase removed some 100 tons of earth from beneath the foundation. Reservations, which are essential, can be made online or by calling the Museo dell'Opera del Duomo; it's also possible to arrive at the ticket office and book for the same day. Note that children under eight years of age are not allowed to climb. ✉*Piazza del Duomo* ☎*050/3872210* 🌐*www.opapisa.it* 🎟*€17* ⏱*Mar. 21–Sept., daily 8:30–8:30; Oct., daily 9–7; Nov.–Feb., daily 10–5; Mar. 1–Mar. 13, daily 9–6; Mar. 14–Mar. 20, daily 9–7.*

ALSO WORTH SEEING

❶ Camposanto. According to legend, the cemetery—a walled structure on the western side of the Campo dei Miracoli—is filled with earth that returning Crusaders brought back from the Holy Land. Contained within are numerous frescoes, notably *The Drunkenness of Noah*, by Renaissance artist Benozzo Gozzoli (1422–97), presently under restoration; and the disturbing *Triumph of Death* (14th century; artist uncertain), whose subject matter shows what was on people's minds in a century that saw the ravages of the Black Death. ⊠*Piazza del Duomo* ☎*050/3872210* ⊕*www. opapisa.it* ✉*€5, discounts available if bought in combination with tickets for other monuments* ⊙*Mar. 1–13, daily 9–6; Mar. 14–20, daily 9–7; Mar. 21–Sept., daily 8–8; Oct., daily 10–7; Nov.–Feb., daily 10–5.*

WORD OF MOUTH

"At Pisa we discovered a peaceful haven with relatively few tourists compared with Florence, and a magnificent lawn you could actually walk and sit on. I lay down in the lovely grass and slept in the sun until I was awakened by the cool shadow of the Leaning Tower. It was magic and peaceful and beautiful."   –Jo

⑤ Museo dell'Opera del Duomo. At the southeast corner of the sprawling Campo dei Miracoli, this museum holds a wealth of medieval sculptures and the ancient Roman sarcophagi that inspired Nicola Pisano's figures. ⊠*Piazza del Duomo* ☎*050/3872210* ⊕*www.opapisa.it* ✉*€5, discounts available if bought in combination with tickets for other monuments* ⊙ *Mar. 1–13, daily 9–6; Mar. 14–20, daily 9–7; Mar. 21–Sept., daily 8–8; Oct., daily 10–7; Nov.–Feb., daily 10–5.*

⑦ Museo Nazionale di San Matteo. On the north bank of the Arno, this museum contains some incisive examples of local Romanesque and Gothic art. ⊠*Lungarno Mediceo* ☎*050/541865* ✉*€5* ⊙*Tues.–Sat. 9–7, holidays 9–2.*

⑥ Piazza dei Cavalieri. The piazza, with its fine Renaissance **Palazzo dei Cavalieri, Palazzo dell'Orologio,** and **Santo Stefano dei Cavalieri,** was laid out by Giorgio Vasari in about 1560. The square was the seat of the Ordine dei Cavalieri di San Stefano (Order of the Knights of St. Stephen), a military and religious institution meant to defend the coast from possible invasion by the Turks. Also in this square is the prestigious **Scuola Normale Superiore,** founded by Napoléon in 1810 on the French model. Here graduate students pursue doctorates in literature, philosophy, mathematics, and science. In front of the school is a large statue of Ferdinando I de' Medici dating from 1596. On the extreme left is the tower where the hapless Ugolino della Gherardesca (died 1289) was imprisoned with his two sons and two grandsons; legend holds that he ate them. Dante immortalized him in Canto XXXIII of *his Inferno.* Duck into the **Church of Santo Stefano** and check out Bronzino's *Nativity of Christ* (1564–65).

WHERE TO EAT

$$–$$$ ✕**Beny.** Apricot walls hung with etchings of Pisa make this small, single-room restaurant warmly romantic. Husband and wife Damiano and Sandra Lazzerini have been running the place for two decades, and it shows in their obvious enthusiasm while talking about the menu and daily specials. Beny specializes in fish: its *ripieno di polpa di pesce a pan grattato con salsa di seppie e pomodoro* (fish-stuffed ravioli with tomato-octopus

sauce) is a delight. Another flavorful dish is the *sformato di verdura* (a flan with Jerusalem artichokes), which comes embellished with sweet *gamberoni* (shrimp). ✉*Piazza Gambacorti 22* 🕾*050/25067* ⊟*AE, DC, MC, V* ⊘*Closed Sun. and 2 wks in mid-Aug. No lunch Sat.*

$$ ✕**Osteria dei Cavalieri.** This charming white-wall restaurant, a few steps
★ from Piazza dei Cavalieri, is reason enough to come to Pisa. They can do it all here—serve up exquisitely grilled fish dishes, please vegetarians, and prepare *tagliata* (thin slivers of rare beef) for meat lovers. Three set menus, from the sea, garden, and earth, are available, or you can order à la carte. For dinner there's an early seating (around 7:30) and a later one (around 9); opt for the later if you want time to linger over your meal. ✉*Via San Frediano 16* 🕾*050/580858* ⚿*Reservations essential* ⊟*AE, DC, MC, V* ⊘*Closed Sun., 2 wks in Aug., and Dec. 29–Jan. 7. No lunch Sat.*

WHERE TO STAY

$$$$ 🖫**Hotel Relais dell'Orologio.** What used to be a private family palace opened as an intimate hotel in spring of 2003. Eighteenth-century antiques fill the rooms and public spaces; some rooms have stenciled walls and wood-beam ceilings. On the third floor, sloped ceilings add romance. A large shared sitting room, complete with fireplace, provides a relaxing spot to read or sip a glass of wine. **Pros:** Location—in the center of town, but on a quiet side street. **Cons:** Breakfast costs extra. ✉*Via della Faggiola 12/14, off Campo dei Miracoli, Santa Maria,* 🕾*050/830361* 🖷*050/551869* ⊕*www.hotelrelaisorologio.com* 🛏*16 rooms, 5 suites* ⚴*In-room: safe, refrigerator, dial-up. In-hotel: restaurant, room service, bar, concierge, laundry service, parking (fee), some pets allowed, no-smoking rooms* ⊟*AE, DC, MC, V* ❢⊙*EP.*

$$ 🖫**Royal Victoria.** In a pleasant palazzo facing the Arno, a 10-minute walk from the Campo dei Miracoli, this comfortably furnished hotel has been in the Piegaja family since 1837. That continuity may help explain why such notables as Charles Dickens and Charles Lindbergh enjoyed staying here. Antiques and reproductions are in the lobby and in some rooms, whose style ranges from the 1800s, complete with frescoes, to the 1920s. Ask for a room in the charming old tower. There's also a pretty rooftop garden where you can order cocktails. **Pros:** Friendly staff; free use of a Lancia that seats five—a great vehicle for tooling around Pisa. **Cons:** Rooms vary significantly in size; all are a little worn. ✉*Lungarno Pacinotti 12,* 🕾*050/940111* 🖷*050/940180* ⊕*www.royalvictoria.it* 🛏*48 rooms, 40 with bath* ⚴*In-room: no a/c (some), dial-up. In-hotel: room service, bicycles, concierge, laundry service, parking (fee), some pets allowed* ⊟*AE, DC, MC, V* ❢⊙*BP.*

THE CINQUE TERRE

FIVE REMOTE VILLAGES MAKE ONE MUST-SEE DESTINATION

"Charming" and "breath-taking" are adjectives that get a workout when you're traveling in Italy, but it's rare that both apply to a single location. The Cinque Terre is such a place, and this combination of characteristics goes a long way toward explaining its tremendous appeal.

The area is made up of five tiny villages (Cinque Terre literally means "Five Lands") clinging to the cliffs along a gorgeous stretch of the Ligurian coast. The terrain is so steep that for centuries footpaths were the only way to get from place to place. It just so happens that these paths provide beautiful views of the rocky coast tumbling into the sea, as well as access to secluded beaches and grottoes.

Backpackers "discovered" the Cinque Terre in the 1970s, and its popularity has been growing ever since. Despite summer crowds, much of the original appeal is intact. Each town has maintained its own distinct charm, and views from the trails in between are as breathtaking as ever.

Monterosso

Corniglia

Terracing around Corniglia

HIKING THE CINQUE TERRE

Monterosso—Vernazza Trail
The most demanding portion of the trail. Often narrow, with significant climbs and descents, particularly near Vernazza. Your labors are rewarded with the Trail No. 2's best views.

Vernazza—Corniglia Trail
Ups and downs interspersed with olive groves and terraced vineyards.

Mount Malpertuso

Mount Castello

Le Stalle

Trail No 8a

Mount Gaginara

Drignana

(Red Trail)

38

370

Madonna di Soviore
1hr 30min

Trail No 89

Trail No 1

51

Trail No 8

Santuario del Reggio
1hr

S. Bernardo
Trail No 8

Santuario Bernardino
1hr

Trail No 7

3 km/2 mi—1 hr 30 min

Trail No 2 (Blue Trail)
3 km/2 mi—2 hrs

Guvano Beach

Palma Pt

Vernazza

Molinara Pt

del Frate Island

Monterosso al Mare

FERRY TO LEVANTO

0   1 mi

0   1 km

Monterosso
The most resort-like of the villages, with the largest beach.

Vernazza
Pretty and visitor-friendly. The best spot for lingering in a café and watching waves crash against the shore.

THE CLASSIC HIKE

Hiking is the most popular way to experience the Cinque Terre, and Trail No. 2, the Sentiero Azzurro (Blue Trail), is the most traveled path. To cover the entire trail is a full day: it's approximately 13 km (8 mi) in length, takes you to all five villages, and requires about five hours, not including stops, to complete. The best approach is to start at the eastern-most town of Riomaggiore and warm up your legs on the easiest segment of the trail. As you work your way west, the hike gets progressively more demanding. For a less strenuous experience, you can choose to skip a leg or two and take the ferry (which provides its own beautiful views) or the inland train running between the towns instead.

Manarola

Along Trail No.2

Via dell'Amore

Corniglia–Manarola Trail
Runs through the hills near Manarola, descends to rocky beach near Corniglia.

Manarola–Riomaggiore Trail
Known as the Via dell'Amore (Lovers' Lane). A wide, paved, flat path with fine views.

KEY

:::::::::::::::	*Major footpaths*
- - - - - - - -	*Sanctuary footpaths*
— - — - — -	*Connecting footpaths*
45min	*Hiking times*
☦	*Sanctuaries*

4

IN FOCUS THE CINQUE TERRE

Mount Capri

Mount Cuna

No 1 (Red Trail)

Trail No 6

Mount Galera

Mount Grosso

51

Trail No 7a

Trail No 6d

1hr 30min

Madonna della ☦ Salute

1hr

Trail No 02

Volastra

3 km/2 mi–1 hr
Trail No 2 (Blue Trail)

51

Trail No 3

Madonna di Montenero
☦ 45min

370

370

TO LA SPEZIA

Spiaggione di Corniglia

Corniglia

del Luogo Pt

Ligurian Sea

Manarola

Buonfiglio Pt

30min

•• Via dell' Amore

Riomaggiore

Trail No 2 (Blue Trail)

Torre Guardiola

C di M Nero

Corniglia
Perched on a cliff 500 ft. above the sea, reached by a switchback path (or by shuttle bus).

Manarola
The most photogenic of the villages, best seen from the cemetery a few minutes up the path toward Corniglia.

Riomaggiore
Cliff-clinging buildings are almost as striking as those in Manarola. Stairs to the left of the train station entrance cross over the tracks and lead to the trailhead.

BEYOND TRAIL NO.2

Trail No. 2 is just one of a network of trails crisscrossing the hills. If you're a dedicated hiker, spend a few nights and try some of the other routes. Trail No. 1, the Sentiero Rosso (Red Trail), climbs from Portovenere (east of Riomaggiore) and returns to the sea at Levanto (west of Monterosso al Mare). To hike its length takes from 9 to 12 hours; the ridge-top trail provides spectacular views from high above the villages, each of which can be reached via a steep path. Other shorter trails go from the villages up into the hills, some leading to religious sanctuaries. Trail No. 9, for example, starts from the old section of Monterosso and ends at the Madonna di Soviore Sanctuary.

FODOR'S FIRST PERSON

Angelo Benvenuto
Fisherman,
Monterosso al Mare

Angelo Benvenuto is a 10th-generation fisherman from Monterosso who organizes special boating excursions along the Cinque Terre in his *lampara* (wooden anchovy fishing boat).

Q: Although hiking the Cinque Terre has become a favorite with travelers, you and others maintain that the "way of life" in the Cinque Terre is really that of the sea....

A: For nearly one thousand years Monterosso has been a fishing village. We eat, live, and breathe the sea. In fact, when the barbarians invaded Italy during the middle ages, they did not come down to Monterosso because they were afraid of the sea. Because of this Monterosso as well as the other villages were protected and untouched. Everyday life is always connected to the sea.

Yet, the *sentiri* (trails) were also essential to our livelihood. They provided access to the elements we needed on land such as produce, animals, and of course wine! Now

they are a source of entertainment and beauty for our visitors.

Q: How has the Cinque Terre changed over the past 20 years?

A: There are obviously more people visiting, but everyday life has remained the same. I still go out to fish for the majority of our meals, and my wife works in the garden to provide us with fresh vegetables, fruit, even eggs. It is this way for most of the Cinque Terre.

Of course, many of us have gone into the tourism business—hotels, restaurants, cafes. The tourists have brought us opportunity and some financial stability which is very good for us, for all of the villages.

Q: What is your perfect day in the Cinque Terre?

A: Take a hike up to the garden (located on the slopes above town) or maybe even to Vernazza to visit friends. Then after a nice fresh seafood lunch, glass of *Sciacchetra'* (local dessert wine) and a short *pisolino* (nap), I would then head out to sea on my lampara and enjoy the silence of the sea and the beautiful landscape, and catch some fish for dinner!

PRECAUTIONS

If you're hitting the trails, you'll want to carry water with you, wear sturdy shoes (hiking boots are best), and have a hat and sunscreen handy. ⚠ Check weather reports before you start out; especially in late fall and winter, thunderstorms can send townspeople running for cover and make the shelterless trails slippery and dangerous. Rain in October and November can cause landslides and close the trails. Note that the lesser-used trails aren't as well maintained as Trail No. 2. If you're undertaking the full Trail No.

1 hike, bring something to snack on as well as your water bottle.

ADMISSION

Entrance tickets for use of the trails are available at ticket booths located at the start of each section of Trail No. 2, and at information offices in the Levanto, Monterosso, Vernazza, Corniglia, Manarola, Riomaggiore, and La Spezia train stations.

A one-day pass costs €5, which includes a trail map and a general information leaflet. Information about local train and boat schedules is also available from the information offices.

Working Cinque Terre's vertical vineyards

GETTING THERE & GETTING AROUND

The local train on the Genoa–La Spezia line stops at each of the Cinque Terre, and runs approximately every 30 minutes. Tickets for each leg of the journey (€1.30) are available at the five train stations. In Corniglia, the only one of the Cinque Terre that isn't at sea level, a shuttle service (€1) is provided for those who don't wish to climb (or descend) the hundred-or-so steps that link the train station with the cliff-top town.

Along the Cinque Terre coast two ferry lines operate. From June to September, Golfo Paradiso runs from Genoa and Camogli to Monterosso al Mare and Vernazza. The smaller, but more frequent, Golfo dei Poeti stops at each village from Portovenere (east of Riomaggiore) to Monterosso, with the exception of Corniglia, four times a day. A one-day ticket costs €22.

WHEN TO GO

The ideal times to see the Cinque Terre are September and May, when the weather is mild and the summer tourist season isn't in full swing.

SWIMMING & BEACHES

Each town has something that passes for a beach, but there are only two options where you'll find both sand and decent swimming. The more accessible is in Monterosso, opposite the train station; it's equipped with chairs, umbrellas, and snack bars. The other is the secluded, swimwear-optional Guvano Beach, between Corniglia and Vernazza. To reach it from the Corniglia train station, bypass the steps leading up to the village, instead following signs to an abandoned train tunnel. Ring a bell at the tunnel's entrance, and the gate will automatically open; after a dimly lit 10-minute walk, you'll emerge at the beach. Both beaches have a nominal admission fee.

Monterosso al Mare

THE TOWNS

Riomaggiore

At the eastern end of the Cinque Terre, Riomaggiore is built into a river gorge (thus the name, which means "river major") and is easily accessible from La Spezia by train or car. It has a tiny harbor protected by large slabs of alabaster and marble, which serve as as tanning beds for sunbathers, as well as being the site of several outdoor cafes with fine views. According to legend, settlement of Riomaggiore dates far back to the 8th century, when Greek religious refugees came here to escape persecution by the Byzantine emperor.

Manarola

The enchanting pastel houses of Manarola spill down a steep hill overlooking a spectacular turquoise swimming cove and a bustling harbor. The whole town is built on black rock. Above the town, ancient terraces still protect abundant vineyards and olive trees. This village is the center of the wine and olive oil production of the region, and its streets are lined with shops selling local products.

Corniglia

The buildings, narrow lanes, and stairways of Corniglia are strung together amid vineyards high on the cliffs; on a clear day views of the entire coastal strip are excellent. The high perch and lack of harbor make this farming community the most remote of the Cinque Terre. On a pretty pastel square sits the 14th-century church of **San Pietro**. The rose window of marble imported from Carrara is impressive, particularly considering the work required to get it here. ⊠ *Main Sq.* ☎ *0187/3235582* ⊘ *Wed. 4–6, Sun. 10–noon.*

Vernazza

With its narrow streets and small squares, Vernazza is arguably the most charming of the five towns. Because it has the best access to the sea, it became wealthier than its neighbors—as evidenced by the elaborate arcades, loggias, and marblework. The village's pink, slate-roof houses and colorful squares contrast with the remains of the medieval fort and castle, including two towers, in the old town. The Romans first inhabited this rocky spit of land in the 1st century.

Today Vernazza has a fairly lively social scene. It's a great place to refuel with a hearty seafood lunch or linger in a café between links of the hike on Trail No. 2.

Monterosso al Mare

Beautiful beaches, rugged cliffs, crystal-clear turquoise waters, and plentiful small hotels and restaurants make Monterosso al Mare, the largest of the Cinque Terre villages (population 1,730), the busiest in midsummer. The village center bustles high on a hillside. Below, connected by stone steps, are the port and seaside promenade, where there are boats for hire. The medieval tower, Aurora, on the hills of the Cappuccini, separates the ancient part of the village from the more modern part. The village is encircled by hills covered with vineyards and olive groves, and by a forest of scrubby bushes and small trees.

Monterosso has the most festivals of the five villages, starting with the Lemon Feast on the Saturday preceding Ascension Sunday, followed by the Flower Festival of Corpus Christi, celebrated yearly on the second Sunday after Pentecost. During the afternoon, the streets and alleyways of the *centro storico* (historic center) are decorated with thousands of colorful flower petals set in beautiful designs that the evening procession passes over. Finally, the Salted Anchovy and Olive Oil Festival takes place each year during the second weekend of September.

Thursday, the **market** attracts mingled crowds of tourists and villagers from along the coast to shop for everything from pots and pans and underwear to fruits, vegetables, and fish. Often a few stands sell local art and crafts as well as olive oil and wine. ⊠ *Old town center* ☼ *Thurs. 8–1.*

The **Chiesa di San Francesco**, was built in the 12th century in the Ligurian Gothic style. Its distinctive black stripes and marble rose window make it one of the most photographed sites in the Cinque Terre. ⊠ *Piazza Garibaldi* ☎ *No phone* ✉ *Free* ☼ *Daily 9–1 and 4–7.*

Main Square, Vernazza

WHERE TO STAY & EAT

From June through September, reservations are essential if you plan to stay in a hotel or B&B here. *Affitacamere* (rooms for rent in private homes) are a more modest alternative, often indicated by a simple sign on the front door. At agencies in Riomaggiore and Monterosso you can book officially licensed affitacamere. These rooms vary considerably in comfort, amenities, and cost; arrive early for a good selection.

Riomaggiore

$$–$$$ ✗ **La Lanterna.** Colorful chalkboards out in front of this small trattoria by the harbor list the day's selection of fresh fish; the set-up might sound modest, but this is arguably the finest restaurant in the Cinque Terre. Over the winter, Chef Massimo serves as a teacher at the Culinary Academy in Switzerland, and he always returns with new ideas for his menu. When available, their *cozze ripiene* (stuffed mussels) shouldn't be missed. Other offerings may be a touch exotic, such sting ray with ligurian herbs and white wine. ✉ *Via San Giacomo 10* ☎ *0187/920589* ☰ *AE, DC, MC, VC* ✪ *Closed Jan and 2 wks in Nov.*

$ ▦ **Due Gemelli.** Set above the sea, this small hotel has fabulous views of the turquoise water. The rooms have simple, mismatched furnishings, but they all have balconies, making them bright and airy. ✉ *Via Litoranea 1, 19017* ☎ *0187/920111* ☎ *0187/920678* ⊕ *www.duegemelli.it* ➳ *14 rooms* ⌂ *Restaurant, bar; no a/c* ☰ *AE, DC, MC, V* ⦿ *BP.*

Manarola

$ ▦ **Ca' d'Andrean.** If you want to stay in one of the less crowded of the Cinque Terre, this tiny, simple hotel is one of your best options. White-tile floors cool off the rooms, some of which have balconies. In summer, breakfast, an optional extra at €6 per person, is served in a flower garden. ✉ *Via Discovolo 101, 19010* ☎ *0187/920040* ☎ *0187/920452* ⊕ *www.cadandrean.it* ➳ *10 rooms* ⌂ *Bar; no a/c* ☰ *No credit cards* ✪ *Closed mid-Nov.–mid-Dec.*

Corniglia

$–$$ ✗▦ **Cecio.** On the outskirts of Corniglia, many of the spotless rooms at the family-run Cecio have spectacular views of the town clinging to the cliffs above the bay. The same memorable vista can be enjoyed from the hotel's restaurant, which serves inexpensive and well-prepared local seafood dishes. Try the delicious lasagna with pesto sauce as a first course. ✉ *Via Serra 58, 19010, toward Vernazza* ☎ *0187/812043* ☎ *0187/812138* ➳ *12 rooms* ⌂ *Restaurant; no a/c, no room phones, no TV in some rooms* ☰ *DC, MC, V* ⦿ *BP.*

DID YOU KNOW

Tiny Manarola is the best spot for purchasing the wine and olive oil produced in the Cinque Terre.

Vernazza

$$–$$$ ✕ **Gambero Rosso.** Relax on Vernazza's main square at this fine trattoria looking out at a church. Enjoy such delectable dishes as shrimp salad, vegetable torte, and squid-ink risotto. The creamy pesto, served atop spaghetti, is some of the best in the area. End your meal with Cinque Terre's own *sciacchetrà*, a dessert wine served with semisweet biscotti. Don't drink it out of the glass—dip the biscotti in the wine instead. ✉ *Piazza Marconi 7* ☎ *0187/812265* ▭ *AE, DC, MC, V* ⊙ *Closed Mon. Jan. and Feb.*

$–$$ ✕▦ **Trattoria Gianni Franzi.** Order your pesto with *fagiolini* (green beans), a Ligurian specialty that somehow tastes better when you're eating it outside in a beautiful *piazzetta* (small square) with a view of the port, as you can here. Above the restaurant, a number of simply furnished, economical rooms are available. Your choice here is between the smaller, older rooms without private bathrooms, but with tiny balconies and great views of the port, or those in the newer section, with bathrooms but no view. ✉ *Via G. Marconi 1, 19018* ☎ *0187/821003* 🖷 *0187/812228* ⊕ *www.giannifranzi.it* 🛏 *20 rooms, 12 with bath* ♨ *Restaurant, bar* ▭ *AE, DC, MC, V* ⊙ *Closed Jan. 8–Feb.; restaurant closed Wed. early Mar.–mid-July and mid-Sept.–early Jan.* ⦿ *BP.*

$$$ ✕▦ **La Malà.** A cut above other lodging options in the Cinque Terre, this family-run B&B has only four rooms, and they fill up quickly. The rooms are small but well equipped, with flat screen TVs, a/c, marble showers, and comfortable bedding. Two of the rooms have sea views; the other two face the port of Vernazza. There's a shared terrace literally suspended over the Mediterranean. Book early! ✉ *Giovanni Battista 29, 19018* ☎ *334/2875718* ⊕ *www.lamala.*

it 🛏 *4 rooms* ♨ *In-room: safe, refrigerator, satellite TV, hairdryer, tea & coffee maker.* ▭ *AE, DC, MC, V* ⊙ *Closed Jan. 10–Mar.*

Monterosso al Mare

★ **$$$** ✕ **Miki.** Specialties here are anything involving seafood. The *insalata di mare* (seafood salad), with squid and fish, is more than tasty; so are the grilled fish and any pasta with seafood. If you're in the mood for a pizza, you can order that here as well. Miki has a beautiful little garden in the back, perfect for lunch on a sunny day. ✉ *Via Fegina 104* ☎ *0187/817608* ▭ *AE, DC, MC, V* ⊙ *Closed Nov. and Dec., and Tues. Sept.–July.*

$ ✕ **Enoteca Internazionale.** Located on the main street in centro, this wine bar offers a large variety of vintages, both local from further afield, plus delicious light fare; its umbrella-covered patio is a perfect spot to recuperate after a day of hiking. The owner, Susanna, is a certified sommelier who's always forthcoming with helpful suggestions on local wines. ✉ *Via Roma 62* ☎ *0187/817278* ▭ *AE, MC, V* ⊙ *Closed Tues., Jan–Mar.*

$$ ✕▦ **Il Giardino Incantato.** This small B&B in the historic center of Monterosso oozes comfort and old-world charm. The building dates back to the 16th century and still maintains its wood beam ceiling and stone walls. Each room has been impeccably restored with modern amenities. Breakfast is served either in your room on request or in their lovely private garden under the lemon trees. The owner, Maria Pia, goes out of her way to make you feel at home and whips up a fabulous frittata for breakfast. ✉ *Via Mazzini 18, 19016* ☎ *0185/818315* ⊕ *www.ilgiardinoincantato.net* 🛏 *3 rooms, 1 junior suite* ♨ *In-room: safe, refrigerator, satellite TV, hairdryer, tea & coffee maker. In-hotel: private garden.* ▭ *AE, DC, MC,*

Between Florence & Venice

HIGHLIGHTS OF EMILIA-ROMAGNA & THE VENETO, PLUS MILAN

WORD OF MOUTH

"Ah, Bologna . . . one of Italy's truly underrated gems. Sitting in an outdoor café in Piazza Maggiore is a true Italian experience."
—HowardR

WELCOME TO EMILIA–ROMAGNA & THE VENETO

TOP REASONS TO GO

★ **The signature foods of Emilia-Romagna:** This region's food—the *prosciutto crudo,* the Parmigiano-Reggiano, the balsamic vinegar, and perhaps above all, the pasta—alone makes the trip to Italy worthwhile.

★ **Mosaics that take your breath away:** The intricate tile creations in Ravenna's Mausuleo di Galla Placidia, in brilliantly well-preserved primary colors, depict pastoral scenes that transport you to another age.

★ **Villa Barbaro in Maser:** Master architect Palladio's graceful creation meets Veronese's splendid paintings in a one-time-only collaboration.

★ **Giotto's frescoes in the Capella degli Scrovegni:** At this chapel in Padua, Giotto's innovations in painting technique helped to launch the Renaissance.

★ **Opera in Verona's ancient arena:** Even if the music doesn't move you, the spectacle will.

1 Bologna. In Emilia—Romagna's cultural and intellectual center, rows of street arcades wind around ancient university buildings, grandiose towers—and some of the best restaurants in Italy.

2 Ravenna. It's worth a detour off the path between Florence and Venice to visit this well-preserved city with its remarkable mosaics—glittering treasures left from Byzantine rule.

3 Ferrara. This wonderfully characteristic medieval city north of Bologna is, among other things, home to the world's oldest wine bar, Osteria Al Brindisi, where they've been pour since 1435.

4 Padua. Bustling with bicycles and lined with frescoes, Padua has long been a cultural centers of northern Italy. It's home to Europe's second-oldest university (after the one in Bologna), and you can feel the youthful student energy everywhere.

Ravenna

GETTING ORIENTED

Stretching between Florence and Venice, the region of Emilia-Romagna is Italy's bread basket. The flat expanses of farmland can't compete with the spectacular natural beauty of Tuscany and Umbria; the appeal instead lies in its prosperous, highly cultured midsize cities, where the locals seem to have mastered the art of living—and especially eating—well. The same holds true when you enter the Veneto region: lined up in a row to the west of Venice are three beautiful, artistically rich cities that compete for your attention.

5 **Vicenza.** The elegant art city of Vicenza, nestled on the green plain reaching inland from Venice's lagoon, is most noted for its palaces designed by the great 16th-century architect Andrea Palladio.

6 **Verona.** Shakespeare placed Romeo, Juliet, and a couple of gentlemen in Verona, one of the oldest, best-preserved, and most beautiful cities in Italy. Try to catch Aida at the gigantic Roman arena.

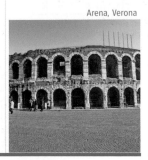

Arena, Verona

EMILIA–ROMAGNA & THE VENETO PLANNER

Making the Most of Your Time

Each city in this chapter has at least one world-class sight that's reason enough to merit a visit, but once you've arrived, you're likely to be won over by the cities as a whole. Many travelers come to Italy to see Florence or Venice, only to fall in love with Bologna or Vicenza.

Bologna makes sense as a base in Emilia–Romagna—there's a lot to do in the city, and you can make easy day trips east to Ravenna and Ferrara.

In the Veneto, Padua, Vicenza, and Verona are all within day-trip distance of Venice. Or, if staying in Venice turns you off, you can make one of these cities your base and visit La Serenissima during the day.

Typical Travel Times

Hours by Car/Train

Florence–Venice	3:15/3:00
Florence–Bologna	1:30/1:00
Bologna–Ravenna	1:00/1:15
Venice–Bologna	2:15/2:00
Venice–Padua	1:15/0:30
Venice–Vicenza	1:30/0:45
Venice–Verona	2:00/1:30

Getting Around

The cities in these regions are connected by well-maintained highways and an efficient railway system. A car provides added freedom, but it's not essential, and it can be a headache. (See below.)

Going by Car: Italy's major north–south highway, A1, runs from Florence to Bologna, then makes a left and continues to Milan. From Bologna, A13 runs north through Ferrara to Padua. If you're driving from Florence to Venice and want to see the cities of the Veneto, continue on A1 past Bologna to A22 (just beyond Modena), which takes you north to Verona. From there A4 leads to Vicenza, Padua, and Venice.

Going by Train: There's frequent train service between the cities covered here. Travel times vary depending on the type of train: Eurostars are the fastest; avoid regionale trains, which stop at every town along the line.

The Challenges of City Driving

When deciding whether to rent a car, keep in mind that driving in Italian cities is a trial: streets are difficult to navigate, congestion can be fierce, and drivers aren't known for their patience. In addition, Padua, Vicenza, and Verona sporadically limit car access—sometimes permitting only cars with plates ending in an even number on even days, odd on odd, or prohibiting cars altogether on weekends. There's no central source for such information; the best strategy is to check with your hotel. In Emilia–Romagna, Bologna's historic center is closed to cars during the day, and the center of Ravenna is closed to cars at all times.

Getting Here

Aeroporto Malpensa, 50 km (31 mi) northwest of Milan, is the major northern Italian hub for intercontinental flights and also sees substantial European and domestic traffic. Venice's **Aeroporto Marco Polo** also serves international destination, mainly from other European cities, though there are direct flights from New York's JFK.

There are regional airports in Bologna and Verona, and Milan has a secondary airport, Linate—all three can be reached on connecting flights from within Italy and from other European cities. If you fly into Malpensa but you don't plan to spend time in Milan, you can also continue your trip by train, using the Italian national rail system, **Ferrovie dello Stato** (☎892021 *toll-free within Italy* ⊕*www.trenitalia.com*). Shuttle buses run three times an hour between Malpensa and Milan's main train station, Stazione Centrale; the trip takes about 75 minutes, depending on traffic. Note that the Malpensa Express Train, which takes 40 minutes, delivers you to Cadorna station, from which you have to take the metro or a taxi across town to reach Stazione Centrale.

How's the Weather?

The ideal times to visit are late spring and early summer (May and June) and in early fall (September and October). Summers tend to be hot and humid—though if you're an opera buff, it's worth tolerating the heat in order to see a performance at the Arena di Verona (where the season runs from July through September).

Winter is a good time to avoid travel to these regions: although the dense fog can be beautiful, it makes for bad driving conditions, and wet, bone-chilling cold isn't unusual from November through March.

Finding a Place to Stay

The hotels in these regions are run with uncommon efficiency; even the smallest and most remote places usually have high standards of quality and service. Many cater to the business traveler, but there are smaller, more intimate options as well. It's a trend for hotels to renovate and subsequently hike their prices, but good low-cost lodgings can still be found. Ask about weekend discounts, which are often available at business-oriented hotels. It's always smart to book in advance—the regions host many fairs and conventions that can fill up hotels even during low season.

DINING & LODGING PRICE CATEGORIES (IN EUROS)

¢	$	$$	$$$	$$$$
Restaurants				
under €15	€15–€25	€25–€35	€35–€45	over €45
Hotels				
Under €70	€70–€110	€110–€160	€160–€220	over €220

Restaurant prices are for a first course (*primo*), second course (*secondo*), and dessert (*dolce*). Hotel prices are for two people in a standard double room in high season, including tax and service.

Planning Ahead

Three top sights in the region demand advance planning:

Reservations are required to see the Giotto frescoes in Padua's **Cappella degli Scrovegni**—though if there's space, you can "reserve" on the spot. On the outskirts of Vicenza, Palladio's **Villa La Rotonda** is open to the public only on Wednesday from mid-March through October. (Hours for visiting the grounds are less restrictive.) Another important Palladian villa, **Villa Barbaro** near Maser, is open from March through October on Tuesday, Saturday, and Sunday afternoons. For the rest of the year, it's open only on weekends.

EMILIA-ROMAGNA

Updated
by Patricia
Rucidlo

The region of Emilia–Romagna, made up predominantly of the Po River plain, doesn't have the drop-dead good looks that you'll find in many Italian landscapes. Instead, it wins your heart through your stomach. Many of Italy's signature food products come from here, including Parmigiano-Reggiano cheese (aka Parmesan), prosciutto di Parma, and balsamic vinegar. The pasta is considered Italy's finest—a reputation the region's chefs earn every day. But food isn't Emilia-Romagna's be-all and end-all. Attractive cities dot the map: Bologna is the principal cultural and intellectual center, with rows of street arcades winding through grandiose towers. The mosaics in Ravenna are glittering treasures left from the era of Byzantine rule, and Ferrara is a meticulously maintained medieval city with a youthful spirit.

BOLOGNA

Bologna, a city rich with cultural jewels, has long been one of the best-kept secrets in northern Italy. Tourists in the know can bask in the shadow of its leaning medieval towers, devour the city's wonderful food, and spend a little less than elsewhere.

The charm of the centro storico, with its red-arcaded sidewalks and passageways, can be attributed to wise city counselors who, at the beginning of the 13th century, decreed that roads could not be built without *portici* (porticoes). Were these counselors to return to town eight centuries later, they would marvel at how little has changed.

The feeling of a university town permeates the air in Bologna. Its population is about 373,000, and it feels young and lively in a way that many other Italian cities do not. It also feels full of Italians in a way that many other towns, thronged with tourists, do not. Known as "Bologna the Fat" from as early as the Middle Ages, the town's agricultural prosperity led to a well-fed population, one that survives into the 21st century. Bolognesi food is, arguably, the best in Italy. With its sublime food, lively spirit, and largely undiscovered art, Bologna is well worth a visit.

GETTING HERE

Frequent train service from Florence to Bologna makes getting here easy. Eurostar and Intercity trains run several times an hour, and take about an hour. Trains from Milan run as frequently, and take about an hour and 45 minutes on the Eurostar, two hours on the Intercity. The historic center is an easy and interesting walk from the station. If you're driving from Florence, take the A1, exiting onto the A14 and then catching the RA1 to Uscita 7–Bologna Centrale. The trip takes about an hour. From Milan, take the A1, exiting to the A14 as you near the city; from there, take the A13 and exit at Bologna, then follow the RA1 to Uscita 7–Bologna Centrale. The trip is just under three hours.

VISITOR INFORMATION

Bologna tourism offices (⊠*Aeroporto Guglielmo Marconi, Via Triumvirato 84 ✛10 km [6 mi] northwest of Bologna* ☎*051/239660* ⊠*Stazione Centrale,* ☎*051/239660* ⊠*Piazza Maggiore 1,* ☎*051/239660* ⊕*www.bolognaturismo.info*).

EXPLORING BOLOGNA

Piazza Maggiore and the adjacent Piazza del Nettuno are the historic centers of the city. Arranged around these two squares are the imposing Basilica di San Petronio, the massive Palazzo Comunale, the Palazzo del Podestà, the Palazzo di Re Enzo, and the Fontana del Nettuno—one of the most visually harmonious groupings of public buildings in the country. From here, sights that aren't on one of the piazzas are but a short walk away, along delightful narrow cobbled streets or under the ubiquitous arcades that double as municipal umbrellas. Take at least a full day to explore Bologna; it's compact and lends itself to easy exploration, but there is plenty to see.

5

THE MAIN ATTRACTIONS

❷ **Basilica di San Petronio.** Construction on this cathedral began in 1390, and work was still in progress on this vast building some 300 years later. It's not finished yet, as you can see: the wings of the transept are missing and the facade is only partially decorated, lacking most of the marble facade the architects had intended. The main doorway was carved in 1425 by the great Sienese master, Jacopo della Quercia. Above the center of the door is a Madonna and Child flanked by Saints Ambrose and Petronius, the city's patrons. Michelangelo, Giulio Romano, and Andrea Palladio (among others) submitted designs for the facade, which were all eventually rejected.

The interior of the basilica is huge: the Bolognesi had planned an even bigger church—you can still see the columns erected to support the larger church outside the east end—but had to tone down construction when the university seat was established next door in 1561. The **Museo di San Petronio** contains models showing how the church was originally intended to look. The most important art in the church is in the fourth chapel on the left; these frescoes by Giovanni di Modena date from 1410–15. ⊠*Piazza Maggiore* ☎*051/225442* ⊠*Free* ☉*Church: Apr.–Sept., daily 7:45–12:30 and 3:30–6; Oct.–Mar., daily 7:30–1 and 2:30–6. Museum: Mon.–Sat. 9:30–12:30 and 2:30–5:30, Sun. 2:30–5:30.*

Fontana del Nettuno. Sculptor Giambologna's elaborate 1563–66 baroque fountain and monument to Neptune occupying Piazza Nettuno has been aptly nicknamed *Il Gigante* (The Giant). Its exuberantly sensual mermaids and undraped God of the sea drew fire when it was constructed, but not enough, apparently, to dissuade the populace from using the fountain as a public washing stall for centuries. ⊠*Piazza Nettuno, next to Palazzo Re Enzo, Piazza Maggiore area.*

★ ❻ **Le Due Torri.** Two landmark towers, mentioned by Dante in *The Inferno,* stand side by side in the compact Piazza di Porta Ravegnana. Every family of importance had a tower as a symbol of prestige and power, and as a potential fortress; only 60 remain out of more than 200 that once presided over the city. **Torre Garisenda** (from the late 11th century), which tilts 10 feet off perpendicular, was shortened to 165 feet in the 1300s and is now closed to visitors. **Torre degli Asinelli** (circa 1109) is 320 feet tall and leans 7½ feet. If you're up to a serious physical challenge—and you're not claustrophobic—you may want to climb the 500 narrow, wooden steps to get to the view over Bologna. ⊠*Piazza di Porta Ravegnana, east of Piazza Maggiore* ⊠€3 ⊙*Torre degli Asinelli: daily 9–5.*

☺ ❼ **Santo Stefano.** This splendid and unusual basilica actually contains
FodorsChoice between four and seven connected churches (authorities differ). Origi-
★ nally on this site there was a 4th-century pagan temple to Isis, though much of what you see dates from the 10th through the 12th centuries. The oldest existing building is **Santi Vitale e Agricola,** parts of which date from the 5th century. It contains a 14th-century Nativity scene

EMILIA-ROMAGNA THROUGH THE AGES

Ancient History. Emilia-Romagna owes its beginnings to a road. In 187 BC the Romans built the Via Aemilia, a long road running northwest from the Adriatic port of Rimini to the central garrison town of Piacenza, and it was along this central spine that the primary towns of the region developed.

Despite the unifying factor of what came to be known as the Via Emilia, the region has had a fragmented history. Its eastern part, roughly the area from Faenza to the coast, known as Romagna, first looked to the Byzantine east and then to Rome for art, political power, and, some say, national character. The western part, Emilia, from Bologna to Piacenza, had a more-northern, rather dour sense of self-government and dissent.

Bologna was founded by the Etruscans and eventually came under the influence of the Roman Empire. The Romans established a garrison here, renaming the old Etruscan settlement Bononia. It was after the fall of Rome that the region began its fragmentation. Romagna, centered in Ravenna, was ruled from Constantinople. Ravenna eventually became the capital of the empire in the west in the fifth century, passing to papal control in the 8th century.

Even today, the city is still filled with reminders of two centuries of Byzantine rule.

Family Ties. The other cities of the region, from the Middle Ages on, became the fiefs of important noble families—the Este in Ferrara and Modena, the Pallavicini in Piacenza, the Bentivoglio in Bologna, and the Malatesta in Rimini. Today all these cities bear the marks of their noble patrons. When in the 16th century the papacy managed to exert its power over the entire region, some of these cities were divided among the papal families—hence the stamp of the Farnese family on Parma, Piacenza, and Ferrara.

A Leftward Tilt. Bologna and Emilia-Romagna have established a robust tradition of rebellion and dissent. The Italian socialist movement was born in the region, as was Benito Mussolini—in keeping with the political climate of his home state, he was a firebrand socialist during the early part of his career. Despite having Mussolini as a native son, Emilia-Romagna did not take to fascism: it was here that the antifascist resistance was born, and during World War II the region suffered terribly at the hands of the Fascists and the Nazis.

much loved by Bologna's children, who come at Christmastime to pay their respects to the Christ Child. Within the church of **San Sepolcro** (probably dating from the 5th century, but remodeled in the late 11th and early 12th centuries) is the **Cortile di Pilato** (Pilate's Courtyard), named for the basin in its center that's said to be where Pontius Pilate washed his hands after condemning Christ—despite the fact that the basin was probably crafted around the 8th century. Also in the building is a **museum** displaying various medieval religious works and with a shop where you can buy honey, shampoos, and jams made by the monks. ⊠ *Via Santo Stefano 24, Piazza Santo Stefano, University area* ☎ *051/223256* ▱ *Free* ⊙ *Daily 9–noon and 3:30–6.*

9 **Univerìà di Bologna.** Take a stroll through the streets of the university area, a jumble of buildings, some dating as far back as the 15th century and most to the 17th and 18th. The neighborhood, as befits a college town, is full of bookshops, coffee bars, and inexpensive restaurants. None of them are particularly distinguished, but they're all characteristic of student life in the city. Try eating at the *mensa universitaria* (cafeteria) if you want to strike up a conversation with local students (most speak English). Political slogans and sentiments are scrawled on walls all around the university and tend to be ferociously leftist, sometimes juvenile, often entertaining. Among the university museums, the most interesting are the **Musei di Palazzo Poggi,** which display scientific instruments and paleontological, botanical, and university-related artifacts. ⌧ *Via Zamboni 33, University area* ☎ *051/2099610* ⊕ *www. museopalazzopoggi.unibo.it* ☑ *Free* ⊙ *Tues.–Fri. 10–1 and 2–4, weekends 10:30–1:30 and 2:30–5:30.*

ALSO WORTH SEEING

8 **Museo Internazionale della Musica.** The music museum in the spectacular Palazzo Aldini Sanguinetti, with its 17th- and 18th-century frescoes, offers among its exhibits a 1606 harpsichord and a collection of beautiful musical manuscripts dating from the 1500s. ⌧ *Strada Maggiore 34, University area* ☎ *051/2757711* ⊕ *www.museomusicabologna.it* ☑ *Free* ⊙ *Oct.–July, Tues.–Fri. 10–1, weekends 10–5.*

3 **Palazzo Comunale.** A mélange of building styles and constant modifications characterize this huge palace dating from the 13th to 15th centuries. When Bologna was an independent city-state, this was the seat of government, a function it still serves today. Over the door is a statue of Bologna-born Pope Gregory XIII (reigned 1572–85), most famous for reorganizing the calendar. There are good views from the upper stories of the palace. The first-floor **Sala Rossa** (Red Room) is open on advance request and during some exhibitions, while the **Sala del Consiglio Comunale** (City Council Hall) is open to the public for a few hours in the late morning. The old stock exchange, part of the Palazzo Comunale which you enter from Piazza Nettuno, has been turned into a library, the **Sala Borsa** (⊕ *www.bibliotecasalaborsa.it*), which has an impressive interior courtyard. Within the palazzo there are also two museums. The **Collezioni Comunali d'Arte** exhibits paintings from the Middle Ages as well as some Renaissance works by Luca Signorelli (circa 1445–1523) and Tintoretto (1518–94). The **Museo Giorgio Morandi** (⊕ *www.museomorandi.it*) is dedicated to the 20th-century still-life artist Giorgio Morandi; in addition to his paintings, there's a re-creation of his studio and living space. Underground caves and the foundations of the old cathedral can be visited by appointment made through the tourist office. ⌧ *Piazza Maggiore 6* ☎ *051/203111 Palazzo, 051/203526 Collezioni, 051/203332Museo* ☑ *Free, except during special art exhibitions* ⊙ *Sala del Consiglio Comunale: Tues.–Sat. 10–1. Sala Borsa: Mon. 2:30–8, Tues.–Fri. 10–8, Sat. 10–7. Collezioni and Museo: Tues.–Fri. 9–3, weekends 10–6:30.*

4 **Palazzo del Podestà.** This classic Renaissance palace facing the Basilica di San Petronio was erected in 1484, and attached to it is the soaring **Torre**

dell'Arengo. The bells in the tower have rung whenever the city has celebrated, mourned, or called its citizens to arms. ⊠*Piazza Nettuno, Piazza Maggiore area* ☎*051/224500* ⊙*During exhibitions only.*

❺ Palazzo Re Enzo. Built in 1244, this palace became home to King Enzo of Sardinia, who was imprisoned here in 1249 after he was captured during the fierce battle of Fossalta. He died here 23 years later in 1272. The palace has other macabre associations: common criminals received last rites in the tiny courtyard chapel before being executed in Piazza Maggiore. The courtyard is worth peeking into, but the palace merely houses government offices. ⊠*Piazza Re Enzo, Piazza Maggiore area* ☎*051/224500* ⊙*During exhibitions only.*

❿ Pinacoteca Nazionale. Bologna's principal art gallery contains many works by the immortals of Italian painting spanning the 13th to the 19th centuries. Its prize possession is the famous *Ecstasy of St. Cecilia* by Raphael (1483–1520). There's also a beautiful multipanel painting by Giotto (1267–1337), as well as *Madonna and Saints* by Parmigianino. ⊠*Via delle Belle Arti 56, University area* ☎*051/4209411* ⊕*www.pinacotecabologna.it* 💶*€4* ⊙*Tues.–Sun. 9–7.*

❶ San Domenico. The tomb of St. Dominic, who died here in 1221, is called the **Arca di San Domenico** and is found in this church in the sixth chapel on the right. Many artists participated in its decoration, notably Niccolò di Bari, who was so proud of his contribution that he changed his name to Niccolò dell'Arca to recall this famous work. The young Michelangelo (1475–1564) carved the angel on the right. In the right transept of the church is a tablet marking the last resting place of the hapless King Enzo, the Sardinian ruler imprisoned in the Palazzo Re Enzo. The attached **museum** displays religious relics and art. ⊠*Piazza San Domenico 13, off Via Garibaldi, south of Piazza Maggiore* ☎*051/6400411* ⊙*Church: daily 8–12:30 and 3:30–6:30. Museum: weekdays 10–noon and 3:30–6, Sat. 9:30–noon and 3:30–5:30, Sun. 3:30–5:30.*

OFF THE BEATEN PATH
Museo del Patrimonio Industriale. Offering a refreshing change from all the art museums, this museum's displays document the development of Bologna's industries and industrial technologies from the 16th to 21st centuries, including fascinating examples of antique machinery, scientific devices, and cars. ⊠*Via della Beverara 123, northwest of city center* ☎*051/6356611* ⊕*www.comune.bologna.it/patrimonio industriale* 💶*Free* ⊙*Oct.–May, Tues.–Fri. 9–1, Sat. 9–1 and 3–6, Sun. 3–6; June–Sept. weekdays 9–1.*

WHERE TO EAT

$$$$ ✕ **Bitone.** It's hard to get good value for your money on the top end in Bologna, but if you are committed to the idea of sitting down at one of the city's most prestigious tables, this restaurant, which dates to 1834, is a good way to go. An airy atrium, ringed by greenery, provides a good foil for the white-tablecloth setting. You might try the *fagottino*

EATING & DRINKING WELL IN EMILIA-ROMAGNA

Italians rarely agree about anything, but most would say that the best food in the country is in Emilia-Romagna. Tortellini, fettucine, Parmesan cheese, and balsamic vinegar are just a few of the Italian delicacies born here.

One of the beauties of Emilia-Romagna is that its exceptional food can be had without breaking the bank. Many *trattorie* and *osterie* serve up classic dishes, mastered over the centuries, at reasonable prices. Cutting-edge restaurants and wine bars are often more expensive; their inventive menus are full of *fantasia*—reinterpretations of the classics. Bologna is a student-oriented town and has great places for those on shoestring budgets.

Between meals, you can sustain yourself with the region's famous sandwich, the *piadina*. It's made with pita-thin bread, usually filled with prosciutto or mortadella, cheese, and vegetables. It's put under the grill and served hot, with the cheese oozing at the sides. These addictive sandwiches can be had at sit-down places or ordered to go.

THE REAL RAGÙ

Emilia-Romagna's signature dish is *tagliatelle al ragù* (flat noodles with meat sauce), known as "spaghetti Bolognese" everywhere else. This primo is on every menu, and no two versions are the same. The sauce starts in a sauté pan with pancetta or guanciale, butter, and minced onions. Purists use nothing but beef, but some mix it with sausage, veal, or chicken. Regular ministrations of broth are added, and sometimes wine, milk, or cream. After a couple of hours of cooking, the ragù is ready to be joined with pasta and Parmesan and brought to the table.

PORK PRODUCTS

It's not just mortadella and cured pork products like prosciutto and *culatello* that Emilia-Romagnans go crazy for— they're wild about the whole hog.

You'll frequently find *cotechino* and *zampone*, both secondi, on menus; cotechino, photo below, is a savory, thick, fresh sausage served with lentils on New Year's Day (the combination is said to augur well for the new year) and with mashed potatoes year-round. *Zampone*, a stuffed pig's foot, is redolent of garlic, and is deliciously fatty.

BOLLITO MISTO

The name means "mixed boil," and they do it exceptionally well in this part of Italy. According to Emilia-Romagnans, it was invented here (its true origins are up for grabs, as other northern Italians, especially from Milan and the Piedmont, would argue this point). Chicken, beef, tongue, and zampone are tossed into a stockpot and boiled; they are then removed from the broth and served with a fragrant *salsa verde* (green sauce), made green by parsley and spiced with anchovies, garlic, and capers. This simple yet rich dish is usually served with mashed potatoes on the side, and savvy diners will mix some of the piquant *salsa verde* into the potatoes as well.

STUFFED PASTA

Among the many Emilian variations on stuffed pasta, *tortellini*, pictured at left, are the smallest. *Tortelli*, photo upper right, and *cappellacci* are larger pasta "pillows," about the size of a Brussels sprout, but with the same basic form as tortellini; they're often filled with pumpkin or spinach and cheese.

Tortelloni are, in theory, even bigger, although their sizes vary. Stuffed pastas are generally served simply, with melted butter, sage, and (what else?) Parmigiano-Reggiano cheese, or (in the case of tortellini) *in brodo* (in beef or chicken broth), which brings out the subtle richness of the filling.

WINES

Emilia-Romagna's wines accompany the region's fine food rather than vying with it for accolades. The best known is Lambrusco, a sparkling red produced on the Po Plain that has some admirers and many detractors. It's praised for its tartness and condemned for the same quality. The region's best wines include Sangiovese di Romagna, somewhat similar to Chianti, from the Romagnan hills, and Barbera, from the Colli Piacetini and Apennine foothills. Castelluccio, Bonzara, Zerbina, Leone Conti, and Tre Monti are among the region's top producers—keep an eye out for their bottles.

croccante di formaggio caprino con fonduta di formaggi ed erba cipollina (a crunchy pasta stuffed with goat cheese, topped with melted cheese and chives) or the legendary tortelli all'erbette (with ricotta, herbs, and hazelnut butter). If you're undecided, the eight-course tasting menu (€70) provides a taste of just about everything. ⊠ Via Emilia Levante 111, San Lazzaro ☎051/546110 ⊕www.ristorantebitone.it ⊟AE, MC, V ⊗Closed Mon. and Tues., and Aug.

$$$

Fodor'sChoice

★

✗**Drogheria della Rosa.** Chef Emanuele Addone, who presides over his intimate little restaurant, hits the food markets every day and buys what looks good. This brings a seasonality to his exceptional menu; he sauces his tortelli stuffed with squacquerone and stracchino (two creamy, fresh cow's-milk cheeses) with artichokes, zucchini flowers, or mushrooms depending on the time of year. In order to do this place justice, you need to come with an appetite—you won't want to skip a course. Kick off the proceedings with a glass of prosecco and a plate of affettati misti (mixed cured meats, a local specialty). Among the secondi, the tender filetto al balsamico (filet mignon with marvelous balsamic vinegar sauce on top) is exquisite. So is the wine list. ⊠ Via Cartoleria 10, University area ☎051/222529 ⊕www.drogheria dellarosa.it ⊟AE, DC, MC, V ⊗Closed Sun.

$$$

✗**Godot Wine Bar.** It's beloved by locals and visitors alike, perhaps because the kitchen stays open until 2 am. The wine list is long and full of temptations, as is the menu. The chef offers four menus—meat, fish, vegetarian, and the intriguing tradizione un po' rivisitata (loosely, "slightly updated tradition"). They're also masters of Bolognese classics, including a mean tagliatelle al ragù. ⊠ Via Cartoleria 12, University area ☎051/226315 ⊟AE, MC, V ⊗Closed Sun. and 3 wks in Aug.

★ $$-$$$

✗**Da Cesari.** It's the creative menu options—delicate squash gnocchi, a slowly braised veal cheek—that make Da Cesari truly memorable. Local standards such as veal cutlet Bolognese (with ham and melted cheese) are also reasonably priced and well executed. Accompany your meal with wine made by the owner's brother: the Liano is excellent. The gentle romantic buzz in the dining room is warm and welcoming; the restaurant is in the very heart of the centro storico. ⊠ Via de' Carbonesi 8, south of Piazza Maggiore ☎051/237710 ⚐Reservations essential ⊟AE, DC, MC, V ⊗Closed Sun., Aug., and 1 wk in Jan.

$$-$$$

✗**È Cucina.** Stark white walls, paintings with oversize sculpted spoons, and an (empty) clawfoot bathtub greet you as you enter this intimate restaurant. Such setting provides a dramatically simple and whimsical backdrop for chef Cesare Marretti's short menu of artfully presented dishes that changes daily; a typical offering might be the creative insalatina di astice con radicchini di campo (lobster-and–wild radicchio salad). A four-course tasting menu for a reasonable €40 (meat, fish, or vegetarian) is a great gustatory and financial deal; prices are even better at lunch. ⊠ Piazza Aldrovandi, Via San Vitale 21/c, University area ☎051/2750069 ⊟MC, V ⊗Closed Mon.

$$

✗**Da Gianni a la Vecia Bulagna.** Locals simply call it "da Gianni," and they fill these two unadorned rooms at lunch and at dinner. Though the decor is plain and unremarkable, it doesn't much matter—this place

CLOSE UP

Cooking alla Bolognese

A hot travel trend in Italy is spending a day at a cooking school to learn local recipes and techniques—and where better to do it than in Bologna? Barbara Bertuzzi, the author of cookbook *Bolognese Cooking Heritage*, teaches classes at **La Vecchia Scuola Bolognese** *(the Old Bolognese Cooking School)*. Her four-hour sessions focus on pasta making and are offered daily; they begin at 9:30 AM and continue to lunchtime, when you can eat the fruits of your labor. Evening courses are available, and Bertuzzi also offers lunches and dinners without the lessons. These tastings of traditional Bolognese recipes cost €30; Tuesday night is a traditional deep-fried meat, vegetable, and fruit dinner. The school is near the Ospedale Maggiore—take Bus 19 from Via Rizzoli near Piazza Maggiore, or a €15 taxi from the *centro storico.* If you're the only aspiring chef in your party, the rest can join after the lesson for dinner at €20 each. ⊠ *Via Malvasia 49* ☎ *051/6491576* ⊕ *www.*

lavecchiascuola.com ☎ *€70 per person, €90 with meal.*

If you prefer your cooking classes in a truly regal setting, you might want to try **La Tavola della Signoria**, held in the spectacular 17th-century rooms of the **Palazzo Albergati** (⊕ *www. palazzoalbergati.it*). These classes are offered only four or five times per month and are more expensive than some others, but they're also longer and more serious. Class starts at 8:30 AM and runs until 5:30 PM; you can choose between different modules, such as bread making, pasta making, desserts, and so on. For the true aficionados, two- and three-day fruit-and-vegetable courses are offered periodically. It's 10 km (6 mi) west of the city center; to get here take SS569, get off at the last Zona Predosa exit, and follow signs for the Palazzo Albergati. You can sign up via the Web site. ⊠ *Via Masini 46* ☎ *051/750247* ⊕ *www.tavoladellasignoria.it* ☎ *€170–€200 per person for 1 day; up to €480 for 3 days.*

is all about food. The usual starters such as a tasty tortellini in brodo are on hand, as are daily specials such as gnocchi made with pumpkin, then sauced with melted cheese. *Bollito misto* (mixed meats boiled in a rich broth) is a fine option here, and the *cotechino con purè di patate* (a deliciously oily sausage with mashed potatoes) elevated to sublimity by the accompanying *salsa verde* (green sauce). ⊠ *Via Clavature 18, Piazza Maggiore area* ☎ *051/229434* ⚐ *Reservations essential* ⊟ *AE, DC, MC, V.*

$$ ✕ **Victoria.** It's not unusual for this unpretentious and charming trattoria-pizzeria off Via dell'Indipendenza to have lines, so reserve ahead. Locals come for the cheap pizzas, which are indisputably the highlight—*mozzarella di bufala* (buffalo mozzarella) is an excellent topping choice—and much less expensive than the primi and secondi on the menu. The back room has a lovely 17th-century painted wooden ceiling. ⊠ *Via Augusto Righi 9/c, north of Piazza Maggiore* ☎ *051/233548* ⊟ *AE, DC, MC, V* ⊘ *Closed Thurs.*

$ ✕ **Trattoria del Rosso.** Though the decor's nothing to write home about ★ (slightly glaring yellow walls with the oddly placed ceramic plate), the place teems with locals, mostly young folks, chowing down on delicious basic Bolognese fare at rock-bottom prices. The nimble staff bearing multiple plates sashays neatly between the closely spaced tables delivering such standards as *crescentine con salumi e squacquerone* (deep-fried flour puffs with cured meats and soft cheese) and tortellini in brodo. This is the kind of place where they don't glare at you if you only order a plate of pasta and little more, perhaps another reason why it's a favorite of university students. ⊠ *Via Augusto Righi 30, University area* ☎ *051/236730* ⊟ *AE, DC, MC, V* ⊗ *Closed Thurs.*

¢ ✕ **Tamburini.** Two small rooms inside, and kegs and bar stools outside comprise the seating arrangements at this lively, packed little wine bar. At lunchtime, office workers swarm at the "bistrot self service" with remarkably tasty primi and secondi. After lunch, it becomes a wine bar with a vast array of selections by the glass and the bottle. The overwhelming plate of affettati misti is crammed with top-quality cured local ham products and succulent cheeses (including, sometimes, a goat Brie). ⊠ *Via Drapperie 1, Piazza Maggiore area* ☎ *051/234726* ⊟ *AE, MC, V* ⊗ *No dinner.*

WHERE TO STAY

$$$$ 📷 **Art Hotel Novecento.** A 2003 overhaul has given a great lift to this
★ swank place inspired by the 1930s Viennese Secession movement. It's in a remarkably serene cul-de-sac just minutes from Piazza Maggiore. Clean lines and elegant restraint are the hallmarks of the rooms, the lobby, and even the elevators, and equally svelte, well-dressed people like to stay here. It's well worth the extra €20 or so to upgrade from a basic double, as the rooms are that much bigger. The copious breakfast includes eggs, and happy hour comes with free wine and snacks. **Pros:** Spacious single rooms ideal for solo travelers; friendly, capable concierge service. **Cons:** Some standard doubles are small. ⊠ *Piazza Galileo 4/3i, Piazza Maggiore area,* ☎ *051/7457311* 🖨 *051/7457322* ⊕ *www.bolognarthotels.it/novecento* ⇨ *24 rooms, 1 suite* ⚒ *In-room: safe, Ethernet. In-hotel: bar, bicycles, concierge, laundry service, public Internet, parking (fee), some pets allowed* ⊟ *AE, DC, MC, V* ⍟ *BP.*

$$$$ 📷 **Art Hotel Orologio.** The location can't be beat: it's right around the corner from Piazza Maggiore, tucked in a quiet little side street. Reception is on the ground floor, and a flight of stairs takes you up to the second floor to the elevator and the charming breakfast room. The rooms are mostly painted yellow, with hardwood floors, and some have tremendous views of 14th-century Palazzo Comunale just across the way. A couple of rooms are ideally suited to families, as they're spacious and have extra beds. **Pros:** Central location; great views. **Cons:** Short flight of steps to elevator. ⊠ *Via IV Novembre 10, Piazza Maggiore area,* ☎ *051/7457411* 🖨 *051/7457422* ⊕ *www.bolognarthotels.it/orologio* ⇨ *29 rooms, 5 suites, 1 apartment* ⚒ *In-room: safe, Ethernet, Wi-Fi. In-hotel: restaurant, bicycles, public Internet, public Wi-Fi, parking (fee), some pets allowed* ⊟ *AE, DC, MC, V* ⍟ *BP.*

$$$$ 📷 **Corona d'Oro 1890.** The Azzaguidi family lived here in the 15th cen-
★ tury, and though little traces of their palace remain, the place still has an aristocratic glow. The interior's been redone in art nouveau, and

the airy, light-filled white atrium provides a perfect place to read a newspaper or enjoy a glass of wine. Rooms have floral lithographs on the walls; cool, muted earth-tone colors; and bathrooms with heated towel racks. Some have their own private balcony. The English-speaking staff are courteous and helpful, and are delighted when children are their guests. **Pros:** Stuffed animals for kids; great location. **Cons:** Street-facing rooms can get a bit noisy. ⊠ *Via Oberdan 12, north of Piazza Maggiore* ☎*051/7457611* 🖷*051/7457622* ⊕*www.bolognarthotels. it/corona* ↻*37 rooms, 3 suites* ⚐*In-room: safe, Ethernet, Wi-Fi. In-hotel: bar, bicycles, public Internet, public Wi-Fi, parking (fee), some pets allowed* ☰*AE, DC, MC, V* ⊘*Closed 1st 3 wks in Aug.* ◎*BP.*

$$$ 🏨 **Accademia.** A mid-range, comfortable base for exploring the area, this small hotel is right in the center of the university quarter. The rooms are adequate, the staff friendly. Look for discounted prices on the Web site. A few of the less-expensive rooms have a shared bath. **Pros:** Rates are very low in off-season; children under 5 sleep for free; good group rates. **Cons:** Rooms are mostly utilitarian; popular with groups. ⊠ *Via delle Belle Arti 6, at Via delle Moline, University area,* ☎*051/232318* 🖷*051/263590* ⊕*www.hotelaccademia.com* ↻*28 rooms, 24 with bath* ⚐*In-room: safe, refrigerator. In-hotel: bar, public Internet, public Wi-Fi, parking (fee), some pets allowed* ☰*MC, V* ◎*BP.*

$ 🏨 **San Vitale.** Modern furnishings and a garden distinguish this modest hostelry, about 1 km (½ mi) east of the center of town. The service is courteous, and rooms are clean and bright. There are private bathrooms, but facilities are very basic. **Pros:** A good budget option. **Cons:** Location removed from the sights. ⊠ *Via San Vitale 94, University area,* ☎*051/225966* 🖷*051/239396* ↻*17 rooms* ⚐*In-hotel: no elevator, public Internet, parking (fee)* ☰*No credit cards* ◎*BP.*

NIGHTLIFE & THE ARTS

THE ARTS

Bologna's arts scene is one of the liveliest in Italy. Opera, ballet, rock concerts, and theatrical extravaganzas happen year-round, as do food festivals. The **Bologna tourism office** (☎*051/239660* ⊕*www.bolognaturismo.info*) has information on performances and events.

MUSIC & OPERA

The 18th-century **Teatro Comunale** (⊠*Largo Respighi 1, University area* ☎*199/107070* ⊕*www.comunalebologna.it*) presents concerts by Italian and international orchestras throughout the year, but is dominated by the highly acclaimed opera performances November–May, so reserve seats well in advance. The ticket office is open Tuesday–Saturday 11–6:30.

NIGHTLIFE

As a university town, Bologna has long been known for its busy nightlife. As early as 1300 it was said to have had 150 taverns. Most of the city's current 200-plus pubs and bars are frequented by Italian students, young adults, and international students, with the university district forming the hub. In addition to the university area, the pedestrians-only zone on Via del Pratello, lined with plenty of bars, is also a hopping night scene, as is Via delle Moline, with cutting-edge cafés and bars. A more upmarket, low-key evening experience can be had at one of Bologna's many wine bars that are also restaurants. And then there are the hypertrendy bar-lounges that represent the newest of Bologna's many faces.

BARS

If you want a night out at a trendy spot, Bologna offers a lot to choose from.

Elegant **Bar Calice** (✉ *Via Clavature 13/a, at Via Marchesana, Piazza Maggiore area* ☎*051/264508*) runs an indoor-outdoor operation year-round (with heat lamps). It's extremely popular with thirtysome-things. At **Le Stanze** (✉ *Via del Borgo di San Pietro 1, University area* ☎*051/228767* ⊕*www.lestanzecafe.com* ⊙*Closed Mon., and July and Aug.*) you can sip an *aperitivo* or a late-night drink at a modern bar. The decor includes 7th-century frescoes in what was once the private chapel of Palazzo Bentivoglio. The adjoining avant-garde restaurant serves modern Italian fusion cooking. Buca San Petronio, an arcaded tunnel street tucked near the Piazza Maggiore, has become quite the evening scene. The loud **Nu Bar Lounge** (✉ *Off Buca San Petronio, Via de' Musei 6, Piazza Maggiore area* ☎*051/222532* ⊕*www.nu-lounge. com*) draws a cocktail-loving crowd, who enjoy the free snacks that show up around 8 PM.

MUSIC VENUES

It's not hard to find drinks accompanied by live music in the city. **Bal-moral** (✉ *Via de' Pignattari 1, Piazza Maggiore area* ☎*051/228694*), a restaurant right near Piazza Maggiore, has good live music most nights, and a vaguely Middle Eastern theme. With live jazz staged every night (€4 cover), **Cantina Bentivoglio** (✉ *Via Mascarella 4/b, University area* ☎*051/265416*) is one of Bologna's most appealing nightspots. You can enjoy light meals and nibbles as well. **Osteria Buca delle Campane** (✉ *Via Benedetto XVI 4/a, University area* ☎*051/220918*), an underground tavern in a 13th-century building, has good, inexpensive food and a lively after-dinner scene popular with locals, including students who come to listen to live music.

WINE BARS

Bologna has one of Italy's highest concentrations of wine bars. A wine bar with romantic ambient lighting and a good draft beer selection, **Con-tavalli** (✉ *Via Belle Arti 2, University area* ☎*051/268395*) is a relaxing choice. The casually hip **Divinis** (✉ *Via Battibecco 4/c, University area* ☎*051/2961502*) wine bar has a remarkable, if pricey, selection by the glass (as well as high-end food) served in chichi surroundings until 1:30 AM. Don't overlook **Godot Wine Bar** *(⇨ Where to Eat, above)*, whose wine list is even more exciting than its food menu.

SHOPPING

WINE & FOOD

Bologna is a good place to buy wine. Several shops have a bewilderingly large selection—to go straight to the top, ask the managers which wines have won the prestigious *Tre Bicchieri* (Three Glasses) award from Gambero Rosso's wine bible, *Vini d'Italia.*

Repeatedly recognized as one of the best wine stores in Italy, **Enoteca Italiana** (⊠ *Via Marsala 2/b, north of Piazza Maggiore* ☎*051/235989*) lives up to its reputation with shelves lined with excellent selections from all over Italy at reasonable prices. Their delicious sandwiches with wine by the glass also make a great stand-up light lunch. Friendly owners run the midsize, down-to-earth **Scaramagli** (⊠*Strada Maggiore 31/d, University area* ☎*051/227132*) wine store. **La Boutique del Formaggio** (⊠ *Viale Oriani 16/a, Piazza Maggiore area* ☎*051/347813*) is a cheese shop from another era, a place where time stands still and where all revolves around the nuances of esoteric cheeses. To shop here is to remember that there are still pockets of Italy where food is life. **La Baita** (⊠*Via Pescherie Vecchia 3/a, Piazza Maggiore area* ☎*051/223940*) sells fresh tagliolini, tortellini, and other Bolognese pasta delicacies, as well as sublime food to take away. Their cheese counter teems with local cheeses of superlative quality.

If you favor sweets, head to **Le Dolcezze** (⊠ *Via Murr 21i, Piazza Maggiore area* ☎*051/444582*), a top local *pasticceria* (pastry shop) whose cakes are excellent, and whose *panettone,* the sweet bread produced only around the holiday season, is considered by some to be the best in town. **Roccati** (⊠*Via Clavature 17/a, Piazza Maggiore area* ☎*051/261964* ⊕*www.roccaticiocccolato.com*) has been crafting sculptural works of chocolate, as well as basic bonbons and simpler stuff since 1909. For fresh produce, meats, and other foods, head to **Via Oberdan** (⊠*Piazza Maggiore area*), the street just off Via dell'Indipendenza downtown. The **Mercato delle Erbe** (⊠ *Via Ugo Bassi, Piazza Maggiore area* ☎*051/230186*) is an equally bustling food market, open Monday through Wednesday, and Friday 7–1:15 and 5–7:30 (4:30–7:30 October–March), Thursday and Saturday 7–1:15. The **Mercato di Mezzo** (⊠*Via Peschiere Vecchie, Piazza Maggiore area*), which sells specialty foods, fruits, and vegetables, is an intense barrage of sights and smells. It's open Monday through Saturday 7–1 and 4:15–7:30, with the exception of Thursday afternoon, when it's closed.

RAVENNA

76 km (47 mi) east of Bologna, 93 km (58 mi) southeast of Ferrara.

A small, quiet, well-heeled city, Ravenna has brick palaces, cobbled streets, magnificent monuments, and spectacular Byzantine mosaics to remind you of its storied past. The high point in Ravenna's history occurred in the fifth century, when Pope Honorious moved his court here from Rome. Gothic kings Odoacer and Theodoric ruled the city until it was conquered by the Byzantines in AD 540. Ravenna then fell under the sway of Venice, and then, inevitably, the Papal States.

Because Ravenna spent much of its past looking to the East, its greatest art treasures show that influence. Churches and tombs with the most unassuming exteriors contain within them walls covered with sumptuous mosaics. These beautifully preserved Byzantine mosaics put great emphasis on nature, which you can see in the delicate rendering of sky, earth, and animals. Outside Ravenna, the town of Classe hides even more mosaic gems.

GETTING HERE
By car from Bologna, take the SP253 to the RA1, and then follow signs for the A14/E45 in the direction of Ancona. From here, follow signs for Ravenna, taking the A14dir Ancona–Milano–Ravenna exit. Follow signs for the SS16/E55 to the center of Ravenna. It's a more convoluted, but more interesting, drive from Ferrara: take the SS16 to the RA8 in the direction of Porto Garibaldi taking the Roma/Ravenna exit. Follow the SS309/E55 to the SS309dir/E55, taking the SS253 Bologna/Ancona exit. Follow the SS16/E55 into the center of Ravenna.

VISITOR INFORMATION
Ravenna tourism office (⊠ *Via Salara 8,* ☏ *0544/35404* ⊕ *www.turismo. ravenna.it*).

EXPLORING RAVENNA

A combination ticket (available at ticket offices of all included sights) admits you to six of Ravenna's important monuments: the Mausoleo di Galla Placidia, the Basilica di San Vitale, the Battistero Neoniano, Sant'Apollinare Nuovo, the church of Spirito Santo, and the Museo Arcivescovile e Cappella Sant'Andrea. Start out early in the morning to avoid lines (reservations are necessary for the Mausoleo and Basilica in May and June). A half day should suffice to walk the town alone; allow an hour each for the Mausoleo, the Basilica, and the Museo Nazionale. Ticket offices often close 15 to 30 minutes before the sights themselves.

THE MAIN ATTRACTIONS
❷ **Basilica di San Vitale.** The octagonal church of San Vitale was built in AD 547, after the Byzantines conquered the city, and its interior shows a strong Byzantine influence. In the area behind the altar are the most famous works in the church, depicting the emperor Justinian and his retinue on one wall, and his wife, Empress Theodora, with her retinue, on the opposite wall. Notice how the mosaics seamlessly wrap around the columns and curved arches on the upper sides of the altar area. Reservations are recommended from March through mid-June. ⊠ *Via San Vitale off Via Salara* ☏ *0544/541688 reservations, 800/303999 toll-free information* ⊕ *www.ravennamosaici.it* ✉ *Combination ticket €8.50* ☉ *Nov.–Feb., daily 9:30–5; Mar. and Oct., daily 9–5:30; Apr.– Sept., daily 9–7.*

❹ Battistero Neoniano. The baptistry, next door to Ravenna's 18th-century cathedral, is one of the town's most important mosaic sights. It dates from the beginning of the fifth century AD, with work continuing through the century. In keeping with the building's role, the great mosaic in the dome shows the baptism of Christ, and beneath are the Apostles. The lowest register of mosaics contains Christian symbols, the Throne of God, and the Cross. Note the naked figure kneeling next to Christ—he is the personification of the River Jordan. ⊠ *Via Battistero* ☎ *0544/541688 reservations, 800/303999 toll-free information* ⊕ *www.ravennamosaici.it* ⊡ *Combination ticket €8.50* ⊙ *Nov.–Feb., daily 10–5; Mar. and Oct., daily 9:30–5:30; Apr.–Sept., daily 9–7.*

❸ Mausoleo di Galla Placidia. The little tomb and the great church stand
Fodor'sChoice side by side, but the tomb predates the Basilica di San Vitale by at least
★ a hundred years. These two adjacent sights are decorated with the best-known, and most elaborate, mosaics in Ravenna. Galla Placidia was the sister of Rome's emperor, Honorius, the man who moved the imperial capital to Ravenna in AD 402. She is said to have been beautiful and strong-willed, and to have taken an active part in the governing of the crumbling empire. This tomb, constructed in the mid-5th century, is her memorial.

Viewed from the outside, the tomb is a small, unassuming redbrick building; the exterior's seeming poverty of charm only serves to enhance by contrast the richness of the interior mosaics, in deep midnight blue and glittering gold. The tiny, low central dome is decorated with symbols of Christ and the evangelists and striking gold stars. Over the door is a depiction of the Good Shepherd. Eight of the Apostles are represented in groups of two on the four inner walls of the dome; the other four appear singly on the walls of the two transepts. Notice the small doves at their feet, drinking from the water of faith. Also in the tiny transepts are some delightful pairs of deer (representing souls), drinking from the fountain of resurrection. There are three sarcophagi in the tomb, none of which are believed to contain the remains of Galla Placidia. She died in Rome in AD 450, and there is no record of her body having been transported back to the place where she wished to lie. Reservations are required for the Mausoleo from March through mid-June. ⊠ *Via San Vitale off Via Salara* ☎ *0544/541688 reservations, 800/303999 toll-free information* ⊕ *www.ravennamosaici.it* ⊠ *€2 supplement in addition to obligatory €8.50 combination ticket Mar. 1–June 15* ◷ *Nov.–Feb., Mon.–Sat. 9:30–5, Sun. 9:30–5:30; Mar. and Oct., Mon.–Sat. 9–5:30, Sun. 9–6; Apr.–Sept., daily 9–7.*

> ## WORD OF MOUTH
>
> "Much of Ravenna is car-free, so we were on foot. Many local people rode bicycles; some of them smoked as they rode. Bikes for hire are parked in blue holders. One rents a key, and can take a bike from any holder and leave it at any holder, like luggage carts at an airport."   –smalti

❻ Sant'Apollinare Nuovo. The mosaics displayed in this church date from the early 6th century, making them slightly older than those in San Vitale. Since the left side of the church was reserved for women, it's only fitting that the mosaics on that wall depict 22 virgins offering crowns to the Virgin Mary. On the right wall are 26 men carrying the crowns of martyrdom. They are approaching Christ, surrounded by angels. ⊠ *Via Roma at Via Guaccimanni* ☎ *0544/219518, 0544/541688 reservations, 800/303999 toll-free information* ⊕ *www.ravennamosaici.it* ⊠ *Combination ticket €8.50* ◷ *Nov.–Feb., daily 10–5; Mar. and Oct., daily 9:30–5:30; Apr.–Sept., daily 9–7.*

ALSO WORTH SEEING

Domus dei Tappeti di Pietra *(Ancient Home of the Stone Carpets).* This underground archaeological site was uncovered during the course of routine maintenance work by the city in 1993 and opened to the public in 2002. Below ground level (10 feet down) lie the remains of a sixth-century AD Byzantine palace, in which a beautiful and well-preserved network of floor mosaics display themes that are fascinatingly un-Christian. ⊠ *Via Barbiani, enter through Sant'Eufemia* ☎ *0544/32512* ⊕ *www.domusdeitappetidipietra.it* ⊠ *€3.50* ◷ *Sun.–Fri. 10–6:30, Sat. 10–4:30.*

❶ Museo Nazionale. The National Museum of Ravenna, next to the Church of San Vitale, contains artifacts from ancient Rome, Byzantine fabrics

The mosaic of Empress Theodora in Ravenna's Basilica di San Vitale

and carvings, and pieces of early Christian art. The collection is housed in a former monastery, but is well displayed and artfully lighted. ⊠ *Via Fiandrini* ☎ *0544/34424* ⊠ *€4* ⊙ *Tues.–Sun. 8:30–7:30.*

⑤ **Tomba di Dante.** The tomb of Dante is in a small neoclassical building next door to the large church of St. Francis. Exiled from his native Florence, the author of *The Divine Comedy* died here in 1321. The Florentines have been trying to reclaim their famous son for hundreds of years, but the Ravennans refuse to give him up, arguing that since Florence did not welcome Dante in life it does not deserve him in death. ⊠ *Via Dante Alighieri 4 and 9* ☎ *0544/30252* ⊠ *Tomb free, museum €2* ⊙ *Tomb: daily 9–noon and 2–5. Museum: Tues.–Sun. 9–noon.*

OFF THE BEATEN PATH
Sant'Apollinare in Classe. This church, about 5 km (3 mi) southeast of Ravenna, is landlocked now, but when it was built it stood in the center of the busy shipping port known to the ancient Romans as Classis. The arch above and the area around the high altar are rich with mosaics. Those on the arch, older than the ones behind it, are considered superior. They show Christ in Judgment and the 12 lambs of Christianity leaving the cities of Jerusalem and Bethlehem. In the apse is the figure of Sant'Apollinare himself, a bishop of Ravenna, and above him is a magnificent Transfiguration against blazing green grass, animals in skewed perspective, and flowers. ⊠ *Via Romea Sud, Classe* ☎ *0544/473569* ⊠ *€3* ⊙ *Mon.–Sat. 8:30–7:30, Sun. 1–7:30.*

WHERE TO EAT

$$ ✕ **Bella Venezia.** Graceful low archways lead into this attractive pink-and-white restaurant's two small, brightly lighted dining rooms. Try the beans with olive oil and *bottarga* (cured roe) or the owner's special risotto with butter, Parmesan, cured ham, mushrooms, and peas to start. For the second course, the *fegato alla Veneziana* (grilled liver with onions) is a good choice. The outdoor garden is quite pleasant in season. ⊠ *Via IV Novembre 16* ☎*0544/212746* ⊕*www.bellavenezia.it* ▤*AE, DC, MC, V* ⊗*Closed Sun. and 3 wks in Dec. and Jan.*

$$ ✕ **Locanda del Melarancio.** This contemporary inn, in a palazzo in the
★ heart of the centro storico, has a pub on the ground floor, a restaurant on the second, and rooms on the third. Decor is minimalist without being stark, and modern artwork on the walls doesn't take away from the warm, traditional feeling. So, too, for the menu, which makes brilliant use of modern techniques to harness traditional Romagnan ingredients: *formaggio di fossa* (cheese aged in a cave) is made into a *sformato* (like a firm mousse) with julienned salami, honey, and balsamic vinegar, while cappellacci are filled with mascarpone and truffle under a sauce of porcini mushrooms. ⊠*Via Mentana 33* ☎*0544/215258* ⊕*www.locandadelmelarancio.it* ▤*AE, DC, MC, V.*

$ ✕ **Ca' de Ven.** A vaulted wine cellar in the heart of the old city, the Ca'
★ de Ven is great for a hearty meal. You sit at long tables with other diners and feast on platters of delicious cold cuts, flat breads, and cold, heady white wine. The tortelli *di radicchio e pecorino* (stuffed with radicchio and goat cheese) makes the best first course. ⊠ *Via C. Ricci 24* ☎*0544/30163* ▤*AE, DC, MC, V* ⊗*Closed Mon., 3 wks in Jan. and Feb., and 1st wk in June.*

$ ✕ **La Gardèla.** The kitchen seems to operate with an otherworldly efficiency, making this bright, bustling downtown restaurant extremely popular with the local business crowd—especially at lunch (always a good sign). The place is best for classics like tagliatelle al ragù and Adriatic fish, such as *sardoncini* (tiny sardines, breaded and fried). ⊠*Via Ponte Marino 3* ☎*0544/217147* ▤*AE, DC, MC, V* ⊗*Closed Thurs. and 10 days in Jan.*

WHERE TO STAY

$$–$$$ ▦ **Hotel Bisanzio.** Steps from San Vitale and the Tomb of Galla Placidia, this Best Western hotel is the most convenient lodging for mosaic enthusiasts. The exterior is drab, but rooms are comfortable and modern; the lobby's Florentine lamps add a touch of style. Ask to be on the top floor and you may get a view of the basilica. **Pros:** No-smoking rooms. **Cons:** Part of a chain; popular with groups. ⊠*Via Salara 30,* ☎*0544/217111* ᵬ*0544/32539* ⊕*www.bisanziohotel.com* ⇗*38 rooms* ⚘*In-room: safe, Wi-Fi. In-hotel: restaurant, bar, public Wi-Fi, parking (fee), some pets allowed* ▤*AE, DC, MC, V* ⦿*BP.*

$–$$ ▦ **Sant'Andrea.** This simple B&B offers an absolutely prime location, steps away from the Basilica di San Vitale. It's like staying in a well-appointed house—rooms are big, bright, and clean, done up in primary colors. The lobby is decked out with homey furniture, and breakfast can be taken in the breakfast room, or in the garden in good weather. Bathrooms are spotless and modern. A suite only costs €30 extra and can accommodate a family of four or five. **Pros:** Children under 12 sleep free; breakfast outdoors when it's warm; discounts for stays of three nights or more. **Cons:** Can get a little noisy; groups favor the place. ⊠ *Via Carlo Cattaneo 33,* ☎🖷*0544/215564* ⊕*www.santandrea hotel.com* ⇆*10 rooms, 2 suites* ☐*In-room: safe. In-hotel: bar, parking (fee)* ⊟*AE, DC, MC, V* ⦿*BP.*

$ ⊡**Hotel Centrale Byron.** Tranquillity is assured here in the center of Ravenna's old town, because it's in a pedestrian zone. The old-fashioned, well-managed hotel has spotless if uninspired rooms. You can drop off your luggage at the door, but you have to park your car in one of the nearby garages or lots. **Pros:** Plenty of triples and quads—great for families and friends. **Con:** Rooms are nothing special. ⊠ *Via IV Novembre 14,* ☎*0544/212225* 🖷*0544/34114* ⊕*www.hotelbyron. com* ⇆*54 rooms* ☐*In-room: safe. In-hotel: bar, parking (fee)* ⊟*AE, DC, MC, V* ⦿*BP.*

$ ⊡ **Hotel Ravenna.** A functional stopover near the train station, the Ravenna is still only a few minutes' walk from the center. This modern hotel has smallish rooms. Service is friendly and helpful. **Pros:** Good budget option; near train station. **Con:** Rooms are short on character. ⊠ *Via Maroncelli 12,* ☎*0544/212204* 🖷*0544/212077* ⊕*www.hotel ravenna.ra.it* ⇆*26 rooms* ☐ *In-hotel: bar, no elevator, parking (fee)* ⊟*MC, V* ⦿*BP.*

NIGHTLIFE & THE ARTS

Friday nights from June to August bring **Mosaics by Night,** when the Byzantine mosaic masterpieces in town are illuminated. The event is also held on certain Tuesdays; to check, call the tourist office, which also offers guided tours. The **Ravenna Festival** is a musical extravaganza held every year in June and July. Orchestras from all over the world come to perform in Ravenna's churches and theaters.

FERRARA

47 km (29 mi) northeast of Bologna, 74 km (46 mi) northwest of Ravenna.

When the legendary Ferrarese filmmaker Michelangelo Antonioni called his beloved hometown "a city that you can see only partly, while the rest disappears to be imagined," perhaps he was referring to the low-lying mist that rolls in off the Adriatic each winter and shrouds Ferrara's winding knot of medieval alleyways, turreted palaces, and ancient wine bars—once inhabited by the likes of Copernicus—in a ghostly fog. But perhaps Antonioni was also suggesting that Ferrara's striking beauty often conceals a dark and tortured past.

Though it was settled as early as the sixth century ad, Ferrara's history really begins with the arrival of the Este, who first made their appearance in the city in 1196. For more than three centuries the dynasty ruled with an iron fist; brother killed brother, son fought father, husband murdered wife. The majestic moated castle, now the architectural gem of the historic center, was originally built as a fortress to protect the ruthless Este dukes from their own citizens; deep within the castle the Este kept generations of political dissidents in dank cells. The greatest of the dukes, Ercole I (1433–1505), attempted to poison a nephew who challenged his power, and when that didn't work he beheaded him. Though the Jews were already well established in Ferrara as early at the 1380s, it is Ercole I who invited Sephardic Jews exiled from Spain to settle in Ferrara, thus giving form to one of the liveliest Jewish communities in western Europe. The maze of twisting cobblestone streets in the ghetto witnessed the persecution of its Jews once Fascist Italy was officially at war with Nazi Germany in October 1943. This tragedy was documented in Giorgio Bassani's semi-autobiographical book and Vittorio De Sica's film, *The Garden of the Finzi-Continis*.

Today you are likely to be charmed by Ferrara's prosperous air and meticulous cleanliness, its excellent restaurants and coffeehouses, and its lively wine bar scene. You'll find aficionados gathering outside any of the wine bars near the Duomo even on the foggiest of weekend evenings. Though Ferrara is a UNESCO World Heritage site, the city still draws amazingly few tourists—which only adds to its appeal.

GETTING HERE
Train service is frequent from Bologna (usually three trains per hour) and takes either a half hour or 45 minutes, depending upon which train type you take. It's a two-hour ride from Florence, and trains go just about every hour. The walk from the train station is easy but not particularly interesting. If you're driving from Bologna, take the RA1 out of town, take the A13 in the direction of Padova, and exit at Ferrara Nord. Follow the SP19 directly into the center of town. The trip should take about 45 minutes.

VISITOR INFORMATION
Ferrara tourism office (⊠ *Castello Estense,* ☎ *0532/299303* ⊠ *Piazza Municipale 11,* ☎ *0532/419474* ⊕ *www.ferrarainfo.com*).

EXPLORING FERRARA

If you plan to explore the city fully, consider buying a Card Musei ("museum card"; €14) at the Palazzo dei Diamanti or at any of the museums around town; it grants admission to every museum, palace, and castle in Ferrara. The first Monday of the month is free at many museums.

THE MAIN ATTRACTIONS
★ Massive **Castello Estense**, the former seat of Este power, dominates the center of town. The building was a suitable symbol for the ruling family: cold and menacing on the outside, lavishly decorated within. The public rooms are grand, but deep in the bowels of the castle are chilling dungeons where enemies of the state were held in wretched conditions—a function these quarters served as recently as 1943, when

antifascist prisoners were detained there. In particular, the **Prisons of Don Giulio, Ugo, and Parisina** have some fascinating features, like 15th-century graffiti protesting the imprisonment of lovers Ugo and Parisina, who were beheaded in 1425 because Ugo's father, Niccolò III, didn't like the fact that his son was cavorting with Niccolò's wife.

The castle was established as a fortress in 1385, but work on its luxurious ducal quarters continued into the 16th century. Representative of Este grandeur are the **Sala dei Giochi,** extravagantly painted with athletic scenes, and the **Sala dell'Aurora,** decorated to show the times of the day. The tower, the terraces of the castle, and the hanging garden—once reserved for the private use of the duchesses—have fine views of the town and the surrounding countryside. You can cross the castle's moat, traverse its drawbridge, and wander through many of its arcaded passages at any time. Do note that the entrance price is substantially higher if there is a special exhibition on. ⊠ *Piazza Castello* ☎ *0532/299233* ⊕ *www.castelloestense.it* ⊠ *Castle €7, tower €1 extra* ⊙ *Castle: Tues.–Sun. 9:30–5:30. Tower: Tues.–Sun. 10–4:45. Ticket office closes at 4:45.*

5

■ **NEED A BREAK?**
Caffetteria Castello (⊠ *Largo Castello 1* ☎ *0532/299337* ⊙ *Tues.–Sun. 9:30–5:30*) is spectacularly situated amid centuries of history. The second floor provides a great place to break for coffee while touring the castle, or to mingle with locals enjoying the lunchtime buffet. Right next door is a small book and gift shop.

★ The magnificent Gothic **Duomo,** a few steps from the Castello Estense, has a three-tier facade of slender arches and beautiful carvings over the central door. Work began in 1135 and took more than 100 years to complete. The interior was completely remodeled in the 17th century. ⊠ *Piazza Cattedrale* ☎ *0532/207449* ⊙ *Mon.–Sat. 7:30–noon and 3–6:30, Sun. 7:30–12:30 and 3:30–7:30.*

The collection of ornate religious objects in the **Museo Ebraico** *(Jewish Museum)* bears witness to the long history of the city's Jewish community. This history had its high points—1492, for example, when Ercole I invited the Jews to come over from Spain—and its lows, notably 1627, when Jews were enclosed within the **ghetto,** where they were forced to live until the advent of a united Italy in 1859. The triangular warren of narrow, cobbled streets that made up the ghetto originally extended as far as Corso Giovecca (originally Corso Giudecca, or Ghetto Street); when it was enclosed, the neighborhood was restricted to the area between Via Scienze, Via Contrari, and Via di San Romano. The museum, in the center of the ghetto, was once Ferrara's synagogue. All visits are led by a museum guide. ⊠ *Via Mazzini 95* ☎ *0532/210228* ⊕ *www.comune.fe.it/museoebraico* ⊠ *€4* ⊙ *Sept.–July, guided tours Sun.–Thurs. at 10, 11, and noon.*

The **Palazzo dei Diamanti** *(Palace of Diamonds)* is so called because of the 12,600 small, pink-and-white marble pyramids ("diamonds") that stud the facade. The building was designed to be viewed in perspective—both faces at once—from diagonally across the street. Work began in the 1490s, and finished around 1504. Today the palazzo contains the **Pinacoteca Nazionale,** which has an extensive art gallery and rotating exhibits. ⊠ *Corso Ercole I d'Este 19–21* ☏*0532/205844* ⊕*www.artecultura.fe.it* ☐*€4* ☉*Tues.–Sun. 9–7.*

WORD OF MOUTH

"Check out what special exhibits are at Ferrara's Palace of Diamonds at the time of your visit. We were lucky enough to hit a John Singer Sargent exhibit, exclusively his work in Italy."

–Ralstonlan

The oldest and most characteristic area of Ferrara is south of the Duomo, stretching between the Corso Giovecca and the city's ramparts. Here various members of the Este family built pleasure palaces, the most famous of which is the **Palazzo Schifanoia** (*schifanoia* means "carefree" or, literally, "fleeing boredom"). Begun in the late 14th century, the palace was remodeled between 1464 and 1469. The lavishly decorated interior, particularly the **Salone dei Mesi,** with an extravagant series of frescoes showing the months of the year and their mythological attributes, is well worth visiting. ⊠ *Via Scandiana 23* ☏*0532/244949* ⊕*www.artecultura.fe.it* ☐*€10* ☉*Tues.–Sun. 10–8.*

One of the streets most characteristic of Ferrara's past, the 2-km-long (1-mi-long) **Via delle Volte** is also one of the best preserved medieval streets in Europe. The series of ancient *volte* (arches) along the narrow cobblestone alley once joined the merchants' houses on the south side of the street to their warehouses on the north side. The street ran parallel to the banks of the Po River, which was home to Ferrara's busy port.

ALSO WORTH SEEING

One of the loveliest of the Renaissance palaces along Ferrara's old streets is the charming **Casa Romei.** Mid-15th-century frescoes decorate rooms on the ground floor; the *piano nobile* (main floor) contains detached frescoes from local churches as well as lesser-known Renaissance sculptures. ⊠ *Via Savonarola 30* ☏*0532/240341* ⊕*www.artecultura.fe.it* ☐*€3* ☉*Tues.–Sun. 8:30–7:30.*

On the busy Corso Giovecca is the **Palazzina di Marfisa d'Este,** a grandiose 16th-century palace that belonged to a great patron of the arts. It has painted ceilings, fine 16th-century furniture, and a garden containing a grotto and an outdoor theater. ⊠ *Corso Giovecca 170* ☏*0532/207450* ⊕*www.artecultura.fe.it* ☐*€3* ☉*Tues.–Sun. 9–1 and 3–6.*

WHERE TO EAT

$$$$
★
✕ **Il Don Giovanni.** Just down the street from Castello Estense, and inside a lovely 17th-century palace, this warm and inviting restaurant has a handful of tables and top-notch service. Chef Pier Luigi Di Diego and partner Marco Merighi pay strict attention to what's seasonal, and the menu reflects this. Complex mozzarella di bufala is paired with raw shrimp so fruity it's like a dab of marmalade. Melt-in-your-mouth-tender

raw scallops reveal just a whisper of sweetness. Cooked fish is equally impressive: juicy, well-seasoned *branzino* (striped sea bass) sits daringly atop chili peppers. Next door, the same proprietors run the less-expensive **La Borsa** wine bar, which has excellent cured meats, cheeses, and a fantastic wine-by-the-glass list. It's open for lunch. ✉ *Corso Ercole I d'Este 1* ☎ *0532/243363* ⊕ *www.ildongiovanni.com* Ⓐ *Reservations essential* ☰ *AE, DC, MC, V* ☷ *Closed Mon. No lunch.*

$$
×L'Oca Giuliva.** Food, service, and ambience unite in blissful harmony at this casual yet elegant restaurant minutes from Piazza Repubblica. Two small rooms in a 12th-century building provide the backdrop for exquisitely prepared local foods. The chef has a deft hand with local specialties, and executes them either in *tradizionale* (traditional) or *rivisitata* (updated) style. Particularly impressive are the primi, especially the cappellacci di zucca al ragù. It might be the best version in town. Meat-and-potatoes folk can opt for the salama da sugo with mashed potatoes, and adventuring sorts might try the *trancio di anguilla* (roast eel) with polenta on the side. The amazing wine list is complemented by a terrific cheese plate. ✉ *via Boccanale di Santo Stefano 38* ☎ *0532/207628* ☰ *AE, DC, MC, V* ☷ *Closed Mon. No lunch Tues.*

$$ ×Osteria Al Brindisi.** Ferrara is a city of wine bars, beginning with this, Europe's oldest, which opened in 1435. Copernicus drank here while a student in the late 1400s, and the place still has a somewhat undergraduate aura. Perfectly dusty wine bottles line the walls, and there are wooden booths in another small room for those who want to eat while they drink. A young staff pours terrific wines by the glass, and offers three different sauces (butter and sage, tomato, or ragù) with its cappellacci di zucca. Those in search of lighter fare might enjoy any of the salads or the grilled vegetable plate with melted pecorino. ✉ *Via degli Adelardi 11* ☎ *0532/209142* ☰ *AE, DC, MC, V* ☷ *Closed Mon.*

$$ × **Trattoria La Romantica.** The former stables of a 17th-century merchant's house have been transformed into this welcoming restaurant, which is a great favorite among local cognoscenti. Although the decor—warm light and wood-beam ceilings, incongruous prints, and a piano—seems to be in perpetual transition, the rustic food is fully realized. Ferrarese specialties like cappellacci di zucca are served side by side with French oysters. ✉ *Via Ripagrande 36* ☎ *0532/765975* ☰ *AE, DC, MC, V* ☷ *Closed Wed., Jan. 7–17, and Aug. 1–15.*

WHERE TO STAY

The city-run **Prenotel hotel reservation hot line** (☎ *0532/462046*) helps you make reservations at any place in town.

$$$ ▥ **Annunziata.** The flower-covered mini-balconies of this hotel could hardly be any closer to the castle and Ferrara's old town—this might just be the best location in the city. The building feels like an old private home, the lobby is inviting, and the pleasantly understated rooms have ceilings with old wooden beams. **Pros:** American-style breakfast (with eggs). **Cons:** Noise can be a problem. ✉ *Piazza Repubblica 5,* ☎ *0532/201111* ▤ *0532/203233* ⊕ *www.annunziata.it* ⬚ *26 rooms*

&In-room: safe, Wi-Fi. In-hotel: room service, bar, bicycles, parking (fee) ⊟AE, DC, MC, V ⊙IBP.

$$$
Fodor's Choice
★

⚏ **Hotel Ripagrande.** The courtyards, vaulted brick lobby, and breakfast room of this 15th-century noble's palazzo retain much of their lordly Renaissance flair. Rooms are decidedly more down-to-earth, but standard doubles and some of the enormous bi- and tri-level suites have faux-Persian rugs, tapestries, and cozy antique furniture; top-floor rooms and suites resemble a Colorado ski lodge, with terraces, and are roomy—especially good for families. Everything here, including the room service, is impeccable. The location is quiet but fairly convenient. **Pros:** Beyond-helpful staff; good choice for families. **Cons:** Staff goes home at midnight. ✉ Via Ripagrande 21, ☎0532/765250 ⊞0532/764377 ⊕www.ripagrandehotel.it ⇆20 rooms, 20 suites &In-room: safe, Wi-Fi. In-hotel: restaurant, room service, bar, laundry service, public Wi-Fi, parking (no fee), some pets allowed ⊟AE, DC, MC, V ⊙IBP.

$

⚏ **Locanda Borgonuovo.** This old-fashioned but lovely bed-and-breakfast is in a 17th-century monastery on a quiet but central pedestrians-only street. It books up months in advance, partly because it's very small and because musicians and actors from the local theater make this their home away from home. Rooms are furnished with antiques, and one has its own kitchen for longer stays. Summer breakfasts are served in the leafy courtyard. **Pros:** Kindly staff. **Cons:** Steep stairs to reception and rooms. ✉ Via Cairoli 29, ☎0532/211100 ⊞0532/246328 ⊕www.borgonuovo.com ⇆4 rooms, 2 apartments &In-room: safe, kitchen (some), Wi-Fi. In-hotel: restaurant, bicycles, no elevator, public Internet, public Wi-Fi, parking (no fee) ⊟AE, MC, V ⊙IBP.

THE VENETO

Updated
by Bruce
Leimsidor

The green plains stretching west of Venice hold three of northern Italy's most appealing midsize cities: Padua, Vicenza, and Verona. Each has notable artistic treasures and an attractive historic center; Padua is famous for its Giotto frescoes, Vicenza for its Palladian villas, and Verona for its ancient arena. All three were once under the control of Venice, and one of the pleasures of exploring them is discovering the traces of Venetian influence—still evident in everything from food to architecture.

PADUA

A romantic warren of arcaded streets, Padua has long been one of the major cultural centers of northern Italy. It's home to Italy's second-oldest university, founded in 1222, which attracted such cultural icons as Dante (1265–1321), Petrarch (1304–74), and Galileo Galilei (1564–1642), thus earning the city the sobriquet *La Dotta* (The Learned). Padua's Basilica di Sant'Antonio, begun around 1238, is dedicated to St. Anthony, and it attracts droves of pilgrims, especially on his feast day, June 13. Three great artists—Giotto (1266–1337), Donatello (circa 1386–1466), and Mantegna (1431–1506)—left significant works here, with Giotto's Scrovegni Chapel one of the best-known, and most meticulously preserved, works of art in the country. Today, a cycle-happy student body—some 50,000 strong—flavors every aspect of local culture. Don't be surprised if you spot a *laurea* (graduation) ceremony marked by laurel leaves, mocking lullabies, and X-rated caricatures.

GETTING HERE

Many people visit Padua from Venice: the train trip between the cities is short and regular bus service originates from Venice's Piazzale Roma. By car from Milan or Venice, Padua is on the Autostrada Torino Trieste A4/E70. Take the San Carlo exit and follow Via Guido Reni to Via Tiziano Aspetti into town. From the south, take the Autostrada Bologna Padova A13 to its Padua terminus at Via Ballaglia. Regular bus service connects Venice's Marco Polo airport with downtown Padua.

Padua is a pedestrian's city. If you arrive by car, leave your vehicle in one of the parking lots on the outskirts, or at your hotel. Unlimited bus service is included with the Padova Card (€14, valid for 48 hours), which allows entry to all the city's principal sights. It is available at tourist information offices and some museums.

VISITOR INFORMATION

Padua tourism office (⊠ *Padova Railway Station,* ☎ *049/8752077* ⊠ *Galleria Pedrocchi,* ☎ *049/8767927* ⊕ *www.turismopadova.it*).

5

THE VENETIAN ARC, PAST & PRESENT

Long before Venetians made their presence felt on the mainland in the 15th century, Ezzelino III da Romano (1194–1259), a larger-than-life scourge who was excommunicated by Pope Innocent IV, laid claim to Verona, Padua, and the surrounding lands and towns. After he was ousted, powerful families such as Padua's Carrara and Verona's della Scala (Scaligeri) vied throughout the 14th century to dominate these territories. With the rise of Venetian rule came a time of relative peace, when noble families from the lagoon and the mainland commissioned Palladio and other accomplished architects to design their palazzi and villas. This rich legacy, superimposed upon medieval castles and fortifications, is central to the identities of present-day Padua, Vicenza, and Verona. The region remained under Venetian control until the Napoleonic invasion and the fall of the Venetian Republic in 1797. The Council of Vienna ceded it, along with Lombardy, to Austria in 1815. The region revolted against Austrian rule and joined the Italian Republic in 1866.

Friuli–Venezia Giulia has a diverse cultural history that's reflected in its architecture, language, and cuisine. It's been marched through, fought over, hymned by patriots, and romanticized by James Joyce, Rainer Maria Rilke, and Jan Morris. Trieste was also vividly depicted in the novels of the towering figure of early-20th-century Italian letters, Italo Svevo. The region has seen Fascists and Communists, Romans, Habsburgs, and Huns. It survived by forging sheltering alliances—Udine beneath the wings of San Marco (1420), Trieste choosing Duke Leopold of Austria (1382) over Venetian domination.

Some of World War I's fiercest fighting took place in Friuli–Venezia Giulia, where memorials and cemeteries commemorate hundreds of thousands who died before the arrival of Italian troops in 1918 finally liberated Trieste from Austrian rule. Trieste, along with the whole of Venezia Giulia was annexed to Italy in 1920. During World War II, the Germans occupied the area and placed Trieste in an administrative zone along with parts of Slovenia. One of Italy's two concentration camps, still visitable, was near Trieste. After the war, during a period of Cold War dispute, Trieste was governed by an allied military administration; it was officially reannexed to Italy in 1954, when Italy ceded the Istrian peninsula to the south to Yugoslavia. These arrangements, long de facto in effect, were ratified by Italy and Yugoslavia in 1975.

EXPLORING PADUA

THE MAIN ATTRACTIONS

 Basilica di Sant'Antonio *(Basilica del Santo).* Thousands of faithful make the pilgrimage here each year to pray at the tomb of St. Anthony. The huge church was probably begun around 1238, seven years after the death of the Portuguese-born saint, and completed in 1310, with structural modifications added from the end of the 14th century into the mid-15th century; it combines elements of Byzantine, Romanesque, and Gothic styles. The imposing interior contains works by the 15th-century Florentine master Donatello. He sculpted the series of bronze reliefs illustrating the miracles of St. Anthony, as well as the bronze statues of the Madonna and saints, on the high altar. But because of the site's popularity with pilgrims, masses are held in the basilica almost constantly, which makes it difficult to see these works. The more accessible **Cappella del Santo** housing the tomb of the saint dates from the 16th century. Its walls are covered with impressive reliefs by various important Renaissance sculptors, including Jacopo Sansovino (1486–1570), the architect of the library in Venice's Piazza San Marco, and Tullio Lombardo (1455–1532), the greatest in a family of sculptors who decorated many churches in the area, among them Venice's Santa Maria dei Miracoli. In front of the church is an undisputed masterpiece of Italian Renaissance sculpture, Donatello's equestrian statue (1453) of the *condottiere* (mercenary general) Erasmo da Narni, known as Gattamelata. Inspired by the ancient statue of Marcus Aurelius in Rome's Campidoglio, it is the first in a series of Italian Renaissance monumental equestrian statues. ✉*Piazza del Santo* ☎*049/8789722* ⊕*www.santantonio.org* ☉*Sept.–May, daily 6:30* AM*–7* PM*; June–Aug., daily 6:30* AM*–8* PM*.*

❶ **Cappella degli Scrovegni** *(The Arena Chapel)*. This world-famous cha-
Fodor's Choice pel and its frescoes were commissioned by Enrico Scrovegno to atone
★ for the sins of his deceased father, Reginaldo, the usurer encountered
by Dante in the Seventh Circle of the Inferno in his Divine Comedy.
Giotto and his assistants decorated the interior from 1303 to 1305
with a universally acclaimed fresco cycle illustrating the lives of Mary
and Jesus. The 38 panels are arranged in tiers and are to be read from
left to right. The spatial depth, emotional intensity, and naturalism of
these frescoes—note the use of blue sky instead of the conventional,
depth-destroying gold background of medieval painting—broke new
ground in Western art. Opposite the altar is a *Last Judgment*, most
likely designed and painted by Giotto's assistants, where Enrico offers
his chapel to the Virgin, celebrating her role in human salvation—particularly appropriate, given the penitential purpose of the chapel.

Mandatory reservations, which should be made at least two days ahead
online or by phone, are for a specific time and are nonrefundable.
Reservations are necessary even if you have a Padova Card. In order
to preserve the artwork, doors are opened only every 15 minutes. A
maximum of 25 visitors at a time must spend 15 minutes in an acclima-
tization room before making a 15-minute (20-minute in winter) chapel
visit. Punctuality is essential; it's best to arrive at the chapel before your
reservation time. If you don't have a reservation, it's sometimes possible to buy your chapel admission on the spot—but you might have to
wait a while until there's a group with an opening. You can see fresco
details as part of a virtual tour at Musei Civici degli Eremitani. A good
place to get some background before visiting the chapel is the multimedia room, which offers films and interactive computer presentations. ⊠*Piazza Eremitani 8* ☎*049/2010020 for reservations* ⊕*www.
cappelladegliscrovegni.it* 🎫*€12 includes Musei Civici, or €1 with
Padova Card* ☉*Daily 9* AM*–7* PM, *entry by appointment only.*

★ ❹ **Palazzo della Ragione.** Also known as Il Salone, this spectacular arcaded
reception hall, which divides the Piazza delle Frutta from the Piazza
delle Erbe, was built between 1303 and 1309, with later 15th century
additions. Giotto painted the original frescoes, which were destroyed
in a fire in 1420. In the Middle Ages, as its name implies, the building
housed Padua's law courts; today, its street-level arcades shelter shops
and cafés. Art shows are often held upstairs in the frescoed **Salone**, at
85 feet high one of the largest and most architecturally pleasing halls
in Italy. In the Salone there's an enormous wooden horse, crafted for
a 15th-century public tournament, with a head and tail later remodeled to replicate the steed from Donatello's *Gattamelata*. In the piazza
surrounding the building are Padua's colorful open-air fruit and vegetable markets. ⊠*Piazza della Ragione* ☎*049/8205006* 🎫*Salone €4
or Padova Card* ☉*Feb.–Oct., Tues.–Sun. 9–7; Nov.–Jan., Tues.–Sun.
9–6.*

❺ **Piazza dei Signori.** Some fine examples of 15th- and 16th-century buildings line this square. On the west side, the **Palazzo del Capitanio** (facade
constructed 1598–1605) has an impressive **Torre dell'Orologio,** with
an astronomical clock dating from 1344 and a portal made by Fal-

conetto in 1532 in the form of a Roman triumphal arch. The **Battistero del Duomo** (12th century, with frescoes by Giusto de Menabuoi, 1374–78) is just a few steps away.

🐚 ❾ **Villa Pisani.** Extensive grounds with rare trees, ornamental fountains, and garden follies surround this extraordinary palace built in 1721 for the Venetian doge Alvise Pisani in Stra, 13 km (8 mi) southeast of Padua. Recalling Versailles more than it does a Veneto villa, it was one of the last and grandest of many stately residences constructed along the Brenta River from the 16th to 18th centuries by wealthy Venetians for their *villeggiatura*—vacation and escape from the midsummer humidity. Tiepolo's (1696–1770) spectacular frescoes on the ballroom ceiling alone are worth the visit. If you have youngsters in tow surfeited with old masters, explore the gorgeous **park** and **maze**. To get here from Venice, you can take the Brenta River bus that leaves from Piazzale Roma. ✉ *Via Doge Pisani 7, Stra* ☎ *049/502074* 💶 *Villa, maze, and park €5; maze and park only €2.50* ⏱ *Apr.–Sept., Tues.–Sun. 9–7; villa and park only: Oct.–Mar., Tues.–Sun. 9–4. Last entry 1 hr before closing.*

ALSO WORTH SEEING

❷ **Musei Civici degli Eremitani** *(Civic Museum).* What was once a monastery now houses works of Venetian masters, as well as fine collections of archaeological pieces and ancient coins. Notable are the Giotto Crucifix, which was once in the Scrovegni Chapel, and the *Portrait of a Young Senator* by Giovanni Bellini (1430–1516). ✉ *Piazza Eremitani 10* ☎ *049/8204551* 💶 *€10, €12 with Scrovegni Chapel, or free with Padova Card* ⏱ *Tues.–Sun. 9–7.*

❽ **Orto Botanico** *(Botanical Garden).* The Venetian Republic ordered the creation of Padua's botanical garden in 1545 to supply the university with medicinal plants. You can stroll the arboretum and wander through hothouses and beds of plants that were first introduced to Italy in this Renaissance garden, which still maintains its original layout. A St. Peter's palm, planted in 1585, stands protected in its own private greenhouse. ✉ *Via Orto Botanico 15* ☎ *049/8272119* ⊕ *www.orto botanico.unipd.it* 💶 *€4 or free with Padova Card* ⏱ *Apr.–Oct., daily 9–1 and 3–7; Nov.–Mar., Mon.–Sat. 9–1.*

❸ **Palazzo del Bo'.** The University of Padua, founded in 1222, centers around this 16th-century palazzo with an 18th-century facade. It's named after the Osteria del Bo' (*bo'* means "ox"), an inn that once stood on the site. It's worth a visit to see the exquisite and perfectly proportioned anatomy theater (1594), the beautiful "Old Courtyard," and a hall with a lectern used by Galileo. You can enter only as part of a guided tour. Most guides speak English, but it is worth checking ahead by phone. ✉ *Via VIII Febbraio* ☎ *049/8273044* ⊕ *www.unipd. it* 💶 *€5* ⏱ *Nov.–Feb., Mon., Wed., and Fri. at 3:15 and 4:15; Tues.,*

Thurs., and Sat. at 10:15 and 11:15; Mar.–Oct., Mon., Wed., and Fri. at 3:15, 4:15, and 5:15; Tues., Thurs., and Sat. at 9:15, 10:15, and 11:15.

Chiesa degli Eremitani houses substantial fragments of Andrea Mantegna's frescoes (1448–50), damaged by allied bombing in World War II. Despite their fragmentary condition, Mantegna's still beautiful and historically important frescoes depicting the martyrdom of St. James and St. Christofer show the very young artist's mastery of extremely complex problems of perspective. ⊠*Piazza degli Eremitani* ☎*049/8756410* ⊙*Daily 8–noon and 4–7.*

WHERE TO EAT

$$$$ ✕**Le Calandre.** A must on any serious gastronomic tour of Italy, Le Calandre is consistently judged by all major Italian restaurant critics as one of the three best restaurants in the entire country. The restaurant is quietly elegant and the service is almost perfect. The food is based on traditional Veneto recipes but given a highly sophisticated and creative treatment. The traditional Venetian squid in its ink, for example, is served as a "cappuccino," in a glass with a crust of potato foam. The menu changes seasonally, and with owner-chef Massimiliano Alajmo's creative impulses. Alajmo considers food to be an art form, not nourishment, so be prepared for small portions at high prices.Make reservations well in advance. Le Calandre is in the village of Sarmeola di Rubano, a few kilometers west of Padua and easily reached by taxi. ⊠ *Via Liguria 1, Sarmeola di Rubano* ☎*049/630303* ⊛*www.calandre. com* ▭*MC, V*⊙*Closed Sun. and Mon. and mid-Aug.–early Sept.*

$$–$$$$ ✕**Antico Brolo.** One of Padua's top restaurants lets you choose between pampered elegance in an historic 16th-century formal dining room, or more casual dining in the cantina or on the terrace. The seasonal menu changes daily. The traditional Veneto combination of radicchio di Treviso and taleggio cheese is transformed into a delicate taleggio-stuffed homemade ravioli topped with the sautéed radicchio. Or you can try a tour de force presentation of four different variations on baccalà, the Veneto's famous dried cod. This very distinguished restaurant also serves pizza in the evening (amazingly at regular pizzeria prices) and stays open late to accommodate the post-theater crowd (it's across from Padua's main theater). Whether you have a pizza on the terrace or a full meal in the formal dining room, you'll receive the same attentive friendly service. The cantina, stocked with more than 600 labels, is a more than adequate complement to the exceptional food. ⊠*Corso Milano 22* ☎*049/664555* ⊛*www.anticobrolo.it*▭*AE, MC, V*⊙*No lunch Mon.*

★ $$–$$$ ✕**Osteria Dal Capo.** A friendly trattoria in the heart of what used to be Padua's Jewish ghetto, Osteria Dal Capo serves almost exclusively traditional Veneto dishes and does so with refinement and care. The Venetian liver and onions is extraordinarily tender. Even the accompanying polenta is grilled to perfection—slightly crisp on the outside and moist on the inside. And the desserts are nothing to scoff at, either. Word is out among locals about this hidden gem, and the tiny place fills up quickly, so reservations are necessary. ☒ *Via degli Oblizzi 2* ☎ *049/663105* ⊟ *AE, DC, MC, V* ⊙ *No lunch Sun. and Mon. Closed 3 wks in Aug.*

$–$$ ✕ **Gigi Bar.** Simple and unpretentious: yellow walls and tablecloths brighten this inexpensive restaurant where high ceilings open up to a second-floor seating area. The central kitchen is behind a counter low enough for the convivial owner-chef Ferruccio to see and supervise the equally friendly dining-room staff. The terrific and popular fish soup is one of the affordable seafood dishes that keep locals queuing up. There are also tasty steaks, salads, vegetable plates, and pizzas with a surprisingly light crust. ☒ *Via Verdi 18/20* ☎ *049/8760028* ⊟ *DC, MC, V* ⊙ *Closed Tues. and 2 wks in July.*

★ $–$$ ✕ **L'Anfora.** This mix between a traditional Veneto bacaro (wine bar) and an *osteria* (tavernlike restaurant) is a local institution. Stand at the bar shoulder to shoulder with a cross section of Padovano society, from construction workers to professors, and let the friendly and knowledgeable proprietors help you choose a wine. The reasonably priced menu offers simple *casalinga* (home-cooked dishes), plus salads and a selection of cheeses. Portions are ample, and no one will look askance if you don't order the full meal. The place is packed with loyal regulars at lunchtime, so come early or expect a wait; if you come alone, you'll probably end up with a table of friends before you leave. ☒ *Via Soncin 13* ☎ *049/656629* ⊟ *AE, V* ⊙ *Closed Sun. (except in Dec.), 1 wk in Jan., and 1 wk in Aug.*

WHERE TO STAY

★ $$$ ⊡ **Majestic Toscanelli.** The charming entrance, with potted evergreens flanking the steps, sets the tone in this pleasant, central hotel close to the Piazza delle Erbe (it's easily the best-located hotel in the city). The cozy bedrooms are furnished in different styles from 19th-century mahogany and brass to French Empire. Your very welcoming hosts offer discounts to seniors, AAA members, and those carrying Fodor's guidebooks. **Pros:** Excellent location; attentive staff; pleasant and warm atmosphere. **Cons:** Rooms, while ample, are not large; little natural light and few views (hotel is on a narrow street); some street noise at night, especially on weekends; hefty parking fee (€19 per night). ☒ *Via dell'Arco 2, near Piazza delle Erbe,* ☎ *049/663244* ⊟ *049/ 8760025* ⊕ *www.toscanelli.com* ⇄ *26 rooms, 6 suites* ⊘ *In-room: safe (some), refrigerator, dial-up, Wi-Fi. In-hotel: restaurant, bar, public Internet, parking (fee), some pets allowed (fee), no-smoking rooms* ⊟ *AE, DC, MC, V* ⏐⊙⏐ *BP.*

★ $$$ ⊡ **Methis.** The strikingly modern Methis takes its name from the Greek word for style and spirit. Four floors of sleekly designed guest rooms reflect the elements: gentle earth tones, fiery red, watery cool blue, and airy white (in the top-floor suites). Rooms have Japanese-style tubs, and four are equipped for guests with disabilities. The lobby has one lounge and a quieter reading room. There's a pleasant view from the front rooms, which face the canal. **Pros:** Rooms are very attractive; staff is helpful and attentive; pleasant little extras like umbrellas are provided free of charge; views from some rooms. **Cons:** Although in

EATING & DRINKING WELL IN VENETIAN ARC

With the decisive seasonal changes of the Venetian Arc, it's little wonder that many restaurants shun printed menus. Elements from field and forest define much of the region's cuisine, including white asparagus, wild herbs, chestnuts, radicchio, and mushrooms.

Restaurants of the Venetian Arc tend to cling to tradition, not only in the food they serve but how they serve it. This means that from three in the afternoon until eight in the evening most places are closed tight (though you can pick up a snack at a bar during these hours), and on Sunday afternoon restaurants are packed with Italian families and friends indulging in a weekly ritual of lunching out.

One of the prime pleasures of this mellow region is buying provisions at an open-air market or *salumeria* (deli) and relaxing over a picnic. In the countryside, good picnicking spots abound. In the cities, two good spots are the Ponte Scaligero footbridge in Verona, and Padua's Basilica di Sant'Antonio—one of the rare churches in Italy that welcomes picnickers.

THE BEST IN BEANS

Pasta e fagioli, a thick bean soup with pasta, served slightly warm or at room temperature, is made all over Italy, but folks in Veneto are justly proud of their version, featuring beans from around the village of Lamon, near Belluno. Even in the Veneto, the beans from Lamon cost over double the next most expensive variety, but their rich and delicate taste is worth it. You never knew bean soup could taste so good.

PASTA, RISOTTO, POLENTA

For *primi* (first courses), the Veneto dines on *bigoli* (thick whole-wheat pasta) generally served with an anchovy-onion sauce, and risotto—saturated with red wine in Verona and prosecco in Conegliano. Polenta is everywhere, varying from a stiff porridge topped with Gorgonzola or stew, to a patty grilled alongside meat or fis, as in the photo below.

FISH

The catch of the day is always a good bet, whether sweet and succulent Adriatic shellfish, sea bream, bass, or John Dory, or freshwater fish from Lake Garda near Verona. But be sure to note whether the fish is wild or farmed—the taste, texture, and price difference is considerable. A staple in the Veneto is *baccalà*, dried salt cod, soaked in water or milk, and then prepared in a different way in each city. In Vicenza, *baccalà alla vicentina*, pictured at left, is cooked with onions, milk, and cheese, and is generally served with polenta. Locals consider it as central to their city's identity as Palladio.

MEAT

Inland, meat prevails: pork and veal are standards, while goose, duck, and guinea fowl are common poultry options. Lamb is best in the spring, when it's young and delicate. In Friuli–

Venezia Giulia, menus show the influences of Austria-Hungary: you may find deer and hare on the menu, as well as Eastern European–style goulash. Throughout the Veneto an unusual treat is *nervetti*—cubes of gelatin from a cow's knee with onions, parsley, oil, and lemon.

RADICCHIO DI TREVISO

In fall and winter be sure to try the radicchio di Treviso, pictured above, a red endive grown near that town but popular all over the region. It's best in a stew with chicken or veal, in a risotto, or just grilled or baked with a drizzle of olive oil and perhaps a bit of taleggio cheese from neighboring Lombardy.

WINE

Wine is excellent here: the Veneto produces more D.O.C. (Denominazione di Origine Controllata) wines than any other region in Italy. Amarone, the region's crowning achievement, is a robust and powerful red with an alcohol content as high as 16%. Valpolicella and Bardolino are other notable appellations. The best of the whites are Soave; sweet, sparkling prosecco; and pinot bianco (pinot blanc). In Friuli–Venezia Giulia, the local wine par excellence is Tocai Friulano, a dry, lively white made from Tocai grapes that has attained international stature.

CLOSE UP

Cocktail Hour on Padua's Piazzas

One of Padua's greatest traditions is the outdoor en-masse consumption, most nights in decent weather, of **aperitifs**: *spritz* (a mix of Aperol or Campari, soda water, and wine), *prosecco* (sparkling wine), or wine.

It all happens in the Piazza delle Erbe and Piazza delle Frutta. Several bars there provide drinks in plastic cups, so you can take them outside and drink while mingling among the crowds.

The ritual, practiced religiously by students most of all, begins at 6 PM or so, at which hour you can also pick up a snack from one of the outdoor seafood vendors. On weekends, the open-air revelry continues into the wee hours, transitioning from a cocktail hour to a bash.

historic center, hotel is far (15-minute walk) from major sights and restaurants; rooms are beautiful, but public spaces are cold and uninviting. ⊠*Riviera Paleocapa 70,* ☎*049/8725555* 🖷*049/8725135* ⊕*www. methishotel.com* 🖘*52 rooms, 7 suites* ⟠*In-room: safe, refrigerator, Wi-Fi. In-hotel: bar, gym, public Internet, parking (no fee)* ▭*AE, DC, MC, V*⦿*BP.*

$ 🖪 **Al Fagiano.** This delightfully funky budget hotel, near Basilica di Sant'Antonio, has spruced up its existing rooms and added new ones by acquiring an adjacent structure. Artistic decoration includes sponge-painted walls, paintings by the owner, brush-painted chandeliers, and an elevator where self-proclaimed artists can add graffiti to their heart's content. An amiable staff and relatively central location make Al Fagiano pleasant and convenient, and some rooms have views of the basilica's spires and cupolas. Breakfast is available for €7. **Pros:** Large rooms for budget property; youthful, relaxed atmosphere; fairly convenient location. **Cons:** No parking facilities, room service, or help with baggage; some may find the eclectic decor to be a bit much. ⊠*Via Locatelli 45,* ☎*049/8750073* 🖷*049/8753396* ⊕*www.alfagiano.com* 🖘*40 rooms* ⟠*In-room: dial-up. In-hotel: bar, some pets allowed* ▭*AE, DC, MC, V*⦿*EP.*

CAFÉS & WINE BARS

No visit to Padua is complete without a trip to **Caffè Pedrocchi** (⊠*Piazzetta Pedrocchi* ☎*049/8781231*). The café has long been central to the city's social life, and you can still sit here, as the French writer Stendhal did shortly after the café was established in 1831, and observe a good slice of Veneto life, especially, as he noted, the elegant Veneto ladies sipping their coffee. The massive café, built in a style reflecting the fashion set by Napoléon's expeditions in Egypt, has long been central to the city's social life. It also serves lunch and dinner, and is proud of its innovative menu. Open 9 AM to midnight daily from mid-June to mid-September; hours for the rest of the year are Sunday to Wednesday 9 to 9, Thursday to Saturday 9 AM to midnight.

Frequented by a blend of students and an older neighborhood crowd, **Hostaria Ai Do Archi** (✉ *Via Nazario Sauro 23* ☎ *049/652335*) is nothing more—or less—than a Padovan version of the *bacari* that are so typical of the Veneto: wine bars where people sit and stand all day long, sipping wine, tasting local snacks, and talking politics. It's a true experience.

VICENZA

Vicenza bears the distinctive signature of the 16th-century architect Andrea Palladio, whose name has been given to the "Palladian" style of architecture. He effectively emphasized the principles of order and harmony in the classical style of architecture established by Renaissance architects such as Brunelleschi, Alberti, and Sansovino. He used these principles and classical motifs not only for public buildings but also for private dwellings. His elegant villas and palaces were influential in propagating classical architecture in Europe, especially Britain, and later in America—most notably at Thomas Jefferson's Monticello.

In the mid-16th century Palladio was commissioned to rebuild much of Vicenza, which had been greatly damaged during wars waged against Venice by the League of Cambrai, an alliance of the papacy, France, the Holy Roman Empire, and several neighboring city-states. He made his name with the basilica, begun in 1549 in the heart of Vicenza, and then embarked on a series of lordly buildings, all of which adhere to the same classicism and principles of harmony.

GETTING HERE
Vicenza is midway between Padua and Verona, and several trains leave from both cities every hour. By car, take the Autostrada Brescia–Padova/Torino–Trieste A4/E70 to SP247 North directly into Vicenza.

VISITOR INFORMATION
Vicenza tourism office (✉ *Piazza Giacomo Matteotti 12,* ☎ *0444/320854* ✉ *Piazza dei Signori 8* ☎ *0444/544122* ⊕ *www.vicenzae.org*).

EXPLORING VICENZA

Many of Palladio's works are near the Venetian gothic and baroque palaces that line Corso Palladio, an elegant shopping thoroughfare where Vicenza's status as one of Italy's wealthiest cities is evident. Part of this wealth stems from Vicenza's being a world center for gold jewelry.

THE MAIN ATTRACTIONS
② **Teatro Olimpico.** Palladio's last, and perhaps most spectacular work, was
Fodor'sChoice completed after his death by Vincenzo Scamozzi (1552–1616). Based
★ closely on the model of ancient Roman theaters, it represents an important development in theater and stage design and is noteworthy for its acoustics and the cunning use of perspective in Scamozzi's permanent backdrop. The anterooms are frescoed with images of important figures in Venetian history. ✉ *Piazza Matteotti* ☎ *0444/222800* 💶 *€8*

Vicenza

includes admission to Palazzo Chiericati ☉ *Sept.–June, Tues.–Sun. 9–5; July and Aug., Tues.–Sun. 9–7.*

4 Villa della Rotonda (Villa Almerico Capra). This very beautiful Palladian villa, commissioned in 1556 as a suburban residence for Paolo Almerico, is undoubtedly the purest expression of Palladio's architectural theory and aesthetic. Although it seems more of a pavilion showplace, it was in fact commissioned as a residence, and as such demonstrates the priority Palladio gave to architectural symbolism of celestial harmony over practical considerations. It's more a villa-temple than a house to live in, and in this respect, it goes beyond the rational utilitarianism of Renaissance architecture. Although a visit to the interior of the building may be difficult to schedule (it's still privately owned), it is well worth the effort in order to get an idea of how the people who commissioned the residence actually lived. Viewing the exterior and the grounds is a must for any visit to Vicenza. The villa is a 20-minute walk from town or a short ride on the No. 8 bus from Piazza Roma. ⊠ *Via della Rotonda* ☎ *0444/321793* 💶 *€10 grounds and interior, €5 grounds only* ☉ *Grounds: Tues.–Sun. 10–noon and 2:30–6 (5 PM closing mid-Nov.–mid-Mar.); interior: Mar.–Nov., Wed. 10–noon and 2:30–6.*

⑤ **Villa Valmarana ai Nani.** Inside this 17th- to 18th-century country house, named for the statues of dwarfs adorning the garden, is a series of frescoes executed in 1757 by Gianbattista Tiepolo depicting scenes from *The Illiad,* Tasso's *Gerusalemme Liberata,* and Ariosto's *Orlando Furioso.* They include his *Sacrifice of Iphigenia, unanimously acclaimed by critics as a major masterpiece of 18th-century painting.* The neighboring *foresteria* (farmworkers' dormitory) is also part of the museum; it contains frescoes showing 18th-century Veneto life at its most charming, and scenes of *chinoiserie* popular in the 18th century, by Tiepolo's son Giandomenico (1727–1804). The garden dwarves are probably taken from designs by Giandomenico. You can reach the villa on foot by following the same path that leads to Palladio's Villa della Rotonda. ✉ *Via dei Nani 2/8* ☏ *0444/321803* 💶 *€8* 🕐 *Mid-Mar.–Oct., Tues.–Sun. 10–noon and 3–6; Nov.–mid-Mar., weekends 10–noon and 2–4:30.*

ALSO WORTH SEEING

③ **Palazzo Chiericati.** This imposing Palladian palazzo (1550) would be worthy of a visit even if it didn't house Vicenza's **Museo Civico.** Because of the ample space surrounding the building site, Palladio combined here elements of an urban palazzo with those he used in his country villas. The museum's important Venetian collection includes significant paintings by Cima, Tiepolo, Piazzetta, and Tintoretto, but its main attraction is an extensive collection of highly interesting and rarely found painters from the Vicenza area, such as Jacopo Bassano (1515–92) and the eccentric and innovative Francesco Maffei (1605–60), whose work foreshadowed important currents of Venetian painting of subsequent generations. ✉ *Piazza Matteotti* ☏ *0444/321348* 💶 *€8 includes admission to Teatro Olimpico* 🕐 *Sept.–June, Tues.–Sun. 9–5; July and Aug., Tues.–Sun. 9–6.*

① **Piazza dei Signori.** At the heart of Vicenza sits this square, which contains the **Palazzo della Ragione (1549),** commonly known as Palladio's basilica, a courthouse and public meeting hall (the original Roman meaning of the term "basilica"). The previously almost-unknown Palladio made his name by successfully modernizing the medieval building, grafting a graceful two-story exterior loggia onto the existing Gothic structure. Take a look also at the **Loggia del Capitaniato,** opposite, which Palladio designed but never completed. The palazzo and the loggia are open to the public only when there's an exhibition; ask at the tourist office.

WHERE TO EAT

$$ ✗ **Antico Ristorante agli Schioppi.** When they want to eat well, Vicenza's natives generally travel to the adjoining countryside—agli Schioppi is one of the few restaurants in the city frequented by Vicentino families and businessmen. Veneto country-style decor, with enormous murals, matches simple, well-prepared regional cuisine at this family-run restaurant. The risotto, flavored heartily with Savoy cabbage and fresh cheese, is creamy and—a rarity in restaurant risottos—beautifully tex-

tured. This is also an excellent place to try *baccalà* (dried cod), a Vicenza specialty. ✉ *Contrà Piazza del Castello 26* ☏ *0444/543701* ⊕ *www.ristoranteaglischioppi.com* ☰ *AE, DC, MC, V* ⊘ *Closed Sun., last wk of July–mid-Aug., and Jan. 1–6. No dinner Sat.*

★ **$-$$** ✗ **Ponte delle Bele.** Vicenza lies at the foot of the Alps, and many residents spend at least a part of the summer in the mountains to escape the heat. So, Alpine cuisine has been incorporated into the local culture and can be enjoyed at this popular and friendly Veneto trattoria. Your homemade pasta may resemble dumplings or spaetzle and your prosciutto might be made from deer or boar. Try Alpine preparations of game, such as venison in blueberry sauce or guinea fowl roasted with white grapes. The rather kitsch Alpine decor doesn't detract from the good, hearty food. ✉ *Contrà Ponte delle Bele 5* ☏ *0444/320647* ⊕ *www.pontedellebele.it* ☰ *AE, DC, MC, V* ⊘ *Closed Sun. and 2 wks in mid-Aug.*

$ ✗ **Dai Nodari.** A good cross section of Vicenza society, from students to businessmen frequents this popular wine bar, which is also a creative yet economical restaurant. At lunch, there's a choice of fixed-price menus ranging from €7 to €9. At dinner, appetizers include interesting cheeses, such as bastardo del Grappa (aged 60 days). Move on to fish or steak, or try rabbit roasted with juniper berries. There are also several pasta and salad choices. But don't wait until mealtime: from 5:30 until midnight you can stop in to have a glass of wine and sample some of the excellent bar snacks. ✉ *Contrà Do Rode 20* ☏ *0444/544085* ☰ *AE, DC, MC, V* ⊘ *Closed Mon.*

¢-$ ✗ **Righetti.** Stake out your seats, then line up at the self-service food counters here. There's a daily pasta, a risotto, and a hearty soup such as *orzo e fagioli* (barley and bean) on the menu. Vegetables, salads, and baccalà are standards; at dinner, meats are grilled to order. Once you have your meal on your tray, help yourself to bread, wine, and water. After you've finished, tell the cashier what you had and he'll total your (very reasonable) bill. Low prices and simple, enjoyable food has generated a loyal following. ✉ *Piazza Duomo 3* ☏ *0444/543135* ☰ *No credit cards* ⊘ *Closed weekends, 1st wk in Jan., and Aug.*

WHERE TO STAY

During annual gold fairs in January, May, and September, it may be quite difficult to find lodging. Be sure to reserve well in advance and expect to pay higher rates.

$$ 🏨 **Campo Marzio.** A five-minute walk from the railway station, this comfortable hotel is right in front of the city walls. You can borrow a bicycle to tool around town. Rooms are ample and furnished in a pleasant modernized-traditional style, but don't expect anything spectacular or romantic. This is the only full-service hotel in Vicenza, so it fills up quickly during the gold fairs—when rates nearly double. **Pros:** Central location; more amenities than most hotels in the city; set back from the street, so it's quiet and gets natural light. **Cons:** Room decor and public spaces are uninspiring; incredibly expensive during gold fairs. ✉ *Viale Roma 21,* ☏ *0444/5457000* ⊕ *www.hotelcampomarzio.com* ⤳ *36*

Continued on page 360

PALLADIO COUNTRY

Wealthy 16th-century patrons commissioned Andrea Palladio to design villas that would reflect their sense of cultivation and status. Using a classical vocabulary of columns, arches, and domes, he gave them a series of masterpieces in the towns and hills of the Veneto that exemplify the neo-Platonic ideals of harmony and proportion. Palladio's creations are the perfect expression of how a learned 16th century man saw himself and his world, and as you stroll through them today, their serene beauty is as powerful as ever. Listen closely and you might even hear that celestial harmony, the music of the spheres, that so moved Palladio and his patrons.

TOWN & COUNTRY

Although the villa, or "country residence," was still a relatively new phenomenon in the 16th century, it quickly became all the rage once the great lords of Venice turned their eyes from the sea toward the fertile plains of the Veneto. They were forced to do this once their trade routes had faltered when Ottoman Turks conquered Constantinople in 1456 and Columbus opened a path to the riches of America in 1492. In no time, canals were built, farms were laid out, and the fashion for *villeggiatura*—the attraction of idyllic country retreats for the nobility—became a favored lifestyle. As a means of escaping an overheated Rome,

villas had been the original brainchild of the ancient emperors and it was no accident that the Venetian lords wished to emulate this palatial style of country residence. Palladio's method of evaluating the standards, and standbys, of ancient Roman life through the eye of the Italian Renaissance, combined with Palladio's innate sense of proportion and symmetry, became the lasting foundation of his art. In turn, Palladio threw out the jambalaya of styles prevalent in Venetian architecture—Oriental, Gothic, and Renaissance—for the pure, noble lines found in the buildings of the Caesars.

PALLADIO, STAR ARCHITECT

Andrea Palladio (1508–1580)

"Face dark, eyes fiery. Dress rich. His appearance that of a genius." So was Palladio described by his wealthy mentor, Count Trissino. Trissino encouraged the young student to trade in his birth name, Andrea di Pietro della Gondola, for the elegant Palladio. He did, and it proved a wise move indeed. Born in Padua in 1508, Andrea moved to nearby Vicenza in 1524 and was quickly taken up by the city's power elite. He experienced a profound revelation on his first

THE OLD BECOMES NEW

La Malcontenta

Studying ancient Rome with the eyes of an explorer, Palladio employed a style that linked old with new—but often did so in unexpected ways. Just take a look at Villa Foscari, nicknamed **"La Malcontenta"** (Mira, 041/5470012, www.lamalcontenta.com €8. Open May–Oct., Tues. and Sat. 9–noon; from Venice, take an ACTV bus from Piazzale Roma to Mira or opt for a boat ride up on the Burchiello). Shaded by weeping willows and mirrored by the Brenta Canal, "The Sad Lady" was built for Nicolò and Alvise Foscari and is the quintessence of Palladian poetry. Inspired by the grandeur of Roman public buildings, Palladio applied the ancient motif of a temple facade to a domestic dwelling, topped off by a pediment, a construct most associated with religious structures. Inside, he used the technique of vaulting seen in ancient Roman baths, with giant windows and immense white walls ready-made for the colorful frescoes painted by Zelotti. No one knows for certain the origin of the villa's nickname—some say it came from a Venetian owner's wife who was exiled there due to her scandalous behavior. Regardless of the name, it's hard today to associate such a beautiful, graceful villa with anything but harmony and contentment.

trip, in 1541, to Rome, where he sensed the harmony of the ancient ruins and saw the elements of classicism that were working their way into contemporary architecture. This experience led to his spectacular conversion of the Vicenza's Palazzo della Ragione (1545) into a basilica recalling the great meeting halls of antiquity. In years to come, after relocating to Venice, he created some memorable churches, such as S. Giorgio Maggiore (1564). Despite these varied projects, Palladio's unassailable position as one of the world's greatest architects is tied to the countryside villas, which he spread across the Veneto plains like a firmament of stars. Nothing else in the Veneto illuminates more clearly the idyllic beauty of the region than these elegant residences, their stonework now nicely mellowed and suntanned after five centuries.

VICENZA, CITY OF PALLADIO

Palazzo della Ragione

La Rotonda

To see Palladio's pageant of palaces, head for Vicenza. His **Palazzo della Ragione**, or "Basilica," marks the city's heart, the Piazza dei Signori. This building rocketed young Palladio from an unknown to an architectural star. Across the way is his redbrick **Loggia dei Capitaniato.**

One block past the Loggia is Vicenza's main street, appropriately named Corso Andrea Palladio. Just off this street is the Contrà Porti, where you'll find the **Palazzo Barbaran da Porto** (1570) at No. 11, with its fabulously rich facade erupting with Ionic and Corinthian pillars. Today, this is the Centro Internazionale di Studi di Architettura Andrea Palladio (0444/323014, www.cisapalladio. org), a study center which mounts impressive temporary exhibitions. A few steps away, on the Contrà San Gaetano Thiene, is the Palazzo Thiene (1542-58), designed by Giulio Romano and completed by Palladio.

Doubling back to Contrà Porti 21, you find the **Palazzo Iseppo da Porto** (1544), the first palazzo where you can see the neoclassical effects of young Palladio's trip to Rome. Following the Contrà Reale, you come to Corso Fogazzaro 16 and the **Palazzo Valmarana Braga** (1565). Its gigantic pilasters were a first for domestic architecture.

Returning to the Corso Palladio, head left to the opposite end of the Corso, about five blocks, to the Piazza Mattoti and **Palazzo Chiericati** (1550). This was practically a suburban area in the 16th century, and for the palazzo Palladio combined elements of urban and rural design. The pedestal raising the building and the steps leading to the entrance—unknown in urban palaces—were to protect from floods and to keep cows from wandering in the front door. (For opening times and details, see the main text).

Across the Corso Palladio is Palladio's last and one of his most spectacular works, the **Teatro Olimpico** (1580). By careful study of ancient ruins and architectural texts, he reconstructed a Roman theater with archaeological precision. Palladio died before it was completed, but he left clear plans for the project. (For opening times and details, see the main text.)

Although it's on the outskirts of town, the **Villa Almerico Capra**, better known as **La Rotonda** (1566), is an indispensable part of any visit to Vicenza. It's the iconic Palladian building, the purest expression of his aesthetic. (For opening times, details, and a discussion of the villa, see the main text.)

A MAGNIFICENT COLLABORATION

Villa Barbaro

At the **Villa Barbaro** (1554) near the town of Maser in the province of Treviso, 48 km (30 miles) northeast of Vicenza, you can see the results of a one-time collaboration between two of the greatest artists of their age.

Palladio was the architect, and Paolo Veronese decorated the interior with an amazing cycle of trompe l'oeil frescoes—walls dissolve into landscapes, and illusions of courtiers and servants enter rooms and smile down from balustrades.

Legend has it a feud developed between Palladio and Veronese, with Palladio feeling the illusionistic frescoes detracted from his architecture; but there is prac-

tically nothing to support the idea of such a rift.

It's also noteworthy that Palladio for the first time connected the two lateral granaries to the main villa. This was a working farm, and Palladio thus created an architectural unity by connecting with graceful arcades the working parts of the estate to the living quarters, bringing together the Renaissance dichotomy of the active and the contemplative life. *Via Cornuda 7, Maser, 0432/923004 www. villadimaser.it , €5 Open April- October Tues. and weekends 3-6; Nov.- March, weekends 2:30- 5, or by reservation; Closed 24 Dec.- 6 Jan.*

ALONG THE BRENTA CANAL

During the 16th century the Brenta was transformed into a landlocked version of Venice's Grand Canal with the building of nearly 50 waterside villas. Back then, boating parties viewed them in *"burchielli"*—beautiful boats. Today, the Burchiello excursion boat (Via Orlandini 3, Padua, 049/8206910, www.ilburchiello. it) makes full- and half-day tours along the Brenta, from March to November, departing from Padua on Wednesday, Friday, and Sunday and from Venice on Tuesday, Thursday, and Saturday; tickets are €40–€71 and can also be bought at American Express at Salizzada San Moisè in Venice. You visit three houses, including the Villas Pisani and Foscari, with a lunchtime break in Oriago. Another canal excursion is run by the Battelli del Brenta (www.battellidel brenta.it). Note that most houses are on the left side coming from Venice, or the right from Padua.

rooms ♿ *In-room: safe, refrigerator, Ethernet, Wi-Fi. In-hotel: bar, parking (no fee), some pets allowed* ⊟AE, DC, MC, V☺.|O|BP.

$ 🔳 **Due Mori.** Authentic turn-of-the-century antiques fill the rooms at
★   this 1883 hotel Due Mori, one of the oldest in the city. Loyal regulars favor the place, because it's light and airy (with tall ceilings and pale walls), yet cozy. Breakfast is available for €5. This comfortable hotel is a true bargain—rates stay the same throughout the year, with no high-season or gold-fair price hikes. **Pros:** Large rooms, very tastefully furnished; friendly staff; central location off the Piazza dei Signori. **Cons:** No TV or air-conditioning in rooms (although thick walls and ceiling fans minimize the need for a/c); no one to help with baggage. ✉*Contrà Do Rode 24,* ☎*0444/321886* ⊕*www.hotelduemori.com* ⟵*30 rooms* ♿ *In-room: no a/c, no TV. In-hotel: bar, parking (no fee), some pets allowed* ⊟*MC, V* ☺*Closed 1st 2 wks of Aug. and 2 wks in late Dec.* |O|*EP.*

NIGHTLIFE & THE ARTS

Vicenza hosts a jazz festival in May and classical concerts in June, with performances throughout the city. Any event you can catch at **Teatro Olimpico** (✉*Piazza Matteotti* ☎*0444/222800* ⊕*www.comune. vicenza.it*) is especially worth attending. The teatro also hosts classical drama performances in September; even if your Italian is dismal, it can be thrilling to see a performance in Palladio's magnificent theater.

VERONA

On the banks of the fast-flowing River Adige, 60 km (37 mi) west of Vicenza, enchanting Verona has timeless monuments, a picturesque town center, and a romantic reputation as the setting of Shakespeare's *Romeo and Juliet.* With its lively Venetian air and proximity to Lake Garda, it attracts hordes of tourists, especially Germans and Austrians. Tourism peaks during summer's renowned season of open-air opera in the Arena and during spring's Vinitaly (✉*Fiera di Verona, Viale del Lavoro 8* ☎*045/8298170* ⊕*www.vinitaly.com*), one of the world's most important wine expos. For five days you can sample the wines of more than 3,000 wineries from dozens of countries.

Verona grew to power and prosperity within the Roman Empire as a result of its key commercial and military position in northern Italy. With its Roman arena, theater, and city gates, it has the most significant monuments of Italian antiquity north of Rome. After the fall of the Empire, the city continued to flourish under the guidance of barbarian kings such as Theodoric, Alboin, Pepin, and Berenger I, reaching its cultural and artistic peak in the 13th and 14th centuries under the della Scala (Scaligero) dynasty. (Look for the *scala,* or ladder, emblem all over town.) In 1404 Verona traded its independence for security and placed itself under the control of Venice. (The other recurring architectural motif is the lion of St. Mark, a symbol of Venetian rule.)

GETTING HERE

Verona is midway between Venice and Milan. It is served by a small airport, Aeroporto Valerio Catullo, which accommodates domestic and European flights; however, many travelers still prefer to fly into Venice or Milan and drive or take the train to Verona. Several trains per hour depart from any point on the Milan–Venice line. By car, from the east or west, take the Autostrada Trieste–Torino A4/E70 to the SS12 and follow it north into town. From the north or south, take the Autostrada del Brennero A22/E45 to the SR11 East (initially, called the Strada Bresciana) directly into town.

VISITOR INFORMATION

Verona tourism office (⊠*Piazza Brà,* ☎*045/8068680* ⊠*Porta Nuova railway station* ☎*045/8000861* ⊕*www.tourism.verona.it*).

EXPLORING VERONA

5

If you're going to visit more than one or two sights, it's worthwhile to purchase a VeronaCard, available at museums, churches, and tobacconists for €8 (one day) or €12 (three days). It buys a single admission to most of the city's significant museums and churches, plus you can ride free on city buses. A €5 Chiese Vive Card is sold at Verona's major churches and gains you entry to the Duomo, San Fermo Maggiore, San Zeno Maggiore, Sant'Anastasia, and San Lorenzo. Do note that Verona's churches strictly enforce their dress code: no sleeveless shirts, shorts, or short skirts.

THE MAIN ATTRACTIONS

☺ ❸ **Arena di Verona.** Only Rome's Colosseum and Capua's arena surpass this amphitheater in size. Though four arches are all that remain of the arena's outer arcade, the main structure is complete. It dates from the early Imperial age, and was used for gymnastic competitions, choreographed sacrificial rites, and games involving hunts, fights, battles, and wild animals. Unlike at Rome's Colosseum, there is no evidence that Christians were ever put to death here. Today you can visit the arena year-round; in summer, you can join up to 16,000 people packing the stands for one of Verona's spectacular opera productions. Even those who aren't crazy about opera can sit in the stands and enjoy Italians enjoying themselves—including, at times, singing along with their favorite hits. ⊠*Arena di Verona, Piazza Brà 5* ☎*045/8003204* ⊕*www.arena.it* ☞*€5 or VeronaCard, €1 1st Sun. of month* ☉*Mon. 1:30–7:15, Tues.–Sun. 8:30–7:15, 8–3:30 on performance days; last entry 45 mins before closing.*

Fodor's Choice
★

❷ **Castelvecchio** *(Old Castle).* This crenellated, russet brick building with massive walls, towers, turrets, and a vast courtyard was built for Cangrande II della Scala in 1354. It presides over a street lined with attractive old buildings and palaces of the nobility. Only by going inside the **Museo di Castelvecchio** can you really appreciate this massive castle complex with its vaulted halls. You also get a look at a significant collection of Venetian art, medieval weapons, and jewelry. The interior of the castle was restored and redesigned as a museum between 1958

Verona

and 1975 by one of the most important architects of the 20th century, Carlo Scarpa. Behind the castle is the Ponte Scaligero (1355), which spans the River Adige. ⊠*Corso Castelvecchio 2* ☏*045/8062611* 💶*€4 or VeronaCard, free 1st Sun. of month* ⊗*Mon. 1:30–7:30, Tues.–Sun. 8:30–7:30; last entry 6:45.*

❼ Duomo. The present church was begun in the 12th century in the Romanesque style; its later additions are mostly Gothic. On pilasters guarding the main entrance, are 12th-century carvings thought to represent Oliver and Roland, two of Charlemagne's knights and heroes of several medieval epic poems. Inside, Titian's *Assumption* (1532) graces the first chapel on the left. ⊠*Via Duomo* ☏*045/592813* ⊕*www.chie severona.it* 💶*€2.50, €5 for combined churches ticket, or VeronaCard* ⊗*Nov.–Feb., Tues.–Sat. 10–4, Sun. 10–5; Mar.–Oct., Mon.–Sat. 10–5:30, Sun. 1:30–5:30.*

❻ Loggia del Consiglio. This graceful structure on the north flank of the Piazza dei Signori was finished in 1492 and built to house city council meetings. Although the city was already under Venetian rule, Verona still had a certain degree of autonomy, which was expressed by the splendor of the loggia. Very strangely for a Renaissance building of this quality, its architect remains unknown, but it is undoubtedly the finest surviving example of such architecture in Verona. ⊠*Piazza dei Signori* ⊗*Closed to public.*

❺ Palazzo degli Scaligeri (Palazzo di Cangrande). The della Scalas ruled Verona from this stronghold built at the end of the 13th century by Cangrande I. At that time Verona controlled the mainland Veneto as far as Treviso and Lombardy to Mantua and Brescia. The portal facing the Piazza dei Signori was added in 1533 by the accomplished Renaissance architect Michele Sanmicheli.

❹ Palazzo della Ragione. An elegant pink marble staircase leads up from the *mercato vecchio* (old market) courtyard to the magistrates' chambers in the 12th-century palace, built at the intersection of the main streets of the ancient Roman city. Following massive restoration, the building reopened in March 2007 and is now used for art exhibitions. It is also available as a conference center. You can get the highest view in town from atop the attached 270-foot-tall **Torre dei Lamberti,** which attained its present height through a modification in 1452. ⊠*Piazza dei Signori* ☏*045/8032726* 💶*€2, €3 with elevator* ⊗*Mon. 1:30–7:30, Tues.–Sun. 8:30–7:30; last entry 6:45.*

Arche Scaligere. On a little piazza adjacent to the Piazza dei Signori are the fantastically sculpted gothic tombs of the della Scalas, who ruled Verona during the late Middle Ages. The 19th-century English traveler and critic, John Ruskin, described the tombs as graceful places where people who have fallen asleep live. The tomb of Cangrande I, hangs over the portal of the adjacent church and is the work of the Maestro di Sant'Anastasia. The tomb of Mastino II, begun in 1345, has an elaborate baldachino, originally painted and gilded, and is surrounded by an iron grillwork fence and topped by an equestrian statue. The latest and most elaborate tomb is that of Cansignorio (1375), the work

5

principally of Bonino di Campione. The major tombs are all visible from the street.

Piazza delle Erbe. Frescoed buildings surround this medieval square, located on a site where a Roman forum once bustled. During the week it's still bustling, as vendors hawk produce and trinkets. Relax at one of the cafés and take in the chaos.

★ ❶ **San Zeno Maggiore.** San Zeno is one of Italy's finest Romanesque churches. The rose window by the 13th-century sculptor Brioloto represents a wheel of fortune, with six of the spokes formed by statues depicting the rising and falling fortunes of mankind. The 12th-century porch is the work of Maestro Niccolò. Eighteen 12th-century marble reliefs flanking the porch by Niccolò and Maestro Guglielmo depict scenes from the Old and New Testaments and profane scenes from the legend of Theodoric. The bronze doors are from the 11th and 12th centuries; some were probably imported from Saxony and some are from Veronese workshops. They combine allegorical representations with scenes from the lives of saints. Inside, look for the 12th-century statue of *San Zeno* to the left of the main altar. In modern times it has been dubbed the "laughing San Zeno" because of a misinterpretation of its conventional Romanesque grin. A justly famous *Madonna and Saints* triptych by Andrea Mantegna (1431–1506) hangs over the main altar, and a peaceful cloister (1120–38) lies to the north (left) of the nave. The detached bell tower was begun in 1045, before the construction of much of the present church, and finished in 1173. ⊠ *Piazza San Zeno* ☎ *045/592813* ⊕ *www.chieseverona.it* ☜ *€2.50, €5 for combined churches ticket, or VeronaCard* ⊙ *Nov.–Feb., Tues.–Sat. 10–4, Sun. 1–5; Mar.–Oct., Mon.–Sat. 8:30–6, Sun. 1–6.*

❽ **Sant'Anastasia.** Verona's largest church, begun in 1290 but consecrated only in 1471, is a fine example of Gothic brickwork and has a grand doorway with elaborately carved biblical scenes. The main reason for visiting this church, however, is *St. George and the Princess* (1434, but perhaps earlier) by Pisanello (1377–1455) above the Pellegrini Chapel right off the main altar. As you come in, look also for the *gobbi* (hunchbacks) supporting holy-water stoups. ⊠ *Vicolo Sotto Riva 4* ☎ *045/592813* ⊕ *www.chieseverona.it* ☜ *€2.50, €5 for combined churches ticket, or VeronaCard* ⊙ *Nov.–Feb., Tues.–Sat. 10–4, Sun. 1–5; Mar.–Oct., Mon.–Sat. 9–6, Sun. 1–6.*

ALSO WORTH SEEING

🕊 **Ancient City Gates/Triumphal Arch.** In addition to its famous arena and
FodorśChoice Roman theater, two of ancient Verona's city gates and a very beauti-
★ ful triumphal arch have survived from antiquity. These graceful and elegant portals give us an idea of the high aesthetic standards of ancient Verona. The oldest, the Porta dei Leoni (on Via Leoni, just a few steps from Piazza delle Erbe), dates from the 1st century BC, but its original earth-and-brick structure was sheathed in local marble during early Imperial times. The Porta dei Borsari (at the beginning of Corso Porta Borsari, just a few steps from the opposite side of Piazza della Erbe), as its elegant decoration suggests, was the main entrance to ancient

Verona, and, in its present state, dates from the 1st century AD. Continuing down Corso Cavour, which starts on the other (front) side of Porta dei Borsari, you'll find the very beautiful Arco dei Gavi, which is simpler and less imposing, but certainly more graceful, than the triumphal arches in Rome. It was built in the 1st century AD by the architect Lucius Vitruvius Cerdo to celebrate the accomplishments of the patrician Gavia family. It was highly esteemed by several renaissance architects, including Palladio.

9 **Museo Archeologico and Teatro Romano.** Housed in what was a 15th-century monastery, the museum's collections were formed largely out of the donated collections of Veronese citizens proud of their city's classical past. Though there are few blockbusters here, there are some very noteworthy pieces (especially among the bronzes), and it is interesting to see what cultured Veronese from the 17th to 19th centuries collected. The museum sits high above the Teatro Romano, ancient Verona's theater, dating from the 1st century AD. ⊠ *Rigaste del Redentore 2* ☎ *045/8000360* ✉ *€3, free 1st Sun. of month, or VeronaCard* ☉ *Mon. 1:30–7:30, Tues.–Sun. 8:30–7:30; last entry 6:45.*

WHERE TO EAT

Book hotels months in advance for spring's Vinitaly, usually the second week in April, and for opera season. Verona hotels are also very busy during the January, May, and September gold fairs in neighboring Vicenza. Hotels jack up prices considerably during trade fairs and the opera season.

★ $$$$ ✕ **Arquade.** An 8-km (5-mi) trip northwest of the city brings you to one of the region's most esteemed high-end restaurants. Chef Bruno Barbieri has earned commendations for a creative menu that might include foie gras ravioli, *tegame tiepido* (pan-steamed seafood), or a soft-cooked egg, ingeniously poached and then fried, nestled in a bed of spinach. Tasting menus are a great way to sample a variety of Barbieri's creations. The wine list has more than 1,000 labels, including more than 100 of the best local wines. You can choose between dining in a converted chapel or on the beautiful terrace surrounding the 16th-century Villa del Quar, the small hotel where Arquade is located. Driving out for lunch or a pre-opera dinner is a great break from summer in the city. ⊠ *Via Quar 12, Pedemonte di San Pietro in Cariano* ☎ *045/ 6800681* ⌦ *Reservations essential* ▤ *AE, DC, MC, V* ☉ *Closed Mon. and Jan.–mid-Mar. No lunch Tues.*

$$$$ ✕ **Dodici Apostoli.** A Veronese institution, in a city where many high-end restaurants tend toward nouvelle cuisine, this highly esteemed restaurant is an exceptional place to enjoy classic regional dishes made with elegant variations on traditional recipes. Near Piazza delle Erbe, it stands on the foundations of a Roman temple. Specialties include gnocchi *di zucca e ricotta* (with squash and ricotta cheese) and *vitello alla Lessinia* (veal with mushrooms, cheese, and truffles). ⊠ *Vicolo Corticella San Marco 3* ☎ *045/596999* ⊕ *www.12apostoli.it* ▤ *AE, DC, MC, V* ☉ *Closed Mon., Jan. 1–10, and June 15–30. No dinner Sun.*

$$$$ ✗**Il Desco.** *Cucina dell'anima* (food of the soul) is how Chef Elia Rizzo describes his cuisine, which, true to the Italian culinary tradition, preserves natural flavors through quick cooking and limits the number of ingredients per dish. But there is little tradition in the inventive and even daring way in which he combines those few ingredients in dishes such as duck breast with grappa, grapes, and eggplant puree, or beef cheeks with goose liver and caramelized pears. For a gastronomic adventure, order the tasting menu (€125, without wine), which includes appetizers, two first courses, two second courses, and dessert. Decor is elegant, if overdone, with tapestries, paintings, and an impressive 16th-century lacunar ceiling. ✉ *Via Dietro San Sebastiano 7* ☎*045/595358* ⚓*Reservations essential* ▭*AE, DC, MC, V* ☽*Closed Sun. and Mon., Dec. 25–Jan. 8, and June 6–25. Dinner served Sun. in July, Aug., and Dec.*

★ $ ✗**Antica Osteria al Duomo.** This friendly side-street eatery lined with old wooden walls and ceilings, and decked out with musical instruments, serves Veronese food to a Veronese crowd; they come to quaff the local wine (€1–€3 per glass) and to savor excellent versions of local dishes like *bigoli con sugo di asino* (thick whole-wheat spaghetti with sauce made from donkey meat) and *pastisada con polenta* (horse-meat stew with polenta). Don't be put off by the dishes featuring unconventional meats; they're tender and delicious and this is probably the best place in town to sample them. First-rate Veronese home cooking comes at very reasonable prices here and is served by helpful, efficient staff. This is a very popular place, so reservations are recommended. ✉ *Via Duomo 7/a* ☎*045/8004505* ▭*AE, MC, V* ☽*Closed Sun. (except in Dec. and during wine fair).*

$ ✗ **Ristorante Redentore.** Across the Ponte Pietra pedestrian bridge from the heart of historic Verona, Redentore gives you a break from the busy city without quite having to leave it. Tall windows, pale walls, and bright paintings may make the interior inviting, but don't pass up the chance to dine alfresco beside the River Adige. Pizzas are the house special at €4.50–€7, but you can also choose among several homemade pastas or opt for a plate of local salamis and cheeses. ✉ *Via Redentore 15/17* ☎*045/8005932* ▭*MC, V* ☽*Closed Jan. 8–23. No lunch Mon.*

WHERE TO STAY

Book hotels months in advance for spring's Vinitaly, usually the second week in April, and for opera season. Verona hotels are also very busy during the January, May, and September gold fairs in neighboring Vicenza. Hotels jack up prices considerably during trade fairs and the opera season.

★ $$$$ 🏠**Villa del Quar.** Leopoldo and Evelina Montresor spared no expense when converting part of their 16th-century villa into a luxurious hotel oasis. It's surrounded by gardens and vineyards, yet only a 10-minute drive from Verona's city center. It's richly appointed with tapestries, antiques, and marble bathrooms, and the lounge is reminiscent of a castle's great hall. Quar's youthful staff provides attentive but relaxed service whether at the poolside bar or in the acclaimed Arquade restaurant (see review, above). **Pros:** Beautiful grounds; one of Italy's best restaurants is on-site. **Cons:** Outside the city center; very pricey; some rooms are starting to show wear. ✉ *Via Quar 12, Pedemonte di San Pietro in Cariano* ✛ *8 km (5 mi) northwest of Verona* ☎ *045/6800681* 🖷 *045/6800604* ⊕ *www.hotelvilladelquar.it* ⤻ *18 rooms, 10 suites* ♿ *In-room: safe, refrigerator, dial-up, Wi-Fi (some). In-hotel: restaurant, bars, pool, gym, public Internet, public Wi-Fi, parking (no fee), some pets allowed* ▤ *AE, DC, MC, V* ⊗ *Closed Jan.–mid-Mar.* ⍞ *BP.*

$$$ 🛏 **Hotel Victoria.** Busy business executives and tourists demanding comfort and quiet luxury frequent this full-service hotel centrally located near the Piazza delle Erbe. The Victoria offers a modern, sleek entryway and traditionally decorated, comfortable rooms. As is the case with many Verona hotels, lower rates are available depending on the season. Standard rooms are attractive and well proportioned, but the "superior" rooms (€290) are really quite lavish (some have hydro-massage showers). Pros: Quiet and tasteful rooms; very central location; billiards room. Cons: No views; not all standard rooms have Internet; contemporary decor in lobby may not be to everyone's taste. ✉ *Via Adua 8,* ☎ *045/5905664* ⊕ *www.hotelvictoria.it* ⤻ *66 rooms* ♿ *In-room: safe, refrigerator, Ethernet (some). In-hotel: bar, gym, laundry service, public Internet, public Wi-Fi, parking (€35)* ▤ *AE, DC, MC, V* ⍞ *BP.*

$ 🛏 **Torcolo.** At this budget hotel you can count on: a warm welcome from the owners and courteous, helpful service from the staff; pleasant rooms, decorated tastefully with late-19th-century furniture; and a central location close to Piazza Brà and the Arena. Breakfast (optional except for July and August), which costs an extra €7.50–€15, is quite generous and is served outside on the front terrace in summer. Note that during opera season and during the wine fair, the price for a double jumps to €140 (though breakfast is included). **Pros:** Despite the central location, the hotel is very quiet; rooms are decorated very tastefully; staff gives reliable advice on visiting Verona. **Cons:** No Internet; no views; no room service or help with baggage (but there is an elevator). ✉ *Vicolo Listone 3,* ☎ *045/8007512* 🖷 *045/8004058* ⊕ *www.hoteltorcolo.it* ⤻ *19 rooms* ♿ *In-room: safe, refrigerator. In-hotel: bar, parking (fee), some pets allowed* ▤ *AE, DC, MC, V* ⊗ *Closed Dec. 21–27 and 2 wks in Feb.* ⍞ *EP.*

OPERA

Fodor's Choice Milan's La Scala, Venice's La Fenice, and Parma's Teatro Regio offer
★ performances more likely to satisfy serious opera fans, but none offers a greater spectacle than the **Arena di Verona** (*Box office* ✉ *Via Dietro Anfiteatro 6/b* ☎ *045/8005151* ⊕ *www.arena.it* ⍰ *Tickets start at €22* ⊗ *Box office Sept.–June 20, weekdays 9–noon and 3:15–5:45, Sat. 9–noon; June 21–Aug., daily noon–9*). During its summer season (July–September) audiences of as many as 16,000 sit on the original stone terraces or in modern cushioned stalls. The best operas are the big, splashy ones, like *Aïda*, that demand huge choruses, lots of color

and movement, and, if possible, camels, horses, or elephants. Order tickets by phone or online: if you book a spot on the cheaper terraces, be sure to take or rent a cushion—four hours on a 2,000-year-old stone bench can be an ordeal. Sometimes you can even hear the opera from Piazza Brà cafés.

SHOPPING

FOOD & WINE
Salumeria Albertini (⊠ *Corso S. Anastasia 41* ☎ *045/8031074*) is Verona's oldest delicatessen: look for the prosciutto and salami hanging outside. **De Rossi** (⊠ *Corso Porta Borsari 3* ☎ *045/8002489*) sells baked bread and cakes, pastries, and biscotti that are lusciously caloric.

MARKETS
On the third Saturday of every month an antiques and arts-and-crafts market fills **Piazza San Zeno**. The city's main general market takes place at the **Stadio** on Saturday 8:30 AM–1 PM.

MILAN

Updated by
Madeleine
Johnson

Milan isn't between Florence and Venice, but as Italy's transport hub, with the biggest international airport, it may well be your point of entry into the country. It's also Italy's business hub, serving as the capital of commerce, finance, fashion, and media. Leonardo Da Vinci's Last Supper and other great works of art are here, as well as a spectacular Gothic Duomo, the finest of its kind. Milan even reigns supreme where it really counts (in the minds of many Italians), routinely trouncing the rest of the nation with its two premier soccer teams.

And yet, Milan hasn't won the battle for hearts and minds. Most tourists prefer Tuscany's hills and Venice's canals to Milan's hectic efficiency and wealthy indifference, and it's no surprise that in a country of medieval hilltop villages and skilled artisans, a city of grand boulevards and global corporations leaves visitors asking the real Italy to please stand up. They're right, of course. Milan is more European than Italian, a new buckle on an old boot, and although its old city can stand cobblestone for cobblestone against the best of them, seekers of Roman ruins and fairy-tale towns may pass. But Milan's secrets reveal themselves slowly to those who look. A side street conceals a garden complete with flamingoes (Via dei Cappuccini, just off Corso Venezia), and a renowned 20th-century art collection hides modestly behind an unspectacular facade a block from Corso Buenos Aires (the Museo Boschi-di Stefano). Visitors lured by the world-class shopping will appreciate Milan's European sophistication while discovering unexpected facets of a country they may have thought they knew.

Virtually every invader in European history—Gaul, Roman, Goth, Longobard, and Frank—as well as a long series of rulers from France, Spain, and Austria, took a turn at ruling the city. After being completely sacked by the Goths in AD 539 and by the Holy Roman Empire under

Frederick Barbarossa in 1157, Milan became one of the first independent city-states of the Renaissance. Its heyday of self-rule proved comparatively brief. From 1277 until 1500 it was ruled by the Visconti and subsequently the Sforza dynasties. These families were known, justly or not, for a peculiarly aristocratic mixture of refinement, classical learning, and cruelty, and much of the surviving grandeur of Gothic and Renaissance art and architecture is their doing. Be on the lookout in your wanderings for the Visconti family emblem—a viper, its jaws straining wide, devouring a child.

VISITOR INFORMATION

The **tourism office** (⊠ *Piazza Duomo 19/A, Piazza Duomo* ☎ *02/ 74043431* ⊕ *www.visitamilano.it* ⊙ *Mon.–Sat. 8:45–1 and 2–6, Sun. 9–1 and 2–5*) Piazza Duomo is an excellent place to begin your visit. It is now accessible by a stairway under the arches on the north side of Piazza Duomo. You can also enter from the Galleria in front of the Hyatt hotel. The Autostradale bus operator, sightseeing companies, and a few theaters have desks here that sell tickets. There are also free maps on a variety of themes and a selection of brochures about smaller museums and cultural initiatives. Pick up a copy of the English-language *Hello Milano* (ask, if it is not on display). This monthly magazine includes a day-to-day schedule of events of interest to visitors and a comprehensive map.

THE DUOMO & POINTS NORTH

Milan's main streets radiate out from the massive Duomo, a late-Gothic cathedral that was started in 1386. Leading north is the handsome Galleria Vittorio Emanuele, an enclosed walkway that takes you to the world-famous opera house known as La Scala. Beyond are the winding streets of the elegant Brera neighborhood, once the city's bohemian quarter. Here you'll find many art galleries, as well as the academy of fine arts. Heading northeast from La Scala is Via Manzoni, which leads to the *Quadrilatero della moda*, or fashion district. Its streets are lined with elegant window displays from the world's most celebrated designers—the Italians taking the lead, of course.

Leading northeast from the Duomo is Corso Vittorio Emanuele. Locals and visitors stroll along this pedestrians-only street, looking at the shop windows, buying ice cream, or stopping for a coffee at one of the sidewalk cafés. Northwest of the Duomo is Via Dante, at the top of which is the imposing outline of the Castello Sforzesco.

MAIN ATTRACTIONS

★ ❽ **Castello Sforzesco.** For the serious student of Renaissance military engineering, the Castello must be something of a travesty, so often has it been remodeled or rebuilt since it was begun in 1450 by the *condottiere* (hired mercenary) who founded the city's second dynastic family, Francesco Sforza, fourth duke of Milan. Though today the word "mercenary" has a pejorative ring, during the Renaissance all Italy's great soldier-heroes were professionals hired by the cities and principalities that they served. Of them—and there were thousands—Francesco

Milan

TO MALPENSA ✈

Parco Sempione

Stazione Cadorna

TO STAZIONE CENTRALE ↗

TO MILANO LINATE ✈

KEY

Ⓜ Metro stops

🛈 Tourist information

5

Sforza (1401–66) is considered one of the greatest, most honest, and most organized. It is said he could remember the names not only of all his men but of their horses as well. His rule signaled the enlightened age of the Renaissance but preceded the next foreign rule by a scant 50 years. The castle's secret crypts and battlements, including a tunnel that emerges well into the Parco Sempione behind, can be visited with privately reserved guides from **Ad Artem** (☎02/6596937 ✉info@adartem.it) or **Opera d'Arte** (☎02/45487400 ✉info@peradartemilano.it).

WORD OF MOUTH

"What I loved about Milan was: attending a concert at La Scala and taking their backstage tour; walking amidst the marble spires on the roof of the Duomo on a sunny day, gazing at the Dolomites in the distance (a definite wow!); window-shopping in the too-chic-for-words Via Montenapoleone area; and seeing *The Last Supper.*" –Maribel

Since the turn of the 20th century, the Castello has been the depository of several city-owned collections of Egyptian and other antiquities, musical instruments, arms and armor, decorative arts and textiles, prints and photographs (on consultation), paintings, and sculpture. Highlights include the **Sala delle Asse,** a frescoed room still sometimes attributed to Leonardo da Vinci (1452–1519). Michelangelo's unfinished *Rondanini Pietà* is believed to be his last work—an astounding achievement for a man nearly 90, and a moving coda to his life. The *pinacoteca* (picture gallery) features paintings from medieval times to the 18th century, including 230 works by Antonello da Messina, Canaletto, Andrea Mantegna, and Bernardo Bellotto. The Museo dei Mobili (furniture museum), which illustrates the development of Italian furniture from the Middle Ages to current design, includes a delightful collection of Renaissance treasure chests of exotic woods with tiny drawers and miniature architectural details. A single ticket purchased in the office in an inner courtyard admits visitors to these separate installations, which are dispersed around the castle's two immense courtyards. ✉*Piazza Castello, Brera* ☎*02/88463700* ⊕*www.milano castello.it* 🎫*€3, free Fri. 2–5* ☉*Castle: daily 7–6; museums: Tues.– Sun. 9–5:30* Ⓜ*Cairoli; Tram 1, 3, 4, 7, 12, 14, 27.*

★ ❶ **Duomo.** This intricate Gothic structure has been fascinating and exasperating visitors and conquerors alike since it was begun by Galeazzo Visconti III (1351–1402), first duke of Milan, in 1386. Consecrated in the 15th or 16th century, it was not completed until just before the coronation of Napoléon as king of Italy in 1809. Whether or not you concur with travel writer H. V. Morton's 1964 assessment that the cathedral is "one of the mightiest Gothic buildings ever created," there is no denying that for sheer size and complexity it is unrivaled. It is the second-largest church in the world—the largest being St. Peter's in Rome. The capacity is reckoned to be 40,000. Usually it is empty, a sanctuary from the frenetic pace of life outside and the perfect place for solitary contemplation.

Milan's spire-studded Duomo is the second largest church in the world.

The building is adorned with 135 marble spires and 2,245 marble statues. The oldest part is the **apse.** Its three colossal bays of curving and counter-curved tracery, especially the bay adorning the exterior of the stained-glass windows, should not be missed. At the end of the southern transept down the right aisle lies the **tomb of Gian Giacomo Medici.** The tomb owes some of its design to Michelangelo but was executed by Leone Leoni (1509–90) and is generally considered to be his masterpiece; it dates from the 1560s. Directly ahead is the Duomo's most famous sculpture, the gruesome but anatomically instructive figure of **San Bartolomeo** (St. Bartholomew), whose glorious martyrdom consisted of being flayed alive. It is usually said the saint stands "holding" his skin, but this is not quite accurate. It would appear more that he is luxuriating in it, much as a 1950s matron might have shown off a new fur stole.

As you enter the apse to admire those splendid windows, glance at the **sacristy doors** to the right and left of the altar. The lunette on the right dates from 1393 and was decorated by Hans von Fernach. The one on the left also dates from the 14th century and is ascribed jointly to Giacomo da Campione and Giovanni dei Grassi. Don't miss the view from the Duomo's **roof**; walk out the left (north) transept to the stairs and elevator. Sadly, air pollution drastically reduces the view on all but the rarest days. As you stand among the forest of marble pinnacles, remember that virtually every inch of this gargantuan edifice, including the roof itself, is decorated with precious white marble dragged from quarries near Lake Maggiore by Duke Visconti's team along road laid fresh for the purpose and through the newly dredged canals.

At this writing, the facade facing the piazza is shrouded in scaffolding for restoration work. ⊠ *Piazza del Duomo* ☎ *02/86463456* 🎫 *Stairs to roof €3.50, elevator €5* ⊙ *Mid-Feb.–mid-Nov., daily 9–5:45; mid-Nov.–mid-Feb., daily 9–4:15* Ⓜ *Duomo.*

Exhibits at the **Museo del Duomo** shed light on the cathedral's history and include some of the treasures removed from the exterior for preservation purposes. ⊠ *Piazza del Duomo 14* ☎ *02/860358* 🎫 *€6, €7 including ticket for elevator to Duomo roof* ⊙ *Daily 10–1:15 and 3–6.*

★ ❸ **Galleria Vittorio Emanuele.** This spectacular, late-19th-century glass-top, barrel-vaulted tunnel is essentially one of the planet's earliest and most select shopping malls. Like its suburban American cousins, the Galleria Vittorio Emanuele fulfills numerous social functions. This is the city's heart, midway between the Duomo and La Scala. It teems with life, inviting people-watching from the tables that spill from the bars and restaurants, where you can enjoy an overpriced coffee. Books, records, clothing, food, pens, and jewelry are all for sale. Known as Milan's "parlor," the Galleria is often viewed as a barometer of the city's well-being. By the 1990s, the quality of the stores (with the exception of the Prada flagship) and restaurants was uninspired. The city government, which owns the Galleria, and merchants' groups evicted some longtime tenants who had enjoyed anomalously low rents, in favor of Gucci, Tod's, and Louis Vuitton. After the restoration, historic Savini restaurant reopened in 2008, ready to host the beautiful and powerful of the city. Like the cathedral, the Galleria is cruciform in shape. Even in poor weather the great glass dome above the octagonal center is a splendid sight. And the floor mosaics are a vastly underrated source of pleasure, even if they are not to be taken too seriously. They represent Europe, Asia, Africa, and the United States; those at the entrance arch are devoted to science, industry, art, and agriculture. Be sure to follow tradition and spin your heels once or twice on the more "delicate" parts of the bull beneath your feet in the northern apse; the Milanese believe it brings good luck. ⊠ *Piazza del Duomo* Ⓜ *Duomo.*

NEED A BREAK?

One thing has stayed constant in the Galleria: the Caffè Zucca, known by the Milanese as Camparino. Its inlaid counter, mosaics, and wrought-iron fixtures have been welcoming tired shoppers since 1867. Enjoy a Campari or Zucca *aperitivo* (aperitif) as well as the entire range of Italian coffees, served either in the Galleria or in an elegant upstairs room.

❺ **Museo Poldi-Pezzoli.** This exceptional museum, opened in 1881, was once a private residence and collection, and contains not only pedigreed paintings but also porcelain, textiles, and a cabinet with scenes from Dante's life. The gem is undoubtedly the *Portrait of a Lady* by Antonio Pollaiuolo (1431–98), one of the city's most prized treasures and the source of the museum's logo. The collection also includes masterpieces by Botticelli (1445–1510), Andrea Mantegna (1431–1506), Giovanni Bellini (1430–1516), and Fra Filippo Lippi (1406–69). ⊠ *Via Manzoni 12, Brera* ☎ *02/794889* 🌐 *www.museopoldipezzoli.it* 🎫 *€8* ⊙ *Tues.–Sun. 10–6* Ⓜ *Montenapoleone.*

GETTING AROUND MILAN

The city center is compact and walkable, while the efficient Metropolitana (subway), as well as buses and trams, provides access to locations farther afield. Driving the streets of Milan is difficult at best, and parking can be downright miserable, so leave the car behind. In addition, as of January 2008, drivers entering the second ring of streets (the so-called *bastioni)* will have to pay a €2 charge between 7:30 and 7:30, weekdays (⊕ *www.comune.milano.it/ ecopass*). To park on the street (only in blue areas; yellow is for residents), purchase scratch-off cards from tobacconists or parking attendants who are often near busy areas.

BY PUBLIC TRANSIT

Tickets valid for one trip on the subway or 75 minutes on buses and trams must be purchased before you board and then stamped in machines at station entrances or on poles inside trolleys and buses. Standard tickets cost €1 and can be purchased from news vendors, tobacconists, and—at larger stops—machines (some of which require exact change). Buying an all-inclusive subway, bus, and tram pass will save you the hassle of purchasing individual tickets. They cost €3 for 24 hours or €5.50 for 48 hours and are available at Duomo Metro and Stazione Centrale Metro stations. Another option is a ticket for 10 tram or subway rides, called a *carnet,* which can be purchased at a discount. These new electronic tickets are delicate and will not function if bent or demagnetized. For problems, contact station managers, who can usually issue new ones. Trains run from 6 AM to 12:30 AM. For more information, check the Web site of **ATM (Azienda Trasporti Milanesi)** (⊕ *www.atm-*

mi.it), which has an English-language version, or visit the information office at the Duomo stop.

BY TAXI

Taxi fares in Milan are high compared to those in American cities. A short downtown ride will come to about €15. Taxis wait at stands, or you can call one of the city's taxi companies—**Amicotaxi** (☎ *02/4000*), **Autoradiotaxi** (☎ *02/8585*), **Radiotaxi** (☎ *02/6969*), **Taxiblu** (☎ *02/4040*). Dispatchers may speak some English; they'll ask for the phone number you're calling from, and they'll tell you the number of your taxi and how many minutes your wait will be. If you're in a restaurant or bar, ask the staff to call a cab for you. It's not customary to flag taxis down in the street, but drivers do sometimes stop if you hail them.

For car service, contact **Autonoleggio Pini** (☎ *02/29400555* 🖷 *02/2047843* ⊕ *www.pini.it*). English-speaking drivers are available.

TOURS

A refurbished 1920s tramcar operates a hop-on-hop-off tour of the city. Tickets (€20) are valid all day and can be purchased on board. Departures are at 11 and 1 (also at 3, April–October) from Piazza Castello. The organization **A Friend in Milan** (⊕ *www.friendinmilan.co.uk*) conducts walking tours of the city, including a visit to *The Last Supper,* day trips to the lakes, and shopping tours.

⑩ **Triennale Design Museum.** After decades of false starts and controversy, Milan finally opened a real museum in 2007 that honors its design talent. Originally the home of triennial decorative arts shows, a spectacular bridge entrance leads to a permanent collection, an exhibition space, and a stylish café (whose seating is an encyclopedia of design icons). The Triennale also manages the museum-studio of designer Achille Castiglione in nearby Piazza Castello. ⊠ *Via Alemagna 6* ☎ *02/724341* ⊕ *www.triennaledesignmuseum.com/* ⊠ *Variable, according to exhibition* ⊙ *Tues.–Sun. 10:30–8:30*

⑨ **Parco Sempione.** Originally the gardens and parade ground of the Castello Sforzesco, this park was reorganized during the Napoleonic era, when the arena on its northeast side was constructed, and then it was turned into a park during Milan's building boom at the end of the 19th century. The park is still the lungs of the city's fashionable western neighborhoods, and the **Aquarium** (⊠ *Viale Gadio 2* ☎ *02/878459* ⊠ *Free* ⊙ *Tues.–Sun. 9:30–5:30*) still attracts Milan's school children. The park became a bit of a design showcase in 1933 with the construction of the Triennale (*see above*). The Fiat café offers outdoor dining in summer along with a view of De Chirico's sculpture-filled fountain *Bagni Misteriosi* (*Mysterious Baths*), which is currently dry.

Even if a walk in the park is not appealing, it is worth visiting to see the **Torre Branca** (⊠ *Parco Sempione* ☎ *02/3324120* ⊠ *€3* ⊙ *Winter: Wed. 10:30–12:30 and 4–6:30; Sat. 10:30–1, 3–6:30, and 8:30–10:30; Sun. 10:30–2 and 2:30–7:30. Summer: Tues. 9:30* PM*–1* AM*; Wed. 10:30–12:30, 4–6:30, and 9:30–1* AM*; Thurs. 9:30* PM*–1* AM*; Fri. 2:30–6 and 9:30* PM*–1* AM*; Sat. 10:30–2, 2:30–7:30, and 9:30* PM*–1* AM*; Sun. 10:30–2, 2:30–7:30, and 9:30* PM*–1* AM*).* Designed by architect Gio Ponti, who was behind so many of the projects that made Milan the design capital that it is, this steel tower rises 330 feet over the Triennale. Take the elevator up to get a view of the city from a height that offers a sometimes intimate view into the city's topography and hidden spaces and monuments. Then have a drink at the glitzy Just Cavalli Café (Monday–Saturday 8 PM–2 AM) at its base. *Parco Sempione:* ⊠ *Piazza Castello, Brera* ⊙ *Nov.–Feb., daily 6:30–8; Mar. and Apr., daily 6:30–9; May, daily 6:30–10; June–Sept., daily 6:30–9; Oct., daily 6:30–9* Ⓜ *Cadorna; Bus 61.*

★ ⑦ **Pinacoteca di Brera** *(Brera Gallery).* The collection here is star-studded even by Italian standards. The entrance hall (Room I) displays 20th-century sculpture and painting, including Carlo Carrà's (1881–1966) confident, stylish response to the schools of cubism and surrealism. The museum has nearly 40 other rooms, arranged in chronological order—pace yourself.

The somber, moving *Cristo Morto* (*Dead Christ*) by Mantegna dominates Room VI, with its sparse palette of umber and its foreshortened perspective. Mantegna's shocking, almost surgical precision—in the rendering of Christ's wounds, the face propped up on a pillow, the day's growth of beard—tells of an all-too-human agony. It is one of Renaissance painting's most quietly wondrous achievements, finding an

5

unsuspected middle ground between the excesses of conventional gore and beauty in representing the Passion's saddest moment.

Room XXIV offers two additional highlights of the gallery. Raphael's (1483–1520) *Sposalizio della Vergine,* with its mathematical composition and precise, alternating colors, portrays the betrothal of Mary and Joseph (who, though older than the other men gathered, wins her hand when the rod he is holding miraculously blossoms). *La Vergine con il Bambino e Santi (Madonna with Child and Saints),* by Piero della Francesca (1420–92), is an altarpiece commissioned by Federico da Montefeltro (shown kneeling, in full armor, before the Virgin); it was intended for a church to house the duke's tomb. The ostrich egg hanging from the apse, depending on whom you ask, either commemorates the miracle of his fertility—Federico's wife died months after giving birth to a long-awaited male heir—or alludes to his appeal for posthumous mercy, the egg symbolizing the saving power of grace. ✉ *Via Brera 28* ☎ *02/722631* ⊕ *www.brera.beniculturali.it* 💶*€5* ⊙ *Tues.–Sun. 8:30–7:15; last admission 45 mins before closing* Ⓜ *Montenapoleone.*

❹ **Teatro alla Scala.** You need know nothing of opera to sense that, like Carnegie Hall, La Scala is closer to a cathedral than an auditorium. Here Verdi established his reputation and Maria Callas sang her way into opera lore. It looms as a symbol—both for the performer who dreams of singing here and for the opera buff who knows every note of *Rigoletto* by heart. Audiences are notoriously demanding and are apt to jeer performers who do not measure up. The opera house was closed after destruction by Allied bombs in 1943, and reopened at a performance led by Arturo Toscanini in 1946.

If you are lucky enough to be here during the opera season, which runs for approximately six months, do whatever is necessary to attend. Tickets go on sale two months before the first performance and are usually sold out the same day. Hearing opera sung in the magical acoustic of La Scala is an unparalleled experience. ✉*Piazza della Scala* ☎*02/72003744* ⊕*www.teatroallascala.org* Ⓜ*Duomo.*

At **Museo Teatrale alla Scala** you can admire librettos, posters, costumes, instruments, design sketches for the theater, curtains, and viewing-box decorations, along with an explanation of the reconstruction project and several interactive exhibits. Exhibition themes reflect current productions. A highlight is the collection of antique gramophones and phonographs. ✉*Piazza della Scala* ☎*02/43353521* 💶*€5* ⊙*Daily 9–noon and 1:30–5.*

ALSO WORTH SEEING

❷ **Battistero Paleocristiano.** Beneath the Duomo's piazza lies this baptistery ruin dating from the 4th century. Although opinion remains divided, it is widely believed to be where Ambrose, Milan's first bishop and patron saint, baptized Augustine. Tickets are available at the kiosk inside the cathedral. ✉*Piazza del Duomo, enter through Duomo* ☎*02/86463456* 💶*€1.50* ⊙*Daily 9:30–5:15* Ⓜ*Duomo.*

★ ➏ **Villa Belgioioso Bonaparte—Museo dell'Ottocento.** Formerly known as the Galleria di Arte Moderna, this museum is one of the city's most beautiful buildings. An outstanding example of neoclassical architecture, it was built between 1790 and 1796 as a residence for a member of the Belgioioso family. It later became known as the Villa Reale (royal) when it was donated to Napoléon, who lived here briefly with Empress Josephine. Its origins as residence are reflected in the elegance of its proportions and its private garden behind.

Likewise, the collection of paintings is domestic rather than monumental. There are many portraits, as well as collections of miniatures on porcelain. Unusual for an Italian museum, this collection derives from private donations from Milan's hereditary and commercial aristocracies. On display are the collection left by prominent painter and sculptor Marino Marini and the immense *Quarto Stato* (*Fourth Estate*), which is at the top of the grand staircase. Completed in 1901 by Pellizza da Volpedo, this painting of striking workers is an icon of 20th-century Italian art and labor history, and as such it has been satirized almost as much as the *Mona Lisa*. This museum is a unique glimpse of the splendors hiding behind Milan's discreet and often stern facades. ⊠ *Via Palestro 16* ☎ *02/76340809* ⊕ *www.villabelgiojosobonaparte. it* ⊙ *Tues.–Sun. 9–1 and 2–5:30* Ⓜ *Palestro.*

☾ The **Giardini Pubblici** (Public Gardens), across Via Palestro from the Villa Reale, were laid out by Giuseppe Piermarini, architect of La Scala, in 1770. They were designed as public pleasure gardens, and today they still are popular with families who live in the city center. Generations of Milanese have taken pony rides and gone on the miniature train and merry-go-round. The park also contains a small planetarium and the **Museo Civico di Storia Naturale** (Municipal Natural History Museum). One of the unenclosed grassy areas near the fountain on the Via Manin side is set aside for dogs to run free.

Parents may want to visit the garden of the Villa Belgioioso-Bonaparte, on Via Palestro, which is entered from a gate to the building's left. Access to the garden, which has statuary and a water course designed in 1790 (the first English-style garden in Milan), is restricted to children accompanied by an adult. Adults without children wanting to see the garden are tolerated, as long as they do not linger in this protected area.

NEED A BREAK? If your energy is flagging after shopping or chasing children around the park, try some of Milan's best cappuccino and pastry at Dolce In (⊠ *Via Turati 2/3* ⊙ *Closed Mon.*), which is equally close to Via della Spiga and the Giardini Pubblici. It's famous for its pastry and also serves sandwiches and cold plates at lunch. On Sunday mornings, classic-car enthusiasts meet informally here, parking their handsome machines out front while they have coffee.

SOUTH & WEST OF THE DUOMO

If the part of the city to the north of the Duomo is dominated by its shops, the section to the south is famous for its works of art. The most famous is *Il Cenacolo*—known in English as *The Last Supper*. If you have time for nothing else, make sure you see this masterwork, which has now been definitively restored, after many, many years of work. Reservations will be needed to see this fresco, housed in the refectory of Santa Maria delle Grazie. Make these at least three weeks before you depart for Italy, so you can plan the rest of your time in Milan.

There are other gems as well. Via Torino, the ancient road for Turin, leads to a half-hidden treasure: Bramante's Renaissance masterpiece, the church of San Satiro. At the intersection of Via San Vittore and Via Carducci is the medieval Basilica di Sant'Ambrogio, named for Milan's patron saint. Another lovely church southeast of Sant'Ambrogio along Via de Amicis is San Lorenzo Maggiore. It's also known as San Lorenzo alle Colonne because of the 16 columns running across the facade.

MAIN ATTRACTIONS

⑮ Basilica di Sant'Ambrogio *(Basilica of St. Ambrose).* Noted for its medieval architecture, the church was consecrated by Milan's bishop, St. Ambrose, in AD 387 (one of the original Doctors of the Catholic Church), and he is buried here. St. Ambroeus, as he is known in Milanese dialect, is the city's patron saint. Until the construction of the more imposing Duomo, this was Milan's most important church. Much restored and reworked over the centuries (the gold and gem encrusted altar dates from the 9th century), Sant'Ambrogio still preserves its Romanesque characteristics. The church is often closed for weddings on Saturday. ⌂ *Piazza Sant'Ambrogio 15* ☎ *02/86450895* ⊙ *Mon.–Sat. 7–noon and 2:30–7, Sun. 3–8* Ⓜ *Sant'Ambrogio.*

NEED A BREAK?

A bit overcrowded at night, when teenagers virtually block the sidewalk and traffic, the Bar Magenta (⌂ *Via Carducci 13, at Corso Magenta, Sant'Ambrogio* ☎ *02/8053808* Ⓜ *Sant'Ambrogio*) can be a good stop en route during the day. Beyond coffee at all hours, lunch, and beer, the real attraction is its mix of old and new, trendy and aristocratic—a quintessentially Milanese ambience. It celebrated its 100th birthday in 2007 and is open until 2 AM.

⑫ Pinacoteca Ambrosiana. Cardinal Federico Borromeo, one of Milan's native saints, founded this picture gallery in 1618 with the addition of his personal art collection to a bequest of books to Italy's first public library. Recent renovations have reunited the core works of the collection, including such treasures as Caravaggio's *Basket of Fruit* and Raphael's monumental preparatory drawing (known as a "cartoon") for *The School of Athens*, which hangs in the Vatican. Heavy on Lombard artists, there are also paintings by Leonardo, Botticelli, Luini, Titian, and (Jan) Brueghel. Previous renovations done in the 1930s with their mosaics and stained-glass windows are worth a look, as are other odd items, including 18th-century scientific instruments and gloves worn by

Napoléon at Waterloo. Access to the library, the Biblioteca Ambrosiana, is limited to researchers who can apply for entrance tickets. ⊠*Piazza Pio XI 2, near Duomo* ☎*02/806921* ⊕*www.ambrosiana.it* ☎*€80* ⊙*Tues.–Sun. 10–5:30* Ⓜ*Duomo.*

⓱ San Lorenzo Maggiore. Sixteen ancient Roman columns line the front of this sanctuary; 4th-century paleo-Christian mosaics survive in the Cappella di Sant'Aquilino (Chapel of St. Aquilinus). ⊠*Corso di Porta Ticinese 39* ☎*02/89404129* ▤*Mosaics €2* ⊙*Daily 8:30–12:30 and 2:30–6:30.*

★ **⓫ San Satiro.** First built in 876, this architectural gem was later perfected by Bramante (1444–1514), demonstrating his command of proportion and perspective, keynotes of Renaissance architecture. Bramante tricks the eye with a famous optical illusion that makes a small interior seem extraordinarily spacious and airy, while accommodating a beloved 13th-century fresco. ⊠*Via Torino 9, near Duomo* ⊙*Weekdays 7:30– 11:30 and 3:30–6:30, weekends 9–noon and 3:30–7* Ⓜ*Duomo.*

★ **⓮ Santa Maria delle Grazie.** Leonardo da Vinci's *The Last Supper,* housed in the church and former Dominican monastery of Santa Maria delle Grazie, has had an almost unbelievable history of bad luck and neglect—its near destruction in an American bombing raid in August 1943 was only the latest chapter in a series of misadventures, including, if one 19th-century source is to be believed, being whitewashed over by monks. Well-meant but disastrous attempts at restoration have done little to rectify the problem of the work's placement: it was executed on a wall unusually vulnerable to climatic dampness. Yet Leonardo chose to work slowly and patiently in oil pigments—which demand dry plaster—instead of proceeding hastily on wet plaster according to the conventional fresco technique. Novelist Aldous Huxley (1894–1963) called it "the saddest work of art in the world." After years of restorers' patiently shifting from one square centimeter to another, Leonardo's masterpiece is free of the shroud of scaffolding—and centuries of retouching, grime, and dust. Astonishing clarity and luminosity have been regained.

Despite Leonardo's carefully preserved preparatory sketches in which the apostles are clearly labeled by name, there still remains some small debate about a few identities in the final arrangement. But there can be no mistaking Judas, small and dark, his hand calmly reaching forward to the bread, isolated from the terrible confusion that has taken the hearts of the others. One critic, Frederick Hartt, offers an elegantly terse explanation for why the composition works: it combines "dramatic confusion" with "mathematical order." Certainly, the amazingly skillful and unobtrusive repetition of threes—in the windows, in the grouping of the figures, and in their placement—adds a mystical aspect to what at first seems simply the perfect observation of spontaneous human gesture.

Reservations are required to view the work. Viewings are in 15-minute, timed slots, and visitors must arrive 15 minutes before their assigned time if they are not to lose their slot. Reservations can be made via phone (☎*02/89421146*) or online (⊕*www.cenacolovinciano.it*); it is best to call because more tickets are set aside for phone reservations. Call about three weeks ahead to be sure of getting the Saturday slot you want; two weeks before for a weekday slot. The telephone reservation office is open 9 AM–6 PM weekdays and 9 AM–2 PM on Saturday. Operators do speak English, though not fluently, and to reach one, you must wait for the Italian introduction to finish and then press "2." However, you can sometimes get tickets from one day to the next. Some city bus tours include a visit in their regular circuit, which may be a good option.

The painting was executed in what was the order's refectory, which is now referred to as the **Cenacolo Vinciano.** Take a moment to visit Santa Maria delle Grazie itself. It's a handsome church, with a fine dome, which Bramante added along with a cloister about the time that Leonardo was commissioned to paint *The Last Supper.* If you're wondering how two such giants came to be employed decorating and remodeling the refectory and church of a comparatively modest religious order, and not, say, the Duomo, the answer lies in the ambitious but largely unrealized plan to turn Santa Maria delle Grazie into a magnificent Sforza family mausoleum. Though Ludovico il Moro Sforza (1452–1508), seventh duke of Milan, was but one generation away from the founding of the Sforza dynasty, he was its last ruler. Two years after Leonardo finished *The Last Supper,* Ludovico was defeated by Louis XII and spent the remaining eight years of his life in a French dungeon. ⊠*Piazza Santa Maria delle Grazie 2, off Corso Magenta, Sant'Ambrogio* ☎*02/89421146* ⊕*www.cenacolovinciano. org* 🖾€*6.50 plus €1.50 reservation fee* ⊙*Weekdays 9–6, Sat. 9–2* Ⓜ*Cadorna.*

ALSO WORTH SEEING

Museo Boschi-di Stefano *(Boschi-di Stefano Museum).* To most of us Italian art means Renaissance art. But the 20th century in Italy was a productive—if less-well-known—era. Just a block behind the Corso Buenos Aires shopping area, the Museo Boschi-di Stefano is a tribute to the enlightened private collectors who replaced popes and nobles as Italian patrons. An apartment on the second floor of a stunning art deco building designed by Milan architect Portaluppi houses this private collection, which was donated to the city of Milan in 2003. Its walls burst with masterpieces by postwar greats, such as Fontana, De Chirico, and Morandi, collected by the Boschi-di Stefano couple. The works mingle with distinctive postwar furniture and stunning Murano glass chandeliers. ⊠*Via Jan 15, Corso Buenos Aires* ☎*02/20240568* 🖾*Free* ⊙*Wed.–Sun. 2–6; last entry at 5:30.*

⓭ **Museo Civico Archeologico** *(Municipal Archaeological Museum).* Appropriately situated in the heart of Roman Milan, this museum's garden encloses the polygonal Ansperto tower, which was once part of the Roman walls. Housed in a former monastery, this museum has some everyday utensils, jewelry, an important silver plate from the last days of paganism, and several fine examples of mosaic pavement. ⊠*Corso*

Magenta 15, Sant'Ambrogio ☎*02/86450011* ⊡*€2, free Fri. 2–5* ⏱*Tues.–Sun. 9–1 and 2–5:30* Ⓜ*Cadorna.*

♿ ⑯ **Museo Nazionale della Scienza e Tecnica** *(National Museum of Science and Technology).* This converted cloister is best known for the collection of models based on Leonardo da Vinci's sketches (although these are not captioned in English, the labeling in many other exhibits is bilingual). On the ground level—in the hallway between the courtyards—is a room featuring interactive, moving models of the famous *vita aerea* (aerial screw) and *ala battente* (beating wing), thought to be forerunners of the modern helicopter and airplane, respectively. The museum also houses a varied collection of industrial artifacts including trains, a celebrated Italian-built submarine, and several reconstructed workshops including a watchmaker's, a lute maker's, and an antique pharmacy. Displays also illustrate papermaking and metal founding, which were fundamental to Milan's—and the world's—economic growth. There's a bookshop and a bar. ✉ *Via San Vittore 21, Sant'Ambrogio* ☎*02/48555200* ⊕*www.museoscienza.org* ⊡*€8* ⏱*Tues.–Fri. 9:30–5, weekends 9:30–6:30* Ⓜ*Sant'Ambrogio; Bus 50, 58, 94.*

⑱ **Navigli district.** In medieval times, a network of *navigli,* or canals, crisscrossed the city. Almost all have been covered over, but two—Naviglio Grande and Naviglio Pavese—are still navigable. Once a down-at-the-heels neighborhood, the Navigli district has been gentrified over the last 20 years. Humble workshops have been replaced by boutiques, art galleries, cafés, bars, and restaurants. The Navigli at night is about as close as you will get to more-southern-style Italian street life in Milan. On weekend nights, it is difficult to walk (and impossible to park) among the youthful crowds thronging the narrow streets along the canals. Check out the antiques fair on the last Sunday of the month. ✉*South of Corso Porta Ticinese, Porta Genova* Ⓜ*Porta Genova; Tram 3, 9, 15, 29, 30.*

WHERE TO EAT

★ **$$$$** ✕**Antica Osteria del Ponte.** Rich, imaginative seasonal cuisine composed according to the inspired whims of chef Ezio Santin is reason enough to make your way 20 km (12 mi) southwest of Milan to one of Italy's finest restaurants. The setting is a traditional country inn, where a wood fire warms the rustic interior in winter. The menu changes regularly; in fall, wild porcini mushrooms are among the favored ingredients. Various fixed menus (at €110 and €150) offer broad samplings of antipasti, primi, and meat or fish; some include appropriate wine selections, too. ✉*Piazza G. Negri 9 Cassinetta di Lugagnano* ✚*3 km (2 mi) north of Abbiategrasso* ☎*02/9420034* ⌕*Reservations essential*⊟*AE, DC, MC, V* ⏱*Closed Sun. and Mon., Dec. 25–1st wk of Jan., and Aug.*

★ **$$$$** ✕**Cracco.** Although renowned local chef Carlo Cracco has ended his collaboration with the city's top gourmet food store (Peck, around the corner in Via Spadari), the Milan culinary establishment has not begrudged the two Michelin stars that Cracco still receives. (Though they sniff a bit at the underground premises.) The dining room is done in an elegant style that favors cool earth tones. Specialties include Milanese classics revisited—Cracco's take on saffron risotto and breaded veal cutlet should not be missed. Be sure to save room for the light, steam-cooked tiramisu. If you can't decide, opt for one of the tasting menus. ⊠ *Via Victor Hugo 4, near Duomo* ☏ *02/876774* ⟐ *Reservations essential* ⊟ *AE, DC, MC, V* ⊘ *Closed Sun., 10 days in Jan., and 2 wks in Aug. No lunch Sat. No dinner Sat. in July and Aug.* Ⓜ *Duomo.*

★ $$$$ ✕ **Don Carlos.** One of the few restaurants open after La Scala lets out, Don Carlos, in the Grand Hotel et de Milan, is nothing like its indecisive operatic namesake (whose betrothed was stolen by his father). Flavors are bold, their presentation precise and full of flair: broiled red mullet floats on a lacy layer of crispy leeks. Walls are blanketed with sketches of the theater, and the opera recordings are every bit as well chosen as the wine list, setting the perfect stage for discreet business negotiation or, better yet, refined romance. A gourmet menu costs €75 for six courses (two-person minimum), excluding wine. ⊠ *Grand Hotel et de Milan, Via Manzoni 29, Duomo* ☏ *02/723141* ⟐ *Reservations essential* ⊟ *AE, DC, MC, V* ⊘ *Closed Aug. No lunch* Ⓜ *Montenapoleone; Tram 1, 2.*

$$$$ ✕ **Joia.** At this haute-cuisine vegetarian restaurant near Piazza della Repubblica, delicious dishes are artistically prepared by chef Pietro Leemann. Vegetarians, who often get short shrift in Italy, will marvel at the variety of culinary traditions—Asian and European—and artistry offered here. The ever-changing menu offers dishes in unusual formats: tiny glasses of creamed cabbage with ginger, spheres of crunchy vegetables that roll across the plate. Fish also makes an appearance. Joia's restful dining room has been refurbished, another room added, and its kitchen enlarged. The fixed-price lunch "box" is a good value, but be sure to reserve ahead. Multicourse menus range from €60 to €100, excluding wine. ⊠ *Via Panfilo Castaldi 18, Porta Venezia* ☏ *02/29522124* ⊟ *AE, DC, MC, V* ⊘ *Closed Sun., 3 wks in Aug., and Dec. 24–Jan. 7. No lunch Sat.* Ⓜ *Repubblica; Tram 1, 5, 11, 29, 30.*

$$-$$$$ ✕ **Da Giacomo.** The fashion and publishing crowd, as well as international bankers and businessmen, favor this Tuscan/Ligurian restaurant. The emphasis is on fish; even the warm slice of pizza served while you study the menu has seafood in it. The specialty, *gnocchi Da Giacomo,* has a savory seafood-and-tomato sauce. Service is friendly and efficient; the wine list broad; and the dessert cart, with tarte tatin and Sicilian cassata (a concoction of sponge cake, ricotta, and candied fruit), rich and varied. With its tile floor and bank of fresh seafood, it has a refined neighborhood bistro style. Don't even think of trying for same-day reservations during fashion or furniture weeks. ⊠ *Via P. Sottocorno 6, entrance in Via Cellini, Cinque Giornate* ☏ *02/76023313* ⟐ *Reservations essential* ⊟ *AE, DC, MC, V* ⊘ *Closed Mon., Christmas wk, and last 3 wks of Aug. No lunch Tues.* Ⓜ *Tram 9, 29, 30.*

$$-$$$ ✕ **La Libera.** Although this establishment in the heart of Brera calls itself a *birreria con cucina* (beer cellar with kitchen), locals come here for excellent evening meals in relaxed surroundings. A soft current of jazz and sylvan decor soothe the ripple of conversation. The creative cooking varies with the season, but could include linguine *al pescato* (with a fish

sauce); *fritto di gamberi, zucchine e totanetti* (fried shrimp, zucchini, and baby squid); or *rognone alla senape* (veal kidneys cooked in mustard). ☒ *Via Palermo 21, Brera* ☏ *02/8053603 or 02/86462773* ⊟ *AE, DC, MC, V* ⊘ *No lunch* Ⓜ *Moscova.*

$$–$$$ ✗**Paper Moon.** Hidden behind Via Montenapoleone and thus handy to the restaurant-scarce Quadrilatero, Paper Moon is a cross between neighborhood restaurant and celebrity hangout. Clients include families from this wealthy area, professionals, football players, and television stars. What the menu lacks in originality it makes up for in consistency—reliable pizza and cotoletta. Like any Italian restaurant, it's not child friendly in an American sense—no high chairs or children's menu—but children will find food they like. Open until 12:30 AM. ☒ *Via Bagutta 1, Quadrilatero* ☏ *02/76022297* ⊟ *AE, MC, V* ⊘ *Closed Sun., 2 wks in Aug., and Dec. 25–Jan 7* Ⓜ *San Babila.*

$$–$$$ ✗**Trattoria Montina.** Twin brothers Maurizio and Roberto Montina have **Fodor'sChoice** turned this restaurant into a local favorite. Don't be fooled by the "trat-★ toria" name. The sage-green paneling makes it airy and cozy on a gray Milan day. Chef Roberto creates exquisite modern Italian dishes such as warmed risotto with merlot and taleggio cheese, while Maurizio chats with guests, regulars, and local families. Milan's famous cotoletta is light and tasty. Try fish or the *frittura impazzita,* a wild-and-crazy mix of delicately fried seafood. Unlike many Italian menus, there's a fine selection on the hard-to-choose dessert cart. ☒ *Via Procaccini 54, Procaccini* ☏ *02/3490498* ⊟ *AE, DC, MC, V* ⊘ *Closed Sun., Aug., and Dec. 25–Jan. 7. No lunch Mon.* Ⓜ *Tram 1, 19, 29, 33.*

$–$$ ✗**Al Rifugio Pugliese.** Just outside the center of town, this is a fun place to sample specialties from the Puglia region of southern Italy. These include homemade *orecchiette* (a small, car-shaped pasta) with a variety of sauces. There is a choice of 60 first courses, as well as plenty of vegetable and fish dishes. The lunch buffet is a good deal as are the fixed-price menus of €29 and €39 that can include wine, coffee, and after-dinner drinks. ☒ *Via Costanza 2, corner of Via Boni 16, Fiera* ☏ *02/48000917* ⊟ *AE, DC, MC, V* ⊘ *Closed Sun., Aug. 5–25, and Dec. 25–Jan. 7* Ⓜ *Wagner.*

★ $–$$ ✗**Da Abele.** If you love risotto, then make a beeline for this neighborhood trattoria. The superb risotto dishes change with the season, and there may be just two or three on the menu at any time. It is tempting to try them all. The setting is relaxed, the service informal, the prices strikingly reasonable. Outside the touristy center of town but quite convenient by subway, this trattoria is invariably packed with locals. ☒ *Via Temperanza 5, Loreto* ☏ *02/2613855* ⊟ *AE, DC, MC, V* ⊘ *Closed Mon., Aug., and Dec. 22–Jan. 7. No lunch* Ⓜ *Pasteur.*

$–$$ ✗**La Bruschetta.** This tiny, bustling first-class pizzeria near the Duomo serves specialties from Tuscany and other parts of Italy. The wood oven is in full view, so you can see your pizza cooking in front of you. Aside from the pizza, the menu is essentially Tuscan. Try the seasonal specialities: in summer, the *panzanella,* a salad with toasted bread; and in winter, the *ribollita,* a dense soup of vegetables, cabbage, and bread. The *tagliata,* thin slices of grilled Tuscan beef garnished with rosemary and peppercorns or arugula, is another specialty. Reservations are essential on weekends, when two sittings of diners are squeezed in between the cinema showtimes. ⊠*Piazza Beccaria 12, Duomo* ☎*02/ 8692494* ▭*AE, MC, V* ⊘*Closed Mon., 3 wks in Aug., and late Dec.– early Jan.* Ⓜ*Duomo.*

¢–$$ ✕**Joia Leggero.** In the Porta Ticinese area, and near the Navigli district, Joia Leggero (light) is a lower-price, more-informal initiative of innovative chef Pietro Leemann, the man behind Joia. With a pleasant view of the church of St. Eustorgio and a few tables outside, this airy restaurant serves haute-vegetarian food. "Leggero" does not necessarily refer to the calorie content; the offerings—especially the excellent desserts—are often satisfyingly rich. This is not typical sprouts-and-grains health food. Try the well-priced set meals (vegetarian lunch is €11, €14 with fish), which are attractively presented on Japanese-inspired trays. ⊠*Corso di Porta Ticinese 106* ☎*02/89404134* ▭*AE, MC, V* ⊘*Closed Sun. and 3 wks in Aug. No lunch Mon.*

¢–$ ✕**Pizza Ok.** Pizza is almost the only item on the menu at this popular spot near Corso Buenos Aires in the Porta Venezia area. The pizza is extra thin and very good, and possibilities for toppings seem endless. A good choice for families, this dining experience will be easy on your pocketbook. Pizza Ok has added locations in other areas. ⊠*Via Lambro 15, Porta Venezia* ☎*02/29401272* ▭*No credit cards* ⊘*Closed Aug. and Dec. 24–Jan. 7. No lunch Sun.* Ⓜ*Porta Venezia* ⊠*Via San Siro 9, Corso Vercelli* ☎*02/48017132* ⊘*Closed Aug. and Dec. 24–Jan. 7. No lunch Mon. and Sun.* Ⓜ*Buonarotti* ⊠*Via Cenisio 19, Cimitero Monumentale* ☎*02/33614582* ⊘*Closed Aug. and Dec. 24–Jan. 7. No lunch Sun. and Mon.* Ⓜ*Tram 12, 14.*

¢ ✕**Bar Tempio.** This wine bar, not far from Giardini Pubblici and the shops of the Quadrilatero, was once so unprepossessing that it didn't have a name—but it turned out some of Milan's best panini. It's been renovated and given a name, but the same artist is still making the sandwiches. This is a lunch-only establishment, and you might have to wait your turn, as panini are made to order from a list (not in English, so bring your phrase book). They feature cured ham, *cipolle* (onions), and various cheeses (including easily recognizable Brie). ⊠*Piazza Cavour 5enter from Via Turati, near Quadrilatero* ☎*02/6551946* ▭*No credit cards* ⊘*Closed Sun. No dinner* Ⓜ*Turati; Tram 1, 2.*

¢ ✕**Taverna Morigi.** This dusky, wood-panel wine bar near the stock exchange is the perfect spot to enjoy a glass of wine with cheese and cold cuts. At lunch, pasta dishes and select entrées are available; pasta is the only hot dish served in the evening. Platters of cheese and cold cuts are always available; if you're coming for a meal, a reservation is a good idea. ⊠*Via Morigi 8, Sant'Ambrogio* ☎*02/86450880* ▭*AE, DC, MC, V* ⊘*Closed Sun. and Aug. No lunch Sat.* Ⓜ*Cairoli.*

WHERE TO STAY

$$$$ ▦**Four Seasons.** The Four Seasons has been cited more than once by the Italian press as the country's best city hotel—perhaps because once you're inside, the feeling is anything but urban. Built in the 15th century as a convent, the hotel surrounds a colonnaded cloister, and some

rooms have balconies looking on to a glassed-in courtyard. Everything about the place is standard Four Seasons (high) style. The Theater restaurant has some of Milan's best hotel dining. **Pros:** Beautiful setting that feels like Tuscany rather than central Milan. **Cons:** Fodors.com readers find the rooms a little on the sad side. ⊠ *Via Gesù 6–8, Quadrilatero,* ☎ *02/7708167* 🖷 *02/77085000* ⊕ *www.fourseasons.com* 🛏 *77 rooms, 41 suites* ⚒ *In-room: Ethernet, Wi-Fi. In-hotel: 2 restaurants, room service, bar, gym, laundry service, parking (fee)* ⊟ *AE, DC, MC, V* ⏀⊙ *EP* Ⓜ *Montenapoleone.*

$$$$ 🖥 **Grand Hotel et de Milan.** Only blocks from La Scala, this hotel, which opened in 1863, is sometimes called the Hotel Verdi, because the composer lived here for 27 years. His apartment, complete with his desk, is now the Presidential Suite. It's everything you hope for in a traditional European hotel; dignified but not stuffy, elegant but not ostentatious. Moss-green and persimmon velvet enliven the 19th-century look without sacrificing dignity and luxury. The Don Carlos restaurant is one of Milan's best. **Pros:** Traditional and elegant; great location. **Cons:** Fitness center has natural light, but is not well appointed. ⊠ *Via Manzoni 29, Scala,* ☎ *02/723141* 🖷 *02/86460861* ⊕ *www.grandhoteletdemilan.it* 🛏 *87 rooms, 8 suites* ⚒ *In-room: Wi-Fi. In-hotel: restaurant, room service, bar, gym, laundry service, parking (fee)* ⊟ *AE, DC, MC, V* ⏀⊙ *EP* Ⓜ *Montenapoleone.*

$$$$ 🖥 **Hotel Spadari al Duomo.** That this hotel is owned by an architect's family shows in the details, including architect-designed furniture and a fine collection of contemporary art. The owner's idea of creating a hotel/gallery extends to the guest rooms, where paintings by young Milanese artists are on rotating display. For all the artistic accents, this is still a comfortable, homey hotel, with an inviting frescoed breakfast room and many rooms with private terraces. Personal touches, such as a collection of short stories on the turned-down beds, abound. **Pros:** Feedback on Fodor's.com: "excellent breakfast, perfect location, and, above all, staff that seems to care about your having a wonderful experience." **Cons:** Rooms and hallways may seem small to some. ⊠ *Via Spadari 11, near Duomo,* ☎ *02/72002371* 🖷 *02/861184* ⊕ *www. spadarihotel.com* 🛏 *40 rooms, 3 suites* ⚒ *In-room: Ethernet, Wi-Fi. In-hotel: bar, no-smoking rooms* ⊟ *AE, DC, MC, V* ⏀⊙ *BP* Ⓜ *Duomo.*

★ $$$$ 🖥 **Principe di Savoia.** Milan's grande dame has all the trappings of an exquisite traditional hotel: lavish mirrors, drapes, and carpets, and Milan's largest guest rooms, outfitted with eclectic fin de siècle furnishings. Forty-eight Deluxe Mosaic rooms (named for the glass mosaic panels in their ample bathrooms) are even larger, and the three-bedroom Presidential Suite features its own marble pool. The Winter Garden is an elegant aperitivo spot, and the Acanto restaurant has garden seating. Lighter food is served in the Lobby Lounge. **Pros:** Probably the most serious spa/health club (considered very chic by Milanese) in town. **Cons:** Overblown luxury in a not-very-central or attractive neighborhood; close enough to the train station to attract pickpockets. ⊠ *Piazza della Repubblica 17, Porta Nuova,* ☎ *02/62301* 🖷 *02/653799* ⊕ *www. hotelprincipedisavoia.com* 🛏 *269 rooms, 132 suites* ⚒ *In-room: Wi-*

5

Fi. In-hotel: 2 restaurants, room service, bar, pool, gym, spa, laundry service☐*AE, DC, MC, V*❢⦿❘*EP*Ⓜ*Repubblica.*

$$$–$$$$ ☷**Ariston.** This hotel claims it is designed around "bio-architectural" principles. Breakfast offers a selection of organic foods. There's Internet access for free in the lobby (and for a fee in the rooms), and bicycles are available in summer. The location is close to the lively Porta Ticinese shops and restaurants and the young people's fashion mecca, Via Torino. Although a longish walk from the nearest subway stop, the Duomo, it is well served by tram. **Pros:** Although for a fee, it has its own parking. **Cons:** Rooms are characterless. ✉*Largo Carrobbio 2, Duomo,* ☎*02/72000556* 🖷*02/72000914* ⊕*www.aristonhotel. com* ↩*52 rooms* ⚐*In-room: Wi-Fi. In-hotel: bar, bicycles, laundry service, public Wi-Fi, parking (fee)* ☐*AE, DC, MC, V*❢⦿❘*BP*Ⓜ*Duomo; Tram 2, 14.*

$$$ ☷**Hotel Gran Duca di York.** This small hotel has spare but classically elegant and efficient rooms—four with private terraces. Built around a courtyard, the 1890s building was originally a seminary and still belongs to a religious institution. With an ideal location a few steps west of the Duomo, it offers exceptional value for Milan and is managed by the same family that owns the Spadari. **Pros:** Central; airy; a good value. **Cons:** Rooms are simple. ✉*Via Moneta 1/ a, Duomo,* ☎*02/874863* 🖷*02/8690344* ⊕*www.ducadiyork.com* ↩*33 rooms* ⚐*In-hotel: bar, laundry service, parking (fee)* ☐*AE, MC, V*⊘*Closed Aug.*❢⦿❘*EP*Ⓜ*Cordusio.*

$$–$$$ ☷**Alle Meraviglie.** This deluxe bed-and-breakfast shares a reception and breakfast area with the Antica Locanda dei Mercanti around the corner. But its rooms are bigger—in fact they are big by Milan standards in general. Families should ask for Suite 4, with two rooms connected by a single entrance. Each room is tastefully furnished with individual color schemes and an appealing mix of modern and antique furniture. Although several features make this technically a hotel, it is more like staying in a Milan apartment. Though breakfast is served in the room at street level, the reasonable price (€5) and homey feel make room service the almost universal choice. **Pros:** In a great neighborhood. **Cons:** Some visitors may find it old-fashioned. ✉*Via San Tomaso 8, Duomo,* ☎*02/8051023* ↩*10 rooms* ⚐*In-room: Wi-Fi. In-hotel: bar, public Internet* ☐*MC, V*❢⦿❘*EP*Ⓜ*Cordusio; Tram 1, 12, 20, 27.*

★ **$$–$$$**   ☷**Antica Locanda dei Mercanti.** On a quiet side street off Via Dante, this 14-room hotel is minutes—and light-years—away from Milan's bustling downtown. Rooms are on the second and third floors (four have private terraces), but you check in at ground-floor reception and take breakfast in the dining room at number 8. Reserve early for the terrace rooms. **Pros:** Central and cozy. **Cons:** Rooms are scattered around floors. ✉*Via San Tomaso 6, Duomo,* ☎*02/8054080* 🖷*02/ 8054090* ⊕*www.lalocanda.it* ↩*14 rooms* ⚐*In-room: Wi-Fi. In-hotel: bar* ☐*MC, V*❢⦿❘*EP*Ⓜ*Cordusio; Tram 1, 12, 20, 27.*

$$–$$$ ☷**Antica Locanda Leonardo.** Only a block from the church which houses *The Last Supper* and in one of Milan's most desired and historic neighborhoods with elegant shops and bars, it has been family-run for 100 years. Half the rooms face a courtyard and the others a back garden.

Many have balconies and one ground-floor room has a private garden with table and chairs. The hotel has a relaxed feel and the owners who live in the building are helpful. They have a special relationship with a car service that offers moderate-price airport pickups and tours to nearby factory outlets. **Pros:** Very quiet and homey; breakfast is ample. **Cons:** More like a bed-and-breakfast than a hotel. ⊠ *Corso Magenta 78, Sant'Ambrogio,* ☎ *02/463317* 🖷 *02/48019012* ⊕ *www. anticalocandaleonardo.com* ⇆ *20 rooms* & *In-room: Wi-Fi. In-hotel: bar, laundry service* ⊟ *AE, DC, MC, V* ⊙ *Closed Dec. 31–Jan. 7 and 3 wks in Aug.* ¶⊙¶ *BP* Ⓜ *Sant'Ambrogio.*

$$ ▦ **Hotel Vittoria.** You'll forgive this hotel its baroque decor when you see how it reflects the owners' eager-to-please hospitality. Although out of the central tourist area (on a quiet residential street), the Vittoria is on the bus line from Linate Airport and on other major tram lines. It's about a 20-minute walk from the Duomo, and there's a good selection of restaurants nearby. English-speaking staff (not a given in smaller hotels) and spotless, comfortable rooms make this an attractive haven after a day out. **Pros:** Good value; friendly staff. **Cons:** Out of the city center; rooms can seem overly decorated. ⊠ *Via Pietro Calvi 32, East Central Milan,* ☎ *02/5456520* 🖷 *02/55190246* ⊕ *www.hotelvittoriamilano.it* ⇆ *40 rooms* & *In-room: safe, Ethernet. In-hotel: parking (fee)* ⊟ *AE, DC, MC, V* ¶⊙¶ *EP* Ⓜ *Tram 29, 30.*

$–$$ ▦ **Hotel Casa Mia Milan.** Easy to reach from the central train station (a few blocks away) and easy on the budget, this tiny hotel, up a flight of stairs, is family-run. Rooms are simple and clean with individual (small) baths. Although not in the center of things, it is two blocks from transport center Piazza Repubblica (tram and metro lines), which also hosts the doyenne of Milan's palace hotels, the Principe di Savoia. **Pros:** Clean; good value. **Cons:** Neighborhood is not the nicest in Milan. ⊠ *Viale Vittorio Veneto 30, Piazza Repubblica,* ☎ *02/6575249* ⊕ *www.casamiahotel.it* ⇆ *15 rooms* & *In-hotel: no elevator* ⊟ *MC, V* ¶⊙¶ *BP* Ⓜ *Republica.*

NIGHTLIFE & THE ARTS

THE ARTS

For events likely to be of interest to non-Italian speakers, see *Hello Milano* (⊕ *www.hellomilano.it*), a monthly magazine available at the tourist office in Piazza Duomo, or *The American* (⊕ *www.theamerican mag.com*), which is available at international bookstores and newsstands, and which has a thorough cultural calendar. The tourist office publishes the monthly *Milano Mese,* which also includes some listings in English.

MUSIC

The two halls belonging to the **Conservatorio** (⊠ *Via del Conservatorio 12, Duomo* ☎ *02/7621101* ⊕ *www.consmilano.it* Ⓜ *San Babila*) host some of the leading names in classical music. Series are organized by several organizations, including the venerable chamber music society, the **Società del Quartetto** (⊕ *www.quartettomilano.it*). The modern **Auditorium di Milano** (⊠ *Largo Gustav Mahler [Corso San Gottardo, at*

CLOSE UP

'Appy Hour

The *aperitivo,* or prelunch or predinner drink, is part of life everywhere in Italy, and each town has its own rites and favorite drinks. Milan bar owners came up with something to fit their city's fast pace and work-oriented culture. They enriched the nibbles from olives, nuts, and chips into full finger (and often fork) buffets serving cubes of pizza and cheese, fried vegetables, rice salad, sushi, and even pasta, and they baptized it 'Appy Hour—with the first "h" dropped and the second one pronounced. For a fixed fee per drink (around €8), you can fill yourself up—don't be rude; remember Italian standards are moderate—on hors d'oeuvres and make a meal of it.

There are 'Appy Hours and *aperitivi* for all tastes and in all neighborhoods. Changes happen fast, but these are reliable: The elegant **Hotel Sheraton Diana Majestic** (✉ *Viale Piave 42* ☎ *02/20582081*) attracts a young professional crowd in good weather to

its beautiful garden, which gets yearly thematic transformations. **Arthé** (✉ *Via Pisacane 57* ☎ *02/29528353*) is a chic enoteca with fresh and fried vegetables and pasta. **G Lounge** (✉ *Via Larga 8* ☎ *02/8053042*) has rotating DJs and quality music. The **Capo Verde** (✉ *Via Leoncavallo 16* ☎ *02/26820430*) is in a greenhouse/nursery and is especially popular for after-dinner drinks. In the Brera neighborhood, the highly rated enoteca **'N Ombra de Vin** (✉ *Via S. Marco 2* ☎ *02/6599650*) serves wine by the glass and, in addition to the plates of sausage and cheese nibbles, has light food and not-so-light desserts. Check out the impressive vaulted basement where the bottled wine and spirits are sold. **Peck** (✉ *Via Cesare Cantù 3* ☎ *02/8693017*), the Milan gastronomical shrine near the Duomo, also has a bar that serves up traditional—and excellent—pizza pieces, olives, and toasted nuts in a refined setting.

Via Torricelli], Conchetta ☎*02/83389201 up to 03* ⊕*www.laverdi. org*), known for its excellent acoustics, is home to the **Orchestra Verdi,** founded by Milan-born conductor Richard Chailly. The season, which runs from September to June, includes many top international performers and rotating guest conductors. The **Teatro Dal Verme** (✉ *Via San Giovanni sul Muro 2, Castello* ☎*02/87905201* ⊕*www.dalverme. org* Ⓜ*Cairoli*) stages frequent classical music concerts from October to May.

OPERA

Milan's hallowed **Teatro alla Scala** (✉*Piazza della Scala* ☎*02/72003744* ⊕*www.teatroallascala.org* Ⓜ*Duomo*) has undergone a complete renovation, with everything refreshed, refurbished, or replaced except the building's exterior walls. Special attention was paid to the acoustics, which have always been excellent. The season runs from December 7, the feast day of Milan patron St. Ambrose, through June. Plan well in advance, as tickets sell out quickly. For tickets, visit the **Biglietteria Centrale** (✉*Galleria del Sagrato, Piazza Del Duomo* ⊘*Daily noon–6* Ⓜ*Duomo*), which is in the Duomo subway station. To pick up tickets for performances from two hours prior until 15 minutes after the start of a performance, go to the box office at the theater, which is around the corner in Via Filodrammatici 2. Although you might not get seats for the more-popular operas with big stars, it is worth trying; ballets are easier. The theater is closed from the end of July through August and on national and local holidays.

NIGHTLIFE

BARS

Milan has a bar somewhere to suit any style; those in the better hotels are respectably chic and popular meeting places for Milanese as well as tourists. The bar of the **Sheraton Diana Majestic** (⊠ *Viale Piave 42*

"LET'S GO TO THE COLUMNS"

Andiamo al Le Colonne in Milanese youthspeak means to meet up at the sober Roman columns in front of the Basilica San Lorenzo Maggiore. Attracted by the bars and shops along Corso di Porta Ticinese, the young spill out on the street to chat and drink. Neighbors may complain about the noise and confusion, but students and night hawks find it indispensable for socializing at all hours. It's a street—no closing time.

5

☎*02/20581*), which has a splendid garden, is a prime meeting place for young professionals and the fashion people from the showrooms of the Porta Venezia neighborhood. **Brellin Caffé** (⊠ *Vicolo Lavandai at Alzaia Naviglio Grande* ☎*02/58101351*) in the arty Navigli district has live music and serves late-night snacks. In Brera, check out the **Giamaica** (⊠ *Via Brera 32* ☎*02/876723*), a traditional hangout for students from the nearby Brera art school. On summer nights this neighborhood pulses with life; street vendors and fortune-tellers jostle for space alongside the outdoor tables. For a break from the traditional, check out ultratrendy **SHU** (⊠ *Via Molino delle Armi, Ticinese* ☎*02/58315720*), whose gleaming interior looks like a cross between *Star Trek* and Cocteau's *Beauty and the Beast*. The **Trussardi Bar** (⊠*Piazza della Scala 5, Duomo* ☎*02/80688295*) has an enormous plasma screen that keeps hip barflies entertained with video art. Open throughout the day, it's a great place for coffee. **Blue Note** (⊠ *Via Borsieri 37, Garibaldi* ☎*02/69016888* ⊕*www.bluenotemilano.com*), the first European branch of the famous New York nightclub, features regular performances by some of the most famous names in jazz, as well as blues and rock concerts. There's a popular jazz brunch on Sunday. Monday evenings are reserved for Italian musicians. For an evening of live music—predominantly rock to jazz—head to perennial favorite **Le Scimmie** (⊠ *Via Ascanio Sforza 49, Navigli* ☎*02/89402874* ⊕*www.scimmie.it*). It features international stars, some of whom jet in to play here, while others, including Ronnie Jones, are longtime residents in Milan.

NIGHTCLUBS

La Banque (⊠ *Via Bassano Porrone 6, Scala* ☎*02/86996565* ⊕*www.labanque.it*) is an exclusive and expensive bar, restaurant, and dance club in a converted early-20th-century bank. Enjoy anything from an aperitivo to a night on the town among its marble columns. There's a €15–€20 cover. The hip **Café l'Atlantique** (⊠ *Viale Umbria 42, Porta Romana* ☎*02/55193906* ⊕*www.cafeatlantique.com*) is a popular place for dancing the night away and enjoying a generous buffet brunch on Sunday afternoon. The €20 cost of admission varies by the evening and the show. To its regular discotheque fare, **Tocqueville** (⊠ *Via Alexis de Tocqueville, Corso Como* ☎*02/29002973* ⊙*Closed Mon.*) has added two nights per week of live music, featuring young and emerging talent. The cover at this ever-popular Milan club is €10–€13.

For nightclubs, note that the cover charges can change depending on the day of the week. **Hollywood** (⊠ *Corso Como 15/c, Centro Direzionale* ☎*02/6598996* ⊕*www.discotecahollywood.com*) continues to be one of the most popular places for the sunglasses set. The €16–€20 cover includes a drink. **Magazzini Generali** (⊠ *Via Pietrasanta 14, Porta Vigentina* ☎*02/55211313* ⊕*www.magazzinigenerali.it*), in what was an abandoned warehouse, is a fun, futuristic venue for dancing and concerts. The €20 cover charge includes a drink. Its venerable age notwithstanding, **Plastic** (⊠ *Viale Umbria 120* ☎*02/733996*), closed Monday through Wednesday and some Thursdays, is still considered Milan's most transgressive, avant-garde, and fun club, complete with drag-queen shows. The action starts late, even by Italian standards—don't bother going before midnight. Cover is €15–€20. **Rolling Stone** (⊠ *Corso XXII Marzo 32, Porta Vittoria* ☎*02/733172* ⊕*www. rollingstone.it* ⊙*Closed Mon.–Wed.*) has been Milan's temple of rock since 1982, hosting the best of foreign and local talent. It reopened with a new sound system and renewed commitment to rock and roll in 2007. Check the Web site for the concert schedule. The €14 cover includes a drink.

SPORTS

SOCCER

AC Milan and Inter Milan, two of the oldest and most successful teams in Europe, vie for the heart of soccer-mad Lombardy. For residents, the city is *Milano* but the teams are *Milan,* a vestige of their common founding as the Milan Cricket and Football Club in 1899. When an Italian-led faction broke off in 1908, the new club was dubbed F.C. Internazionale (or "Inter") to distinguish it from the bastion of English exclusivity that would become AC Milan (or simply "Milan"). Since then, the picture has become more clouded: although Milan prides itself as the true team of the city and of its working class, Inter can more persuasively claim Pan-Italian support.

AC Milan and Inter Milan share the use of **San Siro Stadium (Stadio Meazza)** (⊠ *Via Piccolomini*) during their August through May season. With more than 60,000 of the 85,000 seats appropriated by season-ticket holders and another couple thousand allocated to visiting fans, tickets to Sunday games can be difficult to come by. You can purchase advance AC Milan tickets at Cariplo bank branches, including one at Via Verdi 8, or at the club's web site (⊕*www.acmilan.com*). Inter tickets are available at Banca Popolare di Milano branches, including one at Piazza Meda 4, or at the club's web site (⊕*www.inter.it*). To reach

CLOSE UP

Calcio Crazy

For the vast majority of Italians, *il calcio* (soccer) is much more than a national sport—it's a way of life. The general level of passion for the game exceeds that expressed by all but the most die-hard sports fans in the United States. In a country that's fine-tuned to nuance and inclined to see conspiracy around every corner, controversial referee calls can spark arguments that last weeks. In 2006, a game-fixing scandal that involved Turin's Juventus team convulsed Italy. For weeks on the eve of Italy's victory in the 2006 World Cup, the scandal, known as Moggi-gate in honor of a key fixer whose intercepted telephone calls opened it up, obsessed Italy's people and press.

Nowhere is the passion for the game more feverish than in big soccer cities, of which Milan is the prime example. It's home to two of the country's dominant teams: AC Milan (pronounced with the accent on the "MI") and F.C. Internazionale (aka, Inter). With Turin's Juventus ("la Juve"), they form Italy's ruling football triumvirate. At the stadium, even the most innocuous games are events where chants, insults, and creative banners make crowd-watching an appealing sideshow—especially the banners, whose legendary inside jokes are collected in anthologies.

5

San Siro, take subway Line 1 (red) toward Molino Dorino, exit at the Lotto station, and board a bus for the stadium.

If you're a soccer fan but can't get in to see a game, you might settle for a **stadium tour** (☎*02/4042432* ⊕*www.sansirotour.com*), which includes a visit to the Milan-Inter museum. Tours are available every half hour from Gate 21 from 10 AM to 5 PM, except on game Sundays; they cost €12.50. Call for reservations a few days before your visit.

SHOPPING

The heart of Milan's shopping reputation is the **Quadrilatero della moda** district north of the Duomo. Here the world's leading designers compete for shoppers' attention, showing off their ultrastylish clothes in stores that are works of high style themselves. You won't find any bargains, but regardless of whether you're making a purchase, the area is a great place for window-shopping and people-watching. But fashion is not limited to one neighborhood, and there is a huge and exciting selection of clothing that is affordable, well made, and often more interesting than what is offered by the international luxury brands with shops in the Quadrilatero.

Wander around the **Brera** to find smaller shops with some appealing offerings from lesser-known names that cater to the well-schooled taste of this upscale neighborhood. The densest concentration is along Via Brera, Via Solferino, and Corso Garibaldi. For inexpensive and trendy clothes—for the under-25 set—stroll **Via Torino,** which begins in Piazza Duomo. Stay away on Saturday afternoon if you don't like crowds. Milan has several shopping streets that serve nearby residential concentrations. In the Porta Venezia area, visit **Corso Buenos Aires,** which

Continued on page 396

THE FASHIONISTA'S MILAN

Opera buffs and lovers of Leonardo's *Last Supper,* skip ahead to the next section. No one else should be dismayed to learn that clothing is Milan's greatest cultural achievement. The city is one of the fashion capitals of the world and home base for practically every top Italian designer. The same way art aficionados walk the streets of Florence in a state of bliss, the style-conscious come here to be enraptured.

It all happens in the *quadrilatero della moda,* Milan's toniest shopping district, located just north of the Duomo. Along the cobblestone streets, Armani, Prada, and their fellow *stilisti* sell the latest designs from flagship stores that are as much museums of chic as retail establishments. Any purchase here qualifies as a splurge, but you can have fun without spending a euro—just browse, window-

FLORENCE HAS THE *DAVID.*

ROME HAS THE PANTHEON.

MILAN HAS THE CLOTHES.

shop, and people-watch. Not into fashion? Think of the experience as art, design, and theater all rolled into one. If you wouldn't visit Florence without seeing the Uffizi, you shouldn't visit Milan without seeing the quadrilatero.

On these pages we give a selective, street-by-street list of stores in the area. Hours are from around 10 in the morning until 7 at night, Monday through Saturday.

VIA DELLA SPIGA
(east to west)

Dolce & Gabbana
(No. 2)
☎ 02/795747
www.dolcegabbana.it
women's accessories

Gio Moretti (No. 4)
☎ 02/76003186
women's and men's
clothes: many labels,
as well as books,
CDs, flowers, and an
art gallery

Bulgari Italia (No. 6)
☎ 02/777001
www.bulgari.com
jewelry, fragrances,
accessories

Malo (No. 7)
☎ 02/76016109
www.malo.it
everything cashmere

cross Via Sant'Andrea

Sergio Rossi (No. 15)
☎ 02/76002663
www.sergiorossi.com
women's shoes

Fay (No. 15)
☎ 02/76017597
www.fay.it
women's and men's
clothes, accessories: a
flagship store, designed
by Philip Johnson

Prada (No. 18)
☎ 02/76394336
www.prada.com
accessories

Giorgio Armani (No. 19)
☎ 02/783511
www.giorgioarmani.com
accessories

Tod's (No. 22)
☎ 02/76002423
www.tods.com
shoes and handbags:
the Tod's flagship store

Dolce & Gabbana (No. 26)
☎ 02 76001155
www.dolcegabbana.it
women's clothes, in a
baroque setting

✔ **Just Cavalli** (No. 30)
☎ 02/76390893
www.robertocavalli.net
women's and men's
clothes, plus a café
serving big salads
and carpaccio. It's
the offspring of the
Just Cavalli Café
in Parco Sempione,
one of the hottest
places in town for

drinks (with or without
dinner).

Moschino (No. 30)
☎ 02/76004320
www.moschino.it
women's, men's, and
children's clothes: Chic
and Cheap, so they say

Roberto Cavalli
(No. 42)
☎ 02/76020900
www.robertocavalli.net
women's and men's
clothes, accessories:
3,200 square feet of
Roberto Cavalli

I Pinco Pallino (No.
42) ☎ 02/781931
www.ipincopallino.it
extravagant children's
clothing

Marni (No. 50)
☎ 02/76317327
www.marni.com
women's clothes

VIA MONTENAPOLEONE
(east to west)

Fratelli Rossetti
(No. 1)
☎ 02/76021650
www.rossetti.it
shoes

Louis Vuitton (No. 2)
☎ 02/7771711
www.vuitton.com
leather goods, accessories, women's clothes

Armani Collezioni
(No. 2)
☎ 02/76390068
www.giorgioarmani.com
women's and men's clothes: the "white label"

Etro (No. 5)
☎ 02/76005049
www.etro.it
women's and men's clothes, leather goods, accessories

Agnona (No. 21)
☎ 02/76316530
www.agnona.com
women's clothes: Ermenegildo excellence for women

Bottega Veneta (No. 5)
☎ 02/76024495
www.bottegaveneta.com
leather goods: signature woven-leather bags

Gucci (No. 5/7)
☎ 02/771271
www.gucci.com
women's and men's clothes

Prada (No. 6)
☎ 02/76020273
www.prada.com
men's clothes

Prada (No. 8)
☎ 02/7771771
www.prada.com
women's clothes and accessories

Ermenegildo Zegna
(No. 27A)
☎ 02/76006437
www.zegna.com.
men's clothes, in the finest fabrics

cross Via Sant'Andrea

Armani Junior (in galleria) (No. 10)
☎ 02/783196
www.giorgioarmani.com
children's clothes: for the under-14 fashionista

Versace in Via Montenapoleone

Versace (No. 11)
☎ 02/76008528
www.versace.com
everything Versace, except Versus and children's clothes

FASHION SHOPPING, ACCESSORIZED

Milan's most ambitious shops don't just want to clothe you— they want to trim your hair, clean your pores, and put a cocktail in your hand. Some "stores with more" in and around the quadrilatero are indicated by a ✔.

Corneliani (No. 12)
☎ 02/777361
www.corneliani.com
men's clothes: bespoke tailoring excellence

Aspesi (No. 13)
☎ 02/76022478
www.aspesi.it
low-key local design genius

Lorenzi (No. 9)
☎ 02/76003390
unique Milan—cutlery, razors, gifts

REFUELING

If you want refreshments and aren't charmed by the quadrilatero's in-store cafés, try **Cova** (Via Montenapoleone 8, ☎ 02/76000578) or **Sant'Ambroeus** (Corso Matteotti 7, ☎ 02/76000540). Both serve coffee, tea, aperitifs, sandwiches, and snacks in an ambience of starched tablecloths and chandeliers.

Cova's courtyard café

When the hurly-burly's done, head for the **Bulgari Hotel** (Via Fratelli Gabba 7b, ☎ 02/8058051), west of Via Manzoni, for a quiet (if pricey) drink, In summer, the bar extends into a beautiful, mature garden over an acre in size.

Valentino
corner Via Santo Spirito
☎ 02/76020285
www.valentino.it
women's clothes: elegant designs for special occasions

Loro Piana (No. 27c)
☎ 02/7772901
www.loropiana.it
women's and men's clothes, accessories: cashmere everything

VIA SAN PIETRO ALL'ORTO
(east to west)

Pomellato (No. 17)
☎ 02/76006086
www.pomellato.it
classic Milan—style jewelry

Belfe-Postcard
(No. 7)
☎ 02/781023
www.belfe.it
chic sport and skiwear

Jimmy Choo (No. 17)
☎ 02/45481770
www.jimmychoo.com
women's and men's shoes

CORSO VENEZIA
(south to north)

Prada Linea Rossa
(No. 3)
☎ 02/76001426
www.prada.com
Prada's sports line for men and women

D&G (No. 7)
☎ 02/76004095
www.dolcegabbana.it
swimwear, underwear, accessories: Dolce & Gabbana's younger line

✔ **Dolce & Gabbana**
(No. 15)
☎ 02/76028485
www.dolcegabbana.it
Men's clothes, sold in a four-story, early 19th-century patrician home. Added features are a barbershop (☎ 02/ 76408881), a beauty parlor (☎ 02/ 76408888), and the Martini Bar, which also serves light lunches.

VIA VERRI
(south to north)

cross Via Bigli

Etro Profumi
corner Via Bigli
☎ 02/76005450
www.etro.it
fragrances

D&G in Via della Spiga

VIA SANT'ANDREA
(south to north)

✔ **Trussardi** (No. 5)
☎ 02/76020380
www.trussardi.com
Women's and men's clothes. The nearby flagship store (Piazza della Scala 5) includes the Trussardi Marino alla Scala Café (☎ 02/80688242), a fashion-forward bar done in stone, steel, slate, and glass. For a more substantial lunch, and views of Teatro alla Scala, head upstairs to the Marino alla Scala Ristorante (☎ 02/80688201), which serves creative Mediterranean cuisine.

Banner (No. 8/A)
☎ 02/76004609
women's and men's clothes: a multibrand boutique

Giorgio Armani
(No. 9)
☎ 02/76003234
www.giorgioarmani. com
women's and men's clothes: the "black label"

Moschino (No. 12)
☎ 02/76000832
www.moschino.it
women's clothes: world-renowned window displays

BARGAIN-HUNTING AT THE OUTLETS

Milan may be Italy's richest city, but that doesn't mean all its well-dressed residents can afford to shop at the boutiques of the quadrilatero. Many pick up their designer clothes at outlet stores, where prices can be reduced by 50 percent or more.

Salvagente (Via Bronzetti 16, ☎ 02/76110328, www.salvagentemilano.it) is the top outlet for designer apparel and accessories from both large are small houses. There's a small men's department. To get there, take the 60 bus, which runs from the Duomo to the Stazione Centrale, to the intersection of Bronzetti and Archimede. Look for the green iron gate with the bronze sign, between the hairdressers and an apartment building. No credit cards.

DMagazine Outlet (Via Montenapoleone 26, ☎ 02/76006027, www.dmagazine.it) has bargains in the

✔ **Gianfranco Ferré**
(No. 15)
☎ 02/794864
www.gianfrancoferre.com
Everything Ferré, plus a spa providing facials, Jacuzzis, steam baths, and mud treatments. Reservations are essential (☎ 02/76017526), preferably a week in advance.

Miu Miu (No. 21)
☎ 02/76001426
www.prada.com
Prada's younger line

VIA MANZONI
(south to north)

Valextra (No. 3)
☎ 02/99786000
www.valextra.it
glamorous bags and luggage

Armani in Via Manzoni

✔ **Armani Megastore**
(No. 31)
☎ 02/72318600
www.giorgioarmani.com
The quadrilatero's most conspicuous shopping complex. Along with many Armani fashions, you'll find a florist, a bookstore, a chocolate shop (offering Armani pralines), the Armani Caffè, and Nobu (of the upscale Japanese restaurant chain). The Armani Casa furniture collection is next door at number 37.

CORSO COMO
✔ **10 Corso Como**
☎ 02/29000727
www.10corsocomo.com
Outside the quadrilatero, but it's a must see for fashion addicts. The bazaar-like 13,000-square-foot complex includes women's and men's boutiques, a bar and restaurant, a bookstore, a record shop, and an art gallery specializing in photography. You can even spend the night (if you can manage to get a reservation) at Milan's most exclusive B&B, Three Rooms (P 02/626163). The furnishings are a modern design-lover's dream.

Prada store in the Galleria

GALLERIA VITTORIO EMANUELE
(not technically part of the quadrilatero, but nearby)

✔ **Gucci**
☎ 02/8597991
www.gucci.com

Gucci accessories, plus the world's first Gucci café. Sit outside behind the elegant boxwood hedge and watch the world go by.

Prada (No. 63-65)
☎ 02/876979
www.prada.com
the original store:

look for the murals downstairs.

Louis Vuitton
☎ 02/72147011
www.vuitton.com
accessories, women's and men's shoes, watches

Tod's
☎ 02/877997
www.tods.com
women's and men's shoes, leather goods, accessories

Borsalino (No. 92
☎ 02/804337
www.borsalino.com
hats

Galleria Vittorio Emanuele

midst of the quadrilatero. Names on sale include Armani, Cavalli, Gucci, and Prada.

DT-Intrend (Galleria San Carlo 6, ☎ 02/76000829) sells last year's Max Mara, Max & Co, Sportmax, Marella, Penny Black, and Marina Rinaldi. It's just 300 meters from the Max Mara store located on Corso Vittorio Emanuele at the corner of Galleria de Cristoforis.

At the **10 CorsoComo** outlet (Via Tazzoli 3, ☎ 02/29015130, www.10corsocomo.com) you can find clothes, shoes, bags, and accessories.

Fans of **Marni** who have a little time on their hands will want to check out the outlet (Via Tajani 1, ☎ 02/70009735 or 02/71040332, www.marni.com). Take the 61 bus to the terminus at Largo Murani, from which it's about 200 meters on foot.

Giorgio Armani has an outlet, but it's way out of town—off the A3, most of the way to Como. The address is Strada Provinciale per Bregnano 13, in the town of Vertemate (☎ 031 887373, www.giorgioarmani.com).

runs northeast from the Giardini Pubblici. The wide and busy street is lined with affordable shops. It has the highest concentration of clothing stores in Europe, so be prepared to give up halfway. Avoid Saturday after 3 PM, when it seems the entire city is here looking for bargains. Near the Corso Magenta area, walk a few blocks beyond *The Last Supper* to **Corso Vercelli,** where you will find everything from a branch of the Coin department store to the quintessentially Milanese **Gemelli** (⊠ *Corso Vercelli 16* ☎ *02/48004689* ⊕ *www.gemelli.it*).

NEED A BREAK?

Pasticceria Biffi (⊠ *Corso Magenta 87* ☎ *02/48006702*) is a Milan institution and the official pastry shop of this traditionally wealthy neighborhood. Have a coffee or a rich hot chocolate in its paneled room before facing the crowds in Corso Vercelli.

MARKETS

Weekly open markets selling fruits and vegetables—and a great deal more—are still a regular sight in Milan. Many also sell clothing and shoes. Bargains in designer apparel can be found at the huge **Mercato Papiniano** (⊠ *Porta Genova*) on Saturday and Tuesday from about 9 to 1. The stalls to look for are at the Piazza Sant'Agostino end of the market. It's very crowded and demanding—watch out for pickpockets. Monday- and Thursday-morning markets in **Mercato di Via S. Marco** (⊠ *Brera*) cater to the wealthy residents of this central neighborhood. In addition to food stands where you can get cheese, roast chicken, and dried beans and fruits, there are several clothing and shoe stalls that are important stops for some of Milan's most elegant women. Check out the knitwear at Valentino, about midway down on the street side. Muscle in on the students from the prestigious high school nearby who rush here for the french fries and potato croquettes at the chicken stand at the Via Montebello end.

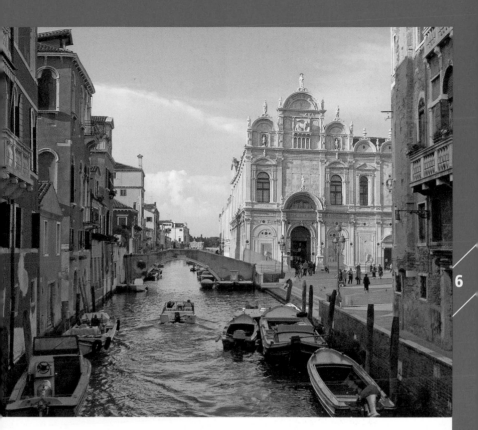

Venice

WORD OF MOUTH

"There's no way to adequately describe the uniqueness, the beauty, and the charm that is Venice. It's like the Grand Canyon. It doesn't matter how many pictures you've seen, until you've come face to face with her, you can't begin to imagine her splendor."

—dcd

WELCOME TO VENICE

TOP REASONS TO GO

★ **Basilica di San Marco:** Whether its opulence seduces you or overwhelms you, it's a sight to be seen.

★ **Gallerie dell'Accademia:** It only makes sense that you find the world's best collection of Venetian paintings here.

★ **Santa Maria Gloriosa dei Frari:** Of Venice's many gorgeous churches, this one competes with San Marco for top billing.

★ **Cruising the Grand Canal:** Whether seen by gondola or by water bus, Venice's Main Street is something from another world.

★ **Snacking at a bacaro:** The best way to sample genuine Venetian cuisine is to head for one of the city's classic wine bars.

1 **The Grand Canal.** Venice's major thoroughfare is lined with grand palazzos that once housed the city's richest families.

2 **San Marco.** In the city's center, this sestiere is one of Italy's most expensive neighborhoods. Its streets are lined with fashion boutiques, art galleries, and grand hotels. Piazza San Marco, called by Napoléon "the world's most beautiful drawing room," is the heart of Venice and the location of its two most distinctive sights, the **Basilica di San Marco and the Palazzo Ducale.**

3 **Dorsoduro.** This elegant residential area is home to the **Gallerie dell'Accademia** and the **Peggy Guggenheim Collection.** The Zattere promenade is one of the best spots to stroll with a gelato or linger at an outdoor café.

4 **Santa Croce and San Polo.** These neighboring sestieri are largely commercial districts, with many shops, several major sights, and the Rialto fish and produce markets.

5 **Castello.** Along with Cannaregio, this area is home to most of the locals. It's the sestiere that's least influenced by Venice's tourist culture—except when the Biennale art festival is on.

Bridge to Mainland

Stazione
Ferrovia
Santa Luca

Canal Della Giudecca

6 **Cannaregio.** Short on architectural splendor, this sestiere provides some of the prettiest canal-side walks in town. **The Fondamenta della Misericordia** is a nightlife center, and the **Jewish Ghetto** has a fascinating history and tradition all its own.

GETTING ORIENTED

Seen from the window of an airplane, central Venice looks like a fish laid out on a blue platter. The train station at the western end is the fish's eye, and the Castello *sestiere* (neighborhood) is the tail. In all, the "fish" consists of six sestieri—Cannaregio, Santa Croce, San Polo, Dorsoduro, San Marco, and Castello. More sedate outer islands swim around them—San Giorgio Maggiore and the Giudecca just to the south, beyond them the Lido, and to the east Murano, Burano, and Torcello.

6

6 CANNAREGIO

Fond d Misericordia

THE JEWISH GHETTO

Grande

Canal

Canal Grande

Ca' d'Oro

SANTA CROCE

4

SAN POLO

Santa Maria
Gloriosa dei Frari

Basilica di
San Marco

5

2

SAN MARCO

Piazza
San Marco

Palazzo Ducale

CASTELLO

1

Canal Grande

Gallerie dell'
Accademia

Peggy
Guggenheim
Collection

Santa Maria
della Salute

3 DORSODURO

*Zatterre
Promenade*

SAN GIORGIO MAGGIORE

LA GIUDECCA

0   1/4 mi

0   1/4 km

VENICE PLANNER

Festivals to Build a Trip Around

Venice's most famous festival is **Carnevale**, drawing revelers from all over the world. For 10 days leading up to Ash Wednesday, it takes over the city—think Mardi Gras meets Casanova.

The prestigious **Biennale** is a century-old international art festival held in late summer and early fall of odd-number years. It's spawned several other festivals, including the **Biennale Danza, Biennale Musica,** and, most famously, **Biennale Cinema**, also known as the Venice Film Festival, held every year at the end of August.

The **Festa Redentore** (Feast of the Redeemer), on the third Sunday in July, is the biggest celebration of the year among locals, who float out in boats on Bacino San Marco and watch midnight fireworks displays.

There are three noteworthy annual contests of Venetian-style rowing: the **Regata delle Bafane**, on January 6; **Vogalonga** (long row), on a Sunday in May; and **Regata Storica**, on the first Sunday in September.

Making the Most of Your Time

A great introduction to Venice is a ride on *vaporetto* (water bus) Line 1 from the train station all the way down the Grand Canal. If you've just arrived and have luggage in tow, you'll need to weigh the merits of taking this trip right away versus getting settled at your hotel first. (Crucial factors: your mood, the bulk of your bags, and your hotel's location.)

Seeing Piazza San Marco and the sights bordering it can fill a day, but if you're going to be around awhile, consider holding off your visit here—the crowds can be overwhelming, especially when you're fresh off the boat. Instead, spend your first morning at Santa Maria Gloriosa dei Frari and the Scuola Grande di San Rocco, then wander through the Dorsoduro sestiere, choosing between visits to Ca' Rezzonico, the Gallerie dell'Accademia, the Peggy Guggenheim Collection, and Santa Maria della Salute—all A-list attractions. End the afternoon with a gelato-fueled stroll along the Zattere boardwalk. Then tackle San Marco on Day 2.

If you have more time, make these sights your priorities: the Rialto fish and produce markets; Ca' d'Oro and the Jewish Ghetto in Cannaregio; Santa Maria dei Miracoli and Santi Giovanni e Paolo in Castello; and, across the water from Piazza San Marco, San Giorgio Maggiore. (In Venice, there's a spectacular church for every day of the week, and then some.) A day on the outer islands of Murano, Burano, and Torcello is good for a change of pace.

Tourist Offices

The multilingual staff of the **Venice tourism office** (☎041/5298711 ⊕ www.turismovenezia.it) can help you out with directions and up-to-the-minute information about events in the city and sight closures. There are office branches at Marco Polo Airport; the train station; Procurate Nuove, near Museo Correr on Piazza San Marco; Garage Comunale, on Piazzale Roma; the Venice Pavilion, near Ghardini Reali in San Marco; and Santa Maria Elisabetta 6/a, on the Lido. The train-station branch is open daily 8–6:30; other branches generally open at 9:30.

Sight Passes & Discount Cards

Sixteen of Venice's most significant churches (noted throughout this chapter) are part of an umbrella group known as the **Chorus Foundation** (☎041/2750462 ⊕ www.chorusvenezia.org), which coordinates their administration, including hours and admission fees. Churches in the group are open to visitors all day except Sunday morning, and usually someone there can provide information and a free leaflet in English. Single church entry costs €3, or you can visit them all with a €9 Chorus pass. Note that the Baslica di San Marco is not part of the Chorus group.

Eleven museums make up Venice's **Musei Civici** (☎041/2715911 ⊕ www.museicivicineziani.it). A museum pass costing €18 and valid for six months lets you make one visit to each museum. A Museum Card, good only at the Piazza San Marco museums —Palazzo Ducale, Museo Correr, Museo Archeologico, and Biblioteca Nazionale Marciana—costs €12.

The **VENICEcard** (☎041/2424 ⊕ www.venicecard.it) offers discounts on a variety of services throughout the city. It is available in two versions—blue or orange. The first includes reductions on public transport fares and discounts at some shops, restaurants, and hotels. In addition to these discounts, the orange card provides free entrance to museums and the Chorus churches. The passes are valid for durations of 12 hours, 48 hours, or 7 days, with blue costing €18.50, €34, or €55, and orange €30, €55, or €81. Cards can be purchased online, at the welcome desks of VeneziaSi at the airport, Tronchetto parking garage, the train station, and at the ACTV/Vela ticket office at Piazzale Roma. Although the cards are convenient, you'll have to do some calculating to see if they're really a money saver for you.

Venetian Vocabulary

Venetians use their own terms to describe their unique city. In fact, they have their own dialect; if you have an ear for Italian, you'll notice a distinct difference in the language. Here are some key words to know:

Sestiere: A neighborhood in central Venice. (There are six of them.)

Rio: A small canal.

Riva: A street running along a canal.

Fondamenta: Another name for a riva.

Calle: A street not running along a canal.

Campo: A square—what elsewhere in Italy would be called a piazza. (The only piazza in Venice is Piazza San Marco.)

Bacaro: A wine bar.

Ombra: A glass of wine served at a bacaro.

Cicchetto (pronounced "chick-ay-toh"): A snack served at a bacaro—roughly the Venetian equivalent of tapas.

GETTING HERE & AROUND

Getting Here by Car

Venice is on the east–west A4 autostrada, which connects with Padua, Verona, Brescia, Milan, and Turin. If you bring a car to Venice, you will have to pay for a garage or parking space.

A warning about parking: don't be waylaid by illegal touts, often wearing fake uniforms, who may try to flag you down and offer to arrange parking and hotels; drive on to one of the parking garages. Parking at **Autorimessa Comunale** (☎ *041/2727211* ⊕ *www.asmvenezia.it*) costs €21 for 24 hours. The private **Garage San Marco** (☎ *041/5232213* ⊕ *www.garagesanmarco.it*) costs €20 for up to 12 hours and €26 for 12–24 hours. You can reserve a space in advance at either of these garages; you'll come upon both immediately after crossing the bridge from the mainland. Another alternative is **Tronchetto** (☎ *041/5207555*) parking (€20 for 1–24 hours); watch for signs for it coming over the bridge—you'll have to turn right before you get to Piazzale Roma. Many hotels have negotiated guest discounts with San Marco or Tronchetto garages; get a voucher when you check in at your hotel and present it when you pay the garage.

Getting Here by Air

Venice's **Aeroporto Marco Polo** (☎ *041/2609260* ⊕ *www.veniceairport.it*) is 10 km (6 mi) north of the city on the mainland. It's served by domestic and international flights, including connections from 21 European cities, plus direct flights from New York's JFK.

From Marco Polo terminal it's a €10 taxi ride or a 10-minute walk to the dock where public and private boats depart for Venice's historic center. **Alilaguna** (☎ *041/2401701* ⊕ *www.alilaguna.it*) has regular ferry service from pre-dawn until nearly midnight. The charge is €12 per person, including bags, and it takes about an hour to reach the landing near Piazza San Marco, with a stop at the Lido on the way. A *motoscafo* (water taxi) carries up to four people and four bags to the city center in a sleek, modern powerboat. The base cost is €90, and the trip takes about 25 minutes. Each additional person, bag, and stop costs extra, so it's essential to agree on a fare before boarding.

Blue buses run by **ATVO** (☎ *0421/383672* ⊕ *www.atvo.it*) make a less scenic but quicker (20-minute) and cheaper (€3) nonstop trip from the airport to Piazzale Roma, from where you can get a vaporetto to the landing nearest your hotel. Tickets are sold at the airport ticket booth (open daily 9 to 7:30), and on the bus when the booth is closed. A land taxi to Piazzale Roma costs about €40.

Getting Here by Train

Venice has rail connections with every major city in Italy and Europe. Note that Venice's station is **Stazione Ferroviaria Santa Lucia,** not to be confused with Stazione Ferroviaria Venezia-Mestre, which is on the mainland 12 km (7 mi) outside of town. Some Continental trains stop only at the Mestre station; in such cases you can catch the next Venice-bound train. Be aware that if you change from a regional train to an Intercity or Eurostar, you'll need to upgrade with a *supplemento* (extra charge) or be liable for a hefty fine. You're also subject to a fine if before boarding you don't validate your ticket in one of the yellow machines found on or near platforms.

Getting Around by Vaporetto

Venice's primary means of public transportation is by vaporetto (water bus). **ACTV** (☎ 041/2424 ⊕ www.hello venezia.it) operates vaporetti on several routes through and around the city. Beginning at 11 PM there is limited service through the night. Landing stages are clearly marked with name and line number, but check before boarding to make sure the boat is going in your direction. Line 1 is the Grand Canal local, calling at every stop and continuing via San Marco to the Lido. The trip takes about 35 minutes from Ferrovia to Vallaresso, San Marco.

A vaporetto ticket for all lines costs €6 one-way (children under four ride free). Another option is a Travel Card: €15 buys 24 hours and €30 buys 72 hours of unlimited travel. For travelers between ages 14 and 29, the 72-hour pass is €18 with the Rolling Venice card. Ask for the card (€4) before buying your tickets. A shuttle ticket allows you to cross a canal, one stop only, for €2.

Line information is posted at each landing, and complete timetables for all lines are available for €0.60 at ACTV/ Vela ticket booths, located at most major stops. Buy your ticket before getting on the boat and validate it in the yellow time-stamp machine. Tickets are also sold on the boat; you must ask to buy one immediately upon boarding, which can be a hassle. When inspectors come aboard, ticketless riders are fined, as are those who haven't validated their tickets. The fine is €35, and pleading ignorance will not spare you. The law says you must also buy tickets for bags more than 28 inches long (there's no charge for your bag if you have a Travel Card), but this is generally enforced only for very bulky bags.

Getting Around by Water Taxi

A *motoscafo* (water taxi) isn't cheap; you'll spend about €60 for a short trip in town, €75 to the Lido, and €90 per hour to visit the outer islands. The fare system is convoluted, with luggage handling, waiting time, early or late hours, and even ordering a taxi from your hotel adding expense. Always agree on the price before departing.

Getting Around by Gondola

As your gondola glides away from the fondamenta, a transformation takes place. To some it feels like a Disney ride, but if you insist that your gondolier take you through the tiny side canals, you'll get an intimate glimpse of the city that can't be experienced any other way.

San Marco is loaded with gondola stations, but to get off the circuit, try the San Tomà or Santa Sofia (near Ca' d'Oro) stations. The price of a 40-minute ride is supposed to be fixed at €80 for up to six passengers, rising to €100 between 7:30 PM and 8 AM, but these are minimums and you may have difficulty finding a gondolier who will work for that unless the city is empty. Come to terms on cost and duration before you start, and make it clear that you want to see more than just the Grand Canal.

Getting Around by Traghetto

Many tourists are unaware of the two-man gondola ferries that cross the Grand Canal at numerous strategic points. At €0.50, they're the cheapest and shortest gondola ride in Venice, and they can save a lot of walking. Look for TRAGHETTO signs and hand your fare to the gondolier when you board.

EATING & DRINKING WELL IN VENICE

The catchword in Venice, at both fancy restaurants and holes-in-the-wall, is fish, often at its tastiest when it looks like nothing you've seen before. How do you learn firsthand about the catch of the day? An early-morning visit to the Rialto's *pescheria* (fish market) is more instructive than any book.

Dining options in Venice range from the ultrahigh end, where jackets and ties are required, to the supercasual, where the clientele (almost all of them tourists) won't notice if you're wearing shorts. Some of Venice's swankiest restaurants—the ones that usually have only male waiters wearing white jackets and bow ties—trade on long-standing reputations and might seem a little stuffy and faded. The food at such places tends toward interpretations of international cuisine and, though often expertly prepared, can seem as old-fashioned as the waiters who serve it. On the other hand, mid-range restaurants are often more willing to break from tradition, incorporating ingredients such as ginger and wasabi in their creations.

GOING BACARO

You can sample wines of the region in *bacari* (wine bars), which are a great Venetian tradition. For centuries, locals have gathered at these neighborhood spots to chat and have a glass of wine (known as an *ombra* in Venetian dialect) accompanied by *cicchetti* (snacks), often substantial enough for a light meal. *Crostini*, toast topped with a fish, meat, or vegetable spread, is a popular cicchetti, as are small sandwiches, crescents of melon wrapped with prosciutto, marinated seafood salads, and toothpick-speared items like roasted peppers, marinated artichokes, deep-fried mozzarella balls, and meatballs.

SEAFOOD

Venetian cuisine is based on seafood—*granseola* (crab), *moeche* (soft-shell crab), and *seppie* or *seppioline* (cuttlefish) are all prominently featured—and trademark dishes include *sarde in saor* (fried sardines with olive oil, onions, pine nuts, and raisins), photo right, and *baccalà mantecato* (cod creamed with milk and olive oil).

When served whole, fish is usually priced by the *etto* (100 grams, about ¼ pound) and can be quite expensive.

RISOTTO, PASTA, POLENTA

As a first course, Venetians favor risotto, the creamy rice dish, prepared with vegetables or shellfish. Pasta, too, is paired with seafood sauces: *pasticcio di pesce* is pasta baked with fish, usually baccalà, and *bigoli* is a strictly local pasta shaped like short, thick spaghetti, usually served with *nero di seppia* (squid-ink sauce).

A classic first course is pasta e fagioli (thick bean soup with pasta). Polenta (creamy cornmeal) is another pillar of regional cooking; it's often served with *fegato alla veneziana* (calves' liver and onions).

VEGETABLES

The salty soil of the larger islands of the lagoon is legendary for the fine vegetables that grow from it. Now just a few

stalls at the Rialto Market sell locally grown crops, but produce from the surrounding regions is of high quality. Spring treats are the fat white asparagus from Bassano and artichokes, usually sautéed with olive oil, parsley, and garlic. From December to March, red radicchio from Treviso is grilled or used as a base for risotto. Fall brings small, brown wild mushrooms called chiodini and zucca barucca, a bumpy squash often baked, used in soups, or stuffed into ravioli.

TIRAMISU

Tiramisu, pictured below, is the most popular dessert in town, but no matter how many times you try it, it's always a bit different, as each restaurant follows its own tiramisu creed. Just to mention a few of the possible variations: sweet liqueur can be added to the coffee, whipped cream or crème anglaise can be stirred into the basic mascarpone and egg-yolk filling, or bits of bitter chocolate can be scattered on top instead of cocoa.

WINES

Local wines are the dry white tocai and pinot grigio from the Friuli region and the bubbly white prosecco, a naturally fermented sparkling wine that is a shade less dry. Popular red wines include merlot, cabernet, raboso, and refosco.

Updated by
Pamela Santini

IT'S CALLED LA SERENISSIMA, "THE MOST SERENE," a reference to the majesty, wisdom, and monstrous power of this city that was for centuries the unrivaled mistress of trade between Europe and the Orient and the bulwark of Christendom against the tides of Turkish expansion. "Most serene" could also describe the way lovers of this miraculous city feel when they see it, imperturbably floating on its calm blue lagoon.

Built entirely on water by men who defied the sea, Venice is unlike any other town. No matter how many times you've seen it in movies or on TV, the real thing is more dreamlike than you could ever imagine. Its landmarks, the Basilica di San Marco and the Palazzo Ducale, seem hardly Italian: delightfully idiosyncratic, they are exotic mixes of Byzantine, Gothic, and Renaissance styles. Shimmering sunlight and silvery mist soften every perspective here, and you understand how the city became renowned in the Renaissance for its artists' rendering of color. It's full of secrets, inexpressibly romantic, and at times given over entirely to pleasure.

You'll see Venetians going about their daily affairs in *vaporetti* (water buses), aboard the *traghetti* (traditional gondola ferries) that carry them across the Grand Canal, in the *campi* (squares), and along the *calli* (narrow streets). They are nothing if not skilled—and remarkably tolerant—in dealing with the veritable armies of tourists from all over the world who fill the city's streets for most of the year.

PIAZZA SAN MARCO

One of the world's most evocative squares, Piazza San Marco (St. Mark's Square) is the heart of Venice, a vast open space bordered by an orderly procession of arcades marching toward the fairy-tale cupolas and marble lacework of the Basilica di San Marco. Perpetually packed by day with people and fluttering pigeons, it can be magical at night, especially in winter, when mists swirl around the lampposts and the Campanile.

If you face the basilica from in front of the Correr Museum, you'll notice that rather than being a strict rectangle, this square opens wider at the basilica end, creating the illusion that it's even larger than it is. On your left, the long, arcaded building is the Procuratie Vecchie, built in the early 16th century as offices and residences for the powerful procurators (magistrates) of San Marco.

On your right is the Procuratie Nuove, built half a century later in a more-grandiose classical style. It was originally planned by Venice's great Renaissance architect, Jacopo Sansovino (1486–1570), to carry on the look of his Libreria Sansoviniana (Sansovinian Library), but he died before construction on the Nuove had begun. Vincenzo Scamozzi (circa 1552–1616), a neoclassicist pupil of Andrea Palladio (1508–80), completed the design and construction. Still later, the Procuratie Nuove was modified by architect Baldassare Longhena (1598–1682), one of Venice's baroque masters.

Continued on page 414

CRUISING THE GRAND CANAL

THE BEST INTRODUCTION TO VENICE IS A TRIP DOWN MAIN STREET

Venice's Grand Canal is one of the world's great thoroughfares. It winds its way in the shape of a backward "S" from Ferrovia (the train station) to Piazza San Marco, passing 200 palazzos born of a culture obsessed with opulence and fantasy. There's a theatrical quality to a boat ride on the canal: it's as if each pink- or gold-tinted facade is trying to steal your attention from its rival across the way.

The palaces were built from the 12th to 18th centuries by the city's richest families. A handful are still private residences, but many have been converted to other uses, including museums, hotels, government offices, university buildings, a post office, a casino, and even a television station.

It's romantic to see the canal from a gondola, but the next best thing, at a fraction of the cost, is to take the Line 1 *vaporetto* (water bus) from Ferrovia to San Marco. The ride costs €6 and takes about 35 minutes. Invest in a Travel Card (€15 buys 24 hours of unlimited passage) and you can spend the better part of a day hopping on and off at the vaporetto's 16 stops, visiting the sights along the banks.

Either way, keep your eyes open for the highlights listed here; the major sites also have fuller descriptions later in this chapter.

FROM FERROVIA TO RIALTO

Palazzo Labia
On September 3, 1951, during the Venice Film Festival, the Palazzo Labia hosted what's been dubbed "the party of the century." The Aga Khan, Winston Churchill, Orson Welles, and Salvador Dalí were among those who donned 18th-century costume and danced in the Tiepolo-frescoed ballroom.

Santa Maria di Nazareth

Ponte di Scalzi

R. DI BIASIO

FERROVIA

SANTA CROCE

Stazione Ferrovia Santa Lucia

As you head out from Ferrovia, the baroque church immediately to your left is **Santa Maria di Nazareth**. Its shoeless friars earned it the nickname Chiesa degli Scalzi (Church of the Barefoot).

One of the four bridges over the Grand Canal is the **Ponte di Scalzi**. The original version was built of iron in 1858; the existing stone bridge dates from 1934.

After passing beneath the Ponte di Scalzi, ahead to the left you'll spy **Palazzo Labia**, one of the most imposing buildings in Venice, looming over the bell tower of the church of San Geremia.

A hundred yards or so further along on the left bank, the uncompleted façade of the church of **San Marcuola** gives you an idea of what's behind the marble decorations of similar 18th-century churches in Venice.

Across the canal, flanked by two *torricelle* (side wings in the shape of small towers) and a triangular *merlatura* (crenellation), is the **Fondaco dei Turchi,** one of the oldest Byzantine palaces in Venice; it's now a natural history museum. Next comes the plain brick **Depositi del Megio**, a 15th-century granary—note the lion marking it as Serenissima property—and beyond it the obelisk-topped **Ca' Belloni-Battagia**. Both are upstaged by the **Palazzo Vendramin-Calergi** on the opposite bank: this Renaissance gem was built in the 1480s, at a time when late-Gothic was still the prevailing style. A gilded banner identifies the palazzo as site of Venice's casino.

CANNAREGGIO

Palazzo Vendramin-Calergi
The German composer Richard Wagner died in Palazzo Vendramin-Calergi in 1883, soon after the success of his opera Parsifal. His room has been preserved—you can visit it on Saturday mornings by appointment.

Church of San Marcuola

GHETTO

S. MARCUOLA ▲

Ca' Belloni-Battagia

Ca' d'Oro
Ca' d'Oro means "house of gold." but the gold is long gone—the gilding that once accentuated the marble carvings of the facade has worn away over time.

S. STAE ▲

Ca' Pesaro

Fondaco dei Turchi

Depositi del Megio

San Stae Church

▲ **CA' D'ORO**

SAN POLO

Ca' Corner della Regina

Pescheria
The pescheria has been in operation for over 1,000 years. Stop by in the morning to see the exotic fish for sale—one of which may wind up on your dinner plate. Produce stalls fill the adjacent fondamenta, and butchers and cheesemongers occupy the surrounding shops.

Fondaco dei Tedeschi

Ca' dei Camerlenghi

▲ **RIALTO**

SAN MARCO

The white, whimsically baroque church of **San Stae** on the right bank is distinguished by a host of marble saints on its facade. Further along the bank is another baroque showpiece, **Ca' Pesaro**, followed by the tall, balconied **Ca' Corner della Regina**. Next up on the left is the flamboyant pink-and-white **Ca' d'Oro**, arguably the finest example of Venetian Gothic design.

Across from Ca' d'Oro is the loggia-like, neo-Gothic **pescheria**, Venice's fish market, where boats dock in the morning to deliver their catch.

The canal narrows as you approach the impressive Rialto Bridge. To the left, just before the bridge, is the **Fondaco dei Tedeschi**. This was once the busiest trading center of the republic—German, Austrian, and Hungarian merchants kept warehouses and offices here; today it's the city's main post office. Across the canal stands the curiously angled **Ca' dei Camerlenghi**. Built in 1525 to accommodate the State Treasury, it had a jail for tax evaders on the ground floor.

FROM RIALTO TO THE PONTE DELL' ACCADEMIA

SAN POLO

Ponte di Rialto

▲ **RIALTO**

Palazzo Barzizza

Ca' Loredan

▲ **S. SILVESTRO**

Ca' Farsetti

Ca' Foscari
Positioned at one of the busiest junctures along the Grand Canal, Ca' Foscari was recently restored after suffering severe foundation damage as a result of the relentless wake from passing boats.

Palazzo Pisani Moretta

Ca' Grimani

▲ **S. ANGELO**

TOMA ▲

Ca' Garzoni

Ca' Corner-Spinelli
If Ca' Corner-Spinelli has a familiar look, that's because it became a prototype for later Grand Canal buildings—and because its architect, Mauro Codussi, himself copied the windows from Palazzo Vendramin-Calergi.

Palazzo Grassi

Ca' Rezzonico

Palazzo Falier
Palazzo Falier is said to have been the home of Doge Martin Fallier, who was beheaded for treason in 1355.

SAN MARCO

REZZONICO ▲

ACCADEMIA ▲

Gallerie dell'Accademia

DORSODURO

Until the 19th century, the shop-lined **Ponte di Rialto** was the only bridge across the Grand Canal.

Rialto is the only point along the Grand Canal where buildings don't have their primary entrances directly on the water, a consequence of the two spacious *rive* (waterside paths) once used for unloading two Venetian staples: coal and wine. On your left along Riva del Carbon stand **Ca' Loredan** and **Ca' Farsetti**, 13th-century Byzantine palaces that today make up Venice's city hall. Just past the San Silvestro vaporetto landing on Riva del Vin is the 12th- and 13th-century facade of **Palazzo Barzizza**, an elegant example of Veneto-Byzantine architecture that managed to survive a complete renovation in the 17th century. Across the water, the sternly Renaissance **Ca' Grimani** has an intimidating presence that seems appropriate for today's Court of Appeals. At the Sant'Angelo landing, the vaporetto passes close to another massive Renaissance palazzo, **Ca' Corner-Spinelli**.

Back on the right bank, in a salmon color that seems to vary with the time of day, is elegant **Palazzo Pisani Moretta**, with twin water entrances. To your left, four-storied **Ca' Garzoni**, part of the Universita di Venezia Ca' Foscari, stands beside the San Toma *traghetto* (gondola ferry), which has operated since 1354. The boat makes a sharp turn and, on the right, passes one of the city's tallest Gothic palaces, **Ca' Foscari**.

The vaporetto passes baroque **Ca' Rezzonico** so closely that you get to look inside one of the most fabulous entrances along the canal. Opposite stands the Grand Canal's youngest palace, **Palazzo Grassi**, commissioned in 1749. Just beyond Grassi and Campo San Samuele, the first house past the garden was once Titian's studio. It's followed by **Palazzo Falier**, identifiable by its twin loggias (windowed porches).

Approaching the canal's fourth and final bridge, the vaporetto stops at a former church and monastery complex that houses the world-renowned **Gallerie dell'Accademia**.

The wooden pilings on which Venice was built (you can see them at the bases of the buildings along the Grand Canal) have gradually hardened into mineral form.

ARCHITECTURAL STYLES ALONG THE GRAND CANAL

BYZANTINE: 12th and 13th centuries. **Distinguishing characteristics:** high, rounded arches, relief panels, multicolored marble. **Examples:** Fondaco dei Turchi, Ca' Loredan, Ca' Farsetti, Palazzo Barzizza (and, off the canal, Basilica di San Marco).

GOTHIC: 14th and 15th centuries. **Distinguishing characteristics:** Pointed arches, high ceilings, and many windows. **Examples:** Ca' d'Oro, Ca' Foscari, Ca' Franchetti, Palazzo Falier (and, off the canal, Palazzo Ducale).

RENAISSANCE: 16th century. **Distinguishing characteristics:** classically influenced emphasis on order, achieved through symmetry and balanced proportions. **Examples:** Palazzo Vendramin-Calergi, Ca' Grimani, Ca' Corner-Spinelli, Ca' dei Camerlenghi (and, off the canal, Libreria Sansoviniana on Piazza San Marco and the church of San Giorgio Maggiore).

BAROQUE: 17th century. **Distinguishing characteristics:** Renaissance order wedded with a more dynamic style, achieved through curving lines and complex decoration. **Examples:** churches of Santa Maria di Nazareth and San Stae, Ca' Pesaro, Ca' Rezzonico (and, off the canal, the church of Santa Maria della Salute).

FROM THE PONTE DELL'ACCADEMIA TO SAN ZACCARIA

Ca' Franchetti
Until the late 19th century, Ca' Franchetti was a *squero* (gondola workshop). A few active *squeri* remain, though none are on the Grand Canal. The most easily spotted is Squero di San Trovaso, in Dorsoduro on a small canal near the Zattere boat landing.

Ca' Barbaro
Monet, Henry James, and Cole Porter are among the guests who have stayed at Ca' Barbaro. Porter later lived aboard a boat in Giudecca Canal.

S A N   M A R C O

Ponte dell' Accademia

Casetta Rossa

Ca' Pisani-Gritti

ACCADEMIA

S. M. DEL GIGLIO

D O R S O D U R O

Ca' Barbarigo

SALUTE

Palazzo Venier dei Leoni
When she was in residence at Palazzo Venier dei Leoni, Peggy Guggenheim kept her private gondola parked at the door and left her dogs standing guard (in place of Venetian lions).

Palazzo Salviati

S. Maria della Salute

Ca' Dario
However tilted Dario might be, it has outlasted its many owners, who seem plagued by misfortune. They include the Italian industrialist Raul Gardini, whose 1992 suicide followed charges of corruption and an unsuccessful bid to win the America's Cup.

 The wooden **Ponte dell' Accademia**, like the Eiffel Tower (with which it shares a certain structural grace), wasn't intended to be permanent. Erected in 1933 as a quick replacement for a rusting iron bridge built by the Austrian military in 1854, it was so well liked by Venetians that they kept it. (A perfect replica, with steel bracing, was installed 1986.)

You're only three stops from the end of the Grand Canal, but this last stretch is packed with sights. The lovely **Ca' Franchetti**, with a central balcony made in the style of Palazzo Ducale's loggia, dates from the late Gothic period, but its gardens are no older than the cedar tree standing at their center.

Ca' Barbaro, next door to Ca' Franchetti, was the residence of the illustrious family who rebuilt the church of Santa Maria del Giglio.

Farther along on the left bank, a garden, vibrant with flowers in summer, surrounds **Casetta Rossa** (small red house) as if it were the centerpiece of its bouquet. Across the canal, bright 19th-century mosaics on

Ca' Barbarigo give you some idea how the frescoed facades of many Venetian palaces must have looked in their heyday. A few doors down are the lush gardens within the walls of the unfinished **Palazzo Venier dei Leoni**, which holds the **Peggy Guggenheim Collection** of contemporary art.

Basilica di S. Marco

SAN ZACCARIA

CASTELLO

Palazzo Ducale

PIAZZA SAN MARCO

S. ZACCARIA

VALLARESSO

Punta della Dogana

The Grand Canal is 2½ miles long, has an average depth of 9 feet, and is 76 yards wide at its broadest point and 40 yards at its narrowest.

SAN GIORGIO MAGGIORE

Lovely, leaning **Ca' Dario** on the right bank is notable for its colorful marble facade.

Past the landing of Santa Maria del Giglio stands the 15th-century **Ca' Pisani-Gritti**, now the Gritti Palace Hotel. On the other bank, narrow **Palazzo Salviati**, with its 20th-century mosaic facade, was among the last glass factories to operate within the Venice city center. At this point the cupola of **Santa Maria della Salute** dominates the scene, but spare a glance for picturesque Rio di San Gregorio and what remains of its Gothic abbey. At **Punta della Dogana** on the tip of Dorsoduro, note the former custom-house, topped by Palla della Fortuna—a golden ball and a weather vane depicting Fortune. At the Vallaresso vaporetto stop you've left the Grand Canal, but stay on board for a view of the **Palazzo Ducale**, with **Basilica di San Marco** behind it, then disembark at San Zaccaria.

When Napoléon (1769–1821) entered Venice with his troops in 1797, he called Piazza San Marco "the world's most beautiful drawing room"—and promptly gave orders to redecorate it. His architects demolished a 16th-century church with a Sansovino facade in order to build the Ala Napoleonica (Napoleonic Wing), or Fabbrica Nuova (New Building), which linked the two 16th-century procuratie and effectively enclosed the piazza.

Piazzetta San Marco, the "little square" leading from Piazza San Marco to the waters of Bacino San Marco (St. Mark's Basin), is a *molo* (landing) that was once the grand entryway to the republic. It's distinguished by two columns towering above the waterfront. One is topped by the winged lion, a traditional emblem of St. Mark that became the symbol of Venice itself; the other supports St. Theodore, the city's first patron, along with his dragon. Between these columns the republic traditionally executed convicts.

TIMING

It takes a full day to take in everything on the piazza thoroughly; so if time is limited you'll have to prioritize. Plan on 1″ hours for the basilica and its Pala d'Oro, Galleria, and Museo di San Marco. You'll want at least two hours to appreciate the Palazzo Ducale. Do take time to enjoy the piazza itself from a café table, or on a clear day, from atop the Campanile.

THE MAIN ATTRACTIONS

❶ Basilica di San Marco. An opulent synthesis of Byzantine and Romanesque styles, Venice's gem is laid out in a Greek-cross floor plan and topped with five plump domes. It didn't become the cathedral of Venice until 1807, but its role as the Chiesa Ducale (doge's private chapel) gave it immense power and wealth. The original church was built in 828 to house the body of St. Mark the Evangelist. His remains, filched from Alexandria by the doge's agents, were supposedly hidden in a barrel under layers of pickled pork to sneak them past Muslim guards. The escapade is depicted in the 13th-century mosaic above the door farthest left of the front entrance, one of the earliest mosaics on the heavily decorated facade; look closely to see the church as it appeared at that time.

Fodor's Choice
★

A 976 fire destroyed most of the original church. It was rebuilt and reopened in 1094, and for centuries it would serve as a symbol of Venetian wealth and power, endowed with all the riches admirals and merchants could carry off from the Orient, to the point where it earned the nickname Chiesa d'Oro (Golden Church). The four bronze horses that prance and snort over the doorway are copies of sculptures that victorious Venetians took from Constantinople in 1204 after the fourth crusade (the originals are in the Museo di San Marco). The rich, colorful exterior decorations, including the numerous different marble columns, all came from the same source. Look for a medallion of red porphyry in the floor of the porch inside the main door. It marks the spot where, in 1177, Doge Sebastiano Ziani orchestrated the reconciliation between Barbarossa—the Holy Roman emperor—and Pope Alexander III. Dim lighting, galleries high above the naves—they served as the *matroneum* (women's gallery)—the *iconostasis* (altar screen), and the single massive Byzantine chandelier all seem to wed Christianity with the Orient, giving San Marco its exotic blend of majesty and mystery.

The basilica is famous for its 43,055 square feet of mosaics, which run from floor to ceiling thanks to an innovative roof of brick vaulting. Many of the original windows were filled in to make room for even more artwork. At midday, when the interior is fully illuminated, the mosaics truly come alive, the shimmer of their tiny gold tiles becoming nothing short of magical. The earliest mosaics are from the 11th and 12th centuries, and the last were added in the early 1700s. One of the most recent is the *Last Judgment,* believed to have been designed by Tintoretto (1518–94), on the arch between the porch and the nave. Inside the main entrance, turn right on the porch to see the Book of Genesis depicted on the ceiling. Ahead through a glass door, 13th-century mosaics depict St. Mark's life in the **Cappella Zen** (Zen Chapel). The **Cappella della Madonna di Nicopeia,** in the left transept, holds the altar icon that many consider Venice's most powerful protector. In nearby **Cappella della Madonna dei Mascoli,** the life of the Virgin Mary is depicted in fine 15th-century mosaics, believed to be

The golden mosaics of Basilica di San Marco

based on drawings by Jacopo Bellini (1400–71) and Andrea Mantegna (1431–1506).

In the **Santuario** (Sanctuary), the main altar is built over the tomb of St. Mark, its green marble canopy lifted high on carved alabaster columns. Perhaps even more impressive is the **Pala d'Oro**, a dazzling gilt silver screen encrusted with 1,927 precious gems and 255 enameled panels. Originally commissioned in Constantinople by Doge Orseolo I (976–978), it was enlarged and embellished over four centuries by master craftsmen and wealthy merchants. The bronze door leading from the sanctuary into the sacristy is by Jacopo Sansovino. In the top left corner the artist included a self-portrait, and above that, he pictured friend and fellow artist Titian (1485–1576). The **Tesoro** (Treasury), entered from the right transept, contains many treasures carried home from conquests abroad.

Climb the steep stairway to the **Galleria** and the **Museo di San Marco** for the best overview of the basilica's interior. From here you can step outdoors for a sweeping panorama of Piazza San Marco and out over the lagoon to San Giorgio. The displays focus mainly on the types of mosaic and how they have been restored over the years. But the highlight is a close-up view of the original gilt bronze horses that were once on the outer gallery. The four were most probably cast in Rome and taken to Constantinople, where the Venetians pillaged them after sacking that city. When Napoléon sacked Venice in 1797, he took them to Paris. They were returned after the fall of the French Empire, but came home "blind"—their big ruby eyes had been sold.

Be aware that guards at the basilica door turn away anyone with bare shoulders or knees; no shorts, short skirts, or tank tops are allowed. If you want a free guided tour in English during summer months (less certain in winter, as the guides are volunteers), look for groups forming on the porch inside the main door. You may also arrange tours by appointment. ⊠ *Piazza San Marco* ☎*041/2708311 basilica, 041/2702421 for free tours Apr.–Oct., call weekday mornings* ☝*Basilica free, Tesoro €2, Santuario and Pala d'Oro €1.50, Galleria and Museo di San Marco €3* ⊙ *May–Sept., Mon.–Sat. 9:45–5:30, Sun. 2–4; Oct.–Apr., Mon.– Sat. 9:45–4:30, Sun. 2–4. Last entry ½ hr before closing* Ⓥ *Vallaresso/ San Zaccaria.*

★ ❷ **Palazzo Ducale** *(Doge's Palace).* Rising above the Piazzetta San Marco, this Gothic-Renaissance fantasia of pink-and-white marble is a majestic expression of the prosperity and power attained during Venice's most glorious period. Some architectural purists find the building top-heavy—its hulking upper floors rest upon a graceful ground-floor colonnade—but the design is what gives the palace its distinctive identity; it's hard to imagine it any other way. Always much more than a residence, the palace was Venice's White House, Senate, torture chamber, and prison rolled into one.

Though a fortress for the doge stood on this spot in the early 9th century, the building you see today was begun in the 12th century, and, like the basilica next door, was continually remodeled over the centuries. Near the basilica you'll see the ornately Gothic **Porta della Carta** (Gate of the Paper), where official decrees were traditionally posted, but visitors enter under the portico facing the water. You'll find yourself in an immense courtyard with the **Scala dei Giganti** (Stairway of the Giants) directly ahead, guarded by Sansovino's huge statues of Mars and Neptune. Though ordinary mortals must use the central interior staircase, its upper flight is the lavishly gilded **Scala d'Oro** (Golden Staircase), also by Sansovino. It may seem odd that you have to climb so many steps to reach the government's main council rooms and reception halls, but imagine how this extraordinary climb must have impressed, and perhaps intimidated, foreign emissaries.

The palace's sumptuous chambers have walls and ceilings covered with works by Venice's greatest artists. Visit the **Anticollegio,** a waiting room outside the Collegio's chamber, where you'll see the *Rape of Europa* by Veronese (1528–88) and Tintoretto's *Bacchus and Ariadne Crowned by Venus.* Veronese also painted the ceiling of the adjacent **Sala del Collegio.** The ceiling of the **Sala del Senato** (Senate Chamber), featuring *The Triumph of Venice* by Tintoretto, is magnificent, but it's dwarfed by his masterpiece *Paradise* in the **Sala del Maggiore Consiglio** (Great Council Hall). A vast work commissioned for a vast hall, this dark, dynamic piece is the world's largest oil painting (23 by 75 feet). The room's carved, gilt ceiling is breathtaking, especially with Veronese's majestic *Apotheosis of Venice* filling one of the center panels. Around the upper walls, study the portraits of the first 76 doges, and you'll notice one picture is missing near the left corner of the wall opposite *Paradise.* A black painted curtain, rather than a portrait, marks Doge

6

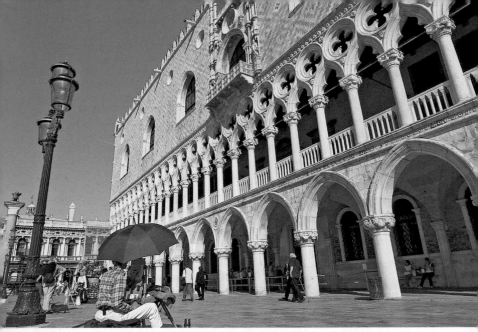
Palazzo Ducale, the massive palace that was Venice's seat of power

Marin Falier's fall from grace; he was beheaded for treason in 1355, which the Latin inscription bluntly explains.

A narrow canal separates the palace's east side from the cramped cell blocks of the **Prigioni Nuove** (New Prisons). High above the water arches the enclosed marble **Ponte dei Sospiri** (Bridge of Sighs), which earned its name from the sighs of those being led to their fate. Look out its windows to see the last earthly view these prisoners beheld.

The palazzo's "Secret Itinerary" tour takes you to the doge's private apartments, through hidden passageways to the interrogation (torture) chambers, and into the rooftop *piombi* (lead) prison, named for its lead roofing. Venetian-born writer and libertine Giacomo Casanova (1725–98), along with an accomplice, managed to escape from the piombi in 1756, the only men ever to do so. ⊠*Piazzetta San Marco* ☎*041/2715911, 041/5209070 "Secret Itinerary" tour* 🎟️*Piazza San Marco museum card €12, Musei Civici museum pass €18, "Secret Itinerary" tour €16* 🕑*Apr.–Oct., daily 9–7; Nov.–Mar., daily 9–5. Last tickets sold 1 hr before closing. English "Secret Itinerary" tours in morning; reservations advisable* Ⓥ*Vallaresso/San Zaccaria.*

NEED A BREAK?

Caffè Florian (☎ *041/5205641*), in the Procuratie Nuove, has served coffee to the likes of Casanova, Charles Dickens, and Marcel Proust. It's Venice's oldest café, continuously in business since 1720 (though you'll find it closed Wednesday in winter). Counter seating is less expensive than taking a table, especially when there's live music. In the Procuratie Vecchie, Caffè Quadri (☎ *041/5289299*) exudes almost as much history as Florian across the way, and is similarly pricey. It was shunned by 19th-century Venetians when the occupying Austrians made it their gathering place. In winter it closes Monday.

ALSO WORTH SEEING

Campanile. Venice's famous brick bell tower (325 feet tall, plus the angel) had been standing nearly 1,000 years when in 1902, practically without warning, it collapsed, taking with it Jacopo Sansovino's 16th-century marble loggia at the base. The crushed loggia was promptly restored, and the new tower, rebuilt to the old plan, reopened in 1912. In the 15th century, clerics found guilty of immoral behavior were suspended in wooden cages from the tower. Some were forced to subsist on bread and water for as long as a year, and others were left to starve. The stunning view from the tower on a clear day includes the Lido, the lagoon, and the mainland as far as the Alps, but, strangely enough, none of the myriad canals that snake through the city. ⊠ *Piazza San Marco* 🕾 *041/5224064* 💶 *€6* 🕑 *Apr.–June, daily 9:30–5; July–Sept., daily 9:45–8; Oct.–Mar., daily 9:45–4. Last entry ½ hr before closing* Ⓥ *Vallaresso/San Zaccaria.*

❹ Museo Correr. Exhibits in this museum of Venetian art and history range from the absurdly high-soled shoes worn by 16th-century Venetian ladies (who walked with the aid of a servant) to the huge *Grande Pianta Prospettica* by Jacopo de' Barbari (circa 1440–1515), which details in carved wood every nook and cranny of 16th-century Venice. The city's proud naval history is evoked in several rooms through highly descriptive paintings and numerous maritime objects, including ships' cannons and some surprisingly large iron mast-top navigation lights. The Correr has a room devoted entirely to antique games, and its second-floor **Quadreria** (Picture Gallery) has works by Venetian, Greek, and Flemish painters. The Correr exhibition rooms lead directly into the **Museo Archeologico** and the **Stanza del Sansovino**, the only part of the **Biblioteca Nazionale Marciana** open to visitors. ⊠ *Piazza San Marco, Ala Napoleonica* 🕾 *041/2405211* 💶 *Piazza San Marco museum card €12, Musei Civici museum pass €18* 🕑 *Apr.–Oct., daily 9–7; Nov.–Mar., daily 9–5. Last tickets sold 1 hr before closing* Ⓥ *Vallaresso/San Zaccaria.*

NEED A BREAK? If you'd like to attend happy hour with the ghosts of Ernest Hemingway, Aristotle Onassis, and Orson Welles, head to Harry's Bar (🕾 *041/5285777*). Walk out Piazza San Marco near the Correr Museum and turn left at Calle Vallaresso; you'll find the legendary hangout right at the vaporetto landing. Harry's still boasts Venice's driest martinis and freshest Bellinis (white peach juice and sparkling *prosecco* wine).

❺ Torre dell'Orologio. Five hundred years ago, when this enameled clock was built, twin Moor figures would strike the hour, and three wise men with an angel would walk out and bow to the Virgin Mary on Epiphany (January 6) and during Ascension Week (40 days after Easter). An inscription on the tower reads HORAS NON NUMERO NISI SERENAS ("I only count happy hours"). After years of painstaking work, the clock

VENICE THROUGH THE AGES

Up from the Muck. Venice was founded in the 5th century when the Veneti, inhabitants of the mainland region roughly corresponding to today's Veneto, fled their homes to escape invading Lombards. The unlikely city, built atop wooden posts driven into the marshes, would evolve into a great maritime republic. Its fortunes grew as a result of its active role in the Crusades, beginning in 1095 and culminating in the Venetian-led sacking of Constantinople in 1204. The defeat of rival Genoa in the Battle of Chioggia (1380) established Venice as the dominant sea power in Europe.

Early Democracy. As early as the 7th century, Venice was governed by a participatory democracy, with a ruler, the doge, elected to a lifetime term. Beginning in the 12th century, the doge's power was increasingly subsumed by a growing number of councils, commissions, and magistrates. In 1268 a complicated procedure for the doge's election was established to prevent nepotism, but by that point power rested foremost with the Great Council, which at times numbered as many as 2,000 members.

Laws were passed by the Senate, a group of 200 elected from the Great Council, and executive powers belonged to the College, a committee of 25. In 1310 the Council of Ten was formed to protect state security. When circumstances dictated, the doge could expedite decision making by consulting only the Council of Ten. To avoid too great a concentration of power, these 10 served only one year and belonged to different families.

A Long Decline. Venice reached its height of power in the 15th and 16th centuries, during which time its domain included all of the Veneto region and part of Lombardy. But beginning in the 16th century, the tide turned. The Ottoman Empire blocked Venice's Mediterranean trade routes, and newly emerging sea powers such as Britain and the Netherlands ended Venice's monopoly by opening oceanic trading routes. The republic underwent a slow decline. When Napoléon arrived in 1797, he took the city without a fight, eventually delivering it to the Austrians, who ruled until 1848. In that tumultuous year throughout Europe, the Venetians rebelled, an act that would ultimately lead to their joining the Italian Republic in 1866.

Art Stars. In the 13th through 15th centuries the influence of Gothic architecture resulted in palaces in the florid Gothic style, for which the city is famous. Renaissance sensibilities arrived comparatively late. Early Venetian Renaissance artists—Carpaccio, Giorgione, and the Bellini brothers, Giovanni and Gentile—were active in the late 15th and early 16th centuries. Along with the stars of the next generation—Veronese, Titian, and Tintoretto—they played a key role in the development of Western art, and their best work remains in the city.

Like its dwindling fortunes, Venice's art and culture underwent a prolonged decline, leaving only the splendid monuments to recall a fabled past. The 18th-century paintings of Canaletto and Tiepolo were a glorious swan song.

CLOSE UP

Wading Through the Acqua Alta

You have to walk almost everywhere in Venice, and where you can't walk, you go by water. Occasionally you walk *in* water, when normally higher fall and spring tides are exacerbated by falling barometers and south-easterly winds. The result is *acqua alta*—flooding in the lowest parts of town, especially Piazza San Marco, which lasts a few hours, until the tide recedes.

Venetians handle the high waters with aplomb, donning waders and erect-ing temporary walkways, but they're well aware of the damage caused by the flooding and the threat it poses to their city. Work has begun on the Moses Project, a plan that would close off the lagoon when high tides threaten, but it's a much-debated response to an emotionally charged problem. Protecting Venice and its lagoon from high tides—as well as high use and the damaging wave action caused by powerboats—is among the city's most contentious issues.

tower has been reassembled and returned to its former glory. Visits in English are offered daily and must be booked in advance. ⊠ *North side of Piazza San Marco* ☎ *041/5209070* ⊕ *www.museicivicivenezian.it* 🎫 *€12* ⏱ *Tours in English Mon.–Wed. at 10 and 11; Thurs.–Sun. at 1, 2, and 3* Ⓥ *Vallaresso/San Zaccaria.*

DORSODURO

The sestiere Dorsoduro (named for its "hard back" solid clay founda-tion) is across the Grand Canal to the south of San Marco. It is a place of monumental churches, meandering canals, the city's finest art muse-ums, and a boardwalk called the Zattere, where on sunny days you'll swear half the city is out for a *passeggiata*, or stroll. The eastern point of the peninsula, Punta della Dogana, has one of the best views in town. The Stazione Marittima, where in summer cruise ships line the dock, lies at the western end. Midway between these two points, just off the Zattere, is the Squero di San Trovaso, where gondolas have been built and repaired for centuries.

Dorsoduro is also home to the Gallerie dell'Accademia, which has an unparalleled collection of Venetian painting, and Ca' Rezzonico, which houses the Museo del Settecento Veneziano. Another of its landmark sites, the Peggy Guggenheim Collection, has a fine selection of 20th-century art.

TIMING

The Gallerie dell'Accademia demands a few hours, but if time is short an audio guide can help you cover the highlights in about an hour. Give yourself at least 1″ hours for the Guggenheim Collection. Ca' Rezzo-nico deserves a couple of hours.

THE MAIN ATTRACTIONS

★ ❸ **Ca' Rezzonico.** Designed by Baldassare Longhena in the 17th century, this palace was completed nearly 100 years later by Giorgio Massari and became the last home of English poet Robert Browning (1812–89). Elizabeth Taylor and Richard Burton danced in the baroque ballroom in the 1960s. Today Ca' Rezzonico is the home of the **Museo del Settecento** (Museum of Venice in the 1700s). Its main floor is packed with period furniture and tapestries in gilded salons (note the four Tiepolo ceiling frescoes) and successfully retains the feel of an old Venetian palazzo. Upper floors contain hundreds of paintings, most from Venetian schools of artists. There's even a restored apothecary, complete with powders and potions. ⊠*Fondamenta Rezzonico, Dorsoduro 3136* ☎*041/2410100* 💷*€6.50, Musei Civici museum pass €18* ⊙*Apr.–Oct., daily 10–6; Nov.– Mar., daily 10–5. Last entry 1 hr before closing* Ⓥ*Ca' Rezzonico.*

★ ❼ **Gallerie dell'Accademia.** Napoléon founded these galleries in 1807 on the site of a religious complex he'd suppressed, and what he initiated now amounts to the world's most extraordinary collection of Venetian art. Jacopo Bellini is considered the father of the Venetian Renaissance, and in Room 2 you can compare his *Madonna and Child with Saints* with such later works as *Madonna of the Orange Tree* by Cima da Conegliano (circa 1459–1517) and *Ten Thousand Martyrs of Mt. Ararat* by Vittore Carpaccio (circa 1455–1525). Jacopo's son Giovanni (circa 1430–1516) draws your eye not with his subjects but with his rich color. Rooms 4 and 5 are full of his Madonnas; note the contrast between the young Madonna and child and the neighboring older Madonna after the crucifixion—you'll see the colors of dawn and dusk in Venice. Room 5 contains *Tempest* by Giorgione (1477–1510), a work that was revolutionary in its time and has continued to intrigue viewers and critics over the centuries. It depicts a storm approaching as a nude woman nurses her child and a soldier looks on. The overall atmosphere that Giorgione creates is as important as any of his figures.

In Room 10, *Feast in the House of Levi*, commissioned as a Last Supper, got Veronese dragged before the Inquisition over its depiction of dogs, jesters, and German (therefore Protestant) soldiers. The artist saved his neck by simply changing the title, so that the painting represented a different biblical feast. Titian's *Presentation of the Virgin* (Room 24) is the collection's only work originally created for the building in which it hangs. Don't miss Rooms 20 and 21, with views of 15th- and 16th-century Venice by Carpaccio and Gentile Bellini (1429–1507), Giovanni's brother—you'll see how little the city has changed.

Booking tickets in advance isn't essential but helps during busy seasons and costs only an additional €1. Booking is necessary to see the **Quadreria**, where additional works cover every inch of a wide hallway. A free map names art and artists, and the bookshop sells a more-informative English-language booklet. In the main galleries a €4 audio guide saves reading but adds little to each room's excellent annotation. ⊠*Campo della Carità, Dorsoduro 1050* ☎*041/5222247, 041/5200345 reservations* ⊕*www.gallerieaccademia.org* 💷*€6.50, €11 includes Ca' d'Oro and Museo Orientale* ⊙*Tues.–Sun. 8:15–7:15, Mon. 8:15–2* Ⓥ*Accademia.*

Dorsoduro

SAN MARCO

Piazza San Marco

S. MARCO GIARDINETTI

S. MARCO VALLARESSO

S.M. DEL GIGLIO

SALUTE

DORSODURO

S.S. SAMUELE

CA' REZZONICO

ACCADEMIA

ZATTERE

S. BASILIO

Canale della Giudecca

Canale della Lavraneri

Grand Canal

KEY

♦ Vaporetto Stop

6

0   1/8 mile

0   1/8 km

NEED A BREAK?

There's no sunnier spot in Venice than Fondamenta delle Zattere, along the southern edge of Dorsoduro. It's the city's gigantic public terrace, with bustling bars and gelato shops; come here to stroll, read in the open air, and play hooky from sightseeing. The Zattere's most decadent treat is found at Gelateria Nico (⊠*Dorsoduro 922* ☎*041/5225293*)—order their famous *gianduiotto*, a nutty slab of chocolate ice cream floating on a cloud of whipped cream, and relax on the big, welcoming deck.

8 Peggy Guggenheim Collection. A small but choice selection of 20th-century painting and sculpture is on display at this gallery in the heiress Guggenheim's former Grand Canal home. Through wealth and social connections, Guggenheim (1898–1979) became a serious art patron, and her collection here in Palazzo Venier dei Leoni includes works by Picasso, Kandinsky, Pollock, Motherwell, and Ernst (at one time her husband). The museum serves beverages, snacks, and light meals in its refreshingly shady, artistically sophisticated garden. On Sunday at 3 PM the museum offers a free tour and art workshop for children 12 and under. ⊠*Fondamenta Venier dei Leoni, Dorsoduro 701* ☎*041/5209083* ⊕*www.guggenheim-venice.it* ☞*€10* ⊙*Wed.–Mon. 10–6* Ⓥ*Accademia.*

9 Santa Maria della Salute. The view of La Salute (as this church is commonly called) from the Riva degli Schiavoni at sunset or from the Accademia bridge by moonlight is unforgettable. Baldassare Longhena was 32 years old when he won a competition to design a shrine honoring the Virgin Mary for saving Venice from a plague that killed 47,000 residents. Outside, this simple white octagon is adorned with a colossal cupola lined with snail-like buttresses and a Palladian-style facade; inside are a polychrome marble floor and six chapels. The Byzantine icon above the main altar has been venerated as the Madonna della Salute (of health) since 1670, when Francesco Morosini brought it here from Crete. Above it is a sculpture showing Venice (left) on her knees while the plague (right) is driven from the city. The **Sacrestia Maggiore** contains a dozen works by Titian, including his *San Marco Enthroned with Saints* altarpiece. You'll also see Tintoretto's *The Wedding at Canaan*, and on special occasions the altar displays a 15th-century tapestry depicting the Pentecost. For the Festa della Salute, held November 21, Venetians make a pilgrimage here and light candles in thanksgiving for another year's health. ⊠*Punta della Dogana, Dorsoduro* ☎*041/2743928* ☞*Church free, sacristy €1.50* ⊙*Apr.–Sept., daily 9–noon and 3–6:30; Oct.–Mar., daily 9–noon and 3–5:30* Ⓥ*Salute.*

NEED A BREAK?

Filled with cafés and restaurants, Campo Santa Margarita also has produce vendors, pizza by the slice, and benches where you can sit and eat. For more than a portable munch, bask in the sunshine at popular Il Caffè (☎*041/5287998*), commonly called Caffè Rossa for its bright red exterior. It's open past midnight, serving drinks and light refreshment every day except Sunday.

ALSO WORTH SEEING

1 **Campo Santo Stefano.** In Venice's most prestigious residential neighborhood, you'll find one of the city's busiest crossroads just over the Accademia bridge; it's hard to believe this square once hosted bullfights, with bulls (or oxen) tied to a stake and baited by dogs. For centuries the campo was grass except for a stone avenue called the *liston*. It was so popular for strolling that in Venetian dialect *"andare al liston"* still means "to go for a walk." A sunny meeting spot popular with Venetians and visitors alike, the campo also hosts outdoor fairs during Christmas and Carnevale seasons. Check out the 14th-century **Chiesa di Santo Stefano** and its ship's-keel roof, created by shipbuilders. You'll see works by Tintoretto and the tipsiest bell tower in town—best appreciated from nearby Campo San Angelo. ✉ *Campo Santo Stefano, San Marco* ☎ *041/2750462 Chorus* 🎫 *€3, Chorus pass €9* ⊙ *Mon.–Sat. 10–5, Sun. 1–5* Ⓥ *Accademia.*

6 **Gesuati.** When the Dominicans took over the church of Santa Maria della Visitazione from the suppressed order of Gesuati laymen in 1668, Giorgio Massari was commissioned to build this structure. It has a score of works by Giambattista Tiepolo (1696–1770), Giambattista Piazzetta (1683–1754), and Sebastiano Ricci (1659–1734). ✉ *Zattere, Dorsoduro* ☎ *041/2750462 Chorus* 🎫 *€3, Chorus pass €9* ⊙ *Mon.–Sat. 10–5, Sun. 1–5* Ⓥ *Zattere.*

2 **Palazzo Grassi.** This 18th-century palazzo, which was once owned by auto magnate Giovanni Agnelli, was bought by the French businessman François Pinaut in 2005 to house his collection of modern and contemporary art. Japanese architect Tadao Ando was brought in for the latest restoration of the interior. Check the Web site for a schedule of temporary exhibitions. ✉ *Campo San Samuele, San Marco* ☎ *041/5231680* ⊕ *www.palazzograssi.it* 🎫 *€10* ⊙ *Daily 9–6* Ⓥ *San Samuele.*

5 **San Sebastiano.** Paolo Veronese (1528–88) established his reputation while still in his twenties with the frescoes at this, his parish church, and for decades he continued to embellish them with amazing trompel'oeil scenes. Don't miss his altarpiece *Madonna in Glory with Saints.* Veronese is buried beneath his bust near the organ. ✉ *Campo San Sebastiano, Dorsoduro* ☎ *041/2750462 Chorus* 🎫 *€3, Chorus pass €9* ⊙ *Mon.–Sat. 10–5, Sun. 1–5* Ⓥ *San Basilio.*

4 **Scuola Grande dei Carmini.** When the order of Santa Maria del Carmelo commissioned Baldassare Longhena to build Scuola Grande dei Carmini in the late 1600s, their brotherhood of 75,000 members was the largest in Venice and one of the wealthiest. Little expense was spared in the decorating of stuccoed ceilings and carved ebony paneling, and the artwork was choice, even before 1739, when Tiepolo painted the **Sala Capitolare.** In what many consider his best work, Tiepolo's nine great canvases vividly transform some rather unpromising religious themes into flamboyant displays of color and movement. ✉ *Campo dei Carmini, Dorsoduro 2617* ☎ *041/5289420* 🎫 *€5* ⊙ *Daily 10–5* Ⓥ *Ca' Rezzonico.*

Touring Venice

If you want some expert guidance around Venice, you have several options to choose from. **Cooperativa Guide Turistiche Autorizzate** (⊠ *San Marco 750, near San Zulian* ☎ *041/5209038* ⊕ *www.guidevenezia.it*) has a list of more than 100 licensed guides. Tours lasting about two hours with an English-speaking guide start at €125 for up to 30 people. Agree on a total price before you begin, as there can be some hidden extras. Guides are of variable quality.

More than a dozen major travel agents offer a two-hour walking tour of the San Marco area (€30), which ends with a glassblowing demonstration daily (no Sunday tour in winter). From April to October there's also an afternoon walking tour that ends with a gondola ride (€40). **Venicescapes** (⊠ *Campo San Provolo, Castello 4954* ☎ *041/5206361* ⊕ *www.venices-*

capes.org), an Italo-American cultural association, offers several themed itineraries focusing on history and culture as well as tourist sights. Their three- to seven-hour tours are in small groups (generally six to eight people). Reservations are recommended during busy seasons, and prices start at €240 for two people. **Walks Inside Venice** (☎ *041/5202434* ⊕ *www. walksinsidevenice.com*) also does several themed tours for small groups starting at €70 per hour and lasting up to three hours.

Serenaded gondola trips, with or without dinner (€73, €35), can be purchased at local travel agencies or at **American Express** (⊠ *Salizzada San Moisè, San Marco 1471* ☎ *041/5200844* ☎ *041/5229937*). Nightly tours leave at 7:30 and 8:30 April–September, at 7:30 only in October, and at 3:30 November–March.

SAN POLO & SANTA CROCE

The two smallest of Venice's six sestieri, San Polo and Santa Croce were named after their main churches, though the Chiesa di Santa Croce was demolished in 1810. The city's most famous bridge, the Ponte di Rialto, unites sestiere San Marco (east) with San Polo (west). The Rialto Bridge takes its name from Rivoaltus, the high ground on which it was built. San Polo has two other major sites, Santa Maria Gloriosa dei Frari and the Scuola Grande di San Rocco, as well as some worthwhile but lesser-known churches.

Shops abound in the area surrounding the Rialto Bridge. On the San Marco side you'll find fashions, on the San Polo side food. Chiesa di San Giacometto, where you see the first fruit vendors as you come off the bridge on the San Polo side, was probably built in the 11th and 12th centuries, about the time the surrounding market came into being. Public announcements were traditionally read in the church's campo; its 24-hour clock, though lovely, has rarely worked.

TIMING

To do the area justice requires at least half a day. If you want to take part in the food shopping, come early to beat the crowds. Bear in mind that a *metà kilo* is about a pound and an *etto* is a few ounces. The

San Polo
& Santa Croce

KEY	
◆	*Vaporetto Stop*

campo of San Giacomo dell'Orio, west of the main thoroughfare that takes you from the Ponte di Rialto to Santa Maria Gloriosa dei Frari, is a peaceful place for a drink and a rest. The museums of Ca' Pesaro are a time commitment—you'll want at least two hours to see them both.

THE MAIN ATTRACTIONS

★ **1** **Ponte di Rialto** *(Rialto Bridge)*. The competition to design a stone bridge across the Grand Canal (replacing earlier wooden versions) attracted the late-16th-century's best architects, including Michelangelo, Palladio, and Sansovino, but the job went to the less-famous but appropriately named Antonio da Ponte. His pragmatic design featured shop space and was high enough for galleys to pass beneath; it kept decoration and cost to a minimum at a time when the republic's coffers were low due to continual wars against the Turks and the opening of oceanic trade routes. Along the railing you'll enjoy one of the city's most famous views: the Grand Canal vibrant with boat traffic. Ⓥ*Rialto*.

7 **Santa Maria Gloriosa dei Frari.** This immense Gothic church of russet-color brick, completed in the 1400s after more than a century of work, FodorśChoice ★ is deliberately austere, befitting the Franciscan brothers' insistence on spirituality and poverty. However, *I Frari* (as it's known locally) contains some of the most brilliant paintings in any Venetian church. Visit the sacristy first, to see Giovanni Bellini's 1488 triptych *Madonna and Child with Saints* in all its mellow luminosity, painted for precisely this spot. The Corner Chapel on the other side of the chancel is graced by Bartolomeo Vivarini's (1415–84) 1474 altarpiece *St. Mark Enthroned and Saints John the Baptist, Jerome, Peter, and Nicholas,* of similar exquisite detail and color. There is also a fine sculpture of St. John the Baptist here by Jacopo Sansovino. You can see the rapid development of Venetian Renaissance painting by contrasting Bellini and Vivarini with the heroic energy of Titian's *Assumption,* over the main altar, painted only 30 years later. Unveiled in 1518, this work was not initially accepted by the church, precisely because of the innovative style and bright colors, especially Titian's trademark red, which would make it famous.

Titian's beautiful *Madonna di Ca' Pesaro,* in the left aisle, was modeled after his wife, who died in childbirth. The painting took almost 10 years to complete, and in it Titian totally disregarded the conventions of his time by moving the Virgin out of center frame and making the saints active participants. On the same side of the church look at the spooky, pyramid-shaped monument to the sculptor Antonio Canova (1757–1822). Across the nave is a neoclassical 19th-century monument to Titian, executed by two of Canova's pupils. ✉ *Campo dei Frari, San Polo* ☎ *041/2728618, 041/2750462 Chorus* 💳*€3, Chorus pass €9* 🕙 *Mon.–Sat. 9–6, Sun. 1–6* Ⓥ *San Tomà.*

NEED A BREAK?

On a narrow passage between the Frari and San Rocco, Gelateria Millevoglie (*Thousand Desires* ☎ *041/5244667*) has pizza slices, calzones, and gelato so popular it backs up traffic. It's closed December and January, but it's open seven days a week—10 AM to midnight in summer and until 9 PM October–March. Just off Campo San Tomà is the decadent Vizio Virtù (☎ *041/2750149* ⊕ *www.viziovirtu.com*). If it's too cold for a gelato, have a hot chocolate to go or choose from a selection of gourmet chocolate creations.

---

❽ **Scuola Grande di San Rocco.** St. Rocco's popularity stemmed from his miraculous recovery from the plague and his care for fellow sufferers. Throughout the plague-filled Middle Ages, followers and donations abounded, and this elegant example of Venetian Renaissance architecture was the result. Although it is bold and dramatic outside, its contents are even more stunning—a series of more than 60 paintings by Tintoretto. In 1564 Tintoretto edged out competition for a commission to decorate a ceiling by submitting not a sketch, but a finished work, which he moreover offered free of charge. *Moses Striking Water from the Rock, The Brazen Serpent,* and *The Fall of Manna* represent three afflictions—thirst, disease, and hunger—that San Rocco and later his brotherhood sought to relieve. ✉ *Campo San*

WORD OF MOUTH

"Scuola Grande di San Rocco is absolutely mind-boggling. It is near Santa Maria Gloriosa dei Frari—also well worth a visit. The bonus is that in the small street between these two places is Millevoglie, a sandwich/pizza shop with *the best* gelato." –Rosemary

Rocco, San Polo 3052 ☎*041/5234864* ⊕*www.scuolagrandesanrocco.
it* ≌*€7* ☉*Apr.–Oct., daily 9–5:30; Nov.–Mar., daily 10–5. Last entry
½ hr before closing* Ⓥ*San Tomà.*

**NEED A
BREAK?**

Just over the bridge in front of the Frari church is Caffè dei Frari (✉*Fondamenta dei Frari, San Polo* ☎*041/5241877*), where you'll find a delightful
assortment of sandwiches and snacks. Established in 1870, it's one of the
last Venetian tearooms with its original decor. Pasticceria Tonolo (✉*Calle
Crosera, Dorsoduro 3764* ☎*041/5237209*) has been fattening up Venetians
since 1886. During Carnevale it's still the best place in town for *fritelle*, fried
doughnuts (traditional raisin or cream-filled); during *acqua alta* flooding,
the staff dons rubber boots and keeps working. The place is closed Monday,
and there's no seating anytime.

ALSO WORTH SEEING

❻ Campo San Polo. Only Piazza San Marco is larger than this square,
where not even the pigeons manage to look cozy, and the echo of children's voices bouncing off the surrounding palaces makes the space
seem even more cavernous. Not long ago Campo San Polo hosted bull
races, fairs, military parades, and packed markets, but now it only
really comes alive on summer nights, when it hosts the city's outdoor
cinema. The **Chiesa di San Polo** has been restored so many times that
little remains of the original 9th-century church, and sadly, 19th-cen-
tury alterations were so costly that the friars sold off many great paintings to pay bills. Though Giambattista Tiepolo is represented here,
his work is outdone by 16 paintings by his son Giandomenico (1727–
1804), including the *Stations of the Cross* in the oratory to the left
of the entrance. The younger Tiepolo also created a series of expressive and theatrical renderings of the saints. Look for altarpieces by
Tintoretto and Veronese that managed to escape auction. San Polo's
bell tower remained unchanged through the centuries—don't miss the
two lions guarding it, playing with a disembodied human head and a
serpent. ✉*Campo San Polo* ☎*041/2750462 Chorus* ≌*€3, Chorus
pass €9* ☉*Mon.–Sat. 10–5, Sun. 1–5* Ⓥ*San Tomà.*

❸ Ca' Pesaro. Baldassare Longhena's grand baroque palace is the beautifully restored home of two impressive collections. The **Galleria Internazionale d'Arte Moderna** has works by 19th- and 20th-century artists
such as Klimt, Kandinsky, Matisse, and Miró. It also has a collection
of representative works from Venice's Biennale art show that amounts
to a panorama of 20th-century art. The **Museo Orientale** has a small
but striking collection of Oriental porcelains, musical instruments,
arms, and armor. ✉*San Stae, Santa Croce 2076* ☎*041/721127 Galleria, 041/5241173 Museo Orientale* ≌*€5.50 includes both museums*
☉*Apr.–Oct., daily 10–6; Nov.–Mar., daily 10–5* Ⓥ*San Stae.*

❺ San Giacomo dell'Orio. It was named after a laurel tree *(orio)*, and today
trees give character to this square. Add benches and a fountain (with
a drinking bowl for dogs), and the pleasant, oddly shaped campo
becomes a welcoming place for friendly conversation, picnics, and
neighborhood kids at play. Legend has it the **Chiesa di San Giacomo**

Venice's Scuola Days

An institution you'll inevitably encounter from Venice's glory days is the *scuola* (plural *scuole*). These weren't schools, as the word today translates, but an important network of institutions established by different social groups—enclaves of foreigners, tradesmen, followers of a particular saint, and parishioners.

For the most part secular despite their devotional activities, the scuole concentrated on charitable work, either helping their own membership or assisting the city's neediest citizens.

The tradesmen's and servants' scuole formed social security nets for elderly and disabled members. Wealthier scuole assisted orphans or provided dowries so poor girls could marry. By 1500 there were more than 200 major and minor scuole in Venice, some of which contributed substantially to arts and crafts guilds. The republic encouraged their existence—the scuole kept strict records of the names and professions of contributors to the brotherhood, which helped when it came time to collect taxes.

dell'Orio was founded in the 9th century on an island still populated by wolves. The current church dates from 1225; its short unmatched Byzantine columns survived renovation during the Renaissance, and the church never lost the feel of an ancient temple sheltering beneath its 15th-century ship's-keel roof. In the sanctuary, large marble crosses are surrounded by a bevy of small medieval Madonnas. The altarpiece is *Madonna with Child and Saints* (1546) by Lorenzo Lotto (1480–1556), and the sacristies contain works by Palma il Giovane (circa 1544–1628). ⊠*Campo San Giacomo dell'Orio, Santa Croce* ☎*041/2750462 Chorus* ⬛€*3, Chorus pass €9* ◷*Mon.–Sat. 10–5, Sun. 1–5* Ⓥ*San Stae.*

❷ **San Giovanni Elemosinario.** Storefronts make up the facade, and the altars were built by market guilds—poulterers, messengers, and fodder merchants—at this church intimately bound to the Rialto Market. It's as rich inside as it is simple outside. During San Giovanni Elemosinario's restoration, workers stumbled upon a frescoed cupola by Pordenone (1484–1539) that had been painted over centuries earlier. Don't miss Titian's *St. John the Almsgiver* and Pordenone's *Sts. Catherine, Sebastian, and Roch*, which in 2002 were returned after 30 years by the Gallerie dell'Accademia, a rare move for an Italian museum. ⊠*Rialto Ruga Vecchia San Giovanni, Santa Croce* ☎*041/2750462 Chorus* ⬛€*3, Chorus pass €9* ◷*Mon.–Sat. 10–5, Sun. 1–5* Ⓥ*San Silvestro/Rialto.*

❹ **San Stae.** The most renowned Venetian painters and sculptors of the early 18th century—known as the Moderns—decorated this church with the legacy left by Doge Alvise Mocenigo II, who's buried in the center aisle. A broad sampling of these masters includes works by Tiepolo, Ricci, Piazzetta, and Lazzarini. ⊠*Campo San Stae, Santa Croce* ☎*041/2750462 Chorus* ⬛€*3, Chorus pass €9* ◷*Mon.–Sat. 9–5, Sun. 1–5* Ⓥ*San Stae.*

CASTELLO & CANNAREGIO

Twice the size of tiny San Polo and Santa Croce, Castello and Cannaregio combined spread east to west from one end of Venice to the other. From working-class shipbuilding neighborhoods to the world's first ghetto, here you see a cross section of city life that's always existed beyond the palace walls. There are churches that could make a Renaissance pope jealous and one of the Grand Canal's prettiest palaces, Ca' d'Oro, as well as detour options for leaving the crowds behind.

TIMING

Visiting both sestieri involves a couple of hours of walking, even if you never enter a building, and there are few chances to hop a boat and save your legs. Some sights have restricted hours, making it virtually impossible to see everything even in a full day. Your best bet is to choose a few sights as priorities, time your tour around their open hours, and then drop in at whatever others happen to be open as you're passing by. If you're touring on Friday, keep in mind that synagogues close at sunset.

THE MAIN ATTRACTIONS

 ⑬ Arsenale. The Venetian Republic never could have thrived without the Arsenale shipyard. Today it belongs to the Italian Navy and isn't regularly open to the public, but it opens for the Biennale and for Venice's festival of traditional boats, held every May. If you're here during those times, don't miss the chance for a look inside. At other times, it's still worthwhile to walk by and observe the place from the outside.

The Arsenale is said to have been founded in 1104 on twin islands. The immense facility that evolved was given the old Venetian dialect name *arzanà*, borrowed from the Arabic *darsina'a*, meaning "workshop." At times it employed as many as 16,000 *arsenalotti*, workers who were among the most respected shipbuilders in the world. (Dante immortalized these sweating men armed with pitch and boiling tar in his *Inferno*.) Their diligence was confirmed time and again—whether building 100 ships in 60 days to battle the Turks in Cyprus (1597) or completing one perfectly armed warship—start to finish—while King Henry III of France attended a banquet.

The Arsenale's impressive Renaissance **gateway** (1460) is guarded by four lions, war booty of Francesco Morosini, who took the Peloponnese from the Turks in 1687. The 10-foot-tall lion on the left stood sentinel more than 2,000 years ago near Athens, and experts say its mysterious inscription is runic "graffiti" left by Viking mercenaries hired to suppress 11th-century revolts in Piraeus. If you look at the winged lion above the doorway, you'll notice that the Gospel at his paws is open but lacks the customary *Pax* inscription; praying for peace perhaps seemed inappropriate above a factory that manufactured weapons. ⊠ *Campo dell'Arsenale, Castello* Ⓥ *Arsenale.*

★ ❹ **Ca' d'Oro.** This exquisite Venetian Gothic palace was once literally a "Golden House," when its marble traceries and ornaments were embellished with pure gold. Created in 1434 by the enamored patrician Marino Contarini for his wife, Ca' d'Oro became a love offering a second time when a 19th-century Russian prince gave it to Maria Taglioni, a celebrated classical dancer who collected palaces along the Grand Canal. The last proprietor, perhaps more taken with Venice than with any of his lovers, left Ca' d'Oro to the city, after having had it carefully restored and filled with antiquities, sculptures, and paintings that today make up the **Galleria Franchetti.** Besides Andrea Mantegna's celebrated *St. Sebastian* and other first-rate Venetian works, the Galleria Franchetti contains the type of fresco that once adorned the exteriors of Venetian buildings (commissioned by those who could not afford a marble facade). One such detached fresco displayed here was made by a young Titian for the (now grayish-white) facade of the Fondaco dei Tedeschi, now the main post office. ⊠*Calle Ca' d'Oro, Cannaregio 3933* ☎*041/5222349* ⊕*www.cadoro.org* ✆*€6 includes Museo Orientale, €11 includes Gallerie dell'Accademia and Museo Orientale* ⊙*Tues.–Sun. 8:15–7, Mon. 8:15–2; last entry ½ hr before closing* Ⓥ*Ca' d'Oro.*

② **Jewish Ghetto.** The neighborhood that gave the world the word *ghetto* is today a quiet warren of backstreets that is still home to Jewish institutions, a kosher restaurant, a rabbinical school, and five synagogues. Though Jews may have arrived earlier, the first synagogues weren't built and a cemetery wasn't founded until the Askenazim, or Eastern European Jews, came in the late 1300s. Dwindling coffers may have prompted the republic to sell temporary visas to Jews, but over the centuries they were alternately tolerated and expelled. The Rialto commercial district, as vividly recounted in Shakespeare's *The Merchant of Venice*, depended on Jewish merchants and moneylenders for trade, and to help cover ever-increasing war expenses.

In 1516 relentless local opposition forced the Senate to confine Jews to an island in Cannaregio, named for its *geto* (foundry), which produced cannons. Gates at the entrance were locked at night, and boats patrolled the surrounding canals. The German accents of early residents changed the soft g sound of "geto" (pronounced zheto) into the hard g in "ghetto." Jews were allowed only to lend money at low interest, operate pawnshops controlled by the government, trade in textiles, or practice medicine. Jewish doctors were highly respected and could leave the ghetto at any hour when on duty. Though ostracized, Jews were nonetheless safe in Venice, and in the 16th century the community grew considerably, with refugees from the Near East, southern and central Italy, Spain, and Portugal. The ghetto was allowed to expand twice, but it still had the city's densest population and consequently ended up with the city's tallest buildings (nine stories); notice the slanting apartment blocks on Campo del Ghetto Nuovo. Although the gates were pulled down after Napóleon's 1797 arrival, the Jews realized full freedom only in the late 19th century with the founding of the Italian state. On the eve of World War II there were about 1,500 Jews left in the ghetto: 247 were deported by the Nazis; 8 returned.

The area has Europe's highest density of Renaissance-era synagogues, and visiting them is a unique cross-cultural experience. Though each is marked by the tastes of its individual builders, Venetian influence is evident throughout. Women's galleries resemble those of theaters from the same era, and some synagogues were decorated by artisans who were simultaneously active in local churches.

The small but well-arranged **Museo Ebraico** highlights centuries of Jewish culture with splendid silver Hanukkah lamps and Torahs, and handwritten, beautifully decorated wedding contracts in Hebrew. Tours of the ghetto in Italian and English leave hourly from the museum. ⊠*Campo del Ghetto Nuovo, Cannaregio 2902/b* ☎*041/715359* ⊕*www.museoebraico.it* 🖾*Museum €3, museum and synagogues €8.50* 🕙*June–Sept., Sun.–Fri. 10–7, last tour 5:30; Oct.–May, Sun.– Fri. 10–6, last tour 3:30* Ⓥ*San Marcuola/Guglie.*

You might complete your circuit of Jewish Venice with a visit to the **Antico Cimitero Ebraico** *(Ancient Jewish Cemetery)* on the Lido, full of fascinating old tombstones half hidden by ivy and grass. The earliest grave dates from 1389; the cemetery remained in use until the late 18th century. ⊠*Via Cipro, Lido* ☎*041/715359* 🖾*€8.50* 🕙*Tours Apr.– Oct., Sun. at 2:30; call for arrangements* Ⓥ*Lido/S. Maria Elisabetta.*

★ **Santa Maria dei Miracoli.** Tiny yet perfectly proportioned, this early-Renaissance gem is sheathed in marble and decorated inside with exquisite marble reliefs. Architect Pietro Lombardo (circa 1435–1515) miraculously compressed the building into its confined space, then created the illusion of greater size by varying the color of the exterior, adding extra pilasters on the building's canal side, and offsetting the arcade windows to make the arches appear deeper. The church was built in the 1480s to house *I Miracoli,* an image of the Virgin Mary that is said to perform miracles—look for it on the high altar. ⊠*Campo Santa Maria Nova, Cannaregio* ☎*041/2750462 Chorus* ✉*€3, Chorus pass €9* ⊙ *Mon.–Sat. 10–5, Sun. 1–5* Ⓥ*Rialto.*

★ ❾ **Santi Giovanni e Paolo.** This massive Dominican church, commonly called San Zanipolo, contains a wealth of art. The 15th-century stained-glass window near the side entrance is breathtaking for its brilliant colors and beautiful figures, made from drawings by Bartolomeo Vivarini and Gerolamo Mocetto. The second official church of the republic after San Marco, San Zanipolo is the Venetian equivalent of London's Westminster Abbey, with a great number of important people, including 25 doges, buried here. Artistic highlights include an outstanding polyptych by Giovanni Bellini (right aisle, second altar); Alvise Vivarini's *Christ Carrying the Cross* (sacresti); and Lorenzo Lotto's *Charity of St. Antonino* (right transept). Don't miss the *Cappella del Rosario* (Rosary Chapel), off the left transept, built in the 16th century to commemorate the 1571 victory of Lepanto, in western Greece, when Venice led a combined European fleet to defeat the Turkish Navy. The chapel was devastated by a fire in 1867 and restored in the early years of the 20th century with works from other churches, among them the sumptuous Veronese ceiling paintings. However quick your visit, don't miss the Pietro Mocenigo tomb to the right of the main entrance, a monument built by the ubiquitous Pietro Lombardo and his sons. ⊠*Campo dei Santi Giovanni e Paolo, Castello* ☏*041/5235913* ☜*€2.50* ☉*Mon.– Sat. 9:30–6:30, Sun. noon–5:30* Ⓥ*Fondamente Nuove/Rialto.*

NEED A BREAK?

To satisfy your sweet tooth, head for Campo Santa Marina and the family-owned and -operated Didovich Pastry Shop (☏*041/5230017*). It's a local favorite, especially for Carnevale-time *fritelle* (fried doughnuts). There is limited seating inside, but in the warmer months you can sit outside. Bar ai Miracoli (☏*041/5231515*) in Campo Santa Maria Nova is a good place to grab a quick bite and gaze across the canal at Santa Maria dei Miracoli, Lombardo's miracle in marble.

ALSO WORTH SEEING

⑤ Gesuiti. Extravagantly baroque, this 18th-century church completely abandons classical Renaissance straight lines in favor of flowing, twisting forms. Its interior walls resemble brocade drapery, and only touching them will convince skeptics that rather than paint, the green-and-white walls are inlaid marble. Over the first altar on the left, the *Martyrdom of St. Lawrence* is a dramatic example of Titian's feeling for light and movement. ⊠*Campo dei Gesuiti, Cannaregio* ☏*041/5286579* ☉*Daily 10–noon and 4–6* Ⓥ*Fondamente Nuove.*

☾ ⑫ Museo Storico Navale *(Museum of Naval History).* The boat collection here includes scale models such as the doges' ceremonial *Bucintoro,* and full-size boats such as Peggy Guggenheim's private gondola complete with romantic *felze* (cabin). There's a range of old galley and military pieces, and also a large collection of seashells. ⊠*Campo San Biagio, Castello 2148* ☏*041/2441399* ⊕*www.marina.difesa.it/venezia/* ☜*€1.55* ☉*Weekdays 8:45–1:30, Sat. 8:45–1* Ⓥ*Arsenale.*

① Palazzo Labia. Once the home of 18th-century Venice's showiest family, this palace is now the Venetian headquarters of the Italian media giant RAI—modern broadcasting goes baroque. In the **Tiepolo Room,** the Labia's gorgeous ballroom, the final flowering of Venetian painting is seen in Giambattista Tiepolo's playful frescoes of Antony and Cleopatra among dwarfs and Barbary pirates. You have to call ahead to arrange a visit here. ⊠*Campo San Geremia, Cannaregio 275* ☏*041/781277* ☜*Free* ☉*Wed.–Fri. 3–4, by appointment* Ⓥ*Ferrovia.*

③ Palazzo Vendramin-Calergi. This Renaissance classic with an imposing carved frieze is the work of Mauro Codussi (1440–1504). You can see some of its interior by dropping into the **Casinò di Venezia.** Fans of Richard Wagner (1813–83) might enjoy visiting the **Sala di Wagner,** the room (separate from the casino) in which the composer died. Though rather plain, it's loaded with music memorabilia. ⊠*Cannaregio 2040* ☏*041/5297111 Casino, 041/2760407 by Fri.* AM *to reserve Wagner*

CLOSE UP

Let's Get Lost

Getting around Venice presents some unusual problems: the city's layout has few straight lines; house numbering seems nonsensical; and the *sestieri* (six districts) of San Marco, Cannaregio, Castello, Dorsoduro, Santa Croce, and San Polo all duplicate each other's street names. The numerous vaporetto lines can be bewildering, and often the only option for getting where you want to go is to walk. Yellow signs, posted on many busy corners, point toward the major landmarks—San Marco, Rialto, Accademia, etc.—but don't count on finding such markers once you're deep into residential neighborhoods. Even buying a good map at a newsstand—the kind showing all street names and vaporetto routes—won't necessarily keep you from getting lost.

Fortunately, as long as you maintain your patience, getting lost in Venice can be a pleasure. For one thing, being lost is a sign that you've escaped the tourist throngs. And although you might not find the Titian masterpiece you'd set out to see, instead you could wind up coming across an ageless bacaro or a quirky shop that turns out to be the highlight of your afternoon. Opportunities for such serendipity abound. Keep in mind that the city is nothing if not self-contained: sooner or later, perhaps with the help of a patient native, you can rest assured you'll regain your bearings.

Room tours ✉*Casino €10, tour €5 suggested donation* ☉*Slots: daily 2:45* PM–*2:30* AM; *tables: daily 3:30* PM–*2:30* AM; *Wagner Room: Tues., Thurs., Sat.* AM *by appointment* Ⓥ*San Marcuola.*

8 **Querini-Stampalia.** The art collection at this Renaissance palace includes Giovanni Bellini's *Presentation in the Temple* and Sebastiano Ricci's triptych *Dawn, Afternoon, and Evening.* Portraits of newlyweds Francesco Querini and Paola Priuli were left unfinished on the death of Giacomo Palma il Vecchio (1480–1528); note the groom's hand and the bride's dress. Original 18th-century furniture and stuccowork are a fitting background for Pietro Longhi's portraits. Nearly 70 works by Gabriele Bella (1730–99) capture scenes of Venetian street life. Admission Friday and Saturday includes concerts with antique instruments at 5 and 8:30. ✉*Campo Santa Maria Formosa, Castello 5252* 🕾*041/2711411* ⊕*www.querinistampalia.it* ✉*€8* ☉*Tues.–Thurs. and Sun. 10–6, Fri. and Sat. 10–10* Ⓥ*San Zaccaria.*

7 **Santa Maria Formosa.** Guided by his vision of a beautiful Madonna, 7th-century St. Magno is said to have followed a small white cloud and built a church where it settled. Gracefully white, the marble building you see today dates from 1492, built by Mauro Codussi on an older foundation. The interior is a blend of Renaissance decoration, a Byzantine cupola, barrel vaults, and narrow-columned screens. Of interest are two fine paintings: *Our Lady of Mercy* by Bartolomeo Vivarini and *Santa Barbara* by Palma il Vecchio. The surrounding square bustles with sidewalk cafés and a produce market on weekday mornings. ✉*Campo Santa Maria Formosa, Castello* 🕾*041/5234645,*

041/2750462 Chorus 💳*€3, Chorus pass €9* 🕐*Mon.–Sat. 10–5, Sun. 1–5* 🅅*Rialto.*

🔟 **Scuola di San Giorgio degli Schiavoni.** Founded in 1451 by the Dalmatian community, this small scuola was, and still is, a social and cultural center for migrants from what is now Croatia. It's dominated by one of Italy's most beautiful rooms, lavishly yet harmoniously decorated with the *teleri* (large canvases) of Vittore Carpaccio. A lifelong Venice resident, Carpaccio painted legendary and religious figures against backgrounds of Venetian architecture. Here he focused on saints especially venerated in Dalmatia: St. George, St. Tryphone, and St. Jerome. He combined observation with fantasy, a sense of warm color with a sense of humor (don't miss the priests fleeing St. Jerome's lion, or the body parts in the dragon's lair). ✉*Calle dei Furlani, Castello 3259/a* 📞*041/5228828* 💳*€3* 🕐*Tues.–Sat. 9:15–1 and 2:45–6, Sun. 9:15–1; last entry ½ hr before closing* 🅅*Arsenale/San Zaccaria.*

SAN GIORGIO MAGGIORE & THE GIUDECCA

Beckoning travelers across St. Mark's Basin, sparkling white through the mist, is the island of San Giorgio Maggiore, separated by a small channel from the Giudecca. A tall brick campanile on that distant bank perfectly complements the Campanile of San Marco. Beneath it looms the stately dome of one of Venice's greatest churches, San Giorgio Maggiore, the creation of Andrea Palladio.

You can reach San Giorgio Maggiore via vaporetto Line 82 from San Zaccaria. The next three stops on the line take you to the Giudecca. The island's past may be shrouded in mystery, but today it's about as down to earth as you can get and one of the city's few remaining neighborhoods that feels truly Venetian.

TIMING
A half day should be plenty of time to visit the area. Allow about a half hour to see each of the churches, and an hour or two to look around the Giudecca.

THE MAIN ATTRACTIONS
Giudecca. The island's name is something of a mystery. It may come from a possible 14th-century Jewish settlement, or because 9th-century nobles condemned to *giudicato* (exile) were sent here. It became a pleasure garden for wealthy Venetians during the republic's long and luxurious decline, but today, like Cannaregio, it's largely working class. The Giudecca provides spectacular views of Venice and is becoming increasingly gentrified. While here, visit the **Santissimo Redentore** church, designed by Palladio and built to commemorate a plague. The third weekend in July it's the site of the Venetians' favorite festival, Redentore, featuring boats, fireworks, and outdoor feasting. Thanks to

several bridges, you can walk the entire length of the Giudecca's promenade, relaxing at one of several restaurants or just taking in the lively atmosphere. Accommodations run the gamut from youth hostels to the city's most exclusive hotel, Cipriani. ⊠ *Fondamenta San Giacomo, Giudecca* ☎*041/5231415, 041/2750462 Chorus* ⬚*€3, Chorus pass €9* ⊙ *Mon.–Sat. 10–5, Sun. 1–5* Ⓥ *Redentore.*

San Giorgio Maggiore. There's been a church on this island since the 8th century, with a Benedictine monastery added in the 10th century (closed to the public). Today's refreshingly airy and simply decorated church of brick and white marble was begun in 1566 by Palladio and displays his architectural hallmarks of mathematical harmony and classical influence. *The Last Supper* and the *Gathering of Manna*, two of Tintoretto's later works, line the chancel. To the right of the entrance hangs *The Adoration of the Shepherds* by Jacopo Bassano (1517–92); his affection for his foothills home, Bassano del Grappa, is evident in the bucolic subjects and terra-firma colors he chooses. The monks are happy to show Carpaccio's *St. George and the Dragon,* hanging in a private room, if they have time. The campanile is so tall that it was struck by lightning in 1993. Take the elevator to the top for some of the finest views in town. ⊠ *Isola di San Giorgio Maggiore* ☎*041/5227827* ⬚*Church free, campanile €3* ⊙ *Daily 9–12:30 and 2:30–6* Ⓥ *San Giorgio.*

ISLANDS OF THE LAGOON

The perfect vacation from your Venetian vacation is an escape to Murano, Burano, and sleepy Torcello, the islands of the northern lagoon. Torcello offers greenery, breathing space, and picnic opportunities (remember to pack lunch). Burano is a toy town of houses painted in a riot of colors—blue, yellow, pink, ocher, and dark red. Visitors still love to shop here for "Venetian" lace, even though the vast majority of it is machine-made in Taiwan. Murano is renowned for its glass, but also notorious for the high-pressure sales on its factory tours, even those organized by top hotels. Vaporetto connections to Murano aren't difficult, and for the price of a boat ticket you'll buy your freedom and more time to explore. The Murano "guides" herding new arrivals follow a rotation so that factories take turns giving tours, but you can avoid the hustle by just walking away.

TIMING

Hitting all the sights on all the islands takes a full day. If you limit yourself to Murano and San Michele, a half day will suffice. In summer San Zaccaria is connected to Murano by express vaporetto Line 5; the trip takes 25 minutes. In winter the local Line 41 takes about 45 minutes. The boat leaves San Zaccaria (in front of the Savoia e Jolanda hotel) every 20 minutes, circling the east end of Venice and stopping at Fondamente Nuove before making the five-minute hop to the San Michele island cemetery and then heading on to Murano. To see glassblowing, get off at Colonna; the Museo stop will put you near the Museo Vetrario.

Venetian Lagoon

Line LN goes from Fondamente Nuove direct to Murano, Burano, and Torcello every 30 minutes, and the full trip takes 45 minutes each way. To get to Burano and Torcello from Murano, pick up Line LN at the Faro stop (Murano's lighthouse), which runs to Burano before continuing on to Torcello, only five minutes away.

THE MAIN ATTRACTIONS

★ ❸ **Burano.** Cheerfully painted houses line the canals of this quiet village where lace making rescued a faltering fishing-based economy centuries ago. As you walk the 100 yards from the dock to Piazza Galuppi, the main square, you pass stall after stall of lace vendors. These good-natured ladies won't press you with a hard sell, but don't expect precise product information or great bargains—real handmade Burano lace costs $1,000 to $2,000 for a 10-inch doily.

The **Museo del Merletto** (*Lace Museum*) lets you marvel at the intricacies of Burano's lace making. It's also a skills center—more sewing circle than school—where on weekdays you'll usually find women carrying on the tradition. They sometimes have authentic pieces for sale privately. ✉*Piazza Galuppi 187* ☎*041/730034* 🎟€4, Musei Civici pass *€18* ⊙*Apr.–Oct., daily 10–5; Nov.–Mar., daily 10–4* ▼*Burano.*

☕ ❷ **Murano.** As in Venice, bridges here link a number of small islands, which are dotted with houses that once were workmen's cottages. In the 13th century the republic, concerned about fire hazard, moved its glassworks to Murano, and today you can visit the factories and watch glass being made. Many of them line the Fondamenta dei Vetrai, the canal-side walkway leading from the Colonna vaporetto landing.

Before you reach Murano's Grand Canal (a little more than 800 feet from the landing) you'll pass **Chiesa di San Pietro Martire.** Reconstructed in the 16th century, it houses Giovanni Bellini's *Madonna and Child* and Veronese's *St. Jerome.* ✉*Fondamenta dei Vetrai* ☎*041/739704* ⊙*Weekdays 9–6, Sat. 2–6, Sun. 11:30–5* ▼*Colonna.*

The collection at the **Museo Vetrario** (*Glass Museum*) ranges from priceless antiques to only slightly less-expensive modern pieces. You'll see authentic Venetian styles and patterns, including the famous Barovier wedding cup (1470–80). ✉*Fondamenta Giustinian 8* ☎*041/739586* 🎟€5.50, Musei Civici museum pass €18 ⊙Apr.–Oct., daily 10–6; Nov.– Mar., daily 10–5. Last tickets sold ½ hr before closing* ▼*Museo.*

The **Basilica dei Santi Maria e Donato,** just past the glass museum, is among the first churches founded by the lagoon's original inhabitants. The elaborate mosaic pavement includes the date 1140; its ship's-keel roof and Veneto-Byzantine columns add to the semblance of an ancient temple. ✉*Fondamenta Giustinian* ☎*041/739056* 🎟*Free* ⊙*Mon.– Sat. 8–6, Sun. 2–6* ▼*Museo.*

★ ❹ **Torcello.** In their flight from barbarians 1,500 years ago, the first Venetians landed here, prospering even after many left to found the city of Venice. As malaria took its toll and the island's wool manufacturing was priced out of the market, Torcello became a ghost town. In the 16th century there were 10 churches and 20,000 inhabitants; today you'll be lucky to see one of the island's 16 permanent residents.

Santa Maria Assunta was built in the 11th century, and Torcello's wealth at the time is evident in the church's high-quality Byzantine mosaics. The massive *Last Judgment* shows sinners writhing in pain, while opposite, above the altar, the Madonna looks calmly down from her field of gold. Ask to see the inscription dated 639 and a sample of mosaic pavement from the original church. The adjacent **Santa Fosca** church, added when the body of the saint arrived in 1011, is still used for religious services. It's worth making the climb up the adjacent **campanile** for an incomparable view of the lagoon wetlands. ✉*Torcello* ☎*041/730119* 🎟*Santa Maria Assunta €4, campanile €4* ⊙*Basilica: Mar.–Oct., daily 10:30–6; Nov.–Feb., daily 10–5. Campanile: Mar.– Oct., daily 10:30–5:30; Nov.–Feb., daily 10–4:30. Last entry ½ hr before closing* ▼*Torcello.*

NEED A BREAK? Locanda Cipriani (☎ *041/730150*), closed Tuesday and January, is famous for good food and its connection to Ernest Hemingway, who often came to Torcello seeking solitude. Today the restaurant (not to be confused with the Giudecca's Cipriani hotel) is busy, with well-heeled customers speeding in for lunch (dinner also on weekends). Dining is pricey, but you can relax in the garden with just a glass of prosecco.

ALSO WORTH SEEING

❶ **San Michele.** This cypress-lined island is home to the pretty Renaissance church of **San Michele in Isola**—and to some of Venice's most illustrious deceased. The church was designed by Codussi; the graves include those of poet Ezra Pound (1885–1972), impresario and art critic Sergey Diaghilev (1872–1929), and composer Igor Stravinsky (1882–1971). Surrounded by the living sounds of Venice's lagoon, this would seem the perfect final resting place. However, these days newcomers are exhumed after 10 years and transferred to a less-grandiose location. ☎*041/7292811* ☒*Free* ☉*Apr.–Sept., daily 7:30–6; Oct.–Mar., daily 7:30–4* Ⓥ*San Michele.*

WHERE TO EAT

Updated by Shannon Essa & Ruth Edenbaum

The catchword in Venice, at both fancy restaurants and holes-in-the-wall, is fish, often at its tastiest when it looks like nothing you've seen before. How do you learn firsthand about the catch of the day? An early-morning visit to the Rialto's *pescheria* (fish market) is more instructive than any book.

There's no getting around the fact that Venice has more than its share of overpriced, mediocre eateries that prey on tourists. Avoid places with cajoling waiters standing outside, and beware of restaurants that don't display their prices. At the other end of the spectrum, showy *menu turistico* (tourist menu) boards make offerings clear in a dozen languages, but for the same 15–20 euros you'd spend at such places you could do better at a *bacaro* (the local version of a wine bar) making a meal of *cicchetti* (savory snacks).

Dining options in Venice range from the ultrahigh end, where jackets and ties are required, to the supercasual, where the clientele (almost all of them tourists) won't notice if you're wearing shorts. Some of Venice's swankiest restaurants—the ones that usually have only male waiters wearing white jackets and bow ties—trade on long-standing reputations and might seem a little stuffy and faded. The food at such places tends toward interpretations of international cuisine and, though often expertly prepared, can seem as old-fashioned as the waiters who serve it. On the other hand, mid-range restaurants are often more willing to break from tradition, incorporating ingredients such as ginger and wasabi in their creations.

Budget-conscious travelers, and those simply looking for a good meal in unpretentious surroundings, might want to stick to trattorias and bacari. Trattorias often serve less-highfalutin versions of classic Vene-

6

tian dishes at substantially reduced prices; bacari offer lighter fare, usually eaten at the bar (though sometimes tables are available), and wine lists that offer lots of choices by the glass.

WHAT IT COSTS IN EUROS				
	¢	$	$$	$$$	$$$$
At Dinner	under €15	€15–€25	€25–€35	€35–€45	over €45

Prices are for a first course (primo), second course (secondo), and dessert (dolce).

CANNAREGIO

$$$ ✕ **Al Fontego dei Pescaori.** Having had a stall at the Rialto fish market for over 25 years, Lolo, the proprietor, really knows fish, and diners fill two cheerful dining rooms to savor what might just be the freshest fish in Venice. There are several spectacular offerings of pesce crudo (raw fish) among the antipasti. Pastas are excellent and the fish entrées are prepared simply but with a twist. Branzino (sea bass) may be topped with its own crispy skin and a frizzle of zucchini or wrapped around itself with the succulent skin becoming the stuffing. Meat dishes are available, but the wine list is built around local wines that go best with fish. ⊠ *Sottoportego del Tagiapier, Cannaregio 3711* ☎ *041/5200538* ▭ *MC, V* ⊙ *Closed Mon., 3 wks in Jan., 2 wks in Aug.* Ⓥ *Ca' d'Oro.*

★ **$$–$$$**   ✕ **Vini da Gigio.** This family-run trattoria on the San Felice Canal is deservedly popular with Venetians and visitors. Homemade pastas, such as rigatoni with duck sauce and arugula-stuffed ravioli nestled in a rich cheese sauce, are excellent. Fish is well represented on the menu, but the meat dishes steal the show: the Burano-style duck is a flavorful fricassee, the steak with red-pepper sauce and the lamb with a heavenly crusty coating are both superb, and the *fegato alla Veneziana* (Venetian style liver with onions) is among the best in Venice. Desserts are worth every luscious calorie. The wine list of over one thousand bottles is a major attraction; an oenophile will be in ecstasy here. ⊠ *Fondamenta de la Chiesa, Cannaregio 3628/a* ☎ *041/5285140* ▭ *DC, MC, V* ⊙ *Closed Mon. and Tues., 2 wks in Jan., and 3 wks in Aug.* Ⓥ *Ca' d'Oro.*

$–$$$ ✕ **Algiubagiò.** A waterfront table is still relatively affordable here on Venice's northern Fondamente Nuove, where you can gaze out toward San Michele and Murano—on a clear day, you can even see the Dolomites. Algiubagiò has a dual personality: pizzas and big, creative salads at lunch; elegant secondi such as Angus fillets and duck with prunes and rosemary at dinner. (There's no fish on the dinner menu.) The young, friendly staff also serves ice cream, drinks, and sandwiches all day. A table here is worth the walk. ⊠ *Fondamente Nuove, Cannaregio 5039* ☎ *041/5236084* ▭ *MC, V* Ⓥ *Fondamente Nuove.*

$$ ✕ **Anice Stellato.** Hidden away on one of the most romantic *fondamente* (canal-side streets) of Cannaregio, this family-run *bacaro*-trattoria is the place to stop for fairly priced, great-tasting food, though service can feel indifferent. The space has plenty of character: narrow columns rise from the colorful tile floor, dividing the room into cozy sections. Tradi-

BEST BETS VENICE DINING

With hundreds of restaurants to choose from, how will you decide where to eat? Fodor's writers and editors have selected their favorite restaurants by price and experience in the Best Bets lists below. In the first column, Fodor's Choice properties represent the "best of the best."

Fodor's Choice ★

Al Paradiso p.450
Cantinone Gia Schiavi p.450
La Zucca p.452
Ristorante Riviera p.447

Best by Price

BEST ¢

Cantinone Gia Schiavi p.450
Enoteca al Volto p.450

BEST $

Al Prosecco p.452
Antica Birreria La Corte p.451
Ostaria al Garanghelo p.451

BEST $$

Bancogiro p.451
Anice Stellato p.446
La Zucca p.452

BEST $$$

Al Fontego dei Pescaori p.444
Antiche Carampane p.451
Vecio Fritolin p.452
Vini da Gigio p.444

BEST $$$$

Alle Testiere p.446
Al Paradiso p.450
Osteria da Fiore p.450
Ristorante Riviera p.447

Best Experiences

OUTDOOR DINING

Algiubagiò p.444
Bancogiro p.451
Ristorante Riviera p.447

ROMANTIC

Al Paradiso p.450
Osteria da Fiore p.450
Ristorante Riviera p.447

GOOD FOR KIDS

Antica Birraria La Corte p.451
Ostaria al Garanghelo p.451

IF YOU DON'T WANT FISH

Antica Birraria La Corte p.451
La Bitta p.447
La Zucca p.452
Vini da Gigio p.444

GREAT VIEWS

Algiubagiò p.444
Bancogiro p.451
Ristorante Riviera p.447

EXCEPTIONAL WINE LIST

Antiche Carampane p.451
Osteria da Fiore p.450
Vini da Gigio p.444

GOOD FOR LUNCH

Alla Vedova p.446
Antica Birraria La Corte p.451
La Zucca p.452
Vecio Fritolin p.452

ALTA CUCINA (SOPHISTICATED CUISINE)

Alle Testiere p.446
Osteria da Fiore p.450

CASALINGA (HOME COOKING)

La Bitta p.447
Ostaria al Garanghelo p.451

6

tional Venetian fare is enriched with such offerings as *carpacci di pesce* (thin slices of raw tuna, swordfish, or salmon dressed with olive oil and fragrant herbs), tagliatelle with king prawns and zucchini flowers, and several tasty fish stews. Meat dishes are also served, including a tender beef fillet stewed in Barolo wine with potatoes. ✉*Fondamenta de la Sensa, Cannaregio 3272* ☎*041/720744* ⊟*MC, V* ☺*Closed Mon. and Tues., 1 wk in Feb., and 3 wks in Aug.* Ⓥ*S. Alvise.*

★ $ ✗**Alla Vedova.** This warm trattoria not far from the Ca' d'Oro (it's also known as Trattoria Ca' d'Oro) was opened as a *bacaro* by the owner's great-grandparents. A Venetian terrazzo floor, old marble counter, and rustic furnishings lend a pleasant authenticity that's matched by the food and service. Cicchetti include tender *seppie roste* (grilled cuttlefish), *polpette* (meatballs), and *baccalà mantecato* (cod creamed with milk and olive oil). The house winter pasta is the *pastisso de radicio rosso* (lasagna with sausage, radicchio, and béchamel sauce). In spring the chef switches to pastisso *de asparagi* (with asparagus). ✉*Calle del Pistor, Cannaregio 3912* ☎*041/5285324* ⊟*No credit cards* ☺*Closed Thurs. No lunch Sun.* Ⓥ*Ca' d'Oro.*

CASTELLO

★ $$$$ ✗**Alle Testiere.** A strong local following can make it tough to get one of the 22 seats at this tiny trattoria near Campo Santa Maria Formosa. With its decidedly unglamorous ceiling fans, the place feels as informal as a bistro (or a saloon); the food, however, is much more sophisticated. Chef Bruno Gavagnin's dishes stand out for lightness and balance: try the *gnocchetti con moscardini* (little gnocchi with baby octopus) or the linguine with *coda di rospo* (monkfish), or inquire about the carpaccio of the day. The wine list is particularly strong on local whites. ✉*Calle del Mondo Novo, Castello 5801* ☎*041/5227220* ⚭*Reservations essential* ⊟*MC, V* ☺*Closed Sun. and Mon., 3 wks Jan.–Feb., and 4 wks July–Aug.* Ⓥ*Rialto/San Zaccaria.*

$$$$ ✗**Do Leoni.** The Two Lions, in the Hotel Londra Palace, is a sumptuous candlelit setting in which to sample modern and traditional Venetian and other Italian cuisine. The kitchen turns out creative dishes like tagliatelle with chicory, Gorgonzola, and peanuts. The summer terrace occupies a good portion of the Riva. ✉*Riva degli Schiavoni, Castello 4171* ☎*041/5200533* ⚭*Reservations essential* ⊟*AE, DC, MC, V* Ⓥ*San Zaccaria.*

★ $$–$$$ ✗**Corte Sconta.** You're close to seafood heaven at this firm favorite on the Venetian dining scene. Simple wooden tables are arranged around an open courtyard with outdoor seating in summer. You could make a meal of the seafood antipasti alone, but you'd miss out on such delights as spaghetti *neri con scampi e spinaci* (cuttlefish-ink pasta with scampi and spinach) and *vongole veraci spadellate allo zenzero* (clams sautéed in ginger). The house dessert is a warm zabaglione with Venetian cookies, and the house pour is a smooth, still prosecco, backed up by a good range of bottled wines. ✉*Calle del Pestrin, Castello 3886* ☎*041/5227024* ⚭*Reservations essential* ⊟*MC, V* ☺*Closed Sun. and Mon., 3 wks in Jan., and 4 wks in July and Aug.* Ⓥ*Arsenale.*

DORSODURO

★ $$$$ ✕**Ristorante Riviera.** Two lovely dining rooms and a canal-side terrace with an exquisite view, combined with truly inspired cuisine, make a visit to Riviera one to remember. Chef Monica Scarpa brings her creative touch to both traditional and contemporary dishes. Fish lovers will enjoy the tuna tartare, seafood risotto, or a mixed fish platter, while carnivores can dig into prosciutto with figs and pecorino cheese followed by a plate of succulent lamb chops with blueberry sauce. Host Luca excels at selecting the perfect wine for any combination of foods. Desserts include a plate of homemade cookies served with vin santo (sweet wine). A simple but appealing children's menu is offered. ⊠*Zattere, Dorsoduro 1473* ☎*041/5227621* ⚓*Reservations essential* ⊟*MC, V* ⊗*Closed Mon., 4 weeks in Jan. and Feb.* Ⓥ*San Basilio.*

★ $$$–$$$$ ✕**Avogaria.** In terms of both food and architecture, ultrafashionable Avogaria lends modern flavor to the Venice restaurant scene. The clean, elegant design of the dining room and garden leaves no doubt that here, you're in the Venice of the present, not the past. The cuisine is Pugliese (from the region in the heel of Italy's boot); highlights among the primi include *orecchiette* (small, round pasta) with turnip tops, and zucchini *involtini* (roll-ups) made with fresh stracciatella cheese. Pugliese cooking, like Venetian, reveres fresh seafood, and you can taste this sensibility in the slow-cooked, sesame-encrusted tuna steak. ⊠*Calle Avogaria, Dorsoduro 1629* ☎*041/2960491* ⊟*AE, DC, MC, V* ⊗*Closed Tues.* Ⓥ*S. Basilio.*

★ $$ ✕**La Bitta.** The decor is more discreet, the dining hours longer, and the service friendlier and more efficient here than in many small restaurants in Venice—and the creative nonfish menu is a temptation at every course. You can start with a light salad of Treviso radicchio and crispy bacon, followed by smoked-beef carpaccio or *gnocchetti ubriachi al Montasio* (small marinated gnocchi with Montasio cheese). Then choose from secondi such as lamb chops with thyme, *anatra in pevarada* (duck in a pepper sauce), or Irish Angus fillet steak. Secondi are served with vegetables, which helps bring down the price. The restaurant is open only for dinner, but serves much later than most, continuously from 6:30 to 11. ⊠*Calle Lunga San Barnaba, Dorsoduro 2753/a* ☎*041/5230531* ⊟*No credit cards* ⊗*Closed Sun. and July. No lunch* Ⓥ*Ca' Rezzonico.*

$ ✕**Ai 4 Feri.** The paper tablecloths and cozy, laid-back ambience are part of this small restaurant's charm. The menu varies according to what's fresh that day; imaginative combinations of ingredients in the primi—herring and sweet peppers, salmon and radicchio, giant shrimp and broccoli (with pumpkin gnocchi)—are the norm. A meal here followed by after-dinner drinks at Campo Santa Margherita, a five-minute walk away, makes for a lovely evening. The kitchen is open until 10:30 PM. ⊠*Calle Lunga San Barnaba, Dorsoduro 2754/a* ☎*041/5206978* ⊟*No credit cards* ⊗*Closed Sun. and 2 wks in June* Ⓥ*Ca' Rezzonico.*

¢ ✕**Cantinone Già Schiavi.** This beautiful 19th-century *bacaro* opposite the *squero* (gondola repair shop) of San Trovaso has original furnishings and one of the best wine selections in town—the walls are covered floor to ceiling by bottles for purchase. Cicchetti here are some

Where to Stay & Eat in Venice

CIMITERO

Cimitero
San
Michele

Sacca
della
Misericordia

Canale delle Fondamente Nuove

FOND. NUOVE

20

4

5

17 19 6

18

7

CA' D'ORO

Campo d.
Pescheria

8

OSPEDALE
CIVILE

15

Ponte di
Rialto

14 RIALTO

16

21

San
Zaccaria

CELESTIA

9

15

14

Piazza
San Marco

13 22

11

12

Castello

23

Darsena
Grande

Rio d. Vergini

16

SAN MARCO
GIARDINETTI

S. ZACCARIA

S. ZACCARIA JOLANDA

S. ZACCARIA
DANIELI

ARSENALE

VALLARESSO

SALUTE

18

10

GIARDINI

Bacino San Marco

S. GIORGIO

S. Giorgio
Maggiore

ZITELLE

Calle Michelangelo

30

31

TO CHIESA DEL
RENDENTORE

KEY

1 Hotels

1 Restaurants

i Tourist information

◆ Vaporetto stop

of the most inventive in Venice: try the crostini-style layers of bread, smoked swordfish, and slivers of raw zucchini, or pungent slices of parmeggiano, fig, and toast. They also have a creamy version of baccalà mantecato spiced with herbs. There are nearly a dozen open bottles of wine for experimenting at the bar. ⊠ *Fondamenta Maravegiei, Dorsoduro 992* 🕾 *041/5230034* ⊟ *No credit cards* ⊘ *Closed 2 wks in Aug.* Ⓥ *Zattere.*

SAN MARCO

¢–$ ✕ **Enoteca al Volto.** A short walk from the Rialto Bridge, this bar has been around since 1936; the fine cicchetti and primi have a lot to do with its staying power. Two small, dark rooms with wooden tables and chairs are the backdrop for the enjoyment of simple fare. The place prides itself on its considerable wine list of both Italian and foreign vintages; if you stick to the *panini* (sandwiches) and a cicchetto or two, you'll eat well for relatively little. If you opt for one of the primi of the day, the price category goes up a notch. ⊠ *Calle Cavalli, San Marco 4081* 🕾 *041/5228945* ⊟ *No credit cards* ⊘ *Closed Sun.* Ⓥ *Rialto.*

SAN POLO

★ $$$$ ✕ **Osteria da Fiore.** Tucked away on a little calle near Campo San Polo, da Fiore is a favorite among high-end diners for its superbly prepared Venetian cuisine and refined yet relaxed atmosphere. The Martin family are hands-on owners, with Mara in the kitchen and Maurizio running every aspect of the dining room. A superlative seafood lunch or dinner here might include delicate hors d'oeuvres of soft-shell crab, scallops, and tiny octopus, followed by a succulent risotto or pasta *con scampi e radicchio* (with shrimp and radicchio), and a perfectly cooked main course of *rombo* (turbot) or *tagliata di tonno* (tuna steak). The formerly all-fish menu has been expanded to include dishes such as a sublime risotto made with butternut squash and balsamic vinegar and a buffalo burger. A jacket is not required, but is highly recommended. ⊠ *Calle del Scaleter, San Polo 2202* 🕾 *041/721308* ⚒ *Reservations essential* ⊟ *AE, DC, MC, V* ⊘ *Closed Sun. and Mon., Aug., and Dec. 24–Jan. 15* Ⓥ *San Silvestro/San Stae.*

$$$–$$$$ ✕ **Al Paradiso.** In a small dining room made warm and cozy by its pleasing and unpretentious decor, proprietor Giordano makes all diners feel like honored guests. Pappardelle "al Paradiso" takes pasta with seafood sauce to new heights while risotto with shrimp, champagne, and grapefruit puts a delectable twist on a traditional dish. The inspired and original array of entrées includes meat and fish selections such as a salmon with honey and balsamic vinegar in a stunning presentation. Desserts include a perfect panna cotta. There's an inspired wine list, but the house wines are infinitely better than those in other restaurants. ⊠ *Calle dei Paradiso, San Polo 767* 🕾 *041/5234910* ⚒ *Reservations essential* ⊟ *AE, MC, V* ⊘ *Closed Mon. and 3 wks in Jan. and Feb.* Ⓥ *San Silvestro.*

$$$–$$$$ ✕ **Antiche Carampane.** Since its appearance in the first of Donna Leon's Inspector Brunetti mysteries, Piera Bortoluzzi Librai's trattoria has lost

none of its charm but gained considerably in elegance. You'll find all the classic Venetian fish dishes ranging from a mixed seafood antipasto to fish soups, pasta, and perfectly grilled fish. Updated plates such as seafood and fruit salads for starters and entrées like turbot with citrus sauce also delight diners. Chocolate mousse, panna cotta, and sweet wine with biscotti make delectable desserts. Francesco, the son of Franco and Piera, whose family recipes elevate many of the classics, is responsible for some of the new presentations. ⊠ *Rio Terà della Carampane, San Polo 1911* ☎ *041/5240165* ⚓ *Reservations essential* ⊟ *AE, MC, V* ⊘ *Closed Sun. and Mon., 10 days in Jan., 3 wks in July and Aug.* Ⓥ *San Silvestro.*

★ $–$$$ ✕ **Bancogiro.** Come to this casual spot in the heart of the Rialto Market in a 15th-century loggia for a change from standard Venetian food. Yes, fish is on the menu, and some of the dishes are Venice classics; but highlights such as mousse *di gamberoni con salsa di avocado* (shrimp mousse with an avocado sauce) and Sicilian-style *sarde incinte* (stuffed, or "pregnant," sardines) are far from typical fare, though portions can be small. The wine list and cheese plate are both divine. There are tables upstairs in a carefully restored room with a partial view of the Grand Canal; when it's warm you can sit outdoors and get the full canal view. ⊠ *Campo San Giacometto, San Polo, 122 under the porch* ☎ *041/5232061* ⊟ *No credit cards* ⊘ *Closed Mon.* Ⓥ *Rialto.*

$–$$ ✕ **Antica Birreria La Corte.** Locals, students, and tourists flock here daily not only for the dazzling list of pizzas (including one topped with porcini mushrooms and wild-boar salami) but also for starters such as a salad of arugula and pecorino with a drizzle of chestnut honey. Gnocchi with white meat sauce or a rich creamy risotto can be followed with one of several excellent meat and fish entrées. Two kitchens—one for pizza and one for everything else—can result in courses arriving haphazardly. Beer's a better bet than wine here, thanks to the large selection on tap. ⊠ *Campo San Polo, San Polo 2168* ☎ *041/2750570* ⊟ *MC, V* Ⓥ *San Silvestro/San Tomà.*

★ $–$$ ✕ **Ostaria al Garanghelo.** Superior quality, competitive prices, and great ambience means this place is often packed with Venetians, especially for lunch and an after-work *ombra* (small glass of wine) and cicchetti. Chef Renato takes full advantage of the fresh ingredients from the Rialto Market, located a few steps away, bakes his own bread daily, and prefers cooking many dishes *al vapore* (steamed). The spicy *fagioli al uciletto* (literally beans, bird-style) has an unusual name and Tuscan origins; it's a perfect companion to a plate of fresh pasta. Don't confuse this centrally located restaurant with one of the same name in Via Garibaldi. ⊠ *Calle dei Boteri, San Polo 1570* ☎ *041/721721* ⊟ *MC, V* ⊘ *Closed Sun.* Ⓥ *Rialto.*

SANTA CROCE

$$$ ✕ **Vecio Fritolin.** At this tidy *bacaro con cucina* (with kitchen) you can have a traditional meal featuring such dishes as *bigoli in salsa* (thick spaghetti with anchovy sauce), baked fish with herbs, and ravioli with scampi and chicory. The name, which translates as "Old Fry Shop," refers to a bygone Venetian tradition of shops selling fried fish "to go," like in Lon-

don, except paired with polenta rather than chips. For €8, you can still get a paper cone of *fritto* here. ⊠*Calle della Regina, Santa Croce 2262* ☎*041/5222881* ▤*AE, DC, MC, V* ✆*Closed Mon.* Ⓥ*San Stae.*

$$ ✕**La Zucca.** The simple place settings, lattice-wood walls, canal window, and mélange of languages make this place feel as much like a typical vegetarian restaurant as you could expect to find in Venice. Though the menu does have superb meat dishes such as the *piccata di pollo ai caperi e limone con riso* (sliced chicken with capers and lemon served with rice), more attention is paid to dishes from the garden: try the radicchio *di Treviso con funghi e scaglie di Montasio* (with mushrooms and shavings of Montasio cheese) or the *finocchi piccanti con olive* (fennel in a spicy tomato-olive sauce). ⊠*Calle del Tintor, Santa Croce 1762* ☎*041/5241570* ⚄*Reservations essential* ▤*AE, DC, MC, V* ✆*Closed Sun. and 1 wk in Dec.* Ⓥ*San Stae.*

$–$$ ✕**Al Prosecco.** Locals stream into this friendly wine bar, down a "Spritz" (a combination of white wine, Campari or Aperol, and seltzer water), and continue on their way. Or they linger over a glass of one of the numerous wines on offer, perhaps also tucking into a tasty panino, such as the *porchetta romane verdure* (roasted pig, Roman style, with greens). Proprietors Davide and Stefano preside over a young and friendly staff who reel off the day's specials with ease. There are a few tables in the back room, and when the weather's warm you can eat outside on the lively campo. ⊠*Campo San Giacomo dell'Orio, Santa Croce 1503* ☎*041/5240222* ▤*No credit cards* ✆*Closed Sun.* Ⓥ*San Stae.*

WHERE TO STAY

Updated by
Nan McElroy

Most of Venice's hotels are in renovated palaces, but space is at a premium—and comes for a price—and even relatively ample rooms may seem cramped by American standards. The most exclusive hotels are indeed palatial, although they may well have some small, dowdy rooms, so it's best to verify ahead of time that yours isn't one of them. Also, not all hotels have lounge areas, and because of preservation laws, some hotels are not permitted to install elevators, so if these features are essential, ask ahead of time. Although the city has no cars, it does have boats plying the canals and pedestrians chattering in the streets sometimes late into the night (most likely along principal thoroughfares, in San Marco and near the Rialto), so ask for a quiet room if noise bothers you.

In temperate weather, be careful about leaving room lights on and your window wide open: mosquitoes can descend en masse. If you find that these creatures are a problem, ask for a Vape, a plug-in anti-mosquito device (or head for the nearest hardware store and pick one up yourself).

From April through November, and during holiday periods, well-reputed hotels fill up well in advance, particularly over weekends, so book as far ahead as you can.

Many travelers assume a hotel near Piazza San Marco will give them the most convenient location, but keep in mind that Venice is scaled to humans (on foot) rather than automobiles; it's difficult to find a location that's *not* convenient to most of the city. Areas away from San Marco may also offer the benefit of being less overrun by day-trippers whose primary destination is the Piazza.

It is essential to have detailed directions to your hotel when you arrive. Arm yourself with not only a detailed map and postal address (Dorsoduro 825), but the actual street name (Fondamenta San Trovaso). Transfer options range from the luxurious, private water taxi to the more economical water bus combined with on-foot navigation, which can be accompanied by the more than occasional occurrence of déjà vu if you don't know exactly where you are going.

Many hotels accept reservations from their personal Web site and will guarantee the lowest prices there. Book ahead using any of the numerous Web booking portals; ⊕*www.venezia.net* is unusual in that it furnishes hotels' official Web site links. **Venezia Si** (☎*39/041/5222264 from abroad, 199/173309 from Italy* ⊙ *Mon.–Sat. 9 AM–11 PM* ⊕*www. veneziasi.it*) can also help for last-minute reservations, as their Web site lists most hotels in town (with some photographs), and they offer a free reservation service over the phone. It's the public relations arm of **AVA** *(Venetian Hoteliers Association)* and has booths where you can make same-day reservations at **Piazzale Roma** (☎*041/5231397* ⊙*Daily 9 AM–10 PM*), **Santa Lucia train station** (☎*041/715288 or 041/715016* ⊙*Daily 8 AM–9 PM*), and **Marco Polo Airport** (☎*041/5415133* ⊙*Daily 9 AM–10 PM*).

PRICES

Venetian hotels cater to all tastes and come in a variety of price ranges. Rates are about 20% higher than in Rome and Milan, but can be reduced by as much as half off-season, from November–March (excluding Christmas, New Year's, and Carnevale), and likely in August as well.

WHAT IT COSTS IN EUROS				
	¢	$	$$	$$$	$$$$
Hotels	under €80	€80–€140	€140–€210	€210–€290	over €290

Prices are for a standard double room in high season.

CANNAREGIO

$$$$ 🖼 **Palazzo Abadessa.** At this elegant late-16th-century palazzo, you'll
Fodor's Choice   experience gracious hospitality and a luxurious atmosphere in keep-
★   ing with Venice's patrician heritage. You'll feel like nobility yourself as you ascend the majestic staircase and enter the expansive piano nobile which overlooks a side canal. Unusually spacious rooms are well-appointed with antique furniture, frescoed ceilings, and fine silk fabrics. The location is remote enough to escape the San Marco throngs while still within striking distance of all of major sights, and there's a private dock for taxi arrival. In summer, breakfast is served in a walled garden complete with sculptures and marble benches. **Pros:** A unique, historic

lodging; spacious rooms and garden; superb guest service. **Con:** Not the best choice for families with young children, who may have difficulty dodging the antique accessories sprinkled throughout. ✉ *Calle Priuli off Strada Nova, Cannaregio 4011,* ☎ *041/2413784* ⊕ *www.abadessa. com* ↻ *5 palazzo rooms, 3 palazzo deluxe, 4 suites, 1 presidential suite* ♿ *In-room: safe, refrigerator, Wi-Fi. In-hotel: room service, bar, no elevator, concierge, laundry service, public Internet, public Wi-Fi, some pets allowed* ⊟ *AE, DC, MC, V* ❍❘*BP* ✅ *Ca' d'Oro.*

$$$–$$$$ ⊞ **Hotel Antico Doge.** Once the home of Doge Marino Falier, this palazzo has been modernized in an elegant Venetian style, with a wealth of textiles and some fine original furnishings. Some rooms have *baldacchini* (canopied beds) and views; all have fabric walls and hardwood floors. The location, on the main thoroughfare from the station to San Marco, is handy but can stay quite lively well into the night, especially during festivals. An ample buffet breakfast is served in a room with a frescoed ceiling and a Murano chandelier. **Pros:** Convenient to the Rialto. **Cons:** On a busy street; no outdoor garden or terrace. ✉ *Campo SS. Apostoli, Cannaregio 5643,* ☎ *041/2411570* ⊕ *www.anticodoge.com* ↻ *8 standard, 2 superior, 9 junior suites, 1 suite* ♿ *In-room: safe, dial-up, Wi-Fi. In-hotel: room service, bar, no elevator, concierge, laundry service, public Internet, public Wi-Fi* ⊟ *MC, V* ❍❘*BP* ✅ *Ca' d'Oro/Rialto.*

$$–$$$$ ⊞ **Ca' Gottardi.** Ca' Gottardi is part of a new generation of small hotels that refresh traditional Venetian style with contemporary design. The clean white-marble entrance leading up to the luminous piano nobile (main floor) of the 15th-century palace gracefully contrasts the opulent Murano chandeliers and rich wall brocades in the guest rooms. Some rooms have canal views, bathrooms are large and modern, and a rich breakfast is served in a bright salon that overlooks a wide canal. Location, just off the Grand Canal near the Ca' d'Oro and a variety of good eateries, is another plus. Do confirm the type of room (suite or standard, with or without a view) and its location (in the annex or the main hotel) when booking. **Pros:** Location; mix of old and new styles; canal views. **Cons:** No outdoor garden or terrace. ✉ *Strada Nova, Cannaregio 2283,* ☎ *041/2759333* ⊕ *www.cagottardi.com* ↻ *14 rooms, 2 junior suites, 3 suites, 9 annex rooms* ♿ *In-room: safe, refrigerator, dial-up. In-hotel: bar, no elevator, concierge, public Wi-Fi* ⊟ *DC, MC, V* ❍❘*BP* ✅ *Ca' d'Oro.*

$$$ ⊞ **Hotel ai Mori d'Oriente.** The theme here, reflected in the decor, is Venice's connection with the exotic East. Some rooms and suites overlook the expansive canal along the Fondamenta della Sensa, one of the bright, broad byways typical of the upper Cannaregio district. In good weather, you can also take breakfast or a Venetian Spritz cocktail at a sunny table along the canal. Though the atmosphere hearkens back to Venice's past, facilities and amenities are everything you'd expect from a 21st-century establishment, and the staff is accommodating. Ask about the type and location of room you're reserving when booking. **Pros:** Modern construction; nice for families; large number of rooms makes it a good last-minute option. **Cons:** Some might consider the hotel remote from the Piazza. ✉ *Fondamenta della Sensa, Cannaregio 3319,* ☎ *041/711001* ⊕ *www.morihotel.com* ↻ *58 rooms, 2 suites*

&In-room: safe, refrigerator, DVD, dial-up. In-hotel: room service, bar, concierge, laundry facilities, laundry service, public Internet, some pets allowed ⊟AE, DC, MC, V �𝄇BP ☑San Marcuola/Madonna dell'Orto.

$$$ ⊞**Hotel Giorgione.** Family-owned and -operated, this quietly elegant hotel charms guests with its original terrazzo flooring, gracious courtyard and marble fountain, and billiard salon. The staff is professional and helpful, and the location is convenient for exploring in any direction. Rooms are decorated with traditional Venetian fabric and furniture, are comfortably appointed, and have either rooftop or courtyard views. Room sizes vary considerably, so book early and ask about the size and view if this is important. Seasonal refreshments are offered each afternoon. **Pros:** Family run; unique ambience; elegant garden. **Cons:** No canal views. ⊠Off Campo Santi Apostoli, Cannaregio 4587, ☎041/5225810 ⊕www.hotelgiorgione.com ☚76 rooms &In-room: safe, refrigerator, dial-up. In-hotel: bar, concierge, laundry service, public Internet ⊟AE, DC, MC, V ⟨◯⟩BP ☑Ca' d'Oro/Fondamente Nuove.

$–$$$ ⊞**Locanda le Vele.** Gracious yet understated Venetian decor, original open-beam ceilings, spotless marble baths, and friendly, attentive service are the hallmarks of this intimate, family-owned locanda. The rooms overlooking the canals are the best in terms of size as well as view. A tasty breakfast is served in your room. The location is tranquil, but still handy to the Ca' d'Oro stop, the traghetto across to the Rialto Market, and the San Marco area. Spring for the airy suite if it's available. **Pros:** Standout service; canal views from some rooms. **Cons:** Not for modern-decor lovers. ⊠Calle delle Vele, Cannaregio 3969, ☎041/2413960 ⊕www.locandalevele.com ☚6 rooms, 1 junior suite, 1 suite, 1 apartment &In-room: safe, refrigerator, Ethernet, dial-up, Wi-Fi. In-hotel: no elevator, laundry facilities, public Wi-Fi ⊟AE, DC, MC, V ⟨◯⟩BP ☑Ca' d'Oro.

★ **$$** ⊞**3749 Ponte Chiodo.** This cheery, homey bed-and-breakfast takes its name from the bridge leading to its entrance (one of the only two left in the lagoon without hand railings). Attentively appointed rooms with geranium-filled window boxes overlook either the bridge and expansive canals below or the spacious enclosed garden. It's a family-owned operation, and service is accommodating and friendly; you'll get lots of suggestions for dining and sightseeing. The private garden and patio are perfect for a relaxing breakfast or scribbling postcards or e-mails to the folks back home. Some bathrooms are smallish, but overall it's an excellent value. The location is also handy to the Ca' d'Oro vaporetto. **Pros:** Highly attentive service; warm, relaxed atmosphere; canal views. **Cons:** No elevator will be a problem for some. ⊠Calle Racchetta, Cannaregio 3749, ☎041/2413935 ⊕www.pontechiodo.it ☚6 rooms &In-room: no phone, safe, refrigerator, Wi-Fi. In-hotel: room service, bar, kitchen, no elevator, public Internet, public Wi-Fi ⊟MC, V ⟨◯⟩BP ☑Ca' d'Oro.

$ ⊞**Ca' San Marcuola.** Tucked in a busy area of shops, trattorias, and wine bars frequented by Venetians and tourists alike, this family-owned hotel stands out for its relaxed and familiar atmosphere. The comfort-

6

able rooms are furnished in delicate pastel colors and full of light; spacious bathrooms are a plus. An elevator that provides access to all floors and a convenient location close to a water-bus stop on the Grand Canal make this a good choice if you have limited mobility. ⊠*Campo San Marcuola, Cannaregio 1763,* ☎*041/716048* 🖷*041/2759217* ⊕*www. casanmarcuola.com* ⇦*12 rooms* ⚹*In-room: safe, refrigerator, dial-up. In-hotel: bar, concierge, room service, public Internet* ⊟*AE, MC, V* ⊙*Closed 4 wks in Dec.–Jan.* ⎮O⎮*BP* ⊻*San Marcuola.*

CASTELLO

$$$$ 🖾**Hotel Londra Palace.** A wall of windows makes this the hotel of choice for soaking up extraordinary, sweeping views of the lagoon and the island of San Giorgio. The downstairs restaurant is all glass, light, and water views, and the superior rooms and junior suites offer the same spectacle. The vista must have been pleasing to Tchaikovsky, who wrote his 4th Symphony here in 1877. Neoclassical public rooms, with splashes of blue-and-green glass suggesting the sea, play nicely off guest rooms, which have fine fabric, damask drapes, Biedermeier furniture, and Venetian glass. The staff is top-notch, as are the restaurant and the bar. **Pros:** Superlative views; professional service. **Cons:** The Riva's liveliness extends late into the evening. ⊠*Riva degli Schiavoni, Castello 4171,* ☎*041/5200533* ⊕*www.hotelondra.it* ⇦*36 standard and deluxe rooms, 17 suites* ⚹*In-room: safe, refrigerator, dial-up, Wi-Fi. In-hotel: restaurant, room service, bars, concierge, laundry service, public Internet, public Wi-Fi* ⊟*AE, DC, MC, V* ⎮O⎮*BP* ⊻*San Zaccaria.*

★ **$$$$**   🖾**Metropole.** Eccentrics, eclectics, and fans of Antonio Vivaldi (who taught music here) love the Metropole, a labyrinth of intimate, opulent spaces featuring exotic Eastern influences and jammed with cabinets displaying collections of ivory-adorned cigarette cases, antique corkscrews, beaded bags, and more. The owner, a lifelong collector of odd objects, fills common areas and the sumptuously appointed guest rooms with endless antiques. The best rooms are up on the roof, where there are also two spacious rooftop terraces. Only six of the standard double rooms offer lagoon views. Suites feature sparkling mosaic sunken baths, Fortuny fabrics, and other notable architectural details that commingle to create a unique atmosphere highlighting colorful aspects of Venice's exotic past. **Pro:** Owner has exquisite taste and collections. **Con:** The Riva is one of the most densely touristy spots in the city. ⊠*Riva degli Schiavoni, Castello 4149,* ☎*041/5205044* ⊕*www. hotelmetropole.com* ⇦*67 rooms, 13 junior suites, 5 suites, 4 exclusive suites* ⚹*In-room: safe, refrigerator, dial-up. In-hotel: restaurant, room service, bar, concierge, laundry service, public Wi-Fi, some pets allowed* ⊟*AE, DC, MC, V* ⎮O⎮*BP* ⊻*San Zaccaria.*

$$$$ 🖾**Palazzo Contarini della Porta di Ferro.** Formerly the residence of the Contarini family, one of Venice's most powerful families, this late-14th-century palace has been a hotel since 2001. The building's aristocratic past shows in the elegant inner courtyard with a majestic marble staircase. All uniquely furnished, the spacious, light-filled rooms have high wood-beam ceilings and Venetian terrazzo or wood flooring; apartments have kitchens, dining rooms, and open mezzanines. The large

Torcello Suite also has a wooden roof terrace from which you can take in a spectacular view of the city. In sunny weather breakfast is served in the small garden. Private dinners, meetings, and small conferences are sometimes held in a large, well-appointed hall overlooking the garden. **Pros:** Spacious; residential neighborhood; good for longer stays. **Cons:** May be a bit remote for some. ⊠*Salizzada San Giustina, Castello 2926,* ☎*041/2770991* ⊕*www.palazzocontarini.com* ⊲*6 rooms, 11 apartments* ⅋*In-room: safe, kitchen (some), refrigerator, dial-up. In-hotel: room service, concierge, laundry service, public Internet, some pets allowed* ⊟*AE, MC, V* ¶⊚|*BP* Ⓥ*Celestia/San Zaccaria.*

$$$–$$$$ 🔲**Ca' Formenta.** This simple 15th-century building underwent a complete makeover before opening as a hotel in 2003. Located in residential rather than tourist Venice, Ca' Formenta offers high-quality services and a canal-side entrance for guests arriving by water taxi; front rooms have a wonderful view of the lagoon. The 15-minute stroll along the waterfront between Piazzo San Marco and this friendly gem of a hotel is through a genuinely "local" part of the city, with plenty of cafés and restaurants. One of the rear rooms has direct access to a pleasant rooftop terrace with tables. **Pros:** Castello area still feels like authentic Venice; convenient to the Piazza, the Lido, and the north Lagoon islands. **Cons:** Not as convenient to San Polo or upper Dorsoduro. ⊠*Via Garibaldi, Castello 1650,* ☎*041/5285494* ⊕*www.hotelcaformenta.it* ⊲*12 rooms, 2 junior suites* ⅋*In-room: safe, refrigerator, dial-up. In-hotel: room service, bar, concierge, laundry service, public Wi-Fi, some pets allowed* ⊟*AE, DC, MC, V* ¶⊚|*BP* Ⓥ*Arsenale/Giardini.*

$$ 🔲**Santa Maria della Pietà.** Though this *casa per ferie* (vacation house) is more spartan than sumptuous, there's more light and space here than in many of Venice's four-star hotels. The hotel, which occupies the upper floors of two historic palaces, opened 10 years ago; it has big windows, restored Venetian terrazzo floors, and a huge rooftop terrace with a coffee shop, bar, and unobstructed lagoon views. On top of these advantages, it's well situated—just 100 yards from the main waterfront and about a 10-minute walk from St. Mark's—which means you'll have to book early to stay here. The shared bathrooms are plentiful, spacious, and scrupulously clean. Some rooms have been remodeled to include en-suite baths, and family rooms with up to six beds are available. **Pros:** Space, light, and views at a bargain price. **Cons:** Not luxurious. ⊠*Calle della Pietà, Castello 3701,* ☎*041/2443639* ⊕*www. pietavenezia.org/casaferie.htm* ⊲*15 rooms* ⅋*In-room: no phone, no TV. In-hotel: bar* ⊟*No credit cards* ¶⊚|*BP* Ⓥ*Arsenale/San Zaccaria.*

DORSODURO

★ $$$$ 🔲**Ca' Maria Adele.** Venice's most elegant small hotel is an updated mix of classic style—terrazzo floors, dramatic Murano chandeliers, antique furnishings—and touches of the contemporary, found in the African-wood reception area and breakfast room. Five dramatic "concept rooms" take on themes from Venetian history; the Doge's Room is draped in deep red brocades, while the Oriental Room is inspired by the travels of Marco Polo. Ca' Maria Adele's location is a tranquil yet convenient spot near the church of Santa Maria della Salute. **Pros:** Quiet and romantic;

imaginative, contemporary furnishings and decor. **Cons:** More formal atmosphere may not be ideal for those with young children. ⊠*Campo Santa Maria della Salute, Dorsoduro 111,* ☏*041/5203078* ⊕*www.camariaadele.it* ⌨*12 rooms, 4 suites* ⚭*In-room: safe, refrigerator, Wi-Fi. In-hotel: room service, bar, concierge, laundry service, some pets allowed* ▤*AE, DC, MC, V* ⦿*BP* ▼*Salute.*

★ $$$$ ⚏**Charming House DD 724.** This ultramodern boutique hotel abandons all things traditionally Venetian, opting instead to create the air of a stylish residence. With impeccable, minimalist decor, Charming House has a contemporary, warmly romantic, and occasionally even dramatic atmosphere. Some rooms overlook small canals and side calli; apartment options with kitchenettes are available for families or small groups. The location is convenient to the Guggenheim, Accademia, Zattere, and San Marco. There are also art exhibits borrowed from neighboring museums on display in common areas. See their Web site for additional locations and apartments with similar ambience located in Castello. **Pros:** Unique décor; variety of lodging options. **Cons:** Not for those who prefer more traditional Venetian style. ⊠*Ramo da Mula off Campo San Vio, Dorsoduro 724,* ☏*041/2770262* ⊕*www.thecharminghouse.com* ⌨*5 rooms, 2 junior suites, 2 suites* ⚭*In-room: safe, refrigerator (some), Wi-Fi. In-hotel: room service, concierge, laundry service, public Internet, public Wi-Fi, some pets allowed* ▤*AE, DC, MC, V* ⦿*BP* ▼*Accademia.*

$$$$ ⚏**Hotel American–Dinesen.** This quiet, family-run hotel has a yellow
Fodor's Choice   stucco facade typical of Venetian houses. A hall decorated with repro-
★   duction antiques and Oriental rugs leads to a breakfast room reminiscent of a theater foyer, with red velvet chairs and gilt wall lamps. Guest rooms are spacious and tastefully furnished in sage-green and delicate pink fabrics with lacquered Venetian-style furniture throughout. Some front rooms have terraces with canal views. A water taxi can deposit you directly in front of the hotel on arrival, and although the four-story building has no elevator, you'll have assistance with your luggage if needed. The exceptional service will help you feel at home at the hotel and in Venice. **Pros:** High degree of personal service; located on a quiet, exceptionally picturesque canal. **Cons:** Lack of elevator will be a problem for some. ⊠*San Vio, Dorsoduro 628,* ☏*041/5204733* ⊕*www.hotelamerican.com* ⌨*28 rooms, 2 suites* ⚭*In-room: safe, refrigerator, Wi-Fi. In-hotel: room service, bar, no elevator, concierge, laundry service, public Wi-Fi, some pets allowed* ▤*AE, MC, V* ⦿*BP* ▼*Accademia/Salute.*

★ $$–$$$$ ⚏**La Calcina.** In 1877, Stones of Venice author John Ruskin lodged at the eclectic La Calcina, which sits in an enviable position along the sunny Zattere, and has front rooms offering heady vistas across the expansive Giudecca Canal. You can sunbathe on the *altana* (wooden roof terrace) or enjoy an afternoon tea in one of the lounge's reading corners with flickering candlelight and barely perceptible classical music. A stone staircase leads to the rooms upstairs, which have parquet floors, original art deco furniture, and firm beds. Besides full meals at lunch and dinner, the Piscina bar and restaurant offers drinks and fresh snacks all day in the elegant dining room or on the waterside terrace. A variety of apartments are also available. One single room does not have a private bath. **Pros:** A historic and perennial favorite; rare rooftop altana; panoramic views from some rooms. **Cons:** Not for travelers who want for contemporary surroundings; no elevator. ⊠*Zattere, Dorsoduro 780,* ☎*041/5206466* ⊕*www.lacalcina.com* ⊅*27 rooms, 5 suites* ⚐*In-room: safe, refrigerator, dial-up, Wi-Fi. In-hotel: restaurant, room service, bar, no elevator, concierge, laundry service, public Wi-Fi* ⊟*AE, DC, MC, V* ⦿|*BP* ⩒*Zattere.*

$$–$$$$ 🖵**Pensione Accademia Villa Maravege.** Aptly nicknamed "Villa of the
Fodor's Choice   Wonders," this patrician retreat once served as the Russian embassy
★   and was the fictional residence of Katharine Hepburn's character in the film *Summertime.* Outside, a secret garden awaits just beyond an iron gate, complete with a mini Palladian-style villa, flower beds, stone cupids, and verdant trees—all rarities in Venice. The hotel is located on a peaceful promontory where two side canals converge with the Grand Canal. The conservative rooms are outfitted with Venetian-style antiques and fine tapestry. Book well in advance. **Pros:** A historic, classic Venetian property. **Cons:** Formal surroundings with lots of antiques are not well suited to families with young children. ⊠*Fondamenta Bollani, Dorsoduro 1058,* ☎*041/5210188* ⊕*www.pensione accademia.it* ⊅*27 rooms, 2 suites* ⚐*In-room: safe, dial-up. In-hotel: bar, no elevator, concierge, laundry service* ⊟*AE, DC, MC, V* ⦿|*BP* ⩒*Accademia.*

6

★ **$$$**   🖵**Locanda San Barnaba.** In contrast to the recent onslaught of international chain hotels, the Locanda San Barnaba, housed in a 16th-century palazzo, is a welcome, family-run find. It's handy, too, just off the Ca' Rezzonico vaporetto stop, and you'll cross no bridges to reach it. The arches in the garden walls peek through to the side canal and there's a rooftop terrace for soaking up Venetian sunsets. There's no elevator, but there are some ground floor rooms available and the staff will happily assist with your luggage. The two superior rooms have original 18th-century frescoes, and one of the junior suites has two small balconies and is exceptionally luminous, but all the rooms are spacious and attractive. There's a water entrance for taxi arrival. **Pros:** Outdoor space; a variety of room options; excellent value. **Cons:** Lack of elevator will be a drawback for some. ⊠*Calle del Traghetto, Dorsoduro 2785–2786* ☎*041/2411233* ⊕*www.locanda-sanbarnaba. com* ⊅*1 single, 8 double, 2 superior, 2 junior suites* ⚐*In-room: safe, dial up. In hotel: room service, bar, no elevator, concierge* ⊟*AE, DC, MC, V* ⦿|*BP* ⩒*Ca' Rezzonico.*

$$ 🖵**Casa Rezzonico.** Rooms here are the rarest site in Venice: good value. A bright canal graces the hotel entrance, and a private garden (where breakfast is served in temperate weather) makes the inner courtyard particularly inviting. Rooms vary in size but are pleasant and comfortable, and overlook either the garden or the canal. Young owners Matteo and Mattia are attentive and helpful, and the location is convenient for exploring the sights from the Rialto to the Salute, hopping the vaporetto at Ca' Rezzonico for any San Marco location. The hotel is easily reachable on foot from Piazzale Roma as well, for coming and going by car. **Pros:** A garden for relaxing; canal views at a reasonable rate; convenient to many locations; great for families. **Con:** s The six rooms fill up early, especially on weekends. ✉*Fondamenta Gherardini, Dorsoduro 2813,* ☎*041/2770653* ⊕*www.casarezzonico. it* ⬆*6 rooms, from single to quad* ♿*In-room: safe, dial-up. In-hotel: room service, no elevator* ☰*AE, MC, V, cash preferred* 🍴*BP* Ⓥ *Ca' Rezzonico.*

GIUDECCA

$$$$ ☷**Cipriani.** It's impossible to feel stressed in this oasis of stunning rooms and suites, some with garden patios. The hotel launch whisks you to Giudecca from San Marco and back at any hour; those opting for a cocktail at the patio bar before dinner can use it as well. Rooms of extraordinary luxury are available both in the main building and in the adjoining 16th-century-style annexes, Palazzo Vendramin and Palazzetto, which offer views across to Piazza San Marco. Prices are high even by Venetian standards, but this is the only place in town with such extensive facilities and services, from an Olympic-size pool and tennis courts to cooking courses, a beauty-and-wellness center, fitness programs, and even a vineyard. **Pros:** Many amenities; private getaway feeling. **Cons:** Even with the hotel taxi, coming and going can be somewhat inconvenient. ✉*Giudecca 10,* ☎*041/5207744* ⊕*www. hotelcipriani.it* ⬆*46 rooms, 58 suites* ♿*In-room: safe, refrigerator, Wi-Fi. In-hotel: 4 restaurants, room service, bar, tennis courts, pool, gym, spa, concierge, laundry service, public Wi-Fi* ☰*AE, DC, MC, V* ☾*Main hotel closed Nov.–Mar.; Palazzo Vendramin and Palazzetto closed 4 wks in Jan. and Feb.* 🍴*BP* Ⓥ*Zitelle.*

LAGOON

$$$$ ☷**San Clemente Palace.** If you prefer wide-open spaces to the intimacy of Venice, this is your hotel. This massive complex occupies an entire island, about 15 minutes from Piazza San Marco by (free) shuttle launch, with acres of parkland, a swimming pool, tennis courts, a wellness center, and four restaurants. The 19th-century buildings are on the site of a 12th-century monastery, of which only the chapel remains. They form a large quadrangle and contain spacious, modern rooms. The view back to Venice with the Dolomites behind on a clear day is stunning. This hotel, open since 2003, offers all the five-star comforts: it even has three holes of golf. **Pro:** True five-star service and amenities. **Con:** Quite remote. ✉*Isola di San Clemente 1,* ☎*041/2445001* ⊕*www.sanclemente.thi.it* ⬆*107 rooms, 96 suites* ♿*In-room: safe, refrigerator, Ethernet, dial-up. In-hotel: 4 restaurants, bar, golf course, tennis courts, pool, gym, spa, laundry service, public Wi-Fi, some pets allowed* ☰*AE, DC, MC, V* 🍴*BP.*

SAN MARCO

★ **$$$$**   ☷**Bauer Il Palazzo.** Il Palazzo, under the same management as the larger Bauer Hotel, is the ultimate word in luxury. Tufted Bevilacqua and Rubelli fabrics cover the walls, and no two rooms are decorated the same. What they have in common, however, are high ceilings, Murano glass, marble bathrooms, and damask drapes. Many have sweeping views. Breakfast is served on Venice's highest rooftop terrace, appropriately named Il Settimo Cielo (Seventh Heaven). The outdoor hot tub, also on the seventh floor, offers views of La Serenissima that will leave you breathless, and personable, professional staff will accommodate your every whim. **Pros:** Il Palazzo will pamper you while making you feel right at home. **Cons:** Located in one of the busiest areas of the city. ⊠*Campo San Moisè, San Marco 1413/d,* ☎*041/5207022* ⊕*www. ilpalazzovenezia.com* ⤳*44 rooms, 38 suites* &*In-room: safe, refrigerator, DVD, Wi-Fi. In-hotel: restaurant, room service, bars, gym, concierge, laundry service, public Internet, public Wi-Fi, some pets allowed* ▤*AE, DC, MC, V* ⓔ*EP* Ⓥ*San Marco/Vallaresso.*

★ \$\$\$\$ 🏨**Locanda Orseolo.** This cozy, elegant hotel offers a welcome respite from the throngs churning around Piazza San Marco. Family owned, it has an attentive staff and comfortable, well-appointed rooms. Classic Venetian designs are given a Carnevale theme, with each room's decor dedicated to one of the traditional masks. The relaxed atmosphere pervades at breakfast, where it's common to get engrossed in conversation with the other guests. **Pros:** Intimate and romantic; extraordinarily friendly staff. **Cons:** Located in the one of the busiest and most commercial areas of the city. ⊠*Corte Zorzi off Campo San Gallo, San Marco 1083,* ☎*041/5204827* ⊕*www.locandaorseolo.com* ⤳*12 rooms* &*In-room: safe, refrigerator, Wi-Fi. In-hotel: room service, concierge, laundry facilities, laundry service, public Internet, public Wi-Fi* ▤*AE, DC, MC, V* ⊘*Closed Jan.* ⓔ*BP* Ⓥ*Rialto/Vallaresso.*

\$\$\$\$ 🏨**Novecento.** This small, family-run hotel is nestled away on a quiet street just a 10-minute walk from the Piazza San Marco. Inspired by the style of Mariano Fortuny, the early-1900s Spanish artist and fashion designer who made Venice his home, the intimate rooms are a surprisingly elegant mélange of multiethnic and exotic furnishings. The Mediterranean, Indian, and Venetian fabrics, silverware, chandeliers, and furniture create a sensual turn-of-the-20th-century atmosphere. In fine weather, breakfast is served in the inner courtyard. **Pro:s** Intimate atmosphere and unusual decor make this a particularly romantic nest. **Cons:** A bit of a walk from the Piazza. ⊠*Calle del Dose, Campo San Maurizio, San Marco 2683/84,* ☎*041/2413765* ⊕*www.novecento. biz* ⤳*9 rooms* &*In-room: safe, refrigerator, dial-up, Wi-Fi. In-hotel: bar, laundry service, public Internet, public Wi-Fi, some pets allowed* ▤*AE, DC, MC, V* ⓔ*BP* Ⓥ*Santa Maria del Giglio.*

★ \$\$\$\$ 🏨**Palazzo Sant'Angelo sul Canal Grande.** There's a distinguished yet comfortable feel to this elegant palazzo, which is large enough to deliver expected facilities and services, but small enough to pamper its guests. Rooms have tapestry-adorned walls and Carrara and Alpine marble in the bath; those facing the Grand Canal have balconies that practically bring the Canal to you. Common areas include an entrance hall with original Palladian flooring, a bright front lounge, and an intimate bar that puts the Canal almost at arm's length. Ask ahead for a room with a view if it's important. **Pros:** Nearby Sant'Angelo vaporetto stop is convenient for visiting the city. **Cons:** Some rooms have no particu-

6

lar view. ⊠*Campo Sant'Angelo, San Marco 3488,* 🕾*041/2411452* ⊕*www.palazzosantangelo.com* ⥥*14 rooms* &*In-room: safe, refrigerator, Ethernet. In-hotel: room service (limited), bar, concierge, laundry service, some pets allowed* ⊟*AE, DC, MC, V* ❖|EP ☑*Sant'Angelo.*

$$$ ⌸**Al Teatro.** Nestled behind the Fenice Theater, just off the Maria Callas bridge, this small B&B is the renovated home of owners Fabio and Eleonora—in fact, it's where Eleanora was born. There are three spacious, comfortable, and conscientiously-appointed rooms with private baths, each overlooking a gondola-filled canal; the largest room has a broad balcony. An ample breakfast (served at a common table) and exceptional service make Al Teatro an excellent value and a relaxing choice in the sometimes-frenetic San Marco atmosphere. Book well in advance, especially for weekend stays. **Pros:** Airy rooms; convenient San Marco location; nice for families. **Cons:** The intimacy of a three-room B&B is not for everyone. ⊠*Fondamenta della Fenice, San Marco 2554,* 🕾*041/5204271* ⊕*www.bedandbreakfastalteatro.com* ⥥*3 rooms* &*In-room: safe, refrigerator, Wi-Fi. In-hotel: room service, no elevator, public Internet, public Wi-Fi* ⊟*AE, MC, V* ❖|BP ☑*Santa Maria del Giglio.*

$$ ⌸**Ca' dei Dogi.** In the crush of hotels in and around Piazza San Marco, there are many undesirables, since the location alone attracts lodgers. This delightful gem, eked out of a 15th-century palace and located in a quiet courtyard secluded from the melee, is one notable exception. The thoughtful, personal touches added by owners Stefano and Susanna are evident everywhere, from the six individually decorated rooms (some with private terraces), to the carefully chosen contemporary furniture, to classic Venetian elements such as wall tapestries and mosaic tiles. There's highly personal service; guests are often welcomed by one of the owners. There's a courtyard where you can enjoy breakfast or an evening interlude, and one attic apartment is available. **Pros:** Terraces, with views of the Doge's Palace, are a definite plus. **Cons:** Rooms are not expansive. ⊠*Corte Santa Scolastica, Castello 4242,* 🕾*041/2413751* ⊕ *www.cadeidogi.it* ⥥*6 rooms* &*In-room: safe, dial-up. In-hotel: room service, no elevator, public Internet, public Wi-Fi, some pets allowed* ⊟*AE, DC, MC, V* ❖|BP ☑*San Zaccaria.*

SAN POLO

★ **$$$–$$$$** ⌸**Oltre il Giardino—Casaifrari.** It's easy to overlook (and can be a challenge to find) this secluded palazzo, sheltered behind a brick wall not far from the Frari church. Especially in high season, the six-room hotel with a pleasant, expansive garden is an oasis of peace. The prevalent white-and-pastel color scheme and elegant, understated decor contribute to the relaxed environment. The house was once the residence of Alma Mahler, widow of composer Gustav Mahler and a fascinating woman in her own right; it still conveys her style and charm today. Service and professional attention is as conscientious as the renovation. **Pros:** A peaceful, gracious setting. **Cons:** No Grand Canal views. ⊠*San Polo 2542,* 🕾*041/2750015* ⊕*www.oltreilgiardino-venezia. com* ⥥*4 rooms, 2 suites* &*In-room: safe, refrigerator, dial-up, Wi-*

Fi. In-hotel: room service, bar, no elevator, public Internet, some pets allowed ☐*AE, DC, MC, V* ⊙|*BP* ☑*San Tomà.*

$$–$$$$ 🔲 **Ca' Angeli.** The heirs of a Venetian architect have transformed his former residence, located on the third and top floors of a palace along the Grand Canal, into an elegant B&B. It retains the classic style of its former owner—most of the furniture was his, including an 18th-century briarwood bureau, an original icon, as well as 18th- and 19th-century art. The five rooms and two suites have views of either the Grand Canal or a side canal—or in the case of the smallish Room 6, rooftops from a terrace twice the size of the room. A rich breakfast, including select cheeses and meats from local producers, is served in a salon overlooking the Grand Canal. There's also an attic apartment option for groups or small families. **Pros:** Historic residence with Grand Canal views; helpful staff. **Cons:** A bit of a walk from the vaporetto stop to the hotel. ✉*Calle del Traghetto della Madoneta, San Polo 1434,* ☎*041/5232480* ⊕*www.caangeli.it* ⬧*5 rooms, 1 junior suite, 1 suite* ♿*In-room: safe, refrigerator, Wi-Fi. In-hotel: public Wi-Fi* ☐*No credit cards* ⊙|*BP* ☑*San Silvestro.*

$$$ 🔲 **Corte 1321.** If you're looking for something more up-to-date than the 18th-century-style decor that predominates in Venetian hotels, try Corte 1321, which is nestled away off the main drag. It has friendly, personal service; spacious, carefully renovated rooms with sparkling baths and "ethnic-chic" decor; and an intimate garden. Unwind here after a long day of exploring, perhaps sharing discoveries of the day with other guests or using the public Wi-Fi to catch up on e-mails. Corte 1321's owner is an American of Italian decent. **Pros:** Lively, eclectic atmosphere great for meeting other guests. **Cons:** No canal views. ✉*Campiello Ca' Bernardi, San Polo 1321,* ☎*041/5224923* ⊕*www.corte1321.com* ⬧*4 rooms, 1 miniflat* ♿*In-room: safe, Ethernet, Wi-Fi. In-hotel: bar, no elevator, laundry service, public Internet, public Wi-Fi* ☐*MC, V* ⊙*Closed Jan.* ⊙|*BP* ☑*San Silvestro.*

$$ 🔲 **Acca Hotel.** This small hotel is one of Venice's better moderately priced options, with bright, well-appointed rooms and simple but attentive service. There's no staff on hand in the evening, but you get your own key. The location is good, and breakfast is served in the courtyard, weather permitting. **Pros:** Lots of amenities; new construction; an excellent value. **Cons:** No canal views; no night porter. ✉*Calle Pezzana, San Polo 2160,* ☎*041/2440126* ⊕*www.accahotel.com* ⬧*8 rooms, 1 suite* ♿*In-room: safe, refrigerator, Wi-Fi. In-hotel: no elevator, laundry service, public Internet, public Wi-Fi* ☐*MC, V* ⊙|*BP* ☑*San Silvestro.*

SANTA CROCE

★ $$$ 🔲 **Hotel al Ponte Mocenigo.** A columned courtyard welcomes you to this elegant, charming palazzo, former home of the Santa Croce branch of the Mocenigo family (the same for which the nearby Museo is named, not to mention a few dogi). The meticulously renovated interior has an updated 18th-century Venetian feel, incorporating a number of distinctive architectural elements such as open-beam ceilings, fireplaces transformed into writing nooks, and Murano chandeliers. The courtyard offers an ideal ambience both for breakfast or to enjoy an aperitivo, and there's even a Turkish sauna that guests may take advantage of after a day of intensive sightseeing. The hotel is located on a side-canal and the delightful surrounding area is convenient to any number of popular sights, eateries, and shopping. **Pros:** Enchanting courtyard; water access; personable staff. **Cons:** Rooms do not overlook a canal. ✉ *Fondamento de Rimpeto a Ca' Mocenigo, Santa Croce 2063,* ☎ *041/5244797* ⊕ *www.alpontemocenigo.com* ⤳*10 rooms, 1 junior suite* ⚄ *In-room: safe, refrigerator, Wi-Fi. In-hotel: room service, bar, public Internet, public Wi-Fi* ▤*AE, DC, MC, V* ⦿ 🏠🏠 ☑*San Stae.*

NIGHTLIFE & THE ARTS

THE ARTS

A Guest in Venice, a monthly bilingual booklet free at most hotels, is your most accessible, up-to-date guide to Venice happenings. It also includes information about pharmacies, vaporetto and bus lines, and the main trains and flights. You can visit their Web site, ⊕ *www.aguestin venice.com,* for a preview of musical, artistic, and sporting events. *Venezia News,* available at newsstands, has similar information but also includes in-depth articles about noteworthy events. The tourist office publishes *Leo* and *Bussola,* bimonthly brochures in Italian and English listing events and updated museum hours. *Venezia da Vivere* is a seasonal guide listing nightspots and live music. Several Venice Web sites allow you to scan the cultural horizon before you arrive; try ⊕ *www. ombra.net* (which has a fantastic map function to find any address in Venice), ⊕ *www.veniceonline.it,* and ⊕ *www.venicebanana.com.* Last but not least, don't ignore the posters you see everywhere in the streets. They're often the most up-to-date information you can find.

CARNEVALE

The first historical evidence of Carnevale (Carnival) in Venice dates from 1097, and for centuries the city marked the days preceding *quaresima* (Lent, the 40 days of abstinence leading up to Palm Sunday) with abundant feasting and wild celebrations. The word *carnivale* is derived from the words for meat (*carne*) and to remove (*levare*), as eating meat was prohibited during Lent. Venice earned its international reputation as the "city of Carnevale" in the 18th century, when partying would begin right after Epiphany (January 6) and the city seemed to be one continuous decadent masquerade. With the republic's fall in 1797, the city lost a great deal of its vitality, and the tradition of Carnevale celebrations was abandoned.

Carnevale was revived in the 1970s when residents began taking to the calli and campi in their own impromptu celebrations. It didn't take long for the tourist industry to embrace the revival as a means to stimulate business during low season. The efforts were successful. Each year over the 10- to 12-day Carnevale period (ending on the Tuesday before Ash Wednesday) more than a half million people attend concerts, theater and street performances, masquerade balls, historical processions, fashion shows, and contests. *A Guest in Venice* (⊕*www.aguestinvenice. com*) gives free advertising to public and private event festivities and is therefore one of the most complete Carnevale guides. For general Carnevale information, contact **Consorzio Comitato per il Carnevale di Venezia** (⊠*Santa Croce 1714,* ☎*041/717065, 041/2510811 during Carnevale* 🖨*041/5200410* ⊕*www.carnevale.venezia.it*). The **Tourist Office** (☎*041/5298711*) has detailed information about daily events. If you're not planning on joining in the revelry, you'd be wise to choose another time to visit Venice. Enormous crowds clog the streets (which become one-way, with police directing foot traffic), bridges are designated "no-stopping" zones to avoid gridlock, and prices absolutely skyrocket.

FESTIVALS

The **Biennale** (⊕*www.labiennale.org*) cultural institution organizes events year-round, including the Venice Film Festival, which begins the last week of August. The Biennale international exhibition of contemporary art is held in odd-numbered years, usually from mid-June to early November, at the Giardini della Biennale, and in the impressive Arsenale. On the third weekend of July, the **Festa del Redentore** *(Feast of the Redeemer)* commemorates the end of a 16th-century plague that killed about 47,000 city residents. Just as doges have done annually for centuries, you, too, can make a pilgrimage across the temporary bridge connecting the Zattere to the Giudecca. Venetians take to the water to watch fireworks at midnight, but if you can't find a boat, the Giudecca is the best place to be. Young people traditionally greet sunrise on the Lido beach while their elders attend church.

MUSIC

Although there are occasional jazz and Italian pop concerts in clubs around town, the vast majority of music you'll hear is classical, with Venice's famed composer, Vivaldi, frequently featured. A number of churches and palazzi regularly host concerts, as do the Ca' Rezzonico and Querini-Stampalia museums. You'll find these events listed in publications such as *A Guest in Venice*; also try asking the tourist information office or your concierge. The **Vela Call Center** (☎*041/2424* ⊙*Daily 8–8*) has information about musical events, and you can buy tickets at Vela sales offices in Piazzale Roma, Ferrovia, and Calle dei Fuseri (a 10-minute walk from San Marco). (When busy, the Vela Call Center number doesn't give a signal, but instead is silent.)

The travel agency **Kele & Teo** (⊠*Ponte dei Bareteri, San Marco 4930* ☎*041/5208722*) has tickets for a number of venues and is conveniently located midway between Rialto and San Marco.

OPERA

Teatro La Fenice (⊠*Campo San Fantin, San Marco* ☎*041/786511* ⊕*www. teatrolafenice.it*), one of Italy's oldest opera houses, has witnessed many memorable premieres, including the 1853 first-night flop of Verdi's *La Traviata*. It's also had its share of disasters, the most recent being a terrible fire, deliberately set in January 1996. It was completely and luxu-

riously restored, and reopened to great fanfare in 2004. Visit the Fenice Web site for a schedule of performances and to buy tickets.

NIGHTLIFE

Piazza San Marco is a popular meeting place in nice weather, when the cafés stay open late and all seem to be competing to offer the best live music. The younger crowd, Venetians and visitors alike, tends to gravitate toward the area around Rialto Bridge, with Campi San Bartolomeo and San Luca on one side and Campo Rialto Nuovo on the other. Especially popular with university students are the bars along Cannaregio's Fondamenta della Misericordia and around Campo Santa Margarita and San Pantalon. Pick up a booklet of *2Night* or visit their Web site ⊕*www.2night.it* for nightlife listings and reviews.

BARS
Bàcaro Jazz (⊠*Across from Rialto post office* ☎*041/5285249*) has music (not usually live) and meals until 2 AM, and its gregarious staff is unlikely to let you feel lonely. Nothing special by day, **Bar Torino** (⊠*Campo San Lucaz* ☎*041/5223914*) is one of Venice's liveliest nightspots, open late and spilling out onto the campo in summer. **L'Olandese Volante** (⊠*Campo San Lio near Rialto* ☎*041/5289349*) is a popular hangout for many young Venetians. The **Martini Scala Club** (⊠*Campo San Fantin, San Marco 1983* ☎*041/5224121*), the Antico Martini restaurant's elegant bar, has live music from 10 PM to 3:30 AM. Full meals are served until 2 AM. One of the hippest bars for the late-night chill-out crowd, **Centrale** (⊠*Piscina Frezzeria, San Marco 1659/B* ☎*041/2960664*) is in a former movie theater—and the crowd does look more Hollywood than Venice. Excellent mojitos and other mixed drinks, black-leather couches, and dim lighting strike a loungey note, and the DJ keeps the beats cool. Hidden in plain sight behind the plate-glass windows of a Mondadori bookstore, the simply named **Bacaro** (⊠*Piscina Frezzeria, San Marco 1345* ☎*041/2960687*) adds a much-needed dash of modern to the antiquities surrounding Piazza San Marco. The circular bar is more crowded and lively than the restaurant upstairs, and serves strong cocktails until 2 AM.

Campo Santa Margarita is a student hangout all day and late into the night. Try **Orange** (⊠*Campo Santa Margarita, Dorsoduro 3054/a* ☎*041/5234740*) for *piadine* sandwiches, drinks, and soccer games on a massive screen. Bohemian **Il Caffè** (⊠*Campo Santa Margarita, Dorsoduro 2963* ☎*041/5287998*), also known as Caffè Rosso for its red exterior, is especially popular in nice weather.

6

WORD OF MOUTH

"Piazza San Marco is a unique and romantic experience at night—with the beautiful architecture and orchestras playing, it's like traveling back in time a few centuries. The cost is free—unless you want to sit outside at one of the famous and historic cafés, in which case you will pay a hefty price for a drink." —Nicole

CASINOS

The city-run casino in the splendid **Palazzo Vendramin-Calergi** is a classic scene of well-dressed high-rollers playing French roulette, Caribbean poker, chemin de fer, 30–40, and slots. You must be 18 to enter, and men must wear jackets; no sneakers allowed. ✉ *Cannaregio 2040* ☎ *041/5297111* ⬛*€10 entry includes €10 in chips* ⊙*Slots: daily 2:45* PM–*2:30* AM, *tables: daily 3:30* PM–*2:30* AM Ⓥ*San Marcuola.*

Mestre's **Ca' Noghera** casino, near the airport, has slots, blackjack, craps, poker, and roulette. Minimum age is 18. A free shuttle bus runs from Piazzale Roma from 4:05 PM until closing. ✉ *Via Triestina 222, Tessera Mestre* ☎*041/5297111* ⬛*€10 entry includes €10 in chips* ⊙*Slots: daily 11* AM–*3:30* AM, *tables: daily 3:30* PM–*3:30* AM.

SHOPPING

Updated by
Pamela Santini

Alluring shops abound in Venice. You'll find countless vendors of trademark Venetian wares such as glass and lace; the authenticity of some goods can be suspect, but they're often pleasing to the eye regardless of their place of origin. For more-sophisticated tastes (and deeper pockets), there are jewelers, antiques dealers, and high-fashion boutiques on a par with those in Italy's larger cities but often maintaining a uniquely Venetian flair. There are also some interesting craft and art studios, where you can find high-quality, one-of-a-kind articles, from handmade shoes to decorative lamps and mirrors.

It's always a good idea to mark on your map the location of a shop that interests you; otherwise you may not be able to find it again in the maze of tiny streets. Regular store hours are usually 9–12:30 and 3:30 or 4–7:30; some stores are closed Saturday afternoon or Monday morning. Food shops are open 8–1 and 5–7:30, and are closed Wednesday afternoon and all day Sunday. Many tourist-oriented shops are open all day, every day. Some shops close for both a summer and a winter vacation.

FOOD MARKETS

The morning open-air fruit-and-vegetable market at **Rialto** offers animated local color and commerce. On Tuesday through Saturday mornings the **fish market** (adjacent to the Rialto produce market) provides an impressive lesson in ichthyology, with species you've probably never seen before. In the Castello district you'll find a lively food market weekday mornings on **Via Garibaldi.**

SHOPPING DISTRICTS

The **San Marco** area is full of shops and couture boutiques such as Armani, Missoni, Valentino, Fendi, and Versace. **Le Mercerie,** along with the Frezzeria and Calle dei Fabbri, leading from Piazza San Marco, are some of Venice's busiest shopping streets. Other good shopping areas surround Calle del Teatro and Campi San Salvador, Manin, San Fantin, and San Bartolomeo. Less-expensive shops are between the Rialto Bridge and San Polo.

SPECIALTY STORES

GLASSWARE

Glass, most of it made in Murano, is Venice's number one product, and you'll be confronted by mind-boggling displays of traditional and contemporary glassware, much of it kitsch. Take your time and be selective. You will probably find that prices in Venice's shops and the showrooms of Murano's factories are pretty much the same. However, because of competition, shops in Venice with wares from various glassworks may charge slightly less.

Domus (⊠*Fondamenta dei Vetrai, Murano 82* ☎*041/739215*) has a selection of smaller objects and jewelry from the best glassworks.

For chic, contemporary glassware, Carlo Moretti is a good choice; his designs are on display at **L'Isola** (⊠*Campo San Moisè, San Marco 1468* ☎*041/5231973* ⊕*www.carlomoretti.com*). **Marina Barovier** (⊠*Calle delle Botteghe off Campo Santo Stefano, San Marco 3216* ☎*041/5236748* ⊕*www.barovier.it*) has an excellent selection of contemporary collectors' glass. Go to Michel Paciello's **Paropàmiso** (⊠*Frezzeria, San Marco 1701* ☎*041/5227120*) for stunning Venetian glass beads and traditional jewelry from all over the world. **Pauly** (⊠*Piazza San Marco 73, 77, and 316; Ponte dei Consorzi* ☎*041/5209899* ⊕*www.paulyglassfactory.com*) has four centrally located shops with an impressive selection of glassware at better prices than for Murano. **Venini** (⊠*Piazzetta dei Leoncini 314, San Marco* ☎*041/5224045* ⊕*www.venini.com*) has been an institution since the 1930s, attracting some of the foremost names in glass design.

LACE & FABRICS

Much of the lace and embroidered linen sold in Venice and on Burano is really made in China or Taiwan. However, at **Il Merletto** (⊠*Sotoportego del Cavalletto under the Procuratie Vecchie, Piazza San Marco 95* ☎*041/5208406*), you can ask for the authentic, handmade lace kept in the drawers behind the counter. This is the only place in Venice connected with the students of the Scuola del Merletto in Burano, who, officially, do not sell to the public. Hours of operation are daily 10 to 5. A top address for linen is **Jesurum** (⊠*Cannaregio 3219, Fondamenta della Sensa* ☎*041/5242540* ⊕*www.jesurum.it*). Go to **Lorenzo Rubelli** (⊠*Palazzo Corner Spinelli, San Marco 3877* ☎*041/5236110* ⊕*www.rubelli.it*) for the same brocades, damasks, and cut velvets used by the world's most prestigious decorators. **Venetia Studium** (⊠*Calle Larga XXII Marzo, San Marco 2403* ☎*041/5229281* ⊠*Calle Larga XXII Marzo, San Marco 723* ☎*041/5229859* ⊕*www.venetiastudium.com*) sells silk scarves, bags, and cushion covers, as well as the famous Fortuny lamps.

6

MASKS

Guerrino Lovato, proprietor of **Mondonovo** (✉ *Rio Terà Canal, Dorso-duro 3063* ☎ *041/5287344* ⊕ *www.mondonovomaschere.it*) is one of the most respected mask makers in town. He was called on to oversee reconstruction of reliefs and sculptures in Teatro La Fenice after it burned to the ground in 1996.

ITALIAN VOCABULARY

ENGLISH	ITALIAN	PRONOUNCIATION
BASICS		
Yes/no	Sí/No	see/no
Please	Per favore	pear fa-**vo**-ray
Yes, please	Sí grazie	see **grah**-tsee-ay
Thank you	Grazie	**grah**-tsee-ay
You're welcome	Prego	**pray**-go
Excuse me, sorry	Scusi	**skoo**-zee
Sorry!	Mi dispiace!	mee dis-spee-**ah**-chay
Good morning/ afternoon	Buongiorno	bwohn-**jor**-no
Good evening	Buona sera	**bwoh**-na **say**-ra
Good-bye	Arrivederci	a-ree-vah-**dare**-chee
Mr. (Sir)	Signore	see-**nyo**-ray
Mrs. (Ma'am)	Signora	see-**nyo**-ra
Miss	Signorina	see-nyo-**ree**-na
Pleased to meet you	Piacere	pee-ah-**chair**-ray
How are you?	Come sta?	**ko**-may **stah**
Very well, thanks	Bene, grazie	**ben**-ay **grah**-tsee-ay
Hello (phone)	Pronto?	**proan**-to
NUMBERS		
one	uno	**oo**-no
two	due	**doo**-ay
three	tre	tray
four	quattro	**kwah**-tro
five	cinque	**cheen**-kway
six	sei	say
seven	sette	**set**-ay
eight	otto	**oh**-to
nine	nove	**no**-vay
ten	dieci	dee-**eh**-chee
eleven	undici	**oon**-dee-chee

ENGLISH	ITALIAN	PRONOUNCIATION
twelve	dodici	**doe**-dee-cee
thirteen	tredici	**tray**-dee-chee
fourteen	quattordici	kwa-**tore**-dee-chee
fifteen	quindici	**kwin**-dee-chee
sixteen	sedici	**say**-dee-chee
seventeen	diciassete	dee-cha-**set**-ay
eighteen	diciotto	dee-**cho**-to
nineteen	diciannove	dee-cha-**no**-vay
twenty	venti	**vain**-tee
twenty-one	ventuno	vain-**too**-no
twenty-two	ventidue	vain-tee-**doo**-ay
thirty	trenta	**train**-ta
forty	quaranta	kwa-**rahn**-ta
fifty	cinquanta	cheen-**kwahn**-ta
sixty	sessanta	seh-**sahn**-ta
seventy	settanta	seh-**tahn**-ta
eighty	ottanta	o-**tahn**-ta
ninety	novanta	no-**vahn**-ta
one hundred	cento	**chen**-to
one thousand	mille	**mee**-lay
ten thousand	diecimila	dee-eh-chee-**mee**-la

USEFUL PHRASES

Do you speak English?	Parla inglese?	**par**-la een-**glay**-zay
I don't speak Italian	Non parlo italiano	non **par**-lo ee-tal-**yah**-no
I don't understand	Non capisco	non ka-**peess**-ko
Can you please repeat?	Può ripetere?	pwo ree-**pet**-ay-ray
Slowly!	Lentamente!	**len**-ta-men-tay
I don't know	Non lo so	non lo **so**

ENGLISH	ITALIAN	PRONOUNCIATION
I'm American	Sono americano(a)	**so**-no a-may-ree-**kah**-no(a)
I'm British	Sono inglese	so-no een-**glay**-zay
What's your name?	Come si chiama?	**ko**-may see kee-**ah**-ma
My name is . . .	Mi chiamo . . .	mee kee-**ah**-mo
What time is it?	Che ore sono?	kay **o**-ray **so**-no
How?	Come?	**ko**-may
When?	Quando?	**kwan**-doe
Yesterday/today/ tomorrow	Ieri/oggi/domani	**yer**-ee/**o**-jee/ do-**mah**-nee
This morning/	Stamattina/Oggi	sta-ma-**tee**-na/**o**-jee
afternoon	pomeriggio	po-mer-**ee**-jo
Tonight	Stasera	sta-**ser**-a
What?	Che cosa?	kay **ko**-za
What is it?	Chee cos'é?	kay ko-**zay**
Why?	Perché?	pear-**kay**
Who?	Chi?	kcc
Where is . . .	Dov'è . . .	doe-**veh**
the train station?	la stazione?	la sta-tsee-**oh**-nay
the subway	la metropolitana?	la may-tro-po-lee-**tah**-na
the terminal?	il terminale?	eel ter-mee-**nah**-lay
the post office?	l'ufficio postale?	loo-**fee**-cho po-**stah**-lay
the bank?	la banca?	la **bahn**-ka
the . . . hotel?	l'hotel . . .?	lo-**tel**
the store?	il negozio?	eel nay-**go**-tsee-o
the cashier?	la cassa?	la **kah**-sa
the . . . museum?	il museo . . .?	eel moo-**zay**-o
the hospital?	l'ospedale?	lo-spay-**dah**-lay
the first-aid station?	il pronto soccorso?	Eel **pron**-to so-**kor**-so
the elevator?	l'ascensore?	la-shen-**so**-ray
a telephone?	un telefono?	oon tay-**lay**-fo-no

ENGLISH	ITALIAN	PRONOUNCIATION
the restrooms?	Dov'è il bagno?	do-**vay** eel **bahn**-yo
Here/there	Qui/là	kwee/la
Left/right	A sinistra/a destra	a see-**neess**-tra/ a **des**-tra
Straight ahead	Avanti dritto	a-**vahn**-tee **dree**-to
Is it near/far?	È vicino/lontano?	ay vee-**chee**-no/ lon-**tah**-no
I'd like . . .	Vorrei . . .	vo-**ray**
a room	una camera	**oo**-na **kah**-may-ra
the key	la chiave	la kee-**ah**-vay
a newspaper	un giornale	oon jor-**nah**-lay
a stamp	un francobollo	oon frahn-ko-**bo**-lo
I'd like to buy . . .	Vorrei comprare . . .	vo-**ray** kom-**prah**-ray
How much is it?	Quanto costa?	**kwahn**-toe **coast**-a
It's expensive/ cheap	È caro/economico	ay **car**-o/ ay-ko-**no**-mee-ko
A little/a lot	Poco/tanto	**po**-ko/**tahn**-to
More/less	Più/meno	pee-**oo**/**may**-no
Enough/too (much)	Abbastanza/troppo	a-bas-**tahn**-sa/**tro**-po
I am sick	Sto male	sto **mah**-lay
Call a doctor	Chiama un dottore	kee-**ah**-mah oon doe-**toe**-ray
Help!	Aiuto!	a-**yoo**-toe
Stop!	Alt!	ahlt
Fire!	Al fuoco!	ahl **fwo**-ko
Caution/Look out!	Attenzione!	a-ten-**syon**-ay

DINING OUT

A bottle of . . .	Una bottiglia di . . .	**oo**-na bo-**tee**-lee-ahdee
A cup of . . .	Una tazza di . . .	**oo**-na **tah**-tsa dee
A glass of . . .	Un bicchiere di . . .	oon bee-key-**air**-ay dee
Bill/check	Il conto	eel **cone**-toe
Bread	Il pane	eel **pah**-nay

ENGLISH	ITALIAN	PRONOUNCIATION
Breakfast	La prima colazione	la **pree**-ma ko-la-**tsee**-oh-nay
Cocktail/aperitif	L'aperitivo	la-pay-ree-**tee**-vo
Dinner	La cena	la **chen**-a
Fixed-price menu	Menù a prezzo fisso	may-**noo** a **pret**-so **fee**-so
Fork	La forchetta	la for-**ket**-a
I am diabetic	Ho il diabete	o eel dee-a-**bay**-tay
I am vegetarian	Sono vegetariano/a	**so**-no vay-jay-ta-ree-**ah**-no/a
I'd like . . .	Vorrei . . .	vo-**ray**
I'd like to order	Vorrei ordinare	vo-**ray** or-dee-**nah**-ray
Is service	Il servizio è	eel ser-**vee**-tzee-o
included?	incluso?	ay een-**kloo**-zo
It's good/bad	È buono/cattivo	ay **bwo**-no/ka-**tee**-vo
It's hot/cold	È caldo/freddo	ay **kahl**-doe/**fred**-o
Knife	Il coltello	eel kol-**tel**-o
Lunch	Il pranzo	eel **prahnt**-so
Menu	Il menù	eel may-**noo**
Napkin	Il tovagliolo	eel toe-va-lee-**oh**-lo
Please give me . . .	Mi dia . . .	mee **dee**-a
Salt	Il sale	eel **sah**-lay
Spoon	Il cucchiaio	eel koo-kee-**ah**-yo
Sugar	Lo zucchero	lo **tsoo**-ker-o
Waiter/Waitress	Cameriere/ cameriera	ka-mare-**yer**-ay/ ka-mare-**yer**-a
Wine list	La lista dei vini	la **lee**-sta **day**-ee **vee**-nee

Italy
Essentials

PLANNING TOOLS, EXPERT INSIGHT, GREAT CONTACTS

There are planners and there are those who, excuse the pun, fly by the seat of their pants. We happily place ourselves among the planners. Our writers and editors try to anticipate all the issues you may face before and during any journey, and then they do their research. This section is the product of their efforts. Use it to get excited about your trip to Essential Italy, to inform your travel planning, or to guide you on the road should the seat of your pants start to feel threadbare.

GETTING STARTED

We're really proud of our Web site: Fodors.com is a great place to begin any journey. Scan Travel Wire for suggested itineraries, travel deals, restaurant and hotel openings, and other up-to-the-minute info. Check out Booking to research prices and book plane tickets, hotel rooms, rental cars, and vacation packages. Head to Talk for on-the-ground pointers from travelers who frequent our message boards. You can also link to loads of other travel-related resources.

WORD OF MOUTH

After your trip, be sure to rate the places you visited and share your experiences and travel tips with us and other Fodorites in Travel Ratings and Talk on www.fodors.com.

∎ RESOURCES

ONLINE TRAVEL TOOLS

Currency Conversion Google (⊕www.google.com) does currency conversion. Just type in the amount you want to convert and an explanation of how you want it converted (e.g., "14 Swiss francs in dollars"), and then voilà. **Oanda.com** (⊕www.oanda.com) also allows you to print out a handy table with the current day's conversion rates. **XE.com** (⊕www.xe.com) is a good currency conversion Web site.

Maps Google (⊕www.google.com) can give you a road map, a satellite view of the terrain, or a hybrid of both. The site can also provide you with directions for getting from place to place. **ViaMichelin** (⊕www.viamichelin.com) is easy to use to find a small town or a small street in a large city on a printable map, to get directions for both driving and walking routes, as well as to discover the distances, travel time, and estimated cost to drive from one location to another.

Safety Transportation Security Administration (TSA ⊕www.tsa.gov)

Time Zones Timeanddate.com (⊕www.timeanddate.com/worldclock) can help you figure out the correct time anywhere in the world.

Weather Accuweather.com (⊕www.accuweather.com) is an independent weather-forecasting service with especially good coverage of hurricanes. **Weather.com** (⊕www.weather.com) is the Web site for the Weather Channel.

Other Resources CIA World Factbook (⊕www.odci.gov/cia/publications/factbook/index.html) has profiles of every country in the world. It's a good source if you need some quick facts and figures.

VISITOR INFORMATION

Contacts at Home Italian Government Tourist Board (ENIT ⊠New York ☎212/245–4822 🖷212/586–9249 ⊠Chicago ☎312/644–0990 🖷312/644–3019 ⊠Los Angeles ☎310/820–0098 🖷310/820–6357).

Tourist Offices in Italy Each city or town has a tourist information office (usually operated by the national Agenzia Per il Turismo (APT) and most of them have Web sites. See contact information at the beginning of town listings throughout this guide.

∎ THINGS TO CONSIDER

PASSPORTS & VISAS

U.S. citizens need only a valid passport to enter Italy for stays of up to 90 days.

PASSPORTS

We're always surprised at how few Americans have passports—only 25% at this writing. This number is expected to grow in coming years, when it becomes impossible to reenter the United States from trips to neighboring Canada or Mexico without one. Remember this: a passport verifies both your identity and nationality—a great reason to have one.

U.S. passports are valid for 10 years. You must apply in person if you're getting a passport for the first time; if your previous passport was lost, stolen, or damaged; or if your previous passport has expired and was issued more than 15 years ago or when you were under 16. All children under 18 must appear in person to apply for or renew a passport. Both parents must accompany any child under 14 (or send a notarized statement with their permission) and provide proof of their relationship to the child.

There are 13 regional passport offices, as well as 7,000 passport acceptance facilities in post offices, public libraries, and other governmental offices. If you're renewing a passport, you can do so by mail. Forms are available at passport acceptance facilities and online.

The cost to apply for a new passport is $97 for adults, $82 for children under 16; renewals are $67. Allow six weeks for processing, both for first-time passports and renewals. For an expediting fee of $60 you can reduce this time to about two weeks. If your trip is less than two weeks away, you can get a passport even more rapidly by going to a passport office with the necessary documentation. Private expediters can get things done in as little as 48 hours, but charge hefty fees for their services.

■TIP➜Before your trip, make two copies of your passport's data page (one for someone at home and another for you to carry separately). Or scan the page and e-mail it to someone at home and/or yourself.

VISAS

When staying for 90 days or less, U.S. citizens are not required to obtain a visa prior to traveling to Italy. If you plan to travel or live in Italy or the European Union for longer than 90 days, you must acquire a valid visa from the Italian consulate serving your state before you leave the United States. Plan ahead because the process of obtaining a visa will take at least 30 days and the Italian government does not accept visa applications submitted by visa expediters.

U.S. Passport Information U.S. Department of State (☎877/487-2778 ⊕www.travel.state.gov/passport).

U.S. Passport Expediters A. Briggs Passport & Visa Expeditors (☎800/806-0581 or 202/338-0111 ⊕www.abriggs.com). **American Passport Express** (☎800/455-5166 or 603/559-9888 ⊕www.americanpassport.com). **Passport Express** (☎800/362-8196 or 401/272-4612 ⊕www.passportexpress.com). **Travel Document Systems** (☎800/874-5100 or 202/638-3800 ⊕www.traveldocs.com). **Travel the World Visas** (☎866/886-8472 ⊕www.world-visa.com).

SHOTS & MEDICATIONS

No immunizations, inoculations, or health certificates are needed to travel in Italy. Bring a supply of your personal medications—enough to cover your entire vacation plus any travel days. Bring a copy of each of your prescriptions in case you lose medications during your stay. *For more information see Health under On the Ground in Italy, below.*

■TIP➜If you travel a lot internationally—particularly to developing nations—refer to the CDC's *Health Information for International Travel* (aka Traveler's Health Yellow Book). Info from it is posted on the CDC Web site (⊕www.cdc.gov/travel/yb), or you can buy a copy from your local bookstore for $24.95.

Health Warnings National Centers for Disease Control & Prevention (CDC ☎877/394-8747 international travelers' health line ⊕www.cdc.gov/travel). **World Health Organization** (WHO ⊕www.who.int).

BOOKING YOUR TRIP

Italy is an easy destination to plan for without the use of a travel agent. Booking flights, making hotel reservations, and reserving museum tickets are all things that can be done online or by telephone before you leave home.

In certain cases, however, a travel agent can provide specific assistance. Making train reservations online during peak times can be difficult to manage, and a travel agent can help. A travel agent who specializes in Italy may also have contacts with private tour guides for individual and small-group custom tours.

Agent Resources American Society of Travel Agents (☎703/739–2782 ⊕www. travelsense.org).

Italy Travel Agents Century Travel (☎512/327–8760 ⊕www.sallywatkins.com). **Ciao Bambino** (☎866/802–0300 ⊕www. ciaobambino.com). **Select Italy** (☎800/877–1755 ⊕www.selectitaly.com). **Zurer Travel** (☎202/210–6975 ⊕www.zurer.com).

▮ ACCOMMODATIONS

Italy has a varied and abundant number of hotels, bed-and-breakfasts, *agriturismi (farm stays),* and rental properties. Throughout the cities and the countryside you can find very sophisticated, luxurious palaces and villas as well as rustic farmhouses and small hotels. Six-hundred-year-old palazzi and converted monasteries have been restored as luxurious hotels, while retaining the original atmosphere. At the other end of the spectrum, boutique hotels inhabit historic buildings using chic Italian design for the interiors. Increasingly, the famed Italian wineries are creating rooms and apartments for three-day to weeklong stays.

The lodgings we list are the cream of the crop in each price category. We always list the facilities that are available, but we don't specify whether they cost extra;

when pricing accommodations, always ask what's included and what costs extra. Properties are assigned price categories based on the range between their least and most expensive standard double room at high season (excluding holidays).

Hotels with the designation BP (for Breakfast Plan) at the end of their listing include breakfast in their rate; offerings can vary from coffee and a roll to an elaborate buffet. Those designated EP (European Plan) have no meals included; MAP (Modified American Plan) means you get breakfast and dinner; FAP (Full American Plan) includes all meals.

APARTMENT & HOUSE RENTALS

More and more travelers are turning away from the three-countries-in-two-weeks style of touring and choosing to spend a week in one city or a month in the countryside. Renting an apartment, a farmhouse, or a villa can be economical depending on the number of people in your group and your budget. All are readily available throughout Italy. Most are owned by individuals and managed by rental agents who advertise available properties on the Internet. Many properties are represented by more than one rental agent, and thus the same property is frequently renamed ("Chianti Bella Vista," "Tuscan Sun Home," and "Casa Toscana Sole" are all names of the same farmhouse) on the various Internet rental sites. The rental agent may meet you at the property for the initial check-in or the owner may be present, while the rental agent only handles the online reservation and financial arrangements.

Issues to keep in mind when renting an apartment in a city or town are the neighborhood (street noise and ambience), the availability of an elevator or number of stairs, the furnishings (including pots and pans and linens), and the cost of utilities (are they included in the rental rate?). Inquires about countryside properties should also include how isolated the property is. (Do you have to drive 45 minutes to reach the nearest town?)

Contacts At Home Abroad (☎212/421–9165 ⊕www.athomeabroadinc.com). **Barclay International Group** (☎800/845–6636 or 516/364–0064 ⊕www.barclayweb.com). **Drawbridge to Europe** (☎888/268–1148 or 541/482–7778 ⊕www.drawbridgetoeurope. com). **Homes Away** (☎800/374–6637 or 416/920–1873 ⊕www.homesaway.com). **Rent A Villa** (☎800/964–1891 or 206/417–3444 ⊕www.rentavilla.com). **Suzanne B. Cohen & Associates** (☎207/622–0743 ⊕www.villaeurope.com). **Italy Rents** (☎800/844-6939 ⊕www.italyrents.com). **Tuscan House** (☎800/844-6939 ⊕www. tuscanhouse.com). **Villas & Apartments Abroad** (☎800/433–3020 or 212/213–6435 ⊕www.vaanyc.com). **Villas International** (☎800/221–2260 or 415/499–9490 ⊕www. villasintl.com). **Villas of Distinction** (☎800/289–0900 or 707/778-1800 ⊕www. villasofdistinction.com). **Wimco** (☎800/449–1553 ⊕www.wimco.com).

CONVENTS & MONASTERIES

Throughout Italy, tourists can find reasonably priced lodging at convents, monasteries, and religious houses. Religious orders usually charge from 30 to 60 euros per person per night for rooms that are clean, comfortable, and convenient. Most have private bathrooms; spacious lounge areas and secluded gardens or terraces are standard features. A continental breakfast ordinarily comes with the room. Sometimes, for an extra fee, family-style lunches and dinners are available.

Be aware of three issues when considering a convent or monastery stay: most have a curfew of 11 PM or midnight; you need to book in advance, because they fill up quickly; and your best means of booking is usually e-mail or fax—the person answering the phone may not speak English. For a list of convents throughout Italy, go to ⊕www.hospites.it.

FARM HOLIDAYS & AGRITOURISM

Rural accommodations in the *agriturismo* (agricultural tourism) category are increasingly popular with both Italians and visitors to Italy; you stay on a working farm or vineyard. Accommodations vary in size and range from luxury apartments, farmhouses, and villas to very basic facilities. Agriturist has compiled *Agriturism*, which is available only in Italian, but includes more than 1,600 farms in Italy; pictures and the use of international symbols to describe facilities make the guide a good tool. Local APT tourist offices also have information.

Information Agriturist (☎06/6852342 ⊕www.agriturist.it). **Agriturismo.net** (⊕ www.agriturismo.net). **Italy Farm Holidays** (☎914/631–7880 ☐914/631–8831 ⊕www. italyfarmholidays.com). **Italy Tourist: Farm Holiday** (⊕www.italytourist.it).

HOME EXCHANGES

With a direct home exchange you stay in someone else's home while they stay in yours. Some outfits also deal with vacation homes, so you're not actually staying in someone's full-time residence, just their vacant weekend place.

Italians have historically not been as enthusiastic about home exchanges as others have been; however, there are many great villas and apartments in Italy owned by foreigners, such as Americans, who use the home exchange services.

Exchange Clubs Home Exchange.com (☎800/877-8723 ⊕www.homeexchange.com); $99 for a one-year online listing. **HomeLink International** (☎800/638-3841 ⊕www. homelink.org); $110 yearly for Web-only membership; $170 includes Web access and two catalogs. **Intervac U.S.** (☎800/756–4663 ⊕www.intervacus.com); $95 for Web-only international membership; $140 includes Web access and a catalog.

HOSTELS

Hostels offer bare-bones lodging at low, low prices—often in shared dorm rooms with shared baths—to people of all ages, though the primary market is young travelers, especially students. Most hostels serve breakfast; dinner and/or shared cooking facilities may also be available. In some hostels you aren't allowed to be in your room during the day, and there may be a curfew at night. Nevertheless, hostels provide a sense of community, with public rooms where travelers often gather to share stories. Many hostels are affiliated with Hostelling International (HI), an umbrella group of hostel associations with some 4,500 member properties in more than 70 countries. Other hostels are independent and may be nothing more than a really cheap hotel.

Membership in any HI association, open to travelers of all ages, allows you to stay in HI-affiliated hostels at member rates. One-year membership is about $28 for adults; hostels charge about $20–$40 per night. Members have priority if the hostel is full; they're also eligible for discounts around the world, even on rail and bus travel in some countries.

Hostels in Italy run the gamut from low-end hotels to beautiful villas. In Florence, the campground and hostel near Piazzale Michelangelo has a better view of the city than any luxury hotel in town.

Information Hostelling International—USA (☎ 301/495–1240 national office, check online for the phone number of the office in your state ⊕ www.hiusa.org). **Hostel World** (⊕ www.hostelworld.com). **Ostelli on Line** (☎ 06/48907740 ⊕ www.ostellionline.org).

∎ RENTAL CARS

When you reserve a car, ask about cancellation penalties, taxes, drop-off charges (if you're planning to pick up the car in one city and leave it in another), and surcharges (for being under or over a certain age, for additional drivers, or for driving across state or country borders or beyond a specific distance from your point of rental). All these things can add substantially to your costs. Request child

car seats and extras, such as GPS, when you book.

Rates are sometimes—but not always—better if you book in advance or reserve through a rental agency's Web site. There are other reasons to book ahead, though: for popular destinations, during busy times of the year, or to ensure that you get certain types of cars (vans, SUVs, exotic sports cars).

∎**TIP➔**Make sure that a confirmed reservation guarantees you a car. Agencies sometimes overbook, particularly for busy weekends and holiday periods.

Renting a car in Italy is helpful for exploring the countryside, but not if you plan to stick to the cities. The Italian countryside has an intricate network of *autostrade* routes (toll highways), good highways, and secondary roads, making renting a car a better but expensive alternative (because of high gas prices and freeway tolls) to public transportation. A rental car can be a good investment for carefree countryside rambles, offering time to explore more-remote towns. Signage on country roads is usually good, but be prepared for fast and impatient fellow drivers.

Having a car in major cities, however, often leads to parking and traffic headaches, plus the additional expense of garage and parking fees. In major cities, such as Rome, Milan, Florence, and Siena, there are restricted zones for cars. These areas are monitored by camera. If you have to drive to your hotel in the city center of these cities, inquire at the front desk of your hotel as to whether your rental car's license tag number must be submitted by the hotel to the police or traffic authority. Failure to do this may result in a large fine being levied on your car-rental company and passed on to you at a later date.

Fiats and Fords in a variety of sizes are the most typical rental cars. Remember that most Italian cars have standard transmission. If you want to rent an automatic, be specific when you reserve the car. Higher rates will apply.

Most American chains have affiliates in Italy, but the rates are usually lower if you book a car before you leave home. A company's rates are the same throughout the country: you will not save money, for example, if you pick up a vehicle in a city rather than at an airport.

In Italy a U.S. driver's license is acceptable to rent a car, but consider getting an International Driver's Permit (IDP). Italy, by law at least, requires non-Europeans to carry an IDP along with their domestic license because the IDP states in Italian (and a dozen other languages) that your license is valid. In practice, it depends on the police officer who pulls you over whether you will be penalized for not carrying the IDP. Check the AAA Web site for more info as well as for information on obtaining an IDP ($15).

In Italy you must be 18 years old to drive a car. Most rental companies will not rent to someone under age 21 and also refuse to rent any car larger than an economy or subcompact car to anyone under age 23, and, further, require customers under age 23 to pay by credit card. Additional drivers must be identified in the contract and must qualify with the age limits. There may be an additional daily fee for more than one driver. Upon rental, all companies require credit cards as a warranty; to rent bigger cars (2,000 cc or more), you must often show two credit cards. There are no special restrictions on senior citizen drivers. Book car seats, required for children under age three, in advance (the cost is generally about €36 for the duration of the rental).

Hiring a car with a driver can come in handy, particularly if you plan to do some wine tasting or drive along the Amalfi Coast. Ask at your hotel for recommended drivers, or inquire at the local tourist office. Drivers are paid by the day, and are usually rewarded with a tip of about 15% upon completion of the journey.

CAR-RENTAL INSURANCE

All rental agencies operating in Italy require that you buy CDW and a theft-protection policy, but those costs will already be included in the rates you are quoted. Be aware that coverage may be denied if the named driver on the rental contract is not the driver at the time of the incident. In Sicily there are some roads for which rental agencies deny coverage; ask in advance if you plan to travel in remote regions. Also ask your rental company about other included coverage when you reserve the car and/or pick it up.

▌ TRAIN PASSES

If you plan to travel by rail, know that there are many different train passes available to help you save money. Some require purchase before you leave home, while others can be bought when you arrive in Italy. Both Eurail Passes and the Eurail Italy Pass require advance purchase in the United States. If Italy is your only destination in Europe, **consider purchasing a Eurail Italy Pass** (aka Trenitalia Pass or Italian Flexi Rail Card), which allows a limited number of travel days within one month. Four days of travel cost $278 (first class) or $223 (second class); additional days cost $30 (first class) or $25 (second class). If you are traveling with others, you should consider the discounted **Italian Flexi Rail Card Saver** (aka Trenitalia Pass Saver), which allows a limited number of travel days within one month for groups of two to five people. Four days of travel, for instance, cost $238 (first class) or $190 (second class); additional days are $27 (first class) and $20 (second class).

Italy is one of 17 countries that accept Eurail Pass, which allows unlimited first-class travel. Order the passes online before you leave for Europe. If you plan to rack up the miles, get a standard Eurail Pass.

The Eurail Select Pass allows for travel in three to five contiguous countries. In addition to standard Eurail Passes, ask about special plans. Among these are the Eurail Youth Pass (for those under 26), the Eurail Flexipass (which allows a certain number of travel days within a set period), the Eurail Saver Flexipass (which gives a discount for two or more people traveling together), and the Eurail Drive Pass (which combines travel by train and rental car).

Remember that you need to reserve seats even if you are using a rail pass. *For more information on traveling by rail in Italy, see By Train in Transportation, below.*

Contacts Europe on Rail (☎866/858–6854 ⊕ www.europeonrail.com). **Rail Europe** (☎800/438–7245 or 877/257–2887 ⊕www. raileurope.com). **RailPass** (☎877/724–5727 ⊕www.railpass.com).

∎ GUIDED TOURS

Guided tours are a good option when you don't want to do it all yourself. You travel along with a group (sometimes large, sometimes small), stay in prebooked hotels, eat with your fellow travelers (the cost of meals sometimes included in the price of your tour, sometimes not), and follow a schedule. But not all guided tours are an if-it's-Tuesday-this-must-be-Belgium experience. A knowledgeable guide can take you places that you might never discover on your own, and you may be pushed to see more than you would have otherwise. Tours aren't for everyone, but they can be just the thing for trips to places where making travel arrangements is difficult or time consuming (particularly when you don't speak the language). Whenever you book a guided tour, find out what's included and what isn't. A "land-only" tour includes all your travel (by bus, in most cases) in the destination, but not necessarily your flights to and from or even within it. Also, in most cases prices in tour brochures don't

include fees and taxes. And remember that you'll be expected to tip your guide (in cash) at the end of the tour.

Also keep in mind that every province and city in Italy has tour guides licensed by the government. Some are eminently qualified in relevant fields such as architecture and art history; others have simply managed to pass the test. Many local guides have Web sites: check online before you leave home. Tourist offices and hotel concierges, also, can provide the names of knowledgeable local guides and the rates for certain services. Before you hire a local guide, ask about their background and qualifications and make sure you can understand each other. Tipping is appreciated, but not obligatory, for local guides.

Recommended Generalists Abercrombie & Kent (☎800/554–7016 ⊕www.abercrombiekent.com). **CIE Tours International** (☎800/243–8687 ⊕www.cietours.com). **Maupin Tour** (☎800/255–4266 ⊕www. maupintour.com). **Perillo Tours** (☎800/431–1515 ⊕www.perillotours.com). **Travcoa** (☎866/591-0070 ⊕www.travcoa.com).

Biking & Hiking Tour Contacts Backroads (☎800/462-2848 ⊕www.backroads.com). **Butterfield & Robinson** (☎866/551–9090 ⊕www.butterfield.com). **Ciclismo Classico** (☎800/866-7314 ⊕www.ciclismoclassico.com).

Culinary Tour Contact Epiculinary (☎888/380-9010 ⊕www.epiculinary.com).

Golf Tour Contact Rosso Soave (☎039/0552305210 ⊕www.rossosoave.com).**Tuscany Golf & Tourism** (☎039/0574600269 ⊕www. tuscanygolftourism.com).

Volunteer Programs Elderhostel (☎800/454-5768 ⊕www.elderhostel.com).

Wine Tour Contacts Cellar Tours (☎034/915-213-939 ⊕www.cellartours.com). **Food & Wine Trails** (☎800/367-5348 ⊕www. foodandwinetrails.com).

TRANSPORTATION

It is not difficult to see two or three diverse parts of Italy in a one-week vacation because of the ease of travel by car on the fast freeway system, via the comprehensive railway with the speedy Eurostar trains, and lastly, by air from the two major airports in Milan and Rome to the smaller efficient airports serving Venice, Florence, Pisa, Naples, and Palermo. While you are planning your itinerary, remember that Italy is a long narrow country and that you don't want to spend your entire vacation in transit. When traveling by car along the smaller country roads or by train on local lines that stop at every station, it will probably take you longer than you think to get from place to place.

▌BY AIR

Air travel to Italy is frequent and virtually problem-free, except for airport- or airline-related union strikes that may cause delays. Alitalia, Italy's national flag carrier, has the most nonstop flights to Rome and Milan. Many travelers to Florence and Tuscany find it much more convenient to bypass the Rome and Milan airports and fly to Florence or Pisa. The airport in Venice also caters to international carriers.

Flying time to Milan or Rome is approximately 8–8½ hours from New York, 10–11 hours from Chicago, and 11½ hours from Los Angeles.

Confirm flights within Italy the day before travel. Labor strikes are frequent and can affect not only air travel, but also the local trains that serve the airport. Your airline will have information about strikes directly affecting its flight schedule. If you are taking a train to get to the airport, check with the local tourist agency or rail station about upcoming strikes.

Airline Security Issues Transportation Security Administration (⊕ www.tsa.gov) has answers for almost every question that might come up.

Contact Italy Air Travel Resources A helpful Web site for information (location, phone numbers, local transportation, etc.) about all of the airports in Italy is ⊕ www.travel-library.com.

AIRPORTS

The major gateways to Italy include Rome's Aeroporto Leonardo da Vinci (FCO), better known as Fiumicino, and Milan's Aeroporto Malpensa (MIL). Most flights to Venice, Florence, and Pisa make connections at Fiumicino and Malpensa or another European airport. You can also take the FS airport train to Rome's Termini station or a bus to Milan's central train station (Centrale) and catch a train to any other location in Italy. It will take about one hour to get from either Fiumicino or Malpensa to the appropriate train station.

Alitalia and other European carriers fly into the smaller airports. Venice is served by Aeroporto Marco Polo (VCE), Naples by Aeroporto Capodichino (NAP), and Palermo by Aeroporto Punta Raisi (PMO). Florence is serviced by Aeroporto A. Vespucci (FLR), which is also called Peretola, and by Aeroporto Galileo Galilei (PSA), which is about a mile outside the center of Pisa and about one hour from Florence. The train to Florence stops within 100 feet of the entrance to the Pisa airport terminal.

Italy's major airports are not known for being new, fun, or efficient. Airports in Italy have been ramping up security measures, which include random baggage inspection and bomb-detection dogs. All of the airports have restaurants and snack bars, and there is Internet access. Each airport has at least one nearby hotel. In the case of Florence and Pisa, the city centers are only a 15-minute taxi ride away—so if you encounter a long delay, spend it in town.

When you take a connecting flight from a European airline hub (Frankfurt or Paris, for example) to a local Italian airport (Florence or Venice), be aware that your luggage might not make it onto the second plane with you. The airlines' lost-luggage service is efficient, however, and your delayed luggage is usually delivered to your hotel or holiday rental within 12 to 24 hours.

Departure taxes from Italian destinations are included in the price of your airline ticket.

Airport Information Aeroporto A. Vespucci (FLR, also called Peterola ✈6 km [4 mi] northwest of Florence ☎055/3061300 ⊕www.aeroporto.firenze.it). **Aeroporto di Venezia** (VCE, also called Marco Polo ✈6 km [4 mi] from Venice ☎041/2609240 ⊕www.veniceairport.it). **Aeroporto Galileo Galilei** (PSA ✈2 km [1 mi] south of Pisa, 80 km [50 mi] west of Florence ☎050/849300 ⊕www.pisa-airport.com). **Aeroporto Leonardo da Vinci** (FCO, also called Fiumicino ✈35 km [20 mi] southwest of Rome ☎06/65951 ⊕www.adr.it). **Aeroporto Malpensa** (MIL ✈45 km [28 mi] north of Milan ☎02/74852200 ⊕www.sea-aeroportimilano.it). **Naples International Airport** (NAP, also called Capodichino ✈7 km [4 mi] northeast of Naples ☎081/7896272 ⊕www.naples-airport.com). **Palermo International Airport** (PMO, also called Punt Raisi ✈32 km [19 mi] northwest of Palermo ☎050/500707 ⊕www.gesap.it).

FLIGHTS

When flying internationally, you must usually choose between a domestic carrier, the national flag carrier of the country you are visiting (Alitalia for Italy), and a foreign carrier from a third country. National flag carriers have the greatest number of nonstops. Domestic carriers may have better connections to your hometown and serve a greater number of gateway cities. Third-party carriers may have a price advantage.

On flights from the United States, Alitalia and Delta Air Lines serve Rome, Milan, and Venice. The major international hubs in Italy, Milan and Rome are also served by Continental Airlines and American Airlines, and US Airways serves Rome. From April through October, the Italy-based EuroFly has nonstop flights from New York to Rome, Naples, Bologna, and Palermo.

Alitalia and British Airways have direct flights from London to Milan, Venice, Rome, and 10 other locations in Italy. Smaller, no-frills airlines also provide service between Great Britain and Italy. EasyJet connects Gatwick with Milan, Venice, Rome, and Bologna. British Midland connects Heathrow and Milan (Linate), Naples, and Venice. Ryanair, departing from London's Stansted airport, flies to Milan, Rome, Pisa, and Venice. Meridiana has flights between Gatwick and Olbia on Sardinia in summer, and flights to Rome and Florence throughout the year.

Tickets for flights within Italy, on Alitalia and small carriers, such as EuroFly, Meridiana, and Air One, cost less when purchased from agents within Italy. Tickets are frequently sold at discounted prices, so check the cost of flights, even one-way, as an alternative to train travel.

Airline Contacts Alitalia (☎800/223-5730 in U.S., 06/65641 in Rome, 848/865641 elsewhere in Italy ⊕www.alitalia.it). **American Airlines** (☎800/433-7300, 02/69682464 in Milan ⊕www.aa.com). **British Airways** (☎800/403-0882 in U.S., 06/52492800 in Italy ⊕www.britishairways.com). **British Midland** (☎0807/6070-222 for U.K. reservations, 1332/64-8181 callers outside U.K. ⊕www.flybmi.com). **Continental Airlines** (☎800/523-3273 for U.S. reservations, 800/231-0856 for international reservations, 02/69633256 in Milan, 800/296230 elsewhere in Italy ⊕www.continental.com). **Delta Air Lines** (☎800/221-1212 for U.S. reservations, 800/241-4141 for international reservations, 06/65954406 in Italy ⊕www.delta.com).

com). **EasyJet** (☎0870/607–6543 in U.K., 848/887766 in Italy ⊕www.easyjet.com). **Euro-Fly** (☎800/459–0581 in U.S., 199/509960 in Italy ⊕www.euroflyusa.com). **Northwest Airlines** (☎800/225–2525 ⊕www.nwa. com). **Ryanair** (☎08701/56–569 in U.K., 199/114114 in Italy ⊕www.ryanair.com). **United Airlines** (☎800/864–8331 for U.S. reservations, 800/538–2929 for international reservations ⊕www.united.com). **US Airways** (☎800/428–4322 for U.S. reservations, 800/622–1015 for international reservations, 848/813177 in Italy ⊕www.usairways.com).

National Carriers Air One (☎06/488800 in Rome, 800/900966 elsewhere in Italy ⊕www. flyairone.it). **Meridiana** (☎199/111333 in Italy ⊕www.meridiana.it).

∎ BY BUS

Italy's regional bus network, often operated by private companies, is extensive, although buses are not as attractive an option as in other European countries, partly because of cheap, convenient train travel. Schedules are often drawn up with commuters and students in mind and may be sketchy on weekends. Regional bus companies often provide the only means (not including car travel) of getting to out-of-the-way places. Even when this isn't the case, buses can be faster and more direct than local trains, so it's a good idea to compare bus and train schedules. SITA operates throughout Italy; Lazzi Eurolines operates in Tuscany and central Italy.

Most of the major cities in Italy have urban bus services. These buses are inexpensive, but they can become jammed, particularly at rush hours.

No buses permit smoking, and both public and private buses offer only one class of service. Cleanliness and comfort levels are high on private buses, which have plenty of legroom and comfortable seats, but no toilets. Private bus lines usually have a ticket office in town or allow you to pay when you board. When traveling on city buses, you must buy your ticket from a machine, newsstand, or tobacco shop and stamp it after you board.

Bus Information ATAC (✉Rome ☎800/431784 or 06/46952027 ⊕www.atac.roma.it [info not in English]). **ATAF** (✉Stazione Centrale di Santa Maria Novella, Florence ☎055/5650642 or 055/5650222 ⊕www.ataf.net). **Lazzi Eurolines** (✉Via Mercadante 2, Florence ☎055/363041 ⊕www.lazzi.it). **SITA** (✉Via Santa Caterina da Siena 17/r, Florence ☎055/214721 ⊕www.sitabus.it).

∎ BY CAR

Italy has an extensive network of autostrade, complemented by equally well-maintained but free *superstrade* (expressways). Save the ticket you are issued at an autostrada entrance, as you need it to exit; on some shorter autostrade, you pay the toll when you enter. Viacards, on sale for €25 at many autostrada locations, allow you to pay for tolls in advance. At special lanes you simply slip the card into a designated slot.

An *uscita* is an "exit." A *raccordo* is a ring road surrounding a city. *Strade regionale* and *strade provinciale* (regional and provincial highways, denoted by S, SS, SR, or SP numbers) may be two-lane roads, as are all secondary roads; directions and turnoffs aren't always clearly marked.

GASOLINE

Gas stations are located along the main highways. Those on autostrade are open 24 hours. Otherwise, gas stations generally are open Monday–Saturday 7–7, with a break at lunchtime. At self-service gas stations the pumps are operated by a central machine for payment, which doesn't take credit cards; accepts only bills in denominations of 5, 10, 20, and 50 euros; and does not give change. Those with attendants accept cash and credit cards. It's not customary to tip the attendant.

At this writing, gasoline (*benzina*) costs about €1.40 per liter and is available in unleaded (*verde*) and super-unleaded (*super*). Many rental cars in Italy use diesel (*gasolio*), which costs about €1.10 per liter (ask about the fuel type for your rental car before you leave the agency).

PARKING

Parking is at a premium in most towns, especially in the *centri storici* (historic centers). Fines for parking violations are high, and towing is common. Don't think about tearing up a ticket, as car-rental companies can use your credit card to be reimbursed for any fines you incur. It's a good idea to park in a designated (and preferably attended) lot. And don't leave valuables in your car, as thieves often target rental cars.

In congested cities, indoor parking costs €23–€30 for 12–24 hours; outdoor parking costs about €10–€20. Parking in an area signposted *zona disco* (disk zone) is allowed for short periods (from 30 minutes to 2 hours or more—the time is posted); if you don't have a cardboard disk (check in the glove box of your rental car) to show what time you parked, you can use a piece of paper. The *parcometro*, a central parking meter that, after coins are inserted, prints a ticket that you leave on your dashboard, has been introduced in most metropolitan areas.

ROAD CONDITIONS

Autostrade are well maintained, as are most interregional highways. Most autostrade have two lanes in both directions; the left lane is used only for passing. Italians drive fast and are impatient with those who don't, so tailgating (and flashing with bright beams to signal an intent to pass) is the norm here; the only way to avoid it is to get out of the way.

The condition of provincial (county) roads varies, but road maintenance at this level is generally good in Italy. In many small hill towns the streets are winding and extremely narrow; consider parking at the edge of town and exploring on foot.

Driving on the back roads of Italy isn't difficult as long as you're on the alert for bicycles and passing cars. In addition, street and road signs are often missing or placed in awkward spots, so a good map and patience are essential.

Be aware that some maps may not use the *SR* or *SP* (*strade regionale* and *strade provinciale*) highway designations, which took the place of the old *SS* designations in 2004. They may use the old *SS* designation or no numbering at all.

ROADSIDE EMERGENCIES

Automobile Club Italiano offers 24-hour road service. English-speaking operators are available. Your rental-car company may also have an emergency tow service with a toll-free call. Be prepared to tell the operator which road you're on, the *verso* (direction) you're headed, and your *targa* (license plate number). Also, in an emergency, call the police (113).

When you're on the road, always carry a good road map, a flashlight, and, if possible, a cellular phone for emergencies. On the autostrade and superstrade, emergency phones are available. To find the nearest one, look on the pavement for painted arrows and the term "SOS."

Emergency Services Automobile Club Italiano (ACI ☎803/116 emergency service ⊕www.aci.it).

RULES OF THE ROAD

Driving is on the right. Speed limits are 110 kph (70 mph) on autostrade and 100 kph (60 mph) on state and provincial roads, unless otherwise marked. Right turns on red lights are forbidden. Headlights are required to be on while driving on all roads (large or small) outside of municipalities. You must wear seat belts and strap young children into car seats at all times. Using handheld mobile phones while driving is illegal; fines can exceed €100. In most Italian towns the use of the horn is forbidden in many areas; a large sign, *zona di silenzio,* indicates a no-honking zone.

The blood-alcohol content limit for driving is 0.5 gr (stricter than U.S. limits) with fines up to €5,000 for surpassing the limit and the possibility of six months' imprisonment. Although enforcement of laws varies depending on the region, fines for speeding are uniformly stiff: 10 kph over the speed limit can warrant a fine of up to €500; greater than 10 kph, and your license could be taken away from you. The police have the power to levy on-the-spot fines.

■ BY TRAIN

In Italy, traveling by train is simple and efficient. Service between major cities is frequent, and trains usually arrive on schedule. For information on train passes, which must be purchased before you leave home, *see* Train Passes *in* Booking Your Trip, *above.*

The fastest trains on the Ferrovie dello Stato (FS), the Italian State Railways, are the Eurostar trains that run between major cities. A high-speed Eurostar called Alta Velocità runs between Rome and Naples and is also planned for Florence, Bologna, Venice, and Milan in the future. Seat reservations are mandatory on the Eurostar trains. You will be assigned a specific seat in a specific coach. To avoid having to squeeze through narrow aisles, board only at your designated coach (the number on your ticket matches the one near the door of each coach).

The next-fastest trains are the *Intercity* (IC) trains. Reservations, required for some IC trains, are always advisable. *Diretto* and *Interregionale* trains make more stops and are a little slower. *Regionale* and *locale* trains are the slowest; many serve commuters. There are refreshments on all long-distance trains, purchased from a mobile cart or a dining car.

Most Italian trains have first and second classes. On local trains a first-class fare gets you little more than a clean doily on your headrest, but on long-distance trains you get wider seats, more legroom, and better ventilation and lighting. At peak travel times, a first-class fare is worth the price as the coaches are less crowded. In Italian, *prima classe* is first class; second is *seconda classe.*

Some cities—Milan, Turin, Genoa, Naples, Florence, and Rome included—have more than one train station, **so be sure you get off at the right place.** When buying train tickets be particularly aware that in Rome and Florence some trains do not stop at all of the cities' train stations and may not stop at the main central station. This is a common occurrence with regional and some Intercity trains. When scheduling train travel on the Internet or through a travel agent, be sure to request a train that goes to the train station closest to your destination in Rome and Florence.

Except for Pisa and Rome, none of the major cities have trains that go directly to the airports, but there are commuter bus lines connecting train stations and airports.

You can pay for your train tickets in cash or with a major credit card such as American Express, Diners Club, MasterCard, and Visa. Always purchase tickets before boarding the train, as you cannot purchase one from a conductor. Fines are steep for passengers without tickets. Trains can be very crowded, so it's always a good idea to make a reservation. You can reserve seats up to two months in advance at the train station or at an Italian travel agency displaying the FS emblem. Remember that you need to reserve seats even if you are using a rail pass. In summer it's fairly common to see people standing for part of the journey.

You must validate your ticket before boarding the train by punching it at a yellow box located in the waiting area of smaller train stations or at the end of the track in larger stations.

Train strikes of various kinds are also common, so it's a good idea to make sure your train is running.

Traveling by night is a good deal, as you do not pay extra for a hotel bed. More-comfortable trains run on the longer routes (Sicily–Rome, Sicily–Milan, Sicily–Venice, Rome–Turin, Lecce–Milan); ask for the good-value T3 (three single beds), Intercity Notte, and Carrozza Comfort. The Vagone Letto Excelsior has private bathrooms and suites with a double bed or two single beds.

Information Trenitalia (☎892021 in Italy ⊕www.trenitalia.com).

Information & Passes *See Train Passes in Booking Your Trip, above.*

■**TIP**➔Ask the local tourist board about hotel and local transportation packages that include tickets to major museum exhibits or other special events.

Travel Times
by Train

Brindisi
Lecce
Bari
Crotone
Catanzaro
TO GREECE
BARI - DUBROVNIK, CROATIA
Taranto
Reggio Calabria
Foggia
Campobasso
< 3hrs 20mn >
Benevento
< 4hrs 45mn >
Potenza
< 5hrs 30mn >
Messina
Catania
Siracusa
Sulmona
Avellino
< 5hrs >
Isernia
Caserta
Salerno
NAPOLI - CATANIA 11HRS
< 3hrs >
Enna
Palermo
< 3hrs 30mn >
< 1hr 15mn >
Napoli
NAPOLI - PALERMO 8HRS
Agrigento
Roma
Trapani
CIVITAVECCHIA - PALERMO 13HRS
Civitavecchia
NAPOLI - OLBIA - 12HRS
LIVORNO - OLBIA - 5HRS
CIVITAVECCHIA - OLBIA - 5HRS
CIVITAVECCHIA - CAGLIARI 15HRS
CAGLIARI - PALERMO 14HRS
Olbia
Sassari
< 4hrs >
Oristano
Cagliari

KEY

○ Major train stations

National train service

Regional train service

- - - Ferry service

MODANE Boarder stations

< time > Eurostar (shortest) travel
time between stations.

ON THE GROUND

■ COMMUNICATIONS

INTERNET

Getting online in Italian cities isn't difficult: public Internet stations and Internet cafés, some open 24 hours, are becoming more and more common. Prices differ from place to place, so spend some time to find the best deal. This isn't always readily apparent: a place might appear to have higher rates, but if it belongs to a chain, it might not charge you an initial flat fee again when you visit a branch in another city.

Wi-Fi hot spots are often within high-end hotels, major airports and train stations, cafés, and shopping centers. Although there is no official map of Italian hot spots, you can check ⊕*www.hotspots.com* for locations in Tuscany and Umbria.

Some hotels have in-room modem lines, but, as with phones, using the hotel's line is relatively expensive. Always check modem rates before plugging in. You may need an adapter for your computer for the European-style plugs. If you are traveling with a laptop, carry a spare battery and an adapter. Never plug your computer into any socket before asking about surge protection. IBM sells a tiny modem tester that plugs into a telephone jack to check whether the line is safe to use.

Contact Cybercafes (⊕ www.cybercafes.com) lists more than 4,000 Internet cafés worldwide.

PHONES

The good news is that you can now make a direct-dial telephone call from virtually any point on Earth. The bad news? You can't always do so cheaply. Calling from a hotel is almost always the most expensive option; hotels usually add huge surcharges to all calls, particularly international ones. Calling cards usually keep costs to a minimum, but only if you purchase them locally. And then there are mobile phones; as expensive as mobile phone calls can be, they are still usually a much cheaper option than calling from your hotel.

When calling Italy from abroad, begin by entering 011 (which gets you an international line), followed by Italy's country code, 39. Note that Italian telephone numbers do not have a standard number of digits (they can range anywhere from four to eight). The area code for Rome is 06, so a call from the United States to Rome would be dialed as 011 + 39 + 06 + phone number.

CALLING WITHIN ITALY

Public pay phones are scarce, although they can be found at train and subway stations, post offices, in hotel lobbies, and in some bars. In rural areas, town squares usually have a pay phone. Pay phones may take coins, but usually require a *carta telefonica* (phone card; ⇨*below*).

For all calls within Italy, whether local or long-distance, dial the area code followed by the number. Rates for long-distance calls vary according to the time of day; it's cheaper to call before 9 AM and after 7 or 8 PM. Italy adopted the prefix "800" for toll-free or "green" numbers.

CALLING OUTSIDE ITALY

Because of the high rates charged by most hotels for long-distance and international calls, you're better off making such calls from public phones with a national or international telephone card, or using a mobile phone *(⇨below)*. If you want to use the hotel phone to make an international call, you'll save money by using an international calling card *(⇨below)*.

To place international calls or collect calls through an operator, dial 170. Rates to the United States are lowest on Sunday around the clock and between 10 PM–8 AM (Italian time) on weekdays and Saturday. You can also place a direct call to the United States using your U.S. phone calling-card number. You automatically reach a U.S. operator and thereby avoid all language difficulties.

The country code for the United States is 1 (dial 00 + 1 + U.S. area code and number).

Access Codes AT&T Direct (☎800/172–444). MCI WorldPhone (☎800/905–825). Sprint International Access (☎800/172–405).

CALLING CARDS

Prepaid *carte telefoniche* (phone cards) are available throughout Italy. Cards in different denominations are sold at post offices, newsstands, tobacco shops, and bars. Cards for calls within Italy are for use with pay phones; tear off the corner of the card and insert it in the phone's slot. When you dial, the card's value appears in a display window. After you hang up, the card is returned.

International calling cards are different; you call a toll-free number and then enter a code found on the back of the card. The best card for calling North America and elsewhere in Europe is the Europa card, which comes in two denominations, €5 for 180 minutes and €10 for 360 minutes.

MOBILE PHONES

If you have a multiband phone (some countries use different frequencies than what's used in the United States) and your service provider uses the world-standard GSM network (as do T-Mobile, Cingular, and Verizon), you can probably use your phone abroad. Roaming fees can be steep, however: 99¢ a minute is considered reasonable. And overseas you normally pay the toll charges for incoming calls. It's almost always cheaper to send a text message than to make a call, since text messages have a very low set fee (often less than 5¢).

If you just want to make local calls, consider buying a new SIM card (note that your provider may have to unlock your phone for you to use a different SIM

card) and a prepaid service plan in the destination. You'll then have a local number and can make local calls at local rates. If your trip is extensive, you could also simply buy a new cell phone in your destination, as the initial cost will be offset over time.

■**TIP**➔If you travel internationally frequently, save one of your old mobile phones or buy a cheap one on the Internet; ask your cell phone company to unlock it for you, and take it with you as a travel phone, buying a new SIM card with pay-as-you-go service in each destination.

The cost of cell phones is dropping; you can purchase a cell phone with a prepaid calling card (no monthly service plan) in Italy for less than €70. Inexpensive cell phones are dual band and will not allow you to call the United States, but using an international calling card and the cell phone solves that problem in a very inexpensive manner. Most medium to large towns have stores dedicated to selling cell phones. You will need to present your passport to purchase the SIM card that goes with the phone.

Rental cell phones are available in cities and large towns. Many Internet cafés offer them, but shop around for the best deal. Most rental contracts require a refundable deposit that covers the cost of the cell phone (€75–€125) and then set up a monthly service plan that is automatically charged to your credit card. Frequently, rental cell phones will be triple band and allow you to call the United States. Be sure to check the rate schedule before you rent a cell phone and commence calling to prevent a nasty surprise when you receive your credit-card bill two or three months later.

■**TIP**➔ Beware of cell phone (and PDA) thieves. Keep your phone or PDA in a secure pocket or purse. Do not lay it on the bar when you stop for an espresso. Do not zip it into the outside pocket of your backpack in crowded cities. Do not leave it in your hotel room. If you are using a phone with a monthly service plan, notify your provider immediately if it is lost or stolen.

Contacts Cellular Abroad (☎800/287–5072 ⊕www.cellularabroad.com) rents and sells GMS phones and sells SIM cards that work in many countries. Mobal (☎888/888–9162 ⊕www.mobalrental.com) rents mobiles and sells GSM phones (starting at $49) that will operate in 140 countries. Per-call rates vary throughout the world. Planet Fone (☎888/988–4777 ⊕www.planetfone.com) rents cell phones, but the per-minute rates are expensive.

■ CUSTOMS & DUTIES

You're always allowed to bring goods of a certain value back home without having to pay any duty or import tax. But there's a limit on the amount of tobacco and liquor you can bring back duty-free, and some countries have separate limits for perfumes; for exact figures, check with your customs department. The values of so-called duty-free goods are included in these amounts. When you shop abroad, save all your receipts, as customs inspectors may ask to see them as well as the items you purchased. If the total value of your goods is more than the duty-free limit, you'll have to pay a tax (most often a flat percentage) on the value of everything beyond that limit.

Travelers from the United States should experience little difficulty clearing customs at any airport in Italy.

Italy requires documentation of the background of all antiques and antiquities before the item is taken out of the country. Under Italian law, all antiquities found on Italian soil are considered state property and there are other restrictions on antique artwork. Even if purchased from a business in Italy, legal ownership of such artifacts may be in question if brought into the United States. Therefore, although they do not necessarily confer ownership, you must have documents such as export permits and receipts when importing such items into the United States.

For returning to the United States, clearing customs is sometimes more difficult. U.S. residents are normally entitled to a duty-free exemption of $800 on items accompanying them. You cannot bring back any of that delicious prosciutto or salami or any other meat product. Fresh mushrooms, truffles, or fresh fruits and vegetables are also forbidden. There are also restrictions on the amount of alcohol allowed in duty-free. Generally, you are allowed to bring in one liter of wine, beer, or other alcohol without paying a customs duty.

Information in Italy Dogana Sezione Viaggiatori (☎06/65954343 ⊕www.agenziadogane.it). Ministero delle Finanze, Direzione Centrale dei Servizi Doganali, Divisione I (☎06/50242117 ⊕www.finanze.it).

U.S. Information U.S. Customs and Border Protection (⊕www.cbp.gov).

■ EATING OUT

Italian cuisine is still largely regional. Ask what the local specialties are: by all means, have spaghetti *alla carbonara* (with bacon and egg) in Rome, pizza in Rome or Naples, *bistecca alla fiorentina* (steak) in Florence, *chingale* (wild boar) in Tuscany, truffles in the Piedmont, and risotto *alla milanese* in Milan. Although most restaurants in Italy serve traditional local cuisine, you can find Asian and Middle Eastern alternatives in Rome, Venice, and other cities.

The restaurants we list are the cream of the crop in each price category. Properties indicated by a ✕▣ are lodging establishments whose restaurant warrants a special trip.

MEALS & MEALTIMES
What's the difference between a ristorante and a trattoria? Can you order food at an enoteca? Can you go to a restaurant just for a snack, or order just a salad at a piz-

LOCAL DO'S & TABOOS

GREETINGS

Upon meeting and leave-taking, both friends and strangers wish each other good day or good evening (*buon giorno, buona sera*); *ciao* isn't used between strangers. Italians who are friends greet each other with a kiss, usually first on the left cheek, then on the right. When you meet a new person, shake hands.

SIGHTSEEING

Italy is full of churches, and many of them contain significant works of art. They are also places of worship, however, so be sure to dress appropriately.

Shorts, tank tops, and sleeveless garments are taboo in most churches throughout the country. In summer carry a sweater or other item of clothing to wrap around your bare shoulders before entering a church.

You should never bring food into a church, and do not sip from your water bottle while inside. If you have a cell phone, turn it off before entering. And never enter a church when a service is in progress, especially if it is a private affair such as a wedding or baptism.

OUT ON THE TOWN

Table manners in Italy are formal; rarely do Italians share food from their plates. In a restaurant, be formal and polite with your waiter—no calling across the room for attention.

When you've finished your meal and are ready to go, ask for the check (*il conto*); unless it's well past closing time, no waiter will put a bill on your table until you've requested it.

Italians do not have a culture of sipping cocktails or chugging pitchers of beer. Wine, beer, and other alcoholic drinks are almost always consumed as part of a meal. Public drunkenness is abhorred.

Smoking has been banned in all public establishments, much like in the United States.

Flowers, chocolates, or a bottle of wine are appropriate hostess gifts when invited to dinner at the home of an Italian.

DOING BUSINESS

Showing up on time for business appointments is the norm and expected in Italy. There are more business lunches than business dinners, and even business lunches aren't common, as Italians view mealtimes as periods of pleasure and relaxation.

Business cards are used throughout Italy, and business suits are the norm for both men and women. To be on the safe side, it is best not to use first names or a familiar form of address until invited to do so.

Business gifts are not the norm, but if one is given it is usually small and symbolic of your home location or type of business.

LANGUAGE

One of the best ways to avoid being an Ugly American is to learn a little of the local language. You need not strive for fluency; even just mastering a few basic words and terms is bound to make chatting with the locals more rewarding.

"Please" is *per favore*, "thank you" is *grazie*, and "you're welcome" is *prego*.

In larger cities such as Venice, Rome, and Florence, language is not a big problem. Most hotels have English speakers at their reception desks, and if not, they can always find someone who speaks at least a little English.

You may have trouble communicating in the countryside, but a phrase book and expressive gestures will go a long way.

A phrase book and language-tape set can help get you started.

Fodor's Italian for Travelers (available at bookstores everywhere) is excellent.

zeria? The following definitions should help.

Not too long ago, *ristoranti* tended to be more elegant and expensive than *trattorie* and *osterie*, which serve traditional, home-style fare in an atmosphere to match. But the distinction has blurred considerably, and an osteria in the center of town might be far fancier (and pricier) than a ristorante across the street. In any sit-down establishment, be it a ristorante, osteria, or trattoria, you are generally expected to order at least a two-course meal, such as: a *primo* (first course) and a *secondo* (main course) or a *contorno* (vegetable side dish); an *antipasto* (starter) followed by either a primo or secondo; or a secondo and a *dolce* (dessert).

In an *enoteca* (wine bar) or pizzeria it's common to order just one dish. An enoteca menu is often limited to a selection of cheese, cured meats, salads, and desserts, but if there's a kitchen you'll also find soups, pastas, and main courses. The typical pizzeria fare includes *affettati misti* (a selection of cured pork), simple salads, various kinds of bruschetta, *crostini* (similar to bruschetta, with a variety of toppings) and, in Rome, *fritti* (deep-fried finger food) such as *olive ascolane* (green olives with a meat stuffing) and *supplì* (rice balls stuffed with mozzarella).

The handiest and least expensive places for a quick snack between sights are probably bars, cafés, and pizza *al taglio* (by the slice) spots. Pizza al taglio shops are easy to negotiate but very few have seats. They sell pizza by weight: just point out which kind you want and how much.

Bars in Italy are primarily places to get a coffee and a bite to eat, rather than drinking establishments. Most bars have a selection of *panini* (sandwiches) warmed up on the griddle (*piastra*) and *tramezzini* (sandwiches made of untoasted white bread triangles). In larger cities, bars also serve vegetable and fruit salads, cold pasta dishes, and gelato. Most bars offer beer and a variety of alcohol as well as wines by the glass (sometimes good but more often mediocre). A café (*caffè* in Italian) is like a bar but usually with more tables. Pizza at a café should be avoided—it's usually heated in a microwave.

If you place your order at the counter, ask if you can sit down: some places charge for table service, others do not. In self-service bars and cafés it's good manners to clean your table before you leave. Note that in some places you have to pay a cashier, then place your order and show your *scontrino* (receipt) at the counter. Menus are posted outside most restaurants (in English in tourist areas); if not, you might step inside and ask to take a look at the menu (but don't ask for a table unless you intend to stay). Italians take their food as it is listed on the menu, seldom if ever making special requests such as "dressing on the side" or "hold the olive oil." If you have special dietary needs, however, make them known; they can usually be accommodated. Although mineral water makes its way to almost every table, you can order a carafe of tap water (*acqua di rubinetto* or *acqua semplice*) instead, but keep in mind that such water can be highly chlorinated.

Wiping your bowl clean with a (small) piece of bread is usually considered a sign of appreciation, not bad manners. Spaghetti should be eaten with a fork only, although a little help from a spoon won't horrify locals the way cutting spaghetti into little pieces might. Order your espresso (Italians don't usually drink cappuccino after breakfast time) after dessert, not with it. Don't ask for a doggy bag.

Breakfast (*la colazione*) is usually served from 7 to 10:30, lunch (*il pranzo*) from 12:30 to 2:30, dinner (*la cena*) from 7:30 to 10. Peak times are usually 1:30 for lunch and 9 for dinner. Enoteche and *bacari* (wine bars) are open also in the morning and late afternoon for a snack at the counter. Most pizzerias open at 8 PM and close around midnight—later in summer and on weekends. Most bars and cafés are open from 7 AM until 8 or 9 PM; a few stay open until midnight.

Unless otherwise noted, the restaurants listed in this guide are open daily for lunch and dinner.

PAYING

Most restaurants have a cover charge per person, usually listed at the top of the check as *coperto* or *pane e coperto*. It should be a modest charge (€1–€2.50 per person) except at the most expensive restaurants. Whenever in doubt, ask before you order to avoid unpleasant discussions later. It is customary to leave a small tip (around 10%) in appreciation of good service. If *servizio* is included at the bottom of the check, no tip is necessary. Tips are always given in cash.

The price of fish dishes is often given by weight (before cooking), so the price you see on the menu is for 100 grams of fish, not for the whole dish. (An average fish portion is about 350 grams.) In Tuscany, *bistecca alla fiorentina* (Florentine steak) is also often priced by weight (€4 for 100 grams or €40 for 1 kilogram [2.2 lbs]).

Major credit cards are widely accepted in Italy, though cash is usually preferred. More restaurants take Visa and Master-Card than American Express.

When you leave a dining establishment, take your meal bill or receipt with you; although not a common experience, the Italian finance (tax) police can approach you within 100 yards of the establishment at which you've eaten and ask for a receipt. If you don't have one, they can fine you and will fine the business owner for not providing the receipt. The measure is intended to prevent tax evasion; it's not necessary to show receipts when leaving Italy.

For guidelines on tipping see Tipping below.

■ ELECTRICITY

The electrical current in Italy is 220 volts, 50 cycles alternating current (AC); wall outlets take Continental-type plugs, with two or three round prongs.

Consider making a small investment in a universal adapter, which has several types of plugs in one lightweight, compact unit. Most laptops and mobile phone chargers are dual voltage (i.e., they operate equally well on 110 and 220 volts), so require only an adapter. These days the same is true of small appliances such as hair dryers. Always check labels and manufacturer instructions to be sure. Don't use 110-volt outlets marked FOR SHAVERS ONLY for high-wattage appliances such as hair dryers.

Contacts Steve Kropla's Help for World Traveler's (⊕ www.kropla.com) has information on electrical and telephone plugs around the world. **Walkabout Travel Gear** (⊕ www. walkabouttravelgear.com) has a good coverage of electricity under "adapters."

■ EMERGENCIES

No matter where you are in Italy, you can dial 113 in case of emergency. Not all 113 operators speak English, so you may want to ask a local person to place the call. Asking the operator for *"pronto soccorso"* (first aid and also the emergency room of a hospital) should get you an *ambulanza* (ambulance). If you just need a doctor, ask for *"un medico."*

Italy has the *carabinieri* (national police force) as well as the *polizia* (local police force). Both are armed and have the power to arrest and investigate crimes. Always report the loss of your passport to the police as well as to your embassy. When reporting a crime, you'll be asked to fill out *una denuncia* (official report); keep a copy for your insurance company.

Local traffic officers, known as *vigili*, are responsible for, among other things, giving out parking tickets. They wear white (in summer) or black uniforms. Should you find yourself involved in a minor car accident in town, contact the vigili.

Pharmacies are generally open weekdays 8:30–1 and 4–8, and Saturday 9–1. Local pharmacies cover the off-hours in shifts: on the door of every pharmacy is a list of which pharmacies in the vicinity will be open late.

Foreign Embassies U.S. Consulate Florence (✉Via Lungarno Vespucci 38, Florence ☎055/2398276). **U.S. Consulate Milan** (✉Via Principe Amedeo 2/10, Milan ☎02/290351). **U.S. Consulate Naples** (✉Piazza della Repubblica, Naples ☎081/5838111). **U.S. Embassy** (✉Via Veneto 121, Rome ☎06/46741 ⊕www.usembassy.it).

General Emergency Contacts Emergencies (☎113). **National police** (☎112).

∎ HOURS OF OPERATION

Religious and civic holidays are frequent in Italy. Depending on the holiday's local importance, businesses may close for the day. Businesses do not close on a Friday or Monday when the holiday falls on the weekend.

Banks are open weekdays 8:30–1:30 and for an hour in the afternoon, depending on the bank. Most post offices are open Monday–Saturday 9–12:30; central post offices are open 9–6:30 weekdays, 9–12:30 on Saturday. On the last day of the month all post offices close at midday.

Most churches are open from early morning until noon or 12:30, when they close for three hours or more; they open again in the afternoon, closing at about 6 PM. A few major churches, such as St. Peter's in Rome and San Marco in Venice, remain open all day. Walking around during services is discouraged. Many museums are closed one day a week, often Monday. During low season, museums often close early; during high season, many stay open until late at night.

Pharmacies are generally open weekdays 8:30–1 and 4–8, and Saturday 9–1. Local pharmacies cover the off-hours in shifts: on the door of every pharmacy is a list of which pharmacies in the vicinity will be open late.

Most shops are open Monday–Saturday 9–1 and 3:30 or 4–7:30. Clothing shops are generally closed Monday mornings. Barbers and hairdressers, with some exceptions, are closed Sunday and Monday. Some bookstores and fashion and tourist-oriented shops in places such as Rome and Venice are open all day, as well as Sunday. Large chain supermarkets such as Standa, COOP, and Eselunga do not close for lunch and are usually open Sunday; smaller *alimentari* (delicatessens) and other food shops are usually closed one evening during the week (it varies according to the town) and are almost always closed Sunday.

HOLIDAYS

If you can avoid it, don't travel through Italy in August, when much of the population is on vacation. Most cities are deserted (except for foreign tourists) and many restaurants and shops are closed.

National holidays in 2009 include January 1 (New Year's Day); January 6 (Epiphany); April 12 and April 13 (Easter Sunday and Monday); April 25 (Liberation Day); May 1 (Labor Day or May Day); June 2 (Festival of the Republic); August 15 (Ferragosto); November 1 (All Saints' Day); December 8 (Immaculate Conception); and December 25 and 26 (Christmas Day and the feast of St. Stephen).

Feast days of patron saints are observed locally. Many businesses and shops may be closed in Florence, Genoa, and Turin on June 24 (St. John the Baptist); in Rome on June 29 (Sts. Peter and Paul); in Palermo on July 15 (Santa Rosalia); in Naples on September 19 (San Gennaro); in Bologna on October 4 (San Petronio); in Trieste on November 3 (San Giusto); and in Milan on December 7 (St. Ambrose). Venice's feast of St. Mark is April 25, the same as Liberation Day, so the Madonna della Salute on November 21 makes up for the lost holiday.

▮ MAIL

The Italian mail system is notoriously slow, but it is improving with some privatization. Allow from 7 to 15 days for mail to get to the United States. Receiving mail in Italy, especially packages, can take weeks; so don't forget your medications or other unique necessary items at home.

Most post offices are open Monday–Saturday 9–12:30; central post offices are open weekdays 9–6:30, Saturday 9–12:30. On the last day of the month, post offices close at midday. You can buy stamps at tobacco shops as well as post offices.

Posta Prioritaria (for small letters and packages) is the name of the most commonly used postage. It supposedly guarantees delivery within Italy in three to five business days and abroad in five to six working days. The more-expensive express delivery, *Postacelere* (for larger letters and packages), guarantees one-day delivery to most places in Italy and three- to five-day delivery abroad.

Mail sent as Posta Prioritaria to the United States costs €0.85 for up to 20 grams, €1.50 for 21–50 grams, and €1.85 for 51–100 grams. Mail sent as Postacelere to the United States costs €43–€50 for up to 500 grams.

Other package services to check are Quick Pack Europe, for delivery within Europe; and EMS Express Mail Service, a global three- to five-day service for letters and packages that can be less expensive than Postacelere.

Two-day mail is generally available during the week in all major cities and at popular resorts via UPS and Federal Express. Service is reliable; a Federal Express letter to the United States costs about €35. If your hotel can't assist you, try an Internet café, many of which also offer two-day mail services using major carriers.

SHIPPING PACKAGES

You can ship parcels via air or surface. Air takes about two weeks, and surface anywhere up to three months to most countries. If you have purchased antiques, ceramics, or other objects, ask if the vendor will do the shipping for you; in most cases, this is a possibility. If so, ask if the article will be insured against breakage. When shipping a package out of Italy, it is virtually impossible to find an overnight delivery option—the fastest delivery time is 48 to 72 hours.

▮ MONEY

Prices vary from region to region and are substantially lower in the country than in the cities. Of Italy's major cities, Venice and Milan are by far the most expensive. Resorts such as the Costa Smeralda, Portofino, and Cortina d'Ampezzo cater to wealthy people and charge top prices. Good values can be had in the scenic Trentino–Alto Adige region and the Dolomites and in Umbria and the Marches. With a few exceptions, southern Italy, Sicily, and Sardinia also offer bargains for those who do their homework before they leave home.

▮TIP➔Banks never have every foreign currency on hand, and it may take as long as a week to order. If you're planning to exchange funds before leaving home, don't wait till the last minute.

ATMS & BANKS

An ATM (bancomat in Italian) is the easiest way to get euros in Italy. There are numerous ATMs in large cities and small towns, as well as in airports and train stations. They are not common in places such as grocery stores. Be sure to memorize your PIN in numbers, as ATM keypads in Italy don't always display letters. Check with your bank to confirm that you have an international PIN (*codice segreto*), to find out your maximum daily withdrawal allowance, and to learn what the bank fee is for withdrawing money.

Your own bank may charge a fee for using ATMs abroad or charge for the cost of conversion from euros to dollars. Nevertheless, you'll usually get a better rate of exchange at an ATM than you will at a currency-exchange office or even when changing money inside a bank with a teller. Extracting funds as you need them is a safer option than carrying around a large amount of cash.

CREDIT CARDS

Throughout this guide, the following abbreviations are used: **AE**, American Express; **DC**, Diners Club; **MC**, Master-Card; and **V**, Visa.

It's a good idea to inform your credit-card company before you travel, especially if you're going abroad and don't travel internationally very often. Otherwise, the credit-card company might put a hold on your card owing to unusual activity—not a good thing halfway through your trip. Record all your credit-card numbers—as well as the phone numbers to call if your cards are lost or stolen—in a safe place, so you're prepared should something go wrong. Both MasterCard and Visa have general numbers you can call (collect if you're abroad) if your card is lost, but you're better off calling the number of your issuing bank, since MasterCard and Visa generally just transfer you to your bank; your bank's number is usually printed on your card.

If you plan to use your credit card for cash advances, you'll need to apply for a PIN at least two weeks before your trip. Although it's usually cheaper (and safer) to use a credit card abroad for large purchases (so you can cancel payments or be reimbursed if there's a problem), note that some credit-card companies *and* the banks that issue them add substantial percentages to all foreign transactions,

whether they're in a foreign currency or not. Check on these fees before leaving home, so there won't be any surprises when you get the bill.

■**TIP**➔Before you charge something, ask the merchant whether or not he or she plans to do a dynamic currency conversion (DCC). In such a transaction the credit-card *processor* (shop, restaurant, or hotel, not Visa or MasterCard) converts the currency and charges you in dollars. In most cases you'll pay the merchant a 3% fee for this service in addition to any credit-card company and issuing-bank foreign-transaction surcharges.

Dynamic currency conversion programs are becoming increasingly widespread. Merchants who participate in them are supposed to ask whether you want to be charged in dollars or the local currency, but they don't always do so. And even if they do offer you a choice, they may well avoid mentioning the additional surcharges. The good news is that you *do* have a choice. And if this practice really gets your goat, you can avoid it entirely thanks to American Express; with its cards, DCC simply isn't an option.

MasterCard and Visa are preferred by Italian merchants, but American Express is usually accepted in Italian tourist spots. Credit cards aren't accepted everywhere; if you want to pay with a credit card in a small shop, hotel, or restaurant, it's a good idea to make your intentions known early on.

Reporting Lost Cards American Express (☎800/992–3404 in the U.S., 336/393–1111 collect from abroad ⊕www.americanexpress. com). **Diners Club** (☎800/234–6377 in the U.S., 303/799–1504 collect from abroad ⊕www.dinersclub.com). **MasterCard** (☎800/622–7747 in the U.S., 636/722–7111 collect from abroad ⊕www.mastercard.com). **Visa** (☎800/847–2911 in the U.S., 410/581–9994 collect from abroad ⊕www.visa.com).

CURRENCY & EXCHANGE

The euro is the main unit of currency in Italy, as well as in 12 other European countries. Under the euro system there are 100 *centesimi* (cents) to the euro. There are coins valued at 1, 2, 5, 10, 20, and 50 centesimi as well as 1 and 2 euros. There are seven notes: 5, 10, 20, 50, 100, 200, and 500 euros.

At this writing, the exchange rate was about 0.68 euros to the U.S. dollar.

Post offices exchange currency at good rates, but you will rarely find an employee who speaks English, so be prepared.

■ TIP→Even if a currency-exchange booth has a sign promising no commission, rest assured that there's some kind of huge, hidden fee. As for rates, you're almost always better off getting foreign currency at an ATM or exchanging money at a bank.

▌ TAXES

A 9% V.A.T. (value-added tax) is included in the rate at all hotels except those at the upper end of the range. At luxury hotels a 12% tax is added to the bill.

No tax is added to the bill in restaurants. A service charge of approximately 10%–15% is often added to your check; in some cases a service charge is included in the prices.

The V.A.T. is 20% on clothing, wine, and luxury goods. On consumer goods it's already included in the amount shown on the price tag, whereas on services it may not be. If your purchases total more than €155 you may be entitled to a refund of the V.A.T.

When making a purchase, ask for a V.A.T. refund form and find out whether the merchant gives refunds—not all stores do, nor are they required to. Have the form stamped like any customs form by customs officials when you leave the country or, if you're visiting several European Union countries, when you leave the EU. After you're through passport control, take the form to a refund-service counter for an on-the-spot refund (which is usually the quickest and easiest option), or mail it to the address on the form (or on the envelope with it) after you arrive home. You receive the total refund stated on the form, but the processing time can be long, especially if you request a credit-card adjustment.

Global Refund is a Europe-wide service with 225,000 affiliated stores and more than 700 refund counters at major airports and border crossings. Its refund form, called a Tax Free Check, is the most common across the European continent. The service issues refunds in the form of cash, check, or credit-card adjustment.

V.A.T. Refunds Global Refund (☎800/566–9828 ⊕www.globalrefund.com).

▌ TIME

Italy is in the Central European Time Zone. From March to October it institutes Daylight Saving Time. Italy is 6 hours ahead of U.S. Eastern Standard Time, 1 hour ahead of Great Britain, 10 hours behind Sydney, and 12 hours behind Auckland. Like the rest of Europe, Italy uses the 24-hour (or "military") clock, which means that after noon you continue counting forward: 13:00 is 1 PM, 23:30 is 11:30 PM.

▌ TIPPING

In restaurants a service charge of 10% to 15% may appear on your check. If so, it's not necessary to leave an additional tip. If service is not included, leave a tip of up to 10% in cash. Always leave your tip in cash. Usually there will not be a line item on your credit-card slip for a tip—but even if there is, tip in cash. Tip checkroom attendants €1 per person and restroom attendants €0.50 (more in expensive hotels and restaurants). In major cities tip €0.50 or more for table service in cafés. At a hotel bar tip €1 and up for a round or two of drinks.

Italians rarely tip taxi drivers, which is not to say that you shouldn't. A euro or two is appreciated, particularly if the driver helps with luggage. Service-station attendants are tipped only for special services; give them €1 for checking your tires. Railway and airport porters charge a fixed rate per bag. Tip an additional €0.25 per person, more if the porter is helpful. Give a barber €1–€1.50 and a hairdresser's assistant €1.50–€4 for a shampoo or cut, depending on the type of establishment.

On sightseeing tours, tip guides about €1.50 per person for a half-day group tour, more if they are especially knowledgeable. In monasteries and other sights where admission is free, a contribution (€0.50–€1) is expected.

In hotels give the *portiere* (concierge) about 10% of his bill for services, or €2.50–€5 for help with dinner reservations and such. Leave the chambermaid about €0.75 per day, or about €4.50–€5 a week in a moderately priced hotel; tip a minimum of €1 for valet or room service. Double these amounts in an expensive hotel. In expensive hotels tip doormen €0.50 for calling a cab and €1.50 for carrying bags to the check-in desk and bellhops €1.50–€2.50 for carrying your bags to the room.

INDEX

ABOUT OUR WRITERS

Hailing from Washington, D.C., **Lynda Albertson** relocated to Italy in 2003 to write a monthly wine column, "In Vino Veritas," for *The American* magazine. Updater of our Rome shopping section, she has an uncanny knowledge of where to purchase absolute necessities from truffle oil to that perfect Piranesi print.

After completing his master's degree in art history, **Peter Blackman** settled permanently in Italy in 1986. Since then he's worked as a biking and walking tour guide. When he's not leading a trip, you'll find Peter at home in Chianti.

Martin Wilmot Bennett's vast background in Italian art and civilization made him a natural to write our photo-feature on the Sistine Ceiling. A major contributor to *Fodor's Rome* and a graduate of Cambridge University, he teaches at Rome's University of Tor Vergata.

Shannon Essa and **Ruth Edenbaum** are authors of the food guide *Chow! Venice— Savoring the Food and Wine of La Serenissima.* When not in Venice, Ruth resides in Princeton Junction, New Jersey, where she is the doting grandmother of two. Shannon is a moderator for the travel Web site www.slowtrav.com, and when not traveling lives in San Diego.

Updater of our Rome nightlife/arts pages, **Erica Firpo** writes for *Luxe City Guide, Zing Magazine, Very Style Guide, National Geographic Traveler,* authored the *Rome Little Black Book,* and tracks Rome in her blog, moscerina.com.

Madeleine Johnson, an unrepentant Midwesterner, has lived in Italy—with a two-year break in Paris—since 1988. Her writing has appeared in *Connoisseur, The Journal of Art,* and *The American.*

Updater of our Rome restaurant reviews, **Dana Klitzberg** trained in top restaurant kitchens in New York and Rome and is owner of Blu Aubergine (www.bluaubergine.com) through which she caters, instructs, and writes about food.

Jen Laskey became smitten with Rome during a summer MFA program in 2000; she returned to become a resident five years later. She updated our Rome restaurant and hotel reviews.

Bruce Leimsidor has published articles on political and social issues in the *International Herald Tribune* and the *Frankfurter Allgemeine Zeitung.* He lives in Venice, where he teaches at the university, collects 17th and 18th century drawings, and is rumored to make the best *pasta e fagioli* in town.

Nan McElroy is the author of the highly acclaimed, purely practical travel guide *Italy: Instructions for Use.* She first set foot in Venice in 1995, relocated there in 2004, and now is part of the Your Friend in Venice travel service.

Florence resident **Patricia Rucidlo** holds master's degrees in Italian Renaissance history and art history. When she's not extolling the virtues of a Pontormo masterpiece or angrily defending the Medici, she's leading wine tours in Chianti and catering private dinner parties.

California native **Pamela Santini** came to study art history 15 years ago at Venice's Ca' Foscari University, where she currently teaches. She's also a writer and translator.

Jonathan Willcocks, a Brit by birth with degrees in French and English literature from the Sorbonne, teaches language, literature, and translation at the university in Perugia.

Megan K. Williams is a Rome-based writer and correspondent, covering Italy and Africa in print for many newspapers and magazines, as well as on the radio for the CBC, Marketplace, and NPR. Her short-story collection *Saving Rome* was published in 2006 to rave reviews.